LEMON-AID
NEW CARS
2000

LEMON-AID
NEW CARS
2000

PHIL EDMONSTON

Published in 1999 by Stoddart Publishing Co. Limited
34 Lesmill Road, Toronto, Canada M3B 2T6

Distributed by:
General Distribution Services Ltd.
325 Humber College Boulevard, Toronto, Canada M9W 7C3
Tel. (416) 213-1919   Fax (416) 213-1917
Email customer.service@ccmailgw.genpub.com

Canadian Cataloguing in Publication Data

The National Library of Canada has catalogued this publication as follows:

Edmonston, Louis-Philippe, 1944–
Lemon-aid new cars

1998–
Annual.
Continues: Edmonston, Louis-Philippe, 1944–   .
Lemon-aid new car guide, ISSN 0714-5861.
ISSN 1481-4188
ISBN 0-7737-6066-0 (2000)

1. Automobiles — Purchasing — Periodicals. I. Title.

TL162.E3396   629.2'222'05   C98-901177-1

Cover design: Bill Douglas @ The Bang
Typesetting and text design: Wordstyle Productions
Editorial services: Greg Ioannou, Colborne Communications

THE CANADA COUNCIL | LE CONSEIL DES ARTS
FOR THE ARTS | DU CANADA
SINCE 1957 | DEPUIS 1957

We acknowledge for their financial support of our publishing program the Canada Council, the Ontario Arts Council, and the Government of Canada through the Book Publishing Industry Development Program (BPIDP).

Printed and bound in Canada

CONTENTS

Part Three/NEW-VEHICLE RATINGS
145

American Vehicles
155

Asian Vehicles
298

European Vehicles
416

Key Documents

The following photos, charts, documents, memos, court filings and decisions, and service bulletins are included in this index so that you can easily find and photocopy whichever document will prove helpful in your dealings with automakers, government agencies, dealers, or service managers. Most of the service bulletins outline repairs or replacements that should be done for free.

Part One

Part Two

Part Three

"Secrets" You Should Know

Service Bulletins and Secret Warranties

Appendices

Introduction
NEW MODELS, OLD SCAMS

Lemon-Aid New Cars 2000 is unlike any other auto book on the market. Its main objective, to inform and protect consumers in an industry known for its dishonesty and exaggerated claims, remains unchanged. However, this guide also focuses on secret warranties and confidential service bulletins that automakers swear don't exist, but may be applicable to your trade-in or the new vehicle you wish to buy. That's why you'll be interested in the "Key Documents" list found on the previous pages. There you'll find the exact bulletin, memo, or news clipping reproduced from the original so neither the dealer nor the automaker can weasel out of its obligations.

The book's information is culled from mostly U.S. and Canadian sources and is gathered throughout the year from owner complaints, whistle blowers, lawsuits, and judgments, as well as from confidential manufacturer service bulletins.

Lemon-Aid not only targets abusive auto industry practices, it also lobbies automakers for changes. For example, two years ago we blew the whistle on Chrysler Canada's biodegradable automatic transmissions and brakes, and defective paint. Following *Lemon-Aid*'s downgrading of Chrysler's minivans and cars, company officials met with me and set up a Warranty Review Committee to pay claims previously rejected. After a similar downgrading last year of Ford's Taurus, Sable, and Windstar, Ford officials arranged to see me in February of this year and began giving refunds to owners of the above vehicles with engine and automatic transmission claims, even after their warranty had expired (see Part Two). This year, we tackle GM's Saturn models for engine, drivetrain, and body defects that no amount of hype can hide. Side airbags also come under close scrutiny, particularly due to early indications that they can severely injure children.

The 2000 guide makes a critical comparison of 1999 and 2000 cars and minivans. Safer, cheaper, and more reliable alternatives are given for each vehicle.

Lemon-Aid uses test results, owner complaints, Internet postings, and surveys to determine its ratings. That's where you, dear reader, can help. Please fill out the questionnaire found at the end of this guide. Your data will be kept confidential and will be used in the next edition of *Lemon-Aid New Cars*.

What better way to separate the deals from the steals?

Phil Edmonston
www.lemonaidcars.com
October 1999

Part One
GET THE BEST FOR LESS

"What's the difference between a $30,000 car and one that costs $50,000? A lot of wasted money, according to Steve Sharf, a former Chrysler Corp. manufacturing executive. Sharf says the equipment used to make cheaper cars costs the same as the machines that turn out expensive cars, and autoworkers are not paid according to how expensive their products are. All the amenities like heated steering wheels and leather seats just don't add up to that extra $20,000. Sharf suggests it would be better to buy a pair of gloves and forgo the heated steering wheels. If it's prestige you're looking for, he says, 'it would be cheaper and make more sense to buy $20 cigars.'"

Ward's Auto World

"The only time manufacturers wittingly admitted to marketing a specific car targeted at women, it failed miserably. Fewer than 1,000 of the 1955/56 Dodge La Femme sedans available in pink and lavender with a rosebud interior are believed to have been sold. The cars came equipped with matching purses, umbrellas, raincoats and boots..."

Karen Brown
Ottawa Citizen

It's hard to believe I've been writing *Lemon-Aid* guides for almost 28 years. Imagine, when the first guides were written, car buying was seen as a man's responsibility, auto safety was dependent upon the "nut behind the wheel," and Volkswagen had a monopoly on cold, slow, and unsold Beetles and minivans. Ford was selling biodegradable pickups (and denying they had a J-67 secret warranty to cover rust repairs), and the average new car could be found for less than $3,000.

But times have changed. Women now influence—and make—the majority of car-buying decisions and are extremely thorough in their research, much to the consternation of sellers who see them walk into their showrooms armed to the teeth with *Lemon-Aid, Consumer Reports,* and the CAA's *Autopinion* magazine. Automakers have redesigned their vehicles to make them more crashworthy and have added airbags. Volkswagen and Audi models top the recommended rating charts, and the average price of a new car or minivan now tops $27,000.

Some things don't change for the better, though—as Nick, above, will confirm. He's working on his fifth Chrysler Getrag transmission.

Reasonable prices, safer products

Throughout the 1980s, the quality of imports improved dramatically, with Toyota, Nissan, and Honda leading the pack. American quality, on the other hand, improved at a snail's pace over the same period, because there was no Japanese competition. Today, the Big Three automakers' quality control is about where the Japanese automakers' was in the mid-'80s. Where the gap hasn't narrowed (and a case can be made that it has actually gotten wider) is in powertrain reliability and fit and finish.

In spite of the persistent quality shortcomings noted above that will likely afflict many of the year 2000 models from Ford, Chrysler, and GM, this is, nevertheless, a good time to take the plunge and buy a new car or minivan. Stable European and Asian currencies and GM's desperate efforts to gain back market share by offering substantial rebates will likely keep prices relatively low throughout 2000. Shoppers can also expect to see a few all-new 2000 models that show considerable promise, and a lineup of carried-over 1999 models with more standard convenience and safety features. For example, all 1999 vehicles must be equipped with similar standard safety features, depowered airbags are used more extensively, child safety seat tethers have been made more user-friendly, and overall crashworthiness has improved. All these factors mean that buyers can purchase a safer, upgraded new car or minivan this year for the same amount or about 2–5 percent more than what a 1999 model would have fetched.

Know what you need (bring your spouse, or Mom or Dad along)

There are about 4,000 vehicle dealerships in Canada, and they all want your money—over $27,000, says the Automotive Industries Association of Canada—for the average new vehicle. Before paying these big bucks, you should know what your real needs are and how much you can afford to spend. Don't confuse needs with styling (Do you transport the neighbourhood hockey team? Do you take long holiday trips?) or the trendy with the essential (Can you *really* fit into a Miata? Are you serious about 4X4 off-roading? Will you be towing a trailer?). Visiting the showroom with your spouse, a relative, or a friend will help you steer a truer course among all the non-essential options you'll be offered. Most sales agents admit that women shoppers are far more knowledgeable about what they want and more patient in negotiating the contract's details than males, who tend to be mesmerized by many of the techno-toys available and often skip over the fine print.

Only $599 a month! But did you spot the $475 "administration fee" and $895 "transportation and preparation" charge? Shame on you, BMW!

Most car buyers don't have a clue what they really want, and automakers are cashing in on their confusion by stuffing their cars and minivans with enough extra equipment to overwhelm most mortals— all in order to squeeze as many dollars as possible out of every sale. The automakers load their vehicles up with costly, complicated mechanical and electronic components that compromise the vehicles' original simplicity and easy repairability. Or, buyers are forced to purchase vehicles that are over-engineered for their driving requirements, or equipped with expensive options needed only for hauling heavy cargo or extended driving vacations. Don't fall for the dealer's "must have" song and dance. Instead, ask yourself the following questions about the kind of vehicle you want and at what price.

What can I afford?
Determine how much money you can spend and then decide on what vehicles interest you in that price range. Have several models in mind so that you won't be tempted by one that may be overpriced. Use as

your benchmark the ratings, alternative models, estimated purchase cost, and residual value figures shown in Part Three. Remember, logic and prudence are the first casualties of showroom hype, so carefully consider your actual requirements and how much you can budget to meet them before comparing models and prices at a dealership. Write down your first, second, and third choices relative to each model and the equipment offered. Call the dealership and ask for an appointment to be assured of getting a sales agent's complete attention.

Car ownership is astoundingly expensive and is directly affected by the choice of vehicle and where you live. Among 1999 models, the Saturn, Ford Escort, and Chevy Cavalier cost less than half as much to own and operate on an annual basis than either the Lincoln Town Car or the Cadillac DeVille, and less than one-third than the Mercedes 320S, according to the latest analysis by Runzheimer Canada, the Toronto-based management consulting firm. In an analysis of 14 cars and 9 light trucks, vans, and sport-utility vehicles, the Cavalier shows annual operating or running costs of $3,040 and annual fixed or ownership costs of $7,029, for total annual costs of just over $10,000. The Escort and Saturn are also just over $10,000 in total costs. The Lincoln Town Car Executive and Cadillac DeVille luxury sedans show annual operating costs of $3,664 and $4,320, respectively, and annual fixed costs of $18,084 and $16,766, for total annual costs of more than $21,000 each. Annual costs for the Mercedes 320S are $38,532 (see table on the following page). Other relatively expensive vehicles in the analysis include the Mercury Grand Marquis and Buick LeSabre Ltd., with annual costs exceeding $14,000. At the other end of the scale, cars with annual costs in the $11,000 range include the Chevy Lumina, Toyota Camry, and Honda Accord. Operating costs include fuel, oil, tires, and maintenance. Fixed costs include insurance, depreciation, financing, taxes, and licensing.

"When you examine which car to buy," notes Ann Rayner, a consultant at Runzheimer Canada Inc., "it is not enough to compare only retail prices or even the best negotiated deals. To gain a true understanding of how much it will cost over the life of the vehicle, all the expenses you incur once you drive off the lot, such as finance payments, insurance, fuel efficiency, annual depreciation and the cost of repairs and maintenance, should be part of your equation."

Make & Model	Cylinder	Projected Ownership and Operating Costs for Selected 1999 Cars			
		(Litres) Displace	Annual Costs Operating	Fixed	Total
Mercedes 320S	8	5.0	$4,400	$34,182	$38,532
Lincoln Town Car Exec.	8	4.6	3,664	18,084	21,748
Cadillac DeVille	8	4.6	4,320	16,766	21,086
Mercury Grand Marquis GS	8	4.6	3,632	11,686	15,318
Buick LaSabre Ltd.	6	3.8	3,776	10,881	14,657
Nissan Maxima GXE	6	3.0	3,152	10,749	13,901
Chrysler Intrepid	6	2.7	3,248	9,775	13,023
Ford Taurus SE	6	3.0	3,424	9,131	12,555
Chevrolet Lumina	6	3.1	3,424	8,387	11,811
Honda Accord LX	4	2.2	2,992	8,540	11,532
Toyota Camry CE	4	2.2	2,960	8,253	11,213
Saturn SL2	4	1.9	2,928	7,361	10,289
Ford Escort LX	4	2.0	2,865	7,205	10,070
Chevrolet Cavalier LS	4	2.2	3,040	7,029	10,069

All four-door vehicles similarly equipped including auto transmission, power steering, power disc brakes, air conditioning, tinted glass, AM/FM stereo, body side moldings, speed control, left-hand remote control mirror, rear window defogger, pulse windshield wipers, anti-lock brakes, driver & passenger airbags and tilt steering.

Costs include operating expenses (fuel, oil, maintenance & tires), fixed expenses (insurance, depreciation, financing, taxes and licensing) and are based on a 36-month/ 96,000 kilometre retention cycle.

All values expressed in Canadian dollars.

Among Canada's major cities, Montreal and St. John's are the most expensive places to own and operate a typical 1999 mid-sized vehicle, with yearly costs exceeding $9,000, says a 1999 study done by Runzheimer Canada Inc. Driving a typical mid-sized car (represented by a Ford Taurus four-door sedan) in the Montreal area costs the owner $9,874 per year, with St. John's close behind at $9,840 (see the table on the following page).

Expenses include operating costs and fixed (or ownership) costs. In sharp contrast, driving this same vehicle in Winnipeg, Regina, or Edmonton costs the owner only slightly over $8,000.

The high-cost cities share one common liability—high auto insurance rates. For example, Toronto rates for liability, comprehensive, and collision insurance ("business use" classification, principal operator over age 25, clean driving record) are nearly $1,900 annually, and Montreal rates are about $1,750.

Runzheimer Canada Analyzes Costs for Mid-Size 1999 Vehicle	
Location	**Total Annual Costs**
Montreal, PQ	C$9,874
St. John's, NF	9,840
Toronto, ON	9,655
Halifax, NS	9,293
Ottawa, ON	8,863
Moncton, NB	8,842
Vancouver, BC	8,563
Charlottetown, PE	8,558
Regina, SK	8,333
Edmonton, AB	8,278
Winnipeg, MB	8,198

The costs above are based on a 1999 Ford Taurus SE 3.0 litre, 6-cylinder, 4-door sedan equipped with automatic transmission with overdrive, power steering, power disc brakes, tinted glass, AM-FM stereo, speed control, air conditioning, engine block heater, heavy-duty battery, driver's air bag, and anti-lock brakes. Costs include operating costs: fuel, oil, tires, and maintenance; and fixed costs: insurance, depreciation, taxes, and licence fees. Factors are based on 4-year/96,000 kilometre retention cycle. Vehicles are driven within an 80-kilometre radius of the city. All costs are shown in Canadian dollars.

Natural Resources Canada says that the difference between a vehicle burning 13L of fuel every 100 km and one burning 10L per 100 km is about $1,200 over five years of ownership, given current gas prices and average driving performance.

Will it suit my driving requirements?

In the city, a small wagon is more practical and less expensive than a minivan. However, if you're going to be doing a lot of highway driving, transporting small groups of people (especially kids), and loading up on accessories, a medium-sized wagon or a minivan like the Toyota Sienna could be the more logical choice, considering price, comfort, and reliability. You need an extended minivan or van only if you have to carry at least seven occupants, haul supplies, or get a better view of the road.

Most families who travel less than 20,000 km per year should avoid the smallest and largest engines available with a given model. Less driving will be accommodated by a smaller engine that offers both economy and performance; more than 20,000 km of driving per year demands the cruising performance, extra power for additional accessories, and durability of a larger engine (a 6-cylinder, perhaps). If you spend lots of time on the road or plan on buying a minivan or van, you'll definitely need a large 6- or 8-cylinder powerplant to handle the AC and other power-hungry accessories essential to your driving comfort and convenience. Believe me, fuel savings will be the last thing on your mind if you buy an underpowered car or van.

What about short-term and long-term comfort?

The advantages of many sports cars and vans quickly pale in direct proportion to your tolerance for a harsh ride, noise, a claustrophobic interior, and limited visibility. Minivan and van owners often have to deal with a high step-up, a cold interior, lots of buffeting from wind and passing trucks, and limited rear visibility. With these drawbacks, many buyers find that after falling in love with the showroom image, they end up hating their purchase—all the more reason to test-drive your choice over a period of several days to get a real feel for its positive and negative characteristics. Each year I get dozens of complaints from owners who didn't test-drive their choice sufficiently and must trade in their almost-new vehicle because the seats are torture after a half-hour commute, or the headlights are too dim for night driving.

Does it respond to my special needs?

Auto designers have been more preoccupied with putting cupholders in their minivans, for example, than designing them to be safer, more convenient to use, and more comfortable for women, families, and an aging population.

A survey of 2,400 women by *Chatelaine* magazine concluded that 77 percent play a role in car buying, and 52 percent feel that manufacturers don't adequately consider women's needs in designing vehicles. For example, some women remarked that if men wore skirts it's doubtful that minivans and vans would have such a high step, and if more men hauled their children around it's likely that standard seats would more easily accommodate child safety seats.

Will I have to change my driving habits?

Front-drive braking is quite different from braking with a rear drive, and braking efficiency on ABS-equipped vehicles is compromised if you pump the brakes. Also, rear-drive minivans and vans handle like trucks, and will scrub the right rear tire during sharp right-hand turns until you get the hang of making wider turns.

What safety features do I want?

Anti-lock brakes and airbags have proven to be of limited effectiveness in certain kinds of accidents, and downright deadly for inexperienced drivers or occupants who aren't of ideal stature (yes, even the new depowered airbags have been fatal). If you're of small size, a senior, likely to carry someone small in the front seat, or have recently had upper torso surgery, airbags may pose a serious safety hazard. Since you can't buy a new car or minivan without a driver-side airbag, you'll want to choose a vehicle with an adjustable seat that can travel far enough backwards to keep you at a safe distance (about a foot) from the airbag's explosive 300 km/h deployment. (Some models come equipped with "Second Generation" airbags, which will deploy with a third less force.) Children's safety can be assured by getting a vehicle with an airbag shut-off switch, or by having them sit in the rear middle seat position.

One safety feature that continues to be a lifesaver is a high crash-protection rating. Since some vehicles are more crashworthy than others, and size doesn't always guarantee crash safety, it's important to buy

Don't be a dummy; sit at least a foot away from the airbag and make sure the tilt steering feature doesn't aim the bag at your head.

the vehicle that gives you the best protection from a frontal collision. For example, the Chrysler Caravan and Ford Windstar minivans are similarly designed, but your chances of surviving a high-speed collision with the Windstar are far greater than if you were riding in a Caravan or any other Chrysler minivan. Furthermore, the latest redesigns don't translate into the safest redesigns, judging by the abysmal crash ratings given to GM's new Venture minivan by the Insurance Institute for Highway Safety (IIHS).

Furthermore, be wary of all of the five-star crash-rating hoopla being raised by Ford and Toyota. There isn't any one vehicle that can claim a prize for being safest. Vehicles that do well in the side and front crash tests done by the National Highway Traffic Safety Administration (NHTSA) may not do very well in the IIHS off-set crash test, or may have poorly designed head restraints that would increase the severity of neck injuries. Or a vehicle may have a high number of airbag failures that cause the bags to deploy when they shouldn't—or not deploy when they should.

Before making a final decision on the vehicle you want, look up its crash rating in Part Three and compare that rating with the ratings of similar vehicles.

Is new better than used?
Probably not if you're buying a rapidly depreciating car. Plus, you may be stuck with a vehicle that has no Canadian track record, an uncertain future, and a weak dealer network making for problematic servicing and warranty support. I'd put Daewoo and Kia, Canada's newest South Korean auto importers, in this category.

You can't lose money, however, if you buy a new minivan, van, pick-up, or sport-utility, which depreciate less rapidly than passenger cars. For example, depreciation will knock off less than one-third of your new minivan's value during the first three years of ownership, whereas the average new car will be worth only half its original value over the same period. Even Lada's much maligned Nivea 4X4 depreciates no faster than the average passenger car. Nevertheless, there is an easy way to reduce the depreciation "bite" on a new car: keep it five years or longer and choose a model that is predicted to last that long without requiring expensive repairs.

Daewoo's vehicles, like the Leganza, shown above, are reasonably priced and well equipped. Nevertheless, they are risky buys during their first year in Canada.

Kia's Sephia, shown above, has been on the American market since 1994 and has weathered Kia bankruptcy (it was bought by Hyundai) and an overall "below par" rating by Consumer Reports.

Keep in mind that you begin to save money from the outset when purchasing any used vehicle—whether you keep it a few months or a few years. Once you add federal and provincial taxes, financing costs, maintenance, and a host of other expenses, you'll find that the yearly outlay for a new car is about twice that of a used car.

Can I get the same vehicle for less, elsewhere?
Sure. You can shop on-line and use one dealer's quotes as leverage to get a better deal elsewhere (Hyundai dealers have quoted lower prices to

cybershoppers than to walk-ins, and I expect Daewoo may attempt the same thing). On the other hand, sometimes a cheaper twin or hybrid model will fit the bill. Twins are those nameplates that are virtually identical in body design and mechanical components, like the Ford Sable/Taurus, GM Camaro/Firebird, and the Chrysler Caravan/Voyager.

If a Ford Taurus, shown above, costs too much, try a Mercury Sable; both vehicles are practically identical, although the Sable is being phased out this year in Canada along with the Mercury nameplate.

Perhaps a hybrid or "captive import" will be more to your, and your pocketbook's, liking. American manufacturers have learned to join the Asian automakers instead of competing against them, and vice versa. This has resulted in hybrids whose parentage is impossible to nail down, but which incorporate a high degree of quality control. Suzuki builds the Chevrolet (formerly known as Geo) Tracker 4X4 in Ontario; Mazda and Ford churn out Probes in the U.S.; and Ford's Villager/Quest minivan is a Nissan co-venture.

Sometimes choosing a higher trimline will cost you less when all the standard features are accounted for. (General Motors '"special edition" vehicles, for example, could give you all the options you need for much less than if you ordered them separately on a cheaper model.) It's hard to compare value prices with the manufacturer's base price, though, because the base prices are inflated and can be negotiated downward, while cars that are value priced are offered as a "take it or leave it" proposition.

Twins and hybrids are only two of the many money-saving options available. Minivans, for example, come in two versions: a base commercial version and a more luxurious model for private use. The commercial version doesn't have as many bells and whistles, but it's more likely to be in stock and will probably cost much less. And if you're planning to convert it, all the extras may just get in the way.

Leasing is an alternative often used to make vehicles appear to be more affordable, but it's more expensive than buying, and for most people the pitfalls will far outweigh any advantages. Jim Davidson of Car Smart, a Toronto company that helps people lease new cars, says leasing has grown to 50 percent of total new vehicle transactions in Canada, but feels it's suitable for only 20 percent of drivers. If you have to lease, keep your losses to a minimum by leasing only for the shortest time possible, and by making sure that the lease is closed-ended (meaning that you walk away from the vehicle when the lease period ends).

If long-term leasing looks too expensive, consider purchasing a three- to five-year-old vehicle with 60,000–100,000 km on the clock and some of the original warranty left. Such a vehicle is likely to be just as reliable for less than half the cost of one bought new. Parts will be easier to find, independent servicing should be a breeze, insurance premiums will come down from the stratosphere—and if you get a lemon, your financial risk will be lessened considerably.

Hidden costs

There are a lot of hidden costs in owning a new car or minivan. Automotive magazines don't provide many details about these costs because they don't want to anger their industry sponsors or undercut new-car sales by directing buyers to used cars. Car columnists in particular don't want to offend the manufacturers who supply them with free test cars. This is why most of the motoring press ignore crashworthiness, parts costs and availability, warranty complaints, and depreciation in their new-car ratings. Yet this is precisely the information that most buyers want. Fortunately, there are some exceptions, such as *AutoWeek,* a spinoff of the fiercely independent *Automotive News; Mechanics Illustrated* and its quarterly spinoff *CarSmart,* which have always taken an independent line; and *Consumer Reports,* which spurns paid advertisements.

Don't be taken in by gas mileage figures trumpeted by the manufacturers, either. They're exaggerated by about 10 percent because vehicles are run under optimum conditions by automakers who submit their test results to the government. Sure, good fuel economy is important, but it's hardly worth a harsh ride, highway noise, sidewind buffeting, anemic acceleration, and a cramped interior. You may end up with much worse gas mileage than advertised—as well as a vehicle that's underpowered for your needs.

Tax advantages

Tax rules for cars and minivans are very complex. Nevertheless, whether you have a full-time job or are self-employed, there's a good chance that you can deduct some of your transportation expenses on your income tax return. It all hinges on the quality of your record-keeping—*not* whether you buy or lease, as some salespeople would lead you to believe. If the dealer promises you tax savings with a particular purchase, ask that the amount be included in your contract and verify it with an accountant.

"New" isn't always new

Sorry to burst your bubble, but it's quite probable that the vehicle you bought isn't really new. The odometer may have been disconnected and the vehicle could have been involved in an accident, as was the case with Chrysler cars sold in the late 1980s. Chrysler admitted to disconnecting the odometers on more than 60,000 vehicles. Some of these had been involved in serious accidents, and were repaired and sold as new to unsuspecting Canadian and American buyers. Or, the dealer may have disconnected the odometer and driven the car for several thousand kilometres as a demonstrator. And even if the vehicle hasn't been used it may have been left outdoors for a considerable length of time, causing the deterioration of rubber components; rusting of internal mechanical parts, which leads to brake malfunction and fuel line contamination (hard starting, stalling); and premature body and chassis rusting.

You can check a vehicle's age by consulting the date of manufacture plate found on the driver's side door pillar. If the date of manufacture is 7/99, your car was one of the last 1999 models made before the September changeover to the 2000 models. Exceptions to this rule are those vehicles that are redesigned or new to the market, arriving at dealerships in early spring or mid-summer. They're considered to be next year's models, but depreciate more quickly owing to their earlier launching (a difference that narrows over time).

There's also the very real possibility that the new vehicle you've just purchased was damaged while being shipped to the dealer, and was fixed by the dealer during the pre-delivery inspection. It's estimated that this happens to about 10 percent of all new vehicles. There's no specific Canadian legislation allowing buyers of vehicles damaged in transit to cancel their contracts. However, in a more general sense, Canadian common-law jurisprudence does allow for cancellation or compensation whenever the delivered product differs markedly from what the buyer expected to receive.

Carryovers from previous years generally have fewer problems than vehicles that have been significantly reworked or just introduced to the market. This fact is borne out by a J.D. Power study of 74 vehicle launches from 1989–96, which showed that the Big Three's relaunched models had an 8 percent decline in quality, which turned around to a 19 percent quality improvement in the second year. Among Japanese automakers, Honda, Toyota, and Nissan posted an average 17 percent decline in their first-year offerings, although this decline was wiped out by an average 19 percent improvement in the next year.

Most vehicles assembled between September and February are called "first series" cars because they were the first off the assembly line for that model year. "Second series" vehicles, made between March and August, incorporate more assembly-line fixes and are built better than the earlier models, which depend on ineffective "field fixes" that may only mask the symptoms until the warranty expires. Both vehicles will sell for the same price, but the post-February one will be a far better buy since it benefits from assembly-line upgrades and rebates.

This is particularly true of GM's entire '99 model production, which was delayed several months in the fall of '98 during its model-year changeover due to strike action. Not only did first-series vehicle quality suffer due to the changeover, but the ensuing rushed production forced dealers to repair assembly-line goofs and replace substandard parts from suppliers who weren't "validated" through GM's quality control cycle.

Who Can You Trust?

Car columnists: hear no evil, see no evil

I still find it hard to accept the passivity of Canadian automotive journalists, who by and large have been bought by the Canadian automobile industry through trips and trinkets—or cowed by their editors and producers into believing that their job hinges on how well they kiss advertisers' butts. Unlike the American press, which boasts a number of principled investigative auto writers, few members of the Canadian automotive press will stand up for their constituents. To do so would mean exposing such truths as the outrageously high cost of auto ownership; unsafe safety features like airbags and anti-lock brakes that are poorly designed, prone to malfunction, and capable of killing or maiming drivers or passengers; and national dealer/automaker sales scams, such as leasing, which annually bilk millions out of motorists' pockets. Their silence adds to their complicity.

If you're still not convinced, go ahead and try to decipher the fine print in most newspapers' leasing ads, or better yet, tell me what the fine print scrolled after a national television ad really says. It's probably something to the effect that "everything said or shown before in this ad may or may not be true."

Although car columnists claim that their integrity is not for sale, there's no doubt that it can be rented. Travel junkets, public relations, and advertising contracts all sweeten the honey pot for these pseudo-journalists. A few years ago, CTV's *W5* newsmagazine show ran an exposé on Canadian car columnists and broadcasters ripping off automakers by demanding $3,000 in corporate membership fees to join their Automobile Journalists Association. (Individual memberships cost $100 at the time.) Following the CTV broadcast, the *Toronto Star* required its columnists to indicate in a footnote to their articles, when applicable, that their information came from a travel junket, or that a manufacturer-supplied vehicle was used. General Motors of Canada pulled out of the Association's "Car of the Year" competition held shortly after the broadcast, but has since returned.

The *Toronto Star* also declared that henceforth its columnists would have to indicate in a footnote to their articles if their information came from a travel junket, or if a manufacturer-supplied vehicle was used. Interestingly, although the CBC and the *Globe and Mail* don't accept automaker junkets or free loaners, these not-so-pristine news organs do hire freelance automotive writers, who take the wheels and meals in their own name.

'Forget Paris,' GM Tells Journalists; Instead, They Get to Visit Detroit

By ROBERT L. SIMISON
Staff Reporter of THE WALL STREET JOURNAL

DETROIT—The fallout from the recent strike at General Motors Corp. included a surprise victim: Cadillac's press junket to the Paris auto show next month.

To generate ink back home about their latest new cars and trucks, the Big Three auto makers routinely host expense-paid trips for U.S. journalists to foreign auto shows—most often in Paris, Frankfurt, Geneva and Tokyo. (Some news organizations, including this one, reimburse their reporters' hosts.)

So it was hardly surprising that GM's luxury division invited a score of auto writers and business reporters to join its executives on a five-day Paris fling in late September. After all, Cadillac is trying to position itself as GM's global luxury marque.

But two weeks after the invitations went out, GM management decreed deep cuts in all discretionary spending.

Cadillac won't say how much it had budgeted for plane fare, hotel rooms, meals, wine and its special briefings, but Detroit public-relations veterans say the tab would hit $10,000 to $12,000 per journalist pretty quickly.

All at once, what had seemed like a good idea started to look fiscally irresponsible, says J. Christopher Preuss, Cadillac communications director. Cadillac decided its Paris activities could wait until January and the at-home Detroit auto show. The invitees who had accepted were quietly informed that because of the strike, the trip was off. "It's embarrassing," Mr. Preuss says.

GM cancelled its press junket to Paris for a score of auto writers during the UAW/CAW strike because the company felt it would look "fiscally irresponsible." In doing so, the automaker saved $10,000 to $12,000 per journalist earmarked for the planned five-day stay.

Nevertheless, there are some Canadian auto writers who have distinguished themselves by writing balanced investigative reports on the auto industry. Interestingly, most of them are women, and most hail from Toronto. John Terauds, the *Toronto Star* "Wheels" editor, writes in-depth profiles of the auto industry using a variety of consumer-based resources. Although he's been called on the carpet repeatedly for his jaundiced eye for industry pap and for denouncing dealer sales scams, he's made the "Wheels" section more consumer-friendly, and still kept his job (keep your fingers crossed). *Toronto Star* business columnist Ellen Roseman is also particularly thorough in unearthing stories often missed by others. Denyse O'Leary is a dedicated Toronto-based freelance journalist who's quite resistant to government and corporate BS; she recently dug in her heels when the Ministry of Transport stonewalled her research into the dangers of airbags. There's Maryanna Lewyckyj, a *Toronto Sun* consumer columnist who has taken advanced auto repair classes and won't take any guff from incompetent or evasive automaker PR staffers. They liken being called by her as somewhat akin to a visit to the dentist. And finally, there is Gillian Shaw, a business and consumer reporter for the *Vancouver Province.* She single-handedly forced Chrysler Canada to restructure its customer relations unit and admit its products were defective a few years back by insisting upon answers to her readers' transmission and paint delamination complaints. The Chrysler

Lemon Owners Group (CLOG) in B.C. would never have been so successful if it weren't for Shaw's persistent inquiries.

Unreliable ratings

Once you've established a budget and selected some vehicles that interest you, the next step is to ascertain which ones are rated as reliable and safe. Be wary of the ratings found in some enthusiast magazines; their supposedly independent tests are a lot of baloney. Their test car is supplied by the manufacturer and tuned to just the right specifications. Of course, servicing will be impeccable. Finally, the manufacturer will probably load the car with an assortment of expensive options to compensate for any design faults.

Automakers can't lose with this rigged test. And if the tester wants other free courtesy cars to drive, the published report had better gloss over the vehicle's defects and hype its mediocre features. Also, if the magazine or newspaper receives advertising from the manufacturer, any criticism that gets through the driver's own self-censorship will be muted by the editor. Another very important reason for discounting these tests is that they don't predict a car's vulnerability to rust, poor servicing, crash forces, or inadequate parts distribution.

Take the *Windsor Star*'s strange, unnecessary, and exaggerated apology to car dealers a few years back, made by that paper's publisher, James Bruce. Bruce ran a three-column apology to Windsor-area car dealers for having run a Canadian Press story criticizing Montreal car dealers (that's right, *Montreal* car dealers). The story, based on a survey done by APA president George Iny, questioned the honesty of nine auto dealerships that were surveyed in Montreal. Bruce felt that the story might reflect badly on local dealers and insisted that the following apology be run.

Story Failed to Meet *Star's* Standards

"On rare occasions a story finds its way into the newspaper which does not meet the high ethical and journalistic standards of balance, fairness and factual accuracy which we set for ourselves at the *Windsor Star*... Although the story did not involve any Essex County dealers, it may have by implication, cast aspersions on their business practices. The story was a discredit to the dealers and employees of members of the Windsor Essex County Dealers Association, who adhere to the highest of ethical standards and provide their customers with first rate standards of service...."

As mentioned earlier, don't look to the automakers or their dealers for helpful information relating to the crashworthiness of the vehicles they manufacture and sell. At Toronto's International Auto Show held in February 1995, Richard Martin, a TVOntario field producer, asked automaker representatives how well their vehicles fared in their own or government-run crash tests. With camera crew in tow, he was rebuffed by a half-dozen automakers who said crash information was unavailable or was given out only by head office. Even after calling each company's head office, no crash data was given out. Surprisingly, Volvo and Saturn, two automakers who claim to put their owners' interests and safety first, refused to provide the requested crash test information.

Handling information overload

Funny, as soon as they hear that you're shopping for a new car, everybody wants to tell you what to buy—relatives, co-workers, and friends all think they know what's best for you. After a while you'll get so many conflicting opinions that it'll seem as if any choice you make will be the wrong one. Before making your decision, remember that you should invest a month of research in your $26,000-plus new-car buying project. This includes two weeks for basic research (see below) and another two weeks to actually bargain with dealers to get the right price and equipment. The following sources provide a variety of useful information that will help you ferret out what vehicle best suits your needs and budget.

"Web" shopping

Anyone with access to a computer and a modem can now obtain useful information relating to the auto industry in a matter of minutes and at little cost. This can be accomplished in two ways: by subscribing to one of the two main American on-line services that offer everything from consumer forums to easy Internet access; or by going directly to the Internet through a low-cost Canadian "server" (service provider) and cruising the thousands of sites that interactively summarize the subject matter that's covered or the services offered.

New-car shopping through automaker and independent websites is a quick and easy way to compare prices and model specifications. In fact, buyers now have access to information they once were routinely denied or had trouble finding, such as manufacturers' suggested retail prices, invoice prices, promotional offers, rebates, the book value for trade-ins, and safety data. American shoppers can access invoice data on-line by surfing the Kelly and Edmunds websites, while Canadian shoppers can contact the Automobile Protection Association by phone or fax.

There are other advantages to on-line shopping. Some manufacturers offer a lower price to on-line shoppers (Hyundai, several years ago, Daewoo, expected this year); the entire transaction, including financing can all be done on the net; and, finally, buyers don't have to haggle, but merely post their best offer electronically to a number of dealers in their area code (for more convenient servicing of the vehicle) and await counteroffers. One caveat: As far as bargains are concerned, *Consumer Reports* says its test shoppers found that lower prices are more frequently obtained by personally visiting the dealer showroom and concluding the sale there.

On-line services

If you're new to cruising the Internet, try the two major American on-line services accessible to Canadians—America Online and its affiliated company, CompuServe. Except for minor differences in the way fees are collected, the services are similar.

After only a few days, you will acquire the skills needed to access the Internet on your own, browse the various consumer-advocacy message areas (called forums) and shop the hundreds of auto-related services that simplify buying and owning a car. With the click of a button you can cruise forums; download (transfer data from a host computer via an electronic link) government auto safety defect probes, recall campaigns, and crashworthiness ratings; and find out what dealer incentives and customer rebates are being paid out by automakers. Subscribers can also access sites in order to shop for a new vehicle or accessories; read on-line versions of popular American auto magazines, including *Car and Driver* and *Consumer Reports;* and get industry news and reviews. Without a doubt, the liveliest and most informative sites are the forums on cars and consumer rights. Watched over, but not censored, by a volunteer system operator (sysop), members post hundreds of messages each week responding to questions ranging from how to keep cats off your car (use an open box of mothballs) to what the particulars are of GM's secret paint warranty (a Chevrolet dealer's warranty administrator actually gave out all the details).

Internet

After having their hands held by AOL for a few months, many on-line service subscribers jump ship and strike out on their own by switching to an Internet service provider that doesn't have all the razzle-dazzle of AOL and CompuServe, but provides easier, quicker Internet access at more competitive prices.

A server will give you unlimited access to the Internet at an average cost of $25 a month. Most servers provide test accounts so that you can try out the service before signing up. This allows you to check the number of phone lines your service provider has and the accessibility of phone-in technical support.

Local newspapers or computer publications are a good place to comparison shop for servers in your area. Before signing up, though, talk to your local college, university, or library to find out if they offer free Internet connections to outsiders, or if they can put you in touch with a "freenet" system run largely by volunteers.

Surfing the web requires an entry-level computer ($800–$1,000) and software such as Netscape Navigator, along with a "dial-up" program, both of which can be loaded without much trouble. Your service provider (if it's a good one) will have a technical service line you can call for step-by-step help in downloading the software you need. There are also search engines that will list sites on the web according to subject or name. For example, if you want to find sites related to Chrysler cars, a web search using WebCrawler or Alta Vista will come up with hundreds of sites.

The first website you should access is *www.lemonaidcars.com*, the official site for the *Lemon-Aid* guides. It carries updates and important links to other sites of particular interest to new- and used-car shoppers as well as car owners seeking refunds for factory-related defects.

Consumer Reports vs. CAA's Autopinion

Consumer groups and auto associations are your best bet for the most unbiased auto ratings. They're not perfect, however, so it's a good idea to consult several and look for ratings where they agree. My favourites are *Consumer Reports* and the Canadian Automobile Association's *Autopinion*. Both publications list the Manufacturer's Suggested Retail Price (MSRP), not the invoice price; however, Canadian dealers' higher markup isn't shown and most prices have been boosted by the time these magazines hit the newsstands.

Consumer Reports is an American publication which has a tenuous affiliation with the Consumers Association of Canada. Its ratings, extrapolated from Consumers Union's annual U.S. member survey, accurately mirror the Canadian experience. There are two exceptions, however. Components that are particularly vulnerable to our harsh climate usually perform less well than the *CR* reliability ratings indicate; and poor servicing caused by a weak dealer body in Canada can make some service-dependent vehicles a nightmare to own in Canada, whereas the American experience may have been benign.

Based on 600,000-plus American and Canadian member responses, *CR* lists vehicles that are better or worse than average if owner reports vary from the industry average. Statisticians agree that *CR*'s sampling method has some room for error, but the ratings are good, conservative guidelines for buying a new vehicle that hasn't changed much from year to year, and the ratings have stood up to court challenges from automakers. My only criticism is that many models—like Lada and Jaguar—are excluded from *CR*'s ratings, and its frequency-of-repair ratings for certain components aren't specific enough (a failing of CAA ratings, as well). For example, don't just tell me there are problems with the fuel, or the electrical system. Rather, let me know about specific components—is it the fuel pumps that are failure-prone, or the injectors that clog up, or the battery that suddenly dies?

Consumer Reports *and the CAA's* Autopinion *are two excellent sources for consumer information on the best and worst car buys.*

There's also the Canadian Automobile Association's *Autopinion* magazine (published every January), available from the CAA and newsstands for $6. Kind of like CARP (Canadian Association of Retired Persons) on wheels, CAA is an efficient, competent organization that has reluctantly stuck its big toe into the hot water of consumer advocacy, mostly through promoting auto safety. The group spends much of its time starting and towing cars, selling vacations and preparing trip maps, and decrying gasoline taxes. Much like Canada's Better Business Bureaus, whose noble intentions were compromised early on by a mixture of business-led intimidation, the threat of lawsuits, and the withdrawal of financial support, CAA has traditionally treated consumer advocacy with a mixture of fear and benign neglect.

That said, I must add that some provincial CAA-affiliated groups, such as the Alberta Automobile Motorists Association and Quebec's Club d'automobile du Quebec take their consumer advocacy roles quite seriously, and have vigorously defended their members' rights. Too bad they're the exception, not the rule.

Autopinion mostly contains general-interest articles from auto industry toadies, as well as a summary listing of new cars and trucks. Its used vehicle ratings are based on an owner sampling that's less than 5 percent of *Consumer Reports'*, but at least you know they're all from Canadian drivers. *Autopinion* gives you a good general idea of those vehicles that have generated the most problems for CAA members, but its conclusions should be compared with *CR*'s recommendations. In some cases, CAA editors paint too broad a stroke for vehicles and model years that have an insufficient number of responses.

AutoWeek and *Automotive News* are the best trade and special-interest magazines for objective car-buying information. These publications accept automaker and engine "wonder drug" ads, but they remain relatively independent. Canadian Tire's *Autoroute* magazine is jam-packed with helpful do-it-yourself information and used-car tips targeted to Canadian drivers. *Popular Mechanics* is a similar publication for Americans.

Look Before You Lease

Canadians are reluctant to buy new vehicles because they cost too darned much. Instead of doing the right thing—reducing prices—automakers are offering deceptive buy-back leases that hide padded list prices through longer monthly payments. And the tactic is working—leasing has never been more popular, or more lucrative, for dealers and automakers alike.

Leasing costs more

Lessees pay the full manufacturer's suggested retail price on a vehicle loaded with costly options, plus hidden fees and interest charges that wouldn't be included if the vehicle were purchased instead (see chart on page 68 listing the dealer's MSRP markup for cars, minivans, vans, pickups, and sport-utilities). But you can forget about getting clear information that would permit you to compare the costs of leasing and financing, says DesRosiers Automotive Research Inc., a Toronto consulting firm that studies the leasing industry. DesRosiers found that cheaper cars often cost more to lease than some luxury models. This was confirmed by the Canadian Bankers Association (CBA) after it blasted dealers' leasing contracts for charging interest rates as high as 34 percent and called for consumer protection legislation to regulate the industry. In another survey carried out five years ago by *Les Affaires*, a Montreal-based business weekly, mid-range cars and minivans were shown to cost about $3,000 more if leased rather than financed, and luxury cars about $7,000–$9,000 more.

Rob Lo Presti, a Toronto-based consumer advocate and leasing consultant, has campaigned tirelessly for more disclosure in leasing contracts. He says a few provinces have legislation that requires disclosure and limits contract cancellation penalties, but they don't go far enough. This allows leasing agencies to get away with legalized highway robbery through outrageously excessive hidden leasing charges and loan rates that are practically usurious. In fact, Ford Motor Credit Company, the automaker's leasing finance unit, is under investigation for fraud in Florida and Illinois following complaints by consumers who said they were made to pay $300 to more than $1,000 in hidden charges beyond what they owed. Investigators say the practice was prevalent during the past three years and affected about 15 percent of leases that were paid off early—when people bought their leased cars, traded in their leased cars toward a purchase, or lost the vehicle to theft or accident.

Most people don't have the time or patience to do the complex calculations that leasing contracts require. For them, Lo Presti has created

Sure, you get zero freight, PDI, air tax, and licence transfer—as long as you pay full MSRP and accept an annual limit of 18,000 km.

CarCalculator, an easy-to-use program that runs on any computer with Windows 3.1 or 95. It takes the mystery out of leasing, giving you the annual interest rate you are paying, the total cost of the lease, and how it compares to financing—facts guaranteed to frustrate any fast-talking dealer or leasing agent. It costs $40—including shipping and GST, for *Lemon-Aid* readers—from OrangeSoft Corp., P.O. Box 33518, 1277 York Mills Road, North York, Ontario M3A 1Z5. Callers may dial 1-800-647-8693 (toll-free in Canada). OrangeSoft Corp. will also check a lease quote for $20 ($10 for each additional quote). For more info call the 1-800 number or check out their Internet site at *www.carcalculator.com*.

Leasing advantages

Leasing can be worthwhile for people who frequently trade in their cars, since it's more convenient and results in less sales tax. (This advantage is wiped out, however, if you lease for longer than three years or buy back the car at the end of the lease.) In some cases, you may be paying too much if you don't lease, since leasing enables you to drive a new vehicle without tying up a bundle of money that you could otherwise invest or use to pay down more costly debts. Leasing may also offer some tax advantages if your car expenses are deductible from gross income. However, the savings may be minimal. According to the accounting firm of Price Waterhouse, in 99 percent of the cases it examined, there wasn't much difference in the tax liability if the vehicle was bought or leased. Your chief consideration shouldn't be the tax savings, but rather the difference between the implicit interest rate in the lease and the financing charge.

Leasing disadvantages

Leased vehicles are usually overpriced, jam-packed with nonessential options, and accompanied by a hefty upfront fee. A leased vehicle's residual value gives the leasing agent another avenue to rip you off by setting the vehicle's buy-back value at much more than it's likely to be worth. (Check the "Residual Values" section found in Part Three for a realistic buy-back price for the car or minivan you're thinking of leasing.) It's also a smart idea to buy additional "gap" insurance to cover the balance owed on the lease if the vehicle is stolen or written off in an accident, but most lessors charge too much for it (about $200 is fair). In some cases, the leasing company will throw in gap insurance at no extra cost.

Ask the leasing firm what it's prepared to do if the car turns out to be a lemon. Most companies accept that this happens from time to time, and will simply return the car to the manufacturer and get a replacement. But that's not part of the standard agreement, so be sure that such a clause is included in your lease before you sign it.

Here are two other reasons why you may not wish to lease:

• If you drive more than 18,000–20,000 km a year (you may be charged from 6 to 15 cents per extra kilometre over that limit).
• If you always seem to have dents or scrapes on your car and can't be bothered getting regular maintenance. The vehicle's value at the end of the lease period is probably the single most important factor in computing whether leasing is to the driver's advantage or not. Responsible leasing firms allow for reasonable wear and tear on the vehicle during the leasing contract, but rip-off companies count every scratch and you may have to pay a grossly inflated repair bill.

Ford has recently responded to owner and dealer complaints about the definition of "normal" wear and tear with the follwoing memo to dealers, telling them exactly what should be considered "normal" and "excessive" when a leased vehicle is returned.

Ford Defines "Normal" Wear and Tear

Normal Wear and Tear	Excess Wear and Tear
• Dings • Minor dents • Small scratches • Stone chips in the paint finish • Reduced tread on tires	• Broken or missing parts • Dented body panels or trim • Damaged fabric • Cracked or broken glass • Poor-quality repairs • Unsightly alterations • Tire/wheel damage or less than $1/_8$ inch of tread remaining • Mechanical and electrical malfunctions

About 7 percent of consumers who try leasing don't lease again following disputes over "excess wear and tear" charges, says Art Spinella, vice president of CNW Marketing/Research, a Brandon, Oregon, consulting firm. Two years of study by CNW concluded that one in five leased vehicles were charged an average of $1,647 (U.S.) for excess wear. Mercedes-Benz Credit Corp, the leasing arm of DaimlerChrysler in the States, uses a "credit card test" to determine if charges apply: if the interior or exterior stain, scratch, or blemish can be physically covered by a credit card, there will be no extra charges. In the States, Chase Auto Finance has eliminated large end-of-lease damage charges by waiving excess wear-and-tear costs of up to $1,500 on new leases.

Unfair lease restrictions
Make sure that the lease allows you to service the vehicle yourself at an independent repair facility. A maintenance lease that ties you to the leasing firm's repair shop can lead to outrageous service charges. Use a less expensive independent repair shop for routine servicing, and keep all your receipts to prove that proper maintenance (as required by the manufacturer) was carried out should a warranty dispute arise.

Be wary of unfair restrictions, excessive penalties, and hidden damage charges. Excessive penalty charges for early cancellation of the contract are horrendous and usually require a payout of three to six months' lease payments. Sometimes lessors will put you on a leasing treadmill by waiving the penalty only if another vehicle is leased. Most impose a 20,000 km per year mileage limit and charge a whopping surcharge on the excess. Also, you may be restricted from driving your vehicle outside Canada or lending it to a third party.

The Obscure Language of Leasing

Acquisition fee: Frequently hidden in the body of the contract, this is a $300–$450 extra charge for what is essentially overhead covered in the monthly payment. It's 100 percent profit for the dealer. Save it as the last item to discuss and then refuse to pay it.

Closed-end lease: This lease protects you from a decline in the vehicle's value when the lease expires. Useful with some cars, but a waste of money with slow-depreciating MPVs.

Disposition fee: Another abusive "extra" for preparing the vehicle for resale at the end of the lease. Don't accept this charge.

Early termination penalty: The fee paid by the customer when the lease is broken (see previous comments).

Excess mileage charge: This fee is charged for mileage that exceeds the cap set in the contract. Try to get a cap of 20,000–30,000 km per lease year and a rate that's less than 6 cents per kilometre.

Open-end lease: This lease holds the customer responsible for the difference should a vehicle's value fall below the residual value pre-set when the contract was signed. Not a likely prospect with most sport-utilities, minivans, vans, and pickups that usually depreciate slowly over the years.

Residual value: Think of it as the pre-set trade-in value for a leased vehicle. The lower the residual value, the greater your chance of making money if you purchase the vehicle at the expiration of the lease and then sell it privately a year or two later.

Decoding leasing ads

Take a close look at the small print found in most leasing ads. Pay particular attention to the model year, kind of vehicle (demonstrator or used), equipment, warranty, interest rate, buy-back amount, down payment, security payment, monthly payment, transportation and preparation charges, administration fee ("acquisition" fee), insurance premium, number of free kilometres, and excess kilometre charge.

One final point about leasing. When you take your leased vehicle back at the end of an open lease, and neighbours or relatives have shown interest in buying it, find out how much they're willing to offer and make sure that you get the leasing company or dealer to call them. This could save you thousands of dollars by preventing the leasing agency from making a "lowball" bid and forcing you to make up the difference between the residual value and what the leasing company actually gets for the vehicle. (See "Leasing" jurisprudence in Part Two.)

When and Where to Buy

When to buy

The best time to buy a new car or minivan is in the winter, between January and March, when you get the first series of rebates and dealer incentives, and production quality begins to improve. Try not to buy when there's strike action—it will be especially tough to get a bargain because there's less product to sell and the dealer has to make as much profit as possible on each sale. Furthermore, work stoppages increase the chances that on-line defects will go uncorrected, and the vehicle will be delivered, as is, to product-starved dealers.

Instead, lay low for a while and then return in force in the summer, when you can double dip from additional automakers' dealer incentive and buyer rebate programs, which can average about a thousand dollars each. Remember, too, that vehicles made between March and August offer the most factory upgrades, based on field reports from those unfortunate owners who bought the vehicles when they first came out (fleet managers and rental car agencies fall in this category).

The driver-side doorplate tells you the month and year of manufacture; try to get an upgraded second-series car.

Since dealers have very few customers in the dead of winter, and most buyers are on vacation or moving in the month of August, dealers are anxious to cut prices substantially during these times to keep their inventory and financing costs low. Some automakers cut special deals in December to boost year-end numbers for specific models—as Ford once did with its Sable and Taurus so that it could then proclaim them as outselling Honda's Accord, their closest competitor.

Allow yourself at least two weeks to finalize a deal if you're not trading in your vehicle, and longer if you sell your vehicle privately. Visit the dealer at the end of the month just before closing, when the salesperson will want to make that one last sale to meet the month's quota. If sales have been terrible, the sales manager may be willing to do some extra negotiating.

Where to buy

Good dealers aren't always the ones with the lowest prices. Dealing with someone who gives honest and reliable service is just as important as getting a good price. Check a dealer's honesty and reliability by talking with motorists who drive vehicles purchased from that dealer (identified by the nameplate on the trunk). If these customers have been treated fairly they'll be glad to recommend him. You can also ascertain the quality of new-car preparation and servicing by renting one of the dealer's minivans or pickups for a weekend, or by having him service your trade-in.

How can you tell which dealers are the most honest and competent? Well, judging from the many complaints I receive each year, dealerships in small suburban and rural communities are fairer than big city dealers, because they're more vulnerable to negative word-of-mouth advertising and poor sales. When their vehicles aren't selling, good service takes up the slack. Prices may also be more competitive because overhead is often much lower than in metropolitan areas.

Dealers selling more than one manufacturer's product line presents special problems. Overhead can be quite high, and cancellation of a dual dealership in favour of an exclusive franchise elsewhere is an ever-present threat. Parts availability may also be a problem, because a dealer with two separate car lines must split his inventory, and so may have an inadequate supply on hand.

The quality of new-car service is linked directly to the number and competence of dealerships within the network. If the network is weak, parts are likely to be unavailable, repair costs can go through the roof, and the skill level of the mechanics may be questionable. Among foreign manufacturers, the Japanese automakers have the best overall dealer representation across Canada. The one exception is Mitsubishi, a Japanese automaker represented by Chrysler until a few years ago. Its dealer network is concentrated in the States, but its cars use generic parts that aren't hard to service or find.

European automakers are almost all crowded into Quebec and Ontario, leaving car owners in the Maritimes and western Canada to fend for themselves. This is particularly troublesome, given that most European imports are highly dependent on dealers for parts and servicing.

Dealers offering top-quality repairs are able to keep their commercial fleet customers, so if a dealer has a large volume of commercial work, chances are he's giving good service at a reasonable price.

Patronize dealers that shun "shop supplies" charges and give you the choice of hourly rather than flat-rate time in calculating repair charges. Twenty-four-hour servicing, free loaner cars, and/or a downtown shuttle service make for more convenient servicing. (Make sure the free loaner car is spelled out in the sales contract.)

It's also a good idea to patronize dealerships that are accredited by auto clubs such as the Canadian Automobile Association affiliates, or consumer groups like the Automobile Protection Association (look for the accreditation symbol in their phone book ads, or affixed to the shop window). Auto club accreditation is not an iron-clad guarantee of honest or competent business practices, but if you're cheated or become the victim of poor servicing from one of their recommended garages, you can take your complaint to them to apply additional mediation pressure. As you'll see under "Repairs/Faulty diagnosis" in Part Two, plaintiffs have won in court by pleading that the auto club is legally responsible for the consequences of the recommendations it makes.

Automobile brokers/vehicle buying services
Throughout this book I've tried to give you all the key information you need to get a good deal when buying a new or used vehicle. I understand that this kind of negotiation isn't for everyone, and offer you the following alternative: an auto broker.

Brokers are independent agents who try to find the new or used vehicle you want at a price below what you'd pay at a dealership (including the extra cost of the broker's services). Broker services appeal to buyers who want to save time and money while avoiding most of the stress and hassle associated with the dealership experience, which for many people is like a swim in shark-infested waters.

Brokers get new cars through dealers, while used cars may come from automobile dealers, auctions, private sellers, and leasing companies. Basically, brokers find an appropriate vehicle that meets the client's expressed needs, and then negotiate the purchase (or lease) on behalf of their client. The majority of brokers tend to deal exclusively in new cars, with a small percentage dealing in both new and used vehicles. Ancillary services vary among brokers, and may include such things as comparative vehicle analysis and price research. For example, one Willowdale, Ontario, broker even finds itself battling insurance adjusters to get fair settlements for claimants.

The cost of hiring a broker ranges anywhere from a flat fee of a few hundred dollars to a percentage of the value of the car. Sometimes a car broker may offer his services for a nominal fee, or even tell the buyer that the service is "free." In such cases, it's best to remember that nothing is free in the car business. If the customer isn't paying the fee directly, then the broker's fee is being paid by the dealer, who simply buries that commission in the total price of the car. Ultimately, the customer pays either way. While it's not impossible to get a reasonable deal under such an arrangement, beware that the broker may be unduly biased toward a certain dealer or manufacturer. Reputable brokers are not beholden to any particular dealership or make, and will disclose their flat fee up front or tell the buyer the percentage amount they charge on a specific vehicle.

Finding the right broker
Buyers who are looking for a broker should first ask friends and acquaintances if they can recommend one. Word-of-mouth referrals are often the best, because people won't refer others to a service with which they were dissatisfied. Your local credit union or the regional CAA office are good places to get a broker referral from people who see their work on an everyday basis.

Toronto's Metro Credit Union has recently added a vehicle counselling and purchasing service (Auto Advisory Services Group, comprising CarFacts and AutoBuy) where members can hire an expert "car shopper" who will do the legwork—including the tedious and frustrating dickering with sales staff—and save members time and hassle. This program can also get that new or used vehicle at a reduced (fleet) rate, arrange top-dollar prices for trade-ins, provide independent advice on options like rustproofing and extended warranties, carry out lien searches, and even negotiate the best settlement with insurance agents. The Credit Union also holds regular car-buying seminars throughout the year in the Greater Toronto Area.

Rosemary Edwards, a CarFacts advisor, says Metro's Car Facts program has saved members over $600,000 since its inception. For information on how you can join Metro or start up a similar program with your credit union, contact Rosemary Edwards or David Lawrence at 1-800-777-8506 or 416-252-5621.

Buying clubs: watch out for kickbacks
Be wary of buying clubs or referrals that aren't backed by a national organization. Except for Price Costco, the Internet's Autobytel, and some auto associations, buying clubs that promise huge savings on purchases or claim to get new vehicles at dealer's cost seldom survive close scrutiny. The savings they promote are often illusory at best, because the so-called wholesale or dealer's cost price is usually no different from the regular retail selling price suggested by the manufacturer. Furthermore, many referral agencies make "sweetheart" deals with dealers that send them "under-the-table" kickbacks or predetermined commissions. Whether dealing with the APA, a credit union, or an on-line referral service, find out first if there is a fee received by the agency for giving

out referrals to particular sellers. To its credit, Autobytel is upfront with the fact that it gets a commission from dealers it promotes.

Some credit unions or union buying clubs do a very good job in cutting prices on all vehicles. They use their buying clout in a particular region to exact substantial concessions from local dealers. They generally charge minimal membership fees, and they don't get too "chummy" with the local dealers because they put their members' interests first.

Safety First

How popular are safety features?

Don Esmond, general manager of Toyota's U.S. sales unit, says Toyota market research shows that consumers in the mid-sized family sedan market rank safety features ninth among the top 10 reasons for choosing a car. Minivan buyers apparently place a higher premium on safety, although firm statistics aren't available. That's why you see Ford, Honda, and Toyota touting their five-star ratings in minivan ads.

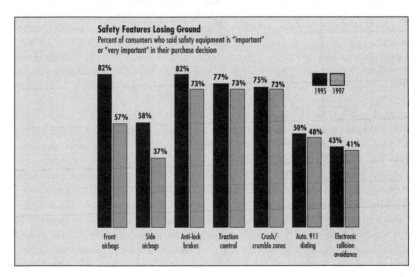

Safety Features Losing Ground
Percent of consumers who said safety equipment is "important" or "very important" in their purchase decision

Safety improvements

Important safety improvements, once found only on luxury vehicles, are working their way down to popular mid-sized family sedans. The 2000 Ford Taurus, for example, will have seatbelt pretensioners, which tighten the seatbelt against the chest. It will also have "thinking" seatbelts that can detect whether a driver has buckled the belt, and can prevent the airbag from deploying in "fender-bender" accidents (or cause it to deploy more slowly in high-speed impacts). The airbags themselves have also been made more benign; they'll come in two parts to protect the head and shoulder area and upper torso area separately. Furthermore, the car's sides have been reinforced to prevent intrusion into the interior, and the

Taurus's armrests have been redesigned to crumple, protecting passengers from possibly severe internal injuries arising from a side-impact.

Canadian and U.S. legislation

Canada's safety legislation is generally a mirror image of U.S. federal regulations, except in the case of recalls. When a recall occurs in Canada, the onus is placed upon automakers to notify owners of a defect, but they do not necessarily have to follow the notice up with a free repair. Canadian regulations are also backwards in another way: they require daylight-running lights, for instance, but don't require airbags or regulate how they should deploy (you won't find an airbag-equipped Lada— hell, you may not find a Lada, anymore, for that matter).

Why not? Here's what Brian Jonah, Transport Canada's director of motor vehicle standards and research, told the *Ottawa Citizen* last year: "We don't dictate the solution when it comes to occupant protection. We don't want to limit a manufacturer's ability to innovate in vehicle design when it comes to protecting passengers." How limp. How Canadian.

If Transport Canada had been on the ball a decade ago, it could have forced automakers to initially make safer airbags. This would have saved over a hundred motorists' lives in North America taken by airbag deployment in fender-bender accidents and reduced the more than 25,000 reports of airbag-induced occupant injuries recorded up to 1991. "We" (read: Canadians) don't dictate, indeed.

Active and passive safety

How safe a vehicle is depends on its active and passive safety features. Active safety components, like radial tires and 4X4 capability, help drivers to avoid accidents. Advocates of active safety stress that accidents are caused by the proverbial "nut behind the wheel" and believe that safe driving courses are the key to fewer accidents.

The theory of active safety has several drawbacks. There is no independent proof that safe driving can be taught successfully. Even if one learns how to master defensive driving techniques, there's still no assurance that this training will be of any use in an emergency situation, where panic reflexes kick in (look at the disappointing ABS findings, discussed in the ABS section below). And what about NHTSA's 1994 study estimating that 41 percent of all fatal accidents are caused by drivers who are under the influence of alcohol or drugs? All the high-performance options and specialized driving courses in the world won't provide much protection for such drivers or their victims.

While professional drivers extol the virtues of active safety features, everyday drivers feel safer with passive safety protection. Passive safety systems, like three-point seatbelts and chassis designed to absorb crash forces and direct them away from a vehicle's occupants, work just as well with skilled and unskilled drivers. Of all the passive safety features one can choose, traction control seems to be the least important because it's so rarely used and its advantages aren't apparent.

Interestingly, anti-lock brake systems (ABS), both an active and passive safety item, have been discredited of late—primarily because drivers use them improperly.

Two accidents per vehicle

According to NHTSA, a new vehicle will be in an average of two accidents from the time it leaves the assembly line (10 percent of all new vehicles sustain some transport damage) to the day it's towed to the junkyard. So crash safety is a major factor that must be taken into consideration when purchasing a new vehicle. NHTSA data show that 51 percent of deaths occur in head-on collisions, 27 percent in side impacts, and barely 4 percent in rear impacts. Rollovers—a frequent occurrence with small sport-utility vehicles—are particularly lethal, especially for occupants who are ejected because they're not wearing their seatbelts. They face a fatality rate 25 times greater than passengers who remain strapped into the vehicle. On the other hand, sport-utilities, trucks, and vans protect passengers better than passenger cars in most collisions.

Traffic safety studies show that women are particularly vulnerable to traffic fatalities and injuries (wait until you read what airbags do to them). The number of women who die behind the wheel has increased 62 percent since 1975, while highway deaths among men are dropping. The reasons given for this difference include the fact that women are driving more, they drive smaller cars, they drive more aggressively, are less tolerant of alcohol than men, and tend to drive on local roads where accident rates are higher. I would also add airbags as a factor.

Secret black boxes

Instead of levelling with government probers, Ford and General Motors have secretly installed "black box" accident data recorders on over six million vehicles sold in North America since 1990. In fact, Canadian motorists were never told that they were, in effect, unwitting test subjects used to amass accident data for American automakers' probing reports of malfunctioning ABS and airbags.

No one will ever know how many litigants lost their cases because the data that could have proven their innocence, or the automakers' negligence, was never divulged by Ford or GM. Nor will anybody be able to calculate the many accident claims paid by rental car companies or provincial insurance corporations for injuries and damages caused by factory-related defects.

The data recorders, known as Sensing and Diagnostic Modules (SDM), are hidden under the front seat of GM and Ford vehicles. It's estimated that GM has installed over six million recorders (mostly in Cadillacs, Corvettes, and Luminas) and Ford has installed several hundred thousand throughout its model lineup. The black boxes, about the size of a VCR, operate in a similar fashion to flight data recorders used in airplanes: they record data during the last five seconds before impact, including the force of the collision, the airbag's performance, when the brakes were applied, engine and vehicle speed, gas pedal position, and whether the driver was wearing a seatbelt.

Apart from the "invasion of privacy" aspect of hiding recorders in customers' vehicles, Ford and GM have systematically hidden their collected data from U.S. and Canadian vehicle safety researchers investigating thousands of complaints relative to airbags that don't deploy when they should (or deploy when they shouldn't), and anti-lock brakes that don't brake.

Anti-lock brake system (ABS)

Anti-lock brakes are impressive on the test track but not on the road. In fact, the Insurance Institute for Highway Safety says that cars with anti-lock brakes are more likely to be in crashes where no other car is involved but a passenger is killed. Insurance claim statistics show that anti-lock brakes aren't producing the overall safety benefits that were predicted by the government and automakers. The latest IIHS study found that a passenger has a 45 percent greater chance of dying in a single-vehicle crash in a car with anti-lock brakes than in the same car with old-style brakes. On wet pavement, where ABS supposedly excels, the chance of being killed increased to 65 percent. In multi-vehicle crashes, ABS-equipped vehicles have a passenger death rate 6 percent higher than vehicles not equipped with ABS.

Essentially, ABS prevents a vehicle's wheels from locking when the brakes are applied in an emergency situation, thus reducing skidding and the loss of directional control. When braking on wet and dry roads, your stopping distance will be about the same as with conventional braking systems. But in gravel, slush, or snow, your stopping distance will be greater.

Automakers have created the impression that cars equipped with ABS will stop on a dime, but they don't fully explain how ABS should be used. For example, many drivers don't know that anti-lock brakes require that they do what driving schools have told them not to do: slam on the brakes in a skid.

The high cost of ABS maintenance is one disadvantage that few safety advocates mention. Consider the following: 1) original equipment parts costs can run five times higher than regular braking components, and 2) many dealers prefer to replace the entire ABS unit rather than troubleshoot its very complex system.

Insurance claims aren't very supportive of assertions that ABS prevents collisions. The Washington-based Highway Loss Data Institute's study of identical vehicles equipped and not equipped with ABS found that the frequency and cost of collision claims were not reduced with ABS. Other studies do show a decrease in crashes, varying between 8 percent (the Markham, Ontario–based Vehicle Information Centre) and 3 percent (General Motors) depending on road conditions. In view of these conflicting studies, insurance companies are backing away from premium reductions for ABS-equipped vehicles.

Transport Canada is concerned about the hype surrounding ABS effectiveness. Its tests indicate that the safety benefits may be compromised by drivers who are less cautious and who tend to drive more aggressively than others. They accelerate more quickly, drive faster, and apply the brakes later than do drivers using vehicles without anti-lock brakes. This contention was confirmed by a paper presented at the 1993 Multidisciplinary Road Safety Conference, which concluded that drivers of vehicles equipped with ABS drove up to 8 km/h faster than people whose cars were not ABS-equipped.

Airbags
I don't trust airbags. Granted they save lives in high-speed collisions, but they also take lives—or leave occupants horribly scarred—in fender-benders. They go off when they shouldn't and don't go off when they should. Depowered and side airbags are also hazardous. I have read the stats and they *are* scary.

True, well-publicized American and Canadian safety studies show convincingly that airbags save lives in high-speed collisions in excess of 39 km/h, but equally thorough, though little-publicized, government-university studies show airbags can maim or kill through inadvertent deployment (1 chance in 30) or in low-speed collisions at speeds as low as 20–39 km/h—particularly if you're a woman, a senior, not of average size, have had upper torso surgery, or use a tilt steering wheel. In fact, the dangers are so great that a recent Transport Canada and George Washington University study of 445 drivers and passengers concludes:

> While the initial findings of this study confirm that belted drivers are afforded added protection against head and facial injury in moderate to severe frontal collisions, the findings also suggest that these benefits are being negated by a high incidence of bag-induced injury…. The incidence of bag-induced injury was greatest among female drivers…. Furthermore, the intervention of the airbag can be expected to introduce a variety of new injury mechanisms such as facial injuries from "bag slap", upper extremity fractures, either directly from the deploying airbag module or from arm flailing, and thermal burns to the face and arms.

**AirBag Deployment Crashes
in Canada**

**Dainius J. Dalmotas
Jean Hurley
Alan German**
Transport Canada
Canada

Kennerly Digges
George Washington University
USA

Preprint

Paper Number 96-S1-O-05

**Fifteenth International Technical Conference
on the Enhanced Safety of Vehicles
Melbourne, Australia,
May 13–16, 1996**

*Don't look for the above study on Transport Canada's website. It's not
there. It can be found, however, in its entirety on the NHTSA website at*
www.nhtsa.dot.gov/esv/16/985007.PDF.

When I accessed the Transport Canada–NHTSA joint study on the
Internet two years ago, I felt a deep sense of betrayal. As I fit together
all the recent accident reports and emergency-room studies, it became
obvious to me that for over two decades engineers, automakers, and
government bureaucrats have lied to us about airbag dangers. Instead
of the promised billowing protective cloud that would gently cushion
us in an accident, we discover that the airbag's 330 km/h deployment
is more like a Mike Tyson right cross. Front airbags have killed 131
people in low-speed collisions or otherwise survivable accidents since
1990. All these deaths came from accidents with speeds as slow as 11 to
12 km/h, and three-quarters of the adults killed were women. Seven of
the first 28 recorded deaths involved 1994–96 Chrysler minivans.

Sexist federal regulations governing automobile airbag design are
the main reason why the safety devices put women, children, and the
aged at risk. The auto industry and government engineers have set federal regulations that aim to protect the average-sized unbelted adult
male in a 57 km/h frontal crash. Meeting that rule requires that the
airbag inflate with sufficient force to kill or seriously injure women,
children, and seniors who don't fit the engineering norm.

A campaign of misinformation

The safety "establishment," composed of government, automakers, and safety advocates, hasn't levelled with the public about airbag dangers inherent in the 60 million airbag-equipped vehicles on North American highways. For example, their admonition that children under the age of 13 should sit in the rear is nonsense, since it's a question of size, not age (a small 18-year-old could be more vulnerable). Actually, no one who is of small stature, child or adult, should sit behind an airbag. The government also has to explain why airbags are of little benefit to seniors 70 and older, and why there have been more than 25,000 injuries resulting from airbag deployment between 1988 and 1991 recorded by NHTSA. There have also been thousands of incidences of airbag malfunctions—causing late deployment or inadvertent deployment— reported to American federal safety regulators, resulting in the recall of 2 million vehicles (1 out of every 38 on the road) since 1993. If the five ongoing investigations also result in recalls, one out of 30 vehicles will be affected.

Most importantly, we have to stop blaming the victims of airbag deployment for sitting too close, not "buckling up," or allowing their children to ride in the front seat. The above-cited Canadian/American airbag study clearly demonstrates that most of the belted drivers and passengers who were injured did nothing to put themselves at risk— except, perhaps, having the wrong gender and a federal ministry of transport that blindly followed Washington's lead.

Federal regulators' efforts to explain away airbag hazards have been a deliberate policy decision: they didn't want to lose their own credibility, alarm the public, or undermine the acceptance of airbags as a supplementary restraint. Well, guess what? The public is more than alarmed; in fact, it's clamouring for retrofitted cut-off switches and looking for new vehicles in which airbags aren't a standard feature. Recent surveys show that the public's confidence in airbags has plummeted following the spate of news stories reporting airbag-induced deaths and injuries.

Despite government and industry promises to the contrary, substantial engineering improvements to airbags won't be built anytime soon. "Smart" airbags won't be generally available until well into the year 2000, and the use of "depowered" airbags will simply reduce fatalities, not eliminate them.

Inadvertent airbag deployment

Airbags frequently go off for no apparent reason due to what Ralph Hoar, a safety adviser to plaintiffs' attorneys, blames on "cheap sensors." Other causes of sudden deployment: passing over a bump in the road in your GM Cavalier or Sunfire, slamming the car door, having wet carpets in your Cadillac or, in some Chrysler minivans, simply putting the key in the ignition. This happens more often than you would imagine, judging by the frequent recalls and thousands of complaints recorded on NHTSA's website at *www.nhtsa.dot.gov/cars/problems/ complain/compmmy1.cfm*. Incidentally, insurers are refusing to pay for car damage or airbag replacements unless there has been a collision. Automakers deny responsibility on the grounds that the vehicle collided with "something." In the end, the driver is faced with a hefty repair bill and no means of proving the automaker's liability.

Airbag deployment—for no apparent reason—is bad enough if the vehicle is parked. However, if it explodes while the vehicle is being driven, it will likely cause an accident and then be of no use during the ensuing impact, as it has already deflated. Says Michael Leshner, a U.S. forensic engineer, "The airbag knocks them silly. Then they have an accident."

Side airbags
Side airbags protect drivers and passengers in side-impact crashes, estimated to account for 30 percent of vehicular deaths. About three-quarters of automakers offer side airbags on some of their models.

NHTSA is concerned that rear side airbag systems offered by Audi, BMW, and Mercedes may be too powerful for rear seat occupants—notably children who must sit in the back to escape the deployment dangers of front seat airbags. Following these findings, BMW has turned off the rear airbags prior to delivery, although it offers owners the option of having them reconnected by the dealer. Side airbags aren't required by federal regulation in the States or in Canada and neither government has developed any tests to measure their safety to children and small adults.

THE WALL STREET JOURNAL FRIDAY, APRIL 9, 1999

Side Air Bags Coming Under Scrutiny For Potential to Hurt Kids in Back Seat

By ANNA WILDE MATHEWS
Staff Reporter of THE WALL STREET JOURNAL
WASHINGTON — Federal regulators have expressed concern that three auto manufacturers' side air bags may deploy with enough force to injure children sitting in the back seat.

The National Highway Traffic Safety Administration believes that, based on test results, side air-bag systems provided by Audi, Mercedes and BMW may be too powerful for the rear seat, where children supposed to sit, according to iar with the matter known to

vices, which are an optional feature, in the rear seats of model year 2000 cars. Buyers will have the choice to turn them back on, the spokesman said. Previously, cars were shipped with the rear side air bags activated, and customers could request that they be turned off.

A spokesman for Mercedes of DaimlerChrysler concerns

Automakers are rushing side airbags into production without fully evaluating their danger to children and small adults. Frankly, I wish manufacturers would prioritize the redesign of head restraints to make them more effective.

Protect yourself

You should take the following steps to lessen the danger from airbag deployment:

- Don't buy a vehicle with side airbags until the federal government comes up with standards.
- Make sure that seatbelts are buckled and all head restraints are properly adjusted (at about ear level).
- Make sure the head restraints are rated "Good" by the Insurance Institute for Highway Safety.
- Insist that passengers who are frail, short, or have recently had surgery sit in the back.
- Make sure that the driver's seat can be adjusted for height and has tracks with sufficient rearward travel to allow short drivers to remain a safe distance away from the bag's deployment and still reach the accelerator and brake. Buy pedal extensions, if needed.
- Have a retrofitted cutoff switch installed by a dealer for your make of vehicle. Be patient: the American government has just sanctioned their use and Canadian dealers and automakers haven't yet worked out the kind of legal waiver that motorists must sign. Canadian federal motor vehicle safety regulations don't require the installation of airbags in motor vehicles. However, because the airbag is an integral part of the vehicle restraint system, provincial statutes in Nova Scotia, P.E.I., New Brunswick, and Alberta make airbag deactivation or removal illegal.
- Buy a vehicle that comes with passenger-side airbag disablers.
- Buy a vehicle that uses sensors to detect the presence of an electronically tagged child safety seat in the passenger seat, and disable the airbag for that seat (already used in the Mercedes SLK).
- If you are short-statured, consider the purchase of aftermarket pedal extensions from auto parts retailers or optional adjustable accelerator and brake pedals from Ford to keep you a safe distance away from a deploying airbag. The pedals are a standard item on some Ford and Chrysler vehicles such as the Dodge Viper and are available from Ford as an optional feature.
- If you feel at risk and live near the American border, you may have your airbag deactivated by an American dealer or independent garage, following factory-approved guidelines (in some cases, it may involve simply removing a fuse). An extensive listing of garages willing to perform this service is available from NHTSA's website found in Appendix I. Cost: about $100 (U.S.). Keep in mind, however, that you may be violating provincial statutes. On the other hand, inspectors can't easily check for compliance, and penalties for deactivation are practically nonexistent.

Childproof locks

Especially important in sport-utility vehicles, minivans, and vans, childproof locks consist of a special control that the driver can trip to prevent the rear doors from being unlocked from the inside while the vehicle is in motion. They offer extra safety and convenience.

Child restraint systems
Every year car accidents in Canada kill almost 70 youngsters under age five and injure another 4,000. The tragedy of this statistic is that parents ignore it; half of the children riding in vehicles still aren't properly secured compared to the 87 percent of adults who wear seatbelts. Seventy percent of these deaths and injuries could have been prevented if children had been properly belted into a safety seat. In recognition of this fact, safety authorities and the courts are cracking down on negligent parents. Provinces with seatbelt laws now require that children, especially infants, travel in an approved safety seat. Drivers who don't protect young passengers may face criminal charges or be held liable for civil damages if a youngster is injured or killed.

Contrary to popular belief, carrying young children on laps in a moving vehicle is not safe. A 9 kg (20 lb.) child will be pulled away with a force of over 270 kg (600 lb.) in a 48 km/h crash. Accident studies show that unrestrained adults can crush their children against the dashboard during a crash. Even in a relatively minor accident or panic stop, a child can be pulled away with surprising force and hit the dashboard or the floor hard enough to be seriously injured or killed.

There are three types of safety seats for children: infant-only carriers for newborns up to about 9 kg (20 lb.) or 69 cm (27 in.) in height; convertible carriers for children from birth up to 18 kg (40 lb.) or 1.02m (40 in.) in height; and booster seats for kids weighing between 18 and 27 kg (40–60 lb.). If you're not sure which seat fits your child's weight and height, check the Transport Canada compliance label affixed to the seat.

There are two sizes of infant carriers—those that are designed only for infants weighing up to 7.9 kg (17 lb.), and others that can handle up to 9 kg (20 lb.). Infant carriers often do double-duty as rockers and baby feeders. The typical carrier is lined with soft padding, has an internal safety harness, and is anchored by the vehicle's safety belt in the rear seat. Extra padding (a rolled-up towel or baby blanket) can be added between the legs or on the sides as long as it's not placed under the harness straps. The baby faces backwards in a semi-reclining position. In an accident, the baby's back absorbs the crash forces rather than its delicate chest and abdomen. These rear-facing infant safety seats should never be used in the front seat of a vehicle equipped with a passenger-side airbag, unless the airbag has a disabler. The force of the airbag inflating is the equivalent of being hit by a vehicle travelling 320 kilometres per hour (200 mph). Put the carrier in the rear outboard seats.

Forward-facing seats are anchored to the vehicle's frame by a tether strap, and they too should always be used in the rear seat. The U.S. Department of Transportation estimates that 80 percent of all child safety seats are improperly secured, so take the extra care needed to make sure that the seat is installed properly. Convertible models are bulky and much less portable than infant seats, but they can be used for a much longer time. Chrysler's built-in child safety seats are an innovative optional safety feature patented by Ontario-based Magna International Ltd., and are now offered by many other automakers. They're convenient to use and may spare you the expense of a convertible or booster seat. Since they can't be faced to the rear, don't use them to carry infants.

A booster seat bridges the gap between a forward-facing seat and the vehicle's standard seatbelt. It consists of a firm cushion that incorporates its own restraining system, which ensures the lap belt doesn't ride up. Instead, the belt fits snugly over the child's lap and the shoulder harness doesn't touch the neck. Remember, booster seats designed for use around the house cannot protect your child in a collision.

Booster seats are needed for children weighing 40–60 pounds, roughly ages four to eight, as they are too big for baby car seats and too small for adult seatbelts. You can discontinue use of the booster seat when the child's height or weight exceeds the compliance label's limits. Safety experts and physicians recommend booster seats be installed in the rear seat, a location considered one-third safer for children. But the problem with this is that if you own a vehicle made before 1988, you won't likely have a rear-seat shoulder belt essential for the proper installation of a booster seat.

Tots that are almost, but not quite, large enough for regular seatbelts may be able to use the "Child Saver," a device that allows adjustment of a three-point seatbelt so that it fits a small child. It sells for under $25 at most auto parts stores.

A variety of child safety seats can be rented from hospitals and provincial safety groups. If you decide to purchase one, be sure to ask the retailer for a registration card. The manufacturer can notify you of a recall that you otherwise might not learn about.

Vehicle size and safety
Insurance Institute for Highway Safety (IIHS) figures show that for every thousand pounds added to a car's mass, driver injury risk is lowered by 34 percent for the unrestrained driver and 25 percent for the restrained driver. This doesn't mean that motorists should drive cars and trucks built like army tanks. In fact, many subcompacts are so well designed to absorb crash forces that they'll allow you to walk away from a frontal collision at 57 km/h (35 mph).

Ergonomics
One of the new catchphrases used in rating vehicles is "ergonomics." Simply put, it means making the vehicle's interior user-friendly. For example, can you reach the controls you'll need without strain, or without taking your eyes off the road? Are the controls just as easy to operate by feel as they are by sight? Can rear-seat passengers enter or exit without becoming contortionists, as is the case with many two-door sport-utility vehicles?

To answer these questions, you need to drive the vehicle over a period of time to test how well it responds to the diversity of your driving needs. If this can't be done, you may find out too late that the climate control system keeps you cold in the winter and hot in the summer, or that the handling is more truck-like than you'd wanted. But you can conduct the following showroom test. Adjust the seat to a comfortable setting, buckle up, and settle in. When you look out the windshield and use the rear- and side-view mirrors, do you detect any serious blind spots? Will optional mirrors give you an unobstructed view? Does the seat feel comfortable enough for long trips? Can you reach important controls without moving off the seatback? If so, then your vehicle has been ergonomically designed. If not, shop for something that better suits your requirements.

Head restraints
Offered as a standard feature on all front and some rear seats, the main function of head restraints is to prevent neck whiplash injuries during a rear collision when the impact forces snap your head back. Whiplash injuries are not only literally a pain in the neck, they're affecting younger, female drivers more than ever before. According to a 1999 joint study carried out by IIHS and State Farm insurance (yep, the same insurance company fined for refusing claims in the United States), over a quarter of accident claims involve neck injury. The study also revealed that in mid-sized vehicle accidents women have more neck injuries than men (30 percent versus 23 percent) and, surprisingly, drivers 65 years and older had lower neck injury rates than younger drivers.

Whiplash injuries are also closely related to head restraint design. Your vehicle's head restraints may be either fixed or adjustable. Fixed restraints are preferred, but adjustable ones are acceptable as long as they're adjusted high enough (at ear level). Make sure that rear visibility isn't obstructed by the front or rear restraints. The State Farm study showed that drivers struck in the rear in cars with head restraints rated "Good" by the IIHS are 24 percent less likely to sustain neck trauma than drivers using head restraints rated "Poor." Unfortunately, 70 percent of head restraints are rated "Poor" by the IIHS; only three percent are rated "Good." Ratings can be found at the IIHS website: *www. highwaysafety.org/vehicle_ratings/head_restraints/head.htm.*

Seats and seatbacks
Seat anchorages have to conform to government load regulations, but the regulations are so minimal that seats can easily collapse or tear loose from their anchorages, leaving drivers and passengers vulnerable in accidents. In fact, NHTSA's complaint database is replete with instances in which occupants report severe injuries caused by collapsing seatbacks that have injured front seat occupants or crushed children in safety seats placed in the rear seat.

Seatbelts
Apart from airbags, seatbelts provide the best means of reducing the severity of injury arising from both low- and high-speed frontal collisions.

In order to be effective, however, seatbelts must be adjusted properly and feel comfortably tight without undue slack. Unfortunately, this is not always the case, and seatbelts rank high in customer complaints: they don't retract enough for a snug fit, are too tight, chafe the neck, and don't properly fit children. Some automakers have corrected these problems with adjustable shoulder-belt anchors that allow both tall and short drivers to raise or lower the belt for a snug, more comfortable fit. Another important seatbelt innovation is front seatbelt pretensioners, devices that automatically tighten the safety belt in the event of a crash. They are offered only as original equipment on a limited number of vehicles and must be replaced once deployed.

Crashworthiness

All things being equal, a heavier vehicle—except for compacts and mid-size sport-utilities—will fare better in a crash than a light one. GM's recent two-car crash tests dramatically confirm this fact. Its engineers concluded that if two cars collide, and one weighs half as much as the other, the driver in the lighter car is ten times as likely to be killed as is the driver in the heavier one.

Chrysler's '99 Caravan crash protection isn't very good, says NHTSA. Occupants face certain, possibly severe, injury.

The Washington-based IIHS says that vehicles in the mid-size and large car class are far safer than smaller ones when crashed at 65 km/h (40 mph)—8 km/h (5 mph) more than in government tests. The IIHS figures show that the fatality rate for the occupants in a small car is roughly twice that of a mid-size car, and three times as high as a big car. What's the cutoff point? A wheelbase of at least 105 inches. Vehicles with wheelbases of 105 inches or more have 1.4 or fewer deaths per 10,000 registered vehicles, while those with 104-inch wheelbases or less have 2.1 or more deaths for the same number of registered vehicles.

The IIHS and NHTSA crashworthiness ratings don't usually differ all that much. However, there are some other factors that can skew both groups' scores: size, height, and frame rail placement, for example. If your Ford Taurus (five-star rating) is clobbered by a Dodge Durango 4X4 (two stars), chances are you'll fare much worse than the sport-utility's occupants simply because it's so much heavier (2148 kg vs. 1579 kg) and may ride over the Taurus' protective frame. On the other hand, some small vehicles are designed better than larger ones to absorb crash forces. VW's New Beetle is a good example. So far, it's the only small car to win a "good" crash rating from the IIHS, while a handful of sport-utilities and even some Cadillacs rate poor at protecting their occupants. Other factors include whether or not occupants are wearing seatbelts, and airbag and head restraint design.

Owners of imports that haven't been crash-tested in the States or Canada (Lada, for example) may access the Federation internationale de l'automobile website (*www.fia.com*) for European crash test scores. Interestingly, the crash data is posted in English, although the website is clearly oriented to the French driver.

Choosing an Inexpensive Vehicle

Know your warranty
There's a big difference between warranty promises and warranty performance. All major automakers offer bumper-to-bumper warranties good for the first 3 years/60,000 kilometres. It's becoming an industry standard for car companies to also pay for roadside assistance, a loaner car, or hotel accommodations if your vehicle breaks down under warranty while you're away from home.

The auto industry's more comprehensive warranties have become an important marketing tool, featured heavily in advertising campaigns. But, like the performance ads you see on TV, what you think you see isn't always what you get. For example, bumper-to-bumper coverage usually excludes tires (GM vehicles are an exception, in that they allow you to claim a refund through the dealer), stereo components, brake pads, clutch disks, and many other expensive components. To really know what the warranty covers on your vehicle, you have to read the fine print. Chrysler, for example, offers a fairly comprehensive powertrain warranty, but major items are excluded and Chrysler is very tightfisted in the interpretation of its obligations (exemplified by its frequent refusal to pay air conditioning, ABS brakes, automatic transmission, and paint delamination claims). Ford has also been less than generous in dealing with premature engine and transmission failures.

Look for "secret" warranties
Automobile manufacturers are reluctant to publicize their secret warranty programs because they feel that such publicity would weaken consumer confidence in their products and increase their legal liability. The closest they come to an admission is to send out a "goodwill policy," "special policy," or "product update" service bulletin for dealers' eyes only. These bulletins admit liability and propose free repairs

for defects running the gamut from fishy-smelling headliners on Chrysler sport-utilities and minivans to transmission failures on Chrysler, Ford, and GM cars and minivans (see Part Three).

When faced with repairs for what is clearly a factory mistake, the only motorists who get compensated are the ones who yell the loudest or threaten to go to small claims court. Uninformed customers who hesitate to complain are forced to pay for the same repairs.

If you're refused compensation, keep in mind that secret warranty extensions are, first and foremost, an admission of manufacturing negligence. You can usually find them in dealer service bulletins (DSBs) that are sent daily to dealers by automakers. Your bottom-line position should be to accept a pro-rata adjustment from the manufacturer, whereby you share a third of the repair costs with the dealer and automaker. If polite negotiations fail, challenge the refusal in court on the grounds that you should not be penalized for failing to make a reimbursement claim under a secret warranty that you never knew existed!

Getting a DSB summary for your vehicle

If you want your own DSB summary, fill out the *Lemon-Aid* Survey/DSB Summary Request found in Appendix II. For a $15 fee (this includes computer time and mailing costs), you'll be faxed or mailed an exhaustive summary of all DSBs that concern your vehicle. For an additional $5 per DSB, you can then order any number of the DSBs listed in the summary that address your concerns. For example, one summary and one specific DSB would cost $20. Remember, there's no extra charge for fax replies. On the other hand, only Visa cards or cheques made out to DSB are accepted.

Service bulletins are great guides for warranty inspections (especially the final one) and they're useful in helping you decide when it's best to trade in your car. They're written by automakers in "mechanic-speak" and republished here unedited because service managers relate better to them that way, and manufacturers can't weasel out of their obligations by claiming that they never wrote such a bulletin.

If your vehicle is out of warranty, show these bulletins to less expensive independent garages. They can quickly find the trouble and order the most recent *upgraded* part so that you don't replace one defective part with another.

Because these bulletins are sent out by U.S. automakers, Canadian service managers will sometimes deny, at first, that they even exist. However, when they're shown a copy they usually find the appropriate Canadian part number or DSB in their files. The problem and its solution don't change from one side of the border to another. Imagine American and Canadian tourists being towed across the border because each country's technical bulletins were different. Mechanical fixes do differ in cases where a bulletin is for California only, or relates to a safety or emissions component used only in the U.S. But these instances are rare indeed.

1999 Ford Truck Windstar V6–232 3.8L VIN 4SFI

Dealer Service Bulletins

Number	Date	Name
99-5-5	Mar 99	A/C–Lack of Temperature Control in All Modes
99-5-3	Mar 99	A/T–Checkiing Transmission Fluid Level Cold
99-7-6	Apr 99	A/T–No Reverse Engagement–AX4S/AX4N Built Thru 2/22/99
98-26-5	Jan 99	Anti-Lock Brake System (ABS) Noise
99-5-1	Mar 99	Calibration Information–Vehicles Built Through 1/29/1999
99-1-8	Jan 99	Diagnostic Service Tips–Passive Anti Theft System (PATS)
99-8-15	May 99	Interior Door Trim Panel Replacement–Service Tip
98-25-9	Dec 98	Interior Trim–Repairs to Vinyl Covered Surfaces
99-6-6	Apr 99	Lack of Cooling–Refrigerant Leak at Condenser Fittings
99-1-9	Jan 99	MIL On/Codes PO442, PO445–No Driveability Concerns
98-23-10	Nov 98	Mass Air Flow Sensor Contamination–Service Tip
99-8-16	May 99	Motor Oil–SAE 5W-30 Viscosity Grade Recommendation
98-24-6	Dec 98	New Electrical Terminal Grease Released For Service
99-3-1	Feb 99	Power Seat Switch Inoperative or Fuse 104 Opens
99-3-6	Feb 99	Power Sliding Door–Summary of Concerns
98-23-17	Nov 98	Product Changes For The 1999 Windstar
99-4-3	Mar 99	Reprogramming Powertrain Control Modules–Out of Vehicle
99-4-10	Mar 99	Reverse Sensing System (RSS)–Service Tips
99-8-4	May 99	Squeaking/Rattling Noise From Left/Right Rear Of Vehicle
98-26-2	Jan 99	Tips To Resolve Volatility Related Driveability Concerns
99-1-13	Jan 99	Trailer Tow Wiring Service Kit Available
99-6-5	Apr 99	Windnoise Around Side Doors–Service Tips
99-2-3	Feb 99	Windshield Sealing For Water Leaks–Service Tip
99-6-3	Apr 99	Wire Splicing And Wire Harness Terminal Repair Kit

Confidential dealer service bulletins pave the road to free repairs because they prove that a part failure is factory-related and not part of normal maintenance; hence the repair cost should be paid by the dealer and manufacturer even if the normal warranty has expired.

The best way to get DSB-related repairs carried out is to visit the dealer and show him the specific DSB covering your vehicle's problems. Direct his attention to all the tech-speak and codes and ask for the Canadian equivalent. If you're refused help:
- Fax the automaker in Canada a copy of the DSB and ask for the appropriate kit or upgraded part number for Canada.
- If the dealer and automaker say that Canadians are excluded, ask why Canadians don't have the same rights as Americans.
- Complain to Transport Canada and your provincial consumer affairs about being refused corrective repairs that are given routinely to American customers.
- Finally, you could visit an American dealer to have the repair carried out during a regularly scheduled vacation trip. Once back in Canada, you can sue the Canadian automaker and its dealer for your costs (including DSB and fax costs) in small claims court, because they gave you the runaround in the first place.

Fuel economy fantasies

Fuel economy figures are published by Transport Canada (a free copy of its *Fuel Consumption Guide* can be obtained by calling 1-800-387-2000) and are based on data supplied by the automakers who follow U.S. Environmental Protection Administration testing guidelines. These figures can be off by 10 to 20 percent depending on the testing method chosen. In fact, a recent Ford bulletin warns dealers that "very few people will drive in a way that is identical to the EPA tests…. These [fuel economy] numbers are the result of test procedures that were originally developed to test emissions, not fuel economy."

If you never quite got the hang of metric fuel economy measurements (like me), use the fuel conversion table that follows to establish how many miles to a gallon of gas your vehicle provides.

Conversion Table					
L/100 km	m.p.g.	L/100 km	m.p.g.	L/100 km	m.p.g.
5.0	56	7.4	38	12.5	23
5.2	54	7.6	37	13.0	22
5.4	52	7.8	36	13.5	21
5.6	50	8.0	35	14.0	20
5.8	48	8.5	33	15.0	19
6.0	47	9.0	31	15.0	18
6.2	46	9.5	30	17.0	17
6.4	44	10.0	28	18.0	16
6.7	43	10.5	27	19.0	15
6.8	42	11.0	26	20.0	14
7.0	40	11.5	25	21.0	13
7.2	39	12.0	24	23.0	12

Insurance costs

Insurance costs can vary between $500 and $5,000 per year, depending on the type of vehicle you own and your personal statistics and driving habits. Multi-purpose vehicles are usually classed in the high-risk category (accident and theft) and therefore usually cost more than passenger cars to insure.

Now that banks are getting into the insurance business, they're heating up the competition by offering lower premium payments through independent agents whom they use as go-betweens. The Canadian Imperial Bank of Commerce, for example, says that it offers low insurance premiums by selling directly to the Ontario public, avoiding the 10–12 percent commission that most insurance brokers charge. The Toronto-Dominion Bank also jumped into the Ontario market several years ago.

Insured depreciation savings

High depreciation losses can be avoided during the first few years by purchasing insurance coverage for an extra $25 a year that will give you the actual purchase price of the vehicle and its equipment. Depreciation charges are limited by a special endorsement on the automobile policy called "Removing Depreciation Deduction" (OPCF43). With this policy rider the insurance company won't charge depreciation within the time specified (usually 24 months). So, if you have an accident, you are refunded the amount you originally paid in addition to all sales taxes—or the Manufacturer's Suggested Retail Price (MSRP) at the time of purchase, whichever amount is lower.

This endorsement can save you thousands of dollars during the first few years if your vehicle is written off in an accident. Unfortunately, few motorists are aware that this cheap extra protection is available. Since these endorsements change periodically and coverage cost may fluctuate, contact your local insurance broker or the Insurance Bureau of Canada (1-800-387-2880) for the latest details.

The dealer network

A weak dealer network drives up maintenance costs, adds to a vehicle's downtime, and makes it difficult for you to go elsewhere when servicing is poor. Also, the more sophisticated and complicated a vehicle's engineering and the farther away its manufacturing plant, the more important it is to have strong dealer service support. Ford Aerostar and GM Astro/Safari minivans, for example, use mostly old truck technology and so can often be repaired anywhere using parts from independent suppliers. The more complicated VW EuroVan, on the other hand, is severely handicapped by a lack of extensive dealer support. The Service Performance chart shows how *Lemon-Aid* readers have rated their vehicle's servicing over the past few years.

Service Performance

❶	❷	③	④	⑤
Unacceptable	Below Average	Average	Above Average	Excellent

	Dealer Network	Parts Cost/ Availability	Warranty Promise/ Performance
ACURA	❷	④/④	③/③
AUDI	③	❷/❷	⑤/⑤
BMW	❷	④/❷	④/③
CADILLAC	⑤	③/③	④/❷
CHRYSLER	⑤	③/⑤	③/③
*DAEWOO	❶	NA/NA	NA/NA
FORD	⑤	⑤/⑤	④/❶
GEO	④	③/③	④/⑤
GM	⑤	③/⑤	④/❷
HONDA	④	⑤/⑤	⑤/⑤
HYUNDAI	③	④/④	④/③
INFINITI	④	③/③	⑤/③
JAGUAR	❷	❷/❷	⑤/④

JEEP	④	④/④	④/❷
*KIA	❶	NA/NA	NA/NA
LADA	❶	NA/NA	NA/NA
LAND ROVER	❶	NA/NA	NA/NA
LEXUS	④	④/⑤	⑤/⑤
LINCOLN	⑤	⑤/⑤	⑤/③
**MAZDA	③	❶/③	⑤/❷
MERCEDES	❷	③/❷	⑤/⑤
NISSAN	④	⑤/⑤	⑤/⑤
SAAB	❷	③/❷	④/③
SATURN	③	③/③	⑤/❶
SUBARU	❷	❷/❷	⑤/⑤
SUZUKI	❷	③/③	④/⑤
TOYOTA	⑤	④/④	⑤/⑤
VOLKSWAGEN	③	③/③	⑤/③
VOLVO	③	④/③	⑤/⑤

* Predicted Service Performance
** Parts prices were just cut substantially.

Sometimes good parts availability exists within a weak dealer network. This occurs when a vehicle has sold quite well or has been on the market for a long time with few changes, thereby creating a good supply of replacement parts and creating a reservoir of knowledgeable technicians.

Parts and service

Parts for imports are generally no more expensive than parts sold by the major American automakers. But when it comes to captive imports, some American automakers have been known to charge twice as much for the same part sold by their Japanese partners.

Here are a two tips that may help cut the high cost of repair parts:

• Try to find good-quality rebuilt parts whenever possible. Generally, rebuilt parts cost anywhere from one-third to one-half the price of new parts and last just as long. A vehicle has to be on the market for at least two years before rebuilt or remanufactured parts become available in sufficient quantities.

• Before authorizing non-warranty repairs at an independent shop, ask the mechanic to compare the parts prices charged by different manufacturers selling the same basic vehicle. For example, a Tracker part may be cheaper at a Suzuki dealership under the Sidekick name than one bought from General Motors.

Even when parts costs aren't deliberately "boosted" by American car manufacturers, prices are unacceptably high. For example, according to the Alliance of American Insurers, the price of original-equipment replacement parts needed to rebuild a vehicle is about 2.5 times the original retail price. In an annual study, a 1999 Ford Taurus SE retailing for $25,000 was rebuilt with Ford-supplied replacement parts. Total cost? More than $72,000 for the parts alone. No labour was included in the estimate.

Consumers have found that automakers are more interested in sales than in ensuring that their dealers give honest, competent service. In fact, I can't recall a single occasion where an automaker terminated a dealership's franchise because of odometer tampering or other dishonest dealings, yet the RCMP reports dozens of odometer fraud convictions every year.

A vehicle can incorporate the best engineering in the world, but it will quickly deteriorate and fall into the lemon category if the servicing is lousy, as may be the case with a used Mazda MPV or Chrysler minivan. The servicing problem is more acute with vehicles that are new on the market, and with South Korean imports. American manufacturers are generally weak in service support, and General Motors is the best example of this deficiency. Its own records show that 70 percent of its customers switch to other repair outlets when their vehicle warranty expires.

The *Wall Street Journal* reports that GM spends about $3.5 billion annually paying 22.5 million warranty claims to correct factory-related defects. For 1999, in a move to cut warranty costs by spotting defect trends earlier, GM standardized reporting of breakdowns and set up sophisticated computerized models similar to the Atlanta-based Center for Disease Control's epidemiological tracking models.

GM says its improved tracking system has been so successful that even "hardy perennials," recurring defects that have defied correction for years, are finally getting fixed. The company cites excessive axle noise in trucks as an example of one nagging problem that was finally fixed at the factory on 1999 models. In the past, GM spent tens of millions of dollars under warranty, or about $924 U.S. per vehicle to reduce the axle noise.

Servicing among European importers has much improved, although customers still complain about the abrasive, arrogant attitude typified by some German and Swedish automakers and service outlets.

Check servicing costs and the quality of repairs with owners who drive similar models, fleet administrators, and rental car counter attendants. They'll be glad to tell you about servicing problems they've encountered. Be sure to question consumer protection groups about which vehicles generate the most complaints and what mechanical components are the most failure-prone and covered by secret warranties. Owner comments found in on-line forums, owners' groups listed in collectors' publications, and car buff magazines are also helpful in giving you a picture of the overall reliability, parts availability, servicing, and price range for specific models.

Finding a Reliable Vehicle

The elusive "American" car

A lot of controversy surrounds the relative quality control of North American and imported vehicles. Before deciding which manufacturer provides the best quality, forget all the popular mythology about what is made in North America and what is "foreign" made. The seesaw value of the dollar and the yen has led to a rush of foreign and American automakers moving production facilities to the U.S., Canada, and Mexico. Surprisingly, this has been accomplished without a corresponding drop in quality control. Toyota's Corolla assembly plant in Cambridge, Ontario, for example, has been rated by J.D. Power and Associates as the highest quality production facility in North America.

American or Japanese?
Despite their improvements over the past several years, American vehicles still don't measure up to the Japanese in quality and technology, especially when it comes to body construction and paint. This is particularly evident in small pickups, where Toyota, Nissan, and Mazda have the highest reliability and dependability ratings. American firms have copied Japanese production methods and their team approach, but the quality of their vehicles hasn't closed the reliability gap except in co-ventures like the Ford/Mazda production of the Probe and Ranger, the Nissan/Mercury Villager, and the GM/Suzuki Tracker.

Japanese vehicles aren't made better or more quickly because of robotics or overworked, low-salaried workers, as American automakers would like us to believe. Actually, American production costs are now lower than what the Japanese and Europeans pay at home. High manufacturing costs in Japan and Europe (due mostly to high taxes and workers' benefits) are forcing European and Japanese automakers to locate plants in Canada and the U.S., where skilled workers are plentiful. The real reasons for the poor quality of American cars are the automakers' blind price-cutting at the expense of quality, and their preference for style over substance.

European quality varies
Motorists' complaints, dealer service bulletins, and auto association membership surveys like those sent out by the CAA confirm that the quality of European vehicles like Mercedes, BMW, VW, and Audi remains quite high, while other European automakers like Lada, Saab, and Jaguar produce vehicles of lesser quality. Lada may be in the worst shape. It didn't import any 1999 vehicles and there is no guarantee that next year will be any different.

Most European automakers are breaking sales records due to their cars' impressive driving performance and comfort. Volkswagen and Audi have become top sellers by dramatically improving the quality of their vehicles over the past few years, offering comprehensive warranties, and holding the line on prices in the mid-range. In comparison, Japanese imports are too pricey and American cars don't perform as well. Luxury and sports car importers, like BMW and Porsche, have also made a remarkable comeback through price cuts and inexpensive new products. Unfortunately, what these companies give they also take away—the last few years have seen steep price increases by both Audi and VW.

Other Buying Considerations

What about Y2K failures?
Should you hold off on buying a new 2000 model because you're fear-
ful its computer could leave you stranded with the arrival of the next
millennium? No, say both the Canadian and American governments,
automakers, and *Consumer Reports*.

According to the automakers, the computers that control a vehicle's
engine, transmission, anti-lock brakes, and heating and air conditioning systems are not calendar and date sensitive. Therefore, they aren't
likely to cause any vehicle to cease to function come January 1, 2000.
Of course, these are the same folks who claim that the airbags and anti-
lock brakes they produce won't "cease to function properly."

Front-wheel drive
Front-wheel drives direct engine power to the front wheels, which *pull*
the vehicle forward while the rear wheels simply support the rear. The
biggest benefit of front-wheel drive (FWD) is foul weather traction.
With the engine and transmission up front there's lots of extra weight
pressing down on the front-drive wheels, increasing tire grip in snow
and on wet pavement. But when you drive up a steep hill or tow a boat
or trailer the weight shifts, and you lose the traction advantage.

Although I recommend a number of FWD vehicles in this *Guide*, I
don't like them as much as rear-drives. Granted, front-drives provide a
bit more interior room (no transmission hump), more car-like handling, and better fuel economy than do rear-drives, but damage from
potholes and fender-benders is usually more extensive, and maintenance costs (especially premature front tire and brake wear) are much
higher than with rear-drives.

Servicing front-wheel drives can be a real nightmare—and a wallet-
buster. Entire steering, suspension, and drivetrain assemblies have to
be replaced when only one component is defective. Downtime is considerable, the cost of parts is far too high, and the drivetrain and its
components aren't designed for the do-it-yourself mechanic. A new
FWD transmission assembly (called a transaxle) can cost about $2,000
to repair, compared to $700 for a rear-drive transmission. And having
to make such a repair isn't that remote a possibility, particularly if you
own a 1989–96 Chrysler minivan or a Ford Taurus or Sable.

Accident repairs are a unique problem. Front-wheel-drive transmissions and steering and suspension components are easily damaged, and
alignment difficulties abound. Repair shops need expensive, specialized
equipment to align all four wheels and square up a badly smashed uni-
body chassis—and even if you manage to get all four wheels tracking
true, the clutch and transaxle can still be misaligned. No wonder many
insurance companies prefer to write off an FWD car rather than repair
it. And when that happens, you wind up eating the difference between
what you paid for the vehicle and what the insurance company says your
vehicle is worth—minus your deductible, of course.

Rear-wheel drive

Rear-drives direct engine power to the rear wheels, which push the vehicle forward. The front wheels steer and also support the front of the vehicle. With the engine up front, the transmission in the middle, and the drive axle in the rear, there's plenty of room for larger and more durable drivetrain components. This makes for less crash damage, lower maintenance costs, and higher towing capacities than front-drives.

On the other hand, rear-drives don't have as much weight over the rear wheels as do the front-drives (no, putting cement blocks in the bed or trunk will only void your transmission warranty), and therefore they can't provide as much traction on wet and icy roads unless they're equipped with an expensive traction-control system.

Finally, rear-drives are scarcer than hens' teeth, so much of the foregoing dissertation may be of little practical value if all you have to pick from are front-wheel drives.

Four-wheel drive

Four-wheel drives direct engine power through a transfer case to all four wheels, which *pull* and *push* the vehicle forward, giving you twice as much traction. The system is activated with either a floor-mounted shift lever or a dashboard button. When the 4X4 drive isn't engaged, the vehicle is essentially a rear-drive truck. The large transfer case housing makes the vehicle sit higher, giving you additional ground clearance. The most fuel-efficient systems disengage the four-wheel drive when extra traction isn't needed. Rear-drives, though, have some of the highest payload and towing capabilities, usually slightly higher than four-wheel drives.

Encouraged by the popularity of 4X4 vehicles in North America, many automakers now offer optional four-wheel drive or all-wheel drive on their more moderately priced family sedans, pickups, and minivans—at jacked-up prices. Nevertheless, despite reports of high repair costs, low rust resistance, fragile mechanical components, and government studies that show poor crashworthiness and an increased risk of rollover accidents, 4X4 and AWD sport-utilities, pickups, and vans are hotter than ever.

All-wheel drive

Essentially, this is four-wheel drive *all* the time. Used mostly in minivans, AWD never needs to be deactivated when running over dry pavement and doesn't require a heavy transfer case (although some sport-utilities and pickups do use a special transfer case) that raises ground clearance and cuts fuel economy. AWD-equipped vehicles aren't recommended for off-roading because of their lower ground clearance and their fragile driveline parts that aren't as rugged as four-wheel drive components.

Surviving the Options Jungle

Dealers make three times as much profit selling options as they do selling most cars (50 percent vs. 15 percent). No wonder their eyes light up when you start perusing their options list. If you must have some options, compare prices with independent retailers and buy where the price is lowest and the warranty is the most comprehensive. Buy as few options as possible from the dealer, since you'll get faster service, more comprehensive guarantees, and lower prices from independent suppliers. Remember, extravagantly equipped vehicles hurt your pocketbook in three ways: they cost more to begin with, they cost more to maintain, and they often consume extra fuel.

Before buying options separately, consider getting a vehicle in a higher trimline or in a "special edition" format, where the options package includes what you want for a lower price. Another possibility is "value pricing," where automakers like GM will offer a package of options on a bare-bones model. Whichever choice you make, don't buy any unnecessary options if the total cost of the package exceeds what you'd pay for the options if purchased separately.

A heavy-duty battery and suspension and perhaps an upgraded sound system will generally suffice for American-made vehicles; most imports already come well equipped. An engine block heater with a timer isn't a bad idea, either. It's an inexpensive investment that ensures winter starting and reduces fuel consumption by allowing you to start out with a semi-warm engine. Factory installed in-line heaters are usually more efficient and durable.

It's hard to buy and even harder to lease a new vehicle that isn't loaded with unnecessary options. This is particularly evident with medium-size vehicles and minivans. If you're unsure as to what optional equipment like sound systems and anti-theft devices should cost, shop around and compare prices with independent suppliers like J.C. Whitney. Their mail order parts catalogue can be ordered by calling 312-431-6102 (Visa and Mastercard accepted).

Smart Options

Air conditioning
Whether or not you choose air conditioning should depend more on where you live and your comfort requirements than on saving money. Just like buying an underpowered car to save on fuel costs and then regretting its poor performance, your savings will be the last thing on your mind when you're sweltering in your vehicle some summer day.

Air conditioning costs between $800 and $1,650, plus a $100 federal excise tax, and may reduce fuel economy by as much as 10 percent in stop-and-go traffic. At highway speeds, air conditioning increases fuel consumption by 3 to 4 percent. It provides extra comfort, reduces wind noise from not having to roll down the windows, and improves window defogging. But because air conditioning units aren't used year-round, they're failure-prone (expect repairs of about $1,500 around the five-year mark), easy prey for premature corrosion, and an excellent incubator for airborne bacteria and allergens. If you must have air conditioning, opt for a factory-installed unit. You'll get a longer warranty and reduce the chance that other mechanical components will be damaged during installation.

Anti-theft systems

Car break-ins and thefts cost Canadians more than $400 million annually, meaning that there's a 1 in 130 chance that your car will be stolen and only a 60 percent chance that you'll ever get it back. It's no wonder that over one-third of new vehicles are equipped with standard or optional alarms, with a clear preference for fuel cut-off devices and electronic alarms among the four main types of security systems: active and passive units either armed by the driver or self-arming, ignition disablers, parts identification, and security keys.

Some automakers have more effective standard alarm systems than others. Volkswagen, for example, was recently singled out for praise by the Canadian Crime Prevention Bureau after its new anti-theft devices and car parts marking resulted in a 75 percent drop in VW thefts.

The most effective theft-deterrent systems aren't always the most expensive ones. Don't waste your money on costly anti-theft devices that depend solely upon your car's horn or lights to scare thieves away. They often go off at the wrong time and can be easily deactivated. Furthermore, they frighten the thief away only after the vehicle has been damaged. When it comes to stealing your car's contents, no alarm system can resist a brick through a side window. It takes just twelve minutes for thieves to strip a car seat, radio, and body parts, and few citizens are brave enough to personally stop a theft or testify in court. Your best protection is discretion: take your radio with you or lock it in the trunk, particularly if you own a Japanese or German car with an upgraded sound system.

Since most cars are stolen by amateurs, the best theft deterrent is a visible device that complicates the job while immobilizing the vehicle and sounding an alarm. For less than $150, you can install both a steering wheel lock and a hidden remote-controlled ignition disabler. These clublike devices cost between $50 and $75, and deter thieves by forcing them to carry a hacksaw and adding about a half-minute to the time it takes to steal the average car (they have to cut through the steering wheel or bust the lock).

Ignition disablers are also inexpensive and very effective. They sell for $30–$90, depending on their sophistication. The Electronic Cop sells for $89.95 and can be purchased from Sequel Security Systems, 853 Sanders Road, Box 278, Northbrook IL 60062 (1-800-215-4100).

Battery (heavy-duty)

The best battery for northern climates is the optional heavy-duty type offered by many manufacturers for about $80. It's a worthwhile purchase, especially for vehicles equipped with lots of electrical options. Most standard batteries last only two winters; heavy-duty batteries give you an extra year or two for about 20 percent more.

Block heater
A block heater is an inexpensive investment at about $75. Factory-installed in-line models are effective and durable. Cheaper ($40 installed) dipstick or freeze plug models are not recommended.

Cellular telephone
This is a recommended option mainly because it provides a greater degree of safety for drivers stuck on the side of the road or threatened by smash-and-grab artists. Buy the cheapest hands-free model available from an independent retailer.

Cellular phones are expensive to operate due to the high rates charged by the phone companies to "carry" calls. Because calls are billed by the minute and according to the distance the caller or receiver is from a given site, charges can vary from $250–$1,000+ a month for a sales agent who uses it extensively. The temptation to use the car phone for nonessential calls is also hard to resist, and expensive in the long run. The average monthly cost for personal calls is about $125. And remember that what's said on a cellular phone can be heard by anyone.

Three independent studies have shown that car phones are a safety hazard. Drivers whose attention is distracted while talking on a cellular telephone have four times as high a risk of having an accident, says a recent University of Toronto study of 699 car crashes reported in the February 1997 issue of *The New England Journal of Medicine*. Drivers using hands-free phones were just as likely as people holding a receiver to be involved in an accident while on the phone or shortly after having used it. The American Automobile Association Foundation for Traffic Safety says that a road hazard is 20 to 30 percent more likely to go unnoticed by someone using a car phone than by a driver who gives full attention to driving. This warning is buttressed by another study done at the Rochester Institute of Technology in Rochester, New York, which found that drivers with cellular phones installed in their vehicles run a 34 percent greater risk of having an accident than other motorists.

If the possibility of crashing into someone isn't scary enough, how about cellular phones that are real heart-stoppers? The U.S. government is looking into allegations that people with heart pacemakers implanted in their chests may experience pacemaker malfunctions as a result of their cell phones. Safety researchers say that if the phone is placed in close proximity to the chest it may cause the pacemaker to stop, restart, or recalibrate itself. The problem is more apparent with the new digital cellular phones than with the older analog models now most commonly used.

One last thing: cellular phones aren't particularly efficient in placing emergency calls through the 911 exchange. Rather than going to a central dispatch centre where the caller's location is indicated on-screen, cell phone calls are often routed to other, distant places where staffers may be unfamiliar with the area from which the call originates.

Central locking control

Costing around $200, this option is most useful for families with small children, car-poolers, or drivers of pickups, minivans, and vans who can't easily slide across the seat to lock the other doors. Look for a remote feature that provides automatic locking and then unlocking when the inside door handle is pulled.

Child safety seat (integrated)

One of the best child safety innovations to come along in decades, integrated safety seats are designed to accommodate any child more than one year old or weighing over 20 pounds. Since it's permanently integrated into the seatback, it takes the fuss out of installing and removing the safety seat and finding some place to store it. When not in use, it quickly folds away out of sight, becoming part of the seatback. Two other safety benefits: you know the seat has been properly installed (which is not the case with 80 percent of the bolt-ons), and your child gets used to having his or her "special" seat in back where it's safest to sit.

Courtesy lights

This option permits the car's lights to stay on a few seconds after the doors are closed. This is particularly convenient when entering your home if the only outside source of illumination is your car's headlights.

Engines

Choose the most powerful 6- or 8-cylinder engine available if you're going to be doing a lot of highway driving, plan to carry a full passenger load and luggage on a regular basis, or intend to load up the vehicle with convenience features like air conditioning. Keep in mind that multipurpose vehicles with larger engines are easier to resell, and retain their value the longest. For example, Honda's '96 Odyssey minivan was a sales dud despite its bulletproof reliability, mainly because buyers didn't want a minivan with an underpowered 4-cylinder powerplant. Some people underpower their vehicles in the mistaken belief that increased fuel economy is a good trade-off for decreased engine performance. It isn't.

Engine and transmission cooling system (heavy-duty)

This relatively inexpensive option provides extra cooling for the transmission and engine. It can extend the life of these components by preventing overheating when heavy towing is required.

Keyless entry (remote)

A safety and convenience option. You don't need to fiddle with the key in a dark parking lot or take off a glove in cold weather to unlock/lock the vehicle. Try to get a keyless entry system combined with anti-theft measures that include an ignition kill-switch or some other disabler.

Mirror options
Power mirrors are particularly convenient on vehicles that have a number of drivers, or on large sedans and wagons, minivans, vans, or trucks.

Navigation aids
Both GM and Ford offer an optional navigation aid, called OnStar and RESCU respectively, which links a GPS satellite unit to the vehicle's cellular phone and electronics. For a monthly fee of about $25, GM's OnStar unit connects Cadillac drivers to live operators who will help them with driving directions, give repair or emergency assistance, or relay messages. And if the airbag deploys or the car is stolen, satellite-transmitted signals are automatically sent from the car to operators who will notify the proper authorities of the vehicle's location.

Power-assisted windows and seats
Merely a convenience feature with cars, power-assisted windows and seats are a necessity with minivans—crawling across the front seat a few times to roll up the passenger-side window or to lock the doors will quickly convince you of their value. Power seats with memory are particularly useful if a vehicle is driven by more than one person. Automatic window and seat controls currently have few reliability problems, and they're fairly inexpensive to install, troubleshoot, and repair.

Running boards
Rather than returning you to '50s styling, running boards are practically essential for climbing into some minivans. They can be purchased from independent suppliers for $65–$200, which is much less than the $500–$700 charged by some automakers.

Seats
Make sure the driver's seat has sufficient rearward travel to keep you out of harm's way (about a foot) should the airbag deploy. Also look for a height adjustment so that you can still see over the hood as the seat is pushed rearward. Make sure the head restraints are properly adjusted and don't block your rear vision. Finally, rent the vehicle overnight to determine if the seats are comfortable after an hour or two of driving. Keep in mind that uncomfortable seats is one of the most frequent complaints heard from new car buyers.

Sound system
Remember when it was just called a radio?
    Three criteria must be considered when buying a sound system: your overall budget, the make of car, and the kind of music that's likely to be played. A simple AM/FM stereo radio with a stereo cassette tape player is sold by GM for less than $500, but most independent after-market stores can easily beat GM's price. Sophisticated, personalized car stereos may cost between $500 and $1,000, and hi-fi fanatics can spend between $2,000 and

$9,000 for a "total sound system" that'll likely get ripped off shortly after leaving the showroom. In addition to getting the best-quality sound for the cheapest price, the stereo buyer should look for features that make it easy and safe to operate—for example, radios that automatically seek out stations and cassette decks with automatic reverse, play, and eject.

In budgeting for a stereo sound system, allocate half the money for the speakers. Pare down the scores of available features to what's essential, like a strong FM receiver (under two decibels), separate controls for treble and bass, auto reverse, and a key-auto-eject to protect the tape when the ignition is turned on and off.

Factory-installed speakers are usually lousy performers, and options are outrageously priced by automakers. For example, an after-market CD player priced at $400 would cost about $1,200 if installed by the factory or dealer. Dealers often say that only the factory's original equipment can overcome electrical interference or provide the appropriate sound for a vehicle's particular interior configuration. This is baloney.

There are, however, some advantages to having a factory-installed sound system. It's usually guaranteed for a much longer period than an independently installed unit, and the dealer is better equipped than a retailer to remove, ship, and reinstall it. A factory unit will also be more cosmetically attractive and less prone to rattle because it fits better when mounted in the dash and door panels.

Once a stereo system has been purchased, it must be protected from theft. Experts recommend the installation of a slider box for about $80–$100. It's the size of a textbook and connects the cassette player and radio to the car's wiring when pushed into place. When the car is parked, the box and unit stereo can be removed from the vehicle.

CD players

Sales of car CD players exceed a million units annually, including at least 140 separate models. Mail-order discount houses offer them for less than $300. Improved vibration dampening has made the players impervious to potholes. Look for:

• repeat functions that allow you to select a mixture of tracks or repeat a particular track;
• anti-theft features that include removing the faceplate or unit; and
• a truck-mounted CD changer, which allows you to play many different CDs.

Suspension (heavy-duty)

Always a good idea, this inexpensive option pays for itself by providing better handling, additional ride comfort (though a bit on the firm side), and extending shock life an extra year or two.

Tires

There are three rules to remember when purchasing tires. First, neither brand nor price is a reliable gauge of performance, quality, and durability. Second, choosing a tire recommended by the automaker may not be in your best interest, since traction and long tread life are often sacrificed for a softer ride and maximum EPA mileage ratings. And third, don't buy any new tire that's older than two years, since the rubber compound may have deteriorated due to poor handling and improper storage (near electrical motors). You can check the date of manufacture on the sidewall.

There are two types of tires: all-season and performance. Touring is just a fancier name for all-season tires. All-season radial tires cost between $90 and $150. They're a compromise, since according to Transport Canada they won't get you through winter with the same margin of safety as will snow tires, and they don't provide the same durability on dry surfaces as do regular summer tires. In low to moderate snowfall areas, however, these tires are adequate as long as they're not pushed beyond their limits.

Mud or snow tires provide the best traction on snowy surfaces, but traction on wet roads is actually decreased. Tread wear is also accelerated by the use of softer rubber compounds. Beware of using wide tires for winter driving; 70-series or wider give poor traction and tend to "float" over snow. Consumers report good performance with Nokia Hakkapellitas snow tires imported from Finland.

Performance tires have a low sidewall profile and a wider and shallower tread. They give good wet and dry traction, but perform poorly on snow and ice. They also wear quickly and tend to give a hard ride. Remember, some sports cars can't be fitted with snow tires unless the rims are changed or a more expensive brand is chosen.

It's a good idea to purchase tires that provide a road hazard warranty. Under the terms of this guarantee, the tire dealer or manufacturer will provide compensation for any tire that's found to be defective. Also, don't pay full list for any tire; just as with cars, prices may vary by as much as 40 percent among retailers. Make sure, though, that the price includes mounting and balancing. Tire dealers are the best place to find a wide selection of tire brands, models, and sizes, and their salespeople are usually more knowledgeable than they are at dealerships, discount houses, or gas stations. Mail-order tire distributors are also quite price competitive and will often deliver your tires to the garage of your choice within a few days of purchase.

Self-sealing tires

A good idea if you don't mind spending from $130–$200 per tire. Uniroyal has introduced its NailGuard tire, available in over 22 different sizes, that can seal up to a 5 mm puncture once the puncturing object has been removed. Remember, self-sealing tires generally don't perform well in wet snow and slush.

Which tires are best?

There is no independent Canadian agency that evaluates tire performance and durability. However, NHTSA, a Washington-based government agency, rates tread wear, traction, and resistance to sustained high temperatures. It posts its findings on the Internet (just enter "NHTSA" after locating the Alta Vista search engine). The tread wear grade is fixed at a base 100 points and the tire's wear rate is measured after the tire is driven through a course that approximates most driving conditions. A tire rated 300 will last three times as long as one rated 100.

I've come up with the following tire ratings after researching government tests, consumer comments, and industry insiders.

Dunlop D65 and D60 A2: Treadware rated 520, this tire is the bargain of the group. It corners well and provides excellent wet braking and good steering response. Cost: $146 list; sells for $100.

Goodrich Comp T/A HR4: Treadwear rated 360, this tire excels at cornering and is bargain priced at $120.

Goodyear Aquatred: Treadware rated 340, this tire is a bit noisy and its higher-rolling resistance cuts fuel economy. Still, it's an exceptional performer on wet roads, and works especially well on front-drive cars where the weight is over the front tires. Average performance on dry pavement. Costs about $130; no discounts.

Goodyear Regatta: Treadware rated 460, this $100 tire does everything well, including keeping tire noise to a minimum.

Michelin MX4: Treadware rated 320, this tire gives a smoother ride and a sharper steering response than the Aquatred. Cost: $144 list; often discounted to $100.

Pirelli P300 and P400: Treadware rated 460 and 420, these are two of the best all-around performing all-season tires. Cost: $173 list; sells for about $120.

Yokohama Avid MD-H4: Treadware rated 300, this is another Aquatred knock-off that performs almost as well for half the price.

The following tires aren't recommended: **Bridgestone Potenza RE 92, Cooper Lifeline Classic II, Firestone Firehawk GTA, Firestone FR680, General XP2000 H4, Hydro 2000** and **Ameri G4S, Goodyear Eagle GA** and **WeatherHandler, Goodrich Advantage, Michelin XGT H4, XW4,** and **MXV4 Green X, Pirelli P4000 Super Touring** (not to be confused with the recommended **P400**), and the **Toyo 800 Plus**.

Trailer-towing equipment

Just because you need a vehicle with towing capability doesn't mean that you have to spend big bucks. The first thing you should do when choosing a towing option is determine if a pickup or small van will do the job and if your tires will handle the extra burden. For most towing needs (up to 900 kg or 2,000 lb.), a passenger vehicle, small pickup, or minivan will work just as well and cost much less than a full-size pickup or van. But if you're pulling a trailer that weighs more than 900 kg, most passenger vehicles won't handle the load, unless they've been specially outfitted according to the automaker's specifications. Pulling a trailer that weighs more (up to 1,800 kg or 4,000 lb.) will likely require a compact passenger van. A full-size van can handle up to 4,500 kg (10,000 lb.), and may be cheaper and more versatile than a multipur-pose vehicle that would have to be equipped with a V8 engine and heavy-duty chassis components.

Don't trust the towing limit found in the owner's manual. Automakers publish tow ratings that are on the optimistic side, and sometimes they're outright wrong. Also, don't take the dealer's word that a vehicle is capable of pulling a particular trailer. Make the claim a condition of the sale by putting it in the sales contract. Check all claims with the trailer manufacturer for an independent assessment of your vehicle's capabilities.

Automakers reserve the right to change limits whenever they feel like it, so make any sales promise an integral part of your contract (see "Misrepresentation" in Part Two). A good general rule is to reduce the promised tow rating by 20 percent. In assessing towing weight, consid-er the cargo, passengers, and equipment of both the trailer and the tow vehicle. Keep in mind that five people and their luggage add 450 kg (1,000 lb.) and that a full 227 litre (50 gallon) water tank adds another 225 kg (500 lb.) to the load. The manufacturer's gross vehicle weight rating (GVWR) takes into account the anticipated average cargo and supplies that your vehicle is likely to carry.

Automatic transmissions are fine for trailering, although there's a slight fuel penalty to pay. Manual transmissions tend to have greater clutch wear from towing than do automatic transmissions. Both trans-mission choices are equally acceptable if the driver is competent. Ford and Chevrolet/GMC give higher tow ratings to their trucks with auto-matics than to those with manual transmissions—they know that driv-ers tend to ride the clutch and generally mess up shifting with a manual. Remember, the best compromise is to shift the automatic man-ually for maximum performance going uphill, and to maintain control while not overheating the brakes when descending.

Unit-body vehicles (without a separate frame) can handle most trai-lering jobs as long as their limits aren't exceeded. Front-drives aren't the best choice for pulling heavy loads in excess of 900 kg, since they lose some steering control and traction with all the weight concen-trated in the rear.

Whatever vehicle you choose, keep in mind that the trailer hitch is cru-cial. It must have a tongue capacity of at least 10 percent of the trailer's weight, otherwise it may be unsafe to use. Hitches are chosen according to the type of tow vehicle and, to a lesser extent, the weight of the load. They fall into the following four classes depending on the weight they can pull:

- Class 1: loads up to 900 kg (2,000 lb.); hooked to the frame or rear bumper of most passenger cars, small pickups, and small vans.
- Class 2: loads up to 1,600 kg (3,500 lb.); attached to a car or MPV frame.

- Class 3: loads up to 3,400 kg (7,500 lb.); also attached to a car or MPV frame.
- Class 4: loads up to 4,500 kg (10,000 lb.); attached to a pickup or MPV frame or incorporated as fifth-wheel hitches used in the beds of large pickups.

Most hitches are factory installed, even though independents can put them on more cheaply. Expect to pay about $200 for a simple boat hitch and a minimum of $600 for a fifth-wheel version.

Equalizer bars and extra cooling systems for the radiator, transmission, engine oil, and steering are a prerequisite for towing anything heavier than 900 kg. Heavy-duty springs and brakes are a big help, too. Separate brakes for the trailer may be necessary to increase your vehicle's maximum towing capacity.

Transmission: automatic, manual, 5-speed, and overdrive automatic
A transmission with four or more forward speeds is usually more fuel efficient than one with three forward speeds, and manual transmissions are usually more efficient than automatics, although this isn't always the case. Nevertheless, most motorists prefer to pay extra to have a transmission that shifts by itself, even though this convenience saps the performance of small engines, requires expensive repairs, and makes you less alert to driving conditions. This last point is particularly important, because a manual transmission makes you aware of the traffic flow and requires that you shift gears in anticipation of changes.

But, if you want a stick shift, you'd better act quickly. Aging knees, cheap gasoline, and the increasing popularity of cell phones have led automakers to curtail their production of stick shift–equipped cars. In fact, J.D. Power & Associates says the percentage of cars and light trucks with manual transmissions has dropped from 17.5 percent in the 1989 model year to 13.6 percent in 1997. Even sports cars have been affected. Only 30 percent of GM's Corvettes carry a manual transmission, Ford's Taurus SHO only comes with an automatic, and both the Porsche 911 and Ferrari F1 are clutchless. Industry experts predict that in the future, manual transmissions may only be offered in a small number of economy cars, trucks, and high-priced sports cars.

Dumb Options

Adjustable steering wheel
This option can be deadly in an airbag-equipped vehicle, since it can tilt the steering so that the deployed airbag could cause severe or fatal head and neck injuries. On the plus side, this option facilitates access to the driver's seat and permits a more comfortable driving position. It's particularly useful if a vehicle will be driven by more than one person.

Automatic level control
A useless option, unless you're planning to carry heavy loads or pull a trailer. It's expensive to repair and not easily adjusted.

Bumper strips and bumper guards
Merely decorative items that give very little real protection from fender-bender accidents.

Cruise control
Mainly a convenience feature, automakers provide this $250–$300 option to motorists who use their vehicles for long periods of high-speed driving. Some fuel is saved owing to the constant rate of speed, and driver fatigue is lessened during long trips. Still, the system is particularly failure-prone and expensive to repair, and it can lead to driver inattention and make the vehicle hard to control on icy roadways. Malfunctioning cruise control units are also one of the major causes of sudden acceleration incidents. At other times cruise control can be just plain annoying, as is the case with Chrysler's current crop, which often "hunt" for the right gear when traversing hilly terrain.

Electronic instrument read-out
If you've ever had trouble reading a digital watch face or re-setting your VCR you'll feel right at home with this electronic gizmo. Gauges are presented in a series of moving digital patterns that are confusing, distracting, and unreadable in direct sunlight. It's often accompanied by a trip computer and a vehicle monitor that computes fuel use and kilometres to empty, indicates average speed, and signals component failures. Figures are frequently in error or slow to catch up.

Foglights
A pain in the eyes for other drivers, foglights aren't necessary for most drivers with well-aimed original-equipment headlights.

Leather upholstery
An expensive option that's too hot in summer, too cold in winter, too slippery, and tough to clean or repair.

Paint and fabric protectors
Paint protectors sold by auto dealers aren't just overpriced—they also don't work. The auto industry's equivalent of the "Emperor's New Clothes," I wouldn't give two cents for paint protector products sold by car dealers. This is said with the knowledge that Chrysler, Ford, and GM factory paint jobs have become less and less durable over the years. Selling for $200–$300, these "sealants" are a waste of money and add nothing to a vehicle's resale value. Although paint lustre may be temporarily heightened, this treatment is less effective and more costly than regular waxing, and may also invalidate the manufacturer's guarantee at

a time when the automaker will look for any pretext at all to deny your paint claim.

According to tests carried out by the Consumers' Association of Canada and the Quebec Consumer Protection Bureau, waxing your vehicle regularly is a much better idea than investing in paint protectors. Certain waxes are better than others, as shown in CAC field tests; Nu Finish gave good paint protection for three to six months after each application and did very well in bringing out paint lustre. Surprisingly, Turtle Wax was one of the poorer performers in the CAC study.

Consumer Reports and the Canadian Automobile Protection Association believe that auto fabric protection products are nothing more than Scotchguard variations, which can be bought in aerosol cans for a few dollars, instead of the $50–$75 charged by dealers. Still, if you want someone else to do the spraying, offer the dealer half of what he asks. Even at that, he should make a small profit.

Radar detectors and "stealth" devices

Another product that targets van vacationers and sports car enthusiasts, radar detectors are a dumb idea for two reasons: they're illegal in most provinces and most U.S. states and, like so-called paint protectors, they aren't always effective. The newest wrinkle is an electronic "stealth" cloaking device that claims to generate a frequency that confuses police radar and laser guns. Mounted on the front end of the vehicle, the $400 (tax and installation included) device failed every test carried out by the *Vancouver Province*. Even if it were effective, motorists would have to buy one for the rear end as well since many laser guns are trained on vehicles after they've gone by.

Roof-top carrier

Although this inexpensive option provides additional baggage space and may allow you to meet all your driving needs with a smaller vehicle, a loaded roof rack can increase fuel consumption by as much as 5 percent. An empty rack cuts fuel economy by about 1 percent.

Rustproofing

The high profits earned from rustproofing cars (over 75 percent in some cases) encourage dealers to sell aftermarket rustproofing, even though automakers like GM and Nissan threaten to void the rust warranty if critical drain holes are plugged. Most automakers will reject all rust warranty claims where holes have been drilled into their cars by aftermarket rustproofers.

Nevertheless, rustproofing is no longer necessary now that the automakers have extended their own rust warranties. In fact, you have a greater chance of seeing your rustproofer go belly-up than having your untreated vehicle ravaged by premature rusting. Even if the rustproofer stays in business, you're likely to get a song and dance about why the warranty won't cover so-called internal rusting, or why repairs

will be delayed until the sheet metal is actually rusted through.

If you live in an area where roads are heavily salted in winter, or in a coastal region, have your vehicle washed every few weeks and undercoated frequently—paying particular attention to rocker panels (door bottoms) and wheel wells. Also, keep your car away from a heated garage in winter; Canadian studies show that a heated garage will accelerate the damage caused by corrosion.

Sunroof

Unless you live in a temperate region, the advantages of a sunroof are far outweighed by its disadvantages. You're not going to get better ventilation than a good air conditioning system would provide, and you'll appreciate that your highway trips aren't accompanied by wind noises, water leaks, and road dust accumulation. Gas consumption is increased, night vision is reduced by overhead highway lights shining through the roof opening, and several inches of headroom can be lost, forcing tall drivers to adopt a hunched-over driving position. Flip-up styles are particularly leak-prone, while electronically-controlled sliding sunroofs often fall prey to short circuits. And without a manual override, your car will be vulnerable to theft and the weather.

Factory installation of a sunroof is far more costly than having it done by an independent—$1,000 vs. $250, with little difference in the quality of the job or the warranty.

Tinted glass

Tinting jeopardizes your safety by reducing night vision. On the other hand, it does keep the interior cool in hot weather, reduces glare, and hides the car's contents from prying eyes. Factory applications are worth the extra cost because cheaper aftermarket products (costing about $100) distort visibility and peel away after a few years. Some tinting done in the U.S. can run afoul of provincial highway codes that require more transparency.

Wheels (aluminum)
Standard equipment on many sporty models, alloy wheels are optional on other cars ($150–$300). They're fragile, frequently leak, corrode easily, and aren't always compatible with snow tires. Unpainted wheels require regular cleaning with acetone and an annual coating with a protective clear spray.

Cutting the Price

Buy by Internet or fax—no more "showroom shakedown"
Of the 15.1 million new vehicles sold in 1998 in North America, 2 million were sold over the Internet. This figure isn't all that surprising when you consider that hundreds of Internet-based new-car shopping services (like Autobytel) have sprung up during the past several years. These services are for consumers who want a fair price, loathe haggling, or are just too busy to visit a number of showrooms. For a service fee, these firms encourage dealers to bid against each other for your business through electronic mail. In other cases, you can go directly to a number of dealer websites and initiate the bidding process on your own. So far, shoppers report impressive savings, particularly in regions where there aren't that many dealers and the local dealer has a "take it or leave it" attitude.

If you don't have a computer or aren't Internet-savvy, don't despair. You can get the same results by using a fax machine. Simply fax an invitation (a cover letter with your company logo would help) for bids to area dealerships, asking them to give their bottom-line price for a specific make and model and clearly stating that all final bids must be faxed within a week. Because no salesperson is acting as a commission-paid intermediary, the dealers' first bids are likely to start off a few hundred dollars less than advertised. When all the bids are received, the lowest bid is faxed to the other dealers to give them a chance to beat that price. After a week of bidding, the lowest price gets your business.

Dozens of *Lemon-Aid* readers have told me how effective buying by fax was in keeping the price down and preventing the showroom song-and-dance routine between the sales agent and sales manager ("he said, she said, they said").

Here's how one Downsview, Ontario, *Lemon-Aid* reader got the bidding started and subsequently paid 18 percent, or $1,995.47, less than the list price of a Nissan Sentra.

FAX TRANSMISSION
Date: November 30, 1994
To: Joe Blow Motors
Att: President

Dear Sir,
  I have decided to buy a new car. What and from whom I buy depends on the responses to this fax.
  I have visited dealerships and have brochures for every car I am considering, and am sending this fax to other dealers. It is now a matter of finding the best deal.
  I will buy either a Nissan Sentra, Honda Civic, Toyota Corolla, or Mazda Protegé. I would like the base model, and the only options that interest me are a full-size spare tire and a block heater. I will accept other features that are already installed, but my decision is going to be based on price. I want a manual transmission, will take either two or four doors, and will accept any color. I will pay by cheque and will not trade in my current car.
  Please fax me an offer. Include the price of the car, the price of all options, PDI, freight, GST, PST, all surtaxes (fuel, etc.), your administration fee, and the licence transfer fee. You should specify the total amount and include the name of the person I should contact if I accept the offer.
  Today is November 30, 1994. I will make my selection at the end of the business day on December 7th. When faxing your offer, please phone me first at 555-1212 so I may connect my modem.
  I want to buy a car. Do you want to sell one?
  Awaiting your earliest convenient response, I remain

Sincerely,
Jane Customer

Several hours after sending this fax, our reader got her first quote. She also received additional bids by phone and mail, including one dealer's promise to beat the lowest price offered. That dealer gave the best price, drove the customer to his dealership, and sold the Sentra.

The myth of "no haggle" pricing
New cars and minivans have no "official" selling price, and most dealers will charge as much as the market will bear. If you let them they'll use any pretext they can to boost prices, including a "no dicker sticker" policy. They'll pretend to have abandoned negotiated prices and high-pressure sales tactics in favour of "no haggle prices," where they give the buyer a better deal.
  Don't believe dealers who say they won't negotiate the MSRP. In effect, all dealers bargain. They hang out the "NO DICKERING, ONE PRICE ONLY" sign simply as a means to discourage customers from asking for a better deal. Like parking lots and restaurants that claim

they won't be responsible for lost or stolen property, in the end they're bluffing. Still, you'd be surprised by how many people believe that if it's posted, it's non-negotiable. Industry figures show that "no dicker" dealers average a 14 percent markup over their cost.

There are several price guidelines, however, and dealers use the one that will make the most profit on each transaction. Take, for example, the following experience one Vancouver shopper relates when he dealt with a major Chevrolet-Oldsmobile dealer in that city:

> Here's one to put in your "Things dealers do to sell cars" file (although you have probably seen this before): [this] Chev Olds [dealer] in Vancouver has been advertising that they are selling Chev Ventures at one dollar below invoice plus freight (which is in fine print). Seeing this, I decided to go down and check out what they are doing to maintain their profit margin. They gladly show you the invoice, which I looked at and confirmed that it was the factory price (based on the APA dealer prices). However, the "invoice price" includes the $840 freight charge and the $100 air conditioning levy. Then they take a dollar off that price and add freight and the levy AGAIN. When I pointed this out to them he said that this was their profit margin (he was quite candid about it). So I said it was a bit of stretching the truth about "a dollar below invoice," why didn't they just advertise that they would sell the vehicle at $840 above invoice? And why did he want to charge me a second air conditioning levy? I didn't get a straight answer on that one, so I left shaking my head at the things dealers do to sell cars...!

Two of the more common prices quoted are the Manufacturer's Suggested Retail Price (what the carmaker advertises as a fair price) and the dealer's invoice cost, which is supposed to indicate how much the dealer paid for the vehicle. Both price indicators leave considerable room for the dealer's profit margin, along with some extra padding in the form of inflated transportation and preparation charges. If presented with both figures, go with the MSRP because it can be verified by calling the manufacturer. Any dealer can print up an invoice and swear to its veracity. If you want an invoice price from an independent source, contact the Automobile Protection Association (see Appendix I).

Residents of rural and western Canada are often faced with car prices that are grossly inflated compared to those charged in major metropolitan areas. A good way to beat this scam without buying out of province is to buy a couple of out-of-town newspapers (the Saturday *Toronto Star* "Wheels" section is especially helpful) and demand that your dealer bring his selling price, preparation, and transportation fees into line with the costs as advertised.

Getting a Fair Price

What's the dealer's cut?

Most new-car salespeople are reluctant to give out information on the amount of profit figured into the cost of each new car, but a few years back *Automotive News* gave the following markups based on the Manufacturer's Suggested Retail Price (MSRP). These percentages may vary a bit from year to year, but they're fairly accurate.

Dealer Markup (American Vehicles)
small cars: 10–12%
mid-size cars: 15–18%
large cars: 20%
sports cars: 17–20%
high-end sports cars: 20+%
luxury cars: 25+%
high-end luxury cars: 20+%
minivans: 18+%
high-end minivans: 21+%
base pickups: 14+%
high-end pickups: 16+%
vans and sport-utility vehicles: 16+%
fully equipped, top-of-the-line vans and SUVs: 21+%

Dealer Markup (Japanese Vehicles)
small cars: 8–12%
midsize cars: 10–15%
large cars: 15–17%
sports cars: 15–17%
high-end sports cars: 18+%
luxury cars: 20%
high-end luxury cars: 20+%
minivans: 15+%
high-end minivans: 17+%
base pickups: 12+%
high-end pickups: 16+%
sport-utility vehicles: 15+%
fully equipped, top-of-the-line vans and SUVs: 18+%

European vehicle markups are slightly lower than the markups charged by American dealers.

In addition to the dealer's markup, some previous-year Big Three vehicles may also have a 3 percent carryover allowance paid out in a dealer incentive program and a holdback allowance of another 2–3 percent (Japanese automakers have no holdback). Some GM dealers maintain that they no longer get a holdback allowance. I suspect the holdback has been added to their annual "incentive" programs, which won't show up on the dealer's invoice. Options are the icing on the cake, with their average 35–65 percent markup.

2000 HONDA AUTOMOBILE PRICE LIST (Confidential)			
MODEL CODE	MODEL	DEALER NET (Exc. Taxes)	SUGGESTED RETAIL (Exc. Taxes)
EJ612YPB	CIVIC COUPE DX 5-SPEED	14,996	16,300
EJ622YPB	CIVIC COUPE DX 4-SPEED AUTO	15,916	17,300
EJ616YE	CIVIC COUPE DX-G 5-SPEED	16,376	17,800
EJ626YE	CIVIC COUPE DX-G 4-SPEED AUTO	17,292	18,800
EJ812YF	CIVIC COUPE SI 5-SPEED	17,368	18,900
EJ822YF	CIVIC COUPE SI 4-SPEED AUTO	18,308	18,900
EJ817YJ	CIVIC COUPE SI-G 5-SPEED	18,768	20,400
EJ827YJ	CIVIC COUPE SI-G 4-SPEED AUTO	19,688	21,400
EM115YJ	CIVIC COUPE SIR 5-SPEED	21,528	23,400
EJ632YB	CIVIC HATCHBACK CX 5-SPEED	13,299	14,300
EJ642YPB	CIVIC HATCHBACK CX 4-SPEED AUTO	14,415	15,500
EJ633YPB	CIVIC HATCHBACK DX 5-SPEED	14,229	15,300
EJ643YPB	CIVIC HATCHBACK DX 4-SPEED AUTO	15,159	16,300
EJ653YX	CIVIC SEDAN LX 5-SPEED	14,812	16,100
EJ663YX	CIVIC SEDAN LX 4-SPEED AUTO	15,782	17,100
EJ651YXV	CIVIC SEDAN SPECIAL EDITION 5-SPEED	15,717	16,900
EJ661YXV	CIVIC SEDAN SPECIAL EDITION 4-SPEED AUTO	16,647	17,900
EJ650YX	CIVIC SEDAN EX 5-SPEED	16,008	17,400
EJ660YX	CIVIC SEDAN EX 4-SPEED AUTO	16,928	18,400
EJ658YX	CIVIC SEDAN EX-G 5-SPEED	17,388	18,900
EJ668YX	CIVIC SEDAN EX-G 4-SPEED AUTO	18,308	19,900
CG314YPB	ACCORD COUPE LX 5-SPEED	21,777	23,800
CG324YPB	ACCORD COUPE LX 4-SPEED AUTO	22,692	24,800
CG315YJN	ACCORD COUPE EX LTH 5-SPEED	25,437	27,800
CG325YJN	ACCORD COUPE EX LTH 4-SPEED AUTO	26,352	28,800
CG225YJN	ACCORD COUPE EX V6 4-SPEED AUTO	28,640	31,300
CF854YPB	ACCORD SEDAN DX 5-SPEED	20,130	22,000
CF864YPB	ACCORD SEDAN DX 4-SPEED AUTO	21,045	23,000
CG554YE	ACCORD SEDAN LX ABS 5-SPEED	22,235	24,300
CG564YE	ACCORD SEDAN LX ABS 4-SPEED AUTO	23,150	25,300
CG556YJN	ACCORD SEDAN EX LTH 5-SPEED	25,437	27,800
CG566YJN	ACCORD SEDAN EX LTH 4-SPEED AUTO	25,352	28,800
CG165YJN	ACCORD SEDAN EX V6 LTH 4-SPEED AUTO	28,640	31,300
RL185YE	ODYSSEY LX-CAPTAIN AUTO	28,182	30,800
RL186YPK	ODYSSEY EX-CAPTAIN AUTO	30,927	33,800
BB614YJ	PRELUDE 5-SPEED	25,529	27,900
BB624YJ	PRELUDE 4-SPEED AUTO	26,444	28,900
BB615YJ	PRELUDE TYPE SH 5-SPEED	29,189	31,900
Issue Date:	September 1, 1999		

Honda dealer markups are exceptionally low.

What's a fair price?

To come up with a fair price, subtract one-half the dealer markup from the MSRP and trade the carryover and holdback allowance for a reduced delivery and transportation fee. Compute the options separately and sell your trade-in privately. Buyers can more easily knock

$1,000–$2,000 off a $20,000 base price if they wait until January or February when sales are stagnant, choose a vehicle in stock, and forego unnecessary options.

Remember, the 7 percent GST and the provincial sales tax must be paid on the *negotiated* price of a new vehicle and not on its suggested selling price. GST is calculated before subtracting the trade-in value from the purchase price. For example, if you buy a vehicle for $20,000 (plus $200 for transport and PDI), and you have a $5,000 trade-in, you must pay 7 percent GST on the $20,200. Taxes that have to be paid are a fuel conservation tax, a $100 federal excise tax on air conditioning, and provincial sales tax calculated on the $20,200 plus the GST. If there's a $1,000 rebate, you deduct the amount from your total. You only pay GST and provincial sales tax once, at the point of purchase. You don't pay it each time you make a loan payment.

Once you and the dealer have settled on the vehicle's price, you aren't out of the woods yet. Like a tag-team wrestling match, you'll then be handed over to an F&I (financing and insurance) specialist, whose main goal is to convince you to buy additional financing, loan insurance, paint and seatcover protectors, rustproofing, and extended warranties. These items will be presented on a computer screen as costing only "a little bit more each month." Compare the dealer's insurance and financing charges with an independent agency that may offer better rates and better service. Often the dealer gets a kickback for selling insurance and financing, and guess who pays for it? Additionally, remember that if the financing rate looks too good to be true, you're probably paying too much for the vehicle. The F&I closer's hard-sell approach will take all your willpower and patience to resist, but when he gives up, your trials are over.

Don't overpay the sales tax. Make sure that each transaction is treated separately and that the trade-in amount is deducted from the new vehicle price before provincial tax is calculated. The federal 7 percent GST will be charged on the full price of the contract, including all options, and provincial tax is then charged only after the trade-in value has been deducted.

Add-on charges are the dealer's last chance to stick it to you before the contract is signed. Dealer preparation PDI and transportation charges, "documentation" fees, and extra handling costs are ways that the dealer gets extra profits for nothing. Dealer preparation is a once-over-lightly affair, with a car seldom getting more than a wash job and a couple of dollars of gas in the tank. It's paid for by the factory in most cases and, when it's not, should cost no more than 2 percent of the car's selling price. Reasonable transportation charges are acceptable, although they're often inflated by dealers who claim that the manufacturer requires the payment.

Wait until management has approved the vehicle's bottom-line price you've agreed upon before rejecting these add-on charges; otherwise the dealership may try to pad the price to get its normal add-on profit. Negotiate delivery and preparation charges down to a strict minimum. Dealers are particularly adept at boosting these charges, but if you head for the door, they'll relent. Remember, the key to keeping costs down is to sell your trade-in privately (see "Selling Your Trade-In"), keep options to a minimum, and don't accept a high markup for low interest rates or a rebate.

Dealer incentives and customer rebates

When vehicles are first introduced in the fall, they're generally overpriced. Later on, near the end of summer, automakers offer customer cash rebates of $750–$3,000, and increased dealer cash incentives for almost as much. Incentives are first offered during the winter months and boosted in late summer or early fall when dealer showroom traffic has fallen off. Smart shoppers who buy during these months can shave an additional 10 percent off a vehicle's list price by double-dipping from both of these automaker rebate programs.

In most cases, the manufacturer's rebate is straightforward and mailed directly to the buyer from the automaker. But there are other rebate programs that require a financial investment on the dealer's part. These shared programs tempt dealers to offset losses by inflating the selling price or pocketing the manufacturer's rebate. Therefore, when the dealer participates in the rebate program, demand that the rebate be deducted from the suggested selling price and not from some inflated invoice price concocted by the dealer.

Some rebate ads will include the phrase "from dealer inventory only." If your dealer doesn't have the vehicle in stock, you won't get the rebate. Keep in mind that the manufacturer's rebate is considered to be part of the fair value and is not deductible from the purchase price prior to determining the retail sales tax payable.

Sometimes automakers will suddenly decide that a rebate no longer applies to a specific model, even though their ads continue to include it. If this happens, take all brochures and advertisements showing your eligibility for the rebate plan to provincial consumer protection officials. They can use false advertising statutes to force automakers to give rebates to every purchaser who was unjustly denied one.

When buying a heavily discounted vehicle, be wary of "option packaging" by dealers who push unwanted protection packages (rustproofing, paint sealants, and upholstery finishes) or levy excessive charges for preparation, filing fees, loan guarantee insurance, and credit life insurance.

Rebate savings

To come out ahead, you have to know how to play the rebate game. Customer and dealer incentives are frequently given out to stimulate sales of year-old models that are unpopular, scheduled to be redesigned, or headed for the axe. By choosing carefully which rebated models you buy, it's easy to achieve important savings with little downside risk. For example, GM's $1,000 incentive on its Cavalier and Sunbird models is a great deal on these inexpensive, slow-depreciating, well-equipped small cars that are also reasonably reliable. On the other hand, GM's Tahoe, Yukon, and Catera rebates ($1,500–$3,000) will barely cover these vehicles' poor performance and high maintenance costs. The same can be said of Ford's $1,500–$2,000 rebates on the Taurus, Sable, Contour, and Mystique. These four vehicles have had serious reliability problems and the Contour and Mystique will be dropped this year.

False bargains, indeed.

Prevailing market value
Generally, vehicles are priced according to what the market will bear. Therefore, a vehicle's stylishness, scarcity, or general popularity can inflate its value considerably. For example, the Dodge Sebring convertible and Ford Explorer sport-utility have a prevailing market value that's higher than their suggested selling price, mainly because they're part of a hot market segment and in short supply. Once sales slow down later in the new year, popular cars will sell at a discount. A good general rule for vehicles that have a high prevailing market value is to wait for their popularity to subside, or to purchase the previous year's version. Don't try this with a Honda Accord or Toyota Camry, however. Their market value generally stays constant throughout the year. On the other hand, if a vehicle has an unusually low market value (like the Chevrolet Astro and Safari), find out why it's so unpopular before buying it. (In the GM example, both mini-vans have a worse-than-deserved reputation for being unreliable.)

Vehicles that don't sell because of their weird styling are no problem, but reports of poor quality control can send prices plummeting. Already, Ford Taurus and Sable owners are finding that dealers are reluctant to take their cars in trade due to reports of serious engine and transmission defects afflicting the 1991–95 models. This perceived lack of quality has carried over to the automaker's new models and resulted in lower-priced '98 models. If consumer confidence isn't restored, buyers will likely see these two Ford models drastically reduced in price this year through rebates and dealer incentives.

Accommodation sales
To carry out an accommodation sale, you must first find a buyer for your trade-in and obtain the cooperation of the dealer who'll be selling you your new vehicle. The dealer reduces the new-car cost by deducting the selling price of the trade-in. This lowers the amount of sales tax you pay on the new car. The buyer of the trade-in pays you through the dealer, and the dealer ends up selling a new car plus receiving an additional small fee (usually $50) for permitting the transaction. The seller pays the dealer's fee and is responsible for any serious problems that the buyer may have with the trade-in.

Leftovers: false bargains?
In the fall, at the beginning of each new model year, most dealers still have a few of last year's cars left. Some are new, some are demonstrators. The factory gives the dealer a 3–5 percent rebate on late-season cars, and dealers will often pass on some of these savings to clients. But are these leftovers really bargains?

They might be, if you can amortize the first year's depreciation by keeping the vehicle for six to ten years. But if you're the kind of driver who trades every two or three years, you're likely to come out a loser by buying an end-of-season car. The simple reason is that as far as trade-ins are concerned, a leftover is a used car that has depreciated at least 10–15 percent. The savings the dealer gives you may not equal that first year's depreciation, a cost you'll incur without getting any of the first year's driving benefits. If the dealer's discounted price matches or exceeds the depreciation, then you're getting a pretty good deal. But if the next year's model is only a bit more expensive, and has been substantially improved or is covered by a more extensive, comprehensive warranty, it could represent a better buy than a slightly cheaper leftover.

Ask the dealer for all work orders relating to the car and make sure that the odometer readings follow in sequential order. Remember as well that most demonstrators have less than 5,000 km on the ticker, and the original warranty has been reduced from the day the vehicle was first put on the road. Have the dealer extend the warranty or lower the price accordingly—about $100 for each month of warranty that has expired. If the vehicle's file shows that it was registered to a leasing agency or any other third party, you're definitely buying a used vehicle disguised as a demo. You should walk away from the sale because you're dealing with a crook.

Mid-year models
Entirely new models often make their debut in mid-summer, and getting any kind of a discount from the dealer for mid-year models is like pulling teeth. Dealers know that a seller's market exists during the first few months of a model's launch, and they're not likely to sell their few sample cars for anything less than full price. Furthermore, you're likely to lose an extra year of depreciation since, over time, mid-year vehicles are depreciated back to the beginning of the model year in which they were introduced.

Paying Cash vs. Getting a Loan

The accounting firm of Price Waterhouse says that it may be smarter to borrow the money to purchase a new vehicle even if you can afford to pay cash, because if you use the vehicle for business a portion of the interest may be tax deductible. The cash that you free up can then be used to repay debts that aren't tax deductible (mortgages or credit card debt, for example).

Hidden loan costs
Decide how much you want to spend and then pre-arrange your loan before you buy the car, so that you'll know in advance if your credit is good enough to qualify for the amount you need. In your quest for an auto loan, remember that the Internet offers help for people who need an auto loan, want quick approval, but don't like to face a banker. The Bank of Montreal (*www.bmo.com*) was the first Canadian bank that accepted

loan applications on its website, and claims to send a loan response within 20 seconds. Other banks, such as Royal Bank, are offering a similar service. Loans are available to any web surfer, including those who aren't current Montreal or Royal customers.

Be sure to call various financial institutions to find out:
• the annual percentage rate on the amount you want to borrow and for the duration of your repayment period;
• the minimum down payment that the institution requires;
• whether taxes and licence fees are considered part of the overall cost, and thus covered by part of the loan;
• whether lower rates are available for different loan periods or for a larger down payment; and
• whether discounts are available to depositors, and if so, how long you must be a depositor before qualifying.

When comparing loans, consider the annual rate and calculate the total cost of the loan offer; that is, how much you'll pay above and beyond the total price of the vehicle.

Don't dismiss dealer financing out of hand. Dealers can finance the cost of a new car at interest rates that are competitive with the banks because of the rebates they get from the manufacturers and some lending institutions. Some dealers, though, mislead their customers into thinking they can borrow money at as much as 5 percentage points below the prime rate. Actually, they're jacking up the retail price to more than make up for the lower interest charges. Sometimes, instead of boosting the price, dealers reduce the amount they pay for the trade-in. In either case, the savings are illusory.

When dealing with banks, keep in mind that the traditional 36-month loan has now been stretched to 48 and 60 months. Longer payment terms make each month's payment more affordable, but over the long run they increase the cost of the loan considerably. Therefore, take as short a term as possible.

Be wary of lending institutions that charge a "processing" or "document" fee, ranging from $99–$150. Sometimes consumers will be charged an extra 1–2 percent of the loan up front in order to cover servicing. This is similar to lending institutions adding "points" to mortgages, and it's totally unjustified.

Some banks will cut the interest rate if you're a member of an automobile owners association, or if loan payments are automatically deducted from your chequing account. This latter proposal may be costly, though, if the chequing account charges exceed the interest rate savings.

Finance companies affiliated with GM, Ford, and Chrysler have been offering low-interest loans many points below the prime rate. In many cases, this low rate is applicable only to hard-to-sell models or cars equipped with expensive options. The low rate frequently doesn't cover the entire loan period. If vehicles recommended in this book are covered by low-interest loans, then the automaker-affiliated finance companies become a useful alternative to regular banking institutions.

TRADE IN DESCRIPTION & LIEN DISCLOSURE			TERMS OF SETTLEMENT		
☐ G.S.T. REGISTRANT	G.S.T. REGISTRANT NO.		TOTAL CASH SALE PRICE	*10800*	*00*
YEAR	MI / KM	ODOMETER READING			
MAKE	MODEL		SUBTOTAL	*10800*	*0·*
SERIAL					
YEAR	MI / KM	ODOMETER READING	TRADE-IN ALLOWANCE		
MAKE	MODEL		SUBTOTAL		
SERIAL					
I HEREWITH TRANSFER TO DEALER ALL MY RIGHTS, TITLE AND OWNERSHIP IN THE ABOVE MOTOR VEHICLE, AND I DECLARE I AM THE SOLE OWNER AND POSSESSOR OF SAME AND THAT THERE IS NO MORTGAGE, LIEN, NOTE OR CLAIM OF ANY KIND OR NATURE ADVERSE TO MY RIGHTS OF, UPON, OR AGAINST SAID VEHICLE OTHER THAN AS STATED BELOW			G.S.T.	*756*	*00*
			SUBTOTAL	*11556*	*00*
I HEREBY STATE THAT TO THE BEST OF MY KNOWLEDGE THE ODOMETER READING AS STATED ABOVE INDICATES THE TOTAL DISTANCE ACTUALLY TRAVELLED BY THE VEHICLE.					
CUSTOMER SIGNATURE X			ADMINISTRATION FEE	99	00
LIEN PAYABLE TO			PAYOUT LIEN ON TRADE-IN		
ADDRESS		$	BALANCE DUE	*11655*	*00*
			DEPOSIT CASH ☐ CHEQUE ☐ VISA	*1000*	*00*
			PAYABLE ON DELIVERY	*10656*	*00*
THIS AGREEMENT SUBJECT TO FOLLOWING ADDITIONAL PROVISIONS. ONLY THESE PROVISIONS WILL BE RECOGNIZED.					

Dealer greed knows no bounds. This buyer was charged a $99 "administration fee" for a USED car!

Loan protection

Credit insurance guarantees that the car loan will be paid if the borrower becomes disabled or dies. There are three basic types of insurance that can be written into an installment contract: credit life, accident and health, and comprehensive. Most bank and credit union loans are already covered by some kind of loan insurance, but dealers sell the protection separately at an extra cost to the borrower. For this service the dealer gets a hefty commission that may vary between 10 and 20 percent. The additional cost to the purchaser can be significant. The federal 7 percent GST is applied to loan insurance, but provincial sales tax is exempted in provinces such as Ontario.

Collecting on these types of policies isn't easy. There's no payment if your illness is due to some condition that existed prior to your taking out the insurance. Nor will the policy cover strikes, layoffs, etc. Generally, credit insurance is unnecessary if you're in good health, have no dependents, and your job is secure.

The Royal Bank has two interesting loan programs. One protects motorists from depreciation losses arising from an accident. For example, if a vehicle is scrapped after an accident, the Royal Bank will reimburse its depreciated value. The other program keeps monthly payments low, except for a final balloon payment.

There are plenty of advantageous programs available elsewhere. Personal loans from financial institutions now offer lots of flexibility. Most offer 100 percent financing (with no down payment), fixed or variable interest rates, a choice of loan terms, and no penalties for prepayment. Precise conditions depend on your personal credit rating. Leasing contracts are less flexible. There's a penalty for any prepayment, and rates aren't necessarily competitive. Finally, credit unions can also underwrite new-car loans that combine a flexible payment schedule with low rates.

Negotiating the Contract

Any document that requires your signature is a contract. Don't sign anything unless all the details are clear to you and all the blanks have been filled in. Don't accept any verbal promises. Remember, too, that your contract doesn't have to include all the clauses found in the dealer's preprinted form. You and the sales representative can agree to strike some clauses and add others. It's up to you to negotiate the best deal for yourself.

When the sales agent asks for a deposit, make sure that it's stated on the contract as a deposit and try to keep it as small as possible (a couple of hundred dollars at the most). If you decide to back out of the deal on a vehicle taken from stock, let the seller have the deposit as an incentive to cancel the contract (believe me, it's cheaper than a lawyer and probably equal to his or her commission).

Scrutinize all references to prices and delivery dates. Delivery can sometimes be delayed three to five months, and you'll have to pay all price increases announced during the interim (3–5 percent) unless you specify a delivery date in the contract that protects the price.

Make sure that the contract indicates your new vehicle will be delivered to you with a full tank of gas. At one time, this was the buyer's responsibility, however, with drivers spending almost $30,000 for the average new vehicle, dealers usually throw in a free tank of gas in the process. In fact, a 1998 Maritz New Vehicle Buyer Study that polled 31,763 Canadian buyers found that 72 percent of buyers left the dealership with a free full tank of fuel (Toyota Canada insists upon it).

Additional clauses

You can put things on a more equal footing by negotiating the inclusion of as many clauses as possible from the sample additional contract clauses found on page 78. To do this, write in a "Remarks" section on your contract, and add "See attached clauses, which form part of this agreement." Then attach a photocopy of the "Additional Contract Clauses" and have the sales agent initial as many of the clauses as you can. Although some clauses may be rejected, the inclusion of just a couple of these clauses can have important legal ramifications later on if you want a full or partial refund. For example, as a result of GM's recent two-month strike, many GM dealers will experience two- and three-month delivery delays and may try to pass on to their customers any price increases announced in the interim. Clauses #2 and #4 will protect you from these delays and price increases.

Don't take the dealer's word that "we're not allowed to do that," heard most often in reference to your cancelling the sale or reducing the PDI/transportation fee. Sales are cancelled all the time. In fact,

Saturn made a big deal of its money-back warranty in which only a few dozen purchasers sought refunds over the several years the program was in effect. If Saturn dealers can do it, other dealers can, too. As far as PDI/transportation fees are concerned, some dealers have been telling *Lemon-Aid* readers that they are "obligated" by the automaker to charge a set fee and could lose their franchise if they charge less. This is pure hogwash. No dealer has ever had their franchise licence revoked for cutting prices, and the automakers clearly state that they don't set a bottom-line price, since that would violate Canada's Competition Act—that's why you always see them putting disclaimers in their ads saying the dealer can charge less.

The pre-delivery inspection
Many new vehicle orders are screwed up by the factory, so the pre-delivery inspection (PDI) is critical for making sure that corrections are made before taking delivery. Also, because about 10 percent of new vehicles are damaged in transit from the factory, the PDI can spot the damage and the extent of repairs needed. If the repair costs are substantial, the dealer can be forced to exchange the vehicle or give the buyer a rebate. Every auto manufacturer expects the dealer to carry out a PDI on each vehicle sold.

The PDI allowance is figured into the suggested retail price, so whatever you pay the dealer is profit. Dealers who don't get top dollar for a vehicle are tempted to skip the PDI. According to testimony before the U.S. Federal Trade Commission and the U.S. Senate Subcommittee on Antitrust and Monopoly, many dealers deliver vehicles straight from the factory to their customers with only a cursory inspection. This practice wouldn't have such serious consequences if vehicles were delivered from the factory in reasonably good shape. The PDI serves as a last stop to catch the three or so major and minor defects that *Consumer Reports* estimates afflict most new vehicles. If they aren't corrected before delivery, there's a good chance the dealer will charge to fix them later. And if these minor defects aren't caught in time, they can quickly become major failures.

The best way to ensure that the PDI will be done is to write in the sales contract that you'll be given a copy of the completed PDI sheet when the vehicle is delivered to you. Then, with the PDI sheet in hand, verify some of the items that were to be checked. If any items appear to have been missed, refuse delivery of the vehicle. Once you get home, check out the vehicle more thoroughly and send a registered letter to the dealer if you discover multiple major defects.

Additional Contract Clauses

1. **Financing:** This agreement is subject to the purchaser obtaining financing at a rate of _____% or less within _____ days of the date below. Failing notification in writing confirming approval of this financing, the contract is automatically cancelled.
2. **Delivery:** The vehicle is to be delivered by _____, failing which the contract is cancelled and the deposit will be refunded.
3. **Cancellation:** (a) The purchaser retains the right to cancel this agreement without penalty at any time before delivery of the vehicle by sending a notice in writing to the vendor.
   (b) Following delivery of the vehicle, the purchaser shall have two days to return the vehicle and cancel the agreement in writing, without penalty. After two days and before thirty-one days, the purchaser shall pay the dealer $25 a day as compensation for depreciation on the returned vehicle.
   (c) Cancellation of contract can be refused where the vehicle has been subjected to abuse, negligence, or unauthorized modifications after delivery.
   (d) The purchaser is responsible for accident damage and traffic violations while in possession of the said vehicle. The purchaser is also responsible for re-registering the vehicle traded in and obtaining reimbursement of the sales tax. If the traded vehicle has been resold, the vendor will remit the monetary value attributed to the vehicle when it was delivered to the vendor.
4. **Protected Price:** The vendor agrees not to alter the price of the new vehicle, the cost of preparation, or the cost of shipping.
5. **Trade-in:** The vendor agrees that the value attributed to the vehicle offered in trade shall not be reduced. An exception may be made when the said vehicle has been significantly modified or has suffered from unreasonable and accelerated deterioration since the signing of the agreement.
6. **Courtesy Car:** (a) In the event the new vehicle is not delivered on the agreed-upon date, the vendor agrees to supply the purchaser with a courtesy car at no cost. If no courtesy vehicle is available, the vendor agrees to reimburse the purchaser the cost of renting a vehicle of equivalent or lesser value than the new car purchased.
   (b) If the vehicle is off the road for more than five days for warranty repairs, the purchaser is entitled to a free courtesy vehicle for the duration of the repair period. If no courtesy vehicle is available, the vendor agrees to reimburse the purchaser the cost of renting a vehicle of equivalent or lesser value.
7. **Work Orders:** The purchaser will receive duly completed copies of all work orders pertaining to the vehicle, including warranty repairs and the original pre-delivery inspection (PDI).
8. **Dealer Stickers:** The vendor will not affix any dealer advertising, in any form, on the purchaser's new vehicle.
9. **Fuel:** Vehicle will be delivered with a free full tank of gas.

_____   _____   _____
Date   **Vendor's Signature**   **Buyer's Signature**

Selling Your Trade-In

Buy, sell, or hold?
It doesn't take a genius to figure out that the longer one keeps a vehicle, the less it costs to own—up to a point. The Hertz Corporation has estimated that a small car equipped with standard options, driven 10,000 miles (16,000 km), and traded each year, costs 9.6 cents more a mile than a comparable car traded after five years. That same car kept for ten years and run 10,000 miles a year would cost 10.8 cents less a mile (6.75 cents less a kilometre) than a similar vehicle kept for five years, and a whopping 20.38 cents less a mile (12.75 cents a kilometre) than a comparable compact traded in each year. That would amount to a savings of $20,380 over a ten-year period.

Shortly after your vehicle's fifth birthday (or whenever you start to think about trading it in), ask a mechanic to look at it to give you some idea of the repairs, replacement parts, and maintenance work it will need in the coming year. Find out if dealer service bulletins show that it will need extensive repairs in the near future. (See Appendix II on how to order a bulletin summary.) If it's going to require expensive repairs, you should trade the car right away, but if expensive work isn't necessary you may want to keep your vehicle. Auto owner associations provide a good yardstick. They estimate that the annual cost of repairs and preventive maintenance for the average car is between $500 and $600. If your vehicle is five years old and you haven't spent anywhere near $3,000 in maintenance, it would pay to invest in your old car and continue using it for another few years.

Consider whether your car can still be serviced easily. If it's no longer on the market, the parts supply is likely to dry up and independent mechanics will be reluctant to repair it.

Don't trade for fuel economy alone. More fuel-efficient vehicles, such as front-wheel drives, offset the savings through higher repair costs. Also, the more fuel-efficient cars may not be as comfortable to drive due to excessive engine noise, lightweight construction, and stiff suspension and torque steer.

Reassess your needs. Does your family growth require a different vehicle? Are you driving less? Are long trips taken less frequently? Let your car rust in peace and pocket the savings if its deteriorating condition doesn't pose a safety hazard or isn't too embarrassing. On the other hand, if you're in sales and are constantly on the road, it makes sense to trade every few years—in that case mechanical reliability becomes a prime consideration, and the increased depreciation costs are mostly tax deductible.

Getting the most for your trade-in
Customers who are on guard against paying too much for a new car often sell their trade-ins for too little. Before agreeing to any trade-in amount, read Part Three of *Lemon-Aid Used Cars 2000* if your trade-in is

a passenger car or minivan. For prices on used pickups, vans, or sport-utilities, consult *Lemon-Aid Used 4X4s, Vans and Trucks 2000*. Both guides give your vehicle's dealer and private selling price, and offer a formula to figure out regional price fluctuations. For a small fee, you can also obtain new and used car prices by calling the Montreal or Toronto office of the Automobile Protection Association (514-273-1733 or 416-964-6774). Keep in mind, however, that the APA can't guarantee that you'll always get the lowest price possible. In fact, some buyers tell me that they've done better buying a new or used car on their own.

Now that you've nailed down your trade-in's approximate value, here are some tips on selling it with a minimum of stress:

• Never sign a new car sales contract unless your trade-in has been sold—you could end up with two cars.

• Negotiate the price from retail (dealer price) down to *wholesale* (private sales).

• If you haven't sold your trade-in after two weekends, you might be trying to sell it at the wrong time of year or have it priced too high.

Private sales

If you must sell your vehicle and want to make the most out of the deal, consider selling it yourself and putting the profits toward your next purchase. You'll likely come out hundreds or thousands of dollars ahead—buyers will pay more for your vehicle, since they won't have to pay the 7 percent GST on a private sale. The most important thing to remember is that there's a large market for used vehicles in good condition in the $7,000–$10,000 range. Although most people prefer buying from individuals rather than from used-car lots, they may still be afraid that the vehicle is a lemon. The following suggestions should enable you to assuage that fear and sell your vehicle quite easily:

1. Know its value. Study dealers' newspaper ads and compare them with the prices listed in this book. Undercut the dealer price by $300–$800, and be ready to bargain down another 10 percent for a serious buyer. Remember that prices can fluctuate wildly depending on which models are trendy, so watch the want ads carefully.

2. Enlist the aid of the salesperson who is selling you your new car. Offer him a couple of hundred dollars if he finds you a buyer. The fact that one sale hinges on the other, and the prospect of making two commissions, may work wonders.

3. Post notices on bulletin boards at your office or local supermarkets, and place a "For Sale" sign in the window of the car itself. Place a newspaper ad only as a last resort.

4. Don't give your address right away to a potential buyer responding to your ad. Instead, ask for the telephone number where you may call that person back.

5. Don't sell to friends or family members. Anything short of perfection, and you can forget Christmas dinner with the family.

6. Don't touch the odometer. You may get a few hundred dollars more—and a criminal record.
7. Paint the vehicle. Some specialty shops charge only $300 and give a guarantee that's transferable to subsequent owners.
8. Make minor repairs. This includes a minor tune-up and patching up the exhaust. Again, if any repair warranty is transferable, use it as a selling point.
9. Clean the vehicle. Go to a reconditioning firm or spend the weekend scrubbing the interior and exterior. First impressions are important. Clean the chrome, polish the body, and peel off old bumper stickers. Remove butts from the ashtrays and clean out the glove compartment. Make sure all tools and spare parts have been taken out of the trunk. Don't remove the radio or speakers. The gaping holes will make the vehicle worth much less than the radio or speakers cost. Replace missing or broken dash knobs and window cranks.
10. Change the tires. Recaps are good buys.
11. Let the buyer examine the vehicle. Insist that the vehicle be inspected by an independent garage, and accompany the prospective buyer to the garage.
12. Keep important documents handy. Show prospective buyers the sales contract, repair orders, owner's manual, and all other documents that show how the vehicle has been maintained. Authenticate your claims about fuel consumption.
13. Don't mislead the buyer. If the vehicle was in an accident, or some financing is still to be paid, admit it. Any misleading statements may be used later in court against you. It's also advisable to have someone witness the actual transaction in case of a future dispute.
14. Sell to a dealer who sells the same make. He'll give you more because he can easily sell your trade-in to customers who are interested only in that make of vehicle.
15. Write an effective ad.

Selling to dealers
Selling to a dealer means that you're likely to get 20 percent less than if you sold your vehicle privately, unless the dealer agrees to participate in an accommodation sale. Most sellers will gladly pay some penalty to the dealer, however, for the peace of mind that comes with knowing that the eventual buyer won't lay a claim against them. This assumes that the dealer hasn't been cheated by the seller—if the car is stolen, isn't paid for, has had its odometer spun back (or forward to a lower setting), or is seriously defective, the buyer or dealer can sue the original owner for fraud.

Drawing up the contract
Draw up a bill of sale in duplicate and date it (photocopy the sample bill of sale on the following page). Identify the vehicle (including the serial number), its price, whether a warranty applies, and the nature of the examination made by the buyer. The buyer may ask you to put in a lower

price than what was actually paid in order to reduce the sales tax. If you agree to this, don't be surprised when a Ministry of Revenue agent comes to your door. Although the purchaser is ultimately the responsible party, you're an accomplice in defrauding the government. Furthermore, if you turn to the courts for redress your own conduct may be put on trial.

Bill of Sale
Used Vehicles

1. The seller agrees to sell, and the buyer agrees to buy a:
   a) _____ , b) _____ .
       Year   Serial Number

2. The seller is selling the motor vehicle:
   ❏ without a warranty
   ❏ with the following warranty _____ .

3. The buyer:
   ❏ has test driven the motor vehicle
   ❏ has not test driven the motor vehicle.

4. The purchase price in full is $_____ .

5. The seller acknowledges receiving from the buyer a deposit in the amount of $_____ .

6. The seller warrants and guarantees that there are no liens, chattel mortgages, or security agreements outstanding with respect to the motor vehicle or any equipment and/or accessories, and that the motor vehicle and any equipment and/or accessories has/have not been given as collateral on any loan.

7. The seller and the buyer agree that the buyer was allowed to take the motor vehicle for an inspection by a mechanic before the signing of this agreement.

8. The seller warrants to the buyer that to the best of his knowledge:
   a) the odometer reading on the motor vehicle is accurate,
   b) the motor vehicle has not been damaged in a collision, and
   c) there are no outstanding traffic violations with respect to the motor vehicle.

_____	_____
Date	City
_____	_____
Buyer	Seller

After the sale
Don't forget to take your licence plates off the car. They're your property and must remain with you once the vehicle has been sold. In most

provinces, your vehicle's registration certificate will have a plate portion and a vehicle portion. When the car is sold, the vehicle portion of the permit must be signed by you and given to the buyer. The remaining portion and your plates must be turned in to your province's Ministry of Transportation if you don't intend to buy another vehicle. You'll get a refund for the unexpired time left on your plates. If you decide to buy another car, you can put your old plates on it (if it's a similar class of vehicle), but it has to be re-registered within a short period (usually a week).

Summary

Purchasing a vehicle used saves you the most money. Paying cash or with the biggest down payment you can afford, and piling up as many kilometres and years as possible on your trade-in, are the next best ways to save money. Remember, too, that safety is another consideration largely dependent on the type of vehicle you choose. Focus on the following objectives.

Buy smart
1. Buy the vehicle you need and can afford, not what someone wants you to buy, or one loaded with options that you'll probably never use. Take your time. Price comparisons and test drives may take a month, but you'll get a better car and price in the long run.
2. Buy in winter or later in the new year to double-dip from dealer incentive and customer rebate programs.
3. Sell your trade-in privately.
4. Arrange financing before buying your vehicle.
5. Test-drive your choice by renting it overnight or for several days.
6. Buy through the Internet, by fax, or use an auto broker if you're not confident in your own bargaining skills, lack the time to haggle, or want to avoid the "showroom shakedown."
7. Ask for at least a 5 percent discount off the MSRP and cut pre-delivery inspection and freight charges by at least 50 percent. Insist on a specific delivery date written in the contract as well as a protected price, in case there's a price increase from the time the contract is signed and when the vehicle is delivered. Plus, ask for a free tank of gas.
8. Order a minimum of options and seek a 30 percent discount on the entire option list. Try not to let the total option cost exceed 15 percent of the vehicle's MSRP.
9. Try to avoid leasing. If you must lease, choose the shortest time possible, drive down the MSRP, and refuse to pay an "acquisition" fee.
10. Japanese vehicles made in North America, co-ventures with American automakers, and re-badged imports often cost less than imports, and are just as reliable. But some Asian and European imports aren't as reliable as you might imagine—Hyundai, Jaguar, and Saab are prime examples. Get extra warranty protection from the automaker if you're buying a model that has a poorer-than-average repair, quality control, or

warranty performance history. Use auto club references to get honest, competent repairs at a reasonable price.

Buy safe
Look for:
1. a high crashworthiness rating and low rollover potential;
2. good quality radial tires—be wary of "all-season" tires;
3. three-point belts with belt pretensioners and adjustable shoulder belt anchorages;
4. integrated child safety seats and seat anchors;
5. depowered dual airbags with a cutoff switch and highly rated, unobtrusive head restraints;
6. front driver's seat with plenty of rearward travel and a height adjustment;
7. good all-around visibility;
8. an ergonomic interior with an efficient heating and ventilation system; and
9. headlights that are adequate for night driving.

Now that you know what the rules of the game are, Part Two will show you how to fight back if that dream car turns into a nightmare and your dealer tells you to get lost.

Inadequate headlight illumination has been a chronic problem since 1993 on Chrysler's Concorde, Intrepid (shown above), LHS, New Yorker, and Vision. Take a test drive at night, before you purchase.

Part Two
FIGHTING BACK

We All Feel Your Pain, Ed

"Let's face it, the manufacturers have expanded coverages and have exaggerated claims that confuse, anger and give the public a perception of warranties that are beyond their actual intent...and the dealer, not the manufacturers, receive the pillorying from the customers."

Ed Mullane, President
Ford Dealers Alliance
July 19, 1999

Both Chrysler and Runzheimer Consultants estimate that 1 out of every 10 American vehicles produced by the Big Three is a "lemon." If you've bought a lemon, or if you've been forced to pay for repairs that shouldn't be your responsibility, this section will help you get your money back—without going to court or getting frazzled by the broken promises or "benign neglect" of the dealer or private party who sold you the vehicle. But if going to court is your only recourse, you'll find the jurisprudence you need to get an out-of-court settlement or to win your case without spending a fortune on lawyers and research.

A paint-delaminated Ford Taurus. Chrysler, Ford, and GM will repaint their vehicles for free, if threatened with a small claims lawsuit.

Subject: Re: defective Chrysler Transaxle
Date: Thu, 12 Feb 1998 19:14:36 –0500

Hi Phil,

Just thought that I would let you know that I received a "goodwill" cheque from Chrysler Canada today in the amount of $1977.34 to cover the cost of transmission parts on my 91 Dodge Caravan. Thanks again for your advice—it sure was worthwhile pursuing the matter!!!

Sincerely,

Wayne Sockovie
Port Robinson, Ont. Canada.

Three Ways to Get Your Money Back

Remember the "money-back" guarantee? Well, with the exception of Saturn, automakers are reluctant to offer any warranty that requires them to take back a defective new car or minivan. Nevertheless, our provincial consumer protection laws have filled the gap so that now, any sales contract for a new or used vehicle can be cancelled—or free repairs can be ordered—if the vehicle:
• is misrepresented;
• is unfit for the purpose for which it was purchased; or
• hasn't been reasonably durable, considering how well it was maintained, the mileage driven, and the type of driving done (particularly applicable to engine, transmission, and paint defects).

Here's what the three legal concepts enumerated above mean in real-life situations: if the seller says that a minivan can pull a 900 kg (2,000 lb.) trailer and you discover that it can barely tow half that weight, you can cancel the contract for misrepresentation. The same principle applies to a seller's exaggerated claims concerning a vehicle's fuel economy or reliability, as well as to "demonstrators" that are in fact used cars with false (rolled back) odometer readings.

It's essential that printed evidence and/or witnesses (relatives are not excluded) are available to confirm that the false representation actually occurred. These misrepresentations must concern an important fact that substantially affects the vehicle's performance, reliability, or value.

When their products fail to live up to the advertised hype, automakers often blame the owner for having pushed the vehicle beyond its limits. Therefore, when you seek to set aside the contract by claiming that the vehicle is unfit for your needs, it's essential that you get the testimony of an independent mechanic and co-workers in order to prove that the vehicle's poor performance isn't caused by negligent maintenance or abusive driving.

The reasonable durability claim is probably the easiest allegation to prove, since all automakers have benchmarks as to how long body components, trim and finish, and mechanical and electronic parts should last (see the durability chart on pages 98–99). Vehicles are expected to be reasonably durable and merchantable. What is reasonably durable depends on the price paid, kilometres driven, purchaser's driving habits, and how well the vehicle was maintained by the owner. Judges carefully weigh all these factors in awarding compensation or cancelling a sale.

Whatever reason you use to get your money back, don't forget to conform to the "reasonable diligence" rule that requires you to file suit within a reasonable time after purchase or after you've discovered the defect. If there have been no negotiations with the dealer or automaker, this delay cannot exceed a few months. If either the dealer or the automaker has been promising to correct the defects for some time, or has carried out repeated unsuccessful repairs, the delay for filing the lawsuit can be extended.

Consequential damages

It's a lot easier to get the automaker to pay to replace a defective part than it is to obtain compensation for a missed day of work or a ruined vacation. Manufacturers hate to pay for consequential expenses under the basic warranty, supplementary warranty, or extended warranty because they can't control the amount of the refund. (Towing expenses, however, are usually accepted.) Courts are more generous, having ruled that all expenses (damages) flowing from a problem covered by a warranty or service bulletin are the manufacturer's/dealer's responsibility under both common law (all provinces except Quebec) and Quebec civil law. Fortunately, when legal action is threatened—usually through small claims court—automakers quickly back down from their refusal to pay consequential damage claims.

Warranties

In addition to the automakers' and dealers' *expressed* warranty, every vehicle sold new or used in Canada is covered by an *implied* warranty— a collection of federal and provincial laws and regulations that protect you from misrepresentation and a host of other evils. Furthermore, Canadian law presumes that car dealers, unlike private sellers, are aware of the defects present in the vehicles they sell. That way, dealers can't just pass the ball to the automakers and walk away from the dispute.

The manufacturer's warranty is a legal promise that its product will perform in the normal and customary manner for which it was designed. Regardless of the number of subsequent owners, this promise remains in force as long as the warranty's original time/kilometre limits haven't expired.

Tires and batteries aren't covered by most car manufacturers' warranties (except for GM's), and are warranted instead by the manufacturer on a pro-rated basis. Batteries are covered for at least a year against defects, and are then usually pro-rated for another 24 months. This isn't such a good deal, because the manufacturer is making a profit by charging you the full list price. If you were to buy the same replacement battery from a discount store you'd likely pay less, even without the pro-rated rebate. The same principle applies to tires, because you're given a pro-rated rebate on the suggested list price, which almost nobody pays.

Safety restraints, such as airbags and safety belts, usually mirror the basic warranty, with coverage extended for the lifetime of the vehicle.

Aftermarket products and services—such as gas-saving gadgets, rust-proofing, paint protectors, air conditioning, and van conversions—can render the manufacturer's warranty invalid, so be sure to check with your dealer before purchasing any optional equipment or services from an independent supplier.

How fairly a warranty is applied is more important than how long it remains in effect. The new warranties are useful to consumers who are making claims before provincial small claims courts, because they prove that the technology exists to make powertrain components and rust resistance/paint adhesion last far longer than admitted in the past. Once you know the normal wear rate for a mechanical component or body part, you can demand proportional compensation when you get less than normal durability—no matter what the original warranty said.

Some dealers tell customers that they need to have original equipment parts installed in order to maintain their warranty. A variation on this theme requires that routine servicing—including tune-ups and oil changes (with a certain brand of oil)—be done by the selling dealer, or the warranty is invalidated.

Nothing could be further from the truth. Canadian law stipulates that whoever issues a warranty cannot make that warranty conditional on the use of any specific brand of motor oil, oil filter, or any other component, unless it's provided to the customer free of charge.

Sometimes dealers will do all sorts of minor repairs that don't correct the problem, and then, after the warranty runs out, they'll tell you that major repairs are needed. You can avoid this nasty surprise by repeatedly bringing in your vehicle to the dealership before the warranty ends. During each visit, insist that a written work order include the specific nature of the problem, *as you see it*, and that it carries the notation that this is the second, third, or fourth time the same problem has been brought to the dealer's attention. Write it down yourself, if need be. This allows you to show a pattern of non-performance by the dealer during the warranty period and establishes that it's a serious and chronic problem. When the warranty expires, you have the legal right to demand that it be extended on those items consistently reappearing on your handful of work orders.

Extended (supplementary) warranties

Supplementary warranties providing extended coverage may be sold by the manufacturer, dealer, or an independent third party and are automatically transferred when the vehicle is sold. They cost between $500 and $1,500 and should be purchased only if the vehicle you're buying is off its original warranty or has a poor repair history (see Part Three), or if you're reluctant to use the small claims courts when factory-related trouble arises. Don't let the dealer pressure you into deciding right away. Generally, you can purchase an extended warranty anytime during the period in which the manufacturer's warranty is in effect.

Because one-third to one-half of the warranty's cost represents dealer markup, dealers love to sell extended warranties. Out of the remainder comes the sponsor's administration costs and profit margin, calculated at another 25 percent. What's left is a minuscule 25 percent of the original amount paid to the dealer. It's estimated that, of the car buyers who purchase an extended service contract, fewer than half actually use it.

It's often difficult to collect on supplementary warranties, because independent companies not tied to the automakers frequently go out of business. When this happens, and the company's insurance policy won't cover your claim, take the dealer to small claims court and ask for the repair cost and a refund of the original warranty payment. Your argument for holding the dealer responsible is a simple one: by accepting a commission for acting as an agent of the defunct company, the selling dealer took on the obligations of the company as well.

Emissions control warranties
These little-publicized warranties can save you big bucks if major engine or exhaust components fail prematurely. They come with all new vehicles and cover the emissions control system for up to 8 years/130,000 km. Unfortunately, although owners' manuals vaguely mention the emissions warranty, most don't specify which parts are covered. Fortunately, the U.S. Environmental Protection Agency has intervened on several occasions with hefty fines against Chrysler and Ford and ruled that all major motor and fuel-system components are covered. These include fuel metering, ignition spark advance, restart, evaporative emissions, positive crankcase ventilation, engine electronics (computer modules), and catalytic converters, as well as hoses, clamps, brackets, pipes, gaskets, belts, seals, and connectors. Canada, however, has no government definition, and it's left up to each manufacturer and the small claims courts to decide which components are covered.

Some of the dealer service bulletins listed in *Lemon-Aid's* bulletin summaries show parts failures that are covered under the emissions warranty. The two recent bulletins that follow, applicable to Ford's trucks, vans, and sport-utilities, are a good example. It is explicitly stated that owners of these vehicles who experience hard starting, chronic stalling, or excessive exhaust noises will get free repairs under the basic warranty, and when the basic warranty expires, under the emissions warranty. Unfortunately, few owners will ever see these bulletins, and will end up paying for repairs that are really Ford's responsibility.

```
Article No.
97-9-5
04/28/97
LONG CRANK - STICKING IDLE AIR CONTROL (IAC) VALVE - VEHICLES BUILT FROM 11/1/94 THROUGH 3/30/96 STALL -
AFTER STARTING WHEN ENGINE ALLOWED TO SOAK FROM 1-4 HOURS - STICKING IDLE AIR CONTROL (IAC) VALVE - VEHICLES
BUILT FROM 1/11/94 THROUGH 3/30/96
1995-96 CONTOUR, CROWN VICTORIA, ESCORT, TAURUS, THUNDERBIRD
1996 MUSTANG
LINCOLN-MERCURY:
1995-96 CONTINENTAL, COUGAR, GRAND MARQUIS, MARK VIII, MYSTIQUE, SABLE, TOWN CAR, TRACER
LIGHT TRUCK:
1995-96 AEROSTAR, BRONCO, ECONOLINE, F-150-350 SERIES, RANGER, WINDSTAR
1996 EXPLORER
ISSUE:
After a 1-4 hour engine soak time, long crank times and/or long crank to start followed by a stall may occur on some vehi-
cles. No further stalling or rough idle will occur after the engine is running. The long crank and/or stall may be due to the
Idle Air Control (IAC) Valve sticking.
ACTION:
Replace the AC Valve with a revised AC Valve if no Diagnostic Trouble Codes (DTCs) are present.
WARRANTY STATUS: Eligible Under The Provisions Of Bumper to Bumper Warranty Coverage And Emissions Warranty
```

This fuel system repair would cost you several hundred dollars, if you didn't have this bulletin in your possession.

```
97-16-6
08/04/97
• EXHAUST SYSTEM - LOOSE CATALYST OR MUFFLER HEAT SHIELDS
• NOISE - "BUZZING" OR "RATTLING" - LOOSE CATALYST OR MUFFLER HEAT SHIELDS
FORD:
1985-94 TEMPO                                    1986-97 TAURUS
1985-97 CROWN VICTORIA, MUSTANG, THUNDERBIRD     1988-93 FESTIVA
1985-98 ESCORT                                   1989-97 PROBE

LINCOLN-MERCURY:
1985-92 MARK VII                                 1987-89 TRACER
1985-94 TOPAZ                                    1991-94 CAPRI
1985-97 CONTINENTAL, COUGAR, GRAND MARQUIS, TOWN CAR   1991-98 TRACER
1986-97 SABLE

MERKUR:
1985-89 XR4TI                                    1988-89 SCORPIO

LIGHT TRUCK:
1985-90 BRONCO II                                1986-97 AEROSTAR
1985-96 BRONCO                                   1988-97 F SUPER DUTY
1985-97 ECONOLINE, F-150, F-250, F-350, RANGER   1991-97 EXPLORER
```

This TSB article is being republished in its entirety to include vehicles built through the 1997 model year.
ISSUE:
A "buzzing or rattling" noise from the exhaust system may be caused by a loose heat shield attachment to the muffler or
catalyst. The noise is noticeable during normal driving conditions or at engine idle.
ACTION:
Install worm clamps to secure the heat shield attachments.
WARRANTY STATUS: Eligible Under Basic Warranty Coverage For 1991 And Prior Models, Bumper to Bumper Warranty Coverage
For 1992-97 Models, And Emissions Warranty Coverage For Catalytic Converters With Welded Heat Shields For All Model Years

Many problems related to the exhaust system are also covered by the emissions warranty.

Make sure you get your emissions system checked out thoroughly by a dealer or independent garage before the emissions warranty expires and before having the vehicle inspected by provincial emissions inspectors. In addition to ensuring you pass provincial tests, this precaution could save you up to $1,000 if both your catalytic converter and your other emissions components are faulty, as the following *Lemon-Aid* reader relates:

Knowing my '96 Pontiac Grand Am has "second level diagnostics" (OBD 2) and has the ability to store intermittent code alerts in its computer, I phoned my brother-in-law, who is an Ontario licenced mechanic, (I'm an Ontario licenced auto body repairer) and asked him to "scan" my car with his Snap-On scanner for any hidden trouble codes.

He did, and sure enough, he found that it had a defective oxygen sensor that never triggered the CHECK ENGINE light to come on. How long it had been defective, I have no idea. But, I knew it was using more gas than it should because I was filling it up every week. (Now a tank of gas lasts two weeks since it's been fixed.)

So I took it to the dealer and explained what we did and showed them the data from the scanner. They fixed it for free, right away. (If they didn't, I was advised to contact Environment Canada.)

Phil, please urge people to have their "second level diagnostics" scanned by an independent garage before the warranty expires, because the cost of the check-out is small compared to the cost of replacing emissions components out of warranty, not to mention the hassle if their cars won't pass an emissions test because of failed components that nobody knew about.

D.R.
St. Catharines, Ontario

Thanks for the tip. By the way, the "check engine" or "service engine soon" lights are notorious for coming on for no apparent reason; GM estimates that 99% of car owners can expect one false warning during the first 16,000 km (10,000 miles). Most motorists ignore the warning since it usually only shows a glitch in the emissions system—not some major engine failure. Common causes are a loose gas cap or failure of an oxygen sensor—a device that double-checks that the emissions controls are working properly.

Secret warranties

Secret warranties have been around since automobiles were first mass-produced. They're set up to provide free repairs of performance-related defects caused by substandard materials, faulty design, or assembly-line errors. In 1974, *Lemon-Aid* exposed Ford's secret J-67 seven-year rust warranty, which covered the company's 1970–74 models. After first denying that it had such a warranty, Ford admitted two years later that it was indeed in place, and negotiated a $2.8 million settlement with this author to compensate owners of rust-cankered Fords. And you know what? Twenty-five years later, hundreds of secret warranties continue to exist among most automakers. *Lemon-Aid* is still the only consumer publication blowing the whistle on hundreds of current programs that secretly allocate funds for the repair of engine, transmission, fuel pump, and paint defects on cars, sport-utilities, trucks, minivans, and vans.

Even mundane little repairs that can still cost you a hundred bucks or more are covered. Take, for example, the elimination of foul, musty, or mildew odors emitted by the air conditioning unit. Despite what the dealer may say, GM, Ford, and Chrysler service bulletins clearly show automakers will pay for AC service adjustments for a reasonable period of time.

As mentioned in Part One, automobile manufacturers are reluctant to make secret warranty extensions public because they feel it would weaken confidence in their product and increase their legal liability. The closest they come to an admission is sending a "goodwill policy," "product improvement program," or "special policy" service bulletin to dealers or first owners of record. Consequently, the only motorists who get compensated for repairs to defective parts are those who are the original owners, who haven't moved or leased their vehicle, or who yell the loudest and present automaker service bulletins (see Appendix II to order your own bulletins).

If you're refused compensation, keep in mind that secret warranty extensions are an admission of manufacturing negligence. Try to compromise with a pro rata adjustment from the manufacturer. A good bottom-line position is to suggest the dealer and manufacturer each pay a third of the cost. If polite negotiations fail, challenge the refusal in court on the grounds that you should not be penalized for failing to make a reimbursement claim under a secret warranty you never knew existed!

Here are a few examples of the latest and most comprehensive secret warranties that have come across my desk in the last several years. Keep in mind that an up-to-date listing of other secret warranties and service programs for every vehicle *Lemon-Aid* rates can be found in Part Three under "Secret Warranties/Service Tips" in *Lemon-Aid Used Cars 2000.*

Chrysler
1991–96 cars, minivans, vans, sport-utilities, and trucks
• **Problem**: Defective automatic transmissions, air conditioners, and brakes; delaminated paint that turns a chalky colour and then peels off.
• **Warranty coverage**: Chrysler has offered full or partial refunds for claims that are within the durability guidelines set out on pages 98–99.

Chrysler set up a special Warranty Review Committee in February 1998 in response to the bad publicity and threats of court action coming from *Lemon-Aid* and the approximately six hundred Chrysler owners who helped form Chrysler Lemon Owners Groups (CLOG) in British Columbia and New Brunswick. These groups submitted the names of irate owners to Chrysler and have succeeded in getting sizeable refunds for brake, transmission, and paint repairs. If you have had any of these problems and want "goodwill" repairs (or a refund for repairs already carried out), go through Chrysler's regular customer relations hot line. If you're not satisfied by the response you get, then phone or fax Lou Spadotto, National Service Manager: tel.: 519-973-2300 (Bob Renaud's old line) or 519-973-2890; fax: 519-973-2318. If you cannot get in touch with Lou Spadotto, phone or fax Larry Latta, Vice President Sales and Marketing: tel.: 519-973-2947; fax: 519-973-2799. Mr. Spadotto confirmed to me earlier this year that the Review Committee continues to review all claims, including those that were previously rejected by customer relations staffers.

Three suggestions if you plan to contact the Review Committee: send Chrysler copies of all your repair bills or independent garage estimates; don't accept a refusal based on the fact that you're not the first owner; and finally, don't let Chrysler turn your claim down because the repairs were carried out by an independent repair facility (see below).

Dear Phil,

I thought you might be interested to learn of the outcome of my troubles with a transmission failure on my 1993 Plymouth minivan. I requested a faxed dealer service bulletin summary from you on August 21 this year. You added a note that I should call a Bob Renaud at Chrysler and start the claim process.

We phoned this gentleman's office and spoke with Sharon McDonald, who assigned us a claim file number and asked that we fax her our bill and a covering letter outlining the circumstances. We sent that off on September 4, and heard nothing until today, the 25th of September. We were actually going through our copy of *Lemon-Aid*, reading up on our next step (threaten court action?) when the mail arrived containing a letter from Chrysler Canada and a cheque to reimburse us for our costs.

We were stunned! Surely it couldn't be this easy! We hadn't even trotted out our list of DSB numbers yet, nor had we mentioned lawyers or Small Claims Court. Chrysler obviously knew they had a problem with the transmissions....

I hope my experiences can be used to help other motorists. They can be summarized thusly:

1. Don't let the dealer brush you off (this is their job)—go to the factory.

2. Just because you chose the short-term warranty option doesn't mean you aren't covered by the long-term—if you fight for it.

Thank you very much for the excellent advice in your book: it gave us the determination to keep on at the problem when it would have been all too easy to let go. Thanks especially for the phone contact at Chrysler. I'm sure that one little piece of information saved us hours of time and many dollars in phone calls to Ontario. Our local dealer certainly wasn't forthcoming with stuff like that. We are definitely a lot more satisfied with Chrysler now, thanks to their willingness to promptly settle a fair claim....

Yours sincerely,
Wally James & Barb Steele

September 12, 1998

Ms. Barbara Steele

Dear Ms. Steele:

We have received your letter of September 4, 1998 which is further to our previous telephone contact regarding your 1993 Plymouth Grand Voyager.

As a goodwill gesture, Chrysler Canada is enclosing a cheque in the amount of
$2,885.73 to reimburse you for the transmission repairs performed by Honest "T"
Repairs Inc. on July 13, 1998. We hope this cheque will convince you of our commitment to quality products and customer service.

The tie rod ends are not a powertrain component, and repairs are the owner's responsibility at the current date and metrage.

We apologize for the inconvenience you encountered, and we appreciate the opportunity
to be of assistance.

Yours very truly

CHRYSLER CANADA LTD.

V. Ryan

V.J. Ryan (Mrs.)
Customer Service Manager

CAIR #5119301

(Encl.)

Chrysler Canada Ltd.
P.O. Box 162
Windsor, Ontario N9A 4H6

The transmission failed at 98,138 km.

Chrysler/Jeep

1989–91 Cherokee and Wagoneer; 1990–93 Dynasty, New Yorker, Salon, Fifth Avenue, and Imperial; 1991–92 Monaco and Premier; and 1991–93 minivans

• **Problem**: Malfunctioning ABS.

• **Warranty coverage**: Chrysler has extended the warranty to up to 10 years/160,000 km (except for the brake actuator piston assembly and the pump motor assembly, which have lifetime warranties). Owners will also be reimbursed for previous ABS repairs.

Ford/Lincoln

1994–95 Taurus, Sable, Windstar; 1994 Lincoln Continental

• **Problem**: Defective 3.8L engine head gaskets may cause loss of coolant, overheating, or destruction of the engine.

• **Warranty coverage**: Ford will replace the defective components at no charge up to 5 years/100,000 km. Vehicles that have exceeded the kilometre limit will still be covered if the problem was reported or repaired before December 31, 1998. Ford is also offering a full refund for repairs performed by independents prior to the issuing of its June 23, 1998, letter. Claims for pre-1994 vehicles and independent repairs carried out after the above date will be reviewed on a case-by-case basis (see following page).

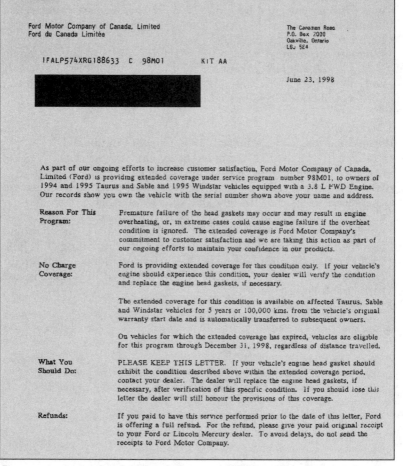

Premature engine head gasket failures are quite common and are expensive to repair. At present, GM Cavaliers and Sunbirds, Saturns, and Toyota 6-cylinder engines are eligible for "goodwill" programs that will pay for head gasket repairs. Symptoms indicating a faulty head gasket include overheating, poor fuel economy, reduced engine power, and coolant leaking into the engine, which then mixes with the ventilation system and causes a film to be deposited on the interior glass surfaces. (At night, the streetlights will look blurry.)

Chrysler/Ford/General Motors

All models, all years

• **Problem**: Faulty paint jobs that cause paint to turn white and peel off of horizontal panels. GM and Ford documents show that the problem is a factory defect.

- **Warranty coverage**: Vehicle will be repainted free for up to six years with no mileage limitation. Thereafter, the automakers usually offer 50–75 percent refunds.

PONTIAC DIVISION
GeneralMotors Corporation
One Pontiac Plaza
Pontiac, Michigan 48340-2952
October 16, 1992

TO: All Pontiac Dealers

SUBJECT: Partners in Satisfaction (PICS)
Dealer Authorization

Pontiac continually reviews the Warranty Management System to ensure that Warranty Administration achieves its purposes, including high levels of customer satisfaction with after sale treatment.

Following a recent review, Pontiac has decided to provide dealers authorization for cases involving paint repairs for vehicles up to six (6) years from the date of delivery, without regard for mileage. This is a change from the current PICS dealer self-authorization which allows paint repair goodwill adjustments to be made up to 6 years/60,000 miles. Dealers who have a deductible override capabilities may also waive deductibles as they see appropriate on this type of repair.

Paint repairs are only to be authorized beyond the warranty period by the Dealership Service Manager on a case-by-case basis as with any other goodwill policy adjustment.

Assistance should only be considered for cases involving evidence of a defect in materials or workmanship by the manufacturer. Assistance should not be considered for conditions related to wear and tear and/or lack of maintenance (such as fading, stone chips, scratches, environmental damage, etc.).

Please contact your Zone representative if you have specific questions.

Perry S. White
Director of Service/
Customer Satisfaction

GM says it has no secret paint warranty, so what's this?

How Long Should Parts/Repairs Last?

Let's say you can't find a service bulletin that says your problem is factory-related or covered by a special compensation program. Or a part lasts just a little longer than its guarantee, but not as long as is generally expected. Can you get a refund if the same problem reappears shortly after it has been repaired? Yes—if you can prove the part failed prematurely.

Automakers, mechanics, and the courts have their own benchmarks as to what a reasonable period of time or amount of mileage is during which one should expect a part or adjustment to last. The following table shows what most automakers consider to be reasonable durability as expressed by their original warranties, as well as their secret warranties (often called "goodwill" or "special policy" programs).

Estimated Part Durability

ACCESSORIES
Air conditioner	7 years
Cellular phone	5 years
Cruise control	5 years/ 100,000 km
Power antenna	5 years
Power doors, windows	5 years
Radio	5 years

BODY
Paint (peeling)	7 years
Rust (perforations)	7 years
Rust (surface)	5 years
Vinyl roof	5 years
Water/wind/air leaks	5 years

BRAKE SYSTEM
Brake drum	120,000 km
Brake drum, turn	40,000 km
Brake drum linings	35,000 km
Disc brake calipers	30,000 km
Disc brake pads	30,000 km
Master cylinder, rebuild	100,000 km
Wheel cylinder, rebuild	80,000 km

ENGINE AND DRIVETRAIN
Constant velocity joint	5 years/ 100,000 km
Differential	7 years/ 150,000 km
Engine (gas)	7 years/ 160,000 km
Radiator	4 years/ 80,000 km
Transfer case	7 years/ 150,000 km
Transmission (auto.)	7 years/ 150,000 km

Transmission (man.)	7 years/ 200,000 km
Transmission oil cooler	5 years/ 100,000 km
Universal joint	5 years/ 100,000 km

EXHAUST SYSTEM
Catalytic converter	5 years/ 100,000 km or more
Muffler	2 years/ 40,000 km
Tailpipe	3 years/ 60,000 km

FUEL SYSTEM
Carburetor	5 years/ 120,000 km
Fuel filter	2 years/ 40,000 km
Fuel pump	5 years/ 80,000 km
Injectors	5 years/ 80,000 km

IGNITION SYSTEM
Cable set	60,000 km
Electronic module	5 years/ 80,000 km
Retiming	20,000 km
Spark plugs	20,000 km
Tune-up	20,000 km

SAFETY COMPONENTS
Airbags	life of vehicle
ABS brakes	7 years/ 150,000 km
ABS computer	10 years/ 160,000 km
Seatbelts	life of vehicle

STEERING AND SUSPENSION

Alignment	1 year/ 20,000 km
Ball joints	80,000 km
Power steering	5 years/ 80,000 km
Shock absorber	2 years/ 40,000 km
Struts	5 years/ 80,000 km
Tires (radial)	5 years/ 80,000 km
Wheel bearing	3 years/ 60,000 km

VISIBILITY

Aim headlights	20,000 km
Halogen/fog lights	3 years/ 60,000 km
Sealed beam	2 years/ 40,000 km
Windshield wiper motor	5 years/ 80,000 km

The previous guidelines are extrapolated from Chrysler's payout to dozens of Chrysler Lemon Owners Group (CLOG) members from December 1997 through 1998, in addition to Chrysler's original seven-year powertrain warranty applicable from 1991–95. Other sources for this chart were the Ford and GM transmission warranties as outlined in their secret warranties, and GM, Mercury, Nissan, and Toyota engine "special programs" laid out in their internal service bulletins.

Safety features generally have a lifetime warranty, with the exception of ABS brakes, which are a wear item. Nevertheless, the Chrysler 10-year "free service program" portion of its ABS recall, announced several years ago, can serve as a handy benchmark as to how long one can expect these components to last.

Airbags are a different matter. Those which deploy in an accident, as well as the personal injury and interior damage their deployment will likely have caused, are covered by your accident insurance policy. However, if there is a sudden deployment for no apparent reason, the automaker and dealer should be held jointly responsible for all injuries and damages caused by the airbag. This will likely lead to a more generous settlement from the two parties and prevent your insurance premiums from being jacked up. Inadvertent deployment may occur after passing over a bump in the road, slamming the car door, having wet carpets in your Cadillac (no kidding), or, in some Chrysler minivans, simply putting the key in the ignition. This happens more often than you might imagine, judging by the hundreds of recalls and thousands of complaints recorded on the U.S. National Highway Traffic Safety Administration's website at *www.nhtsa.dot.gov/cars/problems/complain/compmmy1.cfm*.

Finally, the manufacturer's emissions warranty serves as the primary guideline governing how long a vast array of electronic and mechanical components should last. Look first at your owner's manual for an indication of which parts on your vehicle are covered. If you come up with few specifics, use the provincial government's guidelines in provinces where emissions testing is mandatory. Keep in mind that these durability benchmarks, secret warranties, and emissions warranties all apply to subsequent owners.

Recall Campaigns

Safety- and emissions-recall campaigns confer warranty benefits on owners whereby the manufacturer and dealer are obligated to repair a defect at no charge, no matter how often the vehicle has been sold or what its mileage is. Furthermore, Transport Canada monitors how well automakers carry out recall campaigns and will intervene if any company stonewalls a legitimate request.

Recall repairs

Let the automaker know who and where you are. If you've bought a used vehicle, or if you've moved, it's a smart idea to pay a visit to your local dealer and get a "report card" on which recalls, free service campaigns, and warranties are listed. Simply give the service advisor your vehicle identification number (VIN)—found on the dash just below the windshield on the driver's side, or on your insurance card—and have the number run through the automaker's computer system ("Function 70" for Chrysler, "OASIS" for Ford, and "CRIS" for GM). Ask for a computer printout of the vehicle's history (have it faxed to you, if you're so equipped) and make sure you're listed in the automaker's computer as the new owner. This ensures that you'll receive notices of warranty extensions and emissions and safety recalls.

Still, don't expect to be welcomed with open arms when your vehicle develops a safety- or emissions-related problem that's not yet part of a recall campaign. Automakers and dealers generally take a restrictive view of what constitutes a safety or emissions defect and frequently charge for repairs which should be free under federal safety or emissions legislation. To counter this tendency, look at the following list of typical defects that are clearly safety-related, and if you experience similar problems, tell the dealer you expect your repair to be paid by the manufacturer:

• airbag malfunctions
• corrosion affecting safe operation
• disconnected or stuck accelerators
• electrical shorts
• faulty windshield wipers
• fuel leaks
• problems with original axles, drive shafts, seats, seat recliners, or defrosters
• seatbelt problems
• stalling or sudden acceleration
• sudden steering or brake loss
• suspension failures
• trailer coupling failures

U.S. recall campaigns force automakers to pay the entire cost of fixing a vehicle's safety-related defect. This includes used vehicles, and has no cut-off limitation. Recalls may be voluntary or ordered by the U.S.

Department of Transportation. Canadian regulation has an added twist: Transport Canada can only order automakers to notify owners that their vehicles may be unsafe; it can't force them to correct the problem. Fortunately, most U.S.-ordered recalls are carried out in Canada, and when Transport Canada makes a defect determination on its own, automakers generally comply with an owner notification letter.

Voluntary recall campaigns are a real problem, though. They aren't as rigorously monitored as government-ordered recalls, and dealers and automakers routinely deny there's a recall. Also, the company's so-called "fix" often doesn't correct the hazard. Take, as an example, Chrysler's voluntary recall to strengthen the rear latches on as many as 4.5 million 1984–95 minivans. Almost 50 percent of affected owners were still waiting for Chrysler to fix their minivans nearly two years after the company volunteered to correct the defect.

Safety defect information
If you wish to report a safety defect or want recall info, you may access Transport Canada's website: *www.tc.gc.ca/roadsafety/Recalls/search_e.asp*. You'll get recall information in French or English, as well as general information relating to road safety and importing a vehicle into Canada. Cybersurfers can now access the recall database for 1970–2000 model vehicles, but unlike NHTSA's website, owner complaints aren't listed, defect investigations aren't disclosed, and service bulletin summaries aren't provided. You can also call Transport Canada at 1-800-333-0510 (toll-free within Canada) or 613-993-9851 (within the Ottawa region or outside Canada) to get additional information.

Unfortunately, there are some problems with Ottawa's database—and attitude. First, when calling Ottawa through the toll-free line, Transport Canada bureaucrats insist that the dealer must already have refused you the recall info before they will give it to you. You won't be told if others have reported similar safety problems affecting your vehicle. And more often than not, if you suspect your car has a safety defect, you'll be asked to take it to the dealer for a safety exam (where there's a good chance the problem will be covered up or you'll be blamed for the malfunction).

If you're not happy with Ottawa's treatment of your recall inquiry, try the U.S. government's NHTSA website. It's more complete than Transport Canada's site (NHTSA's database was established in 1972 and is updated daily). You can search the database specific to your vehicle and be thoroughly briefed on recalls, crash ratings, safety and performance defects reported by other car owners, and a host of other safety-related items. The NHTSA website is *www.nhtsa.dot.gov/cars/problems/recalls/recmmy1.cfm* for recalls and *www.nhtsa.dot.gov/cars/problems/complain/compmmy1.cfm* for the complaint database.

NHTSA's fax-back service provides the same info through a local line that can be accessed from Canada—although long-distance charges will apply (most calls take 5–10 minutes to complete). For calls placed within the U.S., the toll-free hot line is 1-800-424-9393 (1-800-424-9153 for the hearing impaired). The following local numbers get you into the automatic response service just as quickly, and can be reached 24 hours a day: 202-366-0123 (202-366-7800 for the hearing impaired).

Three Steps to a Settlement

Step 1: informal negotiations

If your vehicle was misrepresented, has major defects, or wasn't properly repaired under warranty, the first thing you should do is give the seller (the dealer and automaker or a private party) a written summary (by registered mail or fax) of the outstanding problems and stipulate a time period in which they will need to be corrected or your money will be refunded. Keep a copy for yourself along with all your repair records. Be sure to check all of the sales and warranty documents you were given to see if they conform to provincial laws. Any errors, omissions, or violations can be used to get a settlement with the dealer in lieu of making a formal complaint.

When negotiating with the seller, speak in a calm, polite manner and try to avoid polarizing the issue. Talk about how "we can work together" on the problem. Support your position with independent garage reports, service bulletins, and maintenance records. Let a compromise slowly emerge—don't come in with a hard-line set of demands. Don't demand the settlement offer in writing, but make sure you're accompanied by a friend who can confirm the offer in court if it's not honoured (relatives can testify in court). Be prepared to act on the offer without delay, so that you won't be blamed for its withdrawal.

Service managers

Service managers are directly responsible to dealers and manufacturers and make the first determination of what work is covered under warranty. They are paid to save the dealers and automakers money and to mollify irate clients—almost an impossible balancing act, wherein my sympathies are more with the dealers than with the automakers. When service managers agree to warranty coverage, it's because you've convinced them that they must do so. This can be done by getting them to access the vehicle's history from the manufacturer's computer and by presenting the facts of your case in a confident, forthright manner with as many dealer service bulletins and NHTSA owner complaint printouts as you can find for support.

If the service manager can't or won't set things right, your next step is to convene a mini-summit with the service manager, the dealership principal, and the automaker's rep. By getting the automaker involved, you run less risk of having the dealer fob you off on the manufacturer and you can often get an agreement in which the seller and automaker pay two-thirds of the repair cost.

Dealers/automakers

Check all of the sales and warranty documents you were given to see if they conform to provincial laws. Any errors, omissions, or violations can be used to clinch a deal with the dealer in lieu of making a formal complaint, because the dealer could be fined if he's violated provincial protection laws.

You have to make the case that the vehicle's defects were present during the warranty period, or that the vehicle doesn't conform to the way it was represented when it was purchased. Emphasize that you intend to use the courts if necessary to obtain a refund—most dealers would rather settle than risk a lawsuit with all the attendant publicity. An independent estimate of the vehicle's defects and cost of repairs is essential if you want to convince the seller that you're serious in your claim and stand a good chance of winning your case in court. The estimated cost of repairs is also useful in challenging a dealer who agrees to pay half the repair costs and then jacks up the costs a hundred percent so that you wind up paying the whole shot.

If the dealer won't talk with you, write or call the nearest regional office or the manufacturer's head office. The address and telephone numbers can be found in the owner's manual. General Motors, for example, has a toll-free customer hot line (1-800-263-3777) that operates out of Oshawa, Ontario and employs over 30 people (one-third of whom are bilingual) to answer customer inquiries. Don't expect miracles from these people. Each staffer has a guide book showing the appropriate, corporate-approved response for the most frequently asked consumer questions. If you dig too deeply, you'll likely get the cold shoulder or, as one GM owner wrote me, get the receiver hung up in your ear.

If there's a warranty dispute, or if you've found that your service manager can't correct a persistent problem, GM customer relations staff will intervene to set things right, if possible, at the dealership level. Once your name, vehicle identification number (VIN), and dealer's name are punched into the computer, the customer relations rep can tell you if you're eligible for free repairs under a special (i.e., secret) warranty or through a safety/emissions recall campaign. The telephone staff will never mention the phrase "secret warranty," nor will they ever pass you on to someone else in charge. Since they were hired to reduce the number of calls their bosses receive, every call that gets through their screening is a black mark against their job performance.

Ford and GM car owners tell me that the telephone staff have been told to "barter down" owners' requests for warranty compensation involving paint defects and other secret warranty-related problems. Callers are given a "Let's Make a Deal" spiel where the initial offer of 50 percent is often boosted to 75 percent compensation if the customer will agree—at that very moment—to pay 25 percent of the repair.

Factory reps

The factory rep is directly responsible to the manufacturer and has the last word on what work is covered under warranty. Not unlike the customer relations staff, he's paid to save the company money. Every time he says no, he does his job. When he says yes to warranty coverage, it's because you've convinced him he must. Should you see that you're getting nowhere with the factory rep, give him one last chance to make a reasonable offer. Don't threaten him or tip him off to your next move.

Step 2: send a registered letter or fax
This is the next step to take if your claim is refused. Send the dealer and manufacturer a polite registered letter or a fax that asks for compensation for repairs that have been done or need to be done, insurance costs while the vehicle is being repaired, towing charges, supplementary transportation costs like taxis and rented cars, and damages for inconvenience.

Specify five days (but allow ten) for either party to respond. If no satisfactory offer is made, file suit in small claims court. Make the manufacturer a party to the lawsuit, especially if the emissions warranty, a secret warranty extension, a safety-recall campaign, or extensive chassis rusting is involved. Use the sample complaint letter on the following page as a guide for getting compensation. Include a reference in your letter to any court decisions you find in this section of the book that support your claim.

New-Car Complaint Letter/Fax

Without Prejudice

Date: _____
Name and address of dealer: _____
Name and address of manufacturer: _____

Please be advised that I am not satisfied with my _____ (indicate year, make, model, and serial number of vehicle). The vehicle was purchased on _____ (indicate date) and currently indicates _____ km on the odometer. The vehicle presently exhibits the following defects:

      1. Premature rusting
      2. Paint peeling/discoloration
      3. Water leaks
      4. Other defects (explain)

(List previous attempts to repair the vehicle. Attach a copy of a report from an independent garage, showing cost of estimated repairs and confirming the manufacturer's responsibility.)

I hereby request that you correct these defects free of charge under the terms of the implied warranty provisions of provincial consumer protection statutes as applied in *Kravitz v. General Motors* (1979), I.S.C.R., and *Chabot v. Ford* (1983), 39 O.R. (2d).

If you do not correct the defects noted above to my satisfaction and within a reasonable length of time, I will be obliged to ask an independent garage to _____ (choose [a] estimate or [b] carry out) the repairs and claim the amount of $_____ (state the cost, if possible) by way of the courts without further notice or delay.

I have dealt with your company because of its competence and honesty. I close in the hope of hearing from you within five (5) days of receiving this letter, failing which I will exercise the alternatives available to me. Please govern yourself accordingly.

Sincerely,

(Signed, with telephone number)

Step 3: mediation and arbitration
If you have a new- or used-vehicle complaint and the formality of a court-room puts you off, or if you're not sure your claim is all that solid and don't want to pay legal costs to find out, consider using mediation or arbitration sponsored by the Better Business Bureau, the Automobile Protection Association, the Canadian Automobile Association, or provincial and territorial governments.

CAMVAP
Except for Quebec, all provinces and the Northwest Territories adhere to the Canadian Motor Vehicle Arbitration Plan (CAMVAP), which arbitrates disputes between consumers and automakers that result from alleged manufacturing defects. Before you decide to use CAMVAP to resolve your dispute, there is one thing you must keep in mind. Once the CAMVAP arbitrator has made a decision, that decision is final. This means that both you and the manufacturer are subject to very limited rights to have the decision reviewed by a court through judicial review. In applying for judicial review, you should keep in mind that you must pay the costs of initiating this process. Neither party can appeal or seek judicial review just because you do not agree with the arbitrator's decision.

The Provincial and Territorial Arbitration Acts allow judicial review of the arbitration process. This takes place before a judge. If the judge rules that the arbitrator made a mistake or error in law at your hearing, the decision can be set aside or a new hearing may be ordered. The Arbitration Acts also allow the arbitrator to correct minor errors or omissions in the award. The time limit for referring the matter back to the arbitrator varies by province and territory. To be safe, if you believe there is an error or omission in the decision made by the arbitrator, you should communicate your concern in writing to the CAMVAP Administrator for your region within 15 days of receiving the arbitrator's decision.

Arbitrating about 450 cases a year, CAMVAP offers its services free of charge to new- and used-car owners. Lawyers aren't usually involved (so no awards need to be split); binding arbitration by a neutral third party can be arranged within a six- to eight-week period; and all negotiations are carried out informally, allowing plaintiffs to bring along anyone they wish to represent them.

CAMVAP won't consider claims for personal injury, tire defects (except on GM's models), third-party rustproofing or paint protection failure, motor homes, or vehicles used primarily for business purposes, unless the plaintiff owns the business and the vehicle is driven by that person or a member of his or her family.

CAMVAP arbitration is worth serious consideration, particularly now that its rules have been become more user-friendly as a result of *Lemon-Aid* and other consumer group pressures. Access to the program is now much easier and compensation guidelines for plaintiffs have been enhanced. For example, consumers who use the CAMVAP process are no longer sworn to secrecy; the formula for automaker buy-backs now includes freight charges, administration fees, and fuel and tire conservation taxes which could add as much as $1,000 to the award; a new buy-back formula for leased vehicles includes the reimbursement of the down payment and security deposit; and the arbitrator can award out-of-pocket expenses up to $500.

Under CAMVAP's present rules, Canadian residents who own or lease a defective 1995 or later model vehicle with less than 160,000 km must first contact their dealer and automaker to settle the dispute before asking for arbitration. If this doesn't take care of the problem, ask the dealer for the regional CAMVAP phone number and call for an arbitration application form. If the dealer is uncooperative, call CAMVAP toll-free at 1-800-207-0685. If the vehicle has been in service longer than three years or 36,000 km, only repair or repair compensation can be awarded. No buy-backs are possible.

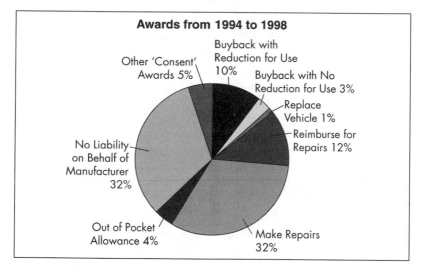

Awards from 1994 to 1998

CAMVAP claims that over the past five years of operation, it has ruled in the consumer's favour 68 percent of the time. Of course, this self-serving figure can't be checked, because CAMVAP put a gag order on all claimants prior to relaxing its rules in June 1999. Nevertheless, the organization says it heard 463 cases last year and ordered the manufacturer to buy back 63 vehicles and repair most of the others. CAMVAP officials have also pledged to post 1999 case results on the CAMVAP website later this year (*www.camvap.ca*).

Getting outside help
Don't lose your case due to poor preparation. Ask government or independent consumer protection agencies to evaluate how well you're prepared before going to your first hearing. Also use the Internet to

ferret out additional facts and gather support (*www.lemonaidcars.com* is a good place to start).

On-line services/Internet/websites
America Online and CompuServe are two on-line service providers with active consumer forums that use experts to answer consumer queries, and to provide legal and technical advice. The Internet offers the same information using a worldwide database. If you or someone you know is able to create a website, you might consider using this site to attract attention to your plight and arm yourself for arbitration or court.

Several years ago, Debra and Edward Goldgehn's 1985 Ford Ranger caught fire and burned completely. The couple's suspicion that it was a factory-related defect was later confirmed by a TV show that reported a series of similar Ford fires. The couple created their own website called "Flaming Fords" and began amassing an incredible database containing reports of similar fires, class action lawsuits, expert witnesses, and actions taken outside the U.S. (For example, Ford had already recalled a number of its vehicles in order to fix the problem here in Canada.) Shortly thereafter, Ford USA recalled 8.7 million cars and trucks, representing the largest recall ever announced by a single auto manufacturer. Ford says that the Internet pressure was coincidental and not a factor in its decision to recall the vehicles in the States.

Right, and Elvis is building Fords in Oakville.

Michael Hos, a dissatisfied Acura owner from the United States, became fed up with what he felt was Acura's stonewalling of his complaints. Rather than getting angry, he got organized and set up a website called "Acura 1997 CL 3.0L: My Lemon" to collect other owners' comments and list some of the most common Acura problem areas. Within six months, Acura settled. Here's what Hos has to say:

> Phil,
> Hi, remember me? I'm the guy that had the 1997 Acura CL lemon. Well, as it turns out Acura settled with me. I got my attorney fees taken care of, and I'm walking away with $4,000 in my pocket after the experience. I was so glad to get rid of this car you have no idea.
> I have pulled down my "anti-Acura" website and washed my hands clean of the entire ordeal. I turned in the CL about two weeks ago, and my checks should be here next week....
> ...At any rate, I wanted to say thanks for all your input into the case and the encouragement to continue on. The last few months of driving the car were horrible, I'm glad it's done.

In a follow-up posting, Hos writes:

> As far as my website goes, I think it was a major part of them settling early. I had a counter placed on it which showed them how

many people had visited the site. Anyone can set up a web page like mine pretty easily. I have web space on my university's computer, so it was free for me to use. Folks without space should expect to spend about $20 a month for space, or if they have their own e-mail account, web space is usually provided for free. If they don't know how to set up their web page, paying someone to do it will be kinda pricey, a few hundred bucks should cover it. The main thing it needs to have is the counter, and it also needs to be slander free. I had only facts on my web page as I didn't want to get involved in a slander suit. They also need to register the site with all the major search engines so it comes up when looking for the manufacturer. *Submitit.com* offers such services for free. Putting in a <Meta> tag into the page also helps move it up the search engines' list of hits. Posting to newsgroups also is helpful. I also wrote to J.D. Power, NHTSA, *Consumer Reports*, and any other consumer-oriented agency I could think of.

When we settled before going to court, I had to sign the settlement papers saying I would pull down my site. They would not settle with me until I did that. This shows how much power the site can have. I would also put the manufacturer's phone number and address on it so viewers of the site can contact the manufacturer.

For the most part everyone who read my site took my side of the story and agreed that Acura should pay up. I did have a few folks that were mad I was slamming Acura, but I wasn't concerned with them. I have about 200 e-mail responses that people have mailed to me over the last few months.

As a side note, I think the only real reason they settled with me, in addition to the page being up, was my attorney. I had seven charges filed against them in Superior Court. Also, keep in mind that I paid nothing for my attorney until after we settled. My bill for him is $1,500, but that's included in the settlement. Also, I'm only 23, so anyone can do this if they are persistent.

Classified ads
Use your local paper's classified section or *The Globe and Mail*'s "National Personals" column to gather data from others who may have experienced a problem similar to your own. This alerts others to the potential problem, helps build a core base for a class action or group meeting with the automaker, and puts pressure on the dealer or manufacturer to settle.

Federal and provincial consumer affairs
The wind left the sails of the consumer movement over a decade ago, leaving provincial consumer affairs offices understaffed and unsupported by the government. This has created a passive mindset among many staffers, who are tired of getting their heads kicked in by businesses and budget-cutters.

110

PROJECTS AND CAUSES

A BAD FIRE occured in our 1994 Jeep Cherokee because of driving with a compact spare tire while in 4WD (could not get out of 4WD). Compact spare is standard equipment but appropriate warning not in Owners Manual. No appropriate answers from Chrysler Canada yet. Seeking others with similar experience.

Consumer affairs offices can still help with investigation, mediation, and some litigation. Strong and effective consumer protection legislation has been left standing in most of the provinces, and resourceful consumers can use these laws in conjunction with media coverage to prod provincial consumer affairs offices into action. Furthermore, provincial bureaucrats aren't as well shielded from criticism as are their federal counterparts. A call to your MPP or MLA, or to the minister's executive assistant, can often get things rolling.

Federal consumer protection is a government-created PR myth. Don't expect the reorganized Consumer and Corporate Affairs staffers to be very helpful—they've been de-fanged and de-gummed through budget cuts and a succession of ineffective ministers. Although the revised Competition Act has some bite concerning misleading advertising and a number of other illegal business practices, the federal government has watered down the act's applicability to consumer groups and individual consumers.

Nevertheless, when used creatively the recently beefed-up Competition Act can be a powerful tool for forcing a formal government investigation and prosecution, attracting media attention, and obtaining individual and collective compensation.

Getting a Secret Warranty Settlement

The following settlement advice applies mainly to paint defects, but you can use these tips for any other vehicle defect that you believe is the automaker's or dealer's responsibility. If you're not sure that the problem is a factory-related deficiency or a maintenance item, have it checked out by an independent garage or get a dealer service bulletin summary for your vehicle. The summary may include specific bulletins relating to the diagnosis, correction, and ordering of upgraded parts needed to fix your problem.

1. If you know the problem is factory related, take your vehicle to the dealer and ask for a written, signed estimate. When you're handed the estimate, ask that the paint job be done for free under the manufacturer's "goodwill" program. (Ford's euphemism for this secret warranty is "Owner Dialogue Program," GM's term is "Special Policy," and Chrysler just calls it "goodwill." Don't use the term "secret warranty" yet, you'll just make the dealer and automaker angry and evasive.)

2. Your request will probably be met with a refusal, an offer to repaint the vehicle for half the cost, or, if you're lucky, an agreement to

repaint the vehicle free of charge. If you accept half-cost, make sure that it's based on the original estimate you have in hand, since some dealers jack up their estimates so that your 50 percent is really 100 percent of the true cost.

3. If the dealer/automaker has already refused your claim and the repair hasn't been done yet, get an additional estimate from an independent garage that shows the problem is factory related.

4. Again, if the repair has yet to be done, send a registered claim letter or fax to the automaker (send a copy to the dealer), claiming the average of both estimates. If the repair has been done at your expense, send a registered claim letter or fax with a copy of your bill.

5. If you don't receive a satisfactory response within a week, deposit a copy of the estimate or paid bill and letter before the small claims court and await a trial date. This means that the automaker/dealer will have to appear, no lawyer is required, costs should be reasonable ($95–$125), and a mediation hearing or trial will be scheduled in a few months followed by a judgment a few weeks later (the time varies among different regions).

Things that you can collect to help your case include photographs, maintenance work orders, previous work orders dealing with your problem, dealer service bulletins, and an independent expert (the garage or body shop that did the estimate or repair is best, but you can also use a local teacher who teaches automotive repair).

Other situations

• If the vehicle has just been repainted but the dealer says that "goodwill" coverage was denied by the automaker, pay for the repair with a certified cheque and write "under protest" on the cheque. Remember, though, if the dealer does the repair, you won't have an independent expert who can affirm that the problem was factory related or that it was a result of premature wearout. Plus, the dealer can say that you or the environment caused the paint problem. In these cases, internal service bulletins can make or break your case.

• If the dealer/automaker offers a partial repair or refund, take it. Then sue for the rest, including any "deductible" you were forced to pay; GM's own memo says the deductible can be waived (see page 97). Remember, if a partial repair has been done under warranty, it counts as an admission of responsibility, no matter what "goodwill" euphemism is used. Also, the repaired component/body panel should be just as durable as if it were new. Hence, the clock starts ticking again until you reach the original warranty parameter—again, no matter what the dealer's repair warranty limit says.

• It's a lot easier to get the automaker to pay to replace a defective part than it is to be compensated for a missed day of work or a ruined vacation. Manufacturers hate to pay for consequential expenses apart from towing bills because they can't control the amount of the refund. Fortunately, the courts have taken the position that all expenses (damages) flowing from a problem covered by a warranty or service bulletin are the manufacturer's/dealer's responsibility under both common law and Quebec civil law. Nevertheless, don't risk a fair settlement for some outlandish claim of "emotional distress," "pain and suffering," etc. If you have invoices to prove actual consequential damages, then use them. If not, don't be greedy.

Very seldom do automakers contest these paint claims before small claims court, opting instead to settle once the court claim is bounced from their customer relations people to their legal affairs department. At that time, you'll probably be offered an out-of-court settlement for 50–75 percent of your claim.

Stand fast and make reference to the service bulletins you intend to subpoena in order to publicly contest in court the unfair nature of this "secret warranty" program (automaker lawyers cringe at the idea of trying to explain why consumers aren't made aware of these bulletins). One hundred percent restitution will probably result. A good example is the *Shields v. General Motors of Canada* judgment rendered January 6, 1998 (see second case in the following section).

Bentley v. Dave Wheaton Pontiac Buick GMC Ltd. and General Motors of Canada, Victoria Registry No. 24779, British Columbia Small Claims Court, December 1, 1998, Judge Higinbotham. This is the third, and most recent, small claims judgment against GM. It builds upon the Ontario *Shields v. General Motors of Canada* decision and cites other jurisprudence as to how long paint should last. If you're wondering why Ford and Chrysler haven't been hit by similar judgments, remember that they usually settle.

Reasons for Judgment

In this case the claimant purchased a vehicle, a pickup truck, from a dealership, Dave Wheaton Pontiac Buick G.M.C. Ltd., a new vehicle, in 1991. There was an admitted defect in the paint which did not become apparent until later. General Motors is also a defendant in this action and discovered in a general sense this problem of delamination in the paint on some vehicles in 1992, about one year after the claimant purchased the vehicle in question.

The specific problem with this vehicle was observed early in 1994. It was brought to the attention of Wheaton when the vehicle was brought in for other maintenance two weeks after the warranty expired. At that time the problem was relatively minor. I say relatively in the sense that compared to what later occurred it was minor.

Mr. Palfry, who is the manager of the paint and body shop for the retailer Wheaton, was made aware of the problem. There is no dispute about that, and he sold the claimant a tub of touch-up paint.

The paint continued to deteriorate and in late 1996 was severely peeled.

In January of 1997, the claimant became aware that this problem was general to certain GM vehicles, vehicles of certain colours produced at a certain time by the defendant company.

The claimant took the vehicle back in but was told that it was too late. The warranty had expired and even the discretionary goodwill warranty was over. I do not think the claimant was told about the discretionary goodwill warranty, but in fact it was a policy of GM to extend the warranty for this sort of claim in certain circumstances, but it was discretionary. In any case, the claimant was told that it was too late for it to be fixed under warranty. Neither the dealership nor the manufacturer would accept responsibility at that time. As a result, this action was commenced.

I make the following findings: There was a latent defect in the vehicle relating to the paint, which revealed itself over time and in far less time than a good paint job would be expected to last.

The dealer or the manufacturer, had the manufacturer been informed by the dealer, ought to have advised the claimant in May of 1994 that they were aware of this general delamination problem and ought to have advised as to what warranty extension might be available. I will say more about this in a moment. In any event, the dealer and the manufacturer, if the dealer had notified the manufacturer of the problem, would have known that the delamination commenced within the three year period and ought to have honoured the warranty.

Despite my findings, as I said earlier that the dealer and manufacturer ought to have given guidance to the claimant in May of 1994 as to a possible warranty claim, I do not find any cause of action arising directly from this finding. It would simply have been good business practice for them to have advised the claimant.

If liability is to be found against General Motors, it must be for a breach of the warranty. On the other hand, if liability is to be found against Dave Wheaton, it must be because as a seller the dealership breached an implied condition of the Sale of Goods Act.

On the issue of the warranty supplied by General Motors, I note that it covers "repairs, or adjustments to correct any vehicle defect related to material or workmanship occurring during the warranty period." It appears from the evidence that General Motors' major concern with this particular case was that the problem with this specific vehicle was not brought to their attention during the warranty period, not that the problem with the paint did not actually arise within the warranty period.

I find the claimant has established that the paint problem was brought to the attention of the dealer in mid-May of 1994. The warranty had expired two weeks earlier. I accept that the defect occurred during the warranty period on two bases. First, as submitted by the claimant, Ms. Bentley, the defect occurred at the time of manufacture and continues to this day.

Similar finding was made in *Shields v. General Motors of Canada*, a decision of the Ontario Court, General Division, number 1398 of 1996.

Secondly, in any event, based on the condition of the paint in mid-May 1994, the defect likely became apparent during the three year warranty period. I therefore find that General Motors has breached the warranty and the claimant is entitled to damages.

As for the dealership, defendant's counsel argues that there has been no breach of the Sale of Goods Act in that the vehicle when sold was of merchantable quality and reasonably fit for the purpose for which it was intended.

I agree as to merchantable quality. And as to the other implied condition, I also agree if what is meant by "reasonably fit for the purpose" is that it was a truck that operated and was capable of hauling cargo and passengers, but I am of the view that every seller of new vehicles knows that the purchaser expects the vehicle to be reasonably fit for the purpose of resale at some future time, depending upon the age and quality of the vehicle. This vehicle was not and is not reasonably fit for resale given those factors. It is not reasonably fit due to the latent defect in its quality, a defect which existed in incipient form at the time of sale.

I note that in *McCready Products v. Sherwin-Williams*, (1984) 53 A.R. 304, a decision of the Alberta Queen's Bench, referred to in the article by Fridman submitted by counsel, in that case paint that weathered and faded in less than three years was found unfit for its purpose. That was house paint. The same is true here. Even though the paint in question here was only a component of the item purchased, it was a very important component having a great deal to do with the value of the vehicle.

I therefore find the defendant Dave Wheaton Pontiac Buick G.M.C. Ltd. also liable for damages. The liability of both defendants is joint and several.

I turn now to the question of damages. The claimants have averaged three estimates they have placed before the court and claim the amount of twenty-three hundred seventy-three dollars and sixty-one cents.

The defendant says damages are lower as a different allowance to dealers are made under the warranty. The defendants cannot now get the benefit of this, in my opinion, as responsibility under the warranty was denied by them.

I prefer to assess damages by taking the defendant's estimate or figure of fifteen hundred eighty-eight dollars twenty-six cents, a sum which the dealer could charge under the warranty to GM, and multiply that figure by a factor admitted to by the defendant as to what another body shop would—the number of hours another body shop would employ in order to obtain a realistic assessment.

It was stated in evidence that twenty-two to twenty-five hours is required to repair this damage, of which two hours are the actual painting.

The defendant's estimate is based on sixteen point one hours, because that's all they can claim under the warranty. There is therefore a difference of approximately nine hours in the estimates based on the upper level of twenty-five hours required by another body shop. I accept the proportion of paint to labour as stated by the witness and therefore accept that the defendant's estimate is based on fourteen point one hours of labour.

I also accept that the acceptable labour rate is fifty dollars and fifty-five cents and the painting rate is twenty-three dollars and seventy-one cents. It is the nine hours of labour that is in issue here in the assessment of damages.

The costs of the paint and materials I accept is two hundred and sixty-two dollars and forty-two cents.

I am therefore going to base damages on the defendant's estimate of one thousand eight hundred and ten dollars and sixty-two cents, which includes taxes, plus an additional nine hours labour at fifty dollars and fifty-five cents per hour, plus taxes, or an additional five hundred eighteen dollars eighty-four cents, bringing the total to two thousand three hundred and twenty-nine dollars and forty-six cents, very close to the estimate given by the claimant.

I am making no adjustment for betterment as it is known because, in my opinion, this is offset by the fact that for seven and a half years, or at least most of those seven and a half years, the vehicle was essentially unmarketable, unsaleable without substantial loss.

The claimant will therefore have judgment against both defendants, joint and several, in the amount of two thousand three hundred twenty-nine dollars forty-six cents, plus costs. No interest is awarded as it is inapplicable to this type of claim.

Shields v. General Motors of Canada, No. 1398/96, Ontario Court (General Division), Oshawa Small Claims Court, 33 King Street West, Oshawa, Ontario L1H 1A1, July 24, 1997, Robert Zochodne, Deputy Judge. The owner of a 1991 Pontiac Grand Prix purchased the vehicle used with over 100,000 km on its odometer. Commencing in 1995, the paint began to bubble, flake, and eventually peel off. Deputy Judge Robert Zochodne awarded the plaintiff $1,205.72 and struck down every one of GM's environmental/acid rain/UV-rays arguments. GM did not appeal any of these important aspects in this 12-page judgment:

1. The judge admitted many of the service bulletins referred to in *Lemon-Aid* as proof of GM's negligence.
2. Although the vehicle had 156,000 km when the case went to court, GM still offered to pay 50 percent of the paint repairs if the plaintiff dropped his suit.

3. Deputy Judge Zochodne ruled that the failure to protect the paint from the damaging effects of UV rays is akin to engineering a car that won't start in cold weather. In essence, vehicles must be built to withstand the rigours of the environment.
4. Here's an interesting twist: the original warranty covered defects that were present at the time it was in effect. The judge, taking statements found in the GM bulletins, ruled the UV problem was factory related, and therefore, *it existed during the warranty period and thereby represented a latent defect* that appeared once the warranty expired.
5. The subsequent purchaser was not prevented from making the warranty claim, even though the warranty had long since expired from a time and mileage standpoint and he was the second owner.

Williams v. General Motors of Canada, October 27, 1997, British Columbia Provincial Small Claims Court, Nanaimo Registry, No. 15691, Presiding Judge J.D. Cowling.

Reasons for Judgment

The claimants sought damages for the paint delamination of a blue 1988 Grand Am which they purchased new on October 1, 1988. They first noticed the paint chipping from their vehicle in September of 1994. They called GM's toll-free customer relations hot line and were told there were no known paint issues regarding their model of vehicle.

By 1995, the chipping problem had expanded into extensive delamination of paint on the upper horizontal surfaces of the car. The Plaintiffs' local dealer then admitted it was a common problem, but added that the "goodwill" program was discontinued as of August 1995. The Plaintiffs were quoted $1,939.60 to have their car repainted.

Subsequent inquiry by the claimants revealed that as of October 1992, the defendant GM had issued a product service bulletin that described the problem as follows:

> Blues, Grays, Silvers, and Black Metallics are the colours that have the highest potential for this condition...may have delamination (peeling) of the paint colourcoat from the ELPO primer depending upon variable factors including prolonged exposure to sunlight and humidity.

> This condition may occur on vehicles produced in plants where the paint process does not call for application of a primer surfacer. Under certain conditions, ultraviolet light can penetrate the colourcoat, sometimes causing a reaction and separation of portions of the colourcoat from the ELPO (electrocoat primer).

Other product service bulletins from the U.S. branch of the defendant indicate the paint delamination problem was not unique to cars in Canada. In the U.S., the Center for Auto Safety negotiated an agreement with GM to implement a post-warranty adjustment program for paint problems described as follows in letter dated February 5, 1993:

- broad dealer discretion
- six years coverage from date of delivery
- unlimited mileage
- deductibles may be waived
- not just delamination

The nature of the delamination problem is such that once detected in a particular vehicle, spot repainting is not a viable remedy but rather the removal of the topcoat and primer surfaces is required.

The purchase of this car by the claimants is a sale by description within the meaning of s. 17 of the Sale of Goods Act. Pursuant to s. 18 (b) of the Act there is an "...implied condition that the goods are of merchantable quality..." and further by virtue of s. 18 (c) an "...implied condition that goods will be durable for a reasonable period of time."

I find that having regard to the type of car purchased by the claimants, the condition in which they have maintained it, the extent of the paint problem it suffers from and the reason for the problem that the claimants have established a breach of the section 18 (b) and (c) warranties. I consider the reasoning of O'Donnell, J, in Thauberger v. Simon Fraser Sales Ltd. et al (1977) 3 B.C.L.R. No. 193 with respect to what was then s. 20 (b) of the Act to be directly on point in this case. I acknowledge that the paint surface in Thauberger failed after 21 months and not six years as here, however, I consider that the buyer of a new car in 1988 may reasonably expect its paint surface not to delaminate under normal use within 6 years. I find that the settlement GM (U.S.) negotiated with the Center for Auto Safety supports that position although not determinative of it.

The claimants are entitled to judgment against the defendant in the sum of $1,229.70. They are entitled to Court Order interest on this amount from September 1, 1995, to the date of judgment to account for any increase in the present cost of a paint job from the date of the 1995 quote. The claimants will also have their costs in this matter for filing and service fees. The judgment is payable within 15 days from its entry.

Launching a Lawsuit

When to sue

If the seller you've been negotiating with agrees to make things right, give him or her a deadline and then have an independent garage check the repairs. If no offer is made within 10 working days, file a suit in court. Make the manufacturer a party to the lawsuit only if the original, unexpired warranty was transferred to you, your claim falls under the emissions warranty, a secret warranty extension or a safety recall campaign exists, or extensive chassis rusting is involved.

There are small claims courts in most counties of each province, and you can make a claim either in the county where the problem occurred or where the defendant lives and carries on business. The first step is to make sure that your claim doesn't exceed the dollar limit of the court. You should then go to the small claims court office and ask for a claim form. (The form includes instructions on how to properly fill it out.) Keep in mind that you must identify the defendant correctly. It's a practice of some dishonest firms to change a company's name in order to escape liability. For example, it would be impossible to sue Joe's Garage (1991) if your contract is with Joe's Garage Inc. (1984).

You're entitled to bring any evidence to court that's relevant to the case, including such written documents as a bill of sale or receipt, a contract, or a letter. If your car has developed severe paint problems, take a photograph to court. Have the photographer sign and date the photo. You may also have witnesses testify in court (a family member may act as a witness). It's important to discuss a witness's testimony prior to the court date. If a witness can't attend the court date, he or she can write a report and sign it for representation in court. This situation usually applies to an expert witness, such as the independent mechanic who evaluated your car's problems.

Be sure to organize your evidence, prepare questions for the witnesses, and write down what you want to tell the court.

Choosing the Right Court

You must decide which remedy to pursue; that is, whether you want a partial refund or a cancellation of the sale. To determine the refund amount, add the estimated cost of repairing existing mechanical defects to the cost of prior repairs. Don't exaggerate your losses or claim for repairs that are considered routine maintenance.

Generally, if the cost of repairs falls within the small claims court limit (discussed later), the case should be filed there to keep costs to a minimum and to obtain a speedy hearing. Small claims court judgments aren't easily appealed, lawyers aren't necessary, filing fees are minimal (about $125), and cases are usually heard within a few months.

If the damages exceed the small claims court limit and there's no way to reduce them, or if you want to cancel the sale, you'll have to go to a higher court—where costs quickly add up and lengthy delays of a few years or more are commonplace. However, some lawyers may take your case on a "contingency fee" basis, where they get nothing if you lose, but take up to a third of the award if you win.

A suit for cancellation of sale involves practical problems. The court requires that the vehicle be "tendered" back to the seller at the time the lawsuit is filed. This means you are without transportation for as long as the case continues, unless you purchase another car in the interim. If you lose the case, you must then take back the old car and pay storage fees. You could go from having no car to having two, one of which is a clunker. For these reasons, try to stay out of the higher courts if at all possible and plead the case yourself (after getting legal advice).

Small claims court

Canadian small claims courts offer simple claim forms, and actions cost only about $50–$125 for a $6,000 claim and take only a few months to be heard. The beauty of a small claims action is that most provincial courts force the automaker into a mediation session with you before proceeding to trial. Many claims are settled through mediation for one-half to two-thirds of the amount demanded in the action.

Sometimes, small claims courts can be used creatively to get as much compensation as would be given by a higher court. For example, the hardship of owning a $6,000 lemon can be eased if the owner sues the dealer in small claims court for the maximum to cover repairs, insurance, rental cars, inconvenience, etc., which may total $3,000. If the court awards this amount, the car can then be sold without the repairs done for about $3,000. Thus, the customer gets back the $6,000 with few legal fees to pay after a delay of only a few months. Furthermore, the car can still be used during the lawsuit, because the plaintiff isn't seeking to set the sale aside.

If the damages exceed the small claims court limit and there is no way to reduce them, you'll have to go to a court with a higher claim limit. This will be costly. Before rushing off to file a lawsuit, consider the following ways in which you can win your case in a higher court and still wind up losing your shirt.

• For a simple case that comes to a short trial, lawyers' fees can vary between $500 and $1,000. These fees must be paid whether the case is won or lost. If you lose, you may have to pay court costs as well.

• The first trial isn't likely to take place for two or three years. Then, even if you win, the judgment is likely to be appealed, thus delaying final judgment for another two to four years, and boosting each side's legal fees.

• Once appeals are exhausted and you've won, the judgment will be paid in depreciated dollars supplemented by a low interest rate—if you can collect.

• Car dealers can avoid judgment by disappearing or closing down and reopening under a new name. It happens quite often, and the courts can do little to stop it.

Class actions

Class action lawsuits allow a single individual to sue a company, government, or other entity on behalf of hundreds or even thousands of others with similar claims. Although class action suits have been used for three decades in the United States, they are a recent arrival in Canada. Quebec was the first province to adopt this legal remedy in the early '80s, and Ontario and British Columbia followed suit in 1992 and 1995, respectively. In fact, both Chrysler and General Motors are facing class action lawsuits in British Columbia, where plaintiffs are seeking compensation for paint-delaminated 1986–97 vehicles.

Class actions allow for contingency fees, where consumers can enter into no-win-no-pay agreements with lawyers. If you lose, you usually pay your expenses and move on. However, Ontario judges can require that losing class action plaintiffs pay the defendant's fees as well, a chilling thought for most plaintiffs. (B.C. legislation requires that both sides pay their own legal costs.)

One of the more recent successful class actions in Canada concerned the recovery of condo owner deposits in Toronto. In *Windisman v. Toronto College Park Ltd.*, 544 condominium residents recovered $2.6 million, representing the interest earned on their deposit payments for apartments, parking spaces, and storage lockers.

How to file a class action
• Like any other lawsuit, a lawyer files the plaintiff's statement of claim against the defendant and the plaintiff applies to the court to certify the lawsuit as a class action.
• The presiding judge will then decide whether there is an "identifiable class of two or more persons," whether a class action is the "preferable procedure," and whether the plaintiff truly represents the class. If you meet all the above criteria, the judge will issue a certification order and designate you as the Class Representative.
• Other class members must be notified of the lawsuit. Small groups can be contacted by mail, but larger groups may require notification through newspaper ads backed up by a toll-free telephone line. Members of the class must then be given an opportunity to opt out of the lawsuit. If they don't, they remain part of the class.

If the class wins, individual cases may then be heard to assess damages, or a notification may be sent to each member to apply for their part of the settlement or award. It may take from three to five years before a final judgment is rendered, and appeals may double that time. Lawyers typically charge the class one-third of the amount obtained.

Trial conduct

Because the cost of defence would be prohibitive and the bad publicity could ruin the dealer's business, lawyers often tell their dealer-clients to settle a small claims case out of court. Lawyers also know that urging their clients to settle out of court means they never lose a case.

Sometimes a dealer's lawyer will threaten to sue the plaintiff for libel or slander if the case is taken to court. This is a move designed to intimidate. No one can be sued for libel or slander merely for exercising his or her rights before the courts. The dealer, however, can be sued for harassment, and the lawyer can be cited for unprofessional conduct if the threat is carried out.

On the day of the trial, bring in a mechanic to confirm that the defects exist and to estimate the cost of repairing them. If the repairs have already been carried out, he can explain what caused the defects and justify his bill for repairing them. This should be done by presenting the defective parts, if possible. He must convince the judge that the defects were present at the time the car was sold, and that they were not caused by poor maintenance or abusive driving habits.

Before the dealer leaves the stand, get him to confirm any representations he or his salespeople made, either verbally or through a newspaper ad, extolling the vehicle's qualities. With witnesses excluded, it's quite likely that the dealer's witnesses will contradict him when their turn comes to testify because they didn't hear the previous testimony. Your own co-workers or friends can testify as to how well you maintained the vehicle and how it was driven, as well as describe the seriousness of the defects.

Dos and don'ts

- Do complain to the provincial Transport and Consumer Affairs ministries about possible violations of provincial laws.
- Do contact local consumer groups and the Automobile Protection Association for recent jurisprudence and help in mediating the complaint.
- Do publicize any favourable court judgment as a warning to other dealers and as encouragement for other consumers.
- Don't sue a car dealer if he is bankrupt, or is willing to negotiate a settlement.
- Don't threaten or insult the dealer. This will only gain sympathy for him and hurt your own credibility.

Remember not to delay in filing a claim once it's obvious that no settlement is forthcoming. A lawsuit should be filed no later than three months after the final registered claim letter has been sent.

Collecting Your Winnings

Settlements

You may be asked to sign a document called a "release," which proves that a final settlement has been made. Generally, once you sign the release you can't sue the other person for that particular debt or injury. If you're the debtor, it's very important that you make sure the other person signs the release when you pay him or her. If you're the creditor collecting on the debt, you must sign the release, but don't do so until you've received the money or verified that the check is good. Also, don't give up any more rights than you have to. Release the debtor from that particular debt, but don't release him or her from all future debts.

Sample Settlement Form

I, John Doe, hereby acknowledge the receipt of $300 plus $10 interest from Jane Smith, in full and final satisfaction of all claims, which I may have against her arising from a sale of a used Ford Mustang by her to me on June 30th, 1996, and from all claims arising from a cheque for $300 dated November 30th, 1993, signed by her and payable to me, which was returned to me marked "Not Sufficient Funds."

_____   _____
Date   John Doe

Name of Witness: _____

Key Court Decisions

The following Canadian lawsuits and judgments cover typical problems that are likely to arise. Put any relevant case in your claim letter as leverage when negotiating a settlement, or as a reference should your claim go to trial. Legal principles are similarly applicable to Canadian and American law. Quebec court decisions, however, may be based on legal principles that don't apply outside that province. Therefore, do what most lawyers do: present all the court judgments that may be helpful and let the presiding judge or the defendant's lawyer sort out those that they feel apply.

Additional court judgments can be found in the legal reference section of your city's main public library or at a nearby university law library. Ask the librarian for help in choosing the legal phrases that best describe your claim.

Drivers who have been charged with a traffic offence and who wish to mount a spirited and well-researched defence should ask the librarian for a copy of *The Law of Traffic Offences (Second Edition)*, by Scott Hutchison, David Rose, and Philip Downes and published by Carswell. Written by three Toronto lawyers, this guide covers radar challenges, fatal prosecutorial flaws, court procedure, objections, appeals, witnesses, and expert testimony, giving relevant case law for almost any situation. First published in 1988, this is an excellent reference guide for laypersons and legal practitioners alike.

Damages (Punitive)

Punitive damages (also known as exemplary damages) allow the plaintiff to get compensation that exceeds his or her losses. In Canada, judges sometimes award punitive damages as a deterrent to those who carry out dishonest or negligent practices; however, these kinds of judgments are more common in the U.S. For example, last July both Ford and GM were hit with huge punitive judgments: the GM plaintiffs were given $4.9 billion by a California jury as compensation for burns sustained when a speeding Mustang rear-ended their 1972 Malibu; and Ford plaintiffs were awarded $295 million for injuries sustained from a Bronco rollover.

Vlchek v. Koshel (1988), 44 C.C.L.T. 314, B.C.S.C., No. B842974. The plaintiff was seriously injured when she was thrown from a Honda all-terrain cycle on which she had been riding as a passenger. The Court allowed for punitive damages because the manufacturer was well aware of the injuries likely to be caused by the cycle. Specifically, the Court ruled that there is no firm and inflexible principle of law stipulating that punitive or exemplary damages must be denied unless the defendant's acts are specifically directed against the plaintiff. The Court may apply punitive damages "where the defendant's conduct has been indiscriminate of focus, but reckless or malicious in its character. Intent to injure the plaintiff need not be present, so long as intent to do the injurious act can be shown."

See also:
- *Granek v. Reiter*, Ont. Ct. (Gen. Div.), No. 35/741.
- *Morrison v. Sharp*, Ont. Ct. (Gen. Div.), No. 43/548.
- *Schryvers v. Richport Ford Sales*, May 18, 1993, B.C.S.C., No. C917060, Judge Tysoe.
- *Varleg v. Angeloni*, B.C.S.C., No. 41/301.

Furthermore, a slew of cases cover specifics in damage claims. Provincial business practices acts cover false, misleading, or deceptive representations, and allow for punitive damages should the unfair practice toward the consumer amount to an unconscionable representation. (See C.E.D. (3d) s. 76, pp. 140–45.) "Unconscionable" is defined as "where the consumer is not reasonably able to protect his or her interest because of physical infirmity, ignorance, illiteracy, or inability to understand the language of an agreement or similar factors."
- Exemplary damages are justified where compensatory damages are insufficient to deter and punish. See *Walker et al. v. CFTO Ltd. et al.* (1978), 59 O.R. (2nd), No. 104 (Ont. C.A.).
- Exemplary damages can be awarded in cases where the defendant's conduct was "cavalier." See *Ronald Elwyn Lister Ltd. et al. v. Dayton Tire Canada Ltd.* (1985), 52 O.R. (2nd), No. 89 (Ont. C.A.).
- The primary purpose of exemplary damages is to prevent the defendant and all others from doing similar wrongs. See *Fleming v. Spracklin* (1921).

- Disregard of the public's interest, lack of preventive measures, and a callous attitude all merit exemplary damages. See *Coughlin v. Kuntz* (1989), 2 C.C.L.T. (2nd) (B.C.C.A.).
- Punitive damages can be awarded for mental distress. See *Ribeiro v. Canadian Imperial Bank of Commerce* (1992), Ontario Reports 13 (3rd) and *Brown v. Waterloo Regional Board of Comissioners of Police* (1992), 37 O.R. (2nd).

Defects (Body/Performance Related)

What's a lemon?
The definitive description of a "lemon" is found in U.S. state law, in which it's defined as a vehicle with problems that can't be repaired after four attempts, keep the vehicle out of service for more than 30 days, or render it unfit for the purpose for which it was purchased.

When a vehicle no longer falls within the limits of the warranty expressed by the manufacturer or dealer, it doesn't necessarily mean that the manufacturer can't be held liable for damages caused by defective design. As mentioned before, the manufacturer is always liable for the replacement or repair of defective parts if independent testimony can show that the part was incorrectly manufactured or designed, and that this "mistake" affects its reliability or durability. The existence of service bulletins indicating upgrades, or a secret warranty extension, will usually help to prove that the part was poorly made (or the paint process was flawed). For example, in *Lowe v. Chrysler*, internal service bulletins were instrumental in showing an Ontario small claims court judge that Chrysler had a history of automatic transmission failures since 1989.

In addition to replacing or repairing the part that failed, an automaker can be held responsible for any damages arising from the part's failure. This means that loss of wages, supplementary transportation costs, and damages for personal inconvenience can be awarded.

Paint delamination or peeling, and rusting
Although this was once a problem with early Hondas, Mazdas, and Nissans, premature paint delamination and peeling now mostly afflicts the Big Three American automakers. Chrysler, Ford, and GM 1984–97 models are equally affected. Each company, however, has responded differently to owners' requests for compensation. To help you prepare the best arguments for negotiations or court, read the following court judgments carefully and frame your claim accordingly.

Chrysler
Because Chrysler has settled most of its paint claims out of court, there aren't any recent judgments against the company. There is, however, a 29-page class action lawsuit filed in the state of Washington which seeks damages for all Chrysler owners who have owned or leased paint-delaminated 1986–97 models: *Schurk, Chanes, Jansen, and Ricker v.*

Chrysler, No. 97-2-04113-9-SEA, filed in the Superior Court of King County, Washington on October 2, 1997 (contact Steve Berman or Clyde Platt with the Seattle, Washington, law firm of Hagens and Berman at 206-623-7292). *Lemon-Aid Used Cars 1999* has much of the text.

Canadian lawyers have filed a class action seeking damages for paint delamination from Chrysler on behalf of British Columbia owners of 1986–97 Chrysler vehicles. What makes this lawsuit particularly important is that the plaintiffs are suing under the provincial Trade Practice Act, alleging that Chrysler and its dealers engaged in a deceptive trade practice due to their knowledge that "the two-stage paint process was defective. In particular, prior to 1986 the defendants knew that exposure to sunlight caused the electrocoat layer to deteriorate and result in failure of the bond between the paint finishes and the vehicle body...."

The lawsuit concludes that the "failure to disclose the defective nature of the two-stage process to the class plaintiffs and, in particular, the representative plaintiffs, constitutes a deceptive trade practice pursuant to section three of the Act." Any B.C. residents who want to join this class action may contact the plaintiffs' attorneys: Joe Fiorante or J.J. Camp at 1-800-689-2322, or *jcamp@campchurch.com* and *jfiorante@campchurch.com*. In the States, Paul Weiss, who is coordinating his efforts with the Canadian lawyers, has already filed similar paint delamination class actions against Chrysler, Ford, and GM on behalf of American owners. Paul Weiss can be reached at *jandpw@ix.netcom.com*.

Ford

Louisiana attorney Danny Becknel, along with other lawyers, has filed three separate class action lawsuits against Chrysler, Ford, and GM. He's also filed suit against PPG Industries, a company out of Pittsburgh that he says sold defective car paint to the three companies.

Becknel also claims in his suits that in the late '80s/early '90s, the Big Three bought a product from PPG Industries called "Uniprime" without thoroughly testing it. He says that when the companies bought "Uniprime," they switched from a three-coat car painting process (bottom coat, spray primer, colour coat) to a two-coat process which eliminated the middle coat. Mr. Becknel claims that eliminating the middle spray primer layer saved Ford anywhere from $6–$16 a car: "This paint seems to be a minor cost, but when you multiply it by 10–15 million times a year, it's a big number."

Faced with an estimated 13 percent failure rate, Ford repainted its delaminated 1983–93 cars, minivans, vans, F-series trucks, Explorers, Rangers, and Broncos free of charge for five years under a secret "Owner Dialogue" program. Ford whistle blowers say the company discontinued the program in January '95 because it was proving to be too costly. Nevertheless, owners who cry foul and threaten small claims action are still routinely given initial offers of 50 percent compensation, and eventually complete refunds if they press further.

General Motors
Confidential U.S. dealer service bulletins and memos confirm the six-year/unlimited mileage benchmark that GM uses to accept or reject secret warranty paint claims (see page 97). As with Ford and Chrysler, GM customers seeking paint compensation are thrust into a "Let's Make a Deal" scenario, where they're usually first offered a 50 percent refund—and then 100 percent, if they stand their ground.

In addition to their Chrysler paint lawsuit, British Columbia lawyers Joe Fiorante and J.J. Camp (see *"Chrysler,"* above, for contact information) also filed a class action against General Motors last May seeking damages for paint delamination from Chrysler on behalf of 1986–97 GM vehicle owners in B.C. Again, they contend that GM violated the provincial Trade Practice Act, claiming the automaker and its dealers engaged in a deceptive trade practice.

Other paint/rust cases
Martin v. Honda Canada Inc., March 17, 1986, Ontario Small Claims Court (Scarborough), Judge Sigurdson. The original owner of a 1981 Honda Civic sought compensation for the premature "bubbling, pitting, cracking of the paint and rusting of the Civic after five years of ownership." Judge Sigurdson agreed and ordered Honda to pay the owner $1,163.95.

Perron v. Vincent Automobile Ltée. (1979), C.P., No. 166. The plaintiff had the dealer rustproof her new car at a cost of $115. This dealer's warranty said that any future rusting would be repaired up to a cost of $115, or the purchase price would be refunded. The dealer interpreted this to mean that $115 would be the total amount that could be claimed while the guarantee was in effect. However, the Court agreed with the plaintiff that she could claim up to $115 each time a warranty claim was made.

Prochera v. Sherwood Chevrolet, November 9, 1978, Saskatoon Small Claims Court, Judge Clifford Peet. In this Blazer paint case, the plaintiff sued for the correction of a mismatched paint job carried out by the dealer to repair delivery damage and the original mismatching of the paint seen when the vehicle was first delivered. The plaintiff was awarded $75 plus court costs.

Rolland v. Chrysler, November 1979, Third Small Claims Court of Lanark County, Ontario, No. 148/79, Judge Thorpe. After Chrysler admitted it had a secret warranty that paid for the replacement of rusted-out front fenders, Judge Thorpe awarded $896.17 to a couple who purchased a used 1976 Chrysler Volaré from a relative in 1978.

Thauberger v. Simon Fraser Sales and Mazda Motors, 3 B.C.L.R., No. 193. This Mazda owner sued for damages caused by the premature rusting of his 1977 Mazda GLC. The Court awarded him $1,000. Mr. Thauberger had previously sued General Motors for a prematurely rusted Blazer truck and was also awarded $1,000 in the same Court. Both judges ruled that the defects could not be excluded from the automaker's expressed warranty or from the implied warranty granted by ss. 20, 20(b) of the B.C. Sale of Goods Act.

Whittaker v. Ford Motor Company (1979), 24 O.R. (2nd), No. 344. A new Ford developed serious corrosion problems in spite of having been rustproofed by the dealer. The Court ruled that the dealer, not Ford, was liable for the damage for having sold the rustproofing product at the time of purchase. This is an important judgment to use when a rust-proofer or paint protector goes out of business or refuses to pay a claim, since the decision holds the dealer jointly responsible.

See also:
• *Danson v. Chateau Ford* (1976) C.P., Quebec Small Claims Court, No. 32-00001898-757, Judge Lande.
• *Doyle v. Vital Automotive Systems*, May 16, 1977, Ontario Small Claims Court (Toronto), Judge Turner.
• *Lacroix v. Ford*, April 1980, Ontario Small Claims Court (Toronto), Judge Tierney.
• *Marinovich v. Riverside Chrysler*, April 1, 1987, District Court of Ontario, No. 1030/85, Judge Stortini.

Performance defects
Bagnell's Cleaners v. Eastern Automobile Ltd. (1991), 111 N.S.R. (2nd), No. 51, 303 A.P.R. 51 (T.D.). This Nova Scotia company found that the new van it purchased had serious engine, transmission, and radiator defects. The dealer pleaded unsuccessfully that the sales contract excluded all other warranties except for those contained in the con-tract. The Court held that there was a fundamental breach of the implied warranty and that the van's performance differed substantially from what the purchaser had been led to expect. An exclusionary clause could not protect the seller, who failed to live up to a funda-mental term of the contract.

Burridge v. City Motor, 10 Nfld. & P.E.I.R., No. 451. This Newfoundland res-ident complained repeatedly of his new car's defects during the warranty period, and hadn't used his car for 204 days after spending almost $1,500 for repairs. The judge awarded all repair costs and cancelled the sale.

Davis v. Chrysler Canada Ltd. (1977), 26 N.S.R. (2nd), No. 410 (T.D.). The owner of a new $28,000 diesel truck found that a faulty steering assembly prevented him from carrying on his business. The Court ordered that the sale be cancelled and $10,000 in monthly payments be reimbursed. There was insufficient evidence to award compensation for business losses.

Fox v. Wilson Motors and GM, February 9, 1989, Court of Queen's Bench, New Brunswick, No. F/C/308/87. A trucker's new tractor-trailer had repeated engine malfunctions. He was awarded damages for loss of income, excessive fuel consumption, and telephone charges under the provincial Sale of Goods Act.

Gibbons v. Trapp Motors Ltd. (1970), 9 D.L.R. (3rd), No. 742 (B.C.S.C.). The Court ordered the dealer to take back a new car that had numerous defects and needed 32 hours of repairs. Refund was reduced by mileage driven.

Johnson v. Northway Chevrolet Oldsmobile (1993), 108 Sask. R. (Q.B.), No. 138. Two years after purchase, the buyer initiated a lawsuit for the purchase price of a new car that had been brought in for repairs on 14 different occasions and for general damages. The Court ordered the dealer to take back the car, and awarded general damages.

Julien v. GM of Canada (1991), 116 N.B.R. (2nd), No. 80. The plaintiff's new diesel truck produced excessive engine noise. The dealer claimed that the problem was caused by the owner's engine alterations. The plaintiff was awarded $5,000—the cost of having the engine repaired by an independent dealer.

Kravitz v. General Motors, January 1979, Supreme Court of Canada, I.R.C.S., No. 393. This owner of a new Oldsmobile was never able to have it properly repaired under warranty. When the warranty period was over, General Motors and the dealer refused to do further free work, or to give him another vehicle. The presiding judge awarded the car owner damages and a refund of the purchase price. This Quebec case is based on articles 1522–1530 of the Quebec Civil Code (hidden defects), but it applies in common-law provinces as well. The Supreme Court ruled that both the dealer and the manufacturer can be held jointly or separately responsible, and that the manufacturer's warranty does not negate the implied legal warranty of fitness.

Lowe v. Fairview Chrysler-Dodge Limited and Chrysler Canada Limited, May 14, 1996, Ontario Court (General Division), Burlington Small Claims Court, No.1224/95. This judgment raises the following important legal principles relative to Chrysler:
• Internal dealer service bulletins are admissible in court to prove that a problem exists and that certain parts should be checked out.
• If a problem is reported prior to a warranty's expiration, its warranty coverage is automatically carried over after the warranty ends.
• It's not up to the car owner to tell the dealer/automaker what the specific problem is.
• Repairs carried out by an independent garage can be refunded if the dealer/Chrysler unfairly refuses to apply the warranty.

- The dealer/Chrysler Canada cannot dispute the cost of the independent repair if they fail to cross-examine the independent mechanic.
- Auto owners can ask for and win compensation for their inconvenience, which in this judgment amounted to $150.
- Court awards aren't simply limited to a refund. The plaintiff was given $1,985.94 plus court costs and prejudgment interest—with costs of inconvenience fixed at $150, the final award amounted to $2,266.04.

MacDonald GMC v. Gillespie, June 3, 1986, New Brunswick Court of Appeal. Compensation of $7,148 was awarded to a new-car buyer after the dealer failed to honour his salesman's verbal promises to repair certain defects at no charge.

Magna Management Ltd. v. Volkswagen Canada Inc., May 27, 1988, B.C.C.A., No. CA006037. This precedent-setting case allowed the plaintiff to keep his new $48,325 VW while awarding him $37,101—three years after the car was purchased. The problems were centred on poor engine performance. The jury accepted the plaintiff's view that the car was practically worthless with its inherent defects.

Maughan v. Silver's Garage Ltd., Nova Scotia Supreme Court, 6 B.L.R. 303, N.S.C. (2nd), No. 278. The plaintiff leased a defective backhoe. The manufacturer had to reimburse the plaintiff's losses because the warranty wasn't honoured. The Court rejected the manufacturer's contention that the contract's exclusion clause protected the company from lawsuits for damages resulting from a latent defect.

Murphy v. Penney Motors Ltd. (1979), 23 Nfld. & P.E.I.R., 152, 61 A.P.R., No. 152 (Nfld. T.D.). This Newfoundland trucker found that the repairing of engine problems took his new trailer off the road for 129 days during a seven-month period. The judge awarded all repair costs, as well as compensation for business losses, and cancelled the sale.

Murray v. Sperry Rand Corp., Ontario Supreme Court, 5 B.L.R., No. 284. The seller, dealer, and manufacturer were all held liable for breach of warranty when a forage harvester did not perform as advertised in the sales brochure or as promised by the sales agent. The plaintiff was given his money back and reimbursed for his economic loss based on what his harvesting usually earned. The Court held that the advertising was a warranty.

Oliver v. Courtesy Chrysler (1983) Ltd. (1992), 11 B.C.A.C., No. 169. This new car had numerous defects over a three-year period, which the dealer attempted to fix to no avail. The plaintiff put the car in storage and sued the dealer for the purchase price. The Court ruled that the car wasn't roadworthy and that the plaintiff couldn't be blamed for putting it in storage rather than selling it and purchasing another vehicle. The purchase price was refunded, minus $1,500 for each year the plaintiff used the car.

Olshaski Farms Ltd. v. Skene Farm Equipment Ltd., January 9, 1987, Alberta Court of Queen's Bench, 49 Alta. L.R. (2nd), No. 249. This Massey-Ferguson combine caught fire after the manufacturer had sent two notices to dealers informing them of a defect that could cause a fire. The judge ruled under the Sale of Goods Act that the balance of probabilities indicated that the manufacturing defect caused the fire, even though there was no direct evidence proving that the defect existed.

Western Pacific Tank Lines Ltd. v. Brentwood Dodge, June 2, 1975, B.C.S.C., No. 30945-74, Judge Meredith. The Court awarded the plaintiff $8,600 and cancelled the sale of a new Chrysler New Yorker with the following defects: badly adjusted doors, water leaks into the interior, and electrical short circuits.

Defects (Safety Related)

More than 250 million cars have been recalled since the late '60s to correct safety-related defects. Under Canadian federal legislation (Canadian Motor Vehicle Safety Act, 1971), car companies don't have to recall their cars, or fix them free of charge within a certain period of time. The law stipulates only that companies have to notify owners that their cars can kill them. American legislation requires notification and free correction unless the NHTSA's defect determination is challenged in the courts.

Motor murder. It's quite common for American juries to award multi-million dollar judgments against automakers for defective components that have killed or injured plaintiffs, but you won't find similar judgments in Canada. Blame it on no-fault insurance.

In provinces where no-fault insurance has been adopted, both consumers and bar associations have discovered that insurance companies or the province—not automakers—must pay for the injuries and deaths caused by defective vehicles. It also shields governments responsible for public roadways.

Says the Saskatchewan Branch of the Canadian Bar Association:

> Given that vehicle manufacturers contribute nothing towards the Saskatchewan insurance system and that their defective products cause serious injury and financial loss to motorists and the health care system, lawyers' organizations have taken particular offence to this aspect of the law....

They must have been clinking champagne glasses in Detroit!

Although your rights to claim for death or injury are limited, use the following court decisions in your claim letter and as a guide to what you can expect when filing a lawsuit against an automobile manufacturer for safety-related defects.

Airbags

The National Highway Traffic Safety Administration says that airbags have saved 2,500 lives and reduce moderate and severe injuries in auto accidents by 25 percent. Unfortunately, says the *Wall Street Journal*, these figures are shaky and not based on real-world experiences.

THE WALL STREET JOURNAL.

MARKETPLACE

WEDNESDAY, JANUARY 22, 1997 **B1**

FLORIDA JOURNAL *(Follows Page B10)*

Rx for HMOs: *Managed health-care industry faces some changes in the Legislature.*

Royal Feud: *Bond forged by King of Beers and home-run king starts to break apart.*

Shaky Statistics Are Driving the Air Bag Debate

By ASRA Q. NOMANI
And JEFFREY TAYLOR
Staff Reporters of THE WALL STREET JOURNAL

How many lives have air bags saved? At a recent Senate hearing, Ricardo Martinez, chief of the National Highway Traffic Safety Administration, had a fairly

AUTOS

precise answer: more than 1,700. In the highly emotional debate over air bags, that number purports to provide a degree of comfort. Auto makers and federal regulators use it frequently to counter concerns about the 55 people killed since 1990 by the explosive force of air bags.

In fact, no one can say with certainty how many lives they have claimed. Was the air bag really to blame in each of the deaths or were other factors involved? Moreover, the 1,700 figure for lives saved is an estimate, generated by a computer model developed by the NHTSA. And the estimate isn't very specific; those who crunch the numbers say the actual tally

could be anywhere from 1,039 to 2,437.

As uncertain as they are, the figures show how pivotal statistics can be in a red-hot safety debate. They also demonstrate how estimates can create a public perception of precision and certainty when neither exist.

"It's a numbers game," says Idaho Republican Sen. Dick Kempthorne, who has been calling for new testing procedures since November, when an infant in his state was decapitated by an air bag in a low-speed fender bender. Both the number of lives saved and lives lost are likely to increase as air bags become more prevalent. By law, all new cars must be equipped with both driver-side and passenger-side bags by next fall.

Even NHTSA officials concede that their air bag "save" figures are far from precise. They are based on an August 1996 report in which a team of researchers used two different methods to estimate fatalities prevented by air bags, then averaged them together. First, the NHTSA researchers looked at how many drivers and front-seat passengers had died in crashes of

KEY DATA MEASURING the efficacy of air bags in a crash often ignore whether passengers were using seat belts.

2,880 cars equipped with air bags, compared with fatalities in crashes of 5,237 cars without air bags. After accounting for the difference in the sample sizes, they found 10% fewer fatalities in cars with air bags.

The NHTSA researchers also compared survival rates with and without air bags in frontal and nonfrontal crashes, and concluded that air bags reduced fatalities by 12%. Then they averaged the two results to derive a best estimate: that air bags bring 11% fewer fatalities. From actual accident statistics, they calculated that there would have been 1,136 additional fatalities between 1986 and 1995 if air bags did not exist. Finally, they estimated the number of 1996 fatalities, factored in the number of new cars equipped with air bags that have

entered the market and projected that the number of lives saved through last year was 1,703.

Still, in calculating those numbers, government researchers don't know for sure whether or not the people "saved" by air bags had been wearing seat belts. If they had been belted, they would have faced less risk of death in the first place, safety experts say. But the federal accident database the researchers used "does not contain accurate information about the belt use of crash survivors, especially in recent years," the report notes.

The seat belt question complicates the count of people "killed" by air bags, as well. Of the 55 people who died, 35 were children sitting on the passenger side. In each case, NHTSA investigators culled accident reports and determined that the air bag itself caused the fatal injuries. But 24 of the 35 children were not wearing seat belts or were improperly restrained. In nine cases, the children were in rear-facing child-seats, which are not supposed to be placed in a front seat.

"The greatest threat to children isn't *Please Turn to Page B11, Column 1*

Although safety experts agree that you are likely to need anti-lock brakes 99 times more often than an airbag, the bag's advantage is that it doesn't depend upon driver skill or reaction time and it deploys when it's too late for braking. Nevertheless, there have been thousands of reports of airbags that have failed to deploy or have accidentally gone off and caused massive injuries. In fact, General Motors recalled almost a million Cadillacs, Cavaliers, and Sunfires for just that problem of accidental deployment—caused by wet carpeting in Cadillacs and passing over a bump in the road for the other vehicles.

Safety experts at NHTSA once estimated that 25,000 people were injured by airbags between 1988 and 1991. Additionally, recent NHTSA-run crash tests indicate that all of Chrysler's minivan airbags produced in 1997 and earlier deploy with such excessive force they may cause disabling or fatal injuries. In February 1999 crash tests, the deploying passenger-side airbag in a 1997 Caravan caused neck injuries to a small, belted, female dummy that, according to the agency, would have disabled or killed a person. The suspect airbags may be in as many as 1.9 million minivans. Coincidentally, a U.S. national auto safety group, the Insurance Institute for Highway Safety (IIHS), has launched an exhaustive investigation into reports that inflating airbags have seriously injured motorists.

Hundreds of lawsuits have been filed claiming airbags don't function as designed (not deploying when they should, or deploying when they shouldn't) and over 60 suits have been filed claiming the device caused or aggravated injuries after actually deploying as designed. Chrysler, the first automaker to install airbags as standard equipment, is the target of most of these lawsuits. So far, the successful suits against Chrysler relate to poor design rather than malfunctions and fall into two categories: severe burns and premature deployment at low speeds.

Severe burns
Claimants have won substantial jury awards for first- or second-degree burns caused by the Thiokol-designed airbag directing hot gases at the driver's hands and wrists. Used on Chrysler's 1988–91 models, these airbags have vent holes that direct hot gases at the three o'clock and nine o'clock hand positions. In late 1990, the vent holes were relocated to the twelve o'clock position. A class action lawsuit asking for damages arising from the earlier Thiokol design was filed in Philadelphia County and has recently resulted in a verdict of $60 million in compensatory damages, and another $3.75 million in punitive damages, for 80,000 Pennsylvania Chrysler owners who purchased their vehicles between 1988 and 1990. The jury ruled that vehicles sold during that time came with airbags that, when deployed, could severely burn the hands and wrists of drivers. Owners were awarded $730 each to replace the defective airbags, although Pennsylvania's Consumer Protection Law could triple the damages. Martin D'Urso from the law firm of Kohn, Swift & Graf and Isaac Green from Moody & Anderson pleaded the case for the plaintiffs.

Collazo-Santiago v. Toyota, July 1998, 1st Circuit Court of Appeals. The driver of a 1994 Corolla suffered minor facial burns and abrasions when her airbag deployed as her car was rear-ended. The court concluded that the airbag's design caused the injuries. Toyota maintained that the airbag deployed as it should, and that it couldn't change the design without reducing the airbag's effectiveness. The plaintiff was awarded $30,000 compensation.

Premature airbag deployment
All automakers are worried they may face a slew of huge damage awards in the future following a $750,000 jury award for damages in the death of a five-year-old from a deploying airbag. In *Crespo v. Chrysler*, a New York jury concluded that the 1995 minivan's airbag design contributed to the child's death because it deployed too early (at a speed of between 9 and 12 mph). Safety experts contend that the airbag should deploy within a range of 15–20 mph (24–32 km/h). Chrysler submitted, however, that there are no standards as to what speeds should trigger the airbag's deployment, and claimed most automakers program their airbags to deploy at crash speeds of 8–14 mph (13–23 km/h). The

jury rejected Chrysler's argument and awarded half the damages sought by the child's family, despite the fact that the child was unbelted and not seated in a safety seat.

Failure to deploy

Taylor v. Ford, Wayne County Circuit Court. American courts are taking a harder look at the automakers' liability when airbags fail to deploy, following a recent Michigan Court of Appeals decision to uphold a lower court's $292,000 verdict against Ford. Although the 1990 Lincoln Continental's driver-side airbag failed to deploy during a frontal collision, the jury found no design defect, but awarded damages against Ford for breach of an implied warranty based on defective manufacturing.

Inadvertent deployment

Perez-Trujillo v. Volvo Car Corp. (*www.law.emory.edu/1circuit/mar98/97-1792. 01a.html*). This lawsuit involves injuries suffered by a dockworker while parking a Volvo on the dock. The case has just been reinstated by a U.S. Appeals Court and provides an interesting, though lengthy, dissertation on the safety hazards that airbags pose and why automakers are ultimately responsible for the injuries and deaths caused by their deployment.

Axle

Fuller v. Ford of Canada Ltd. (1978), 2 O.R. (2nd), No. 764. This new 1974 Econoline truck had an axle failure that caused an accident. The Court held both the manufacturer and seller responsible.

Battery

Marin v. Varta Batteries Ltd. (1983), 28 Sask. R., No. 173; 5 D.L.R. (4th) (Q.B.), No. 427. An exploding battery caused serious injuries to the plaintiff's face. The battery maker admitted liability, and the Court awarded the plaintiff $21,000 in damages.

Brakes

Chrysler and GM have both come under fire over the past several years for installing defective anti-lock brakes in their vehicles. GM has quietly bought back many of its vans and sport-utilities with ABS failures, while Chrysler has initiated a recall campaign and promised free servicing over a 10-year period.

Marton Properties v. Northbridge Chrysler Plymouth Ltd., March 2, 1979, B.C.S.C. The plaintiff's used Chrysler had serious brake defects that warranted cancellation of the sales contract. The Court ordered the vehicle returned and the purchase price refunded.

Phillips v. Ford of Canada and Elgin Motors (1970), 2 O.R., No. 714. Ford was held responsible for the injuries caused by a defect in the power brakes that would not have been apparent to the plaintiff. The dealer and Ford had a duty to warn the plaintiff that if the power-brake unit failed, the back-up brakes would be inadequate.

Santos v. Chrysler Corporation, February 1996, Suffolk County Superior Court. The plaintiff's wife and three children were killed when his 1988 Caravan's rear brakes locked as he applied them to avoid rear-ending another vehicle. The jury award for $19.2 million followed Paul Santos's pleadings that Chrysler "knowingly built the vehicle with a deadly defect that caused the rear brakes to lock before the front brakes." Chrysler's defence was that Santos drove the Caravan 100 miles with a broken windshield wiper and steered directly into oncoming traffic.

Fires
Ford
Brown v. Ford of Canada Ltd. (1979), 27 N.B.R. (2d), 550. While under warranty, the plaintiff's 1977 van suddenly caught fire. The court held the manufacturer only partially negligent because the plaintiff's son, who was a mechanic, should have spotted the defect.

Chabot v. Ford Motor Company of Canada Ltd. (1983), 39 O.R. (2d) 162. This case contains an excellent and exhaustive review of a manufacturer's liability for defectively manufactured vehicles. It establishes liability for losses arising from a defect while the vehicle is being maintained by the dealer. Although the plaintiff could not prove that a defective part caused a fire, Judge Eberle's presumption that the 1979 F-250 truck ignited from some sort of manufacturing defect implied that the manufacturer was negligent (*re ipsa loquitur*).

The court also ruled that Ford breached a fundamental term of the sales contract by providing an unfit vehicle, and that Ford also failed to meet its obligations as set by the Manitoba Sale of Goods Act (Ontario Sale of Goods Act R.S.O. 1980 c 462, 5–15).

In his decision, the judge made a number of interesting and critical observations about the motives and strategies of a large manufacturer like Ford when it prepares for a case and presents expert evidence.

In cases where companies try to avoid liability through their own limited warranties, or through invoking the exclusions expressed in the warranty, this decision confirms the *Kravitz v. General Motors* decision (which struck down these exclusions under Quebec law) from a common-law standpoint.

See also:
- *CPR v. Kerr,* 49 S.C.R., 33 at 36.
- *Gougeon v. Peugeot Canada,* July 20, 1973, Quebec Superior Court, No. 12736, Judge Kaufman.
- *Lazanik v. Ford,* June 15, 1965, C.S.M., No. 623-664, Judge Challies.
- *Parent v. Lapointe* (1952), I S.C.R., No. 381.

- *Rioux v. General Motors*, March 9, 1970, C.S.M., No. 739-005, 6.
- *Touchette v. Pizzagalli* (1938), S.C.R., No. 433.
- *Zelezen v. Model Auto Sales Ltd.*, November 26, 1971, C.S.M., No. 722-487, Judge Nichols.

Chrysler

La Paix v. Chrysler Canada, April 5, 1982, Quebec Provincial Court, No. 500-02-040677-796, Judge Prenouveau. A new 1976 Volaré suddenly caught fire when the owner tried to start the car. It had been in use for only 10 months. Chrysler Canada refused all liability, claiming the fire was probably due to poor starting technique. The court held Chrysler responsible for $4,039 in damages after it was proven that the fire was caused by unburned gasoline catching fire in the muffler.

General Motors

Racine v. Durand Pontiac-Buick and General Motors, December 15, 1977, Quebec Provincial Court, No. 02-015218-774, Judge Lacoste. The plaintiff claimed $700 for a catalytic converter that exploded. General Motors and the dealer claimed that the explosion was due to poor maintenance and that the 5-year/50,000 mile emissions warranty on the converter did not cover such maintenance-related defects. The judge disagreed, stating that the catalytic converter exploded due to a defective PCV valve for which General Motors and the dealer had to take responsibility. The fact that the converter could overheat and catch fire whenever the engine was badly tuned caused the judge to suggest that a warning be placed on all General Motors vehicles with the converter. The plaintiff was awarded $700.

Saab

Delage vs. Saab, San Francisco Superior Court, November 1997. A jury awarded Delage $1.4 million for damages caused by an electrical fire in his 1988 Saab 9000, even though the car was never examined. After hearing testimony from eight other Saab owners whose cars had caught on fire, the jury concluded that a defective fuse box caused the fire. Related to this, the *San Francisco Chronicle* published a Saab internal memo that indicated a main connection in the 9000 box (located behind the glove compartment) could loosen, overheat, and ignite the insulation.

Minivan latches (Chrysler)

Jimenez v. Chrysler, October 8, 1997, South Carolina Federal Court. (For additional information, contact the Jimenez family attorney, Garrick Grobler, at the Washington law firm of Ross, Dixon & Masback. He has another similar case against Chrysler scheduled to be heard in North Carolina.) Chrysler was hit by a $262.5 million South Carolina jury verdict arising from a lawsuit alleging that the plaintiff's son was killed after he was thrown out of a 1985 Caravan because the rear liftgate latch failed following a collision. Chrysler told the jury that its minivan latches weren't defective and that its recent retroactive "fix" of the latches on 4.3 million 1984–95 vehicles was simply a service campaign.

Then a subpeonaed Chrysler internal memo surfaced, showing that top Chrysler officials knew all along that the latch problem was a safety defect. That memo, sent to Chairman Robert Eaton and Chrysler President Robert Lutz on December 9, 1994, confirmed that the latch problem "is a safety defect that involves children."

An incensed jury awarded $12.5 million in actual damages, plus another $250 million in punitive damages against Chrysler.

Parking gear slippage
General Motors v. Colton, October 17, 1980, Quebec Court of Appeal, No. 500-09-000692-772. A 1970 Oldsmobile parked on the plaintiff's inclined driveway rolled backwards and injured the owner. Judgment after appeal was against General Motors for $29,000.

Steering
Holley v. Ford of Canada, June 18, 1980, Nova Scotia Supreme Court, Judge Cowan. The plaintiff purchased a used 1976 Ford Custom 200 truck that was involved in an accident due to steering assembly failure. The plaintiff was awarded $4,100 in damages.

White v. International Harvester (1969), W.W.R., No. 235 (Alta. T.D.). This new truck's steering assembly had problems and was adjusted by the dealer, but 4,200 miles (6,720 km) later it suddenly veered out of control due to a defective steering component. The plaintiff was awarded both costs and damages.

Sudden acceleration
Willar v. Ford (1991), 118 N.B.R. (2nd), No. 323. The owner sued Ford after the throttle jammed open twice, causing several accidents. The Court held that Ford, not the dealer, was responsible for the plaintiff's damages.

Tires
Chase v. Goodyear Tire and Rubber Co. and Goodyear Canada Inc., New Brunswick Court of Queen's Bench, Trial Division, No. S/C/513/89, April 12, 1991. The plaintiff was injured when the tire he was inflating exploded. There was no evidence of a manufacturing defect on the original tire or with the retread. Goodyear was found negligent because it failed to warn its customer of the danger inherent in inflating a retreaded tire with worn-out and damaged radial cords, thereby breaching its duty to warn. The plaintiff was awarded $65,000 for his injuries.

Gagnon v. Canadian Tire (1979), C.P., No. 251. The plaintiff was awarded $1,310 as compensation for a radial tire that exploded when he was rocking his car out of a snowbank.

Murphy v. D. & B. Holdings (1979), 31 N.S.R. (2nd), No. 380; 52 A.P.R. (S.C.), No. 380. The Court held that the manufacturer was liable for damages for permitting a customer to use its tires in a dangerous manner.

Tire iron placement adding to collision injuries

Gallant v. Beitz (1983), 42 O.R. (2nd), No. 86. This judgment states clearly that automakers are presumed to know that their vehicles will be involved in accidents and must take reasonable steps to minimize injuries caused by flaws inherent in the design of their vehicles.

Transmissions jump from Park to Reverse

Automatic transmissions often jump from Park to Reverse or Neutral, causing vehicles to back down under power or roll away. Ford, however, has had a steady stream of complaints and lawsuits targeting its vehicles over the past three decades.

McEvoy v. Ford Motor Company et al., September 6, 1989, B.C.S.C., No. 3841989, Judge Hinds. Mr. McEvoy was killed when his new Ford pickup backed over him after the transmission jumped from Park to Reverse. He had left the engine running and was unloading cargo when the right front wheel crushed his chest.

Justice Hinds found Ford 65 percent negligent for the following reasons:

• The RCMP mechanic testified that the gearshift lever could easily be mispositioned into an "unstable Park" position.
• It was determined that Ford was aware of this defect as early as 1971, according to internal company documents presented during the trial.
• Ford had a duty to warn its customers of the hazard caused by the C-6 automatic transmission; the warning in the owner's manual was deemed insufficient to satisfy this duty.
• Ford and its Canadian distributor had breached their duty to the consumer.

Unger v. Ford. In this Bridgeport, Connecticut, out-of-court settlement, Ford paid $700,000 to the family of a man crushed to death when his 1988 F-series pickup went into Reverse while the gearshift lever was in Park. The plaintiff claimed that the automatic transmission and PRNDL indicator were defective. His lawyer also alleged that Ford had received 26,000 complaints about the transmission defect.

Wheels

Michel Beauregard v. Goyette Auto and General Motors, July 3, 1982, Quebec Provincial Court, No. 500-05-011478-763, Judge Aronovitch. One wheel on a new 1975 Ventura suddenly locked up, causing the vehicle to go out of control. The plaintiff was awarded $3,500.

Nason v. General Motors of Canada Ltd., November 1, 1995, British Columbia Provincial Court (Small Claims Division), No. C93-04200,

Judge C.L. Bagnall. Judge Bagnall awarded the plaintiffs $5,416 plus interest for damages arising from an accident caused by their Reatta's faulty right rear wheel knuckle. Damages included $4,500 for the decrease in the car's value, and $916 for the loss of a safe driving discount offered by the Insurance Corporation of British Columbia.

Delay (in Bringing Lawsuit)

Bouchard v. Vaillancourt (1961), C.S., No. 171. If the seller has defrauded the consumer, delays for initiating a lawsuit are allowed to be longer than in cases where fraud isn't involved.

See also:
• *Ennis v. Klassen,* 70 D.L.R. (4th), No. 325.
• *Ginn v. Canbec Auto* (1976), C.S., No. 416.
• *Lemire v. Pelchat* (1957), R.C.S., No. 823.

False Advertising

False sales prices
R. v. Lanthier and Lalonde, Sessions Court (Montreal). A Montreal Ford dealer was fined $300 for placing ads showing tremendous reductions to the manufacturer's suggested retail price on new cars. After criminal charges were laid, it was shown that the advertised savings were lies (judgment on file with Consumer and Corporate Affairs). Several dozen suburban Toronto Chrysler dealers were fined by the federal government for similar deceptions.

Odometer tampering
Odometer tampering is a criminal offence under the federal Weights and Measures Act. The Department of Consumer and Corporate Affairs uses the RCMP to investigate all such cases. Many violators have been caught and successfully prosecuted. Nevertheless, the federal law is weak because fines are so low that they practically represent a licence to operate illegally, and an individual can escape prosecution by pleading that the odometer was broken and had to be changed.

Bouchard v. South Park Mercury Sales (1978), 3 W.W.R., No. 78. The odometer figure written on the contract was incorrect. The dealer pleaded ignorance, but the judge ruled that the car's owner should receive damages to compensate for the extra mileage.

Used car sold as new (demonstrator)
Leblanc v. Frenette and Chrysler Credit, May 27, 1971, Quebec Provincial Court, No. 279-772, Judge Laurier. The plaintiff's "new" demonstrator was actually a used car with a rolled-back odometer. It had also been in an accident. The Court held the dealer responsible and ordered him to refund the purchase price.

Leasing

Why leasing costs more

Leasing is big business, having grown from just 4 percent in 1990 to over 46 percent of Canadian vehicle sales of about 1.4 million units in 1997 (leasing is less popular in the States, representing only 36 percent of all transactions). In straight dollar figures, Canadian leases accounted for $19 billion of the $31 billion spent in 1997 for auto loan and lease financing. Windfall profits from leases have undoubtedly led to the Big Three American automakers sustaining record profits over the past three years. For example, from 1993–97, Chrysler Credit Canada's profit rocketed from $5.5 million–$34.1 million. GM and Ford did almost as well.

Most of this money went into automakers' pockets, inasmuch as Canadian banks are barred from leasing, unlike their counterparts south of the border. In fact, 80 percent of the Canadian market is held by automaker captive finance companies, whereas only 43 percent of the American market is under automaker dominance (banks make up another 32 percent). Bankers say the increased competition has made leases on average 1.2 percentage points lower in the States than in Canada.

Canadian bankers want to get in on the action (read: profits), but they've been stymied by strong lobbying by Canada's 3,500-strong auto dealers, who frighten the bejeebies out of Ottawa MPs every time they dare breathe the word "competition." Where do they get their power? From their community involvement, where they control lots of the local political establishment and can be counted.

Why you pay more

Lessees pay the full manufacturer's suggested retail price on a vehicle loaded with costly options, plus hidden fees and interest charges that wouldn't be included if the vehicle were purchased instead (see chart on page 68 listing the dealer's MSRP markup for cars, minivans, vans, pickups, and sport-utilities). But you can forget about getting clear information that would permit you to compare the costs of leasing and financing, says DesRosiers Automotive Research Inc., a Toronto consulting firm that studies the leasing industry. DesRosiers found that cheaper cars often cost more to lease than some luxury models.

This was confirmed by the Canadian Bankers Association (CBA) after it blasted dealers' leasing contracts for charging interest rates as high as 34 percent and called for consumer protection legislation to regulate the industry. In another survey carried out six years ago by *Les Affaires,* a Montreal-based business weekly, mid-range cars and minivans were shown to cost about $3,000 more if leased rather than financed, and luxury cars about $7,000–$9,000 more.

Although the state of Florida got a $4.2-million settlement from its Toyota dealers for leasing misrepresentation, the Canadian government hasn't taken similar action, even though the same misleading practices are prevalent here among the major leasing agencies and dealers. Fortunately, Canadian courts are more progressive than the government, and have made several significant rulings that give lessees added clout when seeking refunds for deceptive practices and defective vehicles.

Ford Motor Credit v. Bothwell, December 3, 1979, Ontario County Court (Middlesex), No. 9226-T, Judge Macnab. The defendant leased a 1977 Ford truck that had frequent engine problems, characterized by stalling and hard starting. After complaining for one year and driving 22,000 miles (35,000 km), the defendant cancelled the lease. Ford Credit sued for the money owing on the lease. Judge Macnab cancelled the lease and ordered Ford Credit to repay 70 percent of the amount paid during the leasing period. Ford Credit was also ordered to refund repair costs, even though the corporation claimed that it should not be held responsible for Ford's failure to honour its warranty.

Salvador v. Setay Motors/Queenstown Chev-Olds, Hamilton Small Claims Court, No.1621/95. Robert Salvador, an Ontario consumer advocate and founder of the Consumer Action Group (CAG), was awarded $2,000 plus costs from Queenstown Leasing. The Court found that the company should have tried harder to sell the leased vehicle, and for a higher price, when the "open lease" expired.

Salvador gave Queenstown a list of offers from independent buyers when he returned the vehicle, but they were never contacted. Instead, the leasing agency auctioned off the van to the highest bidder. You guessed it—Queenstown Leasing.

This judgment can also be helpful in cases where a repossessed vehicle is sold or auctioned off for far less than what it's worth, or where the seller is in a conflict of interest by being the buyer as well.

Schryvers v. Richport Ford Sales, May 18, 1993, B.C.S.C., No. C917060, Justice Tysoe. The Court awarded $17,578.47 (including $6,000 in punitive damages) plus costs to a couple who paid thousands of dollars over the purchase price for their Ford Explorer and Escort in unfair and hidden leasing charges. The Court found that this price difference constituted a deceptive, unconscionable act or practice in contravention of the Trade Practices Act, R.S.B.C. 1979, c. 406.

Judge Tysoe concluded that the total of the general damages awarded to the Schryvers for both vehicles would be $11,578.47. He then proceeded to give the following reasons for awarding an additional $6,000 in punitive damages:

> Little wonder Richport Ford had a contest for the salesperson who could persuade the most customers to acquire their vehicles by way of a lease transaction. I consider the actions of Richport Ford to be sufficiently flagrant and high-handed to warrant an award of punitive damages.

There must be a disincentive to suppliers in respect of intentionally deceptive trade practices. If no punitive damages are awarded for intentional violations of the legislation, suppliers will continue to conduct their businesses in a manner that involves deceptive trade practices because they will have nothing to lose. In this case I believe that the appropriate amount of punitive damages is the extra profit Richport Ford endeavoured to make as a result of its deceptive acts. I therefore award punitive damages against Richport Ford in the amount of $6,000...

See also:
- *Barber v. Inland Truck Sales*, 11 D.L.R. (3rd), No. 469.
- *Canadian-Dominion Leasing v. Suburban Super Drug Ltd.* (1966), 56 D.L.R. (2nd), No. 43.
- *Neilson v. Atlantic Rentals Ltd.* (1974), 8 N.B.R. (2nd), No. 594.
- *Volvo Canada v. Fox*, December 13, 1979, New Brunswick Court of Queen's Bench, No. 1698/77/C, Judge Stevenson.
- *Western Tractor v. Dyck*, 7 D.L.R. (3rd), No. 535.

Misrepresentation

Late delivery
When the delivery of a new car is delayed, the customer can either demand that the contract be cancelled or ask for special damages. If the delay was caused by the seller's or manufacturer's negligence, both the contract's cancellation and compensating damages can be claimed.

Manery v. Kampe (1943), 3 W.W.R., No. 687 (B.C.C.A.). The seller delivered the goods 18 days after the contracted delivery date. The buyer refused the merchandise and sued for cancellation of the contract. The Court ordered that the buyer's money be refunded.

"New" car really a used car
Bilodeau v. Sud Auto, Quebec Court of Appeal, No. 09-000751-73, Judge Tremblay. This appellate Court cancelled the contract, and held that a car can't be sold as new or as a demonstrator if it has ever been rented, leased, sold, or titled to anyone other than the dealer.

Rourke v. Gilmore, January 16, 1928 (*Ontario Weekly Notes*, vol. XXXIII, p. 292). Before discovering that his new car was really used, the plaintiff drove it for over a year. For this reason, the contract couldn't be cancelled. However, the Appeals Court instead awarded damages for $500, which was quite a sum in 1928!

Vehicle not as ordered
Whether you're buying a new or used vehicle, the seller can't misrepresent the vehicle. Anything that varies from what one would commonly expect, or from the seller's representation, must be disclosed

prior to signing the contract. Typical scenarios involve odometer turn-backs, accident damage, used or leased cars sold as new, new vehicles that are the wrong colour and the wrong model year, or vehicles that lack promised options or standard features.

Chenel v. Bel Automobile (1981) Inc., August 27, 1976, Quebec Superior Court (Quebec City), Judge Desmeules. The plaintiff didn't receive his new Ford truck with the Jacob brakes essential for transporting sand in hilly regions. The Court awarded the plaintiff $27,000, representing the purchase price of the vehicle less the money he earned while using the truck.

Lasky v. Royal City Chrysler Plymouth, February 18, 1987, Ontario High Court of Justice, 59 O.R. (2nd), No. 323. The plaintiff bought a 4-cylinder 1983 Dodge 600 that was represented by the salesman as being a 6-cylinder model. After putting 40,000 km on the vehicle over a 22-month period, the buyer was given her money back, without interest, under the provincial Business Practices Act.

White v. Munn Motors (1960), 45 M.P.R., No. 253 (Nfld. T.D.). The dealer misrepresented a half-ton truck as having a three-quarter-ton capacity. The buyer was given his money back because he didn't get what he paid for.

Wrong model year
Adelaide Motors v. Alexander (1962), 48 M.P.R., No. 258 (Nfld. T.D.). The customer bought a new 1960 car that was misrepresented as being a 1961 model. The Court ruled that the duped owner was entitled to damages.

Ginn v. Canbec Auto, Quebec Superior Court (Montreal), No. 500-05-014597-74-4. Relying on expert testimony provided by the APA, the Court awarded $10,000 to the purchaser of a new 1972 BMW that was fraudulently sold as a 1973 model. The case demonstrates beyond a doubt that car retailers are culpable for the misrepresentation of their products.

Woods v. Borstel (1962), 34 D.L.R. (2nd), No. 68 (Alta. C.A.). The customer bought a new 1958 car that was misrepresented as being a 1959 model. The Court ruled that the seller's model year representation was a warranty as defined under s. 2(1)(n) of the Alberta Sale of Goods Act. The plaintiff was entitled to all damages, but the contract remained in force.

Secret Warranties

It's common practice for manufacturers to extend their warranties secretly to cover components with a high failure rate. Customers who complain vigorously get extended warranty compensation in the form of "goodwill" adjustments.

François Chong v. Marine Drive Imported Cars Ltd. and Honda Canada Inc., May 17, 1994, British Columbia Provincial Court (Small Claims Division), No. 92-06760, Judge C.L. Bagnall. Mr. Chong is the first owner of a 1983 Honda Accord with 134,000 km on the odometer. He's had six engine camshafts replaced—four under Honda "goodwill" programs, one where he paid part of the repairs, and one via the small claims court judgment below.

In his ruling, Judge Bagnall ordered Honda and the dealer to each pay half of the $835.81 repair bill, for the following reasons:

> The defendants assert that the warranty which was part of the contract for purchase of the car encompassed the entirety of their obligation to the claimant, and that it expired in February 1985. The replacements of the camshaft after that date were paid for wholly or in part by Honda as a "goodwill gesture." The time has come for these gestures to cease, according to the witness for Honda....
>
> The claimant has convinced me that the problem he is having with rapid breakdowns of camshafts in his car is due to a defect, which was present in the engine at the time that he purchased the car. The problem first arose during the warranty period and in my view has never been properly identified nor repaired.

Repairs

Faulty diagnosis

Let's say that before taking a holiday you have your van checked out and are assured that it's in good condition. While en route to your vacation spot, it dies on the highway and ruins your holiday. When the check-up is incorrect and leads to financial losses (damages), the garage owner is responsible for those losses, as well as for refunding the diagnostic costs. Of course, you'd better show that the defect that caused your troubles was present and detectable at the time the vehicle was checked.

Davies v. Alberta Motor Association, August 13, 1991, Alberta Provincial Court, Civil Division, No. P9090106097, Judge Moore. The plaintiff had a used 1985 Nissan Pulsar NX checked out by the AMA's Vehicle Inspection Service prior to buying it. The car passed with flying colours. A month later the clutch was replaced and numerous electrical problems ensued. At that time, another garage discovered that the car had been involved in a major accident, had a bent frame, a leaking radiator, and was unsafe to drive. The Court awarded the plaintiff $1,578.40 plus three years of interest. The judge held that the AMA set itself out as an expert and should have spotted the car's defects. The AMA's defence—that it was not responsible for errors—was thrown out. The Court held that a disclaimer clause could not protect the Association from a fundamental breach of contract.

Flat-rate abuses
R. v. Birchcliff Lincoln Mercury Ltd., July 7, 1987, Ontario Court of
Appeal, 60 O.R. (2nd), No. 610, 220; 220 A.C., No. 274. This new-car
dealer advertised a $38 hourly labour charge and then calculated the
number of hours using a flat-rate guide that allowed more hours than
those actually worked. This was held by the Appeal Court to be false
advertising under the federal Combines Act (Competition Act).

Illegal/Unfair Insurance Company Practices

Inadequate compensation
The following two lawsuits may be helpful in any disputes you may
have with an insurance company over its failure to pay a claim or
use quality replacement parts in repairs. Don't get the impression
that this is just a State Farm problem. These abuses are widespread.
If your insurer tries a similar tactic, contact the provincial
Superintendent of Insurance or sue in small claims court for a refund.

Campbell v. State Farm Mutual Insurance Automobile Insurance Co. This
Utah case saw a $147.6 million jury award against State Farm cut to
$26 million by the presiding judge who didn't want the case over-
turned on appeal because the original award may have been considered excessive.

In his December 19, 1997, verdict, Judge William B. Bohling called
State Farm "greedy, callous, clandestine, fraudulent, and dishonest"
after evidence showed the company refused to pay off a claim until
its own policyholder sued State Farm for bad-faith dealings.

The Campbell attorneys successfully asserted that State Farm
had a national plan to cheat policyholders that included using infe-
rior car parts in repairs, low-balling settlements, and misleading
consumers about policy benefits.

This evidence led the judge to conclude that State Farm
"appeared to have preyed on the weakest of the herd" in cheating
"the most vulnerable" policyholders with its "calculated and callous
attitude towards settling valid claims." He concluded:

> It became a matter of plain evidence that State Farm has sold as
> its product, peace of mind, and has used as its advertising slogan,
> "like a good neighbor." State Farm's action amounts to betraying
> the trust that it invites its policyholders to place in it.

Poor-quality replacement parts
In a $2 billion Illinois class action, State Farm has been found guilty
of breaching its promise to restore policyholders' autos to their
"pre-loss condition," by using aftermarket bumpers, door panels,
and other parts that failed to meet automakers' specifications for
fit, finish, corrosion protection, and safety.

Part Three
NEW-VEHICLE RATINGS

"Only" 10% of Chryslers Cause Repeat Problems

"Out of 100 vehicles, we're apt to build 10 that are as good as any that Toyota has ever built, 80 that are okay and 10 that cause repeated problems for our customers."

Robert Lutz, President
Chrysler U.S.
Chrysler Times, July 17, 1995

Ford Admits Paint Mistake

"In June 1990, a field survey of about 1,000 F-series trucks (1985–1990 models) was conducted in three locations by Body and Chassis Engineering to assess paint durability. Results showed that about 13% of the F-series trucks displayed peeling paint, which would represent about 90,000 vehicles annually...."

Memo to Members of the Finance Committee
A.J. Trottman, Executive Vice President
Ford North American Automotive Operation

That's right, Robert and A.J., and it's *Lemon Aid*'s job to warn buyers to steer clear of that last 10 percent and even reconsider that 80 percent you consider "okay." Buyers need to know which ones pack an airbag "surprise" or are equipped with just "okay" transmissions and paint jobs.

What Makes a Good Car or Minivan?

Your new car or minivan must first live up to the promises made by the manufacturer and dealer. It *must* be safe, crashworthy, reasonably durable (lasting at least 10 years), cost no more than $800 a year to maintain, and provide you with a fair resale value a few years down the road. Parts should be reasonably priced and easily available, and servicing shouldn't be delayed or incompetent.

Lemon-Aid guides try to publish up-to-date photographs of each new model rated, but some automakers disagree with our ratings and refuse to cooperate with us in any manner whatsoever, including sending us recent photos and current technical specifications. We regret any errors or omissions that may result. Our independence is more important than an all-inclusive book with pretty pictures.

Under no circumstances are dealers or manufacturers solicited for free "test" vehicles, as is the case with most auto columnists and some consumer groups. When a test vehicle is needed, it is rented from a major rental agency or borrowed from its owner. I've adopted this prac-

145

tice from my early experience as a consumer reporter, 20 years ago. At that time, Nissan asked me to test-drive their new 1974 240Z—no strings attached. I took the car for a week, had it examined by an independent garage, spoke with satisfied and dissatisfied owners, and accessed internal service bulletins. I came to the conclusion that the car's faulty brakes made it unsafe to drive, and said so in my report. Nissan sued me for $4 million, fixed the brakes through a "product improvement campaign," and dropped the lawsuit two years later. I never went back for another car.

Definitions of Terms

Ratings

This edition makes use of owner complaints, confidential dealer service bulletins, and test-drives to expose serious factory-related defects, design deficiencies, or servicing glitches. It should be noted that customer complaints alone do not make a scientific sampling, and that's why they are used in conjunction with other sources of information. On the other hand, owner complaints combined with inside information found in dealer service bulletins are a good starting point to cut through the automakers' hyperbole and get a glimpse of reality. Since ratings can change dramatically from one year to the next, depending upon the manufacturer's warranty performance, you will want to keep abreast of these changes between editions, by logging onto *www.lemonaidcars.com.*

This edition emphasizes important new features that add to a vehicle's safety, reliability, road performance, and comfort, and points out those changes that are merely gadgets and styling revisions. Also noted are important improvements to be made in the future, or the dropping of a model line. In addition to the "Recommended" or "Not Recommended" rating, each vehicle's strong and weak points are summarized.

Unlike most auto guides, *Lemon-Aid* isn't bedazzled by high-tech wizardry. Almost 30 years of consumer advocacy in the auto industry have taught me that complex components are usually quite troublesome during their first few years on the market (airbags and anti-lock brakes can be particularly dangerous, as GM's recent 3.5 million vehicle recall on 1991–96 pickups, SUVs, and vans for faulty ABS brakes shows). Complexity drives up ownership costs, reduces overall reliability, and puts extra stress on such expensive major parts as the powertrain, fuel system, and emissions components.

Depreciation is the biggest—and most often ignored—expense you encounter when you trade in your vehicle, or when an accident forces you to buy another vehicle before the depreciated loss can be amortized. Most new cars depreciate a whopping 30–40 percent during the first two years of ownership. Fortunately, minivans, vans, trucks, and sport-utilities lose their value at a much slower rate. The best way to use depreciation rates to your advantage is to choose a vehicle listed as being both reliable and economical to own and keep it for five to ten years. Alternatively, you may buy insurance to protect you from depreciation's bite (see page 45).

During a car or minivan's first year on the market it takes about six months to acquire enough information for a fair-minded evaluation, unless it's a hybrid that has been in service under another name or has only been re-badged. Most new cars hit the market before all of the bugs have been worked out, so it would be irresponsible to recommend them before they've been owner-driven, or before the quality of service from the dealer and manufacturer has been customer-tested. The Chrysler Neon is a case in point. Hailed as "Car of the Year" by the motoring press in 1995, it's now noted mostly for its costly engine, AC, electrical, and body deficiencies.

Recommended

This rating indicates a best buy. This category includes new vehicles that combine a high level of crashworthiness with good road performance, decent reliability, and better than average resale value. Servicing must be readily available, and parts inexpensive and easy to find.

A vehicle may lose its "Recommended" rating from the previous edition of *Lemon-Aid* whenever its price becomes unreasonable or its warranty performance inadequate (as with Ford and Chrysler minivans), or when the competition offers a comparable model with a lower price or more standard safety, mechanical, or convenience features.

Above Average

Vehicles in this class exhibit quality construction, durability, and safety features as standard equipment. They may have expensive parts and servicing, an unreasonably high price tag, or only satisfactory warranty performance, one or all of which may have disqualified them from the "Recommended" category.

Average

Vehicles in this group have some deficiencies or flaws that make them a second choice. In many cases, certain components are prone to premature wear or breakdown, or some other positive aspect of long-term ownership is lacking. An "Average" rating can also be attributed to such factors as substandard assembly quality, lack of a solid long-term reliability record, or some flaw in the parts and service network.

Below Average

This rating category denotes a vehicle that may have had a poor reliability record, but where improvements have been made with regard to durability and/or safety features. A "Below Average" vehicle could be a risky buy, but is nevertheless a cut above "Not Recommended." Ensure you get an extended warranty with a vehicle in this category.

Not Recommended
Buy at your own risk. Substandard crashworthiness, poor overall reliability, inadequate road performance, and poor dealer service, among
other factors, can make owning one of these vehicles a traumatic and
expensive experience. It doesn't necessarily follow that every single vehicle produced in a "Not Recommended" model line will have exactly the
same reliability shortcomings, but chances of having trouble are higher
than normal.

Vehicles that have not been on the road long enough to assess, or
that are sold in such small numbers that owner feedback is insufficient,
are "Not Recommended" or left unrated.

Cost analysis/best alternatives
Following an incredibly successful 1999 model year, fall price increases
for the year 2000 models are expected to be relatively restrained, ranging from 1–2 percent for the Big Three and only slightly higher for
most Asian and European makes. Be wary, though, of subsequent price
increases throughout next year that may boost selling prices several
additional percentage points. Also, popular models may have MSRPs
that are 5–10 percent higher than last year's version.

Each model's cost is analyzed in light of cheaper earlier models eligible for substantial rebates, PDI and destination charges, insurance
costs, parts costs, depreciation, and fuel consumption. According to
the CAA, annual maintenance costs average about $800. A listing of
competing recommended models is also included.

Under "Annual fuel cost," we have included Transport Canada's predicted fuel cost for each model vehicle according to its engine size. The
annual fuel cost and consumption estimates are based on a distance
travelled of 20,000 km, with 55 percent city and 45 percent highway driving. A price of 58 cents/L for regular unleaded gasoline, 67 cents/L for
premium unleaded gasoline, and 55 cents/L for diesel fuel was used in
the calculation of the estimated annual fuel cost.

Quality/reliability/safety
Lemon-Aid bases its quality and reliability evaluations on owner comments, confidential manufacturer service bulletins, and government
reports from the NHTSA safety complaint files, among other sources.
This year's edition also draws on the knowledge and expertise of professionals working in the automotive marketplace, including mechanics
and fleet owners. The aim is to have a wide range of unbiased (and
irrefutable) data on quality, reliability, durability, and ownership costs.
Allowances are made for the number of vehicles sold versus the number
of complaints, as well as for the seriousness of problems reported and
the average number of problems reported by each owner.

Manufacturer service bulletins listed in this section give the most
probable cause of factory-related defects on 1999 models that will likely
be carried over to the 2000 version, because manufacturers depend on

the dealer corrections outlined in their bulletins until a permanent, cost-effective engineering solution is found at the factory. This sometimes takes several model years with lots of experimentation.

Many of the bulletins listed in this edition come from American sources and often differ from Canadian bulletins where part numbers are concerned. Nevertheless, the problems and defects they treat are exactly the same on both sides of the border. Some vehicles have more DSBs than others, but this doesn't necessarily mean they're lemons. It may be that the listed problems affect only a small number of vehicles, or are minor and easily corrected. DSBs should also be used to verify that a problem was correctly diagnosed, the correct upgraded replacement part was used, and the billed labour time was fair.

Warranty performance
I'm more impressed by performance than promise. A manufacturer's warranty is a legal commitment that the product it sells will perform in the normal and customary manner for which it is designed. It's an important factor in this edition's ratings, and is judged by how fairly it's applied—not by what's promised. Extended or supplementary warranties provide extended coverage and may be sold by the manufacturer, dealer, or an independent third party. If a part malfunctions or fails (not owing to owner negligence), the dealer will fix, repair, or replace the defective part or parts and bill the automaker or warranty company for the cost.

Most new-vehicle warranties fall into two categories: bumper-to-bumper for a period of three to five years, and powertrain for up to 6 years/130,000 km. Automakers sometimes charge an additional $50–$100 fee for repairs requested by purchasers of used vehicles with unexpired base warranties. For snowbirds, the federal and provincial governments can charge GST and sales tax on warranty and non-warranty repairs done south of the border. Beware.

After using longer, more comprehensive warranties to successfully sell its cars and minivans, Chrysler dropped its generous seven-year warranty in 1995 in favour of rebates and low interest rates, even though its cars and minivans aren't sufficiently reliable to forego the extra protection. Now, much like Ford and GM, Chrysler uses secret warranties to pay for factory defects. Unlike other automakers, however, you rarely see written confirmation of this fact in a service bulletin or dealer memo, leading to incredible variations (injustices?) in the treatment of warranty claims.

ADDENDUM TO BASIC WARRANTY

The following applies to 1993 through 1997 New Yorker, LHS, Concorde, Intrepid, Vision and Grand Cherokee vehicles equipped with factory-installed air conditioning:

The Basic Warranty coverage for the air conditioner evaporator has been extended to 7 years or 115,000 kilometres, whichever occurs first, from the vehicle's warranty start date.

This extended coverage applies to all owners of the vehicle. All of the other warranty terms apply to this extension.

We suggest that you keep this addendum card in your warranty information booklet.

AD9502-B

The above little-known warranty extension was sent to all owners on record, says Chrysler. It's the first time I've seen it. Be that as it may, this special policy confers rights on owners of other Chrysler vehicles with AC problems because it establishes a seven-year benchmark as to what Chrysler sees as normal AC durability.

Chrysler is also unique among automakers in having set up a special Review Committee several years ago to give out compensation to owners who were refused help through normal warranty channels. That committee, available only to Canadians, is still operating today, and is mostly preoccupied with automatic transmission, brake, and paint delamination claims (see Appendix I).

Ford's warranty performance in Canada (not in the States, where owners are treated as serfs) has improved considerably since I called attention to the company's shamefully arrogant and insensitive customer relations staff in last year's *Lemon-Aid*. The company settled close to 100 complaints I submitted and there have been fewer complaints in the last six months. As you may recall, I blasted Ford for waiting until June 1998 to formally extend the warranty retroactively on its 3.8L engine head gasket failures afflicting the Mustang, Taurus, Sable, Lincoln Continental, and Windstar, even though the problem had been evident since 1988. Furthermore, I'm still not pleased that Ford hasn't yet formally extended its warranty on past models to cover automatic transmission failures, caused by an aluminum piston, that affect over a decade's worth of its entire vehicle line.

General Motors is tougher to deal with than Chrysler or Ford. Once it rules on a customer's complaint, the file is closed and won't be reopened unless there's a threat of court action or the media becomes interested in the case. Like other automakers, GM informs its dealers and customers selectively of its goodwill policies through bulletins and memos. Nevertheless, the automaker likes to see its customers squirm, urging dealers to give them the third degree before warranty assistance is forthcoming.

Road performance
The main factors considered in this rating are acceleration and torque, transmission operation, routine handling, emergency handling, steering, and braking.

Every vehicle must at minimum be able to merge safely onto a highway and have adequate passing power for two-lane roads. Steering feel and handling should inspire confidence. The suspension ought to provide a reasonably well-controlled ride on most road surfaces. Ideally, the passenger compartment will be roomy enough to accommodate passengers comfortably on extended trips. The noise level should not become tiresome and annoying. As a rule, handling and ride comfort are inversely proportional—variations from this pattern are reflected in the ratings.

Comfort/convenience
Here we rate a vehicle based on the level of standard equipment offered, driving position comfort, effectiveness of controls, displays, and climate control, ease of entry/exit without running boards, amount of front and rear interior space/comfort, cargo space, trunk space and liftover, and degree of interior quietness.

Driving pleasure is hard to define, but a cramped interior, controls that are hard to see or reach, poor climate control systems, and excessive engine, road, and wind noise can turn that pleasure into a distressing experience.

Cost
Here we list the manufacturer's suggested retail price (MSRP), in effect at press time and applicable to standard models, that price's negotiability, the range of the dealer's markup, and the vehicle's estimated residual value over the next five years (particularly helpful when leasing). Undoubtedly, the MSRP will be a bit higher when the fall prices are announced. However, if the dealer's price is more than 3 percent higher than the price indicated in *Lemon-Aid*, ask for a copy of the manufacturer's notice to the dealer of the MSRP increase. You can confirm the MSRP figure by consulting the latest monthly Red Book under "Suggested Retail Price."

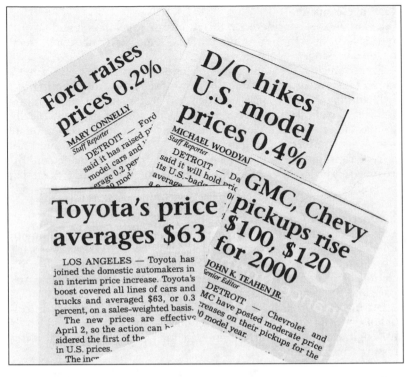

Ford raises prices 0.2%

MARY CONNELLY
Staff Reporter

DETROIT — Ford said it has raised p... model cars and ... erage 0.2 per ... ... mo...

D/C hikes U.S. model prices 0.4%

MICHAEL WOODYA...
Staff Reporter

DETROIT — Da... said it will hold pric... its U.S.-bad... averag...

Toyota's price averages $63

LOS ANGELES — Toyota has joined the domestic automakers in an interim price increase. Toyota's boost covered all lines of cars and trucks and averaged $63, or 0.3 percent, on a sales-weighted basis.

The new prices are effective April 2, so the action can b... sidered the first of the... in U.S. prices.

The inc...

GMC, Chevy pickups rise $100, $120 for 2000

JOHN K. TEAHEN JR.
Senior Editor

DETROIT — Chevrolet and MC have posted moderate price ...reases on their pickups for the ...0 model year.

Once you discover the latest MSRP, negotiate a reduction of the MSRP of at least half the indicated markup percentage, keeping in mind whether the price is "firm" or "negotiable." After reducing the MSRP price, ask the dealer to reduce the price further with whatever rebates or holdbacks apply.

With all the attention given to so-called "no haggle" sticker prices, keep in mind that all dealers "haggle" in one way or another. The substantial gap between the cost of the vehicle to the dealer ("invoice") and the manufacturer's suggested retail price (the "sticker" price) allows for such bargaining. This difference represents the dealer's markup (or gross profit), which is usually augmented by other incentive programs and holdbacks. To help you negotiate the best price, this edition indicates those MSRP prices that are firm and those that are negotiable, and gives the approximate price markup percentage in parentheses.

Destination charges and the PDI fee are outrageous $500–$700 add-ons that you shouldn't pay. In fact, Infiniti dealers have been ordered by Nissan/Infiniti to forego both the delivery and preparation charges on all new models, and Land Rover has these costs built into the selling price (where they belong). If you get tired of haggling with the dealer, agree to pay no more than 1 percent of a vehicle's MSRP for these extra charges. Also, don't fall for the $99–$475 "administration fee" scam.

Technical data

Note that towing capacities differ depending on the kind of powertrain/ suspension package or towing package you buy. Remember that there's a difference between how a vehicle is rated for cargo capacity or payload and how heavy a boat or trailer it can pull. Do not purchase any new vehicle without receiving very clear information, in writing, about a vehicle's towing capacity and the kind of special equipment you need to meet your requirements. Have the towing capacity and necessary equipment written into the contract.

In the ratings, cargo capacity is expressed in cubic feet with the rear seat up. With the rear seat folded or removed, cargo capacity obviously becomes quite larger.

Safety features/crashworthiness

Some of the main features weighed in the safety ratings are a model's crashworthiness and claims experience (as assessed by NHTSA and various insurers' groups, including the Highway Loss Data Institute and the Insurance Institute for Highway Safety), and the availability of seatbelt pretensioners, depowered airbags, airbag disablers, anti- lock brakes (rear-wheel-only systems aren't as effective as the four- wheel ABS), integrated child safety seats, effective head restraints, traction control, and front and rearward visibility. Side airbags won't be considered a safety-plus until real-world crash findings prove their worth and confirm that they're not a danger to children or small- statured adults.

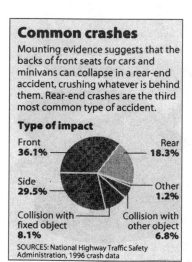

Common crashes

Mounting evidence suggests that the backs of front seats for cars and minivans can collapse in a rear-end accident, crushing whatever is behind them. Rear-end crashes are the third most common type of accident.

Type of impact

Front 36.1%
Rear 18.3%
Side 29.5%
Other 1.2%
Collision with fixed object 8.1%
Collision with other object 6.8%

SOURCES: National Highway Traffic Safety Administration, 1996 crash data

Crash protection figures are taken from NHTSA's New Car Assessment Program. Vehicles are crashed into a fixed barrier, head-on, at 57 km/h (35 mph), in order to evaluate the effects of the consequent forces exert- ed on the specially constructed dum- mies placed in the two front seats. Some 1997–2000 models may have been tested for side impact protection as well. The latest results—even if they may be several years old—have been included in the ratings.

NHTSA shows a vehicle's level of crashworthiness by the likelihood, expressed as a percentage, of the belted occupants being seriously injured. The higher the number of stars, the greater the protection:

NHTSA Front Collision Ratings

★★★★★ — a 10% or less chance of serious injury
★★★★   — an 11% to 20% chance of serious injury
★★★   — a 21% to 35% chance of serious injury
★★   — a 36% to 45% chance of serious injury
★   — a 46% or greater chance of serious injury

NHTSA tests don't necessarily provide an accurate picture of how a given model will perform in every accident; test figures are only valid if they're used to compare vehicles that are of the same size (i.e., compact, mid-size, or large). It's also unfortunate that vehicles aren't tested twice to confirm the validity of the first test.

Mercedes-Benz, proud of its reputation for building crashworthy vehicles of all sorts, hasn't always fared well in the NHTSA head-on collisions, and questions the validity of the ratings. The company claims that its own crash data show that most frontal collisions occur at an angle (offset), and that that's the kind of test wherein its vehicles excel. The Insurance Institute for Highway Safety (IIHS) sides with Mercedes, and crash-tests at an angle and at 64 km/h (40 mph). NHTSA doesn't do front offset testing, but it has tested some 1997–2000 cars for side-impact protection.

NHTSA Side Collision Ratings

★★★★★ — a 5% or less chance of serious injury
★★★★   — a 6% to 10% chance of serious injury
★★★   — an 11% to 20% chance of serious injury
★★   — a 21% to 25% chance of serious injury
★   — a 26% or greater chance of serious injury

Toyota's Sienna minivan has excellent crashworthiness ratings and is far more reliable than Ford's Windstar.

American Vehicles
CHRYSLER

Here's my dilemma: I like Chrysler, but I'm afraid the company has forgotten its roots as a manufacturer of good quality, reasonably priced vehicles. I'm hopeful, however, that being gobbled up by Daimler-Benz will improve assembly-line quality and the company's warranty performance, although I know "sticker shock" will remain as long as the company's profits continue to soar.

So throughout the year 2000 expect to see Chrysler, or DaimlerChrysler, if you wish, making tons of money churning out stylish, roomy, poor-quality cars and minivans (but reasonably reliable and highly profitable trucks and full-sized vans). The odds don't favour Daimler making any short-term quality improvements in Chrysler's products. It didn't work with Saab when GM took them over, Ford's Jaguar quality took almost a decade to improve, and after Chrysler bought out American Motors, its approach to improving AMC and Renault quality was to dump most of the company's models or send them back to France (remember the Eagle 4X4 and Encore?).

Concurrently, there is some good news for Chrysler's customers. As long as profits rise, the company's warranty performance (the manner in which it handles customer complaints) should continue to improve, inasmuch as there are now definite structural improvements in place following two years of angry car owner protests that led to CLOGs (Chrysler Lemon Owners Groups) sprouting up in British Columbia and New Brunswick.

Beset with angry owner protests like the one above in New Brunswick, Chrysler has successfully restructured its customer relations department to give owners a fair hearing. Now, if only they'd improve their products...

Quality problems likely to continue
Although the warranty and post-warranty "goodwill" may be more generous in paying for your repairs in the future, there are no signs whatsoever that Chrysler's poor quality control has been addressed in its '99
and year 2000 model cars and minivans—judging by the automaker's
own service bulletins and press statements.

Chrysler bean-counters still reign supreme—"get the dollars first;
repair the defects later."

Six years ago, the automaker's cost-cutters came up with the not-so-
bright idea that the company could save millions of dollars by cutting
its base warranty down to 3 years/80,000 km, selling the previous seven-
year protection for up to $1,000 extra (now sometimes as high as
$1,400), and squeezing supplier prices, even if quality was compro-
mised. Chrysler complied, and as a result has boasted both record-
breaking profits during the past three years and a steady stream of
complaints from disgruntled owners.

Since the warranty was shortened, most Chrysler products have finished at the bottom of most of the J.D. Power quality and customer satisfaction surveys, and, in light of the shorter warranty and member
complaints, *Consumer Reports* says the company's mid-sized cars are no
longer recommended. Other Chrysler vehicles have been similarly
downgraded.

Now let's look at what Chrysler's failure-prone components mean
from a dollar-and-cents standpoint. Automatic transmission failure—
$3,000; paint delamination—$3,000; AC replacement—$1,500; and
ABS failure—$1,500. That's a total potential cost during the first five
years of $9,000. Now you understand why I don't recommend most
Chrysler products unless they're covered by an optional, comprehensive warranty. Interestingly enough, all of the above problems are covered by Chrysler "goodwill" programs—in some cases, up to 10 years!

It'd be so much simpler if Chrysler would forget the "goodwill" and simply build better vehicles, as it did three decades ago.

Year 2000 products: same old, same old
DaimlerChrysler Canada is eliminating the Plymouth brand in Canada
and halting the sale of some Dodge cars in order to streamline its marketing. Consequently, Canadian dealers will no longer be able to order
the Avenger, Stratus, Breeze, and Voyager, although they'll still be sold
in the States. The Dodge nameplate will remain on vans, trucks, and
sport-utilities.

Chrysler isn't putting much new product into this year's market,
except for a revamped Neon and a four-door Dakota pickup. You'll
have to wait until 2001 to see major redesigns of all minivans, along
with the Stratus, Avenger, Cirrus, Sebring, and Cherokee. The Durango
will also get slight body trim freshening. Additionally, look for the 2001
PT Cruiser to create as much of a stir as the Prowler and Viper did
when first introduced. A retro Neon clone, the PT Cruiser is Chrysler's

$25,000+ mini-minivan, cobbled together with Neon parts and engineering and assembly processes, and aimed to appeal to your primordial "reptilian hot spot" (I swear, that's how the marketing guys talk).

Chrysler's 2000 PT Cruiser: Do you have a "reptilian hot spot" it can grab? Expect to pay $16,000–$21,000 (U.S.) for a base to fully-loaded model. The automaker will build 100,000 per year in Toluca, Mexico, on the former Neon assembly line.

The PT Cruiser is essentially a fuel- and space-efficient hatchback economy car that uses the same nostalgic hot rod flare that's been so successful with the Prowler. It comes with a nice assortment of new parts that includes attractive chrome door handles, a four-spoke steering wheel, and a cue-ball shifter for the 5-speed manual that sits atop a chrome stalk with a vinyl boot. It carries a Dodge Stratus/Plymouth Breeze 150-hp 2.4L 16-valve engine, although, in other markets, a 1.6L and 2.0L 4-cylinder will be offered. Times from 0–100 km/h should average in the eight-second range with the manual gearbox.

Removable seats and a flat floor puts the PT into the truck class for government taxonomists. Seating is midway between a Caravan and a Neon, making access quite easy. Tall, chair-like seats provide lots of leg room, and there's also generous head room, although the Cruiser is a bit narrower than the Neon. Tall drivers beware: the windshield is uncomfortably close, making it impossible to see overhead traffic lights. Higher perched rear seats for two only.

Prowler

Prowler

RATING: Recommended. Neither service bulletins nor owner comments show any problems. **Strong points:** Attractive styling, good acceleration and handling, reasonably priced, and slow to depreciate. **Weak points:** ABS is unavailable, limited visibility, difficult entry/exit, limited storage space, and the car shakes and rattles.

NEW FOR 2000: Suspension revisions to improve ride quality.

OVERVIEW: An aluminum and plastic, rear-drive, two-seat pseudo–hot rod that isn't for introverts. With a $55,000 base price, the Prowler, much like the Viper (another head-turner), is one of Chrysler's most unusual cars. Despite its racy styling, the Prowler's no high-performance muscle car, even though it posts impressive 0–100 km/h acceleration times. With a 253-hp 3.5L V6 engine, the 4-speed automatic comes with AutoStick (also available on the Vision, Intrepid, and Stratus), allowing you to shift the transmission as you would with a manual gearbox. On climbs, it prevents the transmission from changing gears back and forth, and on the downhill you can keep the car in a lower gear to prevent picking up excess speed. This year's model gets an additional colour (yellow), an airbag cut-off switch, and side airbags.

On the downside, the Prowler has a kidney-pounding, stiff ride; no trunk (you have to buy an optional purple mini-trailer); no spare tire; and room only for two—as long as they're not too tall. **Best alternatives:** Mercedes-Benz SLK230, Chevrolet Corvette convertible, and Porsche Boxster.

Viper RT/10

Viper

RATING: Recommended. **Strong points:** Good acceleration and handling. **Weak points:** No ABS, poor fuel economy, and passenger comfort is compromised by excessive wind noise. Only a hundred or so Vipers have been allocated to Canada.

NEW FOR 2000: An additional colour (steel gray).

OVERVIEW: This red-hot $93,255, mid-sized, two-door, rear-drive roadster breaks all the marketing rules—and wins. Basically a limited production of less than 500 a year (only 303 were built in 1994), its awesome 450-hp 8.0L V10 engine, 6-speed manual gearbox, and "in your face" styling aren't equalled by any other vehicle in its class. It also features depowered airbags and an airbag cut-off switch. Interestingly, service bulletins and owner comments paint a positive picture of the Viper's overall dependability. **Best alternatives:** Acura NSX, Chevrolet Corvette, and Porsche Boxster.

Neon

RATING: Not Recommended. **Strong points:** Plenty of interior space, good handling, and a thrifty engine. **Weak points:** Wimpy engine, imprecise manual shifter, clunky 3-speed automatic, mediocre braking, excessive engine, road, and body noise, and a history of failure-prone powertrain and body components.

NEW FOR 2000: The two-door has been dropped, along with the optional 150-hp 2.0L engine. Four-door models get a 1-inch longer wheelbase and a 2.6-inch longer body. There's also more trunk space; full-frame doors (reducing wind noise and water leaks); a redesigned interior that includes a tachometer, a six-speaker stereo, and floormats; optional traction control; and a new Sentry Key security system that will disable the starter, unless the correct ignition key is used. The manual transmission has been upgraded to improve acceleration.

OVERVIEW: The Neon, Chrysler's homegrown small car, is roomy and reasonably powered for urban use. This year's refinements give the Neon a mini-Intrepid styling and a softer, quieter ride while enhancing the car's handling. Interior room is where the Neon shines, though, with front and rear seating that easily accommodates six-footers. Essentially, Chrysler is trying to make its low-end year 2000 Neon more appealing by loading up on features that are usually only seen with higher-priced vehicles—transforming cheap into chic. One side benefit: the Belvedere, Ill., manufacturing plant has fewer different versions of the car to configure (2,792 versus 50,564).

Cost analysis/best alternatives: Forget the '99 version, it doesn't have the refinements (smoother ride, noise suppression, and luxury features) found in this year's Neon. Other cars worth considering are the Ford Escort (great time to buy as its prices have fallen to make room for the Focus), Geo Metro, Honda Civic, Mazda Protegé, and Toyota Corolla. If you're in the market for a sport coupe, make sure that you also check out the VW Golf GTi. **Options:** Built-in child safety seats (if available) and height adjustment for the steering wheel (for short drivers). Don't lament the loss of the optional 150-hp 4-banger—you'll just get a lot more noise and not much more power. ABS is another option that hasn't got the bugs worked out yet. **Rebates:** $1,000–$1,500 rebates. **Delivery/PDI:** $600. **Depreciation:** About average. **Insurance cost:** Average. **Parts supply/cost:** Average. **Annual maintenance cost:** Higher than average. **Warranty:** Bumper-to-bumper 3 years/60,000 km; rust perforation 5 years/160,000 km. **Supplementary warranty:** Don't buy a Neon without extra protection. **Highway/city fuel economy:** 7–9.5L/100 km with the base 2.0L engine, and 7.3–11.2L/100 km with last year's high-output powerplant. **Annual fuel cost:** 2.0L: 1,675L=$921.

Quality/Reliability/Safety

Pro: Front adjustable shoulder belt anchors.

Con: Quality control: It may take longer than the base warranty's three-year limit to correct the Neon's many problems, notably its powertrain, electrical system, and body deficiencies. *Consumer Reports* says that its member survey found that first-year (1995 model) Neons had nearly twice the problems of the average 1995 model car. **Reliability:** When *Autoweek,* an American car enthusiast magazine, tested a '96 Neon Sport Coupe with only 16,566 miles (26,506 km) on the odometer for its March 4th edition, it concluded that "aliens" had invaded the test car. Some of the magazine's "close encounters": a raggedy shifter, premature front brake pad wear, excessive brake fade, a rumbling noise coming from under the car, distorted sound coming from the cassette player, frozen windshield wipers, and a defroster that won't clear the windshield or side windows and that produces a wheezing noise when operating. **Warranty performance:** Chrysler's shortened warranty is far from reassuring when one considers how tough Chrysler has been in interpreting its warranty obligations, and that most powertrain problems occur after the third year of ownership. Fortunately, you can always appeal any warranty repair refusal to the company's Review Committee (see Appendix I). **Owner-reported problems:** A perusal of owner comments confirms that these cars continue to have lots of serious factory-related defects, including engine head gasket failures, an air-conditioning system that often requires expensive servicing, lots of interior noise and leaks, interior window film buildup, exposed screw heads, uneven fit and finish, and poor-quality trim items that break or fall off easily. The finish isn't as good as most other subcompacts, either; the thickness of the coat varies considerably and will chip easily. **Service bulletin problems:** A new engine head gasket has been put into service to address complaints regarding the earlier version; oil seepage at cam position sensor; AC compressor locks up at low mileage; vehicle overheats and radiator fan inoperative, or runs continuously; measures to reduce steering wheel column clunks and rattles; front brake squeaks and groans; front suspension creaking; erratic tachometer; remote keyless transmitter battery failure; water leaks into the left side of the trunk and pools in the spare tire well; sunshade delamination. **NHTSA safety complaints/safety:** Airbags fail to deploy or deploy inadvertently; Michelin tires fail prematurely; engine head gasket, intake manifold, front-end suspension, and drivetrain failure; front and rear head restraints are set too low; headlight switch is a "hide-and-go-seek" affair; ventilation system doesn't contain a mechanism to shut off exterior air flow to prevent exhaust fumes from entering the cabin; horn failures.

Road Performance

Pro: Better than average acceleration (0–100 km/h: 8.1 sec) with plenty of low-end torque. The 2.0L engine's 132 horses and the Neon's low weight give it acceptable performance in lower gear ranges, but restrict it to mainly urban use. **Emergency handling:** Better than average. **Steering:** Precise and easy to control on smooth roads.

Con: Acceleration/torque: Base engine runs out of steam in high gear and is buzzy from 4,000 rpm on up. It runs particularly roughly after 5,000 rpm. This is especially irritating because horsepower and torque peak at 5,000 and 6,000 rpm. Even with the manual transmission, highway passing requires downshifting from fifth gear to third, with the 2.0L engine crying all the way. The optional 150-hp 4-cylinder engine only available on last year's model isn't much better. **Transmission:** The manual transmission is harsh and noisy—no comparison with Honda and Toyota vehicles. The manual gearbox also requires lots of downshifting when going over small hills. The 3-speed automatic transmission lacks sufficient torque in high gear, and shifts abruptly and often. The car cries out for a more economical and efficient 4-speed electronic transmission. **Routine handling:** Definitely improved over last year, but the jittery ride becomes fairly rough when traversing anything but the smoothest roads. Ride deteriorates and the suspension bottoms with a vengeance with a full load. **Braking:** Worse than average (100–0 km/h: 143 ft.).

Comfort/Convenience

Pro: Driving position: Good driving position. The bucket seats are comfortable and there's plenty of head room. **Controls and displays:** Easy-to-operate controls and clear gauges. Easy-to-use and effective heating-and-ventilation system. **Climate control:** Everything's within easy reach and easily read. **Entry/exit:** Good up front; large door openings for long legs. **Interior space/comfort F/R:** The Neon seats five adults and has a spacious interior. Practical cloth bucket seats. Seats are firmer and more comfortable than one would expect. Plenty of rear leg room and elbow room. Rear seat is roomy enough for three adults. Rear seatbacks can be folded down to increase trunk space. **Cargo space:** Lots of little storage areas. Upgraded radio antenna reduces wind noise.

Con: Standard equipment: Low-quality interior appointments. Rear visibility compromised by high rear parcel shelf. Gauges lose contrast in dim light with headlights on. Door-mounted power window switches press uncomfortably against the driver's leg. Rear door shape makes for difficult entry and exit. Hard-to-access rear seat doesn't provide enough thigh support. Inadequate rear head room and toe space. No locks for the inside trunk release or seatback sections that give access to the trunk. Hard-to-operate window cranks and only the front windows are power-assisted. Short, flimsy trunk lid restricts trunk access. **Trunk/liftover:** Narrow trunk with a low sill. Trunk hinges eat up lots of storage space as well as possibly damaging your luggage. **Quietness:** Although there's less noise than on the '99 Neon, you'll still find plenty of engine boom and growling, automatic transmission whine, and tire thumping.

COST

List Price (negotiable)	Residual Values (months)			
	24	36	48	60
'99 2d: $15,775 (12%)	$8,500	$6,500	$5,000	$3,500
LE 4d: $17,995 (13%)	$9,800	$7,900	$6,700	$4,900
LX 4d: $19,995 (14%)	$11,000	$9,000	$7,500	$6,000

TECHNICAL DATA

Powertrain (front-drive)
Engines: 2.0L 4-cyl. (132 hp)
Transmissions: 5-speed man.
• 3-speed auto.
Dimensions/Capacity
Passengers: 5
Height/length/width:
53/171.8/67.5 in.

Head room F/R: 39.6/36.5 in.
Leg room F/R: 42.5/35.1 in.
Wheelbase: 104 in.
Turning circle: 35.4 ft.
Cargo volume: 42.6 cu. ft.
Tow limit: 1,000 lb.
Fuel tank: 47L/reg.
Weight: 2,400 lb.

SAFETY FEATURES/CRASHWORTHINESS

	Std.	Opt.
Anti-lock brakes	❏	■
Seatbelt pretensioners	—	—
Side airbags	—	—
Traction control	❏	■
Head restraints	*	*
Visibility (front/rear)	*****	*
Crash protection (front) D/P	***	****
Crash protection (side) D/P	N/A	
Crash protection (offset)	N/A	
HLDI injury claims (model)	N/A	
HLDI injury claims (all)	N/A	

Avenger, Sebring

Sebring

RATING: Above Average. **Strong points:** Comfortable ride, adequate interior room, and optional ABS. **Weak points:** No manual transmission with the V6, mediocre engine performance, lots of engine and road noise.

NEW FOR 2000: The Avenger is being phased out in Canada. The Sebring convertible gets an upgraded suspension and the hardtop now carries a standard 2.5L engine.

OVERVIEW: The Avenger and its more luxuriously appointed Sebring twin are good buys mainly because they've had fewer new-model "teething" problems than other Chrysler-built compacts. Sebring is a reasonably priced luxury coupe equipped with standard amenities, including AC, bucket seats, and a tilt steering wheel, while the Avenger fills the sport coupe niche with standard tinted glass and an awesome sound system.

Except for the convertible version, these front-drive replacements for the failure-prone Dodge Daytona and LeBaron coupes are built in Normal, Illinois, in the same factory that once produced the Talon. They share many safety features and mechanical components, including standard dual airbags and a 140-hp 2.0L twin cam 4-cylinder engine on the '99 versions. This year's Sebring is powered by a 163-hp 2.5L V6 coupled to an electronically controlled 4-speed automatic transaxle.

The convertible, made in Mexico, is six inches longer than the Sebring coupe and is powered by a standard 2.0L twin cam, while the upscale JXi gets a performance injection with the 2.5L 6-cylinder powerplant coupled to an AutoStick transaxle, 4-wheel disc brakes, ABS, and traction control.

Cost analysis/best alternatives: The 2000 Avenger and Sebring don't cost more than last year's models and the standard 6-cyliner is an additional inducement to buy a 2000 model. Avenger shoppers should take a look at other sporty coupes, including the Honda Accord and Toyota Celica. Convertibles worth a glance: Ford Mustang and Chevrolet Camaro. **Options:** These cars come well-appointed. **Rebates:** $1,000 rebates on the '99s. **Delivery/PDI:** $350. **Depreciation:** Much slower than average. **Insurance cost:** Average. **Parts supply/cost:** Reasonably priced parts are easily found. **Annual maintenance cost:** Average. **Warranty:** Bumper-to-bumper 3 years/ 60,000 km; rust perforation 5 years/160,000 km. **Supplementary warranty:** Not essential. **Highway/city fuel economy:** 7.3–11.2L/100 km with the base 4-cylinder; 8–12L/100 km with the V6. **Annual fuel cost:** 4-cylinder: 1,889L=$1,096; V6: 2,040L=$1,183.

Quality/Reliability/Safety

Pro: Quality control: Quality control is unusually good. Body construction and assembly are solid, with few gaps. **Reliability:** Better than average. **Warranty performance:** Average. This may be because these cars haven't been on the market very long. Remember, you can always appeal any warranty repair refusal to the company's Review Committee (see Appendix I).

Con: Owner-reported problems: Premature brake wear and some electrical glitches. **Service bulletin problems:** Faulty transmission range sensor; oil seepage from cam position sensor; harsh ride, vehicle pull, and brake shudder; tips on correcting brake pedal pulsation and steering wheel shake; headliner sagging above the rear window; sunshade delamination. **NHTSA safety complaints/safety:** Electrical system fire; several brake system failures due to loss of vacuum; space-saver spare tire is only good for a few miles and at slow speeds; seatbelts too tight; chronic dead battery.

Road Performance

Pro: Emergency handling: Better than average. **Steering:** Steering is responsive and light. **Acceleration/torque:** Adequate, but far from sporty acceleration (0–100 km/h: 10 sec. with the V6). The base 4-cylinder is thrifty and adequate for most driving tasks. It works well with both the manual and automatic transmission. **Transmission:** Smooth and quiet operation in all gear ranges. **Routine handling:** Handling is exceptional with either engine, and there's little body lean when cornering under speed. The ride deteriorates only slightly on bad surfaces due to the car's compliant suspension. Jarring is reduced as the weight of passengers is added.

Con: The base 2.0L engine loses power when mated to the 4-speed automatic and, when pushed, it's noisy and less responsive than the V6. Unfortunately, the V6 doesn't come with a manual gearbox, so its extra power doesn't translate into performance thrills. Some front-end plow in turns. The car's large turning circle makes parking a chore. **Braking:** Unimpressive (100–0 km/h: 141 ft.).

Comfort/Convenience

Pro: Standard equipment: Well-appointed with many standard features. **Controls and displays:** Controls and gauges are easily reached and seen. **Entry/exit:** Large doors facilitate entry and exit. **Interior space/comfort F/R:** The rear seating area is more adult-friendly than most sport coupes. Three tall passengers can sit in the rear for short trips, but the seating is really designed for two. **Cargo space:** Limited trunk cargo area can be extended by folding the split seatback. **Trunk/liftover:** Average trunk space with a low liftover. Rear seatback and remote trunk release can be locked.

Con: Driving position: Front seats need additional lateral support, and the seatback bulge is annoying to some drivers. The tilt steering wheel is set too low (almost in the driver's lap). Short drivers may have difficulty with forward vision, even with the seat raised to its maximum setting. **Climate control:** The climate control system is hampered by a noisy fan and uneven air distribution. The rear defroster leaves some of the glass untouched. With rear-quarter windows that won't open and the optional rear deck-lid spoiler cutting rear visibility, it's not hard to feel a bit claustrophobic. **Quietness:** Excessive tire/road noise intrudes into the passenger compartment.

COST

List Price (very negotiable)	Residual Values (months)			
	24	36	48	60
Sebring LX: $23,380 (19%)	$16,000	$15,000	$13,500	$12,000
'99 Avenger: $19,180 (15%)	$13,500	$11,500	$9,500	$8,000

TECHNICAL DATA

Powertrain (front-drive)
Engines: 2.0L 4-cyl. (140 hp)
• 2.5L V6 (163 hp)
Transmissions: 5-speed man.
• 4-speed auto.
Dimensions/Capacity
Passengers: 5
Height/length/width:
53.3/187.2/69.1 in.

Head room F/R: 37.6/36.5 in.
Leg room F/R: 43.3/35 in.
Wheelbase: 103.7 in.
Turning circle: 33.6 ft.
Cargo volume: 13.1 cu. ft.
Tow limit: 1,000 lb.
Fuel tank: 60L/reg.
Weight: 3,000 lb.

SAFETY FEATURES/CRASHWORTHINESS

	Std.	Opt.
Anti-lock brakes	■	■
Seatbelt pretensioners	—	—
Side airbags	—	—

Traction control	■	❑
Head restraints	**	**
Sebring	*****	**
Visibility (front/rear)	****	*****
Crash protection (front) D/P	*****	*****
Convertible	****	****
Crash protection (side) D/P	N/A	
Crash protection (offset)	N/A	
HLDI injury claims (model)	**	
Convertible	***	
HLDI injury claims (all)	***	
Convertible	***	

Breeze, Cirrus, Stratus

Cirrus

RATING: Average. **Strong points:** Plenty of passenger room, well-appointed, and excellent handling. **Weak points:** Insufficient 2.0L engine torque, poor-quality workmanship and reliability.

NEW FOR 2000: The Breeze and Stratus are being phased out in Canada; Cirrus returns unchanged.

OVERVIEW: The Chrysler Cirrus and Dodge Stratus are identical mid-sized, front-drive sedans. The Cirrus LXi comes loaded with standard features that include AC, leather-trimmed interior with adjustable driver's seat, ABS, an upgraded sound system with cassette player, tilt steering, cruise control, and plenty of power-assisted accessories. Breeze, Plymouth's entry-level version, offers an optional 2.4L 4-cylinder engine, but won't carry the V6 in order to keep its base price low. Most of these cars' components have been used for some time on other Chrysler models, particularly the Neon subcompact and Avenger/Sebring sport coupes.

Power is supplied by three engines: a 2.0L 4-cylinder engine shared with the Neon powers the Stratus, while a base 2.4L 4-banger and an optional 2.5L V6, used by the Avenger, propel the high-performance

Cirrus and Stratus ES. Carrying Chrysler's "cab forward" design a step further up the evolutionary ladder, these cars have short rear decks, low noses, and massive sloping grilles. A wheelbase that's two inches longer than the Ford Taurus' makes both cars comfortable for five occupants, with wide door openings and plenty of trunk space.

Cost analysis/best alternatives: Get the '99 models at a discount (about $2,000, not including rebates), since the newer versions don't have that much more to offer. Other vehicles worth considering: Honda Accord, Toyota Camry, and Volvo S70 or V70. **Options:** The 2.5L V6 and an integrated child safety seat for the rear centre seat. **Rebates:** $1,000 rebates on the '99s. **Delivery/PDI:** $375. **Depreciation:** Slower than average. **Insurance costs:** A bit higher than average. **Annual maintenance cost:** Higher than average. **Warranty:** Bumper-to-bumper 3 years/60,000 km; rust perforation 5 years/160,000 km. **Supplementary warranty:** Essential. Invest the money you saved in buying a '99 model on an extended seven-year warranty. **Highway/city fuel economy:** 7.3–11.2L/100 km with the 2.0L; 7.1–11.3L/100 km with the 2.4L; 8–12L/100 km with the 2.5L engine. **Annual fuel cost:** 2.4L: 1,882L=$1,092.

Quality/Reliability/Safety

Pro: Reliability: Average.

Con: Quality control: Spotty. Body construction and powertrain components leave much to be desired. **Warranty performance:** The three-year base warranty is clearly insufficient coverage in view of Chrysler's traditionally poor quality control and sub-par warranty performance. You'll likely wind up appealing for a warranty refund to the company's Review Committee (see Appendix I). **Owner-reported problems:** Engine head gasket failures, AC malfunctions, frequent stalling, myriad body squeaks and rattles, and fragile body hardware. **Service bulletin problems:** New engine head gasket put into production; oil seepage at cam position sensor; transaxle desensitization to intermittent faults causing all sorts of transmission failures (not again!); loose or broken antenna mount; off-centre steering wheel, steering column, wheel clunks and rattles; low frequency rumble, gear noise from front of vehicle; front door snapping on cladding; seat adjuster rises when the seat is unoccupied; wheel covers may fall off. **NHTSA safety complaints/safety:** Airbags failed to deploy; inadvertent airbag deployment knocked out driver and caused a collision; sudden loss of all electrical power; light bulb in the trunk is too intense, caused a foam pillow to ignite.

Road Performance

Pro: Emergency handling: Fairly good, though not as precise as the Ford Contour/Mystique. **Acceleration/torque:** Although the base 2.4L 4-cylinder performs competently, the 2.5L V6 is a better choice from a noise and performance standpoint. It provides plenty of power in all gear ranges (0–100 km/h: 9.8 sec.) and this year's improvements have also reduced engine vibration and noise somewhat. **Routine handling:** Although high-performance handling isn't as sporty as the Contour's and the steering isn't quite as sensitive, overall handling is quite competent. Ride quality is generally smooth and pleasant and doesn't deteriorate as the load increases. **Braking:** Better than average (100–0 km/h: 122 ft.), although there is some brake fade after successive stops.

Con: Forget about the Neon-borrowed 2.0L 4-banger; it's overwhelmed by this car's size and accessories and is quite noisy. The V6 is also a bit noisy when pushed and lacks the aggressiveness of the Ford Contour and Mystique V6, particularly when passing. **Steering:** Steering response is vague and gives little feel of the road. **Transmission:** When passing, the powertrain computer kicks the transmission down to second gear, pushing the tachometer to the redline without gaining much more speed. It's also sometimes slow to downshift.

Comfort/Convenience

Pro: Standard equipment: Attractive, tasteful interior with lots of standard features. **Driving position:** Excellent, with a commanding view of the road. **Controls and displays:** Both tall and short drivers can see and access all controls and gauges. **Climate control:** Efficient and easy to adjust. Rear-seat comfort has been enhanced through floor ducts located under the front seats. The defroster also heats the side mirrors. **Interior space/comfort F/R:** Seats are generally comfortable, with nice side bolsters. They aren't quite as snug as the Contour and Mystique seats, but most drivers prefer the extra room. Plenty of front head and leg room. Rear seating is comfortable only for two adults. **Cargo space:** Rear seatback folds down, extending the trunk cargo space. **Trunk/liftover:** Fairly large with a low liftover.

Con: Front seat bottom cushion is a little short on thigh support for tall drivers. **Entry/exit:** Difficult access to the front seats due to the sharply slanted roof pillars. **Quietness:** In highway cruising between 100 and 120 km/h, the powertrain emits an annoying high-pitched whine. Some suspension noise intrudes into the interior when going over rough surfaces. Noisy heater fan. Narrow rear-door armrests and the lack of a centre armrest leave you without much to lean on. The trunk's cargo net is poorly positioned.

COST				
List Price (very negotiable)	**Residual Values** (months)			
	24	**36**	**48**	**60**
Cirrus LX: $22,500 (18%)	$13,000	$11,500	$9,500	$8,000
Breeze LX: $22,365 (19%)	$13,000	$11,000	$9,000	$8,000

TECHNICAL DATA

Powertrain (front-drive)
Engines: 2.0L 4-cyl. (132 hp)
• 2.4L 4-cyl. (150 hp)
• 2.5L V6 (168 hp)
Transmissions: 5-speed man.
• 4-speed auto.
Dimensions/Capacity
Passengers: 5
Height/length/width:
52.5/186/71.7 in.

Head room F/R: 38.1/36.8 in.
Leg room F/R: 42.3/38.1 in.
Wheelbase: 108 in.
Turning circle: 35.4 ft.
Cargo volume: 15.7 cu. ft.
Tow limit: 1,000 lb.
Fuel tank: 60L/reg.
Weight: 3,100 lb.

SAFETY FEATURES/CRASHWORTHINESS

	Std.	Opt.
Anti-lock brakes	■	■
Seatbelt pretensioners	—	—
Side airbags	—	—
Traction control	—	—
Head restraints	*	*
Stratus	**	*
Visibility (front/rear)	*****	*****
Crash protection (front) D/P	***	****
Crash protection (side) D/P	***	**
Crash protection (offset)	*	
HLDI injury claims (model)	***	
HLDI injury claims (all)	***	

300M, Concorde, Intrepid, LHS

Intreprid

LHS

RATING: *Concorde* and *Intrepid:* Average. These cars give you more room than dependability. *300M* and *LHS:* Below Average. These over-priced, stylish sedans offer a nicely packaged depository of generic components used on the Concorde and Intrepid. This means they will have generic Chrysler-type problems in addition to traditional first-year model snafus (all the more reason to avoid the left over '99s). **Strong points:** *Concorde* and *Intrepid:* Attractive styling, nice riding, easy entry/exit, and lots of passenger and cargo room. *300M* and *LHS:* Attractive styling, good acceleration and handling, plenty of passenger and cargo room, and reasonable price. The LHS also has a large trunk with a wide opening. **Weak points:** *Concorde* and *Intrepid:* Excessive road and wind noise, vague steering, optional ABS, limited rear visibility caused by the cars' high rear end, impractical trunk, poor reliability, and sub-par warranty performance on Chrysler's part. *300M* and *LHS:* Rough-running engine and transmission, excessive road and wind noise, five-passenger capacity, the 300M has limited rear leg room, a narrow rear windshield reduces rear visibility and carries a smaller trunk with a smaller opening than the LHS, no side airbags, mediocre fit and finish, and questionable reliability.

NEW FOR 2000: Intreprid gets an R/T package with a 3.5L engine.

OVERVIEW: *Concorde* and *Intrepid*: These full-sized cars share the same chassis and offer most of the same standard and optional features. Both cars have loads of passenger space and many standard features that usually sell as options, such as four-wheel disc brakes and an inde-pendent rear suspension. The Concorde is marketed to the more con-servative buyer. The Intrepid, the more popular model, is the entry-level version. Base models are equipped with a 2.7L V6 aluminum engine that delivers 200 hp. Higher line variants get a more powerful 3.2L V6 225-hp powerplant, or a 242-hp 3.5L V6.

300M and *LHS:* These two models represent the near-luxury and sport clones of the Chrysler Concorde. Although they use the same front-drive platform as the Concorde, their bodies are shorter and they're styled differently. In fact, the 300M is the shortest of Chrysler's mid-sized sedans. Both cars are powered by a 253-hp 3.5L V6 and mated to Chrysler's AutoStick semi-automatic transmission. Only a few months after their launch in the summer of '98, Chrysler made engineering changes to reduce noise and vibration and smooth out what was thought to be an overly harsh ride. Automatic headlights were added as well.

Cost analysis/best alternatives: Look for a 15 percent discount on the '99 versions before any rebates are applied, and make sure your door-plate shows the '99 was made in late summer or early fall to benefit from Chrysler's interim upgrades. 2000 versions aren't worth the extra cost unless you want the Intrepid's R/T package. If you want first-class quality, though, an Acura RL, Audi A6, Lexus GS 300, Nissan Maxima, or a fully loaded Toyota Camry or Avalon should be your first choice. **Options:** You'd be smart to get any of the two larger V6 engines. Goodyear GA tires provide better handling, but they're noisy. The harsh sports suspension, however, is a waste of money. Opt for the handling package and you get crisper steering response, better brakes and tires, and stiffer springs that eliminate much of the body roll. The large rear windshield may need tinting to protect rear-seat passengers from the sun. **Rebates:** All four models will have $1,000–$1,500 rebates coming into the year 2000. **Delivery/PDI:** $800. **Depreciation:** About average. The Intrepid suffers from a low level of owner loyalty—industry stats show that about nine out of ten Intrepid owners walk away from the model when considering their next vehicle purchase. **Insurance cost:** Higher than average. **Parts supply/cost:** Reasonably priced and easily found. **Annual maintenance cost:** Much higher than average. **Warranty:** Bumper-to-bumper 3 years/60,000 km; rust perforation 5 years/ 160,000 km. **Supplementary warranty:** Don't leave home without it. A wise investment, judging from the serious problems reported on previous models. **Highway/city fuel economy:** 7.2–11.3L/100 km with the 2.7L engine; 7.6–12.5L/100 km with the 3.2L engine; 8.0–13L/100 km with the 3.5L engine. **Annual fuel cost:** 2.7L: 1,891L=$1,097; 3.2L: 2,121L=$1,230; 3.5L: 2,159L=$1,252.

Quality/Reliability/Safety

Pro: Plastic front fenders are dent- and corrosion-resistant. Platinum-tipped spark plugs are expected to last 160,000 kilometres. Improved headlights really illuminate the road, and the upgraded defroster now clears the entire windshield.

Con: Quality control: Below average. **Reliability:** Poor overall. **Warranty performance:** Worse than average. Fortunately, you can always appeal any warranty repair refusal to the company's Review Committee (see Appendix I). **Owner-reported problems:** Glitches in the computerized transmission's shift timing, which cause driveability problems (stalling, hard starts, and surging). Amazingly, the 4-speed LE42 automatic transmission—a spin-off of Chrysler's failure-prone A604—appears to be just as problem-plagued as its predecessor, with reports of driveline shudder during three to four shifts and frequent transmission defaults into second gear (limp-in mode). Other owner-reported defects include premature brake wear and brake malfunctions, electrical problems, and sloppy body construction. For example, owners complain of water and air leaks into the interior, uneven fit and finish, poor-quality trim items that break or easily fall off, exposed screw heads, faulty door hinges that make the doors rattle and hard to open, windows that come off their tracks or are misaligned, and power-window motor failures. **Service bulletin problems:** Transaxle desensitization to intermittent faults causing all sorts of transmission failures; troubleshooting tips for eliminating body panel gaps; faulty wiper switch; exhaust drone; tapping noise originating from the temperature door; and vehicle leads or pulls. **NHTSA safety complaints/safety:** Transmission won't shift to reverse, engine stalls; headlights sometimes shut off on their own; side seatbelts don't retract; front and rear windshields distort view; there may be an annoying reflection on the inside of the windshield, particularly evident on vehicles with beige interiors. 300M and LHS rear visibility compromised by narrow rear windows.

Road Performance

Pro: Emergency handling: Steering is a bit vague and ponderous with some tire squealing, but no worse than the competition. **Acceleration/torque:** The 3.2L and 3.5L V6 engines provide plenty of low-end torque and acceleration (0–100 km/h: 9 sec.). **Routine handling:** Good or better handling and steering response than the Taurus, and the optional AutoStick clutchless manual transmission available with the Intrepid sports package improves overall performance even more. Independent suspension also maximizes control and provides lots of suspension travel so that you don't get bumped around on rough roads. The ride doesn't deteriorate as the load is increased. The best balance between performance and ride is found with the mid-level touring suspension. It's not as harsh as the optional sport suspension, and it's firmer than the standard settings. **Braking:** Good braking performance with standard brakes (100–0 km/h: 125 ft.).

Con: The smaller, 2.7L V6 engine is inadequate to handle a fully loaded Concorde or Intrepid. The traction control system is noisy when activated. The 300M and LHS 3.5L V6 isn't as smooth a performer as the Lexus GS 300 or the Acura TL powerplants. **Transmission:** The 4-speed automatic transmission shifts in and out of overdrive with a jolt. A considerable amount of body roll occurs in tight manoeuvring.

Comfort/Convenience

Pro: Standard equipment: Loaded with standard features. A sleeker, more aerodynamic body than the Taurus/Sable, the Honda Accord, and Chevrolet's Lumina. Excellent visibility due to the large windshield and low front end. **Controls and displays:** Very user-friendly. Analogue instruments are clearly laid out. **Climate control:** Automatic climate-control system is much improved. Efficient and easy to adjust. **Entry/exit:** Excellent front and rear access. The user-friendly interior features passenger grab handles for easy access. **Interior space/comfort F/R:** Extended front seat tracks for long-legged drivers or simply for people wanting to sit away from the airbag. Comfortable front bucket seats and rear seat sits three abreast. **Cargo space:** Lots of storage space, including map pockets in the door.

Con: Driving position: Front seat lacks lateral support and the adjustable lumbar support is uncomfortable. Instrumentation illumination could be brighter and more distinct on the LHS and 300M. The trunk has a high deck lid, making for difficult loading and unloading, and there's no inside access by folding down the rear seat, as in the Camry. **Quietness:** All four vehicles have excessive engine, road, and wind noise that comes mainly from the tires and poor sealing around the doors and windows

COST				
List Price (very negotiable)	**Residual Values** (months)			
	24	**36**	**48**	**60**
Intrepid: $25,520 (21%)	$16,000	$13,000	$11,000	$9,000
Concorde LX: $28,115 (22%)	$17,000	$14,000	$12,000	$10,000
300M: $39,150 (22%)	$28,000	$23,000	$18,000	$15,000
LHS: $39,150 (22%)	$27,000	$22,000	$17,000	$14,000

TECHNICAL DATA	
Powertrain (front-drive)	Head room F/R: 38.3/37.2 in.;
Engines: 2.7L V6 (200 hp)	38.3/37.7 in.
• 3.2L V6 (225 hp)	Leg room F/R: 42.2/41.6 in.;
• 3.5L V6 (242 hp)	42.2/39.1 in.
Transmissions: 5-speed man.	Wheelbase: 113 in.
• 4-speed auto.	Turning circle: 35.4 ft.; 37.6 ft.
Dimensions/Capacity (Concorde;	Cargo volume: 18.7 cu. ft.; 16.8 cu. ft.
300M)	Tow limit: 2,000 lb.
Passengers: 3/3; 2/3	Fuel tank: 68L/reg.; 65L/reg.
Height/length/width:	Weight: 3,550 lb.; 3,567 lb.
55.9/209.1/74.4 in.;	
56/197.8/82.7 in.	

SAFETY FEATURES/CRASHWORTHINESS

	Std.	Opt.
Anti-lock brakes	■	■
Seatbelt pretensioners	—	—
Side airbags	—	—
Traction control	■	■
Head restraints (Concord)	*****	**
Head restraints (300M)	**	**
Head restraints (Intrepid)	*****	**
Head restraints (LHS)	**	**
Visibility (front/rear)		
Concorde and Intreprid	*****	*****
300M and LHS	*****	*
Crash protection (front) D/P	****	****
Crash protection (side) D/P	****	***
Crash protection (offset)	N/A	
HLDI injury claims (model)	N/A	
HLDI injury claims (all)	N/A	

Caravan, Grand Caravan, Voyager, Grand Voyager, Town & Country

Caravan

RATING: Average. Compromised by a history of poor quality control and worse than average reliability, particularly since 1991. Recent service bulletins on the '99 model indicate fewer problems than have been seen on past versions. Not to be bought without an extended warranty, which should be bargained down to about half the asking price. **Strong points:** Comfortable ride, excellent braking, lots of innovative convenience features, user-friendly instruments and controls, driver-side sliding door, and plenty of interior room. **Weak points:** Poor acceleration with the base engine and mediocre handling with the extended versions. Both automatic transmissions perform poorly in different ways.

Headlight illumination is inadequate. Skimpy storage compartments. A chintzy base warranty is inadequate to deal with serious powertrain, ABS, and body defects, and is exacerbated by the automaker's hard-nosed attitude in interpreting its warranty obligations. Crashworthiness has declined.

NEW FOR 2000: A carryover year with no substantive changes. The Voyager will be phased out in Canada.

OVERVIEW: These versatile and stylish minivans return with a wide array of standard and optional features that include AWD, anti-lock brakes, child safety seats integrated into the seatbacks, flush design door handles, and front windshield wiper/washer controls located on the steering column lever for easier use. Childproof locks are standard and the front bucket seats incorporate vertically adjustable head restraints. The Town & Country, a luxury version of the Caravan, comes equipped with a 3.8L V6 and standard luxury features that make the vehicle more fashionable for upscale buyers.

Cost analysis/best alternatives: Chrysler is expected to keep 2000-model price increases within 3 percent through January. Nevertheless, last year's practically identical versions remain the better buy, if you can get a 10 percent discount, plus whatever rebates are offered. Don't look for any bargains among the Japanese imports. The red-hot Honda Odyssey and Toyota Sienna minivans will cost much more by year's end, and Mazda's redesigned MPV probably won't be discounted until well into the year 2000. One small minivan that may be better suited to your needs is the Nissan Quest. You may have better luck bargaining down the Quest's price since Nissan is desperate to make a profit this year. On the other hand, some full-sized GM or Ford rear-drive cargo vans, ripe for conversion, might be a more affordable and practical buy if you intend to haul a full passenger load, do some regular heavy hauling, use lots of accessories, or take frequent motoring excursions. **Options:** As you increase body length you lose manoeuvrability. Don't even consider the 4-cylinder engine—it has no place in a minivan, especially when hooked to the automatic transmission. If you buy a Grand version, stay away from the inadequate 3.0L V6 mated to the 3-speed automatic. That transmission lacks an Overdrive and will shift back and forth as speed varies, and it's slower and noisier than the other optional 6-cylinders when accelerating from a standing start. The 3.3L V6 is a better choice for most city-driving situations, but don't hesitate to get the 3.8L if you're planning lots of highway travel or carrying four or more passengers. Since its introduction, it's been relatively trouble-free, plus it's more economical on the highway than the 3.3L, which strains to maintain speed. The sliding side doors makes it easy to load and unload children, install a child safety seat in the middle, or remove the rear seat. On the downside, they expose kids to traffic and are a costly option. Child safety seats integrated into the rear seatbacks are convenient and reasonably priced but Chrysler's versions have had a history of tightening up excessively or not tightening enough, allowing the child to slip out. Try the seat with your child before buying it. Other important features to consider are the optional defroster, power mirrors, power door locks, and power driver's seat (if you're shorter than 5'9" or expect to have different drivers using the minivan). You may wish to pass on the tinted windshields; they seriously reduce visibility. Town & Country buyers should pass on the optional all-wheel drive coupled with four-wheel disc brakes (instead of the standard rear drums). Although the disc brakes have been improved, Chrysler's large number of ABS failures is worrisome. **Rebates:** Now that foreign minivans are red hot (read Honda Odyssey and Toyota Sienna), look for both '99 and 2000 models getting rebates that top $1,000 to $2,000, depending upon the model year. Furthermore, in an effort to wean buyers away from the Plymouth models, Chrysler is sweetening the pot for Caravan and Grand Caravan buyers. **Delivery/PDI:** $850. **Depreciation:** Slightly slower than average. Resale values have picked up this year as buyers turn away from more expensive sport-utilities and pickups. Dealers from bordering states have also been buying up used minivans and shipping them south. **Insurance cost:** Higher than average, but about average for a minivan. **Parts supply/cost:** Average. Chrysler says that its 3.3L and 3.8L engines won't require tune-ups before 160,000 kilometres. Prepare to be disappointed; many owners have had to tune up their minivans way before then. **Annual maintenance cost:** Repair costs are average during the warranty period. Now that the base warranty has been cut back, owners won't have the luxury of time to get proper warranty servicing through repeat repair-bay visits. If your dealer or Chrysler starts to play the waiting game—waiting for the warranty to expire—don't hesitate to use an independent garage if that's where good service can be found, and take the dealer and Chrysler to small claims court if the defect is factory related. **Warranty:** Base warranty is inadequate, if you plan to keep your minivan five years or more. Bumper-to-bumper 3 years/60,000 km; rust perforation 5 years/160,000 km. **Supplementary warranty:** A must-have—preferably a seven-year powertrain warranty (the bumper-to-bumper extended warranty is simply too expensive). Paying over $1,000 for this protection is ridiculous; settle for a third or half as much. **Highway/city fuel economy:** *Caravan/Voyager:* 9–13L/100 km; *Grand Caravan AWD:* 10–14L/100 km; *Town & Country:* 9–14L/100 km; *Town & Country AWD:* 10–15L/100 km. **Annual fuel cost:** 3.0L: 2,144L=$1,244; 3.3L: 2,284L=$1,385; 3.8L: 2,337L=$1,355. Grand Caravans and the Town & Country have a similar annual fuel bill. The AWD versions, however, cost about $200 a year more to run.

Quality/Reliability/Safety

Pro: ABS improvements made two years ago are promising in that consumer complaints have gone down, though they have not been eliminated entirely. It will take several more years to be sure that these systems are functioning as they should. Dual airbags include knee bolsters to prevent front occupants from sliding under the seatbelts. Side-impact protection has been increased with steel beams in door panels. An innovative engine compartment layout also makes for a larger "crumple zone" in the event of collision. Remote-control power door locks can be programmed to lock when the vehicle is put in gear. Chrysler has developed a mechanism that releases the power door locks and turns on the interior lights when the airbag is deployed. The rear wiper is extraordinarily efficient and the Grand Voyager's heated windshield wiper does a good job of keeping the blades from icing up in nasty weather.

Con: Quality control: There is nothing in the press releases I received from Chrysler or the service bulletins I accessed that reassures me that the year 2000 minivans won't continue to have some powertrain and body deficiencies. Although *Consumer Reports* rates only the extended versions as worse than average, Canadian *Lemon-Aid* readers report that the base versions are just as failure-prone. This isn't surprising—quality control has been below average since these vehicles were first launched 15 years ago, and got much worse after the '90 model year. Quality has improved a bit over the last two years; we no longer have an unending stream of automatic transmission, ABS, and paint delamination complaints. Interestingly, the British Columbia class action against Chrysler for paint delamination includes vehicles only up to the 1997 model year. Hopefully, the worst is behind us—once the warranty expires, these common problems can collectively produce repair bills that will easily reach $5,000. **Reliability:** Has improved of late; approaching average. **Warranty performance:** Has gone from unacceptable to average. In just two years, Chrysler has come a long way in restructuring its customer relations department (it stank two years ago) to handle post-warranty complaints in a fair and efficient manner; you can always appeal any warranty repair refusal to the company's Review Committee (see Appendix I). Many owners have been compensated by the Committee, but compensation cannot replace better quality control and a more comprehensive base warranty. **Owner-reported problems:** Most owner complaints centre upon electrical glitches, premature brake wear, poor body construction, and body creaks, rattles, moans, and groans. Premature wear-out reported on these parts: cooling system, clutch, front suspension components, wheel bearings, front brake rotors, air-conditioning compressor, and body parts (trim, weatherstrip becomes loose and falls off, plastic pieces rattle and break easily). In spite of improvements over the years, the front brakes need constant attention, if not to replace the pads, or warped rotors, then to silence the excessive squeaks when braking. **Service bulletin problems:** Loud moaning and groaning sound from the compressor and reports of low-mileage AC compressor lockup, a honking or squealing noise during parking lot manoeuvres, front door weatherstrip falls off, suspension strut tower chirping or squeaking (see following bulletin), excessive engine ticking, CV boot grease seepage, engine gasket oil seepage, front door glass misadjustment causes excessive wind noise, ticking noise emanating from the top of the left B-pillar, whirling noise coming from the front or side sliding door power lock motors, and faulty transmission range sensors. **NHTSA safety complaints/safety:** Sudden acceleration, first in Reverse and then in Drive; stalling while cruising on the highway; van parked with gear in Park with the ignition off rolled backwards, crashed through a fence and hit a mobile home; five-year-old pulled vehicle shift lever out of Park and into Drive and vehicle took off; sliding door opens when passing over bumps; side power door switch burns out prematurely; right rear brake lockup when backing up; headlights aren't bright enough (a problem common to many Chrysler vehicles of 1993–99 vintage); faulty speedometer. In a side-impact crash test last January, fluid simulating fuel leaked from a 1999 Caravan when the filler hose broke loose. NHTSA researchers are investigating the leakage on 1996–99 models.

Squeaking Noise From Strut Bearings
02-10-98
GROUP: Suspension
DATE: Sept. 25, 1998
SUBJECT:
Squeaking Noise From Strut Bearing(s)
MODELS:
1998–1999 (NS) Town & Country/Caravan/Voyager
1998–1999 (GS) Chrysler Voyager (International Market)
SYMPTOM/CONDITION:
A squeaking/chirping noise is heard (inside or outside the vehicle) from the strut tower area(s) when turning the steering wheel or when the vehicle is driven over any irregularities in the road surface.
DIAGNOSIS:
With the vehicle on a level surface, hold a front suspension coil spring, with your hands near 180° apart, and try to rotate the spring right and left. If a squeaking/chirping noise is heard from the top of the strut tower, perform the Repair Procedure. Repeat for the opposite side strut tower.
Parts Information:
AR(2)   04684418 Bearing, Strut Upper Pivot
POLICY: Reimbursable within the provisions of the warranty.
TIME ALLOWANCE:
Labor Operation No:
02-05-39-93   One Side   0.9 Hrs.
02-05-39-94   Two Sides 1.6 Hrs.
FAILURE CODE: P8 - New Part

This suspension noise problem, present since 1997, will probably remain uncorrected until the next redesign—in 2001!

Road Performance

Pro: Emergency handling: Slow, but acceptable. **Steering:** Precise and predictable. **Acceleration/torque:** The most versatile, though a bit underpowered, powertrain for short-distance commuting is the 3.3L V6 engine coupled with the 4-speed automatic transmission (0–100 km/h: in about

10.8 sec. with a 3.3L-equipped Grand Caravan). Chrysler's top-of-the-line 3.8L engine is a better choice if you intend to do a lot of highway cruising: it's smooth and quiet with lots of much-needed low-end torque. The AWD transfers 90 percent of the engine power to the front wheels during normal driving conditions. It's easy to use and performs well. As the front wheels lose traction, the rear wheels get additional power until traction has been stabilized or the 55/45 percent front-to-rear limit is reached. **Routine handling:** These minivans are the closest thing to a passenger car when it comes to ride and handling. The redesigned chassis and improved steering provide a comfortable, no-surprise ride. Stiff springs greatly improve handling and comfort. Manoeuvrability around town is easy. Remember, the Grand version sacrifices handling for extra interior room. **Braking:** Acceptable ABS braking when it functions as it should (100–0 km/h: 118 ft. with the base Voyager and 132 ft. with the Grand Caravan).

Con: Sluggish highway acceleration until you move up to the 3.8L engine found with the ES package. And at that, you'll have to get used to excessive engine noise when passing. **Transmission:** The 3-speed automatic transmission accelerates poorly and is noisy, while the optional 41TE 4-speed automatic transmission with Overdrive shifts slowly and imprecisely. Excessive transmission whine. It's hard to use engine compression to slow down by "gearing down." Downshifting from the electronic gearbox provides practically no braking effect. Although it works well, the all-wheel drive option is overrated and not worth the fuel penalty for most driving situations. The stretched wheelbase version gives less-than-nimble handling. A large turning radius and long nose can make parking difficult. Power steering is vague and over-assisted as speed increases. Brake pedal feels mushy and the brakes tend to heat up after repeated applications, causing considerable loss of effectiveness (fade) and warping of the front discs. The ABS system has proved unreliable on older vans and repair costs are astronomical. Furthermore, the ABS control unit is located behind a front wheel, where it's susceptible to contamination by road salt and dirt.

Comfort/Convenience

Pro: Standard equipment: This is where Chrysler minivans shine. They offer plenty of standard comfort and versatility features. **Driving position:** Drivers are treated to a car-like driving position. Good overall view of the road. **Controls and displays:** The instrument panel features easy-to-read gauges and warning lights, and radio and heater controls are set close to the driver. The location of the turn signal indicators is particularly well thought out—they're in the lower portion of your field of vision. Lots of cupholders and interior reading lights. **Climate control:** Adequate. Dual-zone AC allows for different temperature settings for the driver and front-seat passenger. Overhead heating and ventilation ducts to the rear seat are well placed. **Entry/exit:** Easy. The step-up height isn't too high for most people. Another nice touch: grab handles on the rear hatch and sliding door. There's convenient "walk through" access to the rear seating area. **Interior space/comfort F/R:** Minivan doesn't mean "mini" in terms of passenger space. The aerodynamic exterior design, increased window area, and lower sills make for an attractive, roomier-feeling vehicle, and the interior is large and versatile with excellent outward visibility. Chrysler has copied the Windstar in providing theatre-type seating; each row is set a little higher than the row in front, giving most passengers a better view. A fairly high roofline—about four inches taller than the Ford Windstar—means that a six-foot-tall passenger will sit comfortably in the back seat, but would touch the roof in a Windstar. The rear seat will accommodate three adults. Chrysler's integrated child safety seat has a reclining back. An optional "Convert-a-Bed" package is available with the seven-passenger seating configuration. **Cargo space:** Plenty and practical. This is where the dual sliding doors come in handy. No longer do you have to walk around to the passenger side to load or unload cargo. Rear seatbacks fold down, and removing the centre and rear seats is a "snap," thanks to the addition of little wheels on the base of the rear seat. Snap them down and you can roll the seat anywhere. Lifting them is a chore, though. **Trunk/liftover:** Easy to load and unload 4x8-foot sheets of plywood thanks to the wide doors and low floor. Courtesy lights in front and on the liftgate are an added convenience. Interestingly, with the rear seat removed, the regular-sized Caravan provides more cargo space than the Grand Caravan. **Quietness:** Better than average, thanks to better body soundproofing with polyurethane foam injected into body cavities (watch those allergies).

Con: Controls and displays: Driver is faced with 44 switches, dials, and buttons on the dash/door panel/console. Centre console is way too low and console storage bin for small objects is sometimes hard to open and close, and the panel dimmer is hidden behind the steering wheel. Wipers obstruct forward vision. **Climate control:** AC and heater take a while to be felt. **Entry/exit:** Both sliding side doors are unwieldy to slide and it takes lots of effort to push the buttons that unlatch them. Rear hatch door is hard to close. **Interior space/comfort F/R:** Front seats lack sufficient lumbar support and the seatback comes up short against the shoulder blades. Tall drivers will find leg room a bit tight without an adequate left footrest. Three adults will find the third-row bench seat a bit cramped and the head restraints set too low. **Cargo space:** Storage space is squandered by an absence of door pouches; skimpy, poorly accessible storage compartments, like the tiny glove compartment; a lack of storage shelves; and coat hooks that can't support a hanger. Removable seats, which weigh 50 to 100 pounds, aren't as easy to remove as Chrysler would have you believe. **Quietness:** Some wind noise intrudes into the interior.

COST

List Price (very negotiable)	Residual Values (months)			
	24	**36**	**48**	**60**
Base Caravan: $24,885 (19%)	$17,000	$14,000	$12,000	$9,000
G. Caravan: $26,580 (20%)	$18,000	$15,000	$13,000	$10,000
Town & Country LXI:				
$41,730 (22%)	$27,000	$24,000	$21,000	$18,000

TECHNICAL DATA

Powertrain (front-drive)
Engines: 2.4L 4-cyl. (150 hp)
• 3.0L V6 (150 hp)
• 3.3L V6 (158 hp)
• 3.8L V6 (180 hp)
Transmissions: 3-speed auto.
• 4-speed auto.
Dimension/Capacity (base)
Passengers: 2/2/3
Height/length/width:
68.5/186.3/76.8 in.

Head room F: 39.8/R1: 40.1/R2: 38.1 in.
Leg room F: 41.2/R1: 36.6/R2: 35.8 in.
Wheelbase: 113.3 in.
Turning circle: 39.5 ft.
Cargo volume: 64 cu. ft.
GVWR: N/A
Payload: N/A
Tow limit: 2,000–3,500 lb.
Fuel tank: 76L/reg.
Weight: 3,985 lb.

SAFETY FEATURES/CRASHWORTHINESS

	Std.	Opt.
Anti-lock brakes (4W)	❏	■
Seatbelt pretensioners	❏	❏
Side airbags	❏	❏
Traction control	■	❏
Head restraints	**	*
Visibility (front/rear)	****	*****
Crash protection (front) D/P		
Caravan	***	***
G. Caravan	****	****
Town & Country	****	****
Crash protection (side) D/P		
G. Caravan	*****	***
Town & Country	*****	***
Crash protection (offset)	**	
HLDI injury claims (model)	***	
HLDI injury claims (all)	*****	

Note: Above data apply to only Caravan and Voyager, unless otherwise specified.

FORD

Ford has more variety in its vehicle lineup than any other automaker. Its vehicles appeal to buyers wanting inexpensive and reliable front-drive econoboxes like the Escort and Focus; those opting for imported and domestic front-drive mid-sized sedans and coupes; muscle car enthusiasts who want a rear-drive machine; and those wanting the comfort and power of traditional rear-drive luxury cars. It is also favoured by Jaguar aficionados and minivan drivers.

Ford's Excursion: just what we need, the mother of all SUVs riding our rear bumper!

The small Escort and large-sized Crown Victoria/Marquis have been particularly successful in fighting imports at both ends of the market while keeping Chrysler and GM on their toes. This is all the more ironic because the Escort is a knock-off of the Mazda 323/Protegé, and the rear-drive Crown Victoria/Marquis and Mustang are restyled 1970s products. The Taurus and Sable duo have also done well against Toyota's Camry, the Honda Accord, and Mazda's 626. But this isn't likely to last, now that Taurus reliability problems keep surfacing and the Camry, Accord, and 626 redesigns attract more buyers.

Ford has followed Daimler-Benz in showing an interest in Burnaby-based Ballard Power System's hydrogen fuel-cell engine, in an effort to produce a zero-emission car. The automaker plans to have a vehicle prototype equipped with the new engine within a year. Less environmentally friendly, however, is Ford's huge year 2000 Excursion sport-utility, an imposing new entry that's been dubbed a "Suburban Assault Vehicle" by environmentalists.

Warranty performance

Ford's warranty performance leaves much to be desired. Although the company has been more forthcoming in admitting its vehicles' failures and has stuck by its commitment to extend post-warranty "goodwill" to some owners to cover its own manufacturing errors, there are still many angry owners who have been denied refunds for defective 3.8L engines, transmissions, and paint jobs.

Taurus, Sable, and Windstar owners may be angry that their vehicles have been downgraded in this year's guide to Below Average, while Chrysler's minivans, faced with similar ongoing transmission failures, are given an Average rating. The ratings differ because Chrysler gives customers a second chance for warranty or post-warranty compensation once their initial claim has been refused. By-passing normal warranty channels, Chrysler's Warranty Review Committee provides an efficient customer relations infrastructure that judges complaints in a reasonably fair, rapid, and consistent manner.

Ford's customer relations, on the other hand, is contracted out to an independent firm. Additionally, this automaker has lost several top administrators during the past six months, throwing the customer relations department into a state of flux, where customer complaints go unanswered, inexcusably long delays for a response are frequent, and claims are routinely dismissed through the recitation of a prepared script.

Finally, Chrysler's powertrain problems are narrow in scope, involving mostly the automatic transmission. Some head gasket failures have begun popping up on 4-cylinder engines, but they're a relatively recent phenomenon. Meanwhile, Ford's engine and transmission deficiencies are broad based and have existed for over a decade.

When Ford of Canada eliminates these quality problems and sets up its own customer relations department that actually *relates* to customers, then its *Lemon-Aid* ratings will improve.

> Your Lemon-Aid 2000 Vans and Trucks has been a huge source of info and encouragement....My next step will probably be small claims court, but right now I'm enjoying my van HUGELY. It is still driveable, but I can't carry a load or go faster than 50 klicks. That's okay. The slower the better, although I'm sorry I can't take it on the highway.
>
> Ford has offered me a deal: (I'll pay) 25% of the cost of a new transmission. Their transmission. You know. The crappy kind. $3,200. I'm afraid this sucks badly, so I'm fighting back. Or so I think. A photo speaks a thousand words.
>
> Have gotten nowhere with Ford: talking with "Customer Assistance" is like running a marathon in chest deep water. The owner of the dealership promised to "get back to me in no more than three days".
>
> Three weeks later his brain went into dysfunctional overload trying to remember who the hell I even was.
>
> Anyway! The World Rowing Finals were in St. Catharines this last weekend. All that SLOW MOVING traffic and ALL DAY driving was exhausting!!! I could fill ten pages with the great reactions I got. Except for one lovely gentleman who set his face up like ten rat traps. Yesterday, when I drove into the dealer to pay my lease it was clear why...he works there. Reception all round was icy. Oooooh.
>
> O. K. So I'm having a little fun with Ford these days. Civility is a useless bargaining strategy...I plan on changing my captions once in a while. After all, I have to keep my public interested.
>
> S. M.
> St. Catharines, Ontario

In the above case, Ford eventually offered the owner a 90% refund.

I'll continue monitoring Ford's treatment of its customers this year through *Lemon-Aid* reader feedback and email reports. If I detect any change in its policies before next year's edition, I'll post the information on *www.lemonaidcars.com*.

Ford's quality control of mechanical and electronic components and body construction is still sub-par. Automatic transmission failures and chronic malfunctions apparently afflict the company's entire model line to such an extent that Chrysler and GM's transmission problems pale in comparison. Premature brake wear, noise, and brake failures are other areas where Ford needs immediate improvement and a more generous policy in handling customer complaints. The quality of body components also remains far below Japanese and European standards. Poor paint quality, a Ford problem for over a decade, was addressed in 1995 by a changeover in suppliers and the use of improved processes. Paint complaints have trailed off since then.

New products

This year will see the debut of a number of new vehicles running the gamut from the small Focus to the outrageously large, "in your face" Excursion sport-utility. Additionally, the Lincoln LS and F-150 SuperCrew pickup will be available for the first time. Taurus returns with a major redesign, the Escort lineup will be pared down to make way for the Focus, and the Expedition and Navigator will get minor body changes.

A number of slow-moving models like the Contour and the Contour SVT may no longer be sold in Canada at the start of the 2000 model year. Also, some more familiar Mercury nameplates will disappear (Mystique and Sable), as Ford further consolidates its distribution after keeping the Mountaineer out of the country and dropping the Villager last year. Only the Mercury Cougar and Grand Marquis will remain in Canada, but all Mercury models will continue to be sold in the States.

Incidentally, Ford Canada Mercury dealers are up in arms over their loss of product and have set up a lobbying association to protect their interests. They vow to petition the courts for an injunction to prevent Ford from jeopardizing their livelihood.

Important safety improvements, once found only on luxury vehicles, are working their way down to Ford's popular mid-sized family sedans. The 2000 Taurus, for example, will have "thinking" seatbelts and airbags that come in two parts to protect head and shoulders and upper torso separately.

Focus

Focus

RATING: Not Recommended during its first year on the market. Ford's first-year models (Escort, Taurus, Contour, and Windstar, for example) have proven to be particularly troublesome.

OVERVIEW: Hailed as Europe's 1999 Car of the Year, Ford's sleek Focus comes to North America this November as an uplevel, premium small car, positioning itself between the entry level four-door Escort and

Contour. Passenger comfort has been enhanced with the high roofline, raised seating position, and tall, wide doors. Two inches taller and almost seven inches longer than the Escort, and embodying Ford's "new edge" styling (read less aero, more creases), are three body styles: a two-door hatchback in sporty ZX3 trim; LX, SE, and upscale ZTS four-door sedans; and a four-door SE wagon. The Escort's base engine, a 107-hp 2.0L four, is carried over to the Focus LX and SE, while the 130-hp twin-cam 2.0L (also used on the Escort ZX2 coupe), is standard on the ZTS and ZX3 and optional on the SE. Either engine can be hooked to a manual or an optional 4-speed automatic transmission. Safety features include standard head/chest front airbags, optional side airbags, optional anti-lock brakes (standard only on the ZTS), and rear child safety seat anchors.

Cost analysis/best alternatives: Prices were not available at press time—however, they are expected to be in the $16,000–$19,000 range. Any '99 or year 2000 Ford Escort variation should be discounted up to $2,000 to make room for the Focus and the '99 Contour and Mystique—two upscale European compacts that perform quite well and may be discounted by as much as $2,500. Other viable alternatives include this or last year's GM Cavalier and Sunfire or Hyundai Accent, accompanied by $1,000–$1,500 rebates early in the year 2000.

Cougar

Cougar

RATING: Average, for what is essentially a Contour spin-off. **Strong points:** Attractive styling and pleasant handling. **Weak points:** So-so acceleration, problematic transmission performance, a four-seater with a narrow, claustrophobic interior, too many decontented standard features, an ugly and superfluous trunklid spoiler, and excessive interior noise.

NEW FOR 2000: A carried over model.

OVERVIEW: Part Contour and part Probe, the 2000 Cougar, like the Contour and Mystique, is based on the European Mondeo sedan and is built at the Mazda-run Auto Alliance plant in Flat Rock, Michigan, once home to the Probe, MX-6, and 626. The redesigned front-drive Cougar, restyled as a hatchback, is priced (including PDI and freight) at $20,595 for the base version, equipped with a 16-valve, 125-hp 2.0L inline-four and $22,635 for a better equipped model carrying a 24-valve, 170-hp 2.5L V6. ABS and side airbags are optional.

Although the Cougar shares the Contour's chassis (with an inch added), base 4-banger, and V6, its suspension and steering are much tighter than what's found on the Contour. The firm suspension and quick, responsive steering make the Cougar both nimble and stable when cornering under speed (especially with the optional Sport Group's wider tires) as long as it's not pushed very hard. Comfortable seatbacks and a split-fold rear seatback make cargo hauling a breeze. Headlight illumination is impressive and braking is quite good with little fading after successive stops.

On the minus side, acceleration is only so-so with either engine and they both run roughly. The automatic transmission tends to "hunt" the proper gear when going over hilly terrain and there's no way to lock out Overdrive in fourth gear. The 5-speed hooked to the V6 also shifted roughly. The base suspension doesn't absorb bumps very well and the optional Sports Group tires produce a busy, jostling ride on any surface that's less than perfect. Steering is a bit heavy in city traffic.

The interior feels narrow and small—the Accord gives a much roomier impression. Short front seat cushions don't give enough thigh support, rear seating is cramped and uncomfortable, and rear-seat access still takes some acrobatic prowess. The tacky-looking cabin houses an overstyled dashboard with controls that are confusing and cheap-looking, the radio is mounted too low and uses small buttons that are the antithesis of user-friendly, and the silly, non-functional rear spoiler is both distracting and cuts rearward vision. There is excessive road rumble and exhaust noise and a few reports of annoying body squeaks and groans. Cargo loading is made difficult by the high liftover.

Rather than raise prices, Ford has reduced content, making optional equipment that should be standard. This includes AC (standard in the States), ABS ($731 extra; standard with the Cavalier and Sunfire), and side airbags ($500 more). **Best alternatives:** Acura CL; GM Cavalier, Sunfire; Dodge Avenger; Honda Accord, Civic, or Prelude; Mazda's 626; or the Toyota Corolla or Camry.

Lincoln LS

RISKY BUY

Lincoln LS

RATING: Not Recommended during its second year on the market. It will take the more expensive V8 LS version to deliver only *some* of the performance of its competitors. In the meantime, stay away from the LS until it overcomes the performance gap and works out the inevitable growing pains (as in defects, inadequate parts supply, and servicing learning curve).

OVERVIEW: Lincoln's $40,595 LS rear-drive sedan comes with a high-performance 200-hp variant of the Taurus 3.0L V6 mated to an optional manual or a standard automatic gearbox. Also available: a 250-hp 3.9L V8 based on the Jaguar XK8 coupe coupled to a semi-automatic transmission. Both engines are identical but produce 30 less horses than the Jag equivalent. The V8 is the engine of choice for moving the LS—however, it falls short of the competition when measured against the 20–40 additional horsepower delivered by competitors' V8s. The V6's performance, on the other hand, is seriously compromised by the Lincoln's heft and turns in 0–100 km/h times that are one to two seconds slower than V6 competitors.

The 5-speed automatic shifts slowly, not as decisively as competitors' gearboxes, and far less smoothly than Lexus drivetrains. A manual transmission (first one since 1951) is available only with the V6-equipped LS. The LS is roomier than both the Bimmer and Mercedes E-Class and a bit longer and taller than the Jaguar S-type. Suspension provides a soft ride and is not as sporty as the competition. Steering is also not as responsive as European and Japanese luxury vehicles. Traction control is optional on the V6 version and standard on the V8. An optional sports package includes thicker anti-roll bars, upgraded brake pads, recalibrated variable-ratio steering, an automanual shifter (if ordered with an automatic), body coloured bumper trim, a full-sized spare, and bigger wheels and tires. **Best alternatives:** Pricing is where the LS excels. The V6 version is priced in the BMW 3 Series, Lexus ES 300, and Mercedes C-Class territory while delivering standard equipment and interior space that rivals the 5 series, GS, and E-Class.

Escort

RATING: Above Average. Ideal for both city and highway use. **Strong points:** Comfortable ride, easy handling, good fuel economy, and excellent reliability. **Weak points:** Slow throttle response, some gear hunting when going uphill, mediocre braking, insufficient front leg room, and only average crash protection. The ZX2 has less cargo space and more difficult rear-seat access due to its sportier styling.

NEW FOR 2000: Escorts return without any significant changes and will remain in the model lineup, minus the two-door wagon and Mercury Tracer, until Ford decides to discontinue the model entirely.

OVERVIEW: Ford's top-selling compacts, the Escort and Tracer underwent significant changes three years ago, making them more attractive and smoother-riding, and giving them better handling. Their latest redesign brings them closer to Ford than ever before. Ford is now responsible for interior and exterior features, the standard 2.0L engine, and the fuel-injection and ignition systems. Escorts for '99 come in three body styles: the similarly equipped sedan and wagon, and a racier-styled, high-performance coupe called the ZX2. Year 2000 models only come as four-door sedans.

Cost analysis/best alternatives: This is your chance to get a real bargain if you buy a discounted '99 Escort or Tracer. There's ample supply and both cars should be discounted 10 percent or more, before rebates kick in. You may also wish to consider the Honda Civic, Mazda Protegé, and Toyota Corolla, but they're unlikely to be eligible for rebates and discounts will be minimal. **Options:** A rear wiper for wagons. Think twice about getting AC—the base engine may not be powerful enough to handle the extra load. Also, considering the limited head room, a sunroof isn't advisable. One optional keyless entry system only locks the driver's door; get a unit that activates both doors. **Rebates:** Look for $1,000–$2,000 rebates early in the year 2000. **Delivery/PDI:** $450. **Depreciation:** Slower than average. **Insurance cost:** Average. **Parts supply/cost:** Parts are easily found, but the CAA says they may cost more than average. Don't worry about finding parts once the Escort is discontinued; so many units have been sold over the past decade that there's a huge supply of parts available. Comparison-shop independent suppliers for the best prices. **Annual maintenance cost:** Below average. **Warranty:** Bumper-to-bumper 3 years/60,000 km; rust perforation 5 years/unlimited km. **Supplementary warranty:** Save your money, it's not needed. **Highway/city fuel economy:** 6–9L/100 km with the base 2.0L engine. The ZX2's high-performance engine only burns about 20 more litres per year than the base powerplant. **Annual fuel cost:** 1,588L=$921.

Quality/Reliability/Safety

Pro: Quality control: Escorts have been recommended since 1991 for their overall reliability, good road manners, and spaciousness. The 2.0L 130-hp ZX2's engine is borrowed from the Contour and has been quite dependable so far. Increased body rigidity means that doors, windows, trunks, hoods, and body panels fit together better, there's minimal body flexing, and most wind and road noise is muted fairly successfully. **Reliability:** Above average. **Warranty performance:** Ford customer relations staffers are generally fair and efficient in handling warranty claims. Insiders tell me that there aren't many Escort warranty claims.

Con: Owner-reported problems: Premature front brake wear, excessive interior noise, minor fuel injection glitches, and electrical shorts leading to hard starts and stalling. **Service bulletin problems:** Cause and correction of vinyl dash abrasions and premature wear; exhaust system "buzzing" or "rattling" (a problem for almost a decade); fuel fill nozzle clicks off too soon when fueling up; positive crankcase ventilation (PCV) freezes up; inoperative CD player; tips on properly adjusting the transmission range sensor. **NHTSA safety complaints/safety:** Fire in the engine compartment (fire officials blame the fuse box); faulty steering wheel assembly; inadvertent airbag deployment; airbags deployed during a minor "fender-bender" collision; airbag deployed and started smoldering; sudden acceleration; chronic engine stalling while parked, cruising down the highway, during rainy weather, or when going uphill; hard starts; brake failure; ABS failure; driver-side seatbelt buckle failure; defective child safety seat harness strap; defective engine mounts cause excessive vibration; faulty air conditioner; poor headlight illumination; horn doesn't operate properly; premature tire wear.

Road Performance

Pro: The ZX2's 0–100 km/h acceleration time of 7.9 seconds is impressive, and there's plenty of bottom-end torque for hill climbing. **Emergency handling:** Better than average. The re-tuned suspension makes for a firmer, more controlled ride with less oversteer. **Steering:** Precise, with lots of road feel. **Routine handling:** Very good. Overall handling and braking have been given a boost with a lighter, more responsive power steering unit, stronger front disc brakes, larger rear drums, and bigger, 14-inch wheels.

Con: Acceleration/torque: Mediocre acceleration with the manual transmission (0–100 km/h: 10.9 sec.) is much worse with the automatic. The engine stumbles and hesitates at idle with the AC system on and the throttle often takes several seconds to close when you take your foot off the pedal to downshift. **Transmission:** Hill climbing leads to annoying gear hunting. **Braking:** Unacceptably long stopping distances (100–0 km/h: 140 ft.) mandate the choice of optional ABS.

Comfort/Convenience

Pro: The sedan and wagon have rounded features similar to the Taurus design; the ZX2's styling resembles Hyundai's Tiburon. **Driving position:** Good, if you don't mind your leg rubbing against the centre console. **Climate control:** Quiet, efficient heating and ventilation system uses four large dash vents to control the temperature. **Entry/exit:** Not difficult. **Interior space/comfort F/R:** The interior isn't expansive, but it's adequate. The wagon borrows the most from Mazda and is the practical choice for interior room. Comfortable front seats with plenty of front leg room. **Cargo space:** Plenty of small storage areas. **Trunk/liftover:** Reasonably sized trunk.

Con: Standard equipment: Just the basics. GT styling is a yawner and the spoiler is out of place on this econobox. **Controls and displays:** Confusing climate control layout forces you to take your eyes off the road. Radio is hard to tune because of small buttons and a long reach. Rear leg room could be better, and three rear passengers will have a tight fit. The doorstops often don't prevent the door from closing. The wagon's raised sill makes cargo loading difficult. The ZX2's trunk has 8 percent less space than the Escort sedan. **Quietness:** Excessive engine noise.

COST				
List Price (very negotiable)	**Residual Values** (months)			
	24	**36**	**48**	**60**
Escort LX: $17,895 (13%)	$12,000	$10,500	$9,000	$7,500
Note: Price includes PDI, freight.				

TECHNICAL DATA

Powertrain (front-drive)
Engines: 2.0L 4-cyl. (110 hp)
• 2.0L 4-cyl. (130 hp)
Transmissions: 5-speed man.
• 4-speed auto.
Dimensions/Capacity (LX)
Passengers: 5
Height/length/width:
53.3/174.7/67 in.

Head room F/R: 39/36.7 in.
Leg room F/R: 42.5/34 in.
Wheelbase: 98 in.
Turning circle: 35.4 ft.
Cargo volume: 12.8 cu. ft.
Tow limit: N/A
Fuel tank: 48L/reg.
Weight: 2,450 lb.

SAFETY FEATURES/CRASHWORTHINESS

	Std.	Opt.
Anti-lock brakes	❑	■
Seatbelt pretensioners	—	—
Side airbags	—	—
Traction control	—	—
Head restraints	*	*
Visibility (front/rear)	*****	*****
Crash protection (front) D/P	***	****
Crash protection (side) D/P	***	***
Crash protection (offset)	***	
HLDI injury claims (model)	***	
HLDI injury claims (all)	**	

'99 Contour, '99 Mystique

Contour

RATING: Average. Once these cars are taken off the market their deficiencies will be amplified and Ford won't care about maintaining owner loyalty with generous post-warranty payouts (remember the Merkur?). **Strong points:** The main advantages of the Contour and Mystique are exceptional handling, a smooth ride, and a powerful, limited-maintenance V6 engine. **Weak points:** An anemic 4-banger, erratic automatic gear shifting, cramped rear seating, and difficult entry/exit.

NEW FOR 2000: Both year 2000 models have been dropped in Canada because they're slow sellers—and also because Ford's closing down its Mercury dealerships and cutting back its Mercury nameplates.

OVERVIEW: These front-drive, mid-sized twin sedans are based on the European-designed Mondeo, which has met with respectable sales after many years on the market. The four-door, five-passenger Contour sells for a bit less than its practically identical Mercury counterpart.

Both vehicles are set on a wheelbase that's slightly larger than the Taurus' and come with two engines and transmissions: a base 16-valve 125-hp 2.0L 4-cylinder, and an optional 24-valve 170-hp 2.5L V6. Either engine can be hooked to a standard 5-speed transaxle or an optional 4-speed automatic. A smooth but firm ride and crisp handling are guaranteed by the standard MacPherson strut front suspension, an anti-roll bar, and fully independent rear suspension.

Other interesting standard features include dual airbags, adjustable head restraints, 60/40 split-fold rear seats, rear heater ducts, and a sophisticated air filtration system for the passenger compartment. Four-wheel disc brakes, a sport-tuned suspension, and high-performance tires are standard features on the V6.

Cost analysis/best alternatives: There are plenty of unsold '99s available; only consider buying one if you can live with the deficiencies noted in this report and the price is cut by at least 15 percent, plus rebates. Marketed to fit between the compact Escort and Tracer and the larger mid-sized Taurus and Sable, their high manufacturer's suggested retail price (MSRP) have put both vehicles far beyond the budget of former Tempo/Topaz owners (whose cars they replaced). Mazda's 626 is a worthwhile alternative to the Contour and Mystique. It's a more stylish, highway-proven sedan with better-than-average reliability and excellent parts supply, and also gets many improvements this year. Other vehicles worth considering include the Nissan Altima, Honda Accord, Toyota Camry, and the '99 Oldsmobile Cutlass (its last year). Be wary of the Chrysler Cirrus: it's roomier and more stylish, but much less reliable. **Options:** The V6 engine—but, if you want better fuel economy, stay with the standard 5-speed transmission. **Rebates:** $1,000–$2,000 by mid-summer. The longer you wait to buy, the greater your chances of snaring a car that's eligible for both a rebate and dealer incentive bonus. **Delivery/PDI:** $375. **Depreciation:** Higher than average. **Insurance cost:** Higher than average. **Parts supply/cost:** Average cost, and not hard to find, so far. Because so many newer products are using generic Contour parts, it's unlikely that mechanical and electronic components will ever be in short supply. Body parts may be more problematic, however. **Annual maintenance cost:** Average. **Warranty:** Bumper-to-bumper 3 years/60,000 km; rust perforation 5 years/unlimited km. **Supplementary**

warranty: A good idea because of the Contour's British heritage and the fact that fewer will be around to service. **Highway/city fuel economy:** 2.0L: 7.1–10.4L/100 km; 2.5L: 7.7–11.9L/100 km. **Annual fuel cost:** 2.0L: 1,783L=$1,034; 2.5L: 2,002L=$1,161.

Quality/Reliability/Safety

Pro: Quality control: Better than average. Ford promises that its new Duratec V6 engine won't require a tune-up before 160,000 km. So far they've kept their word. **Reliability:** Computer glitches and powertrain malfunctions causing stalling and hard starts. **Warranty performance:** Very good, but keep your fingers crossed.

Con: Owner-reported problems: AC and computer module failures, powertrain problems, and unsatisfactory repairs by mechanics who seem unfamiliar with the car. Other, more specific problems are listed on the Contour/Mystique website *(www.contour.org/FAQ/)*. **Service bulletin problems:** Detonation, stalling, exhaust sulfur odour; corrective measures for stalling caused by an overly lean fuel mixture; engine coolant leaks; automatic transmission won't engage forward gears; broken PRNDL indicator; fuel gauge won't read below 1/4 full tank; replacement of the steering column gap hider; engine compartment hooting or moosing noise with AC on; exhaust system "buzzing" or "rattling"; dash and door trim panels may wear out prematurely; left AC vent may be too warm. **NHTSA safety complaints/safety:** Sudden loss of all electrical power while on the highway; headlight illumination inadequate for night driving; airbags failed to deploy; airbag warning light goes on for no reason; passenger and driver seatbelt broke when vehicle was rear-ended; front seatbelt retractors constantly jam; excessive brake wear and noise; premature brake pad replacement.

Road Performance

Pro: Emergency handling: Although traction control is available, the car's front-drive configuration gives good traction on slippery roads without the option. **Steering:** Power steering is quick and precise. **Acceleration/torque:** The base 4-cylinder engine is quiet and smooth-running; acceptable for urban use. Ford's 2.5L dual overhead cam 24-valve Duratec V6 is also reasonably quiet and smooth, and gives plenty of power without hesitation at low and moderate engine speeds (0–100 km/h: 8.8 sec.). **Transmission:** Very smooth and quiet over even terrain. Superb ride and handling qualities. Gear ratios in the 4-speed electronically controlled automatic transmission are well matched to the engine's output. **Routine handling:** Even with an automatic transmission, the Contour slices through corners with limited body roll and excellent control. **Braking:** Braking is acceptable (100–0 km/h: 130 ft.).

Con: The base 4-cylinder engine is a yawner that isn't suited for passing or hilly terrain, particularly when hooked to the automatic transmission, as the following Contour owner discovered: "The trip was a white-knuckler all the way. Foot on the gas, pushing through the firewall, engine wheezing like crazy. Old VW Westphalias went by like we were standing still. The thing was so slow it was scary!" Poorly timed transmission upshifts when traversing hilly terrain.

Comfort/Convenience

Pro: Standard equipment: Well-appointed with lots of standard features. **Driving position:** Very good. The Contour's front seats are first rate, even in the least expensive GL. Along with the more luxuriously upholstered seats in the Mystique, they're the best in their class. Plenty of front seat room for a six-footer. **Controls and displays:** The instrument panel is well laid out—a high-mounted coin bin is a thoughtful touch. **Climate control:** Efficient and easy to adjust. **Cargo space:** Better than average. **Trunk/liftover:** Surprisingly spacious trunk is easy to load.

Con: Entry/exit: Difficult rear seat access. **Interior space/comfort F/R:** Door panels limit leg room. Sport seat bolsters are a bit too snug. The rear seat is inadequate—even with the extra inch added last year. The Mazda Protegé has more rear-seat leg room than the Contour. The heads of tall passengers will hit the headliner/roof where it meets the steeply sloped back window, and despite this year's redesign, rear leg room is still insufficient. Power-window switches are awkward to use and the radio controls are tiny push buttons requiring the driver's full attention, plus a steady hand, to operate when the car is moving. Slow-operating power door locks. **Quietness:** Lots of road noise.

COST

List Price (very negotiable)	Residual Values (months)			
	24	36	48	60
Contour LX: $18,335 (18%)	$13,000	$11,000	$9,500	$8,000
Contour SVT: $28,935 (19%)	$18,000	$16,000	$14,000	$12,000
Note: Price includes PDI, freight.				

TECHNICAL DATA

Powertrain (front-drive)
Engines: 2.0L 4-cyl. (125 hp)
• 2.5L V6 (170 hp)
Transmissions: 5-speed man.
• 4-speed auto.
Dimensions/Capacity
Passengers: 5
Height/length/width:
54.5/183.9/69.1 in.

Head room F/R: 39/36.7 in.
Leg room F/R: 42.9/35.9 in.
Wheelbase: 106.5 in.
Turning circle: 35.4 ft.
Cargo volume: 13.9 cu. ft.
Tow limit: 2,000 lb.
Fuel tank: 55L/reg.
Weight: 2,750 lb.

SAFETY FEATURES/CRASHWORTHINESS		
	Std.	**Opt.**
Anti-lock brakes	❏	■
Seatbelt pretensioners	—	—
Side airbags	—	—
Traction control	❏	■
Head restraints	**	*
Visibility (front/rear)	*****	*****
Crash protection (front) D/P	*****	****
Crash protection (side) D/P	***	****
Crash protection (offset)	*	
HLDI injury claims (model)	***	
HLDI injury claims (all)	***	

Mustang

Mustang

RATING: Recommended. **Strong points:** Fast acceleration, impressive handling, braking, and resale value. Better than average crashworthiness and overall reliability. **Weak points:** Insufficient rear seat room, limited cargo space, fishtails easily when accelerating upon a wet surface or cornering under moderate speed.

NEW FOR 2000: Re-skinned and re-engineered last year, this year's Mustang is a carried-over model without any significant changes. It will be redesigned and given a new platform sometime in 2002.

OVERVIEW: While GM seriously considers dropping its sporty Camaro, Ford has renewed its commitment to the Mustang through a "retro" restyling, using sharp exterior creases that hearken back to the pony car's early years. Last year the Mustang's length and width were increased by almost two inches. The car also got a 40-hp boost to its 3.8L V6 (also used in the Taurus and Windstar) and 25 extra horses to its

4.6L V8 engine. Optional all-speed traction control is also available. A new Cobra with independent rear suspension made its debut in mid-'99.

The Mustang carries a base 3.8L V6 and offers an optional 4.6L V8 along with a high performance, limited-edition Cobra variation that delivers 60 more horses than the stock 4.6L V8. The single and twin cam V8 options make the Mustang a powerful street machine that has far more brawn than finesse (one of its failings when compared with its GM rivals). V6 models are an acceptable compromise, even though the engine fails to deliver the gobs of power expected of a Mustang by most performance enthusiasts. Base models come equipped with a host of luxury and convenience items. Furthermore, the price is hard to beat, and resale value stays relatively high through the fifth year of ownership.

This is definitely not a family car. But for those who want a sturdy and stylish second car, or who don't need room in the back or standard ABS, the Mustang is a less risky buy than most of the Big Three sports cars.

Cost analysis/best alternatives: Get a '99 model for the discounting in the $1,000–$2,000 range on V6-equipped versions. Discounts are rare on the GT and convertible versions. Other cars worth considering are the GM Camaro/Firebird (ample stock of '99s available), and Toyota Celica. **Options:** Traction control, considering this rear-drive's tendency to "spin out" when pushed, and an anti-theft system that includes an engine immobilizer. **Rebates:** $500 rebates to clear out 1999 V6-equipped leftovers. **Delivery/PDI:** $400. **Depreciation:** Much slower than average. **Insurance cost:** Way higher than average. **Parts supply/cost:** Inexpensive and easily found among independent suppliers. **Annual maintenance cost:** Lower than average. Any mechanic is able to fix a Mustang. **Warranty:** Bumper-to-bumper 3 years/60,000 km; rust perforation 5 years/ unlimited km. **Supplementary warranty:** Not necessary, put your money into making the car safe from thieves. **Highway/city fuel economy:** 7–12L/100 km with the 3.8L; 9–14.5L/100 km with the 4.6L. **Annual fuel cost:** 3.8L: 1,998L=$1,159; 4.6L: 2,322L=$1,347. Imagine, less than $200 more in fuel costs for the V8-equipped version. You'll save more than that through the GT's slow depreciation.

Quality/Reliability/Safety

Pro: Quality control: Better than average. The Mustang's repair history has improved greatly and this is likely to continue with the 2000 models, which use parts improved upon from previous years. **Reliability:** Very good. The engines and transmissions are durable, as are most other components. Body assembly has improved of late, with fewer rattles and a more solid feeling. **Warranty performance:** Much improved; few warranty complaints.

Con: Owner-reported problems: The front suspension, brakes, and steering components remain the only consistent weak spots. The engine computer can be temperamental, and electrical problems are common. Keep an eye on the 3.8L engine: head gasket failures may be in the offing. Assembly quality is not up to the level of Japanese vehicles. **Service bulletin problems:** Automatic transmission fluid leak near the radiator; faulty key fob transmitter; premature wearout of some vinyl-covered items like dash cover and door panels; exhaust system "buzzing" or "rattling." **NHTSA safety complaints/safety:** Sudden acceleration; sudden loss of steering when making a left hand turn; car left on an incline with transmission in Park and motor shut off rolled down after 10 minutes and hit a tree; airbags failed to deploy in a frontal collision; emergency brake ratchet assembly broke, making mechanism inoperable; gas spills out of fuel tank due to clams not sufficiently tightened; left front wheel fell off when the lower control arm and ball joint became loose; defective transmission spider gear; seat ratchet assembly teeth broke; chronic stalling; engine produces an annoying "harmonic vibration." A light rear end makes the car dangerously unstable on wet roads or when cornering at moderate speeds.

Road Performance

Pro: Emergency handling: Slow but predictable. **Steering:** Quick and responsive. **Acceleration/torque:** The V8 provides very quick acceleration and smooth power delivery (0–100 km/h: 7.1 sec.), while the V6 performs fairly well with the automatic 4-speed transmission. **Transmission:** The clutch is reasonably smooth and the automatic shifts reasonably well most of the time. **Routine handling:** Models equipped with the sport suspension (which includes larger tires) provide sure and predictable handling on dry roads. The upgraded base suspension also makes the car more stable and controllable on most roads. **Braking:** Excellent braking performance for a car this heavy (100–0 km/h: 123 ft.).

Con: The 3.8L V6 is rough and noisy when pushed. The V8s are a bit too powerful for the amount of traction available to the rear wheels, making for lots of wheelspin and instability on slippery surfaces. The manual transmission is notchy at times and the automatic sometimes hesitates between gears. The rear end tends to slip out under hard cornering. The GT rides harshly on rough roads. These cars are a bit clumsy around town because of a wide turning circle.

Comfort/Convenience

Pro: Standard equipment: Even the base Mustangs come well equipped with lots of standard features. **Driving position:** Excellent, with plenty of head and leg room for tall drivers. **Controls and displays:** First class. Complete and well laid-out dual-cowl dashboard and controls. **Climate control:** Efficient, easy to adjust, and quiet. **Interior space/comfort F/R:** Comfortable front seats on all models. **Cargo space:** The split folding rear seat frees up much-needed trunk storage space. Easy loading, thanks to the low liftover. **Quietness:** Improved body rigidity has reduced interior noise somewhat.

Con: Rear visibility is obstructed by the roof pillars and high parcel shelf. Front seats need at least an inch more travel, and the rear seat is best left to children, especially with the convertible version. **Entry/exit:** The wide doors make for clumsy entry and exit in tight spots. GT ride comfort is below average. **Trunk/liftover:** Very shallow trunk with a small opening. Low liftover.

COST

List Price (negotiable)	Residual Values (months)			
	24	**36**	**48**	**60**
Mustang: $20,995 (18%)	$17,000	$14,000	$11,000	$9,000
Cvt.: $24,995 (20%)	$19,000	$16,000	$14,000	$12,000
GT: $29,995 (21%)	$21,000	$18,000	$16,000	$14,000
Cvt.: $33,000 (22%)	$23,000	$20,000	$18,000	$16,000

Note: Price includes PDI, freight.

TECHNICAL DATA

Powertrain (front-drive)
Engines: 3.8L V6 (190 hp)
• 4.6L V8 (260 hp)
• 4.6L V8 (320 hp)
Transmissions: 5-speed man.
• 4-speed auto.
Dimensions/Capacity
Passengers: 4
Height/length/width:
53.4/181.5/71.8 in.

Head room F/R: 38.2/35.9 in.
Leg room F/R: 42.9/31.3 in.
Wheelbase: 101.3 in.
Turning circle: 35.4 ft.
Cargo volume: 10.3 cu. ft.
Tow limit: 1,000 lb.
Fuel tank: 58L/reg.
Weight: 3,300 lb.

SAFETY FEATURES/CRASHWORTHINESS

	Std.	Opt.
Anti-lock brakes	❑	■
Seatbelt pretensioners	—	—
Side airbags	—	—
Traction control	—	■
Head restraints	*	*
Visibility (front/rear)	*****	**
Crash protection (front) D/P	****	****
Convertible	*****	*****
Crash protection (side) D/P	***	***
Crash protection (offset)	N/A	
HLDI injury claims (model)	***	
HLDI injury claims (all)	**	

Taurus, '99 Sable

RISKY BUY

Taurus

RATING: Below Average. Maybe this year's redesign will improve reliability, maybe it won't. The additional safety features and restyling this year are a nice touch but they fail to convince me that this car's horrendously poor reliability record won't continue. Best bet: buy only with an extended bumper-to-bumper warranty and trade in at the five-year mark—just before the extended warranty expires. **Strong points:** Quiet running, good handling, comfortable ride, better than average crash protection, and bargain prices (we know why). **Weak points:** Insufficient storage space, limited rear head room and access, and serious mechanical and body deficiencies.

NEW FOR 2000: Restyled and important safety improvements, once found only on luxury vehicles, will be available on the new Taurus. The Sable will be phased out in Canada as Mercury dealers are shut down.

OVERVIEW: Despite its deficiencies, the Taurus and Sable are Ford's most popular family cars due to their attractive combination of safety, performance, handling, and comfort. The base 3.0L Vulcan V6 is adequate, though dated, and the high-performing 24-valve V6 provides plenty of power for most driving needs. Other nice standard features include heated outside mirrors, a 60/40 split-fold rear seatback for additional cargo space, a driver's foot rest, and reserve power to operate the power windows and moon roof after the engine is shut off.

The SHO high-performance version returns this year with a 3.4L, 32-valve V8 engine. It delivers sparkling performance and sports car handling—at a price. Acceleration rivals the Mustang GT with a top speed of over 225 km/h, and it comes with an automatic transmission.

Cost analysis/best alternatives: Get the 2000 model for the safety upgrades, and hopefully more durable mechanical and body components. A '99 version discounted by $2,000–$3,000 could be a false bargain for the following reasons: you'll miss out on important new safety features; the extra year's depreciation will take over five years to amortize; and once you get to that fifth year, you're risking expensive powertrain, AC, brake, computer, suspension, and body repairs. Wagons are competent performers, but they're outclassed by some imports and most minivans as far as reliability and overall performance are concerned. The SHO has become a cult car for high-performance fans and its slow depreciation reflects this fact; bargains are hard to find, except on those cars that have been beaten up. Other sedans worth considering are the Honda Accord, Mazda 626, Toyota Camry, and Volvo S70. Wagons worth considering are the Honda Accord EX, Subaru Legacy, Toyota Camry LE V6, and Volvo 940/V90. **Options:** Expect to spend about $300 more for the flexible-fuel Taurus (ethanol or methanol), currently sold only to fleets. The automatic climate control system, a rear integrated child safety seat, power seats, and a heavy-duty suspension are wise choices. Get the optional DOHC V6 variation, but tell the dealer to forget the wagon's uncomfortable rear-facing third seat. Don't buy the optional leather seats, either; they're slippery and not all that durable. The digital instrumentation is another useless option; it's gimmicky and distracting. On the other hand, Ford's optional InstaClear windshield is a boon in Canadian winters. **Rebates:** As the Toyota Camry and Honda Accord eat into Ford's sales and stock continues to pile up in dealers' lots, generous dealer incentives and customer rebates will start kicking in before the year is up. Expect at least $2,000 rebates on the '99s. **Delivery/PDI:** $375. **Depreciation:** Higher than average. **Insurance cost:** Higher than average. **Parts supply/cost:** Parts are easily found, and they are reasonably priced. **Annual maintenance cost:** Average to higher than average as the vehicle ages. **Warranty:** Bumper-to-bumper 3 years/60,000 km; rust perforation 5 years/unlimited km. **Supplementary warranty:** A wise investment, particularly when you replace the AC, automatic transmission, or fuel pump around the fifth year of use. **Highway/city fuel economy:** 7.7–12L/100 km with the 3.0L; 8.5–14.5L/100 km with the SHO V8. **Annual fuel cost:** 3.0L: 2,013L=$1,168; SHO V8: 2,360L=$1,369. Imagine, only $201 more for V8 power!

Quality/Reliability/Safety

Pro: Reliability: The SHO engine has been particularly reliable.

Con: Quality control: Below average for an American car. Ford promises that many of its quality problems have been corrected with this latest redesign. I'm not a believer; I was told the same story when the car was reworked for 1996, and factory-related defects remained practically unchanged. Paint and body assembly is sub-par and body squeaks and rattles are omnipresent. **Reliability:** Mediocre long-term reliability, highlighted by an automatic transmission that Ford apparently still can't build to last or even shift properly. **Warranty performance:** Below average to average. Ford has improved its handling of engine and automatic transmission post-warranty claims during the past year, after *Lemon-Aid* blasted the company both publicly and in private meetings with Ford executives. Nevertheless, the safety risk, outrageously expensive repair costs, and chronic inconvenience and anxiety that these defects create cannot be imagined or easily assuaged merely with "goodwill" reimbursements, as the following July 1999 letter I received from a Toronto owner of a '93 Taurus clearly shows:

Ford Motor Company of Canada
July 9, 1999

To whom it may concern:

I have received your recall notice: Number 98S15—Spring Shield. I have a number of concerns about this recall. I have already had my Ford Taurus fall onto the highway as I was driving at the maximum speed on the Gardiner Expressway in Toronto. After regaining control of the car and narrowly avoiding a semi-trailer, I managed to scrape my way across the highway to pull over under the bridge at Jamieson: a very dangerous spot. There, I was told by a tow truck driver that he could not tow me as the car was almost flat on the ground and he was unable to get his gear underneath it.

I would like the following concerns addressed before I take my car into a dealer:
• the car has already fallen onto the highway once. In the process, the front tire was destroyed...when the left front spring broke and the other tires were prematurely worn, despite hundreds of dollars worth of alignments and wheel balancing. This wear problem was corrected when I took the *Lemon-Aid Used Car Guide* to the dealer and pointed to the bullet indicating I needed a rear suspension adjustable camber kit. I assume that this kit should have been free, yet the dealer charged me $387. By the way, I'm told that breaking *rear* springs is now a common problem.
• the cooling system continually malfunctions. I can't count the number of times the car has overheated. Including on my way to the airport with my children to go on vacation. This breakdown alone cost $250 *just in cab fare*. I've had more than a thousand dollars worth of work done to correct this problem. The car still runs hot, but at least it doesn't spontaneously redline anymore.
• unfortunately the car now decides to stop running every once in awhile. It's fun to stop at the side of the 403, returning from a camping trip with your children, in 90 degree heat, waiting for the car to decide it's ready to continue the trip. This makes taking the car to the airport a tense situation. I'm told "this is a common Ford problem."
• should I mention the air conditioning has cost me almost a thousand dollars over the last two years?
• the car vibrates excessively at speeds over 100 km/hour. I've given up on this. The left rear window no longer works either, but I can't afford to spend money on non-essentials.

I had a previous (yes, another) problem where my light switch caught on fire as I was driving along the 401 near Napanee. It was minor and I had it fixed in Ottawa for something like $100–$150. Later, I received a recall for this defect that told me I could get a refund by taking the receipt into one of your dealerships. I took the receipt to my dealership, but never received the refund. I assume the Ford dealer needed the money more than I did.

Sincerely,

J.W.
Toronto

Owner-reported problems: Automatic transmission, AC, electrical system (lots of blown fuses), steering, fuel system, fuel pumps, front suspension, and ignition problems are frequently reported on these cars. There have been lots of complaints concerning paint delamination (fading, chalking, and peeling) and, surprisingly, premature rusting along the door edges, handles, taillight housings, deck lid, and inside hood area, as this photo of a three-year-old Taurus shows.

Service bulletin problems: Torque converter clutch may not engage; Reverse clutch lip seals shearing, tearing, during Reverse engagement in cold weather; stalling problems related to a too-lean fuel mixture; slow fuel fill or fuel gauge shows FULL too quickly; premature wear of the vinyl dash and door panels; squeaking or popping noise from the front outer tie rods; no Forward/Reverse; intermittent neutral condition; rattling noise during acceleration with the 3.0L engine (bulletins relating to last three problems are reprinted on the next page).

```
Article No.
98-3-7
02/16/98
TRANSAXLE - AX4N - INTERMITTENT NEUTRAL
CONDITION - NO FORWARD OR REVERSE
MOVEMENT - VEHICLES BUILT THROUGH 2/1/98
FORD:
1994–98 TAURUS
LINCOLN-MERCURY:
1994–98 SABLE
1995–98 CONTINENTAL
ISSUE:
Some vehicles may experience an intermittent Neutral condition after driving and coming to a stop. This may be caused by
the bonded seals on the forward clutch piston intermittently not sealing during the 3–2 downshift.
ACTION:
Replace the forward clutch piston with a revised Forward Clutch Piston (F8DZ-7A262-AB). Refer to the following Service
Procedure for details.
SERVICE PROCEDURE:
Clean and reseal the transaxle completely including replacement of the forward clutch piston with revised forward clutch pis-
ton and replace the forward clutch plates if darkened or discolored from heat. Refer to the appropriate Continental Service
Manual, Section 07-01, or the appropriate Taurus/Sable Service Manual, Section 07-013, for details.
Be sure to check end clearance on all three (3) select fit thrust washers (# 16, # 8, 1.02-1.50 mm (0.040-0.059")). Be sure
to clean and inspect the main control (pump and valve body) and servos. Prior to returning vehicle to customer recheck fluid
level at operating temperature.
PART NUMBER        PART NAME
F5DZJ153-AA        Seal And Gasket kit
F8DZ-7A262-AB      Forward Clutch Piston
F8DZ-7B164-AC      Forward Clutch Plates - Friction (4)
F2DZ-7B442-A       Forward Clutch Plates - Steel (4)
OTHER APPLICABLE ARTICLES: NONE
```

The ubiquitous forward clutch piston fails again!

```
Article No.
97-26-11
12/22/97
NOISE - "RATTLING" NOISE DURING
ACCELERATION - ALL ENGINE TEMPERATURES -
3.0L VEHICLES BUILT THROUGH 10/30/97
FORD:
1996-98 TAURUS
LINCOLN-MERCURY:
1996-98 SABLE
ISSUE:
Some vehicles may experience a "baby rattle" noise during acceleration. This noise may be greatest at high engine rpms just
before the transaxle shifts into the next higher gear. This may be caused by exhaust flow within the flex coupling. This rat-
tle should not be confused with spark knock which occurs at low rpm, high engine load conditions.
ACTION:
Replace the exhaust pipe flex coupling. The new coupling has a revised interior to reduce the possibility of rattling. Refer to
the following text for details.
Verify the "rattling" noise occurs only on accelerations just before the transaxle shifts.
Replace the previous flex pine with a new Flex Pipe (F8DZ-5G203-AA). Refer to the Service Procedure outlined in the appro-
priate Taurus/Sable Service Manual.
PART NUMBER        PART NAME
F8DZ-5G203-AA      Flex Pipe
OTHER APPLICABLE ARTICLES:
NONE
WARRANTY STATUS:
Eligible Under The Provisions Of Bumper To Bumper Warranty Coverage
OPERATION     DESCRIPTION        TIME
972S11A       Replace Flex Pipe  0.8 Hr.
```

*Remember, this exhaust pipe replacement is fully covered by the base warranty;
it's not a maintenance item.*

NHTSA safety complaints/safety: Engine fire; sudden acceleration and high idle; many cases reported where the vehicle won't decelerate when you let up on the accelerator (a common problem with many Ford models, sometimes attributed to the cruise control and power control module); car accelerates faster than it should when going downhill, regardless of whether cruise control is activated; ABS brakes locked up when applied, vehicle was rear-ended, and then vehicle accelerated; at highway speeds the Overdrive light flashes and the vehicle stalls; sudden stalling at all speeds; airbags deployed during a "fender-bender" accident; sudden loss of steering when bolt fell out of steering column; while parked in gear, vehicle slipped out of gear and rolled away; chronic fuel pump failures; seatbelt broke; front passenger seatbelt won't retract or lock into position; fuel gauge stuck on FULL (see service bulletins above); excessive windshield glare; windshield wipers jammed. This year's Taurus will have "thinking" seatbelts that can detect whether a driver has buckled the belt and prevent the airbag from deploying in "fender-bender" accidents or cause it to deploy more slowly in high-speed impacts. The airbags now come in two parts to protect head and shoulders and upper torso separately. Furthermore, the car's sides have been reinforced to prevent intrusion into the interior, and the Taurus's armrests have been redesigned to crumple, thereby protecting passengers from possibly severe internal injuries in a side impact.

Road Performance

Pro: Emergency handling: Better than average. **Steering:** The speed-sensitive variable-assist power steering makes the car easier to handle, but not as much as Ford claims. **Acceleration/torque:** Better than average with the 3.0L engine (0–100 km/h: 8.7 sec.). The base 3.0L V6 is a decade-old engine that offers adequate power for most driving situations, while the twin cam Duratec version provides exhilarating, quiet acceleration equal to the European-influenced chassis dynamics. **Transmission:** The 4-speed automatic transmission shifts smoothly and responsively. **Routine handling:** The sedan's handling, both around town and on the highway, is better than average due primarily to its solid suspension and stiff body construction.

Con: Ford's 3.0L Vulcan V6 is okay for rentals and city commuting, but it's unable to take full advantage of the car's excellent handling characteristics. Wagons handle poorly in turns and over uneven terrain. The high-performance SHO doesn't handle well in tight spaces, requiring four more feet to make a U-turn. **Braking:** Unimpressive braking (100–0 km/h: 134 ft.). ABS produces strong pedal pulsations.

Comfort/Convenience

Pro: Standard equipment: Nicely restyled 2000 version with plenty of convenience features, but four-wheel disc anti-lock brakes are still optional. The three-way front-seat console is a nice touch. It's a flip-fold affair that's a regular seat, an armrest, or a cup- and coin-carrying console. Armrest switches make it easy to activate the door locks and power windows. Efficient and quiet climate control system. **Interior space/comfort F/R:** Loads of room both in the front and in the rear. The standard seats are comfortable for most people, but the wagon's fabric-covered seats are more comfortable and supportive than the leather-covered sedan seats. The sedans will seat five in comfort, while the wagons offer an optional third seat. **Cargo space:** There's lots of cargo area in the wagon, and its innovative two-way tailgate allows the entire unit to swing out for large cargo or just the window glass to open for small packages. **Trunk/liftover:** The sedan's huge trunk has a low liftover and split rear seatbacks to facilitate easier loading.

Con: '99 versions have ugly (in my opinion) elliptical styling that makes the car look smaller, even though it's more than five inches longer and almost two inches wider than the original. The SHO sedan is loaded with exterior styling gimmicks that may not be to everyone's taste. The wagon's interior plastic trim is cheap. **Driving position:** Short drivers will have to strain to reach the accelerator and see over the dash and tall drivers will find thigh support lacking. Leather seats offer little lateral support. **Controls and displays:** The massive dash and digital treatment are gimmicky and take getting used to. The radio is set too low and too far forward, and the JBL Premium Sound System's pushbutton controls require a Ph.D. to understand. Radio reception quality is disappointing. The low-fuel warning light comes on with enough fuel to travel 160 km. The wagon's liftgate doesn't rise high enough to clear most people's heads. **Climate control:** The rear window defroster is hard to find on the left side of the steering column. Air conditioning push buttons are difficult to understand and manipulate. **Entry/exit:** Difficult third seat access and limited head room for the third seat passenger. **Quietness:** Both the sedan and wagon's noise levels are unusually high, with lots of wind noise and tire drumming from the rear.

COST

List Price (negotiable)

	Residual Values (months)			
	24	36	48	60
Taurus LX: $24,495 (17%)	$14,000	$12,000	$10,000	$7,500

Note: Price includes PDI, freight.

TECHNICAL DATA

Powertrain (front-drive)
Engines: 3.0L V6 (145 hp)
• 3.0L V6 (200 hp)
• 3.4L V8 (235 hp)
Transmissions: 5-speed man.
• 4-speed auto.

Head room F/R: 39.2/36.2 in.
Leg room F/R: 42.2/38.9 in.
Wheelbase: 108.5 in.
Turning circle: 35.4 ft.
Cargo volume: 15.8 cu. ft.
Tow limit: 1,750 lb.

Dimensions/Capacity (LX)	Fuel tank: 60L/reg.
Passengers: 5	Weight: 3,350 lb.
Height/length/width:	
55.1/197.5/73.1 in.	

SAFETY FEATURES/CRASHWORTHINESS

	Std.	Opt.
Anti-lock brakes	❑	■
Seatbelt pretensioners	—	—
Side airbags	■	❑
Traction control	—	—
Head restraints	*	*
Visibility (front/rear)	*****	*****
Crash protection (front) D/P	*****	*****
Crash protection (side) D/P	***	***
Crash protection (offset)	*****	
HLDI injury claims (model)	****	
HLDI injury claims (all)	****	

Crown Victoria, Grand Marquis, Town Car

Crown Victoria

RATING: Recommended. Best suited for highway cruising and trailer towing. **Strong points:** Lots of interior room, quiet running, easy entry/exit, reliable, and excellent resale value. A natural gas V8 engine is available. **Weak points:** Difficult trunk access and terrible fuel economy.

NEW FOR 2000: Nothing significant. Ford plans to stretch the platform in 2002 to appeal more to fleet buyers, cab companies, and police departments.

OVERVIEW: The industry's lowest-priced six-passenger V8 sedans, the Crown Victoria and Grand Marquis have always been a favourite with police, taxi drivers, farmers, and retirees. Now, with the addition of a

4.6L OHC V8 several years ago, they're likely to stay around a relatively long time without many other changes.

Aside from the sheer wastefulness of the design and the high fuel cost of running one of these boats, they're fairly reliable and predictable highway cruisers. Handling isn't very responsive, but everyone is going to be comfortable inside. The mechanical design is straightforward and easy to troubleshoot (electronic gizmos excepted). The Crown Victoria and Grand Marquis have consistently come out on top in quality surveys of North American cars.

Speed-sensitive variable-assist power steering is a standard feature, as it is with most of Ford's luxury cars. The base model and LX are joined by the Touring Sedan, which offers a firmer ride, a more responsive handling package, and different exterior and interior styling touches. An electronically controlled automatic transmission has been around since early 1992.

The Lincoln Town Car still represents the epitome of large car luxury to many people, and it's a popular rear-drive base for Ford's luxury cars. A stretched version of the Crown Victoria/Marquis, its air-spring rear suspension provides a smooth ride and prevents tail-dragging, even when fully loaded.

Cost analysis/best alternatives: Get the '99 model for the discounts since it's essentially no different than the 2000 version. The Marquis is a slightly more luxurious version of the Crown that costs more but gives little of consequence for the extra expense. Other cars worth considering: Nissan Maxima, Mazda Millenia, Toyota Avalon, and Volvo S90 series. **Options:** Invest in the "Handling and Performance" option to reduce body roll and increase traction, and consider a power seat. **Rebates:** In the late fall expect $2,000 rebates on the '99 Crown Victoria and Grand Marquis. **Delivery/PDI:** $500. **Depreciation:** Slower than average. **Insurance cost:** Higher than average. **Parts supply/cost:** Parts aren't hard to find, but the CAA says that Crown Victoria parts are more expensive than most other cars in this class. **Annual maintenance cost:** Higher than average. Although repairs are relatively easy to carry out, these cars have complicated brake, fuel, and electronic systems that are a pain in the butt and wallet to troubleshoot. **Warranty:** *Crown Victoria and Grand Marquis:* Bumper-to-bumper 3 years/60,000 km; rust perforation 5 years/unlimited km. *Town Car:* Bumper-to-bumper 4 years/80,000 km; rust perforation 5 years/unlimited km. **Supplementary warranty:** A good idea as protection from costly diagnostic procedures. **Highway/city fuel economy:** 9.2–13.9L/100 km. **Annual fuel cost:** 2,357L=$1,367.

Quality/Reliability/Safety

Pro: Quality control: Body components and construction are first rate. **Reliability:** Overall reliability has been above average for the past several years. **Warranty performance:** Very good.

Con: Owner-reported problems: Main problem areas are the engine computer module, the electrical system, air-conditioning compressor, prematurely worn brakes, faulty seat tracks and door mouldings, and the fuel system. **Service bulletin problems:** Vinyl covers on the dash and door panels may wear prematurely; exhaust system "buzzing" or "rattling" noise; engine roughness due to exhaust system resonance; driveshaft vibration or boom during high speed operation; clunk noise coming from the rear of the vehicle. **NHTSA safety complaints/safety:** Fire ignited in engine compartment after car sat parked for two days; faulty rear lower control arm causes excessive vibrations; Crown Victoria's front seats may suddenly come loose and tilt; sharp edges on the Crown Victoria's doors have injured several people; the Grand Marquis' poor gas/brake pedal design caused one minor accident; brakes pull suddenly to one side and front brake pads wear out prematurely.

Road Performance

Pro: Emergency handling: A bit slow, but predictable and sure-footed. Less body lean in corners thanks to the upgraded suspension. **Steering:** Improved steering transmits more road feel than before. **Acceleration/torque:** Respectable, though not impressive, acceleration with plenty of low-end torque (0–100 km/h: 10.2 sec.). The smooth, quiet-running 4.6L V8 provides more than enough power for a comfortable ride. Towing capacity is 2,250 kg (5,000 lb.) with the Class III Towing or Handling and Performance packages offered with the Grand Marquis. **Transmission:** Flawless, most of the time. **Routine handling:** Fairly good for vehicles this large. Ride isn't overly soft. A '98 improvement smoothed out the ride and revised the steering to upgrade the handling. In effect, the rear end no longer sways when you turn the steering wheel. **Braking:** Better than average braking with the four-wheel disc brakes (100–0 km/h: 124 ft.).

Con: Transmission sometimes hesitates between gear changes. Handling still takes a backseat to ride quality. Despite improvements, steering is still rather vague.

Comfort/Convenience

Pro: Standard equipment: Lots of standard convenience features. **Driving position:** Very comfortable driving position. **Controls and displays:** Everything is within easy reach and well presented. **Climate control:** Powerful, quiet ventilation system. **Entry/exit:** Large doors make entry/exit a breeze. **Interior space/comfort F/R:** Spacious interior: three passengers are comfortable in the back, where there's lots of head, leg, and shoulder room. The individual front seats are large, comfortable, and supportive (the power seat option is recommended), particularly in the lumbar region. **Cargo space:** Plenty of storage areas. **Trunk/liftover:** Huge trunk. The Town Car's trunk, for example, is an impressive 22 cubic feet, with a low liftover. **Quietness:** Very quiet interior.

Con: Conservative styling. The driver's right knee frequently hits the dashboard/radio housing. Seatbelt anchor pokes into driver's right hip. Distracting continuous digital readout of your fuel economy. The Town Car's electronic dash is too gimmicky, and its moonroof cuts down on rear head room. Confusing power seat and controls. Climate control system is slow to warm up. Poor rear visibility. The split-bench front seat in the Crown Victoria isn't very comfortable due to its insufficient seatback padding and side support. Rear seats also lack sufficient seatback padding. Heater is a bit slow to warm up. Deep-dish trunk is not very practical for everyday baggage. You have to do some acrobatics to get at the full-sized spare tire, which is placed far forward in the trunk.

COST

List Price (negotiable)	Residual Values (months)			
	24	36	48	60
Crown Victoria:				
$32,095 (20%)	$22,000	$17,000	$14,000	$12,000
Town Car Executive:				
$51,195 (22%)	$36,000	$27,000	$23,000	$19,000
Note: Price includes PDI, freight.				

TECHNICAL DATA

Powertrain (rear-drive)
Engines: 4.6L V8 (175 hp) natural gas
• 4.6L V8 (190 hp)
• 4.6L V8 (200 hp)
• 4.6L V8 (220 hp)
Transmission: 4-speed auto.
Dimensions/Capacity
  (Crown Victoria)
Passengers: 6
Height/length/width:
56.8/212/77.9 in.

Head room F/R: 39.4/38 in.
Leg room F/R: 42.5/39.6 in.
Wheelbase: 114.4 in
Turning circle: 35.4 ft.
Cargo volume: 20.6 cu. ft..
Tow limit: 2,000 lb.
Fuel tank: 75L/reg.
Weight: 3,800 lb.

SAFETY FEATURES/CRASHWORTHINESS

	Std.	Opt.
Anti-lock brakes	■	■
Seatbelt pretensioners	■	❑
Side airbags	■	—
Traction control	■	■
Head restraints	*	*
Visibility (front/rear)	*****	**
Crash protection (front) D/P		
Crown Victoria and Gr. Marquis	*****	*****
Town Car	****	*****
Crash protection (side) D/P	****	****
Crash protection (offset) D/P	N/A	
HLDI injury claims (model)	****	
HLDI injury claims (all)	*****	

Lincoln Continental

RATING: Average. Think of the Continental as a larger, fully loaded Ford Taurus. **Strong points:** Many standard features, comfortable ride, easy access, and lots of cargo room. **Weak points:** Limited rear seat room, delayed transmission engagement, and uncertain long-term reliability.

NEW FOR 2000: A carryover model; a complete redesign is due in 2002.

OVERVIEW: The Continental rests on a modified front-wheel drive Taurus chassis, which is one of the most up-to-date designs on the road. With the addition of a depowered 4.6L V8 used in the Mark VIII as the standard powerplant, performance has improved immeasurably, to the point that it's now comparable to other Lincolns. One of the Continental's strong selling points is its large array of standard features that would cost extra on many other luxury sedans.

Cost analysis/best alternatives: Get the '99 model and whatever discounts you can get in the $2,500–$3,000 range. Other cars you may wish to consider: the Ford Crown Victoria or Marquis, Lincoln Town Car, Infiniti, Lexus, Mercedes-Benz 300 series, or Toyota Avalon. The Continental is less expensive than imported luxury sedans, without sacrificing luxury features or innovative technology. On the other hand, German and Japanese models leave the Continental far behind in handling, braking, engine smoothness, and overall reliability. **Options:** A one-touch panic button (RESCU) that alerts the police, ambulance, or tow truck to your whereabouts through a patch between the cellular phone network and global satellites; and run-flat Michelin ZP tires that can be driven up to 80 km (50 miles) without tire pressure. **Rebates:** Expect $3,000 dealer incentives on the '99s early in the year 2000. **Delivery/PDI:** $600. **Depreciation:** Faster than average. **Insurance cost:** Higher than average. **Parts supply/cost:** Parts are easy to come by and reasonably priced, says CAA. **Annual maintenance cost:** Higher than average. The fuel-injection system is difficult and costly to service when problems arise. **Warranty:** Bumper-to-bumper 4 years/80,000 km; rust perforation 5 years/unlimited km. **Supplementary warranty:** A good idea, not just because of the Continental's uncertain long-term reliability, but because the complicated mechanical and electrical components cost so much to troubleshoot and replace. **Highway/city fuel economy:** 8.8–13.9L/100 km. **Annual fuel cost:** 2,321L=$1,555.

Quality/Reliability/Safety

Pro: **Quality control:** Overall quality control is the best of Ford's domestic luxury cars, which is far from complimentary. **Reliability:** Average; the front brakes and suspension system aren't very durable. **Warranty performance:** Better than average.

Con: **Owner-reported problems:** AC, automatic transmission, and fuel pump failures and lots of body squeaks and rattles. The added complexity of ABS, an electronic air suspension, and all the other high-tech items found on these cars are likely to cause some headaches with age, which is reason enough to buy an extended warranty. **Service bulletin problems:** Intermittent neutral condition; no Forward/Reverse; noise from rear underbody/suspension; torque converter clutch failure; AM band static; possibility of excessive wind and road noise; condensation buildup on inside of windows. **NHTSA safety complaints/safety:** Airbags deployed for no apparent reason; sudden failure of the tie rod; headlights don't illuminate the roadway sufficiently at night.

Road Performance

Pro: **Emergency handling:** Better than average. **Steering:** The variable-ratio power steering gives the right amount of road feel and control. **Acceleration/torque:** Brisk and smooth acceleration with lots of low-end torque (0–100 km/h: 8 sec.). **Routine handling:** Air suspension helps both ride and handling; the car is smooth on all but the worst roads, and cornering at highway speeds remains precise and predictable. **Braking:** Acceptable braking, considering the Continental's size (100–0 km/h: 130 ft.).

Con: **Transmission:** The automatic transmission is sometimes slow to downshift and occasionally has trouble deciding if it wants to be in Overdrive or third gear. Despite its good handling, the Continental does feel clumsy around town. The computer-controlled air suspension emits an irritating hissing sound when it settles after parking. Some torque steer (steering twists a bit) when the accelerator pedal is floored.

Comfort/Convenience

Pro: Standard equipment: A sophisticated air cushion suspension allows the driver to dial in different suspension settings for all driving conditions. **Driving position:** Comfortable seating and good all-around visibility. **Entry/exit:** Easy front and rear access. **Interior space/comfort F/R:** Better than average. The interior is narrower than other domestic cars in this class, but it's plush and comfortable. **Trunk/liftover:** Large trunk and low liftover facilitate loading. **Quietness:** Very little engine, road, or wind noise.

Con: Ford's chintzy side is evident when you open the spacious trunk and find that it houses a temporary-service spare tire. Handset cradle is not user-friendly. The standard leather upholstery is slippery, and it's hot in summer and cold in winter. **Controls and displays:** The digital dash is hard to read, and some operating controls are inconvenient and illogical. For example, you'll have to shut off the ignition and blindly grope inside the glove compartment for the trunk lid remote release and hope you don't hit the fuel-filler door release instead. Confusing power-window switches. Plus, it takes far too many buttons to set the trip computer, suspension mode, and steering effort. Seats aren't as comfortable as the competition's and only two can sit up front. Loading the trunk is made difficult by the protruding rear bumper. **Climate control:** Fresh air ventilation is adequate, but the automatic climate controls tend to overcompensate and perform erratically. The rear seats need more side and lower back support. **Cargo space:** The interior lacks storage bins for small objects.

COST				
List Price (negotiable)	**Residual Values** (months)			
	24	36	48	60
Continental: $52,895 (23%)	$39,000	$27,000	$22,000	$19,000
Note: Price includes PDI, freight.				

TECHNICAL DATA	
Powertrain (front-drive)	Head room F/R: 39/38 in.
Engine: 4.6L V8 (275 hp)	Leg room F/R: 41.9/38.9 in.
Transmission: 4-speed auto.	Wheelbase: 109 in.
Dimensions/Capacity	Turning circle: 35.4 ft.
Passengers: 5	Cargo volume: 18.1 cu. ft.
Height/length/width:	Tow limit: 2,000 lb.
56/206.3/73.6 in.	Fuel tank: 67L/reg.
	Weight: 3,900 lb.

SAFETY FEATURES/CRASHWORTHINESS		
	Std.	**Opt.**
Anti-lock brakes	■	❑
Seatbelt pretensioners	■	❑

Side airbags	❑	∎
Traction control	∎	❑
Head restraints	*	*
Visibility (front/rear)	*****	*****
Crash protection (front) D/P	***	N/A
Crash protection (side) D/P	N/A	
Crash protection (offset)	***	
HLDI injury claims (model)	*****	
HLDI injury claims (all)	*****	

Note: NHTSA rating applies to the '94 model.

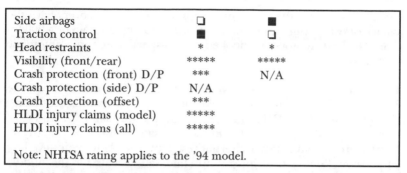

Windstar

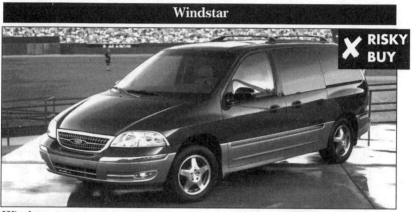

Windstar

RATING: Below Average. I'm not convinced that the '99 model's powertrain defects won't be carried over this year. An extended warranty is strongly recommended. **Strong points:** Comfortable ride; good instrument/controls layout; plenty of passenger space, and a five-star crashworthiness rating. **Weak points:** Automatic transmission and other mechanical components don't hold up well from day one. Mediocre handling and restricted side and rear visibility, lousy horn design, and warranty performance has been problematic in the past.

NEW FOR 2000: Power-adjustable foot pedals and optional on-board video entertainment system.

OVERVIEW: Windstar is a front-drive minivan that looks a bit like a stretched Mercury Villager. It's longer, larger, and lower than most other minivans. It's also one of the few minivans not built on a truck platform (it uses the Taurus platform instead), and as such it has some of the car-like handling characteristics of Chrysler's minivans and some of the engine and automatic transmission problems experienced by Taurus and Sable owners. It's offered in two body styles—a seven-passenger people-hauler and the less expensive basic cargo van. Buyers have the choice of two 6-cylinder engines: a standard 147-hp 3.0L V6 or a 200-hp 3.8L V6. Both motors are hooked to a 4-speed electronic automatic transmission.

Cost analysis/best alternatives: Get the '99 model for the $1,500–$2,000 discounts, but make sure you can handle the horn's eccentricities (see "NHTSA safety complaints/safety"). Chrysler Caravan, '99 Voyager, Honda Odyssey, Nissan Quest, and the Toyota Sienna are recommended alternatives. **Options:** Automatic levelling suspension ($385); dual integrated child safety seats for the middle bench seat; power side windows; and rear air conditioner, defroster, and heater. Don't spring for the centre console option unless you're prepared to sacrifice rear seat access. Most Windstars are the LX, costing about $30,000 with a carefully prepared list of options. Both sliding side doors are powered since the 1999 version and include an override circuit that prevents the door from closing on a hand. This overpriced $1,244 convenience feature is failure-prone and a bit slow in operation. On the other hand, it's amazing the reaction this gadget engenders— buyers' eyes light up when they see the door open automatically with the remote control fob. An argument can be made for the added convenience, but I suspect its chief attraction is to gadget-hungry males who must have the latest eye-popping innovation. Another overpriced feature that has a dubious safety value is Ford's $338 optional reverse sensing system that alerts you to an object behind the vehicle when backing up. Four sonar sensors in the bumpers detect—starting at 1.8m—large stationary objects and emit warning beeps that increase to a steady tone as you get within 25 cm to the object. **Rebates:** $1,500 on the '99s. With minivan sales slowing down, heftier rebates won't be far behind. By the end of the year, look for more generous rebates and dealer incentives. **Delivery/PDI:** $900. **Depreciation:** Much slower than average. **Insurance cost:** Above average. **Parts supply/cost:** Parts are widely available and reasonably priced. **Annual maintenance cost:** Above average. **Warranty:** Bumper-to-bumper 3 years/60,000 km; rust perforation 5 years/unlimited km. **Supplementary warranty:** An extended warranty is a good idea. **Highway/city fuel economy:** With the 3.0L V6: 9.3–14L/100 km; with the 3.8L V6: 9.5–13.3L/100 km. **Annual fuel cost:** 3.0L V6: 2,377L=$1,379; 3.8L V6: 2,318L=$1,344. Interestingly, choosing the more powerful 3.8L engine actually saves on fuel.

Quality/Reliability/Safety

Pro: Warranty performance: Improved a bit over the past 12 months.

Con: Quality control: Below average. The last four years have been a disaster from a quality control standpoint. "Goodwill" payouts can't be used as a substitute for better quality control. **Reliability:** Serious problems affecting the 3.8L engine, and the automatic transmission continues to shift erratically. Ford insiders tell me this transmission problem is both hardware and software in origin and affects most of Ford's model line-up—it's a chronic complaint from owners of '99 models reporting to NHTSA (see below). Electrical system and brake defects also frequently sideline the Windstar. **Owner-reported problems:** As stated above, engine and transmission defects lead the list, but there have also been a worrisome number of complaints concerning the electrical components, AC failures, and premature brake wear. Other problems include: coolant leaks; premature tie rod wear; noisy power steering pumps; a rear heating duct behind the driver's seat that gets so hot it can burn an unsuspecting driver's fingers; rear windows that break suddenly because of auxiliary rear heater overheating; and a front windshield that cracks from the base upwards due to faulty mounting or sudden temperature changes. Ford—not your insurance company—should pay the damage claims arising from these windshield problems. **Service bulletin problems:** Intermittent neutral condition after coming to a stop (a complaint often reported to NHTSA officials); Reverse clutch lip seals shearing, tearing, during Reverse engagement in cold weather; no Reverse gear in cold weather; stalling when decelerating, parking, or coasting; corrective measures for an overly lean fuel mixture; excessive AC odours; inaccurate fuel gauge; rear speakers cut out intermittently; front power door locks ratchet during operation; power door locks grinding or inoperative; premature wear of vinyl on dash, console, and door panels; suspension noise; whistling noise from front AC-heater plenum; rattling, clunking noise from front of vehicle and when moving gearshift lever out of Park; accelerator pedal buzz and exhaust system drone; rattling noise from liftgate area; upper intake manifold rattling; upper radiator hose leaks. **NHTSA safety complaints/safety:** Fire caused by snow short-circuiting the cooling fan; sudden acceleration; accelerator and brake pedal are mounted too close together; chronic stalling, particularly when decelerating or turning (some attribute it to fuel system vapour lock); fuel pump sensor failure causes the fuel pump to shut down; stalling when brakes are applied; automatic transmission failures; transmission jolts continuously; while in Park, vehicle jumped into Reverse and rolled away; when driving or parking on an incline, transmission jumps from Drive to Neutral; driver made a 90-degree right turn and then the axle disconnected from the transmission; when stopping, brake pedal goes all the way to the floor and causes extended stopping distances; left front brake caliper (ABS) locks up and won't retract; driver's side lower brake caliper fell off; sudden brake loss and brake pedal fell off; power steering hose came loose, spewing fluid; vehicle's rear end sways when reaching cruising speeds; driver's seat shifts on its tracks, won't lock when coming to a stop, seat moves forward; sliding side door pops open while driving and slams shut when vehicle's parked on an incline; sliding door handle design allows extended fingers to get caught between the door and door frame; door doesn't automatically retract when closing on one's hand; rear and middle shoulder belts tighten uncomfortably; seat interior and exterior lights pulsate when engine's running; electric windows work only with key off and out of the ignition; trunk lid crashed down upon driver's head while unloading vehicle; catalytic converter heat shield vibrates annoyingly; location of cupholder on the floor, attached to the middle seat, trips occupants as they exit the van. There are many complaints that the driver must hit the horn at the exact spot with extreme force to get it to sound. The "sweet spot" isn't easily found by pressing on the steering wheel—in fact, many Windstar owners greet each other with the question, "Is your horn working?" Ford says its integrated child safety seat will hold a child up to a maximum weight of 60 lb. (27 kg)—however, children up to 43 lb. (20 kg) may not fit; seatbelts in second row middle seat are too tight, and a passenger can't lean forward. Off-centre rear wiper doesn't sweep much of the window, nor does it clean where it should!

Road Performance

Pro: Emergency handling: High-speed handling is acceptably stable and predictable, and the steering is particularly precise and light. **Steering:** Light and responsive, though not as effortless as the competition. **Acceleration/torque:** The 3.8L V6 is usually competent and smooth, with lots of low-end torque (0–100 km/h: 10.7 sec.). **Transmission:** The electronic 4-speed automatic responds well and shifts smoothly, when it's working right (see "Con"). Fourth gear can be locked out for towing. **Routine handling:** Easy to drive. Smooth and supple ride under most driving conditions improves as the load increases.

Con: Engine frequently stalls due to fuel pump, computer module, and electrical system glitches. Erratically performing automatic gearbox often slips out of gear, lurches into gear, or simply refuses to engage whichever gear you choose. The Windstar's city manners aren't impressive: excessive body swish and sway takes its toll on tires and makes highway driving less car-like than the shorter base Chrysler minivans. It also has a large turning radius. Lots of wind noise on the highway. **Braking:** Average braking that's a bit difficult to modulate.

Comfort/Convenience

Pro: Standard equipment: Comfortable and well-appointed interior. Superior sound system. One innovative touch that many families will appreciate: a wide-angle mirror housed in the ceiling console lets the driver watch the little darlings in the rear without turning around. **Driving position:** Excellent driving position gives most drivers a commanding view of the road. **Controls and displays:** Well laid-out instrument panel with easy-to-read gauges. **Climate control:** Adequate and easily adjusted. **Entry/exit:** Acceptable. **Cargo space:** Lots of small storage spaces in addition to the large amount of space for larger items. Another nice touch is the optional power lock switch just inside the rear hatch, which saves you from having to walk to the front of the van to lock up. **Trunk/liftover:** Rear hatch is easy to open and shut, and the low floor improves cargo handling.

Con: There's not a lot of choice when it comes to engine, body format, and cabin layout. The Windstar's driver's seat isn't comfortable for big, tall drivers, who complain of the lack of leg room, seat contouring, and lower back support. The driver's shoulder belt can ride uncomfortably on a tall driver's collarbone because it's anchored too far back. It's also a long reach to put on. Headlight switch is partly obscured by the steering wheel. Tiny, flat buttons on the Windstar's radio make it hard to calibrate. Weak AC and heater airflow to the floor makes an auxiliary heater a good idea. **Interior space/comfort F/R:** Middle and rear seatbenches use short cushions and the rear seat is practically inaccessible. Although the seats are easily removed, getting them in and out of the vehicle is more of a chore than Ford lets on (the rear bench seat alone weighs 110 lb., or almost 50 kg). Restricted side/rear visibility. **Cargo space:** Unlike Chrysler, Ford still hasn't figured out a way to reconfigure the Windstar's storage space so that it will hold bulky items like 4x8 sheets of building material. The right sliding door takes a lot of effort to open and close. Some wind and road noise. **Quietness:** An abundance of clunks, rattles, and wind and road noise.

COST

List Price (negotiable)	Residual Values (months)			
	24	**36**	**48**	**60**
LX: $25,995 (20%)	$18,000	$15,000	$12,000	$10,000
SEL: $31,195 (21%)	$21,000	$18,000	$15,000	$13,000

Note: Price includes PDI, freight.

TECHNICAL DATA

Powertrain (front-drive)
Engines: 3.0L V6 (147 hp)
• 3.8L V6 (200 hp)
Transmission: 4-speed auto.
Dimension/Capacity
Passengers: 2/2/3
Height/length/width:
66.1/200.9/76.6 in.

Head room F: 39.3/R1: 41.1/R2: 37.9 in.
Leg room F:40.7/R1: 36.8/R2: 35.6 in.
Wheelbase: 120.7 in.
Turning circle: 42 ft.
Cargo volume: 66.5 cu. ft.
GVWR: N/A
Payload: 1,800–1,831 lb.
Tow limit: 2,000–3,500 lb.
Fuel tank: 75/94L
Weight: 4,150 lb.

SAFETY FEATURES/CRASHWORTHINESS

	Std.	Opt.
Anti-lock brakes (4W)	■	❑
Seatbelt pretensioners	—	—
Side airbags	—	■
Traction control	❑	■

Head restraints (front/rear)	****	*
Visibility (front/rear)	*****	**
Crash protection (front) D/P	*****	*****
Crash protection (side) D/P	*****	*****
Crash protection (offset)	*****	
HLDI injury claims (model)	*****	
HLDI injury claims (all)	*****	

JAGUAR

Jaguar's name conjures up images of posh sedans and fast sports cars rolling through the English countryside. Jaguars reek of elegance, taste, and money. The car's styling, ride, handling, and comfort still entice motorists full of nostalgia for British cars of the 1960s, but mechanical, electronic, and body problems persist, though there aren't as many as a decade ago. Interestingly, that may explain why Jaguars have such a high rate of depreciation, and why 70 percent of buyers prefer to lease rather than purchase their "Jag."

There are two models to choose from: the XJ8 and the XK8. XJ8s have four variations to choose from: the entry-level XJ8 ($76,900), the long-wheelbase XJ8L, the luxurious long-wheelbase Vanden Plas ($89,900), and the standard-length, supercharged XJR ($92,900). XK8 models are available as coupes or convertibles ($91,900 and $99,900, respectively).

Caught in a dilemma similar to that of the Corvette, the Jaguar's excess weight makes it necessary to install lots of complicated and difficult-to-troubleshoot devices, as well as larger engines, in order to make these cars decent highway performers.

Now that Ford has taken over the company, long-term reliability is still a rather large question mark, even though recent studies show considerable improvement in quality control. Confident that its poor quality cars are past history, Jaguar offers a 30-day, money-back guarantee and a comprehensive 4-year/80,000-km base mechanical warranty. The automaker also provides a 6-year/unlimited-km rust perforation warranty, and Jaguar Club benefits that include no-cost maintenance, roadside assistance, and trip interruption services.

Poor servicing is still a problem, however. Owners report long delays for service appointments and then even longer waits for the right parts to arrive. Unfortunately, there aren't many Jaguar dealers to choose from, so if you don't find a competent and conscientious one it's doubtful that you'll be able to go elsewhere for a second opinion.

S-Type

RATING: Not Recommended during its first year on the market. **Strong points:** Impressive engine performance, superb handling and roadholding, quiet-running, improved reliability, and a well-appointed interior. **Weak points:** Erratic-shifting manual-automatic transmission, not much room for cargo, a cramped interior, limited dealer network, Ford mechanics unfamiliar with this new model, some parts delay, and accelerated depreciation.

NEW FOR 2000: On sale since the summer of 1999 and sharing its rear-drive platform with Ford's new Lincoln LS sedan, the S-Type is Jaguar's smallest luxury car.

OVERVIEW: Finally, Ford comes out with a mid-priced Jaguar, the first product built upon Ford's shared platform concept that will also be used with the 2000 Lincoln LS sedan. So, what's there not to like? How 'bout a transmission that's more suitable to John Deere? Interior room that won't hold three rear occupants in comfort? Plastic trim instead of real wood?

Seen as a "baby Jag," the S-Type has a longer wheelbase than the XJ sedans and is wider and taller. It's just a bit shorter in length, however. Retro styling continues at Ford with the oval grill vertical bars, four round headlights, and bland, pinched-looking taillights. From the side, this "Jag" looks like an Infiniti J30.

Quality control, although improved of late, is likely to still be a long-term problem, particularly in view of this being a new model churned out by Jaguar's old manufacturing complex near Birmingham, England. The car does have four-wheel ABS, traction control, front head/chest side airbags, Ford's Duratec-based 240-hp 3.0L V6, and an optional Jaguar 281-hp 4.0L V8. The only transmission offered, a 5-speed automatic, is a Ford-Jaguar joint venture. It's slow to react to a throttle-induced downshift. Stomp all you want on the gas pedal, the transmission still takes its own sweet time to engage. It also seems to hunt for the proper gear (more pronounced with the V6) and often changes gears for no apparent reason, after hesitating a few seconds.

Other deficiencies: steering is a bit over-assisted for high speeds (the optional Sport Package will help), limited passenger (rear passengers sit knees-to-chin with scrunched toes) and cargo space, an inaccessible glovebox, restricted rear visibility, and a confusing array of audio and climate controls.

Aimed at the BMW 5-series, Mercedes E-Class, and Lexus GS crowd, the S-Type is pricier than its Lincoln LS twin at $59,950 for the V6 and $10,000 more for the V8. This price puts it a few thousand dollars below the Benz, and on par with Lexus and BMW.

Cost analysis/best alternatives: Although sales have been much better than last year, Jaguar still is a low volume seller (629 cars sold during January–June 1999), and discounting is quite common, although the first-year S-Type hoopla will probably lead to less generous reductions. Nevertheless, there isn't any compelling reason to buy or lease a '99 or year 2000 Jaguar when the car is compared with less expensive convertibles/roadsters like the BMW Z3, Mercedes SLK, and Porsche Boxster. Other more reliable luxury cars you may wish to consider, with as much or more cachet, are the Lexus models, the Lincoln Town Car, Infiniti models, Mercedes' S-class, Nissan's Maxima, and the Toyota Camry or Avalon. **Options:** The voice-activation system is a pricey gadget that adds to complexity without providing the convenience promised. **Rebates:** Although you can expect $2,000–$3,000 rebates on other unsold Jags, don't expect any on the S-Type. **Delivery/PDI:** $600. **Depreciation:** Resale values plummet about as quickly as Bre-X stock on most of Jaguar's models; the S-Type may hold its value better during its first year on the market. **Insurance cost:** Higher than average, close to usurious. **Parts supply/cost:** Parts are often back-ordered because not a lot of Ford dealer inventory goes into stocking Jaguar parts. The S-Type will be able to benefit from Ford generic chassis components, but other components will still likely be backordered. Parts are moderately expensive as well, and there aren't any independent suppliers to inject price competition into the equation. **Annual maintenance cost:** Predicted to be higher than average. **Warranty:** Bumper-to-bumper 4 years/80,000 km; rust perforation 6 years/unlimited km. **Supplementary warranty:** Don't leave home without it. **Highway/city fuel economy:** Nothing yet on the S-Type. **Annual fuel cost:** Nothing yet on the S-Type.

SAFETY FEATURES/CRASHWORTHINESS		
	Std.	**Opt.**
Anti-lock brakes	■	❑
Seatbelt pretensioners	■	❑
Side airbags	■	❑
Traction control	■	❑
Head restraints	**	**
Convertible XK8	*	*
Visibility (front/rear)	*****	**

Crash protection (front) D/P	N/A
Crash protection (side) D/P	N/A
Crash protection (offset)	N/A
HLDI injury claims (model)	
XJ8	****
HLDI injury claims (all)	
XJ8	*****

Note: S-class restraints not tested.

GENERAL MOTORS

Fewer buyers, more profits
Ever since GM switched to front-drives over two decades ago, it began losing market share—big time—and earning a reputation for making look-alike, low-quality vehicles. This is one of the main reasons why GM's U.S. market share has plummeted from nearly 50 percent in the late 1970s to its current 29 percent.

Yet, America's largest automaker still manages to make record profits despite selling fewer cars and trucks and losing over $1,000 for every small car it sells. GM makes money because it has cut production costs by closing plants, slashing jobs, reducing the number of parts, using common parts across several product lines, and concentrating on sport-utilities, trucks, and vans, where the most profits are found.

GM knows it has become the marginal car champ, with too many nameplates for models that are both identical and bland. Its various divisions are in serious need of pruning and restructuring. While axing the Olds Cutlass and Riviera was a smart move, GM's entire Olds division should be dropped—it makes no sense at all to have so many Olds nameplates on different model platforms. In fact, Olds sales have declined over the past 10 years almost as much as Saturn sales have increased.

GM's dealers are up in arms over what they see as the company's inefficient vehicle ordering system and disorganized regional advertising. Specifically, dealers complain that GM's new on-line Vehicle Ordering System (VOS) is costing them sales due to delayed deliveries, order mix-ups, and the loading of vehicles with option packages that aren't wanted in certain regions. As far as advertising is concerned, GM's recent takeover of all regional advertising has led to dealers not knowing what GM ads are offering and which vehicles get incentives.

Ronald Zarella, GM's president of North American Operations, has become cognizant that General Motors has serious management deficiencies—serious enough to cause the company's poor product mix and failure to adequately communicate with its dealer body. As a result, he made bold moves earlier this year to streamline decision-making and accountability. Divisional general managers (a vice-president position,

usually) were replaced with lower-ranking managers, North American
and international operations were merged into one group, and the
automaker has pledged to shelve "safe" redesigns and concentrate on
getting more innovative trucks, minivans, and sport-utilities to market
faster.

New products: smoke and mirrors
GM has delayed the redesign of its best-selling Cavalier and Sunfire
until 2004 and says it will put the hundreds of millions of dollars saved
into faster production of new models and the development of daring
new designs. So far, however, GM's new designs appear to be more of
the "same ol', same ol'." Its concept vehicles at this year's Detroit auto
show were particularly uninspiring, generating no product enthusiasm.
DaimlerChrysler's "in your face" Viper, Prowler, and soon-to-be-
launched PT Cruiser exhibits only made GM's designers look like the
bland leading the bland.

Desperate to get new products onto the market, General Motors says
it will reinvent its Cadillac and Saturn divisions over the next five years.
It'll do this by converting most Cadillacs back to rear-drive, expanding
the Saturn model lineup with larger cars, adding a small sport-utility
division that will develop SUTs—sport-utility trucks with pickup beds
(remember the El Camino?), and bringing new sport wagons to the
market. These steps aren't at all innovative; they're merely late efforts
to copy what sold in the distant past (rear-drive) and what has been selling for the past several years while GM fumbled the ball. This is particularly evident in GM's trailing Cadillac sales.

How bad off are American luxury cars? Look at this year's sales stats:
currently Cadillac is third behind Mercedes and Lexus, and Lincoln is
fifth, trailing BMW. In fact, Cadillac was so desperate to show some
sales gains that the company fabricated sales figures earlier this year
and later apologized to journalists for the deception.

The company's promise to bring out daring new designs is, in my opin-
ion similarly deceptive. Nevertheless, here's what GM plans for this year:
• A redesigned Bonneville, DeVille, Impala, LeSabre, and Monte Carlo.
• A redesigned Suburban, Tahoe, and Yukon.
• A redesigned DeVille retaining its front-drive configuration.
• Debut of the Saturn LS (large size).

Additionally, the Cadillac Catera and Saturn S sedan and wagon get
minor styling changes, and the Suburban will also be sold as the Yukon XL.

Cutlass has been cut
How quickly the mighty have fallen—particularly, after the Oldsmobile
Cutlass switched from rear-drive to front-drive in 1986. The Cutlass is
the latest casualty and will be dropped this fall, apparently because it
lacks the style and power of earlier versions and is practically indistin-
guishable from its Chevrolet Malibu twin.

Launched in 1961 as a compact coupe spin-off of the F-85 and carrying a 185-hp V8 engine, the Cutlass quickly embraced the "muscle car" culture of the mid-1960s with its "442." In 1968, a scorching 455-cubic-inch (litres weren't used back then) V8 was introduced that produced 360 horsepower. Power, reliability and roominess all contributed to the Cutlass's popularity—11.9 million units were sold during its 38-year run.

Warranty performance, quality control
With another year of record profits, GM has channelled more money into warranty repairs and empowered its dealers to make most post-warranty decisions on their own. That's why it's not surprising to see that GM warranty complaints have slowed a bit over the past year (it's still high, however). The company has also been more forthcoming in admitting its vehicles' failures, like its recent announcement that it was extending its "goodwill warranty," on 1993–95 Saturns that overheat and blow their engine head gaskets, to six years.

GM's quality control has improved, as well. This is particularly evident in the better-made, redesigned Silverado and Sierra full-sized pickups, and the fewer complaints relating to clunky rear-drive automatic transmissions. Front-drive powertrain and other mechanical and electronic components still aren't as reliable or durable as those produced by the Japanese automakers, but this is a problem shared by all three American automakers. The quality of body components and their assembly also remain far below Japanese and European standards. Poor paint quality, a Ford problem for over a decade, was addressed in 1995 by a changeover in suppliers. Apparently, GM has yet to make that move, in spite of a Canadian class action launched against the company in British Columbia this year—as well as a handful of lengthy, though well-reasoned, small claims court judgments targeting GM paint delamination.

I'll continue monitoring GM's quality control and treatment of its customers this year through *Lemon-Aid* reader feedback and email reports. If I detect any change in its policies before next year's edition, I'll post the information on *www.lemonaidcars.com*.

Metro, Firefly, Swift

Firefly

RATING: Average. Acceptable only for bare-bones city commuting, where fuel savings and agility are paramount. **Strong points:** Cheap to buy and cheap to run, better than average quality control, fun to drive with a manual shifter. **Weak points:** Anemic, noisy engine makes these cars the antithesis of "swift"; harsh, choppy ride; lots of interior noise; a spartan interior; poorly performing original equipment tires; and terrible braking.

NEW FOR 2000: Carried over with few changes; GM plans to drop these cars for the 2001 model year. The Suzuki Swift is also a carried-over model.

OVERVIEW: Good city and commuter cars that are capable of fitting into the tiniest of parking spaces and nipping through narrow city streets, but still provide sufficient room inside for two adults and their cargo. Interestingly, only GM offers optional power steering.

These cars deliver outstanding fuel economy because of an unusual aluminum 1.0L 3-cylinder engine, which is a little rough around the edges but gets the job done efficiently. People who'd like a little more zest from their city scooter can order the fuel-injected 1.3L 4-banger.

Cost analysis/best alternatives: Get the '99 model if it's discounted by at least $1,000. The XFi bare-bones Metro is the fuel economy champion, but it sacrifices an automatic transmission and a host of other amenities. Actually, a better-equipped model would be almost as economical. Convertibles are the best choice for ragtop thrills that won't break your budget. Compare prices with the Suzuki Swift, the Metro's twin; it may offer a longer warranty and more standard features for less. On the other hand, Suzuki dealership servicing and Suzuki's warranty performance are not as good as GM's and its dealers. Other cars to consider are the Honda Civic, Hyundai Accent, and Toyota Tercel. **Options:** The larger engine with fuel injection, a remote trunk release, and split folding rear seats (sedans). Premium tires. **Rebates:** $1,000 on '99 Metros and Fireflys; Swifts may get a $500 dealer incentive. **Delivery/PDI:** $525.

Depreciation: Faster than average. **Insurance cost:** Lower than average. **Parts supply/cost:** Average availability and reasonably priced (power-train components tend to be pricey). Shop around for the best price among GM and Suzuki dealers. **Annual maintenance cost:** Below average. Maintenance is made simple by an uncluttered underhood layout and the availability of two dealer networks for servicing. **Warranty:** *Metro, Firefly:* Bumper-to-bumper 3 years/60,000 km; rust perforation 6 years/160,000 km. *Swift:* Bumper-to-bumper 3 years/80,000 km; rust perforation 5 years/unlimited km. **Supplementary warranty:** Not needed. **Highway/city fuel economy:** 6.2–7.8L/100 km with the 1.3L and 3-speed automatic. **Annual fuel cost:** 1,416L=$821.

Quality/Reliability/Safety

Pro: Quality control: Better than average. This is a low-cost and low-maintenance econobox with a better than average repair record that goes back many years. The trend seems to be continuing, judging by the absence of significant problems reported by owners. **Reliability:** Fairly good, except for some fuel-injection glitches and engine head gasket failures. If not checked often for corrosion and leaks, the cooling system will eventually fail, causing serious damage to the aluminum engine. **Warranty performance:** Average at GM, below average at Suzuki.

Con: Owner-reported problems: Premature brake wear (the front discs warp easily), and the front metallic brake pads are noisy. Some owners complain about fragile body hardware. Stopping distances are greater than average and the car is very sensitive to crosswinds and passing trucks on the highway. **Service bulletin problems:** Inaccurate speedometers. **NHTSA safety complaints:** Sudden acceleration; inadvertent airbag deployment; airbags failed to deploy; fuel tank fuel hose leak; taillight failure when daylight running lights are on; strut failures; transmission failures; clutch failures; brakes are noisy and make for extended stopping distances; emergency brake applied, but vehicle still rolled backwards. Chassis rigidity and crash safety have been enhanced with the placement of a steel beam behind the instrument panel.

Road Performance

Pro: The tiny 1.0L 3-cylinder powerplant has no trouble keeping up with city traffic, but the optional 1.3L 4-cylinder handles the automatic gearbox and highways much better. **Steering:** The non-power steering is fairly precise and always predictable. **Transmission:** The 5-speed manual with Overdrive shifts easily. **Routine handling:** Handling is nimble and stable most of the time, thanks in part to the independent suspension.

Con: Emergency handling: Cornering becomes sloppier and less predictable as speed increases. The added weight of the 4-cylinder engine makes for hard steering while parking. **Acceleration/torque:** Very slow and without much torque (0–100 km/h: 12.3 sec.), which means that you'll quickly become expert at using the manual shifter—and get just as quickly fed up with the constant shifting of the 3-speed automatic. Even with the optional 4-cylinder engine, these cars are not great highway or long-distance cruisers. Some stalling and hesitation under full throttle. If you hear a constant knocking when accelerating or decelerating, blame it on the unusually pliable engine mounts that allow the engine and exhaust system to knock against the floor pan. The clutch is abrupt, and the automatic transmission robs the engine of what little power it produces. The absence of an Overdrive gear on the automatic makes for excessive engine noise at highway speeds. The suspension thumps and bounces in hard turns. Cheap original equipment tires compromise handling, ride, and braking. **Braking:** Incredibly bad without ABS (100–0 km/h: varies between 139 and 152 ft.).

Comfort/Convenience

Pro: Standard equipment: Well-appointed interior with complete instrumentation. **Driving position:** Good. The plunging hood, sweeping window glass, and thin side pillars give the interior an airy look that heightens visibility in all directions. **Controls and displays:** Convenient, easy-to-read controls. **Interior space/comfort F/R:** Despite their diminutive proportions, these cars will easily accommodate tall occupants in front. Standard seats are reasonably comfortable for short rides. **Cargo space:** The area behind the front seats is a compromise; either you get limited space for two people and no room for cargo, or a spacious cargo area with the rear seat folded down. **Trunk/liftover:** Fairly large trunk with a low liftover to facilitate loading.

Con: Coupes don't offer power steering. Some radios furnished by GM dealers are poorly calibrated, producing an irritating, tinny sound. **Climate control:** Mediocre heating and ventilation. Seats become cramped and generally uncomfortable during long trips. **Entry/exit:** Very difficult rear access. Not much room for your feet in the rear. **Quietness:** The interior is quite noisy, due mainly to poor soundproofing and the car's small size.

COST

List Price (firm)	Residual Values (months)			
	24	36	48	60
Firefly: $10,795 (10%)	$8,000	$6,000	$4,000	$3,000
Swift DLX: $11,595 (9%)	$8,500	$7,000	$5,000	$4,000

TECHNICAL DATA

Powertrain (front-drive)
Engines: 1.0L 3-cyl. (55 hp)
• 1.3L 4-cyl. (70 hp)
Transmissions: 5-speed man. OD

Head room F/R: 39.3/37.3 in.
Leg room F/R: 42.5/32.2 in.
Wheelbase: 93.1 in.
Turning circle: 35 ft.

• 3-speed auto.
Dimension/Capacity (Metro LSi)
Passengers: 2/2
Height/length/width:
55.4/164/62.6 in.

Cargo volume: 10 cu. ft.
Tow limit: Not recommended
Fuel tank: 39L/reg.
Weight: 1,792 lb.

SAFETY FEATURES/CRASHWORTHINESS

	Std.	Opt.
Anti-lock brakes	❑	■
Seatbelt pretensioners	—	—
Side airbags	—	—
Traction control	—	—
Head restraints	*	*
Visibility (front/rear)	*****	*****
Crash protection (front) D/P	****	****
Crash protection (side) D/P	N/A	
Crash protection (offset)	N/A	
HLDI injury claims (model)	**	
HLDI injury claims (all)	*	

Saturn S-series, L-series

Saturn

RATING: Average. There have been some improvements, but Saturn's reliability and quality of servicing trail its Asian competitors. *L-series*: Not recommended during its first year on the market. **Strong points:** *S-series*: Comfortable driving position, adequate instrumentation and controls, unobstructed visibility, good braking, dent-resistant body panels, and better than average crashworthiness scores. *L-series*: Well-appointed, comfortable driving position and a roomy interior with a full range of convenience features, instruments, and controls. Excellent powertrain matchup with the V6, firm European ride, impressive high speed stability, and excellent braking. Effective sound-proofing and lots of storage areas, including a large accessible trunk. **Weak points:** *S-series:* Excessive engine noise with the base engine, limited rear seat room, optional ABS and traction control, window of coupe's third door doesn't roll down. *L-Series:* Interior isn't as refined as what you would find in a Toyota or Honda, optional ABS and traction control, limited rear visibility, steering feels heavy at low speeds and too light at higher speeds, small audio controls, and wagons give a jarring ride over bumps.

NEW FOR 2000: A new L-series and a freshening of the S sedan and wagon. In an attempt to save money by adapting a European car to the American market, Saturn's new LS sedan and LW wagon are products of a whole series of cost-cutting compromises as they are spun off the Vectra, made by GM's Opel subsidiary. Some major differences, however, include a lengthened body to give the Saturns additional crashworthiness, a standard ignition theft-deterrent system, a re-engineered chassis to give a more comfortable ride, the continued use of Saturn dent-resistant polymer body panels, the substitution of a Saturn space frame, and the use of a home-grown 137-hp 2.2L 4-banger constructed with aluminum components (remember the Vega?). Other components lifted directly from the European parts bin are Opel's 3.0L V6 engine, a manual transmission from Saab, and German-made braking systems.

Saturn has redesigned the body panels and cabin of its S-series sedan and wagon, giving the vehicles a more angular look and sharing many cockpit components with the new LS-series. These changes give the S-series (except the SC, which gets its makeover next year) a bit over 1.2 inches in extra length, a quieter twin-cam 1.9L engine, door panel-integrated beverage holders, a more user-friendly horn, more front seat travel, better lumbar support, and top tether anchors for child safety seats.

OVERVIEW: Launched in 1992 as an all-American effort to beat the Japanese in the small-car market, the Saturn compact was GM's first totally new car touted as being practically as reliable as the Japanese competition. Is almost as good as Toyota good enough?

No, not when your cars cost almost $20,000!

Here's something to think about the next time those "lovey-dovey" Saturn commercials come on TV extolling Saturn owner loyalty: J.D. Power's Sales Satisfaction Index for 1998 shows the brand has slipped into sixth place and other studies show the majority of 2 million Saturn owners in North American pick non-Saturns for their next vehicle.

Alarmed at the rising tide of defections, Saturn launched the LS, its first mid-sized sedan, last July to compete nose-to-nose with formidable competition like the Honda Accord and Toyota Camry. If this larger Saturn doesn't do well against 20 other mid-sized models, the nameplate will be forever relegated to a shrinking niche small-car market. If sales pick up, GM may spin off a sport-utility variant.

GM's latest $550 million redesign is based on the Opel Vectra, a European mid-sized sedan, which thrusts Saturn into fierce competition with Japanese models that have repeatedly given the Ford Taurus a bloody nose. Most industry watchers felt a sport-utility spin-off would have been a winner. That market has remained strong while small and mid-sized car sales have weakened.

Cost analysis/best alternatives: The SC model doesn't get made over until next year, so buy whichever model year is the cheapest. Other members of the S-series family offer important upgrades on this year's vehicles, which justify a small price increase. The L-series is way overpriced, particularly in view of Saturn's bogus no-haggle policy; only consider a second-series model made after March 2000; earlier models are guaranteed to be glitch-ridden. As alternatives to the S-series, the Honda Civic and Toyota Corolla perform better and offer higher quality vehicles. The Hyundai Tiburon compares well with the Saturn SC. Alternatives to the L-series: the Honda Accord, Mazda's 626, and the Toyota Camry. **Options:** Four-wheel anti-lock brakes and traction control. **Rebates:** Nothing reported yet, but the year 2000 should see $1,000–$1,500 price cutting on all but the LS. **Delivery/PDI:** $475. **Depreciation:** Slower than average. **Insurance cost:** Average. **Parts supply/cost:** Average parts availability. According to CAA, parts are reasonably priced, with heavy discounting by dealers. **Annual maintenance cost:** Average. **Warranty:** Bumper-to-bumper 3 years/60,000 km; rust perforation 6 years/160,000 km. **Supplementary warranty:** A good idea in view of Saturn's poor quality control. **Highway/city fuel economy:** 5.8–8.7L/100 km with the 1.9L engine and an automatic transmission. **Annual fuel cost:** 1,479L=$858.

Quality/Reliability/Safety

Pro: Reliability: Average. Reliability and dealer servicing have been overhyped. You may be surprised to learn that Saturns aren't built that much better than other vehicles.

Con: Quality control: Not up to Japanese car standards. **Warranty performance:** Saturn dealers tell me that GM is no longer as generous in paying warranty goodwill claims. They're worried that this may be a harbinger of a new "tough love" approach advocated by GM dealers in other divisions with better-selling vehicles, who are frustrated by the special treatment given to Saturn customers in the past, using up "goodwill" funds they should be allocated. Sample the Saturn complaint site at *www.pedsweb.com/saturn/*. **Owner-reported problems:** Engine, transmission, fuel system, brake, and body defects. **Service bulletin problems:** Excessive AC odours upon startup, muffler assembly rattling or clunk noise, defective sunroof sunshade fabric, and water leaks into the rear luggage compartment (see bulletin on the following page).

Waterleaks Into Rear Luggage Compartment Area
BULLETIN NO.: 96-T-15A
ISSUE DATE: February, 1999
GROUP/SEQ. NO.: Body-06
CORPORATION NO.: 99-08-57-017
SUBJECT:
Waterleaks into Rear Luggage Compartment Area
(Identify Area of Waterleak and Repair)
Due to a revision under Models Affected, this bulletin supercedes bulletin 96-T-15, which
should be discarded.
MODELS AFFECTED:
1996-1999 Saturn Sedans
CONDITION:
The rear luggage compartment carpet is wet and/or has a musty, mildew odor.
CAUSE:
This condition may be caused by voids in the body seam sealer at either the quarter/
D-ring joint, rear seat-to-back window panel reinforcement joint, and/or tail
panel/quarter joint.
CORRECTION:
Identify waterleak area and repair according to procedure in this bulletin.
CLAIM INFORMATION:

Case Type	Description	Labor Operation Code	Time
VW	Repair Waterleak in Right Rear Luggage Compartment	T9706	1.6 hrs
VW	Repair Waterleak in Left Rear Luggage Compartment	T9707	1.8 hrs

To receive credit for this repair during the warranty coverage period, submit a claim
through the Saturn Dealer System as shown.

This problem has gone uncorrected for four model years.

NHTSA safety complaints/ safety: *SC1*: When applying brakes there's excessive noise coming from the rear end; fuel sloshing sound when fuel tank is half full. *SC2*: Seatbelt tightens on any sudden movement, however slight; the small, recessed horn buttons make it hard to find and activate the horn without looking down. *SL*: Steering wheel came apart while driving; total loss of steering when the retaining clip was omitted during assembly. *SL1*: Windshield wipers fail to adequately clean the windshield; defrosting system doesn't work properly, causing moisture damage and poor visibility. *SL2*: Sudden acceleration; turn signal indicator sticks in the resume position; seatbelts are hard to engage; when driving at night, one sees multiple lights when looking through the rear view mirror at the vehicle in back, as well as the reflection of the defroster lights; during rainy weather, rear windshield view is distorted or wavy; sudden brake failure. *SW2*: Automatic transmission slippage caused collision.

Road Performance

Pro: Emergency handling: Good with the S-series; first class with the L-series. **Steering:** On the S-series it's fairly precise and predictable, with plenty of assist and road feedback. There's no torque steer, owing to the use of equal-length driveshafts. **Acceleration/torque:** Brisk acceleration with both the V6 and the DOHC 124-hp 4-banger (0–100 km/h: 8.5 sec.). The smaller engine delivers excellent fuel economy, as well. **Transmission:** The manual transmission is precise and easily shifted. The automatic shifts smoothly. **Routine handling:** Better than average. The firm suspension gives a comfortable ride. Nimble handling with only a slight tendency to understeer. **Braking:** Fairly good; excellent braking with the optional four-wheel ABS (100–0 km/h: 124 ft.).

Con: Noisy S-series base engine. The 1.9L 100-hp 4-cylinder engine found on the sporty SC coupe gives barely adequate acceleration times (11.5 seconds to reach 100 km/h) with the manual transmission. This time is increased to a near-glacial 13.7 seconds with the 4-speed automatic gearbox, which robs the engine of what little power it produces. Excessive automatic gearbox shudder when the kickdown is engaged while passing. Some wallowing in tight turns, and ride quality deteriorates if the car is loaded. L-series steering could be better tuned and the suspension may be too firm, especially on the wagon.

Comfort/Convenience

Pro: Standard equipment: Base Saturns come with a wide range of standard equipment. Large glove box and convenient door pockets. **Driving position:** Very good. Good all-around visibility on the S-series. **Controls and displays:** Most everything's within easy reach and well presented. **Climate control:** Efficient, quiet, and easy to adjust. **Interior space/comfort F/R:** Comfortable front seats, with a fair amount of head and leg room. **Cargo space:** Plenty of trunk space and storage compartments, particularly with the LS-series. Rear seatbacks fold down 60/40 for cargo flexibility. **Trunk/liftover:** Huge trunk has a large opening and low liftover height.

Con: Interior isn't as refined as that found on the Accord or Camry. GM's too cheap to make ABS a standard feature as it has done with the Cavalier and Sunfire. Steering wheel is too close for comfort and the radio controls are tiny and distracting. LS-series visibility hampered by the high rear deck. Rear fold-down armrest isn't very useful. Coupe's third door window doesn't roll down. **Entry/exit:** Difficult rear access with the S-series. The rear is not the place to be—door sills are high, seat cushions are short, low, and too soft. **Quietness:** Lots of rattles and road and wind noise. Some engine noise at cruising speed.

COST				
List Price (negotiable)	**Residual Values** (months)			
	24	**36**	**48**	**60**
SL1: $13,488 (11%)	$10,000	$9,000	$7,000	$5,500
LS: $19,255 (14%)	$14,000	$12,000	$10,000	$8,500
LS1: $22,440 (17%)	$15,500	$13,500	$11,500	$9,500

LS2: $26,940 (17%)	$17,000	$15,000	$13,000	$11,000
LW1: $25,220 (18%)	$16,500	$14,500	$12,500	$10,500
LW2: $28,630 (18%)	$18,000	$16,000	$13,500	$12,000

TECHNICAL DATA

Powertrain (front-drive)
Engines: 1.9L 4-cyl. (100 hp)
• 1.9L 4-cyl. (124 hp)
• 2.2L 4-cyl. (137 hp)
• 3.0L V6 (182 hp)
Transmissions: 5-speed man.
• 4-speed auto.
Dimension/Capacity (SL/SC)
Passengers: 2/3; 2/2
Height/length/width:
53.8/176.9/66.7 in.

Head room F/R: 39.3/38 in.
Leg room F/R: 42.5/32.8 in.
Wheelbase: 102.4 in.
Turning circle: 41 ft.
Cargo volume: 12 cu. ft.
Tow limit: 1,000 lb.
Fuel tank: 46–49L/reg.
Weight: 2,400 lb.

SAFETY FEATURES/CRASHWORTHINESS

	Std.	Opt.
Anti-lock brakes	❏	■
Seatbelt pretensioners	—	—
Side airbags	—	—
Traction control	—	■
Head restraints	**	*
Visibility (front/rear)		
All excl. L-Series and Saturn SC	*****	*****
L-series	*****	***
Crash protection (front) D/P	*****	*****
Crash protection (side) D/P	***	***
Crash protection (offset)	***	
HLDI injury claims (model)	*****	
Saturn SC	****	
HLDI injury claims (all)	***	
Saturn SC	***	

Note: Only the visibility rating applies to the L-Series.

Cavalier, Sunfire

✓ BEST BUY

Cavalier

RATING: Above Average. **Strong points:** Very reasonably priced, good acceleration with the 2.4L engine, plenty of front passenger and cargo room, comfortable riding, standard ABS, and good fuel economy. **Weak points:** Noisy engine and mediocre steering and handling. Limited rear passenger room. Crash safety and quality control still need some improvement.

NEW FOR 2000: Standard AC and rear defroster, upgraded ABS, a new Getrag 5-speed manual transmission, a redesigned instrument panel and centre console, new body-colour fascias, clear headlight lenses and new taillights. Minor exterior styling tweaks and interior renovations that include an improved dash and sound system, a new remote keyless entry with a panic button, top child-seat anchors for all three rear positions, and a new feature on vehicles equipped with power door locks that prevents accidental lockout with the key in the ignition. Biggest disappointment: no addition of a 6-cylinder powerplant.

OVERVIEW: These twins are two of the lowest-priced cars to come equipped with standard ABS and dual airbags (GM claims to lose $1,000 U.S. on each Cavalier and Sunfire it sells). They have exceptional styling (especially the coupe) and lots of interior room, with a nicely tuned suspension. The ride and handling have also improved markedly over the past three years, with power rack-and-pinion steering, a longer wheelbase, and a wider track. The Sunfire is identical to the Cavalier, except for its more rakish look.

The Cavalier Z24/Sunfire GT are performance versions of the compacts introduced three years ago. They use a reworked version of the failure-prone Quad 4 2.4L DOHC 16-valve 4-cylinder powerplant.

Cost analysis/best alternatives: Get the 2000 model for the upgrades. Also look at the Honda Civic, Hyundai Tiburon, Mazda Protegé, or

Nissan Sentra. **Options:** Four-speed automatic transmission, which will reduce engine noise and make for more responsive performance, a suspension upgrade, traction control, and air conditioning. If you want more performance, the best combination is the 2.4L engine hooked to a 5-speed manual transmission. Of course, you'll have to deal with the engine's uncertain reliability. **Rebates:** $2,000 rebates on the '99 convertibles and $750–$1,000 rebates on the sedans and coupes. **Delivery/PDI:** $620. **Depreciation:** Slower than average. **Insurance cost:** Average. **Parts supply/cost:** Parts are easy to find and CAA says they're reasonably priced, with heavy discounting by dealers. **Annual maintenance cost:** Average. Maintenance on 4-cylinder models is reasonably straightforward. **Warranty:** Bumper-to-bumper 3 years/60,000 km; rust perforation 6 years/160,000 km. **Supplementary warranty:** A wise investment. **Highway/city fuel economy:** 7.5–10.4L/100 km with the 2.2L and automatic 3-speed. **Annual fuel cost:** 1,819L=$1,055.

Quality/Reliability/Safety

Pro: Reliability: Overall reliability has been average. **Warranty performance:** On par with Chrysler; better than Ford.

Con: Failure-prone Getrag maunal gearbox. **Quality control:** Quality control is variable, often leading to poor paint application, inside and outside body panel gaps, and lots of exposed screw heads. Most body hardware is fragile. **Owner-reported problems:** The Quad 4 engine, despite its new refinements, has had a poor reliability history; head gasket failures have been a frequent problem. Computer modules have also been one of the most common sources of complaints; symptoms include stalling and a shaky idle. Fuel-injection and cooling systems are temperamental as well. The power steering may lead or pull, and the steering rack tends to deteriorate quickly, usually requiring replacement some time shortly after 80,000 km. The front MacPherson struts also wear out rapidly, as do the rear shock absorbers. Many owners complain of rapid front brake wear and warped brake discs after a year or so. **Service bulletin problems:** Inaccurate speedometers and trunk deck lid may be hard to open with a key. **NHTSA safety complaints/safety:** *Cavalier.* Engine fires; chronic hesitation or stalling; sudden acceleration; faulty ABS; brake failure due to leaking master cylinder fluid; airbags failed to deploy; transmission failed to engage upon startup; vehicle rolled away even though parked with parking brake engaged; when vehicle is in Drive with foot on the brake it lurches forward, stalls, and produces a crashing sound; during highway driving the vehicle suddenly accelerated without steering control; sudden brake cable breakage while driving; brake grinding noise; warping of the front and rear brakes; when driving with door locked, it came ajar; windshield water leaks. *Sunfire.* Chronic stalling; brake master cylinder leaks; dash warning light indicating time to upshift comes on at the wrong time;

fuel tank leakage; airbags failed to fully inflate; horn only works intermittently; annoying squeak from both doors. On both cars the trunk lid
remains open at such a low angle that it's easy to hit your head.

Road Performance

Pro: Acceleration/torque: Acceptable acceleration with the 2.2L
(0–100 km/h: 9.6 sec.), but the 2.4L is a much better performer. The
fuel-injected 2.2L 4-cylinder engine provides adequate power when
used with the manual transmission or with the smoother, more responsive 4-speed automatic. The 150-hp 2.4L Quad 4 produces lots more
torque, shaving 0–100 km/h times by over a second (to 8 seconds).
Models equipped with an optional suspension package offer the best
handling at highway speeds and the best ride control on bad roads.
Braking: Acceptable (100–0 km/h: 131 ft.).

Con: Even with the torque upgrade this year, when hooked to the
3-speed transaxle the 2.2L 4-cylinder lacks sufficient power to distin-
guish these J-cars from the competition. **Emergency handling:** Excessive
lean when cornering under power and standard tires corner poorly.
Steering: Power steering feels over-assisted, resulting in insufficient
road feel. **Transmission:** The 5-speed manual transaxle has an abrupt
clutch. The 3-speed automatic strains to get into the proper gear range.
Routine handling: Base models don't handle as well as do most other
vehicles in this class.

Comfort/Convenience

Pro: Standard equipment: Nicely equipped, and one of the few entry-
level small cars with standard ABS. **Driving position:** Generous up-front
head room, although tall drivers may find the driving position a bit confining. **Controls and displays:** Well laid-out dashboard and controls.
Entry/exit: Lots of foot space and large door openings make for easy
access into the front or rear areas. **Interior space/comfort F/R:** Interior
room will seat four adults comfortably. **Cargo space:** Fairly generous for
a compact. **Trunk/liftover:** Good-sized trunk with a low liftover.
Quietness: Quiet interior with minimal road/wind noise intrusion.

Con: Poor visibility on the Z24. **Climate control:** Interior ventilation is
feeble without the air conditioning option. Rear seat room is skimpy.
Lots of engine resonance invades the car's interior. Watch out for the
low-hanging trunk lid.

COST				
List Price (firm)	**Residual Values** (months)			
	24	36	48	60
Cavalier Coupe: $15,765 (12%)	$11,000	$8,000	$6,000	$4,500
Sunfire: $16,165 (12%)	$11,000	$7,500	$6,500	$5,000

TECHNICAL DATA

Powertrain (front-drive)
Engines: 2.2L 4-cyl. (120 hp)
• 2.4L 4-cyl. (150 hp)
Transmissions: 5-speed man. OD
• 3-speed auto.
• 4-speed auto.
Dimension/Capacity
Passengers: 2/3
Height/length/width:
54.8/180.3/67.4 in.

Head room F/R: 38.9/37.2 in.
Leg room F/R: 42.3/34.6 in.
Wheelbase: 104.1 in.
Turning circle: 38 ft.
Cargo volume: 14 cu. ft.
Tow limit: 1,000 lb.
Fuel tank: 58L/reg.
Weight: 2,700 lb.

SAFETY FEATURES/CRASHWORTHINESS

	Std.	Opt.
Anti-lock brakes	■	❑
Seatbelt pretensioners	—	—
Side airbags	—	—
Traction control	❑	■
Head restraints	*	*
Visibility (front/rear)	*****	*****
Crash protection (front) D/P		
2d	***	****
4d	****	****
Crash protection (side) D/P		
2d	*	**
4d	*	***
Crash protection (offset)	*	
HLDI injury claims (model)	****	
HLDI injury claims (all)	**	

Grand Am, Alero

Alero

RATING: Average. **Strong points:** Competent V6, good steering and handling, roomy interior, standard ABS and traction control, and average quality control. **Weak points:** Mediocre ride over rough terrain, excessive 4-cylinder noise, noisy interior, difficult rear seat access (coupe), awkward radio controls, and long-term powertrain reliability is still a question mark.

NEW FOR 2000: A Getrag manual gearbox.

OVERVIEW: Taking its styling cues from GM's redesigned Grand Prix, the Grand Am offers a roomy, comfortable interior in two- and four-door body styles. Sharing its platform and mechanical components with the Oldsmobile Alero, the base Grand Am uses a 150-hp Quad DOHC engine; a 170-hp 3.4L V6 engine is optional on the SE1 and standard on the SE2.

The practically identical Alero, Oldsmobile's entry-level model, debuted in 1999 as the replacement for the slow-selling Achieva, often referred to as the "under-Achieva." A V6 engine is optional on the GL and standard on the GLS, but only one transmission is available—a 4-speed automatic.

Cost analysis/best alternatives: Get the '99 model Grand Am if it's discounted by at least 15 percent; get a 2000 Alero, though, just to be sure the first-year bugs have been worked out. Other cars worth considering are the Ford Contour, Honda Accord, Mazda 626, Nissan Altima, Subaru Legacy, Toyota Camry and Avalon, or VW Passat. **Options:** The best engine choice for power, smoothness, and value retention is the 170-hp 3.4L V6; it gives you much needed power and costs only $60 extra per year in fuel. Stay away from the Computer Command Ride option: true, it allows you to choose your own suspension setting, but the settings aren't quite what they pretend to be. **Rebates:** $1,000 on the '99 Grand Am coupe and sedan; nothing on the Alero until next summer. **Delivery/PDI:** $650. **Depreciation:** Faster than average. **Insurance cost:** Higher than average. **Parts supply/cost:** Easy to find parts at reasonable prices. **Annual maintenance cost:** Average. **Warranty:** Bumper-to-bumper 3 years/60,000 km; rust perforation 6 years/ 160,000 km. **Supplementary warranty:** A good idea. **Highway/city fuel economy:** 7.5–11.1L/100 km with the 2.4L and automatic 4-speed, and 7.8–11.8L/100 km with the 3.4L. **Annual fuel cost:** 2.4L: 1,896L=$1,100; 3.4L: 2,000L=$1,160.

Quality/Reliability/Safety

Pro: Quality control: The 4-speed automatic and 5-speed manual have had few major mechanical problems. Rear cornering lights shine at a 45-degree angle and make backing up both easier and safer. **Warranty performance:** Average. Apparently, GM wants to maintain owner loyalty for both the Grand Am and the Alero.

Con: Body assembly and paint application are substandard. **Reliability:** The Getrag manual transmission and Quad 4 engine have proven to be unreliable in the past, and parts are often in short supply. **Owner-reported problems:** Powertrain malfunctions, electrical problems, and substandard body assembly. **Service bulletin problems:** Squawk coming from front suspension or engine area; seatbelt latch slides to anchor sleeve; fuel injector deposits causing chronic stalling, poor idling, or hard starts. **NHTSA safety complaints/safety:** *Grand Am:* Transmission suddenly failed while cruising at speeds over 100 km/h; chronic stalling; vehicle continued accelerating after passing another car on the highway; airbags failed to deploy; inadvertent airbag deployment; inadequate headlight illumination; power steering fluid leakage; steering shudders upon braking, faulty power steering pump; excessive steering vibration when accelerating; premature wearout of the front and rear brake pads; front brake pads wear out every 5,000 km; shoulder belts twist in their housing; power door locks lock on their own, headlights blink on and off, and theft alarm sounds for no reason; middle rear lap seatbelt is too short to secure a child safety seat and GM says an extension isn't available; head restraints and optional rear spoiler blocks rear vision. *Alero:* Engine compartment fire; right front wheel separated because the lug nuts and bolts sheared off; tapped brakes to turn cruise control off and vehicle accelerated; rear main oil seal leak blew oil onto exhaust pipe; electrical shorts cause instrument panel gauges and controls to fail; windshield water leaks cause electrical shorts; side mirror spring mounts break when passing over unpaved roads; seat latch doesn't lock immediately when moved.

Road Performance

Pro: Emergency handling: Better than average. **Steering:** Steering is predictably responsive. **Acceleration/torque:** Fair acceleration (0–100 km/h: 9.9 sec.) with the 4-cylinder engine. V6 acceleration is impressive with power delivered smoothly and quietly. **Transmission:** Well-suited to the V6. **Routine handling:** Better than average on the highway. Suspension improvements have made for better handling and have smoothed out the ride considerably. **Braking:** Reasonably good (100–0 km/h: 121 ft.) with some brake fade after repeated stops.

Con: Transmission: There's been a lot of hype about the Quad 4 engine, but little of this translates into benefits for the average driver. Multi-valve motors produce more power than a standard engine, but always at higher rpms and with a fuel penalty. The Quad 4 is rougher than most multi-valve engines when revved to cruising speed, and so does little to encourage drivers to get the maximum power from it. The Quad 4 powerplant also accentuates the harsh shifting of the 4-speed automatic; it's over-eager to enter lockup mode in high gear, causing sluggish response in city driving. Rough roads aren't completely absorbed by the suspension.

Comfort/Convenience

Pro: Standard equipment: Well-appointed. Nice heavily padded interior. **Driving position:** Comfortable cockpit with an easily adjusted, supportive driver's seat and plenty of head and leg room. Alero's bucket seats are particularly comfortable. **Controls and displays:** Good interior and exterior styling. Well laid-out, user-friendly dash with large, legible gauges. **Climate control:** Efficient heating/defrosting and ventilation system. Rear windows roll all the way down. **Interior space/comfort F/R:** Sedan has better than average room in front and back. Standard split folding rear seats are quite useful. **Trunk/liftover:** Standard split folding rear seatbacks expand cargo space.

Con: Alero's dash vents are rather crude and the seat fabric feels cheap. **Entry/exit:** The doors on two-door models are heavy and awkward to open in tight spaces. The front seatbelts interfere with getting in and out. **Interior space/comfort F/R:** *Coupe:* Back seat will only hold two adults comfortably due to its narrower seats and reduced head room. Rear visibility is also somewhat limited. **Cargo space:** Limited storage space. **Trunk/liftover:** High sill and small opening makes loading difficult. **Quietness:** Excessive road noise and annoying exhaust drone.

COST

List Price (firm)	Residual Values (months)			
	24	36	48	60
Grand Am 2d: $20,495 (16%)	$15,000	$12,000	$9,500	$7,500
Alero: $20,315 (17%)	$16,000	$13,000	$10,500	$8,500
GLS: $27,500 (18%)	$19,000	$16,000	$13,500	$11,000

TECHNICAL DATA

Powertrain (front-drive)
Engines: 2.4L 4-cyl. (150 hp)
• 3.4L V6 (170 hp)
Transmissions: 5-speed man.
• 4-speed auto.
Dimension/Capacity
Passengers: 2/3
Height/length/width:
55.1/186.3/70.4 in.

Head room F/R: 37.8/36.5 in.
Leg room F/R: 43.1/33.9 in.
Wheelbase: 107 in.
Turning circle: 39 ft.
Cargo volume: 14/15 cu. ft.
Tow limit: 1,000 lb.
Fuel tank: 47L/reg.
Weight: 3,066 lb.

SAFETY FEATURES/CRASHWORTHINESS

	Std.	Opt.
Anti-lock brakes (4W)	■	❑
Seatbelt pretensioners	—	—
Side airbags	—	—
Traction control	■	❑
Head restraints	**	**

Visibility (front/rear)	*****	***
Coupes	*****	*
Crash protection (front) D/P	****	****
Crash protection (side) D/P	***	***
Crash protection (offset)	N/A	
HLDI injury claims (model)	N/A	
HLDI injury claims (all)	N/A	

'99 Olds Cutlass, Chevrolet Malibu

Chevrolet Malibu

RATING: Average. **Strong points:** Good V6 powertrain setup. Comfortable ride, easy handling, and precise steering. **Weak points:** Noisy base engine lacks guts, mediocre seats, and uneven quality control.

NEW FOR 2000: *Cutlass:* 1999 was its last model year. *Malibu:* A standard 3.1L V6; a slight makeover is planned for 2001.

OVERVIEW: The Cutlass and Malibu are identical front-drive, five-passenger, mid-sized sedans that replaced the long-discontinued Celebrity and Ciera. They're conventionally styled cars that use a more rigid body structure to cut down on noise and improve handling. Standard mechanical components include a standard 3.1L V6 for both cars. The ignition switch is mounted on the dash (a throwback to your Dad's Oldsmobile). There's plenty of passenger and luggage space. Other points to consider: outside mirrors are too small, the stiffer suspension may be too firm for some, and there's no traction control.

Cost analysis/best alternatives: The Cutlass is by far the better buy with its many standard features, even though it starts out costing more than the Malibu. Fortunately, this price difference will likely be eliminated through rebates and dealer incentive programs, now that it's no longer made. Other cars worth considering: Ford Contour and '99 Mystique,

the '99 Plymouth Breeze, Toyota Camry, Honda Accord, or Mazda 626.
Options: The LS package and premium tires. **Rebates:** $1,000–$1,500
rebates on the Cutlass; $750–$1,000 on the Malibu. **Delivery/PDI:**
$750. **Depreciation:** Average. **Insurance cost:** Higher than average.
Parts supply/cost: These new models use GM generic parts that are
found everywhere and are reasonably priced. **Annual maintenance cost:**
Average. **Warranty:** Bumper-to-bumper 3 years/60,000 km; rust perforation 6 years/160,000 km. **Supplementary warranty:** A wise investment.
Highway/city fuel economy: 7.5–11L/100 km with the 2.4L;
7.4–11.8L/100 km with the 3.1L. **Annual fuel cost:** 2.4L: 1,896L=$1,100;
3.1L: 1,964L=$1,139.

Quality/Reliability/Safety

Pro: Quality control: Average quality control. **Reliability:** Nothing of a
serious nature. **Warranty performance:** Nothing negative, yet. **Safety:**
The automatic headlight control that turns on at dusk is a useful feature.

Con: Owner-reported problems: Some hard starting and stalling; malfunctioning theft lock prevents the car from starting; leaking steering
rack; glove box door won't close; faulty window control pod; and sticking power windows. **Service bulletin problems:** Door handles turn yellow; front and rear doors are hard to open or close; warning chimes
sounds when key is removed from the ignition; inaccurate speedometers. **NHTSA safety complaints:** *Cutlass:* ABS malfunctioned, causing
extended stopping distance and producing a grinding noise; sudden
power steering loss; in a "fender-bender" rear-end collision the driver
and passenger seatbacks collapsed rearward; distracting dash glare in
windshield. *Malibu:* Loose tie rod nut caused steering loss; stalling
caused by fuel line leak; hit a small bump in road and vehicle stalled
with a complete loss of electrical power; tire blew and cruise control
wouldn't disengage; fuel tank filler tube is loosely connected to the
frame; excessive vibration at any speed; transmission doesn't lock when
the key is in the accessory position; very loose steering; faulty high-
beam light switch; original equipment tires don't have gripping power.

Road Performance

Pro: Emergency handling: Very good. Cornering under speed is
well controlled, with little front-end plowing or excessive body roll.
Steering: Quite precise, with lots of road feedback. **Acceleration/torque:**
Brisk acceleration with plenty of low-end torque with the V6 engine
(0–100 km/h: 8.8 sec.) which has the same horsepower as the '99's
4-banger but delivers it in a smoother, quieter manner. **Transmission:**
Smooth and predictable shifting, most of the time. **Routine handling:**
Better than average, thanks to an independent suspension that doesn't
sacrifice solid handling for passenger comfort.

Con: '99 Malibu's base 2.4L engine is noisy and lacks sufficient torque in the higher gear ranges. Push-rod V6 is a bit rougher than the over-head-cam V6s used by the competition. Downshifting is a bit slow when passing other vehicles. **Braking:** Antiquated rear drum brakes provide mediocre braking with standard ABS (100–0 km/h: 128 ft.). Some brake fade after repeated stops.

Comfort/Convenience

Pro: Standard equipment: Well-appointed for the price, but the better-equipped LS version has more of what you need. **Driving position:** Seating is adequate, though a bit low. Large side mirrors help provide good all-around visibility. **Controls and displays:** Very well thought-out instrumentation, and gauges that are easy to access and read. For example, the ignition switch is located on the instrument panel, a radical departure for GM. **Climate control:** Excellent ventilation system and first-class controls that are easy to use. AC vents are mounted high enough to direct cool air at your face. **Entry/exit:** Easy access to both front and rear interiors. **Interior space/comfort F/R:** More head and leg room than the Ford Contour/Mystique or the Chrysler Cirrus/Stratus. Unusually spacious rear seat area can accommodate three adults in comfort. **Cargo space:** Lots of interior storage space. **Trunk/liftover:** Plenty of trunk space that can be expanded through the split folding rear seatbacks. Low liftover and practical cargo net facilitate loading.

Con: Bland styling. Seats could use better lumbar support and side bolstering. Some gauges are hard to read in direct sunlight. Heating to the floor area is a bit slow. Door checks may not hold the doors open when parked facing uphill. Rear seatbacks don't lie flat when folded. Trunk hinges intrude into the trunk area, possibly damaging contents in a stuffed trunk. The 2.4L engine's noise intrudes into the passenger compartment. **Quietness:** Excessive engine noise. Interior not as quiet as GM claims; lots of front suspension squeaks and rattles.

COST				
List Price (negotiable)	**Residual Values** (months)			
	24	36	48	60
Malibu Sedan: $21,920 (18%)	$16,000	$14,000	$12,000	$10,000
'99 Cutlass GL: $23,895 (20%)	$17,000	$13,000	$11,000	$8,500

TECHNICAL DATA	
Powertrain (front-drive)	Head room F/R: 39.4/37.6 in.
Engines: 2.4L 4-cyl. (150 hp)	Leg room F/R: 41.9/38 in.
• 3.1L V6 (170 hp)	Wheelbase: 107 in.
Transmission: 4-speed auto.	Turning circle: 40 ft.
Dimension/Capacity (Malibu)	Cargo volume: 16 cu. ft.
Passengers: 2/3	Tow limit: 1,000 lb.

Height/length/width:	Fuel tank: 58L/reg.
56.4/190.4/69.4 in.	Weight: 3,051 lb.

SAFETY FEATURES/CRASHWORTHINESS

	Std.	Opt.
Anti-lock brakes	■	❑
Seatbelt pretensioners	—	—
Side airbags	—	—
Traction control	—	—
Head restraints	*	*
Head restraints (Malibu)	**	*
Visibility (front/rear)	*****	*****
Crash protection (front) D/P	****	****
Crash protection (side) D/P	*	***
Crash protection (offset)	****	
HLDI injury claims (model)	****	
HLDI injury claims (all)	****	

Century, Grand Prix, Impala, Intrigue, Monte Carlo, Regal

Monte Carlo

RATING: *Century, Grand Prix,* and *Regal:* Average buys; *Intrigue:* Above Average buy; *Impala* and *Monte Carlo:* Not Recommended during their first year on the market with a new platform. **Strong points:** Nice array of standard features on the Impala and Intrigue, good choice of power-trains, comfortable ride, easily accessed, and roomy interior. **Weak points:** Excessive engine noise at high speeds, rear seating uncomfortable for three, and obstructed rear visibility due to high-tail styling.

NEW FOR 2000: The Impala and Monte Carlo were late-summer additions to this growing mid-size family in the late summer. The 3.1L V6 gets 10 more horses (170 hp), some trim changes, standard dual-zone climate control, and an optional driver-side airbag. Intrigue gets an optional anti-skid cornering system to enhance its standard traction control and an optional gold trim package. The Regal LS and LSE get suspension modifications designed to improve ride and handling.

OVERVIEW: These front-drive mid-sized cars share the same platform and mostly exhibit the same performance characteristics with similar powertrains, except for the Intrigue's 3.5L twin-cam V6, which is in a class by itself. *Century:* This is a bland, unexciting sedan, loaded with convenience features and powered by a 3.1L V6. One gets the impression the Century targets young retirees who prefer to be driven, rather than drive. *Grand Prix:* The new sport sedan, it comes as a two- or four-door model and is powered by the Chevy Lumina's 3.1L V6 and an optional 3.8L V6—or supercharged variation—borrowed from the Pontiac Bonneville. Larger brakes, upgraded power steering, and a two-inch longer body, a three-inch longer wheelbase, and a two-inch wider track are also featured. *Impala and Monte Carlo:* Positioned to replace the slightly smaller Lumina sedan, Impala is a more upscale, nicely appointed sedan that seats six and comes equipped with a base 3.4L and an optional 3.8L engine. Surprisingly, ABS is optional on the base model, yet the base Cavalier (a much cheaper car) has it as a standard feature. The Monte Carlo is a mid-sized sport coupe that incorporates more creases in its styling, along with round taillights, a longer wheelbase, and shorter length. Four-wheel ABS is standard, along with a host of other features. Only bucket seats are offered (five-passenger limit) and side airbags aren't available. *Intrigue:* Oldsmobile's near-luxury-class sedan is a much better performer than any of the others. It's got plenty of interior room, a competent base 3.8L V6, and a more powerful optional 3.5L 215-hp 24-valve V6, as well as knockout styling. Initial reports give it high marks for handling and ride comfort, exceptional braking with the AutoBahn package, and a superb suspension that provides a firm, though not unpleasant, ride. *Regal:* GM says the Regal is designed to appeal to younger, more sport-oriented buyers who will appreciate the car's high-performance add-ons.

Cost analysis/best alternatives: Get the 2000 models for the upgrades. Don't buy a first-year '99 model Intrigue; instead, check out the Olds Cutlass: it's only a bit smaller than the Intrigue, but it's much cheaper. Stay away from both the Impala and Monte Carlo until owner feedback and service bulletins confirm that first-year series glitches have been corrected. Consider instead the Acura Integra, Honda Accord, Mazda 626, Nissan Altima and Maxima, and Toyota Camry and Avalon. Intrigue shoppers should also look at the redesigned BMW 3-series. **Options:** The rear-mounted child safety seat. The Intrigue's AutoBahn package with larger brake rotors and better-performing tires, or the GL version, both of which offer lots of useful features for only $2,000 more. **Rebates:** $1,000 on all '99s. Expect $1,500 customer rebates in the year 2000. **Delivery/PDI:** $785. **Depreciation:** A bit slower than average.

Insurance cost: Higher than average. **Parts supply/cost:** Moderately priced parts that aren't hard to find. **Annual maintenance cost:** Higher than average. Servicing can be performed by most neighbourhood mechanics. **Warranty:** Bumper-to-bumper 3 years/60,000 km; rust perforation 6 years/160,000 km. **Supplementary warranty:** Essential, especially after the third year of ownership. **Highway/city fuel economy:** 7.4–11.8L/100 km with the 3.1L for the base sedan; 8–12.7L/100 km with the 3.5L; 7.6–12.3L/100 km with the 3.8L. **Annual fuel cost:** 3.1L: 1,964L=$1,139; 3.5L: 2,117L=$1,228; 3.8L: 2,037L=$1,181. No information available on the Impala and Monte Carlo's 3.4L fuel consumption.

Quality/Reliability/Safety

Pro: Warranty performance: Average. **Safety:** Standard tire-inflation monitor is a good idea.

Con: Quality control: Below average for powertrain and body construction, which puts it on par with Chrysler and a bit better than Ford. **Reliability:** The 3.1L V6 engine has had more than its share of fuel system and engine computer module problems, and the 3.4L engine found in the Impala and Monte Carlo this year have yet to prove themselves. **Owner-reported problems:** Electrical system problems are common on cars loaded with power accessories. The front brakes wear out early and the discs warp far too easily. Shock absorbers and MacPherson struts wear out or leak prematurely. The power rack-and-pinion steering system degenerates quickly after three years and is characterized by chronic leaking. Poor body fit, particularly around the doors, leads to excessive wind noise and water leaks into the interior. Door locks freeze up easily. **Service bulletin problems:** Excessive shaking at 55–90 km/h (see first bulletin on the following page); redesigned front disc brake pads available to reduce brake squealing (see second bulletin on the following page); inaccurate speedometers; door handles turn yellow.

Shaking Sensation When Vehicle Is Between 35–55 MPH
File In Section: 7 - Transmission
Bulletin No.: 83-71-11
Date: September, 1998
Subject:
Shaking Sensation when Vehicle is Operated between 35–55 mph (55–90 km/h) on
Smooth Roads with Curves or Dips (Replace Transmission Mount)
Models:
1997–99 Buick Century, Regal
Condition
Some customers may comment about a shaking sensation when the vehicle is operated
between 35–55 mph (55–90 km/h) on a smooth road surface with curves or dips. This
condition may be further aggravated by elevated ambient temperatures.
Cause
This condition may be caused by the vehicle's engine being vertically displaced or
bounced in its mounts, resulting in the transmitting of a vibration into the body structure.
Correction
Replace existing elastromeric transmission mount with hydraulic transmission mount (P/N
22178939), following applicable Service Manual procedures.
Important:
Transmission mount (P/N 22178939) should NOT be installed in an attempt to correct
any condition other than the vibration described above.

Redesigned Front Disc Pads
File In Section: 5 - Brakes
Bulletin No.: 83-50-25
Date: January, 1999
INFORMATION
Subject:
Front Disc Brake Pads (Shoe/Lining Assemblies) Interim Design Change
Models:
1997–99 Buick Century, Park Avenue, Regal, Riviera
1997–99 Cadillac DeVille, Eldorado, Seville
1997–99 Chevrolet Venture
1997–99 Oldsmobile Aurora, Silhouette
1998–99 Oldsmobile Intrigue
1997–99 Pontiac Grand Prix, Montana, Trans Sport

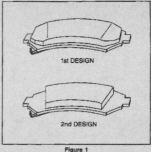

Figure 1

An interim design change was implemented in production that reduces the front brake
pad lining material surface area (see illustration). This pad lining configuration change
has shown to provide a significant reduction in brake squeal during light brake
applications.
A brake pad kit containing these new pad assemblies, P/N 18042214, has been
released for service usage.

NHTSA safety complaints: *Century:* Sudden brake failure; car rolls backward when stopped in gear on an incline; constant reflection of curved dashboard in windshield with or without sunlight; passenger-side windshield wiper channels water directly in the line of vision on the upstroke, temporarily blocking driver's vision; front seat head restraints won't stay in raised position; vent behind shifter handle becomes very hot when heater is on; gear shift lever continually sticks; water leaks onto the interior carpet; air dam deflector on the front of the vehicle is mounted too low; it hits the road on dips; defective radio volume control; horn is hard to find. *Grand Prix:* Chronic stalling; false airbag deployment; airbag failed to deploy; seatbacks designed with an inertia lock that only locks when braking aggressively, allowing unoccupied seatback to flop around and distract driver; ABS failure; prematurely worn rear brake pads create excessive metal-to-metal grinding noise; wheel lug nuts and bolts sheared off causing wheel to fall off; windshield wipers malfunction; windshield wiper system freezes up in cold weather; lap/shoulder seatbelts become twisted when reaching up and pulling down from the guide loop; cruise control suddenly engaged on its own and wouldn't release; sometimes cruise control causes the vehicle to suddenly accelerate and then slow down; right door speaker and dash rattling. *Intrigue:* Fuel leak caused by loose fuel line; cruise control doesn't maintain speeds when going up or down hill; windows fog easily. *Regal:* Vehicle was on a medium incline, with the ignition on and the shift indicator in the Drive position, when driver took foot off the brake pedal and the vehicle rolled backward; excessive shaking on smooth roads; audio speaker failure; loose power steering; passenger-side airbag cover came loose.

Road Performance

Pro: Emergency handling: Better than average, thanks to standard traction control. **Steering:** Precise and predictable. **Acceleration/torque:** The 3.1L V6 engine produces sufficient power for smooth acceleration and works well with the 4-speed automatic transmission (0–100 km/h: 10.5 sec.), but it could use more high-speed torque. For extended highway use, you'll find the 3.8L powerplant better suited to your needs. Intrigue buyers will want to get the 3.5L engine; it's generally smooth and quiet-running (except for some cycling), and has plenty of high-speed torque when you need it. **Transmission:** The automatic transmission is quiet and smooth under most conditions. **Routine handling:** Handling and ride are better than average due to recent suspension and steering refinements. **Braking:** Better than average.

Con: There's excessive engine noise intrusion into the interior when either the 3.1L or 3.8L engine is pushed. There is little information on the 3.4L engine—however, it should be expected to perform similarly to the 3.8L. The 3.5L twin-cam V6 cruising at 100–110 km/h tends to cycle annoyingly. The automatic 4-speed transmission is sometimes slow to downshift.

Comfort/Convenience

Pro: Standard equipment: Reasonably well-appointed, with such innovative features as automatic headlights that turn on at dusk and a system that prevents the doors from locking automatically if the key is in the ignition. Large side mirrors help overcome the obstructed rear view. **Driving position:** The cockpit area is much more user-friendly this year; lots of room; good all-around visibility; optional power driver's seat is a boon for short drivers. A tilt steering wheel is standard. **Controls and displays:** Improved instrumentation and easy-to-read gauges and controls. **Climate control:** Excellent heating-defrosting-ventilation system that even includes a pollen filter. **Entry/exit:** Not difficult. **Interior space/comfort F/R:** Front bench seats accommodate two with plenty of head and leg room. Rear seats have enough space for three adults. Grand Prix seating is quite firm, but not uncomfortable. **Trunk/liftover:** Large trunk and a low liftover. **Quietness:** Fairly quiet, except for some engine noise.

Con: Luxury models use tacky imitation wood and cheap cloth covers. Flimsy cupholders. Climate controls are set too low, interfering with middle passenger's knees, and low dash vents can chill a driver's hands. The Grand Prix sport sedan's head room has been sacrificed to give the car a sleeker appearance. Seats are too soft and lack support on all models, with the exception of the Grand Prix. Insufficient rear leg room. **Cargo space:** Absence of truly functional interior storage areas. There are lots of little storage spaces, but they're generally small and narrow. **Trunk/liftover:** *Century:* Quite a stretch to get over the wide, bumper-level shelf. *Grand Prix:* High trunk sill and narrow opening make for difficult loading and unloading, and large decklid hinges reduce usable trunk space. Rear seatbacks don't fold down to increase trunk space.

COST				
List Price (negotiable)	**Residual Values** (months)			
	24	36	48	60
Century: $25,440 (22%)	$16,000	$13,000	$11,000	$8,000
Grand Prix SE Sedan: $25,775 (22%)	$16,500	$13,500	$11,500	$8,500
Intrigue: $28,365 (23%)	$18,000	$15,000	$13,000	$10,500
Impala: $24,495 (21%)	$16,000	$13,000	$12,000	$9,000
Monte Carlo: $24,715 (22%)	$16,000	$13,000	$11,000	$8,000
Regal: $28,675 (22%)	$17,500	$14,500	$12,500	$9,500

TECHNICAL DATA

Powertrain (front-drive)
Engines: 3.1L V6 (170 hp)
• 3.4L V6 (180 hp)
• 3.8L V6 (200 hp)
• 3.5L V6 (215 hp)
• 3.8L V6 SC (240 hp)
Transmissions: 5-speed man.
• 4-speed auto.
Dimension/Capacity (Grand Prix)
Passengers: 2/3
Height/length/width:
54.7/196.5/72.7 in
Head room F/R: 38.3/36.7 in.
Leg room F/R: 42.4/35.8 in.
Dimension/Capacity (Century)
Passengers: 3/3
Height/length/width:
56.6/194.6/72.7 in.
Head room F/R: 39.3/37.4 in.
Leg room F/R: 42.4/36.9 in.

Dimension/Capacity (Regal)
Passengers: 2/3
Height/length/width:
56.6/196.2/72.7 in.
Head room F/R: 39.3/37.4 in.
Leg room F/R: 42.4/36.9 in.
Dimension/Capacity (Intrigue)
Passengers: 2/3
Height/length/width:
56.6/195.9/73.6 in.
Head room F/R: 39.3/37.4 in.
Leg room F/R: 42.4/36.9 in.
Wheelbase: Grand Prix: 110.5 in.;
  Century, Intrigue, and Regal: 109 in
Turning circle: 40 ft.
Cargo volume: 16/17 cu. ft.
Tow limit: 1,000 lb.
Fuel tank: 62L/reg./prem.
Weight: about 3,400 lb.

SAFETY FEATURES/CRASHWORTHINESS

	Std.	Opt.
Anti-lock brakes (4W)	■	❏
Seatbelt pretensioners	—	—
Side airbags	❏	■
Traction control	■	❏
Head restraints	*	*
Head restraints (Grand Prix)	***	*
Visibility (front/rear)	*****	***
Crash protection (front) D/P		
All excl. Grand Prix and Impala	****	***
Grand Prix	****	*****
Impala	*****	*****
Crash protection (side) D/P		
Century, Impala, Monte Carlo		
and Regal	***	***
Intrigue	***	*
Crash protection (offset)		
Grand Prix	***	
HLDI injury claims (model)		
Century	*****	
HLDI injury claims (all)		
Century	****	

Lumina, '99 Monte Carlo

Monte Carlo

RATING: Below Average. Both vehicles use the same poor-quality components. **Strong points:** Well-matched 3.8L engine and transmission, quiet-running, nicely-tuned suspension provides a comfortable ride, and plenty of front seat and cargo room. **Weak points:** Base, 3.1L engine lacks power, some automatic transmission gear "hunting," light, imprecise steering transmits little road feel, and serious past reliability problems.

NEW FOR 2000: No significant changes for the Lumina; the upsized year 2000 Monte Carlo will share the Impala platform. The Lumina was scheduled to be replaced by the slightly larger Impala, but GM has decided to let the Lumina linger around for another year as a fleet car.

OVERVIEW: The Lumina and Monte Carlo are popular two- and four-door versions of Chevy's mid-sized cars, featuring standard dual airbags, ABS, and 170-hp V6 power. The Monte Carlo was formerly sold as the Lumina Z34. Powertrain enhancements have increased horsepower and fuel efficiency. Each car has been given a slightly different exterior appearance and a distinct "personality." A 3.1L V6 is the standard engine, while a 3.8L V6 equips the more upscale versions.

Cost analysis/best alternatives: The '99 Monte Carlo will likely be the cheapest of the duo as dealers make room for the upsized and upgraded 2000 model set on the Impala platform (see page 245). As far as the Lumina is concerned, expect heavy discounting on both last and this year's models. Other good choices: the Honda Accord, Mazda 626, and Toyota Camry and Avalon. **Options:** Braking is the pits on these cars without ABS, so spring for the $500 or so extra cost. The sunroof option isn't a good idea if you're taller than 5'11". The Lumina's LTZ and the Monte Carlo's Z34 version give you significant performance and comfort upgrades. **Rebates:** $1,500 rebates are currently being offered on the '99 Lumina and $2,500 on the '99 Monte Carlo. These rebates and dealer incentives on the '99s will likely get sweetened further by spring. **Delivery/PDI:** $785. **Depreciation:** About average. **Insurance cost:** Higher than average. **Parts supply/cost:** No problem finding moderately priced parts, especially from independent suppliers. **Annual maintenance cost:** Higher than average. **Warranty:** Bumper-to-bumper 3 years/60,000 km; rust perforation 6 years/160,000 km. **Supplementary warranty:** A good idea, particularly in view of the fact that these cars often develop serious powertrain problems after their third year of use. **Highway/city fuel economy:** 7.4–11.8L/100 km with the 3.1L; 7.6–12.3L/100 km with the 3.8L. **Annual fuel cost:** 3.1L: 1,964L=$1,139; 3.8L: 2,037L=$1,181.

Quality/Reliability/Safety

Pro: Reliability: Overall reliability is better than Chrysler and Ford front-drives, but below the Japanese equivalent.

Con: Quality control: Below average. **Warranty performance:** Mediocre. One gets the impression that GM has written off Lumina owners. **Owner-reported problems:** *Lumina:* In spite of some noise reduction progress, body construction is still below par—loose door panel mouldings, poorly fitted door fabric, and misaligned panels. Other common problems: fuel pump whistling, frequent stalling, vague steering, premature paint peeling on the hood and trunk, heavy accumulation of hard-to-remove brake dust inside the honeycomb design wheels, and front tires that scrape the fenders when the wheel is turned. Despite its own recent redesign, the 3.1L engine isn't entirely problem-free. Electronic fuel-injection systems and engine controls have created many problems for GM owners. The 4-speed automatic transmission still has bugs. The front brakes wear quickly, as do the MacPherson struts and shock absorbers. Steering assemblies tend to fail prematurely. The electrical system is temperamental. The sunroof motor is failure-prone. Owners report water leaks from the front windshield. Front-end squeaks may require the replacement of the exhaust manifold pipe springs with dampers. **Service bulletin problems:** Poor driveability due to fuel-injector deposits; chronic engine misfire calls for the replacement of the ignition control module; inaccurate speedometers. **NHTSA safety complaints/safety:** *Lumina:* Horn button not easily accessible; brake booster diaphragm failure; driver has to keep foot on brake when stopped on a hill; cruise control suddenly cuts out and can't be reset until brake pedal is applied; excessive brake noise when turning while in Reverse; incorrect fuel gauge readings. *Monte Carlo:* During a collision the passenger-side airbag deployed and exploded, burning the driver's face and neck; brakes lose their effectiveness in rainy weather; tires touch the vehicle's body when turning; steering pulls to the right.

Road Performance

Pro: Emergency handling: Better than average. **Acceleration/torque:** Acceptable acceleration with the 3.1L V6 (0–100 km/h: 9.4 sec.). It's the engine of choice for reliability, but it doesn't have enough grunt (particularly in passing power) to handle all highway situations. The 3.8L powerplant is smoother and more powerful, and dealer service bulletins don't show any serious problems. **Routine handling:** Above average. The upgraded suspension has improved both ride and handling under either a light or full load. **Braking:** Acceptable (100–0 km/h: 135 ft.).

Con: Steering: Too light and vague. A fully loaded car causes the back end to sag and makes for a poor ride. Anti-lock brakes control directional stability by preventing wheel lockup, but take an unacceptably long time to work under normal conditions. **Transmission:** The 4-speed automatic occasionally has trouble choosing the right gear.

Comfort/Convenience

Pro: Standard equipment: User-friendly cockpit area. Good visibility. Spacious interior has more room than the Taurus/Sable. The comfortable front bench seats will accommodate just about anyone. **Cargo space:** Plenty of cargo space. **Trunk/liftover:** Large trunk and low liftover. **Quietness:** Very quiet running. Although styling is rather plain, a rigid body structure, thicker side windows, and additional soundproofing material have practically eliminated interior rattles as well as wind and road noise.

Con: Driving position: Uncomfortable driving position without the optional power seat, and the bucket seats are best suited for bucket bottoms. The low-cut side bolstering leaves much of the back unsupported. The seat can't be lowered sufficiently to prevent your head from touching the roof. **Controls and displays:** The interior is too "space age," with omnipresent small buttons and paddle switches that are distracting and difficult to fiddle with, particularly when adjusting the AC system. **Climate control:** Mediocre heating/defrosting. **Entry/exit:** Getting in and out of this car takes real effort and determination, particularly as a result of the heavy, stiff front doors. **Interior space/comfort F/R:** The rear seat isn't very comfortable and there's only marginal room for three adults.

COST				
List Price (negotiable)	**Residual Values** (months)			
	24	**36**	**48**	**60**
Lumina Sedan: $22,329 (20%) $15,000	$11,500	$9,500	$8,000	
'00 Monte Carlo: $25,895 (18%) $15,000	$11,500	$9,500	$8,000	

TECHNICAL DATA

Powertrain (front-drive)
Engines: 3.1L V6 (170 hp)
• 3.8L V6 (200 hp)
Transmissions: 5-speed man.
• 4-speed auto.
Dimension/Capacity
Passengers: 3/3
Height/length/width:
55.2/200.9/72.5 in.

Head room F/R: 38.4/37.4 in.
Leg room F/R: 42.4/36.6 in.
Wheelbase: 107.5 in.
Turning circle: 44/43 ft.
Cargo volume: 16 cu. ft.
Tow limit: 1,000 lb.
Fuel tank: 65L/reg.
Weight: 3,650 lb.

SAFETY FEATURES/CRASHWORTHINESS

	Std.	Opt.
Anti-lock brakes	■	■
Seatbelt pretensioners	—	—
Side airbags	—	—
Traction control	—	—
Head restraints	*	*
Visibility (front/rear)	*****	*****
Crash protection (front) D/P		
Lumina	****	*****
Monte Carlo	****	****
Crash protection (side) D/P		
Lumina	****	***
Crash protection (offset)		
Lumina	*****	
HLDI injury claims (model)		
Lumina	****	
Monte Carlo	***	
HLDI injury claims (all)		
Lumina	****	
Monte Carlo	****	

'99 Bonneville, '99 LeSabre

Bonneville

RATING: Average, but only with an extended warranty. These luxurious family sedans are outclassed by their year 2000 versions and by more reliable and better-performing Japanese competitors. **Strong points:** Well-matched engine and transmission, good braking, easy access, and adequate interior space. **Weak points:** Limited rear visibility, uncomfortable seats, poor fuel economy, and a history of expensive powertrain defects.

NEW FOR 2000: Both models are considerably upgraded and set on the larger Park Avenue/Seville platform. For a comprehensive review of their performance, see Park Avenue's entry.

OVERVIEW: These large, front-wheel drive sedans represent last year's mindset in GM's concept of luxury family motoring, which in turn exemplifies the malaise afflicting the company these days. The LeSabre is the bargain of the two. It offers all the technical features of the more expensive Park Avenue in a smaller package. Pontiac's stylish Bonneville SSE targets those buyers who want more bark and bite, using the same supercharged 240-hp 3.8L engine that powers the Buick Ultra.

   Although the interiors will seat six in a pinch and the decor is suitably "upscale," these large cars still feel as though they got stuck in the 1970s, when conservative styling, uninspiring handling, and a floating, cushiony, extra-quiet ride were the norm. A re-tuned 3800 TPI 3.8L V6 engine and electronically controlled 4-speed transmission form the base drivetrain for both models.

Cost analysis/best alternatives: If you can get a 15–20 percent discount on a '99 model, buy it; there's no reason to pay more for the redesigned year 2000 versions until their first-year bugs have been corrected. Other cars worth considering include the Ford Crown Victoria, Mercury

Grand Marquis, Lincoln Town Car, and Toyota Avalon. **Options:** Traction control, automatic levelling suspension, and power mirrors to compensate for the poor rear visibility. You may wish to buy the optional firmer suspension to counteract the base suspension's unsettling jiggle. It includes quicker-ratio steering, firmer shocks, thicker sway bars, and high-performance Goodyear tires. Stay away from the optional digital cluster—all you get are large digital read-outs and bar graphs. The sports suspension and Grand Touring package also promise much more than they deliver. **Rebates:** Expect $2,000 rebates on '99 models. **Delivery/PDI:** $895. **Depreciation:** Slightly slower than average. **Insurance cost:** Expensive. **Parts supply/cost:** Parts are easily found, but they tend to be fairly expensive. **Annual maintenance cost:** Higher than average. **Warranty:** Bumper-to-bumper 3 years/60,000 km; rust perforation 6 years/160,000 km. **Supplementary warranty:** Should be seriously considered, since these cars tend to incur serious repair expenses after their third year on the road. **Highway/city fuel economy:** *Bonneville:* 7.8–12.4L/100 km and 7.7–13.2L/100 km with the High Output engine. *LeSabre:* 7.6–12.3L/100 km. **Annual fuel cost:** Base Bonneville: 2,066L=$1,198; High Output: 2,145L=$1,437; LeSabre: 2,037L=$1,181.

Quality/Reliability/Safety

Pro: Reliability: The 3.8 V6 engine has proven to be much more reliable than its Quad 4 predecessor.

Con: Quality control: Not very good. Powertrain failures, computer glitches, and body defects indicate poor overall quality. **Warranty performance:** Below average. GM doesn't stand for "generous" motors. **Owner-reported problems:** The electronic controls and sequential fuel-injection system are particularly failure-prone. The electrical system in general is plagued by an alarming frequency of short circuits and other failures, and it's difficult to troubleshoot. Front shock absorbers and steering assembly are likely to wear out quickly. Body hardware is fragile. Many mechanics, including GM's own, find the under-hood systems a mystery—even when there's no problem. Paint application is substandard. **Service bulletin problems:** Outer rear seatbelts are difficult to fasten; inaccurate speedometer; poor AM radio reception. **NHTSA safety complaints/safety:** *Bonneville:* Sudden acceleration; airbag failed to deploy; dash fire ignited behind the radio. *LeSabre:* Throttle sticks, causing high rpms; chronic stalling; inoperative rear seatbelt buckles; turn signal arm doesn't return to Neutral position; plastic part of seatbelt buckle came off when buckling up; location of rear seatbelts makes it difficult to buckle up; parking brake is hard to engage or release and sometimes won't stay locked; broken short steering gear; ABS brake failure; sudden steering failure; when lowering both rear windows while driving, the vehicle begins to vibrate excessively;

when decelerating or stopping the headlights dim or flicker; rear seat-belts are too short for a child safety seat or for some adults.

Road Performance

Pro: Acceleration/torque: The base 3.8L V6 engine is quiet, smooth, and relatively more economical than some competitive V6 powerplants. It provides lots of power through the lower gear ranges, but runs out of steam as it gets to the top end of its power curve (0–100 km/h: 8.2 sec.). **Transmission:** Smooth and quiet shifting with the 4-speed automatic. One major improvement: you can leave the car in Overdrive and drive around town without the transmission constantly shifting up and down. The Olds' suspension is calibrated more on the firm side than most cars in this class. **Braking:** Very good for cars of this heft (100–0 km/h: 127 ft.).

Con: Emergency handling: The ride deteriorates rapidly as the suspension bottoms out on rough roads. This effect worsens as the passenger and cargo loads increase. **Steering:** The power steering transmits very little road feel. **Routine handling:** Highway handling is clumsy, with too much body lean when cornering. The Bonneville SSE handles better than the others, but it still rides harshly for such a large car.

Comfort/Convenience

Pro: Standard equipment: All these cars are loaded with standard features and plush interiors, but their styling is fairly bland—with the exception of the Bonneville. Its SSE interior is stylish, without a lot of steering wheel mounted controls, and its dash layout makes for easy reading of the gauges and controls. The SSEi's trunk contains a road emergency kit and a trunk-mounted air compressor. **Driving position:** Good driving position if your buttocks fit the predefined indents. The optional power seat is essential for a comfortable driving position. **Controls and displays:** A more pleasing and practical half-eyebrow dash copies that of the Japanese and European automakers. User-friendly instruments, climate control system, and radio. **Climate control:** Improved climate controls and a higher-efficiency AC compressor provide excellent ventilation with little noise. You may also choose different temperature settings for either side of the car. **Entry/exit:** Very good. **Interior space/comfort F/R:** The interior feels spacious and airy and will comfortably seat five adults. There's plenty of rear seat leg room, thanks to the limited rearward travel of the front seats. **Cargo space:** Lots of small storage areas, and long objects can be passed from the trunk through the rear-seat armrest port. **Trunk/liftover:** Large trunk with a low liftover. **Quietness:** Quiet ride.

Con: Rear visibility is hampered by the thick rear roof pillars. Front quarter windows don't open. Limited rear travel on the front seats can put the driver too close to the steering wheel. Rear-seat access is a problem. Be wary of GM's claims of a six-passenger carrying capacity; only five passengers will ride in comfort. Front seats require a bit more back support, and the rear seats offer little thigh support and aren't sufficiently padded.

COST

List Price (negotiable)	Residual Values (months)			
	24	36	48	60
'99 Bonneville SE:				
$29,000 (22%)	$23,000	$15,000	$13,000	$11,000
'99 LeSabre Custom:				
$28,845 (23%)	$23,000	$15,000	$13,000	$11,000

TECHNICAL DATA

Powertrain (front-drive)
Engines: 3.8L V6 (205 hp)
• 3.8L V6 (240 hp)
Transmissions: 5-speed man.
• 4-speed auto.
Dimension/Capacity
Passengers: 3/3
Height/length/width:
55.6/200.8/74.4 in.

Head room F/R: 38.8/37.8 in.
Leg room F/R: 42.6/40.4 in.
Wheelbase: 110.8 in.
Turning circle: 42 ft.
Cargo volume: 17 cu. ft.
Tow limit: 2,000 lb.
Fuel tank: 68L/reg.
Weight: 3,450 lb.

SAFETY FEATURES/CRASHWORTHINESS

	Std.	Opt.
Anti-lock brakes	■	❑
Seatbelt pretensioners	—	—
Side airbags	—	—
Traction control	❑	■
Head restraints	*	*
Visibility (front/rear)	*****	**
Crash protection (front) D/P		
Bonneville	*****	***
LeSabre	****	****
Crash protection (side) D/P		
Bonneville	***	**
LeSabre	***	***
Crash protection (offset)	N/A	
HLDI injury claims (model)		
Bonneville	****	
LeSabre	*****	
HLDI injury claims (all)		
Bonneville	****	
LeSabre	*****	

'99 Aurora, '99 Riviera

Riviera

RATING: Average. **Strong points:** Standard ABS and traction control, comfortable ride, good steering and handling, roomy and well-appointed interior. **Weak points:** Underpowered base engine, requires premium fuel, no side airbags, excessive wind noise, and rear seats aren't easy to get into.

NEW FOR 2000: Riviera has been dropped; '99 Aurora is carried over.

OVERVIEW: The Aurora is the epitome of ugly styling. Built on the Park Avenue platform and similar in size to the Lexus LS 400, the Aurora is a five-passenger sports sedan that targets Lexus, Infiniti, Mazda's Millenia, and Toyota's Avalon. GM is shooting at moving targets, however, and has missed the mark with the Aurora. For example, its five-passenger seating can't compete with Avalon's six-passenger capacity; its failure-prone front-drive (based on past complaints when used with other vehicles) competes poorly in a market that has more reliable powertrains and that includes rear-drives; and exterior fit and finish just don't compare.

The Aurora is powered by a 250-hp 4.0L V8 Northstar engine—a smaller version of the Cadillac powerplant—coupled to a standard 4-speed automatic transmission. Standard features include dual airbags, 4-wheel ABS, traction control, adjustable shoulder height manual seatbelts, cruise control, keyless remote entry and security system, and power-assisted everything.

Cost analysis/best alternatives: The 1999 Aurora and Riviera should be discounted by 15 percent or more. Other cars worth considering are the Acura TL, Ford Crown Victoria and Mercury Marquis, Infiniti I30, Lexus ES 300, Lincoln Town Car, Mazda Millenia, Nissan Maxima, and Toyota Avalon. The Olds 88 LSS matches the Aurora's supercharged performance for less money. **Options:** The AutoBahn Package is not for everyone; it makes for a harsher ride than the more forgiving base suspension. Bucket seats provide more comfortable support. **Rebates:** $3,000 on the '99 Riviera; $2,000 on the '99 Aurora. **Delivery/PDI:** $895. **Depreciation:** Faster than average. **Insurance cost:** Higher than average. **Parts supply/cost:** Moderately priced parts that aren't hard to find. **Annual maintenance cost:** Above average. **Warranty:** Bumper-to-bumper 3 years/60,000 km; rust perforation 5 years/160,000 km. **Supplementary warranty:** A good buy. **Highway/city fuel economy:** *Aurora:* 8.4–13.6L/100 km. **Annual fuel cost:** *Aurora:* 2,252L=$1,509.

Quality/Reliability/Safety

Pro: Quality control: It's been spotty so far, but no worse than GM's other models. Improved structural integrity cuts flexing and reduces squeaks and rattles. **Reliability:** Few major reliability problems reported, due to the short time this reworked version has been on the market. The supercharged engine can't be repaired at your corner garage.

Con: Warranty performance: Below average. **Owner-reported problems:** Transmission malfunctions, electrical glitches, and sloppy body construction. **Service bulletin problems:** Excessive shaking and vibration in the steering wheel, floor, and seat at highway speeds (98–115 km/h) and on smooth roads (see Park Avenue entry); brake squealing has been a past problem, though redesigned front disc brake pads should reduce this; water drains into the trunk when the lid is opened; door handles may turn yellow. **NHTSA safety complaints/safety:** Exhaust fumes invade the vehicle's interior; ABS failure.

Road Performance

Pro: Steering: Excellent, with better road feel at high speeds. **Acceleration/torque:** Acceptable acceleration with the base engine; lots of power and torque produced by the supercharged powerplant (0–100 km/h: 8.6 sec.). **Transmission:** Smooth and quiet shifting. **Routine handling:** Better than average handling and ride quality. **Braking:** Excellent braking (100–0 km/h: 123 ft.), although pedal effort is a bit high.

Con: Emergency handling: Some excessive body lean; not as nimble as the competition.

Comfort/Convenience

Pro: Standard equipment: Fairly well-appointed despite some lapses. **Driving position:** Excellent driving position. Impressive styling combined with a roomy interior. Well thought-out interior ergonomics. Plush interior includes comfortable front seats and generous amounts of head and leg room. **Controls and displays:** State of the art, particularly the highly functional analogue instrument cluster. **Climate control:** Efficient, quiet, and easily calibrated. **Interior space/comfort F/R:** Roomy interior provides generous room for five adults. Seating is exceptionally comfortable, with just the right amount of thigh and lumbar support. **Cargo space:** Lots of storage areas that are easily accessed. **Quietness:** Excellent soundproofing and few vibrations.

Con: Lacks some features that are standard with the competition, like side airbags, height-adjustable shoulder belts, fold-away side mirrors, and a passenger-side heated seat. Rear visibility is obstructed by the wide rear pillars, and the undersized door mirrors don't help. **Entry/exit:** The low roof complicates access and creates a claustrophobic interior. This is not a five-passenger car: the middle occupant, front or rear, won't be comfortable for long. **Trunk/liftover:** Although the trunk is huge, the small opening and high liftover make for difficult loading and it's hard to lift the handle-less trunk lid except when it's opened by remote control. Rear seatbacks don't fold flat to expand storage capability.

COST				
List Price (negotiable)	**Residual Values** (months)			
	24	36	48	60
'99 Aurora Sedan:				
$46,190 (25%)	$30,000	$22,000	$19,000	$16,000
'99 Riviera: $44,125 (25%)	$29,000	$21,000	$18,000	$15,000

TECHNICAL DATA	
Powertrain (front-drive)	Head room F/R: 38.2/36.2 in.
Engines: 3.8L V6 (240 hp)	Leg room F/R: 42.6/37.1 in.
• 4.0L V8 (250 hp)	Wheelbase: 113.8 in.
Transmission: 4-speed auto.	Turning circle: 43 ft.
Dimension/Capacity (Aurora)	Cargo volume: 16 cu. ft.
Passengers: 2/3	Tow limit: 3,000 lb.
Height/length/width:	Fuel tank: 76L/prem.
54.4/205.4/74.4 in.	Weight: 3,750 lb.

SAFETY FEATURES/CRASHWORTHINESS		
	Std.	**Opt.**
Anti-lock brakes (4W)	■	❑
Seatbelt pretensioners	—	—
Side airbags	—	—
Traction control	■	❑
Head restraints	*	*
Visibility (front/rear)	*****	*****
Crash protection (front) D/P	***	***
Crash protection (side) D/P	N/A	
Crash protection (offset)	N/A	
HLDI injury claims (model)	*****	
HLDI injury claims (all)	*****	

Note: Crash and insurance data apply to only the Aurora.

Bonneville, LeSabre, Park Avenue, Ultra

Bonneville

RATING: *Park Avenue:* Average; *Ultra:* Above Average; *Bonneville* and *LeSabre:* Not Recommended during their first year using the Park Avenue platform. **Strong points:** Great powertrain performance, standard ABS, well-appointed, and quiet-running. Ultra provides excellent steering and handling. **Weak points:** Ponderous handling caused partly by a mediocre suspension and over-assisted steering with the base model, and no crashworthiness/insurance claim data.

NEW FOR 2000: Big news is the inclusion of the Bonneville and LeSabre into this family of large luxury family sedans. Nothing much new on the Park Avenue and Ultra except for standard front side airbags, child-seat anchors on the rear package shelf, and GM StabiliTrak anti-skid system, standard on the Ultra and optional on the Park Avenue.

OVERVIEW: Full-size luxury sedan aficionados love the flush glass, wrap-around windshield and bumpers, and clean body lines that make for an aerodynamic, pleasing appearance. But these cars are more than a pretty package; they provide lots of room, luxury, style, and—dare I say—performance. Plenty of power is available with the 205-hp 3.8L V6 engine and the 240-hp supercharged version of the same powerplant. It does a 0–100 km/h time in under 9 seconds (an eternity for a Miata, but impressive considering the heft of these vehicles), and improves low- and mid-range throttle response. Power is transmitted to the front wheels through an electronically controlled transmission that features "free-wheeling" clutches designed to eliminate abrupt gear changes. Both the Park Avenue and Ultra use a stretched version of the more rigid Olds Aurora platform.

Cost analysis/best alternatives: Get the year 2000 version for the upgrades. Keep in mind that the '99 Bonneville and LeSabre are entirely different cars. Other vehicles worth considering: the Ford Crown Victoria and Mercury Grand Marquis, Infiniti I30, Lexus ES 300, or Nissan Maxima. **Options:** The Grand Touring suspension is a good middle ground between sporty firmness and luxurious cruising comfort. On the other hand, the Head Up display is more of a gimmick than anything else. **Rebates:** $2,000 applicable to the base '99 Park Avenue; $2,500 for the Ultra. Don't look for much price relief for the Bonneville and LeSabre before mid-summer when rebates and dealer incentives will combine to give about a $1,500 reduction in price. **Delivery/PDI:** $895. **Depreciation:** Faster than average. **Insurance cost:** Higher than average. **Parts supply/cost:** Parts aren't hard to find, but they can be pricey (particularly the supercharged engine components). **Annual maintenance cost:** Higher than average. **Warranty:** Bumper-to-bumper 3 years/60,000 km; rust perforation 5 years/160,000 km. **Supplementary warranty:** It'll come in handy after the third year of use. **Highway/city fuel economy:** 7.8–12.4L/100 km; 7.7–13.2L/100 km with the High Output engine. Supercharged V6 sips fuel, unlike the V8-equipped competition. **Annual fuel cost:** Base model: 2,066L=$1,198; High Output model: 2,145L=$1,437.

Quality/Reliability/Safety

Pro: Quality control: Average. Quality control has improved a lot during the past few years. **Warranty performance:** Better than average. **Safety:** A personalized vehicle security system disables the starting and fuel systems if a non-matching key is used. Rear shoulder belts have a strap to pull the belt away from the neck of small passengers and children. Right-side mirror tilts down when Reverse is engaged (standard on the Ultra).

Con: Reliability: Mediocre. **Owner-reported problems:** Some engine, transmission, and electronic module malfunctions. **Service bulletin problems:** Excessive noise or vibration during low-speed acceleration or braking; excessive shaking and vibration in the steering wheel, floor, and seat at highway speeds (98–115 km/h), and on smooth roads (see following bulletin); redesigned front disc brake pads should reduce brake squealing; poor AM radio reception.

NHTSA safety complaints: False airbag deployment injured driver; airbag deployment when key inserted into the ignition; sudden stalling while driving on the highway; hard-to-read speedometer; difficulty seeing dashboard controls due to dash-top design; a reflection in the windshield coming from the dashboard obstructs view; ABS and service light come on for no reason; intermittent windshield wiper failure; horn is hard to operate.

> **Shake/Vibration in Steering Wheel and Floor**
> File In Section: 3 - Steering/Suspension
> Bulletin No.: 83-30-04
> Date: September, 1998
> Subject:
> Shake/Vibration in Steering Wheel, Floor, Seat at Highway Speeds on Smooth Roads
> (Diagnose/Balance Tires/Wheels)
> Models:
> 1995–99 Buick Riviera
> 1997–99 Buick Park Avenue, Park Avenue Ultra
> 1998–99 Cadillac Seville (SLS, STS)
> 1995–99 Oldsmobile Aurora
> Condition
> Some customers may comment on shaking/vibration in the steering wheel, floor or seat
> at highway speeds, between 60–72 mph (98–115 km/h) on smooth roads. This condi-
> tion may phase in and out.
> Additional Information
> The vehicle structure is very sensitive to rotating corner assembly runout and/or imbal-
> ance and/or tire uniformity/force variation (internal tire structure characteristics) issues.
> This procedure must be completed "step-by-step" to reduce rotating component runout
> and imbalance to a minimum. The majority of the vehicles will be corrected by address-
> ing runout and balance issues with the original tire/wheel assemblies.
> Shortcutting will not repair the condition. This is not, and there is not, an easy fix.

Imagine paying $41,000 plus for a luxury vehicle that shakes and vibrates excessively, and has done so since 1995, for which GM has "no easy fix," wants the District Service Manager "informed," and suggests that "positive communication to the customer is necessary for customer satisfaction." I have a better idea. Ensure "customer satisfaction" by FIXING THE BLOODY PROBLEM!

Road Performance

Pro: Acceleration/torque: The 3.8L V6 engine is competent, quiet, and smooth running, with lots of low-end torque. Impressively fast with the supercharged engine (0–100 km/h: 8 sec.). **Transmission:** The F31 electronic 4-speed transmission works imperceptibly. Cruise control is much smoother without all those annoying downshifts we've learned to hate in GM cars. **Routine handling:** Acceptably predictable, though quite slow with variable-assist power steering and shocks that are a bit firmer than usual. Body roll has been reduced thanks to the re-tuned suspension. With its stiffer suspension the Ultra performs well on wind-ing roads, while the softly sprung Park Avenue is best for city use. **Emergency handling:** Fairly quick and sure-footed. **Braking:** Good brak-ing with or without ABS (100–0 km/h: 135 ft.).

Con: Acceleration/torque: Acceleration isn't breathtaking with the base 3.8L engine; at higher revs torque falls off quickly. **Steering:** Power steering is a bit vague at highway speeds. Panic braking causes consid-erable nose-diving that compromises handling.

Comfort/Convenience

Pro: The entire body has a more solid feel than what one normally finds with GM. **Standard equipment:** Very well equipped, with many performance and convenience features included as standard equipment. **Controls and displays:** Complete and easy-to-read instruments and gauges. **Climate control:** Much improved interior ventilation and AC performance. Easy-to-adjust controls allow the driver and passenger to choose different temperature settings for their own comfort. **Entry/exit:** No problem. **Interior space/comfort F/R:** Exceptionally spacious interior will seat four in total comfort. **Cargo space:** Plenty of storage areas that are easily accessible. **Trunk/liftover:** Huge trunk has a low liftover. **Quietness:** Excellent soundproofing, with minimal wind noise and tire vibration.

Con: Driving position: Driver seat lacks lateral support. Wide rear pillars block visibility, but large side mirrors compensate. **Quietness:** Some wind noise and tire vibration.

COST

List Price (negotiable)	Residual Values (months)			
	24	36	48	60
'00 LeSabre: $30,465 (22%)	$26,000	$22,000	$18,000	$15,000
'00 Bonneville:				
$30,740 (22%)	$26,000	$22,000	$18,000	$15,000
Park Avenue: $41,850 (23%)	$34,000	$30,000	$26,000	$21,000
Park Avenue Ultra:				
$48,310 (23%)	$37,000	$33,000	$29,000	$25,000

TECHNICAL DATA

Powertrain (front-drive)
Engines: 3.8L V6 (205 hp)
• 3.8L V6 (240 hp)
Transmission: 4-speed auto.
Dimension/Capacity
Passengers: 3/3
Height/length/width:
57/206.8/74.7 in.

Head room F/R: 39.8/38 in.
Leg room F/R: 42.4/41.4 in.
Wheelbase: 113.8 in.
Turning circle: 43 ft.
Cargo volume: 19.1 cu. ft.
Tow limit: 3,000 lb.
Fuel tank: 68L/reg./prem.
Weight: 3,950 lb.

SAFETY FEATURES/CRASHWORTHINESS

	Std.	Opt.
Anti-lock brakes	■	❑
Seatbelt pretensioners	—	—
Side airbags	—	—
Traction control	■	❑
Head restraints	*	*
Visibility (front/rear)	*****	***
Crash protection (front) D/P	N/A	
Crash protection (side) D/P	N/A	

Crash protection (offset)	N/A
HLDI injury claims (model)	N/A
HLDI injury claims (all)	N/A

Cadillac Catera

Catera

RATING: Average. If Cadillac is to once again lure luxury buyers into the GM fold, the automaker has to copy its European competitors with something more substantial than a warmed-over Opel. **Strong points:** Well-appointed, good brakes, quiet interior, and a comfortable ride. **Weak points:** Merely adequate acceleration, mediocre handling, numb steering, ponderous cornering, limited rear visibility, bland styling, and an uncertain future.

NEW FOR 2000: A recalibrated suspension, a mild facelift, a new instrument panel, repositioned controls, upgraded audio system, storage compartments with latches, and a new Sport option package. The Catera will be redesigned in 2003.

OVERVIEW: Assembled in Germany and based on the Opel Omega, the rear-drive, mid-sized Catera comes with a 200-hp V6 engine, 4-speed automatic transmission, 16-inch alloy wheels, four-wheel disc brakes, a limited-slip differential, traction control, and standard dual side airbags. The Sport package includes heated sports seats, a firmer suspension, a different grill, rear spoiler (are you kidding?), and alloy wheels.

Cost analysis/best alternatives: Even if it's discounted 20 percent, this is a car to avoid. Other "driver's" cars worth considering: the Audi A6, BMW 328i, Infiniti I30, Lexus ES 300, and Mercedes Benz C280 or CLK. **Options:** The Sport package option isn't worth the extra money. **Rebates:** $3,000 on all models by mid-2000. **Delivery/PDI:** $895. **Depreciation:** Higher than average. **Insurance cost:** Also higher than average. **Parts supply/cost:** Parts are expensive and not easily found. **Annual maintenance cost:** Predicted to be higher than average after the fourth year when the warranty expires. **Warranty:** Bumper-to-bumper 4 years/80,000 km; rust perforation 6 years/160,000 km. **Supplementary warranty:** Essential, until the Catera has proven its long-term reliability, to ensure that you won't be stuck with huge fifth-year repair bills. **Highway/city fuel economy:** 8.8–13.1L/100 km. **Annual fuel cost:** 2,233L=$1,496.

Quality/Reliability/Safety

Pro: Quality control: Average. Just a few computer module and body problems have been reported. **Reliability:** Reliability hasn't been a concern. **Warranty performance:** Unblemished. Now if only all of GM's customers were treated so well.

Con: GM dealers are notoriously bad when it comes to understanding and repairing European-transplanted cars (just ask any Saab owner). **Owner-reported problems:** Premature front brake wear, electrical glitches, and some body imperfections. **Service bulletin problems:** Inaccurate speedometers. **NHTSA safety complaints/safety:** Front seatbelts malfunction; airbag failed to deploy; brakes squeal and pull vehicle sharply to the right when applied; rear visibility is obstructed by a narrow window and large rear head restraints.

Road Performance

Pro: Acceleration/torque: German-built V6 engine has plenty of low-end torque and accelerates smoothly (0–100 km/h: 8.9 sec.). **Transmission:** Smooth and quiet, and the automatic transmission allows for third-gear starts for maximum traction on snow or ice. **Braking:** Respectable for a vehicle this heavy (100–0 km/h: 129 ft.).

Con: Engine runs out of steam in higher gear ranges. **Emergency handling:** Surprisingly slow for a European-bred luxury car. **Steering:** Vague, with little road feel. **Transmission:** The transmission has to kick down two gears to achieve adequate highway passing power. **Routine handling:** Though the "European" ride is comfortable, it has its problems. When you pass over a large expansion joint the floorpan vibrates annoyingly; drive over a bump when turning and the steering wheel kicks back in your hands.

Comfort/Convenience

Pro: Standard equipment: Loaded with convenience and performance features that would be optional on other cars. **Driving position:** Excellent, with good front and rear visibility. **Controls and displays:** Complete, logically presented, and easy to read. **Climate control:** Quite efficient and quiet. **Entry/exit:** Wide door openings make for easy front and rear access. **Interior space/comfort F/R:** Plush interior will seat four adults comfortably. **Cargo space:** Split folding rear seatbacks increase storage capability. **Trunk/liftover:** The large trunk has a low liftover.

Con: The uninspired styling has Lumina written all over it. Unmarked power window switches are mounted on the centre console, where they are less convenient. **Quietness:** Though the interior is fairly quiet, there is some wind noise at highway speeds.

COST				
List Price (very negotiable)	**Residual Values** (months)			
	24	36	48	60
Catera Sedan: $42,310 (30%)	$25,000	$21,000	$17,000	$13,000

TECHNICAL DATA

Powertrain (front-drive)
Engine: 3.0L V6 (200 hp)
Transmissions: 4-speed auto.
Dimension/Capacity
Passengers: 2/3
Height/length/width:
57.4/193.8/70.3 in.

Head room F/R: 38.6/37.8 in.
Leg room F/R: 42/36.2 in.
Wheelbase: 107.4 in.
Turning circle: 37 ft.
Cargo volume: 14 cu. ft.
Tow limit: 2,000 lb.
Fuel tank: 68L/prem.
Weight: 3,800 lb.

SAFETY FEATURES/CRASHWORTHINESS

	Std.	Opt.
Anti-lock brakes	■	❏
Seatbelt pretensioners	■	❏
Side airbags	■	❏
Traction control	■	❏
Head restraints	**	**
Visibility (front/rear)	*****	*
Crash protection (front) D/P	N/A	
Crash protection (side) D/P	N/A	
Crash protection (offset)	N/A	
HLDI injury claims (model)	***	
HLDI injury claims (all)	****	

DeVille DHS, DTS, '99 d'Elegance, '99 Concours

DeVille DHS

RATING: *DeVille DHS* and *DTS*: Not Recommended. Although they show lots of promise, these two models aren't recommended during their first year on the market. *DeVille '99 d'Elegance* and *'99 Concours*: An Average buy. **Strong points:** *DeVille DHS* and *DTS*: It's obvious that Cadillac wants to attract a younger audience through better handling, a well-appointed, spacious interior, and gadgets galore. Well-matched engine and transmission, comfortable riding, better than average body assembly, and many standard safety features. *d'Elegance* and *Concours*: Deeply discounted, nice powertrain performance, good handling, roomy, gives a comfortable, floaty ride, and better than average crash-worthiness and injury claim data. **Weak points:** *DeVille DHS* and *DTS*: Cadillac first-year models are notoriously bug-infested. Plus, these new models house a plethora of complex and fragile electronic systems that have yet to prove themselves. *d'Elegance* and *Concours*: These venerable discontinued models have limited rear and side visibility, base model climate controls that aren't user-friendly, poor fuel economy (premium fuel), and mediocre body assembly quality.

NEW FOR 2000: Cadillac's top seller and biggest sedan gets downsized in a major redesign that adopts the smaller platform used by the Seville and GM's other full-sized models. It is likely to remain Cadillac's only front-drive, once all the other models are converted to the rear-drive Sigma platform over the next four years.

OVERVIEW: The d'Elegance and Concours have been replaced by the DHS (DeVille High Luxury Sedan) and DTS (DeVille Touring Sedan), respectively. The shorter, narrower body uses a front-drive powertrain that includes a 275-horsepower and 300-horsepower V8 Northstar engine coupled to a 4-speed automatic transmission. Other standard features: front side airbags with a head/chest bag for the driver,

Cadillac's StabiliTrak anti-skid system, Variable Road Sensing Suspension, traction control, four-wheel anti-lock brakes, steering wheel audio controls, and separate rear seat temperature controls. Cadillac has also added some rather innovative optional features: rear side torso airbags; a GPS navigation system with touch-screen display; GM's OnStar communication and assistance system; Night Vision—a device that uses infrared technology to detect road hazards beyond headlight range; and Ultrasonic Parking Assist, which uses sensors to warn you both audibly and visually that there's an object behind you when backing up.

Acceleration remains strong with the Northstar still posting 0–100 km/h times under 7 seconds, with regular fuel. The ride is soft, comfortable, and quieter than before thanks to Cadillac's new engine intake system, a tighter chassis, and additional sound-deadening measures. Handling is also much more responsive, particularly with the sportier DTS.

One would think this year's smaller DeVille would sacrifice passenger and storage space—however, this is clearly not the case. There is plenty of room for six passengers (the front middle passenger may be squeezed a bit), the rear bench seat provides loads of head and leg room, and is slightly raised to provide "theatre-like" seating for better visibility. Entry and exit is exceptionally easy due to the large doors that open wide. And as for storage space, the large trunk is easily accessible and opens at bumper level to make loading and unloading a breeze.

d'Elegance and Concours

These two '99 Cadillacs stepped in to replace the rear-drive Fleetwood, and in turn have been replaced by the DHS and DTS. There are really two DeVilles: the Sedan DeVille (GM's most popular Cadillac) aimed at traditional Cadillac buyers, and the Concours, which offers sportier performance. Essentially a front-drive clone of the rear-drive Fleetwood, the sedan is a chrome-ridden, overly large luxury car whose new Northstar powerplant blurs the distinction between it and the Concours. It uses a "brake only" traction-control system, which counters wheelspin at low speeds by applying the front brakes, and a softer suspension. Michelin whitewalls are standard.

The Concours version carries the powerful 4.6L 300-hp Northstar engine and 4-speed automatic transmission, improved traction control, electronic variable-dampening suspension (programmed for a firmer ride), 4-wheel anti-lock disc brakes, and 225/6016 Eagle GA touring tires. Both Cadillacs have moved from GM's C platform—which they used to share with the Buick Park Avenue and Olds Ninety Eight—to a K-Special chassis, a stretched version of the Seville/Eldorado platform.

Cost analysis/best alternatives: Consider a '99 model only if the price is cut at least 20 percent. Other big, traditional luxury cars worth considering: the Ford Crown Victoria and Lincoln's Town Car. **Options:** Stay away from the optional digital cluster; all you get are large digital readouts and bar graphs. Buy the optional firmer suspension to counteract the base suspension's unsettling jiggle. It includes quicker-ratio steering, firmer shocks, thicker sway bars, and high-performance Goodyear tires. **Rebates**: Up to $3,000 on the '99s by next summer. **Delivery/PDI:** $895. **Depreciation:** Predicted to be faster than average. **Insurance cost:** Higher than average. **Parts supply/cost:** Except for engine components, most parts are easily found, though a bit expensive. **Annual maintenance cost:** Average during the first four years of ownership. Engine control and electrical systems are too complicated for most garages to service. **Warranty:** Bumper-to-bumper 4 years/80,000 km; rust perforation 6 years/160,000 km. **Supplementary warranty:** If you plan to keep the car after the fourth year, an extended warranty is essential. **Highway/city fuel economy:** *DeVille d'Elegance* and *Concours*: 8.3–13.9L/100 km; **Annual fuel cost:** 2,276L=$1,525. *DeVille DHS* and *DTS*: fuel economy figures aren't yet available.

Quality/Reliability/Safety ('99 models)

Pro: Warranty performance: Better than average.

Con: Quality control: Assembly quality isn't anywhere near luxury car standards, and paint is often poorly applied. Fragile body hardware. Large gaps between sheet metal panels and doors. **Reliability:** Long-term ownership of any of these models doesn't look promising. Reliability histories are replete with major faults, constant malfunctions, and mind-spinning depreciation. **Owner-reported problems:** The front brakes and shock absorbers wear out quickly. Serious fit and finish deficiencies. Intermittent stalling, rough idling, hesitation, and no-starts. **Service bulletin problems:** Improved on-board diagnostic system (OBD); door handles may turn yellow. **NHTSA safety complaints/safety:** Vehicle suddenly stalls on the highway; stalled while driving uphill and then started rolling backwards; traction control light comes on for no reason; ignition and electronic control module failures; premature brake wear; seats protrude out too far in the back area, preventing passengers from sitting back and making head restraints set too far back; sudden headlight failure; power door locks won't open with remote control device; windshield wipers won't activate unless turned on high.

Road Performance

Pro: Emergency handling: Very good. Road Sensing suspension prevents excessive body lean when cornering at high speed. **Steering:** Speed-sensitive power steering is precise, with lots of road feel. **Acceleration/torque:** Plenty of power and torque with the base 275-hp 4.6L V8 engine, delivered with minimal harshness, vibration, and noise (0–100 km/h: 7.6 sec.). The 300-hp variant is even more impressive. **Transmission:** The 4-speed automatic with Overdrive is responsive, smooth, and quiet. **Routine handling:** Very good. Little body roll and crisp handling. **Braking:** Best in its class (100–0 km/h: 120 ft.).

Con: The 4.6L V8 overpowers the front-drive chassis. Some torque steer is evident. The 44-foot turning radius can make parking a chore.

Comfort/Convenience

Pro: Standard equipment: These cars come equipped with just about every imaginable electrical and power-assisted gadget, in addition to an ultra-plush interior. **Driving position:** Excellent. **Climate control:** Efficient and quiet, though the controls may be hard to reach (Concours). **Entry/exit:** Easy front and rear access. **Interior space/comfort F/R:** This is one huge front-drive Cadillac. Impressively large interior easily accommodates six adults in comfort. **Cargo space:** Lots of storage areas. **Trunk/liftover:** Fairly large trunk has a low liftover. **Quietness:** Very little engine or road noise seeps into the interior.

Con: Tacky imitation wood dash. All seats lack sufficient lumbar support and the front seats lack adequate thigh support. Rear visibility is blocked by wide rear roof pillars, and rear view mirrors are too small to be of much help. **Controls and displays:** Dashboard controls are too fussy for safe operation; the driver must often look away from the road to do such simple things as tune the radio or adjust the climate controls.

COST

List Price (very negotiable)	Residual Values (months)			
	24	36	48	60
DeVille DHS: $49,710 (23%)	$37,000	$26,000	$22,000	$19,000
'99 DeVille: $49,910 (25%)	$35,000	$24,000	$21,000	$18,000

TECHNICAL DATA ('99 MODELS)

Powertrain (front-drive)
Engines: 4.6L V8 (275 hp)
• 4.6L V8 (300 hp)
Transmission: 4-speed auto.
Dimension/Capacity
Passengers: 6
Height/length/width:
56.4/209.7/76.5 in.

Head room F/R: 38.5/38.4 in.
Leg room F/R: 42.6/43.3 in.
Wheelbase: 113.8 in.
Turning circle: 44 ft.
Cargo volume: 20 cu. ft.
Tow limit: 3,000 lb.
Fuel tank: 76L/prem.
Weight: 4,000 lb.

SAFETY FEATURES/CRASHWORTHINESS ('99 MODELS)

	Std.	Opt.
Anti-lock brakes	■	❑
Seatbelt pretensioners	—	—
Side airbags	■	❑
Traction control	■	❑
Head restraints	**	**

Visibility (front/rear)	*****	**
Crash protection (front) D/P	****	****
Crash protection (side) D/P	****	****
Crash protection (offset)	N/A	
HLDI injury claims (model)	****	
HLDI injury claims (all)	*****	

Eldorado, Seville

Seville

RATING: *Eldorado*: Below Average; *Seville*: An Average buy. **Strong points:** *Eldorado*: Impressive engine performance, good handling, and a comfortable ride. *Seville*: Good powertrain matchup, excellent handling, taut ride, responsive steering, lots of storage space, and many standard safety features. **Weak points:** *Eldorado*: Limited rear visibility, rear seating for two, climate controls hard to find on the base model, sloppy body assembly, and poor fuel economy. *Seville*: Limited rear visibility and poor fuel economy.

NEW FOR 2000: An upgraded Northstar V8 and StabiliTrak traction control. The Eldorado's future looks bleak. Poor sales may force GM to drop the "Eldo" next year.

OVERVIEW: The front-drive Eldorado and its sport coupe twin share the same chassis and engine with the Seville. They are both equipped with the Northstar V8 and use the same components. This provides a quiet, comfortable ride along with impressive acceleration.

Two years ago, the Seville was dramatically restyled and adopted GM's G-body, the stiffened chassis created for the Oldsmobile Aurora and Park Avenue. This gave it a wider stance, longer wheelbase, and a bit shorter length.

On the safety front, seatbelts are attached to the seat itself rather than the B-pillar, the tires and rear brakes have been upgraded, and seat-mounted side airbags are standard (Seville only). Other standard safety features include: traction control, an anti-skid system, and anti-lock brakes.

Most Cadillacs offer some sort of performance package, usually in a special model, and the Eldorado and Seville are no different. Granted, this makes them more pleasant to drive, but these are usually only half-hearted efforts when compared to the sterling performance offered by the Japanese and German imports.

Cost analysis/best alternatives: *Eldorado*: Get the '99 model, if the price is cut by at least 20 percent. *Seville*: The '99 Seville, the second year of its redesign, is the better choice for a more refined, high-tech Caddy. Other cars worth considering: a BMW 5-series, Infiniti Q45, Lexus LS 400, or Mercedes-Benz E-class. **Options:** Be wary of the hard-riding ETC package; the base model's standard suspension gives a more comfortable ride and better low-speed performance. **Rebates:** *Eldorado*: $3,000–$4,000 in early 2000; $1,000 on the '99 Seville. **Delivery/PDI:** $895. **Depreciation:** Faster than average. **Insurance cost:** Higher than average. **Parts supply/cost:** Parts aren't hard to find, and they're reasonably priced. **Annual maintenance cost:** Average. **Warranty:** Bumper-to-bumper 4 years/80,000 km; rust perforation 6 years/160,000 km. **Supplementary warranty:** Not necessary. **Highway/city fuel economy:** *Eldorado* and *Seville*: 8.3–13.9L/100 km. **Annual fuel cost:** 2,276L=$1,525.

Quality/Reliability/Safety

Pro: Warranty performance: Better than average. All Cadillacs come with GM's PASS KEY theft-deterrent system that shuts down the starter and fuel system if the right key isn't used. Plastic fuel tanks improve Seville and Eldorado crashworthiness.

Con: Quality control: Assembly quality isn't anywhere near luxury car standards, and paint is often poorly applied. **Reliability:** If you're planning to spend big bucks on either the Eldorado or the Seville, the likelihood of multiple reliability and body problems should make you think twice. Like most of GM's front-drives, these models have amassed a terrible reputation for being unreliable and expensive to maintain. In all, there is little to recommend them; there are cheaper vehicles that offer better performance and interior comfort. Nevertheless, if you have to choose one of the two, go for the Seville—it promises to be around longer than the Eldorado and should have its new platform bugs worked out over the last two years. **Owner-reported problems:** Intermittent stalling, rough idling, hesitation, and no-starts. The front brakes and shock absorbers wear out quickly. Serious fit and finish deficiencies, windshield and trunk leaks, and poor-fitting rear door seals. **Service bulletin problems:** Redesigned front disc pads for quieter braking; door handles may turn yellow; fast flash turn signal arrow; on-board diagnostic (OBD) system improvements; inaccurate speedometer. *Seville*: Excessive shaking, vibration in the steering wheel, floor, and seat at highway speeds, on smooth roads. **NHTSA safety complaints/safety:** *Eldorado*: Shoulder belt chafes the neck and is too tight; *Seville*: water infiltrates through the headlight and taillight lens, causing poor illumination and shorts.

Road Performance

Pro: Emergency handling: Average. Suspension improvements make for much less body roll, more responsive handling, and a softer ride. **Steering:** Steering is crisp and predictable. **Acceleration/torque:** Tire-burning acceleration (0–100 km/h: 7.1 sec.) with gobs of torque and minimal harshness, vibration, and noise. **Transmission:** The 4-speed automatic with Overdrive is responsive, despite occasional confusion about which gear it should be in. **Routine handling:** Better than average, although it floats a bit. Road Sensing suspension prevents excessive body lean in turns. **Braking:** Acceptable, though not impressive (100–0 km/h: 134 ft.).

Con: The 4.6L V8 engine overpowers the Eldorado's front-drive chassis. Some torque steer is evident on both vehicles, but it's particularly strong on the Seville STS. Seville's STS suspension is jarring when passing over bumps.

Comfort/Convenience

Pro: Standard equipment: These cars come equipped with just about every imaginable electrical and power-assisted gadget. **Controls and displays:** Most controls are within easy reach, and instruments aren't hard to decipher. **Interior space/comfort F/R:** Spacious seating due to the Seville's extra length and width, which gives rear passengers considerable room and easy access. The Eldorado also has a surprisingly spacious interior for a coupe, and it actually offers more head room in the rear than up front. **Cargo space:** Plenty of small storage areas that are easily accessed. **Trunk/liftover:** Large trunk with a low liftover. **Quietness:** Better than average. Almost no engine, road, or wind noise finds its way into the passenger compartment.

Con: Driving position: Though the Seville's driving position is quite good, both car's wide rear pillars obstruct the driver's view to the right rear; front seats lack adequate thigh and lumbar support. **Climate control:** Efficient and quiet, but the climate control system has limited manual override and the steering wheel blocks the view of the controls. **Entry/exit:** *Eldorado*: Getting to the back seat requires very inelegant contortions. **Interior space/comfort F/R:** *Eldorado*: Rear seat won't accommodate three adults comfortably.

COST				

List Price (very negotiable) **Residual Values** (months)

	24	36	48	60
Eldorado: $53,230 (25%)	$39,000	$34,000	$29,000	$24,000
Seville SLS: $59,970 (25%)	$45,000	$39,000	$34,000	$29,000

TECHNICAL DATA

Powertrain (front-drive)
Engines: 4.6L V8 (275 hp)
• 4.6L V8 (300 hp)
Transmission: 4-speed auto. OD
Dimension/Capacity (Eldorado; Seville)
Passengers: 2/2; 2/3
Height/length/width:
53.6/200.6/75.5 in.;
55/201/75 in.

Head room F/R: 37.8/38.3 in.;
38/38.3 in.
Leg room F/R: 38/38.3 in.;
43/39.1 in.
Wheelbase: 108/112 in.
Turning circle: 42/44 ft.
Cargo volume: 15/16 cu. ft.
Tow limit: 3,000 lb.
Fuel tank: 76L/prem.
Weight: 3,900/4,010 lb.

SAFETY FEATURES/CRASHWORTHINESS

	Std.	Opt.
Anti-lock brakes	■	❑
Seatbelt pretensioners	—	—
Side airbags	■	❑
Traction control	■	❑
Head restraints	*	*
Visibility (front/rear)	*****	**
Crash protection (front) D/P	N/A	
Crash protection (side) D/P	N/A	
Crash protection (offset)	N/A	
HLDI injury claims (model) Eldorado	*****	
HLDI injury claims (all) Eldorado	*****	

Note: No crash/insurance claim data available for the Seville.

Camaro, Firebird

Camaro

RATING: Recommended. Firebird shares the Camaro's mechanical components, but is styled differently. **Strong points:** High-performance muscle cars with above-average crash protection, a reasonably good reliability record, and high resale value. Good engine performance (Z28) and crisp handling. **Weak points:** Poor wet-weather traction without traction control, limited rear seat room, hard-riding, difficult access, wide rear pillars impede rear visibility, and limited cargo space.

NEW FOR 2000: Nothing significant, except for side airbags. The Camaro may be dropped next year due to poor sales.

OVERVIEW: These sporty convertibles and coupes are almost identical in the features they offer and in their pricing. Both cars were extensively upgraded several years back, making them more powerful and aerodynamic with less spine-jarring performance.

As one moves up the scale, overall performance improves considerably. The aluminum-block LS1 V8 engine gives these cars lots of sparkle and tire-spinning torque, but there's a fuel penalty to pay. A 4-speed automatic transmission is standard on the 5.7L-equipped Z28; other versions come with a standard 5-speed manual gearbox or an optional 6-speed. All cars can be ordered with lots of extra performance and luxury options, including a T-roof package guaranteed to include a full assortment of creaks and groans.

Cost analysis/best alternatives: Last year's models are the better buy if they're discounted by at least 10 percent. Convertibles and V8-equipped models are the best choice for retained value a few years hence. But you can do quite well with the base coupe equipped with the Performance Handling Package (about $800) and 235 tires. Base Camaros usually outperform V6-equipped Mustangs and they get better gas mileage, as well. Other cars worth considering are the Ford Mustang, Honda Prelude, and Toyota Celica. **Options:** Go for GM's Performance Handling Package and 235/55 tires on 16-inch aluminum wheels. Most drivers will find the optional traction control system more useful than the limited-slip differential. **Rebates:** $1,000 rebate for '99 V6 models. **Delivery/PDI:** $700. **Depreciation:** Much slower than average. **Insurance cost:** Much higher than average. Expect to pay about $2,500, or three times the cost of insuring a Japanese econobox. **Parts supply/cost:** No problem finding reasonably priced parts. **Annual maintenance cost:** Average. Servicing the fuel-injection system is an exercise in frustration and drives up maintenance costs. **Warranty:** Bumper-to-bumper 3 years/60,000 km; rust perforation 6 years/160,000 km. **Supplementary warranty:** Not needed. **Highway/city fuel economy:** 7.5–12.4L/100 km with the base 3.8L and automatic; 8.8–14.1L/100 km with the 5.7L and 4-speed automatic. **Annual fuel cost:** 3.8L: 2,039L=$1,183; 5.7L: 2,343L=$1,570.

Quality/Reliability/Safety

Pro: Quality control: Above average. Plastic body panels are dent- and rust-resistant. **Warranty performance:** Above average. Most repairs are simple to perform and relatively inexpensive. **Service bulletin problems:** Nothing significant. Both cars are equipped with an impressively effective PASS KEY theft-deterrent system similar to the one used successfully in the Corvette. A resistor pellet in the ignition disables the starter and fuel system when the key code doesn't match the ignition lock.

Con: Reliability: Powertrain components frequently fail, causing extended periods of downtime while they're repaired. **Owner-reported problems:** The 5.7L V8 fuel and electrical systems have been troublesome in the past. Engine cooling and ignition systems are also bug-plagued. Poor air-conditioner performance is a common complaint. The front brakes and MacPherson struts wear out quickly. Body problems include door rattles, poor fit and finish, misaligned doors and hatch, and a sticking hatch power release. **NHTSA safety complaints/ safety:** *Camaro*: Airbags failed to deploy; driving down the highway, locked T-top flew off. *Firebird*: Airbags failed to deploy.

Road Performance

Pro: Steering: The rack-and-pinion steering is responsive and precise, with lots of road feedback. **Acceleration/torque:** Better than average acceleration with the base V6. Thrilling performance with either the base 305-hp V8 or the optional 320-hp 5.7L V8. Engines start well in cold weather and give ample pulling power. In fact, these cars have so much power in reserve that the automatic transmission doesn't compromise fuel economy or performance. **Routine handling:** Handling is best on the sports models, but even the base coupes perform respectably on the road, and the stiffer suspension makes for much tighter cornering. **Braking:** Much better than average, due primarily to the standard four-wheel anti-lock brakes (100–0 km/h: 117 ft.).

Con: Emergency handling: Without traction control the tires lose traction, and directional stability is compromised on wet pavement. Due to the rear axle suspension, the ride is constantly busy and particularly bouncy on poor roads. A stiffer suspension adds to this effect. These cars cry out for independent rear suspension. **Transmission:** The 6-speed manual transmission's clutch is heavy and gets tiring in city driving—the shifter takes getting used to due to the pattern of the gear throws. Furthermore, it has a fuel-saving feature that automatically shifts to fourth from first gear if you're not driving aggressively enough. The upgraded 4-speed automatic with Overdrive tends to shift late, putting extra strain on the engine.

Comfort/Convenience

Pro: Standard equipment: Even the base models come loaded with such useful features as anti-lock brakes. Most people find the Firebird's front seats more comfortable, but they're comfortable and supportive on both cars. **Controls and displays:** Dash is well laid-out with easy-to-read gauges and complete instrumentation. **Climate control:** Good fresh-air ventilation system. **Cargo space:** Quite limited, but folding back seat expands cargo storage capability. **Quietness:** A tighter chassis has eliminated most of the creaks and groans that have accompanied these cars for decades.

Con: Driving position: Driving position is too low for short drivers and rear visibility is compromised by wide roof pillars and the high rear end. The obtrusive centre console gets in the way when shifting. The front windshield has only a single de-mister vent. **Entry/exit:** Large doors make access into the interior a breeze, but they're a bit unwieldy, especially in tight parking spaces. Very difficult rear seat access. Door detents are too weak to keep the heavy doors open. **Interior space/comfort F/R:** Limited leg room for the front seat passenger. The rear buckets are just that—buckets. Consider this car a two-seater: the split rear seat is a joke (or a place to put people you don't like). **Cargo space:** The cargo area is small and awkwardly shaped. Large objects won't fit under the hatch. **Trunk/liftover:** Small trunk with a high liftover; the convertible has 40 percent less trunk space. Excessive tire, road, and engine noise.

COST				
List Price (very negotiable)	**Residual Values** (months)			
	24	36	48	60
Camaro: $25,890 (18%)	$18,000	$16,000	$13,000	$11,000
Firebird: $27,430 (19%)	$20,000	$18,000	$15,000	$13,000

TECHNICAL DATA

Powertrain (front-drive)
Engines: 3.8L V6 (200 hp)
• 5.7L V8 (305 hp)
• 5.7L V8 (320 hp)
Transmissions: 5-speed man.
• 6-speed man.
• 4-speed auto.
Dimension/Capacity (Z28)
Passengers: 2/2
Height/length/width:
52/193.2/74.1 in.

Head room F/R: 37.2/35.3 in.
Leg room F/R: 42.9/26.8 in.
Wheelbase: 101.1 in.
Turning circle: 42 ft.
Cargo volume: 13 cu. ft.
Tow limit: 1,000 lb.
Fuel tank: 59L/reg.
Weight: 3,600 lb.

SAFETY FEATURES/CRASHWORTHINESS

	Std.	Opt.
Anti-lock brakes	■	❑
Seatbelt pretensioners	—	—
Side airbags	—	—
Traction control	❑	■
Head restraints	*	*
Visibility (front/rear)	**	**
Crash protection (front) D/P	****	*****
Crash protection (side) D/P	***	****
Crash protection (offset)	N/A	
HLDI injury claims (model)	****	
HLDI injury claims (all)	***	

Corvette

Corvette

RATING: Average. A brawny sport coupe that's slowly evolving into a more refined machine. **Strong points:** Powerful powertrain, easy handling, supple ride, attractively styled, user-friendly instruments and controls, and lots of standard convenience features. **Weak points:**

Poorly performing "skip shift" manual gearbox, ride (Z51 suspension), limited rear visibility, inadequate storage space, poor-quality fit and finish, and no crashworthiness or insurance claim data.

NEW FOR 2000: Nothing significant.

OVERVIEW: Introduced in 1953 as a futuristic show car, and the first American car to use fuel-injection (in 1957), Chevrolet has sold more than a million Corvettes over the past 45 years, with an estimated 600,000 still on the roads. Its peak year was 1984, when over 84,000 coupes and convertibles were sold in North America, for about a third of today's price.

This year's Corvette returns with its 345-hp 5.7L LS1 powerplant, harnessed to either a 4-speed automatic or a 6-speed manual transmission. The engine is made from aluminum and most transmission components have been shifted to the rear for better handling and increased passenger room.

The high-performance hardtop version returns along with additional options for the coupe and convertible that include: a head-up display that projects instrumentation readouts onto the windshield, a power telescoping steering column, and an active handling system.

Cost analysis/best alternatives: Get the '99 Corvette if the price is cut 10 percent or more. Keep in mind that premium fuel and astronomical insurance rates will further drive up your operating costs. Other sporty models worth considering are the Dodge Viper and Porsche Boxster. **Options:** The 6-speed manual transmission and Z51 suspension, if you want the extra performance thrills, but you may find the suspension a bit harsh. Run-flat tires from Goodyear are an excellent investment. A dash indicator tells you when the tire is flat, even though you can continue to drive at a steady 90 km/h for 85 kilometres and the only noticeable change you'll feel will be a stiffer ride and less steering response. **Rebates:** The Corvette is so popular that GM doesn't have to offer rebates to boost sales, but dealers have a wide margin for discounting. **Delivery/PDI:** $820. **Depreciation:** Much slower than average. **Insurance cost:** Astronomical. **Parts supply/cost:** Good availability, but parts are pricey. **Annual maintenance cost:** Higher than average. **Warranty:** Bumper-to-bumper 3 years/60,000 km; rust perforation 6 years/160,000 km. **Supplementary warranty:** A smart idea. **Highway/city fuel economy:** 8.8–14.1L/100 km with the automatic. **Annual fuel cost:** 2,343L=$1,570.

Quality/Reliability/Safety

Pro: Warranty performance: Above average. GM has beefed up its warranty and given more authority to its dealers to resolve warranty disputes. Key-controlled lockout feature discourages joy riding by cutting engine power in half. Both Corvette versions are equipped with an impressively effective PASS KEY theft-deterrent system that uses a resistor pellet in the ignition to disable the starter and fuel system when the key code doesn't match the ignition lock. **Safety:** The tires have built-in low-pressure sensors that warn the driver through a light on the centre console. Run-flat tires eliminate the need for a spare tire.

Con: Quality control: Below average, especially body construction. **Reliability:** Spotty. The Corvette's sophisticated electronic and power-train components have low tolerance for real-world conditions. Expect lots of visits to the dealer's repair bays. **Owner-reported problems:** Electronically controlled suspension systems have been glitch-plagued over the past several years. Squeaks and rattles due to the car's structural deficiencies. The car was built as a convertible, and therefore has too much body flex. Servicing the different sophisticated fuel-injection systems isn't easy, even (especially) for GM mechanics. **Service bulletin problems:** Door handles may turn yellow; key warning chimes when key is removed from the ignition; inaccurate speedometer. **NHTSA safety complaints/safety:** Catalytic converter caught fire; steering wheel locked up in Reverse gear and was corrected only when transmission was put into Park and key re-inserted into the ignition; faulty fuel line clip may cause chronic stalling; fuel-injector failures cause vehicle to shudder and stall; engine dies while driving in the rain and brakes don't work; early failure of the engine serpentine belt and tensioner; intermittent electrical problems degrade computer operation; if one wheel loses traction the throttle closes, starving the engine; driver's seat moves while driving; warped trunk door, dash shifting; seatbelts twist easily and tend to pull down uncomfortably against the shoulder; passenger seatbelt jams and won't extend or retract; smelly fumes enter the cabin, causing watery eyes and dizziness; the glass rear view window limits rear vision.

Road Performance

Pro: Emergency handling: Very good. No oversteer, wheel spinning, breakaway rear ends, or nasty surprises. **Steering:** Predictable, with good road feel. **Acceleration/torque:** Gobs of torque and horsepower with a top speed of 172 mph (0–100 km/h: 5 sec.). **Transmission:** The 6-speed gearbox performs well in all gear ranges and makes shifting smooth with short throws and easy entry into all gears. **Routine handling:** Above average. The car's so low that its front air dam scrapes over the smallest rise in the road, but still gives no-surprise handling and responds quickly to the throttle. The Bilstein FX-3 Selective Ride Control suspension can be preset to Touring, Sport, or Performance. Under acceleration, an electronic module automatically varies the suspension as the speed increases. **Braking:** Better than average. The ABS-vented disc brakes are easy to modulate, fade-free, and incorporate a Bosch system that GM engineers claim will pull over 1.0G deceleration rates.

Con: Optional Z51 suspension's ride is too firm for some. This is one large and heavy sports car, whose weight compromises its fuel economy. True, the 6-speed manual does provides quicker acceleration and better fuel economy, but it's not particularly user-friendly.

Comfort/Convenience

Pro: Standard equipment: Attractively styled and full of power-assisted accessories. Rust-resistant fibreglass body. Simple-to-operate convertible top. Innovative Passive Keyless Entry System. **Driving position:** Excellent, with everything within easy reach, good front and rear visibility, and a roomy cockpit. **Controls and displays:** Complete instrumentation that's easy to decipher, and user-friendly controls. **Climate control:** Easy to adjust and quiet. **Entry/exit:** Acceptable. Tall drivers will find the interior confining. **Interior space/comfort F/R:** Snug, but not uncomfortable for two adults.

Con: The electronic dash never quite works right (speedometer lags, for example). Steering wheel hides some controls. No room in the engine compartment for a sophisticated climate control system. Dual-zone climate control system takes time to warm up. Lowering the top takes patience: you release two latches, lift the plastic panel, and manually fold the top into its storage compartment. **Cargo space:** Insufficient storage space, which is no surprise to sports car enthusiasts. The lowered top cuts trunk space in half. **Trunk/liftover:** Skimpy storage space; high sill makes loading baggage difficult. **Quietness:** In addition to an irritating engine boom, there's excessive tire noise, wind whistling through the car's A- and C-pillars, and the all-too-familiar fibreglass body squeaks caused by excessive body flexing on rough surfaces.

COST				
List Price (negotiable)	**Residual Values** (months)			
	24	36	48	60
Corvette: $56,485 (25%)	$41,000	$36,000	$31,000	$26,000

TECHNICAL DATA	
Powertrain (rear-drive)	Head room: 37.8 in.
Engine: 5.7L V8 (345 hp)	Leg room: 42.7 in.
Transmissions: 6-speed man.	Wheelbase: 104.5 in.
• 4-speed auto.	Turning circle: 42 ft.
Dimension/Capacity	Cargo volume: 11 cu. ft.
Passengers: 2/0	Tow limit: N/A
Height/length/width:	Fuel tank: 72L/pre.
47.7/179.7/73.6 in.	Weight: 3,245 lb.

SAFETY FEATURES/CRASHWORTHINESS

	Std.	Opt.
Anti-lock brakes	■	❑
Seatbelt pretensioners	—	—
Side airbags	—	—
Traction control	■	❑
Head restraints	*****	N/A
Visibility (front/rear)	*****	**
Crash protection (front) D/P	N/A	
Crash protection (side) D/P	N/A	
Crash protection (offset)	N/A	
HLDI injury claims (model)	N/A	
HLDI injury claims (all)	N/A	

Montana, Silhouette, Venture

✓ BEST BUY

Venture

RATING: Above Average if you don't overwhelm the engine. **Strong points:** A comfortable ride, easy handling, dual sliding doors, plenty of comfort and convenience features, flexible seating arrangements, and good crash scores. **Weak points:** Average acceleration with a light load; optional traction control; uncomfortable, low rear seats; excessive brake fading; and disappointing fuel economy.

NEW FOR 2000: Dual sliding rear side doors. This trio gets restyled front and rear ends in 2002 and a total redesign (they'll get wider) in 2004.

OVERVIEW: This practically identical threesome of front-drive mini-vans comes in regular and extended wheelbase versions. The extended wheelbase models get more bells and whistles, including optional power slide-open passenger- and driver-side doors. The Venture and Silhouette seat seven, while the Montana manages to squeeze in one more passenger. Longer versions have dual sliding doors with optional power assist.

Cost analysis/best alternatives: Get the '99 minivans if the price is cut 15–20 percent. These minivans are a definite step up from the GM minivans they replaced several years ago. Other vehicles worth considering: Honda Odyssey, Nissan Quest, and Toyota Sienna. **Options:** The power-assisted passenger-side sliding door is both convenient and dangerous (see NHTSA, below)—despite its override circuit that prevents the door from closing on a hand, a number of injuries have been reported. Furthermore, with most sliding doors, mechanical and electronic glitches allow the doors to open when they shouldn't and difficult to close. Overall, this $1,244 convenience feature is overpriced, failure-prone, and a bit slow in operation. An argument can be made for the added convenience, but I suspect its chief attraction is to gadget-hungry males. Consider the $235 load-levelling feature—a must-have for front-drive minivans. It keeps the weight on the front wheels, giving you better steering, traction, and braking. Other options that are worth buying: General XP2000 tires (about $100 for all four), traction control, integrated child safety seats, power side windows, and rear air conditioner, defroster, and heater. The Montana Package offers a firmer suspension and self-sealing tires. **Rebates:** $1,500 on the '99 models. **Delivery/PDI:** $840. **Depreciation:** A bit slower than average. **Insurance cost:** High, but about average for a minivan. **Annual maintenance cost:** Average during the warranty period. Transmission, ABS, and electrical malfunction will likely cause maintenance costs to rise after the third year of ownership. **Parts supply/cost:** Parts are generic to GM's other models, so they should be reasonably priced and not hard to find. Body parts are likely to be more problematic and costly. **Warranty:** Bumper-to-bumper 3 years/60,000 km; rust perforation 6 years/160,000 km. **Supplementary warranty:** An extended warranty is a good idea until long-term reliability has been assessed. **Highway/city fuel economy:** 9.3–13.5L/100 km. **Annual fuel cost:** 2,322L=$1,347.

Quality/Reliability/Safety

Pro: Quality control: Average. Less rattle-prone due to a more rigid body structure than their predecessors. **Reliability:** No serious reliability problems. **Warranty performance:** Average.

Con: Fit and finish is still not up to the Asian competition. Chassis could still use reinforcing to mute the rattles heard when passing over rough roads. **Owner-reported problems:** Electrical glitches, windshield wiper motor failures, excessive front brake noise, power sliding door malfunctions, and assorted body deficiencies. Windshield wipers are frequently frozen into place and the under-hood climate control vents, found at the base of the windshield, freeze up as well. **Service bulletin problems:** An inoperative power sliding door; poor engine performance (hard starts and stalling) due to fuel injector deposits; door handles turn yellow. **NHTSA safety complaints/safety:** Airbag deployed when door was slammed; airbags failed to deploy; windshield suddenly exploded outward while driving with wipers activated; brakes activate on their own, making it appear as if van is pulling a load; steering idler arm fell off due to missing bolt; loose fuel tank due to loose bolts/bracket; plastic tube within heating system fell off and wedged behind the accelerator pedal; bracket weld pin that secures the rear split seat sheared off; vehicle suddenly lost power while going uphill, slid back, and stalled; van will roll back while in gear on an incline; sliding door slams shut on an incline; wrist broken when power sliding door opened; centre rear lap seatbelt isn't long enough to secure a rear-facing child safety seat; middle-row passenger-side seatbelts jam in the retracted position; front passenger shoulder belt cuts into passenger's neck; electrical harness failures result in complete electrical shutdown; headlights and interior lights fail intermittently; excess padding around horn makes it difficult to depress horn button in an emergency; weak-sounding horn; frequent windshield wiper motor failures; heater doesn't warm up vehicle sufficiently.

Road Performance

Pro: Emergency handling: Better than average, due to the responsive powertrain, steering and ABS. **Steering:** The steering takes some effort, but it's responsive and fairly predictable. Longer, loaded versions have a smoother ride than the base versions, which tend to be choppier. **Acceleration/torque:** Nice powertrain setup with smooth acceleration for most light-duty work. The 3.4L engine is smooth and responsive (0–100 km/h: 10.7 sec.). These minivans use the same quiet-running V6 powerplant that harnesses a few more horses than the Chrysler minivans' top-line 3.8L 6-cylinder, providing good mid-range and top-end power. Chrysler's engines do have a bit more torque, however. **Transmission:** The electronically controlled 4-speed automatic transmission shifts smoothly and quietly—another advantage over Chrysler. **Routine handling:** Pretty good. Sedan-like handling is better than most of the competition, particularly when equipped with the load-levelling option. **Braking:** Unimpressive for the Venture (100–0 km/h: 147 ft.), much better with the Montana (100–0 km/h: 134 ft.) and Silhouette (100–0 km/h: 135 ft.).

Con: Some body roll in hard turns. Powertrain isn't suitable for heavy towing or carrying a full passenger load. **Acceleration/torque:** The GM engine is hampered by less torque, making for less grunt when accelerating and frequently downshifting out of Overdrive when climbing moderate grades (there's no Overdrive on/off switch). This is the main reason why owners feel that the GM minivans are underpowered when compared with Chrysler's. **Braking:** Watch out for excessive brake fading; the brakes lose their effectiveness progressively after repeated application.

Comfort/Convenience

Pro: Standard equipment: Fairly well equipped. **Driving position:** Drivers are treated to a car-like driving position. Comfortable left footrest. Concealed windshield wipers, a large windshield, and larger side mirrors enhance visibility fore and aft. **Controls and displays:** Everything is easy to read and within reach. **Climate control:** Efficient and easy to use. AC has a pollen control feature. **Entry/exit:** Easy, especially with the low interior step-in, side interior door handles, power remote sliding door on the curb-side and a manual sliding door on the street-side of extended-wheelbase models. **Interior space/comfort F/R:** Plenty of room in the first two rows, while the third row is more problematic. Comfortable seats, particularly on the Venture. There are two reclining bucket seats in the front row, and the second and third rows can accommodate modular or bench seats. Easy-to-fold seats drop down to increase storage space; the second seat flips forward for access to the third seat. **Cargo space:** Lots of storage bins and compartments. **Trunk/liftover:** A breeze. Dual sliding doors mean that you no longer have to walk around to the passenger side to load or unload cargo. Rear seats can be flipped down to carry a 4x8 sheet of plywood. **Quietness:** One of the quietest minivans in its class.

Con: Tacky plastic interior. **Driving position:** Tall drivers will find insufficient head room and short drivers may find it hard to see where the front ends. **Controls and displays:** Steering column stalk controls are confusing. **Climate control:** These minivans take a while to warm up the interior. **Interior space/comfort F/R:** Uncomfortable centre and rear bench seats; cushions are hard, flat, and too short; and the seatbacks lack sufficient lower-back support. Low rear seats force passengers into an uncomfortable knees-up position. **Cargo space:** One convenience item that can easily become an inconvenience: the two cargo nets found between the front seats and behind the rear seat are easily entangled and complicate the removal of the rear seats. Also, eight of the twelve cupholders are only usable if the seats are folded down. **Trunk/liftover:** Cargo may not slide out easily due to the rear sill sticking up a few inches. **Quietness:** Some wind noise.

COST

List Price (negotiable)	Residual Values (months)			
	24	36	48	60
Montana: $26,625 (20%)	$19,000	$16,000	$14,000	$12,000
Silhouette: $30,630 (20%)	$22,000	$18,000	$16,000	$14,000
Venture SW: $24,895 (20%)	$18,000	$15,000	$11,000	$11,000

TECHNICAL DATA

Powertrain (front-drive)	Head room F: 39.9/R1: 39.3/R2: 38.8 in.
Engine: 3.4L V6 (185 hp)	Head room F: 39.9/R1: 39.3/R2: 38.9 in.

Transmission: 4-speed auto.
Dimension/Capacity
Passengers: 2/2/3; 2/3/3
Height/length/width:
67.4/186.9/72 in.
68.1/187.3/72.7 in.

Leg room F: 39.9/R1: 36.9/R2: 34 in.
Leg room F: 39.9/R1: 39/R2: 36.7 in.
Wheelbase: 112 in.
Turning circle: 42 ft.
Cargo volume: 76 cu. ft.
GVWR: 5,357 lb.
Payload: 1,415–1,577 lb.
Tow limit: 3,500 lb.
Fuel tank: 76/95L
Weight: 3,890 lb./4,005 lb.

SAFETY FEATURES/CRASHWORTHINESS

	Std.	Opt.
Anti-lock brakes (4W)	■	❏
Seatbelt pretensioners	■	❏
Side airbags	■	❏
Traction control	❏	■
Head restraints	*****	*
Head restraints (Venture)	*****	***
Visibility (front/rear)	*****	*****
Crash protection (front) D/P	****	***
Crash protection (side) D/P	*****	*****
Crash protection (offset)	*	
HLDI injury claims (model)	*****	

Astro, Safari

Safari

RATING: Above Average. How come these old dinosaurs rate higher than Ford's and Chrysler's high-tech marvels? Simple: the GM minivans have fewer problems, and those deficiencies that do appear are easier to diagnose and relatively less expensive to repair. **Strong points:** Standard ABS, brisk acceleration, trailer-towing capability, lots of passenger room and cargo space, and improved reliability and quality control. **Weak points:**

Harsh riding, limited front seat room, and excessive fuel consumption made worse by the AWD option.

NEW FOR 2000: Minor engine refinements. Long overdue for a redesign since its 1985 launch, but it may be dropped next year instead.

OVERVIEW: More a utility truck than a comfortable minivan, these boxy, rear-drive minivans are built on a reworked S-10 pickup chassis. As such, they offer uninspiring handling, trouble-prone mechanical and body components, and relatively high fuel consumption. Both Astro and Safari come in a choice of either cargo or passenger van. The cargo van is used either commercially or as an inexpensive starting point for a fully customized vehicle. The Safari is identical to the Astro, except for a slightly higher base price.

The engine is a 4.3L 190-hp V6. Dual airbags are standard. Also offered are an optional rear door and rear bench seats that can be adjusted fore and aft. Carried-over standard features are a 4-speed automatic transmission with Overdrive, power steering, a front stabilizer bar, a 95L fuel tank (a Lumina offers 76L), and anti-lock brakes. All-wheel-drive with a single-speed transfer case with viscous-controlled differential (no switches to throw) is available on the regular length and extended models. The Sport package includes louvred rear-quarter body panels, two-tone paint, fog lights, and a front air dam. With the right options, the Astro and Safari have the advantage of being versatile cargo haulers when equipped with a heavy-duty suspension. In fact, Astro's 5,500-pound trailer-towing capability is 2,000 lb. more than that of the front-drive Venture.

Cost analysis/best alternatives: Get the '99 minivans if they're discounted a few thousand dollars. Front-drive minivans made by Nissan and Toyota have better handling, and are more reliable and economical people carriers; unfortunately, they lack the Astro's considerable grunt essential for cargo hauling and trailer towing. **Options:** Integrated child safety seats, rear AC, and rear Dutch doors. Be wary of the AWD option; it exacts a high fuel penalty. **Rebates:** About $2,000 before year's end on the '99s and possibly half as much on this year's models by mid-summer. **Delivery/PDI:** $845. **Depreciation:** Average. **Insurance cost:** Slightly higher than average. **Annual maintenance cost:** Average. **Parts supply/cost:** Good supply of cheap parts. A large contingent of independent parts suppliers keeps repair costs down. Parts are less expensive than they are for other vehicles in this class according to CAA. **Warranty:** Bumper-to-bumper 3 years/60,000 km; rust perforation 6 years/160,000 km. **Supplementary warranty:** A toss-up. Individual repairs won't cost a lot, but those nickels and dimes can add up. **Highway/city fuel economy:** 10.6–14.6L/100 km for 2-wheel drive and 11.3–15.3L/100 km with AWD. **Annual fuel cost:** 2-wheel drive: 2,560L=$1,485; AWD: 2,700L=$1,566.

Quality/Reliability/Safety

Pro: Quality control: Average. **Reliability:** Average; most of the Astro and Safari's defects are easy to diagnose, leading to a minimum of downtime in the repair bay. **Warranty performance:** Average.

Con: Owner-reported problems: Some problems with the automatic transmission, steering, electrical system, heating and defrosting system, and suspension components. **Service bulletin problems:** GM admits its speedometers may give inaccurate readings. All the automaker has to say is, "THAT'S TOO BAD!" No fix is planned, but the company printed up the following chart to show by how much the readings could be out of line (should be a great help in Traffic Court). **NHTSA safety complaints/safety:** Rear cargo door latch and hinge slipped off and door flew open; sudden total electrical failure, especially when going into Reverse; loss of power steering; sudden brake failure; extended stopping distance with ABS; differential in transfer case locked up while driving; defective axle seals; front passenger seatbelt locked up; fuel gauge failure; faulty AC vents; water can be trapped inside the wheels and freeze, causing the wheels to be out of balance; brake pedal set too high.

Speedometer Accuracy
File In Section: 8 - Chassis/Body Electrical
Bulletin No.: 83-83-16
Date: September, 1998
INFORMATION
Subject:
Speedometer Accuracy
Models:
1997–99 Passenger Cars and Trucks
The speedometers used on most GM vehicles are of the air-core design. This is a moving needle operated by a magnetic coil. Because there is no direct mechanical linkage, there is some variation in accuracy that cannot be eliminated.
Digital readout devices, such as some speedometer displays and HUD's (Head-Up Displays), are direct readouts of the VSS (Vehicle Speed Sensor) and their accuracy is much greater. Tire size, tread life and inflation can cause some variation in the readings. In addition, the Tech 2 device reads the VSS directly and is quite accurate.

MPH - Variation		KPH - Variation	
20	4	32	6
45	3	72	5
65	2	106	3

Any air-core speedometer which reads within these limits should not be returned for service.

Honest, officer, it's the speedometer's fault.

Road Performance

Pro: Acceleration/torque: The V6 engine is more than adequate for most driving chores and has plenty of reserve power for trailer towing and heavy hauling (0–100 km/h: 11.8 sec.). **Braking:** Excellent braking for a minivan (100–0 km/h: 137 ft.). AWD works well.

Con: The V6 is thirsty in city driving. **Emergency handling:** Ponderous, but still fairly predictable. **Steering:** Very light power steering, but still handles and manoeuvres like a large truck. **Transmission:** Clunky automatic transmission. **Routine handling:** Handling isn't very precise; overall behaviour is competent, but sloppy. A heavy-duty suspension will improve both ride and handling. Busy, harsh ride caused by stiff springs.

Comfort/Convenience

Pro: Standard equipment: Adequate. **Controls and displays:** Well laid-out instrument panel with easy-to-read gauges. **Climate control:** Very good climate control system. **Interior space/comfort F/R:** Spacious interior provides plenty of room for passengers. All seats are comfortable, although the front two are the best. The rear seat can be removed by a single person, but not as easily as the automaker's front-drive minivan seats. **Cargo space:** An incredible amount of cargo space can handle all kinds of bulky items, including 4x8 sheets of plywood. **Trunk/liftover:** No problem. In fact, the optional Dutch doors provide better rear-view visibility and include a convenient lift-open glass and defroster.

Con: Driving position: The driving position is awkward for most drivers—more like a truck than a passenger car. Tall drivers will find the pedals too close. Obtrusive engine makes for very narrow front footwells that give little room for the driver's left foot to rest. Some dashboard controls are hard to reach. **Entry/exit:** Difficult due to the high step-up and the intruding wheel well. **Quietness:** Interior noise levels rise sharply at highway speeds.

COST				
List Price (very negotiable)	**Residual Values** (months)			
	24	**36**	**48**	**60**
Base: $24,268 (19%)	$18,000	$14,000	$12,000	$10,500

TECHNICAL DATA	
Powertrain (rear-drive)	Head room F: 39.2/R1: 37.9/R2: 38.7 in
Engine: 4.3L V6 (190 hp)	Leg room F: 41.6/R1: 36.5/R2: 38.5 in.
Transmission: 4-speed auto.	Wheelbase: 111.2 in.
Dimension/Capacity	Turning circle: 45 ft.
Passengers: 2/3/3	Cargo volume: 98 cu. ft.
Height/length/width:	GVWR: 5,950–6,100 lb.
74.9/189.8/77.5 in.	Payload: 1,667–1,764 lb.
	Tow limit: 5,500 lb.
	Fuel tank: 95L
	Weight: 4,520 lb.

SAFETY FEATURES/CRASHWORTHINESS		
	Std.	**Opt.**
Anti-lock brakes (4W)	■	❑
Seatbelt pretensioners	—	—
Side airbags	—	—
Traction control (AWD)	❑	■
Head restraints	**	**
Visibility (front/rear)	*****	**
Crash protection (front) D/P	***	***
Crash protection (side) D/P	N/A	
Crash protection (offset)	*	
HLDI injury claims (model)	****	
HLDI injury claims (all)	****	

SAAB

What's so special about Saabs? Their unusual, aerodynamic styling is (to put it mildly) distinctive; passenger comfort is unbeatable; and they handle very well, with precise steering and lots of road feel. Unfortunately, a lot of less expensive cars offer just as much road performance and are more reliable and easier to repair.

No one can accuse GM of opportunism in buying Saab for $600 million in late 1989—just before the Swedish automaker announced a $380-million operating loss for that year, followed by stunning 1990–91 losses exceeding a billion dollars. Now, after three straight years of losses, Saab says it will be profitable in '99 due to its new products and improved European sales.

Saab's growth has been undeniably slowed by increased competition from European and Japanese luxury sedans that are more smartly styled, have greater market penetration, and are marketed through attractive and innovative leasing plans. Furthermore, Saab's reliability and servicing problems have only begun to be addressed by GM, beset by its own quality and servicing deficiencies.

9-3

RATING: Average. **Strong points:** Many standard safety features, a good highway performer with excellent handling, steering, and braking, comfortable seating, and lots of storage capability. **Weak points:** Turbo lag, and a poor ride with premium tires. Convertible has minimal rear seat room, less comfortable seating, and shakes and rattles. Obstructed rear visibility in both the sedan and convertible, a history of poor quality control, and the servicing network is rather limited.

NEW FOR 2000: The convertible and five-door sedan get "viggen-ized."

OVERVIEW: Selling for about $33,500, the 9-3 is essentially the old 900 loaded with lots of engineering upgrades housed in a two- or four-door hatchback or convertible. The base engine is a 185-hp twin-cam 2.0L four that gets 15 additional horses when turbocharged. A 2.3L 230-hp turbocharged version powers the Viggen, a limited edition coupe. Both the Viggen and the SE High Output Turbo come only with a manual transmission.

Don't expect fast starts uphill. The turbo kicks in at about 3,000 rpm (which means lots of time spent in second gear waiting for a much-needed turbo boost), plus, you'll have to contend with a lurching transmission, uncomfortably long passing times, and sudden torque steer that may tug at the steering wheel.

Notwithstanding the turbo's deficiencies, the 9-3 is a driver's car, with impressive braking performance, sporty handling, and sure-footed cornering. Nevertheless, the SE's high-performance, premium tires accentuate the smallest bumps, and make for a harsh, jiggly ride. The standard V-rated tires give a much smoother ride.

Safety features abound, including "active" head restraints that minimize whiplash injury and thicker headliner padding as cushioning in rollovers. One obvious deficiency is the absence of traction control, a feature offered by almost all of the 9-3's rivals.

There's plenty of cargo space and room for five adults, except in the convertible version, and the soft top is easily raised or lowered electrically. The narrow two-place rear bench seat and manual front passenger seat, however, move slowly to provide rear-seat access. Climate settings on the SE have to be re-adjusted between startups, the ignition is still floor-mounted, rear visibility is not very good in the sedans and even worse in the convertible with the top raised, and the convertible's less-rigid chassis tends to shake and rattle.

The Volvo S70 or V70 are attractive alternatives to the 9-3 hatchbacks; Mercedes' CLK320, the BMW 328i, and the five-cylinder Volvo C70 are credible alternatives to the $53,070 9-3 convertible.

Quality/Reliability/Safety

Pro: Warranty performance: Above average. GM has treated Saab owners more generously than its other divisions with the exception of Saturn and Cadillac.

Con: Quality control: Below average. **Reliability:** Below average; most of the 9-3's defects are electrical in nature, tending to take lots of diagnostic time. **Owner-reported problems:** Electrical and fuel system malfunctions, premature brake wear, and body defects. **Service bulletin problems:** Broken tonneau drive safety pin; soft top won't open; noisy, hard to operate telescopic steering wheel; SID dash display loses memory; ACC panel display malfunctions; excessive front suspension noise; squeaking noise comes from rear of vehicle; with the soft top, no sound from accessory CD changer; loose rear windshield wiper arm nuts. **NHTSA safety complaints/safety:** Side airbag failed to deploy; aluminum hubs may not support the stress of everyday driving; when passing over grooves in the road, vehicle suddenly jerks to the right or left; driver's door lock won't unlock from the inside.

SAFETY FEATURES/CRASHWORTHINESS		
	Std.	**Opt.**
Anti-lock brakes	■	❑
Seatbelt pretensioners	■	❑
Side airbags	■	❑
Traction control	■	■
Head restraints	*****	*****
Visibility (front/rear)	*****	*
Crash protection (front) D/P	****	****
Crash protection (side) D/P	N/A	
Crash protection (offset)	**	
HLDI injury claims (model)	****	
HLDI injury claims (all)	*****	

Note: Safety features also apply to the 9-5; crash and insurance data apply to only the 9-3.

9-5

RATING: Average. **Strong points:** Good acceleration, handling, road-holding, and braking; "smart" head restraints; comfortable seating (lots of room for six-footers plus); lots of storage capability; improved build quality and fit and finish; and good fuel economy. Traction control (V6 only). **Weak points:** Turbo lag, excessive tire noise, the steering feels a bit over-assisted and a bit numb, some body lean when cornering, climate controls aren't very user-friendly, and the servicing network is rather limited.

NEW FOR 2000: The addition of a sporty aero version.

OVERVIEW: The $40,200 9-5 SE replaced the 9000 several years ago. It uses suspension and brake parts taken from GM's Opel Vectra, with a stiffened chassis and added four-wheel independent suspension. It floats less and corners better than the 9000, though there's still too much body lean. Saab has also turbocharged its V6 engine without boosting horsepower, so that it provides lots of low-end torque. It doesn't kick in under 3,000 rpm, however, and comes only with an automatic transmission.

There's plenty of cargo space and room for five adults. In addition to providing a spacious trunk, Saab pays lots of attention to detail. For example: work gloves and a plastic bag are provided so you don't soil your hands when changing the tire; the "smart" head restraint is specially designed to prevent neck injuries; the glove box has an air conditioning duct that keeps drinks cold; there are air vents in the back of the centre console for added comfort; rear seats fold flat for added cargo room; and, for added safety, a passenger-side rear-view mirror automatically tilts down so you can get a better view when you engage Reverse.

Some things you won't like about the 9-5: power steering is over-assisted and doesn't transmit sufficient road feel; only two adults can sit comfortably in the rear; the remote lock/unlock key fob won't fit into the average-sized pocket and is hard to decipher; the outside mirrors are unacceptably small; the in-dash cupholder won't support a tall coffee cup; the fan-cooled seats are more gimmicky than practical; climate controls are set too low to be easily adjusted and have to be recalibrated after each startup; the ignition is still floor-mounted; rear visibility is obstructed; and servicing isn't widely available.

Cost analysis/best alternatives: Choose a discounted second-series '99 model made after March to benefit from the numerous assembly line fixes carried out during the first six months of the model run. Keep in mind that Saabs are cheaper than their European counterparts, like the Audi A6 and Volvo S80, but they depreciate far more quickly. Other cars 9-3 shoppers should consider are the Audi A6, BMW 3-series, Lexus ES 300, Mazda Millenia, and Toyota Avalon. 9-5 shoppers should also look at the BMW 5-series, Lexus GS 300 or 400, or the Mercedes E-class. **Options:** Integrated child safety seats. The V6 engine isn't worth the extra $5,000. It adds additional weight, is fuel-thirsty, and compromises handling. Plus, it's only available with an automatic gearbox. **Rebates:** 9-3 models will likely get $2,000 rebates and dealer incentives early in the year 2000. **Delivery/PDI:** $770. **Depreciation:** Faster than average. Saabs depreciate fairly quickly, so if you plan to keep yours for only a few years and don't want to lose much money through depreciation, choose the convertible; it keeps its value longer. **Insurance cost:** Higher than average. **Parts supply/cost:** Parts are moderately expensive and servicing is a major liability (the dealership network is weak) due to GM's inept administration of its Saab franchises. GM threw out many Saab dealers when it bought the company, and gave the Saab franchise to inexperienced Passport dealers who primarily serviced Isuzus. After fielding a deluge of customer complaints, GM realized this was a mistake and closed a third of its 60 dealerships. Saab owners are feeling GM's pain. **Annual maintenance cost:** Higher than average. **Warranty:** Bumper-to-bumper 4 years/80,000 km; rust perforation 6 years/unlimited km. **Supplementary warranty:** A very good idea, considering that these cars are complicated to diagnose and expensive to repair. **Highway/city fuel economy:** 8.6–12.4L/100 km with the 2.0L, 8.0–12.3L/100 km with the 2.3L, and 8.6–13.3L/100 km with the 3.0L. **Annual fuel cost:** 2.0L: 2,138L=$1,240; 2.3L: 2,073L=$1,202; 3.0L: 2,237L=$1,297.

Quality/Reliability/Safety

Pro: Quality control: Average. Saab 9-5 owners report fewer factory-related defects than owners of the entry-level 9-3. **Reliability:** Average; not much downtime in the repair bay reported, so far. **Warranty performance:** Above average. **NHTSA safety complaints/safety:** Nothing yet.

Con: Owner-reported problems: Electrical and fuel system glitches; some fit and finish complaints. **Service bulletin problems:** AC panel display malfunctions; tips on electrical fault tracing; loose outer door mirror casing; front door window wind noise; alarm siren goes off inadvertently while driving or parked.

Asian Vehicles

With only a few exceptions, Japanese automakers still have a lock on good quality vehicles that are reliable, easy to repair, and slow to depreciate. They're also terribly overpriced, though they have been cheapened during the past few years through "content-cutting" (in Toyota's case) and fewer standard features. South Korean automakers' vehicles, on the other hand, aren't as reliable, even though Hyundai quality control has risen considerably over the past two years. And Daewoo and Kia's products have an even worse reputation, having been rated by their owners as below average in quality. Nevertheless, this year has seen an increase in sales for all three South Korean automakers, after they shifted their marketing strategy to include rock-bottom prices and generous warranties that promise to make up for the quality deficiencies.

Although the Japanese automakers have pledged to keep price increases to a minimum, and in some cases not raise the MSRP on some vehicles, a devalued Canadian and American dollar plus renewed enthusiasm for Japanese and Korean vehicles may push prices higher.

Those automakers likely to be involved in the heaviest discounting are Daewoo, Kia, Mazda, Nissan, and Suzuki. Daewoo and Kia are newcomers to Canada and need to capture market share in order to lure more dealers into their network. Mazda, Nissan, and Suzuki are discounting in order to make up for poor previous-year sales—and, in Nissan's case, get some quick cash to pay off huge debts.

New Products

This year, there will be plenty of new products coming to Canada from Japan and Korea. In addition to Daewoo and Kia bringing their five new vehicles to Canada, Honda will launch its S2000 roadster, Nissan will bring out an Xterra small sport utility, and Toyota's Echo will replace the Tercel. Asian cars that will return redesigned this year are the Hyundai Accent, Infiniti I30, Mazda MPV, Nissan Maxima, Subaru Legacy, and Toyota Celica.

ACURA

When Acura first came to Canada in 1986 it did very well in selling reasonably priced compact cars that many considered to be no more than all-dressed Honda clones. Then the company got cocky and, rather than counting on lower profits and more sales, they raised prices (over dealers' objections) to what the market would bear. Fortunately, competitive pressures—not the least from Lexus and Nissan—forced the automaker to cut Acura prices with cash rebates and low-interest financing programs. Nevertheless, this move was too little, too late, and Acura sales haven't yet fully recovered.

Although they've been somewhat pacified through higher dealer profit margins and an improved product lineup, Canadian Acura dealers are still ticked off by what they consider to be the company's "take it or leave it" attitude toward them. One Canadian Federation of Automobile Dealer Association (FADA) dealer survey blasted Acura management for being insensitive to dealers' concerns and for dragging its feet in launching the 1.6 EL, a Canada-exclusive entry-level model.

Six models are sold under the Acura nameplate: the Integra, CL coupe, TL, RL, SLX sport-utility, and NSX sports car. Except for the SLX sport-utility, which is based on the Isuzu Trooper, Acura's lineup is comprised of overpriced, upscale Honda variants that have been sold and serviced by a separate Acura network since 1986. The NSX and SLX return this year unchanged; the SLX may be dropped in the spring of 2000 when the Alliston, Ontario, Odyssey-based MAV sport-utility debuts.

Acura products are generally good buys even though they're overpriced because maintenance costs are low, reliability is way above average, and Acura's warranty performance has been more generous than that of most automakers.

Asian Vehicles

1.6 EL

1.6 EL

RATING: Above Average. **Strong points:** High level of performance and comfort, slow depreciation, and high-quality construction. **Weak points:** Optional anti-lock brakes (inexcusable, when you consider that GM's $14,915 entry-level Cavalier coupe has standard ABS), no crashworthiness data, limited rear seat room, and difficult rear access.

NEW FOR 2000: Nothing significant.

OVERVIEW: With a $19,700 base price, the 1.6 EL has sold quite well for what is essentially a restyled, luxury version of the Honda Civic Si with the following features: conservative styling, different bumpers and front headlights, upgraded wipers, heated power door mirrors, restyled dash, different seat covers, upgraded soundproofing, 15-inch wheels, and a rear sway bar.

Taken from the Civic Coupe Si, the VTEC 4-cylinder puts out 127 hp, which is 21 more than the base Civics and only three less than the '97 Accord. This gives it good all-around acceleration, but not a sports car personality like that offered by the Integra 1.8, which gives you a sportier 142-hp engine in a two-door body style. (Of course, you're looking at about $6,200 more for the Integra and $500 less for the Civic Si.)

Expect similar performance to that described for the Civic Si. Consumer feedback notes that the 4-speed gearbox is well designed in that it doesn't "hunt" for the right gear when traversing hilly terrain. On the safety front, anti-lock brakes are optional, childproof rear door locks are standard, and no crash tests have yet been carried out.

Some of the 1.6 EL's weak points: relatively expensive for what is essentially a four-door Civic with a bit more horsepower (still, a low depreciation rate may give you back a greater portion of your initial investment); a narrow interior, with seats and seatbacks not to everyone's liking; emergency braking that's only average; head restraints rated "poor" by the IIHS; an average insurance injury claim rate; and excessive engine noise intruding into the passenger compartment despite upgraded soundproofing.

Cost analysis/best alternatives: Get the 2000 model; it's practically identical to last year's version and doesn't cost much more. Other vehicles worth a look: Acura Integra and Honda Civic Si. **Options:** A block heater. **Rebates:** Not likely, but look for 10–15 percent discounts. **Delivery/PDI:** $400. **Depreciation:** Much slower than average. **Insurance cost:** Higher than average. **Parts supply/cost:** Moderately priced parts can be found at Acura or Honda dealers. **Annual maintenance cost:** Lower than average. **Warranty:** Bumper-to-bumper 3 years/60,000 km; powertrain 5 years/100,000 km; rust perforation 6 years/unlimited km. **Supplementary warranty:** Not needed. **Highway/city fuel economy:** 6.8–9.3L/100 km. **Annual fuel cost:** 1,635L=$948.

CL Series

CL

RATING: Average. An attractive, loaded luxury coupe, but you can get the latest redesigned Accord for less. **Strong points:** Styling, plenty of standard features, and comfortable riding. **Weak points:** Engine isn't exactly high-performance, limited rear seat room, and a harsh-shifting automatic transmission (get the manual shifter).

NEW FOR 2000: A redesign next summer will put the CL on the new Accord/TL platform, giving the CL a longer wheelbase and rear-drive for the coupe.

OVERVIEW: Priced from $30,000–$34,000, these cars are stylish, front-drive, five-passenger, American-built and -designed luxury coupes. They have a flowing, slanted back end and no apparent trunk lock (a standard remote keyless entry system opens the trunk from the outside and a lever opens it from the inside). And while other Japanese automakers are taking content out of their vehicles, Acura has put content into the CL, making it one of the most feature-laden cars in its class.

Sure, we all know that the coupe's mechanical components and platform aren't that different from the Accord's, but when you add up all of its standard bells and whistles, you get a fully loaded small car that costs thousands of dollars less than competing luxury coupes such as the BMW 318is and the Lexus SC300. Consider this array of standard features: power windows, power mirrors, power moonroof, six-way power driver seat, a remote keyless entry system, ABS, leather-wrapped steering wheel, simulated wood trim, automatic climate control, dual airbags, tilt steering wheel, cruise control, CD player, and an AM/FM stereo with six speakers.

Although no one would consider the CL a high-performance car, it gets plenty of power from an optional 3.0L 24-valve SOHC Variable Valve Timing and Lift Electronic Control (VTEC) V6, in addition to its base 2.3L, single overhead cam 4-cylinder VTEC engine. Handling is better than average, thanks to upgraded suspension, variable-assisted steering, and 16-inch wheels. Excellent braking (100–0 km/h: 115 ft.).

On the minus side, the automatic transmission shifts are harsh and ill-timed (a good argument for getting a manual gearbox). This is not a car for passengers in the rear, either. Rear windows don't roll down and back seat room is insufficient, unless the front seats are pushed all the way forward. Front shoulder belts have no height adjustment, head restraints are rated "poor" by the IIHS, data indicates only an average insurance injury claim rate, rear entry/exit is a bit difficult, and storage space is skimpy.

Cost analysis/best alternatives: Wait for this summer's redesigned year 2000 model. If you want a CL now, a left over '99 model is your best bet, if the price has dropped at least 20 percent. The only difference between these two coupes is the 3.0/CL's larger engine, different wheels, and larger exhaust tip. Other vehicles worth considering, but with fewer standard features: the BMW 318i, Honda Accord, Lexus SC300, Nissan Maxima, and Toyota Camry. **Options:** The manual transmission. **Rebates:** Likely by the end of 1999. **Delivery/PDI:** $350. **Depreciation:** Much slower than average. **Insurance cost:** Higher than average. **Parts supply/cost:** It's not hard to find moderately priced parts at Acura or Honda dealers. **Annual maintenance cost:** Average. **Warranty:** Bumper-to-bumper 3 years/60,000 km; powertrain 5 years/100,000 km; rust perforation 6 years/unlimited km. **Supplementary warranty:** Not needed. **Highway/city fuel economy:** 7.3–10.6L/100 km with the 2.3L; 7.7–12.0L/100 km with the 3.0L. **Annual fuel cost:** 2.3L: 1,823L=$1,057; 3.0L: 2,013L=$1,168.

TL Series

TL

RATING: Above Average. **Strong points:** Impressive acceleration, handles well, rides comfortably, and is well put-together with quality mechanical and body components. **Weak points:** Suspension may be too firm for some, uncomfortable rear seating, and problematic navigation system controls.

NEW FOR 2000: Wider and longer overall; sportier styling. Also new: a five-speed transmission, front-seat side airbags, and a dual-stage passenger front airbag.

OVERVIEW: Retailing for about $35,320, the base TL combines luxury and performance in a nicely styled front-drive five-passenger sedan that uses the same chassis as the Accord and Odyssey minivan. The only engine available, a 3.2L 225-hp V6 mated to a 4-speed automatic transmission, provides impressive acceleration (0-100 km/h in just over 8 seconds) in a smooth and quiet manner. Handling is exceptional with the firm suspension, and responsive, precise steering makes it easy to toss the TL around turns without losing control. Bumps can be a bit jarring, though, but this is a small price to pay for the car's high-speed stability.

Interior accommodations are better than average up front, but rear occupants may discover that leg room is a bit tight and the seat cushions lack sufficient thigh support. The cockpit layout is very user-friendly due in part to the easy-to-read gauges and accessible controls (far away climate controls, the only exception). Visibility fore and aft is unobstructed; however, the optional navigation system is tough to read, hard to calibrate, and subject to malfunction. Invest in maps instead.

Standard safety features include ABS, traction control, childproof door locks, three-point seatbelts, and a transmission/brake interlock. Crash tests give four stars for driver and passenger crash protection in a frontal collision. On the other hand, head restraints are given a "poor" rating by the IIHS, overall insurance claim rate is average for models in this category, and higher than average for the TL.

Cost analysis/best alternatives: Get the '99 model if it's sufficiently discounted; also consider the Audi A4, BMW's redesigned 3-series, Infiniti's redesigned I30, and the Lexus ES 300. You may want to take a look at the CL coupe: it's not as expensive, and is as close as you can get to the Accord with lots of standard bells and whistles thrown in. **Options:** Don't waste your money on the satellite navigation system; it's confusing to calibrate and hard to see. **Rebates:** No incentives or rebates are likely, but some discounting can be expected early in the year 2000. **Delivery/PDI:** $350. **Depreciation:** Much slower than average. **Insurance cost:** Higher than average. **Parts supply/cost:** Except for some body parts, most mechanical and electronic components are easily found and moderately priced. **Annual maintenance cost:** Less than average. **Warranty:** Bumper-to-bumper 3 years/60,000 km; powertrain 5 years/100,000 km; rust perforation 6 years/unlimited km. **Supplementary warranty:** Not needed. **Highway/city fuel economy:** 8.1–12.6L/100 km. **Annual fuel cost:** 2,115L=$1,417.

Quality/Reliability/Safety

Pro: Quality control: Above average. **Reliability:** Above average. **Warranty performance:** Average.

Con: Owner-reported problems: The only areas that have proven troublesome in the past have been poor body fits, malfunctioning accessories, and premature brake wear. **Service bulletin problems:** Correcting ABS brake problems and diagnosing the cause of steering system scraping noise when turning. **NHTSA safety complaints/safety:** Dashboard display is unreadable in daylight; in a crash, seatbelt did not restrain driver.

Integra

Integra

RATING: Average. The performance and reliability aren't worth $26,000. **Strong points:** Better than average powertrain performance, excellent high-speed handling, good fuel economy, low depreciation, and high-quality construction. **Weak points:** Acceleration compromised by the automatic transmission, skimpy rear seat room, difficult rear access, excessive road noise, and too much low-speed steering effort. Way overpriced; more Honda than Acura.

NEW FOR 2000: No significant changes. A redesign is planned for 2001 when the Integra will be built off of the Civic platform.

OVERVIEW: The Integra doesn't quite fit into any category; it's a comfortable and practical small sedan with a high price. Its sporty pretensions lack the sizzle you'll find with the Mazda Miata or other more stylish small cars. On the whole, there's little to be said against the Integra and little to be said for it. One can get the same size four-door compact with a bit less performance for a lot less money—or a similar car with a lot more performance for just a little more money.

Cost analysis/best alternatives: A '99 model will do; since this year's models don't offer much more to justify a higher price. Other cars worth considering are the Ford Escort ZX2, Honda Prelude, Mazda Miata, or VW Golf or Jetta. **Options:** Don't get the GS-R. You'll quickly tire of its fussy VTEC engine. **Rebates:** Expect sizeable discounts early next year, when the upgraded 2001 models arrive. **Delivery/PDI:** $400. **Depreciation:** Slower than average. **Insurance cost:** Higher than average. **Parts supply/cost:** No problem getting moderately priced parts from Acura or Honda dealers. **Warranty:** Bumper-to-bumper 3 years/60,000 km; powertrain 5 years/100,000 km; rust perforation 6 years/unlimited km. **Supplementary warranty:** Not needed. **Highway/city fuel economy:** 6.7–9.8L/100 km. **Annual fuel cost:** 1,681L=$975.

Quality/Reliability/Safety

Pro: Quality control: Typical Honda (oops—I mean Acura): first class. **Reliability:** Few complaints that affect the Integra's overall reliability. **Warranty performance:** Better than average. Acura has a comprehensive standard warranty, and there have been few occasions where warranty disputes have had to be settled by third parties.

Con: Owner-reported problems: Some body fit and finish deficiencies. **Service bulletin problems:** Sun visor ticking or rattling. **NHTSA safety complaints/safety:** Steering wheel locked up while driving; sunroof suddenly shattered; key can be removed from the ignition without the transmission lever in Park; distorted front windshield; windshield wipers suddenly stop working until you shut off the ignition and wait a few minutes.

Road Performance

Pro: Emergency handling: Better than average, with little body lean or front end plow. **Steering:** Variable-assisted power steering is quick and precise at high speeds. **Acceleration/torque:** Acceptable acceleration from the base engine; more impressive with the high-performance, 170-hp GS-R powerplant (0–100 km/h: 7.2 sec.). **Transmission:** The standard 5-speed manual transmission shifter and clutch mechanism were substantially beefed up last year, giving slightly higher ratios in third and fourth and a taller fifth gear. An optional electronic 4-speed automatic uses "fuzzy logic" to reduce the annoying shifting back and forth over hilly terrain. **Routine handling:** Good handling under almost all circumstances. Gas shocks and improved body rigidity create a smooth and firm ride. Ride doesn't deteriorate as load is increased. **Braking:** Quite respectable (100–0 km/h: 118 ft.).

Con: Base engine whines at high speed. The GS-R's VTEC engine requires expert throttle control, frequent gear shifts, and constant attention in order to work properly. Some torque steer when accelerating. GS-R is hard riding. Steering exhibits a bit of understeer and isn't sufficiently assisted for parking.

Comfort/Convenience

Pro: Driving position: Very good. Comfortable, manually adjusted front bucket seats. **Controls and displays:** The attractive interior includes an easy-to-read dashboard layout with large analogue gauges that are complete and clear, and climate controls that are easy to operate. **Climate control:** The climate control system works flawlessly. **Interior space/comfort F/R:** Plenty of front head and leg room. The coupe's seat cushions provide good thigh support, its windows have frames for better sealing, and a reinforced body makes for a stiffer body shell. The four-door sedan carries four passengers in comfort. The cloth-covered seats are fairly comfortable and supportive for short drives. The sedan has comfortable rear seating for two adults, and the rear seats fold down completely. **Cargo space:** Average.

Con: Standard equipment: Not impressive. A $25,000 base price and anti-lock brakes are optional, and traction control is unavailable. The coupe's four small headlights are a throwback to the Isuzu Impulse, and the side-view mirrors resemble those of both the Prelude and Civic. The sunroof switch is too far from the sunroof, the radio controls aren't easily reached, and the sun visors are cheap-looking. The steering column, even when tilted to the max, practically rests on your kneecaps. Spoiler restricts rear visibility. **Entry/exit:** Entry/exit is made difficult by the curved windows and the doors' awkward design. The three-door model's rear seat is cramped and suitable only for luggage. Seats are lower than usual and tend to be uncomfortable on long trips. **Trunk/liftover:** The trunk on the coupe and sedan is awkward to load because of its narrow opening and high liftover. **Quietness:** Poor sealing around the sedan's side windows. Lots of road and engine noise, especially at full throttle.

COST

List Price (negotiable)	Residual Values (months)			
	24	36	48	60
Integra GS: $25,500 (20%)	$18,000	$15,000	$12,000	$9,000

TECHNICAL DATA

Powertrain (front-drive)
Engines: 1.8L 4-cyl. (139 hp)
• 1.8L VTEC (170 hp)
Transmissions: 5-speed man.
• 4-speed auto.
Dimension/Capacity.
Passengers: 4
Height/length/width:
52.6/172.4/67.3 in.

Head room F/R: 38.6/35 in.
Leg room F/R: 42.7/28.1 in.
Wheelbase: 101.2 in.
Turning circle: 39 ft.
Cargo volume: 13.3 cu. ft.
Tow limit: N/A
Fuel tank: 50L/reg.
Weight: 2,650 lb.

SAFETY FEATURES/CRASHWORTHINESS

	Std.	Opt.
Anti-lock brakes	■	❏
Seatbelt pretensioners	—	—
Side airbags	—	—
Traction control	—	—
Head restraints	***	**
Visibility (front/rear)	*****	**
Crash protection (front) D/P	****	***
Crash protection (side) D/P	N/A	
Crash protection (offset)	N/A	
HLDI injury claims (model)	*****	
HLDI injury claims (all)	***	

DAEWOO

South Korea's debt-ridden conglomerate is seen as a poorly managed company, making wild sales predictions that never materialize. In fact, Daewoo has become South Korea's best-known financial basket case, with the company's shipbuilding, commercial vehicle, automotive-parts, and electronic businesses on the block. Additionally, there's the very real possibility that the company's auto interests will be acquired by General Motors sometime next year.

Although sales have improved of late, Daewoo's two-year foray in the States has been a public relations disaster, characterized by sales way below expectations, a reputation for low-quality vehicles, and angry dealers who claim they've been misled.

Specifically, American dealers accused Daewoo of undercutting them by selling directly to the public at prices they couldn't match. Soon thereafter, the automaker admitted it had made a mistake and stopped the practice after dealers threatened to walk away from their franchises. After settling with its American dealers, the automaker began retailing cars in French markets for about $5,000 less than dealer prices. Now, these franchisees say they were cheated by the parent company and have asked for compensation. Daewoo claims it was simply a marketing mistake.

Now you understand why Canadian dealers are warily eyeing Daewoo's solicitations.

Lanos

RATING: Not Recommended during its first year on the market. **Strong points:** Low base price and relatively fuel-efficient. **Weak points:** Poor acceleration, harsh ride, poor handling, automatic transmission eats into performance, and a cramped interior. Also keep in mind the automaker's uncertain future and small dealer network, which can complicate servicing and warranty support.

OVERVIEW: Daewoo's $13,000 (est.) entry-level, front-drive, subcompact model comes as a five-passenger, two-door hatchback and four-door sedan. The smallest of its three-car lineup, the Lanos is about the size of a VW Golf, with less standard equipment and costing about $6,000 less. The 1.6L 105-hp 16-valve 4-cylinder engine can be mated to a base 5-speed manual transmission or an optional 4-speed automatic. Other standard features: power steering, AM/FM cassette, 60/40 split folding rear seats, and 14-inch tires. The few other options available: a power sunroof, ABS, and air conditioning.

Even though the Lanos looks like a bargain at first glance, it has no track record in Canada or the United States. You can get the more refined Accent or '99 Ford Escort for about the same price.

Nubira

✖ RISKY BUY

Nubia

RATING: The Nubira is another first-year Daewoo that is Not Recommended until the manufacturer, dealer network, and car prove themselves to be more than just hype. **Strong points:** Well appointed, good engine performance, relatively fuel-efficient, competent handling, adequate interior room, and good braking. **Weak points:** Noisy engine, windshield is too close to the driver, steering is over-assisted, predicted rapid depreciation, weak dealer support, and possible bankruptcy.

OVERVIEW: This is a larger, more powerful front-drive (about the Hyundai Elantra's size) that has a few more standard features than the Lanos—as shown by its improved road performance and higher price ($16,500). It's available as a four-door sedan, hatchback, or wagon and will seat five in relative comfort. Standard features include: a twin-cam

129-hp 2.0L, 4-cylinder engine coupled to a 5-speed manual transmission or an optional 4-speed automatic, 4-wheel disc brakes, front and rear anti-sway bars, a fully independent suspension, an AM/FM cassette radio, and foglights.

   The Nubira is a nicely packaged and reasonably priced small car that is outclassed by other small cars with a better track record and a larger dealer network. Alternatives worth considering: the Honda Civic, Mazda Protegé, and Toyota Corolla.

Leganza

RATING: Not Recommended during its first year on the market. You'd have to be crazy to pay $24,495 for a South Korean car that has no past and an uncertain future. **Strong points:** Lots of standard features, adequate acceleration, good braking, and roomy interior. **Weak points:** Noisy engine runs out of steam at higher speeds, mediocre automatic transmission performance, ponderous handling, uncomfortable rear seating, and weak dealer network and warranty support. Power-adjusted driver's seat doesn't adjust the seatback, the leather feels cheap, small vent controls aren't user-friendly, the CD changer skips when the car passes over bumps, and the sound system's graphic equalizer indicator washes out in daylight. Dealers are concentrated in Quebec and Ontario, but don't fret, Daewoo promises to cover all of Canada—by 2003!

OVERVIEW: Daewoo's top-of-the-line luxury sedan, the Leganza is about the size of a Nissan Altima and is loaded to the gills with standard features that enhance performance, convenience, and safety. It uses a 2.2L 131-hp 4-cylinder engine (only two horses more than the Nubira) mated to a standard 5-speed manual transmission or an optional 4-speed automatic. Alternatives worth considering: the Honda Accord, Mazda 626, and Toyota Camry.

Despite its many standard features that would cost extra on its rivals, the Leganza doesn't deliver the performance so apparent with the Accord and Camry. Reliability and durability are also an unknown.

HONDA

Honda continues to set sales records with every one of its cars, trucks, and minivans. Don't look for any bargain prices. The best we can hope for is only moderate increases on the most popular models, like the Accord and Odyssey. This year, Honda launches two new cars—the Insight, Honda's first hybrid powered vehicle, rumoured to get 70 mpg; and the S2000, a limited-production roadster.

Honda S2000
This new world-class sport roadster is lightweight, with a peppy 4-cylinder engine that generates 240 hp and 25 mpg. Its price ($30,000 U.S.) beats out the Porsche Boxster and the 6-cylinder version of the BMW Z3 by $8,000 and $15,000, respectively.

Already sold out in Japan, only 5,000 a year are earmarked for North America (expect less than 500 for Canada).

Honda's S2000: a best-seller even before it's hit the showroom.

The S2000 comes fully equipped with limited-slip differential, anti-lock brakes, AC, cruise control, leather seats, 16-inch wheels, high-intensity headlights, remote door locks with an engine immobilizer, a CD player with remote audio controls, power everything, and an air deflector.

Powered by a 2.0-litre, 16-valve, in-line four, the S2000 will reach 0–100 km/h in about the same time it takes to close the convertible roof—under six seconds. The 6-speed shifter has short throws helped by a direct link with the gearbox, rather than shift-by-wire units used in other cars.

Performance drivers will immediately discover that the S2000 excels at acceleration, braking, cornering, and shifting due in large part to the car's powerful engine, anti-lock brakes, double wishbone body, rigid suspension, and electronically controlled rack and pinion steering, which enhances steering response without compromising stability.

Civic

Civic

RATING: Recommended. New or used, the Honda Civic is one of the best cars money can buy. **Strong points:** Adequate acceleration, smooth-shifting automatic transmission, great handling, comfortable ride, good front and rear visibility (except for the Si's spoiler), high-quality construction, excellent resale value, and bulletproof reliability. **Weak points:** Si suspension may be too firm for some, seats lack sufficient padding, difficult rear access, rear seat room limited to two adults, lots of engine and road noise, and an unusually large number of safety-related complaints covering 1998–99 model years has been reported to NHTSA.

NEW FOR 2000: Minor trim changes. The Civic Si debuts with a more powerful engine, an upgraded exhaust system, a thicker front stabilizer bar, a rear stabilizer bar, and a front tower brace.

OVERVIEW: The Civic is one of the most refined and competent subcompacts on the market today. Few larger and more expensive cars can match its quality, performance, and roominess. The hatchback line is available in a wide range of models: a base CX, a mid-level DX, a VX econobox, and the high-performance Si, powered by the 160-hp VTEC engine resurrected from the defunct del Sol. Sedans are designated in a fashion similar to that of the Accord's, with a base DX, a mid-level LX, and a high-performance EX that carries the most powerful Civic powerplant.

The Civic DX hatchback lacks many of the luxury items that are standard on the LX, but it also lacks the 200–300 pounds in extra curb weight, giving it the performance and handling edge. Civics are easy to resell as used cars and command premium prices. Unfortunately, Civics in any form are now very expensive, especially when compared with domestic offerings. On the other hand, they're stylish, have lots of interior room, and are tops in fuel efficiency, thanks to Honda's new VTEC system.

Cost analysis/best alternatives: Get the '99 model, if it's discounted by about 10 percent. Choose the reasonably priced Civic CX or DX for the best combination of comfort, performance, and fuel economy. Other cars worth considering are the Ford '99 Escort, Mazda Protegé, Nissan Sentra, Hyundai Accent, and Toyota Echo. **Options:** Four-wheel anti-lock brakes are wise buys. Try to get a free extra set of ignition keys written into the contract; Honda's anti-start, theft-protection keys may cost as much as $150 a set. Steer clear of the standard-issue radio. **Rebates:** Not likely. **Delivery/PDI:** $300. **Depreciation:** Much slower than average. **Insurance cost:** High insurance costs: wrote one Elmvale, Ontario, shopper, "I was choosing between a Saturn and a Civic and I simply couldn't afford the insurance costs for the Civic. They were almost three times the cost of the Saturn in our area." **Parts supply/cost:** Moderately priced parts are easily found at dealers and independent suppliers. **Annual maintenance cost:** Less than average. **Warranty:** Bumper-to-bumper 3 years/60,000 km; powertrain 5 years/100,000 km; rust perforation 6 years/unlimited km. **Supplementary warranty:** Not necessary. **Highway/city fuel economy:** 6.0–8.6L/100 km with the base engine and 6.0–9.3L/100 km with the Si. **Annual fuel cost:** Base engine: 1,486L=$862; Si: 1,635L=$948. Imagine, the more powerful engine costs less than $100 more per year to run.

Quality/Reliability/Safety

Pro: Quality control: Assembly, as well as the quality of materials used in these cars, is first class. **Reliability:** Outstanding. Civics have proven to be mostly trouble-free. **Warranty performance:** Not generous, but acceptable. **Owner-reported problems:** Minor fit and finish deficiencies.

Con: Service bulletin problems: Steering pull or drifting; whistling or howling noise coming from the top middle of the windshield at highway speeds; moon roof seal sticks up or leaks; key is difficult to remove from the ignition switch; rear door lock tab is hard to open; warped wheel covers; driver's power mirror vibrations; security system LED malfunction. **NHTSA safety complaints/safety:** Airbags failed to deploy; accelerator pedal sticks to cables mounted too tight; accelerator cable got hung up in the cruise control, causing the vehicle to suddenly accelerate; while driving, vehicle suddenly accelerated due to the throttle sticking open, and brakes couldn't stop the car; car suddenly accelerated when passing another vehicle; gas pedal keeps sticking; while driving at a low speed, transmission popped out of gear and brake pedal went right to the floor without any braking effect; brakes locked up and vehicle pulled to the left when coming to an emergency stop; sudden steering loss while driving; excessive vibration due to engine main bearing failure; transmission sometimes fails to change gear; vehicle suddenly went into Reverse although shift lever was put into Drive; while stopped at a light on a hill, vehicle suddenly shifted into Reverse; another driver had the same thing happen, except this time the transmission shifted into Neutral; transmission was stuck in Reverse; faulty power door lock makes it impossible to open door from the inside or outside; dome light won't work when doors are open; tail-lights don't work when the headlights and dash lights are on; spoiler height prevents a clear line of sight; rear view mirror is poorly located and is non-adjustable, creating a large forward blind spot for tall drivers; sheet metal fatigue on both front fenders; faulty hood support rod causes the hood to come crashing down; exterior rear view mirror becomes loose, despite dealer efforts to tighten it.

Road Performance

Pro: Acceleration/torque: The 1.6L engine is smooth and responsive once it attains cruising speed (0–100 km/h: 9.1 sec.). The only disadvantage with these multi-valve engines is that peak power is developed at high engine rpm. The lack of low-end grunt (torque) means lots of gear shifting. The Si's 160-hp 1.6L 4-cylinder is a tire burner. **Routine handling:** Handling is excellent, and the ride, though stiff, is among the best in the subcompact class. All Civics give a smooth ride over uneven terrain, thanks to a re-tuning of the double-wishbone suspension last year. Si's larger wheels add to its handling prowess. **Braking:** Very good (100–0 km/h: 125 ft.).

Con: It's hard to modulate the throttle without having the car surge or lurch. The base engine loses its pep when the Overdrive gear on the automatic transmission engages in city driving, and the VTEC variant is noisy. Furthermore, get the VTEC option only if you enjoy constant gear shifting and intend to do a lot of highway driving, where it's most useful and less interactive. The VX gets its impressive fuel economy by sacrificing acceleration power through its extremely tall gearing. Unless you want to stall out, get used to using second gear for cornering under speed or passing other cars. **Emergency handling:** Moderate body roll when cornering at highway speeds. Skinny tires add to overall noise and harshness. **Steering:** Optional power steering is imprecise and doesn't communicate much road feel. **Transmission:** The 4-speed automatic transmission jerks into gear during hard acceleration, and the 5-speed manual is hard to shift when it's cold.

Comfort/Convenience

Pro: Driving position: Very good. A large cockpit area, along with interior refinements and the large window area, make for excellent visibility and a feeling of spaciousness. **Controls and displays:** Excellent dashboard design, with easy-to-read gauges and accessible controls. **Climate control:** Heating and ventilation are first class. **Interior space/comfort F/R:** Spacious front seating, less roomy in the rear. **Cargo space:** Versatile and spacious cargo areas. **Quietness:** Engine/road noise has been cut considerably.

Con: Standard equipment: Though it's reasonably well appointed, the base Honda has few standard features in order to keep the base price down. The basic Civic is very plasticky inside. Dual cupholders aren't very accessible. The tiny sun visors are practically useless, tiny horn buttons may be hard to find in an emergency, and the ignition switch is hidden away under the steering wheel. The Targa-style top is tough to remove. Doors give a "tinny" sound when closed. **Entry/exit:** The small door openings and low seating make for difficult entry and exit, and restrict overall visibility. **Interior space/comfort F/R:** Both front and rear seats are uncomfortable on long trips. **Trunk/liftover:** The trunk has limited cargo space and a high sill.

COST				
List Price (firm)	**Residual Values** (months)			
	24	**36**	**48**	**60**
Civic DX: $16,300 (11%)	$12,000	$10,000	$8,000	$6,500

TECHNICAL DATA

Powertrain (front-drive)
Engines: 1.6L 4-cyl. (106 hp)
• 1.6L 4-cyl. (115 hp)
• 1.6L 4-cyl. (127 hp)
• 1.6L 4-cyl. (160 hp)
Transmissions: 5-speed man.
• 4-speed auto.
Dimension/Capacity
Passengers: 5
Height/length/width:
54.7/175.1/67.1 in.

Head room F/R: 38.2/36.2 in.
Leg room F/R: 42.7/34.1 in.
Wheelbase: 103.2 in.
Turning circle: 37 ft.
Cargo volume: 11.9 cu. ft.
Tow limit: N/A
Fuel tank: 45L/reg.
Weight: 2,500 lb.

SAFETY FEATURES/CRASHWORTHINESS

	Std.	Opt.
Anti-lock brakes	■	■
Seatbelt pretensioners	—	—
Side airbags	—	—
Traction control	—	—
Head restraints	**	*
Visibility (front/rear)	*****	***

Crash protection (front) D/P		
2d	****	****
4d	N/A	
Crash protection (side) D/P		
2d	**	***
4d	***	***
Crash protection (offset)	***	
HLDI injury claims (model)	****	
HLDI injury claims (all)	**	

Accord

Accord

RATING: Recommended. Having competed toe-to-toe for over a decade with the Camry and Ford Taurus/Sable, the Accord's incremental upgrades put it in the forefront of mid-sized family sedans. **Strong points:** Excellent V6 acceleration, well equipped with user-friendly instruments and controls, easy handling, a comfortable ride, quiet cabin, good craftsmanship, above average reliability, and high resale value. **Weak points:** Low torque base engine makes for constant highway downshifting, problematic automatic transmission shifts harshly and slowly, average braking, rear passenger room is tight, and an unusually large number of safety-related complaints covering the 1998–99 model years has been reported to NHTSA.

NEW FOR 2000: Standard side airbags.

OVERVIEW: Having undergone a makeover a few years ago, this year's Accord is better than ever. You want performance? Well, you can choose among three engines that include two competent 4-bangers and a powerful V6. You want ride comfort and responsive handling? Accord gives you that too, through a more refined suspension and steering setup. What about space? Look out, Taurus/Sable—the Accord sedans are roomier than ever before, with interior dimension/capacity that provides more interior space than Ford's mid-sized duo. That could be why Honda has regained its lead over Ford in mid-sized sedan sales.

Overall, the Honda Accord is smooth, quiet, mannerly, and predictable. Every time Honda has redesigned this line it not only caught up with the latest advances, but went slightly ahead. Other strong points are ergonomics that prioritize comfort, easy driveability, high-quality fit and finish inside and out, impressive assembly quality, and outstanding reliability.

Fast and nimble without a V6, this is the mid-sized sedan of choice for drivers who want maximum fuel economy and comfort along with lots of space for grocery hauling and occasional highway cruising. With the optional 16-valve 4-cylinder engine or V6, the Accord is one of the most versatile mid-sized cars you can find. It offers something for everyone, and its top-drawer quality and high resale value means there's no way you can lose money buying one.

Cost analysis/best alternatives: Only consider a '99 model if the price is cut by at least 10 percent. Some other vehicles worth considering: the BMW 325i, Mazda Protegé and 626, Toyota Camry, and VW Golf and Jetta. **Options:** V6 for a smoother ride. If you're likely to do a lot of driving in the snow or over wet pavement, don't let the dealer sell you Michelin MXV4 tires—they're terrible snow performers. Choose instead one of the brands recommended in Part One. Try to get a free extra set of ignition keys written into the contract; Honda's anti-start, theft-protection keys may cost as much as $150 a set. **Rebates:** Not likely. **Delivery/PDI:** $500. **Depreciation:** Slower than average. **Insurance cost:** Higher than average. **Parts supply/cost:** Good availability and moderately priced. **Annual maintenance cost:** Less than average. **Warranty:** Bumper-to-bumper 3 years/60,000 km; powertrain 5 years/100,000 km; rust perforation 5 years/unlimited km. **Supplementary warranty:** Not needed. **Highway/city fuel economy:** 7.4–10.5L/100 km with the base engine, 7.1–10.5L/100 km with the 16-valve 2.3L, and 7.8–11.5L/100 km with the V6 engine. **Annual fuel cost:** Base engine: 1,821L=$1,056; 16-valve 2.3L: 1,794L=$1,041; V6: 1,967L=$1,141.

Quality/Reliability/Safety

Pro: Quality control: Traditionally first class. These cars are built with care; rarely is a misaligned piece of trim or a crooked seam to be found. **Reliability:** Excellent for the first five years. **Warranty performance:** Predicted to be average. CAA surveys show that customer satisfaction is an impressive 88 percent, compared to 85 percent for both the Toyota Camry and Mazda 626.

Con: Owner-reported problems: Transmission glitches, brake failures and premature brake wear, electrical short circuits, malfunctioning accessories, and rattles and squeaks. **Service bulletin problems:** Squeaking or groaning when clutch pedal is applied; security system sounds on its own; inaccurate fuel gauge; warped wheel covers. **NHTSA safety complaints:** Airbags failed to deploy; vehicle hit from behind at stoplight and then suddenly accelerated; brake pedal has to be pushed down with both feet to stop vehicle; brake failure caused lengthy stopping distances; emergency brakes failed on an incline; when braking while going downhill, brakes suddenly failed; ABS light continually stays lit; premature brake wear; check engine light stays lit; sudden loss of power steering fluid while driving; loss of power steering fluid when making a U-turn; excessive steering wander that degrades progressively; vehicle suddenly stalls while driving, which dealer says is caused by a faulty computer module; engine hesitates when accelerating to merge with traffic; when cruise control is engaged, the transmission suddenly downshifts; automatic transmission's gears disengage and make a loud noise when engaging while parked on an incline, vehicle rolled forward, despite having gear lever in the Park position; vertical lines distort windshield view; took key out of the ignition and all the accessories still work; due to the design of the dash lighting, it's hard to read the odometer, clock, and radio indicator; speedometer reads 8–10 percent higher than actual speed; fuel tank never shows more than $^2/_3$ when tank is full; turn signal fails to self-cancel on left turns; driver's side seatback rocks; right front passenger-side window suddenly exploded; rear seatbelts lock too tightly around neck and are difficult to loosen; child pulled shoulder belt around neck and head and it locked up when he let the strap go; difficult to secure child safety seat to middle of rear seat; rear seatbelt fails to retract; defective rear computerized motor mounts; excessive wind noise and doors won't close properly due to misaligned body.

Road Performance

Pro: Emergency handling: Very good. A firm but well-controlled ride is achieved through increased body rigidity and a reworked suspension. **Steering:** Improved variable-assist power steering provides excellent road feel. **Acceleration/torque:** Excellent with both the 4- and 6-cylinder engines (0–100 km/h: 7.6 sec. with the V6). The 16-valve 2.3L engine delivers a sportier performance than the more sedate V6. Both engines give sparkling performance with plenty of low-end torque and minimal noise. The new 200-hp V6 doesn't offer a stick shift, but the automatic transmission doesn't sacrifice performance. **Transmission:** The 5-speed manual transmission works very well with smooth and light clutch action. The 4-speed automatic has Overdrive to help save fuel. It also has a Grade Logic feature that reduces gear hunting when climbing hills and automatically downshifts when descending, using engine compression to brake. **Routine handling:** Excellent handling in town or on the highway. It's also amazingly smooth and quiet. There isn't a trace of vibration throughout the operating range, including at idle. Excels in smoothness when passing over freeway expansion joints and potholes, where it damps out the jolts better than most cars in its class. The emphasis on comfort also dominates the Accord's ride and handling. Although its chassis is as good as any, Honda's suspension settings aren't as firm as those of the other cars in this class. **Braking:** Average (100–0 km/h: 133 ft.).

Con: VTEC 150-hp 2.3L engine lacks guts and is a bit buzzy in the higher ranges. Could use a bit more high-end torque. Automatic transmission frequently pops out of gear. No all-wheel drive option, available on many cars in the Accord class. Sometimes, the tall centre console gets in the way of shifting. The four-doors have a less rigid suspension and softer ride than does the coupe. Standard Bridgestone tires don't grip enough in corners.

Comfort/Convenience

Pro: Standard equipment: A nice array of standard features on the base model. Wood and leather on upper-end models. **Driving position:** Excellent driving position and visibility. Very comfortable sporty front seats are well-padded and supportive. Everything is right where it should be, easily seen and easily reached. **Controls and displays:** The well-designed dashboard looks like it's one big moulding, rather than a lot of pieces thrown together. Clear gauges and instruments. User-friendly controls and instrumentation. The radio and AC controls have been moved closer to eye level. **Climate control:** Very user-friendly; quiet, efficient, and easily calibrated. **Entry/exit:** Easy entry and exit. **Interior space/comfort F/R:** More interior space than the BMW 740i, Ford Taurus, or Toyota Camry. Redesigned front seat bases provide more rear foot room. **Cargo space:** The LX and DX sedans' pass-through rear seats allow for more convenient cargo handling. **Trunk/liftover:** Large trunk on sedans and versatile hatchback design; high liftover, however. **Quietness:** Average, with some tire drumming evident.

Con: Si spoiler cuts into rear visibility. Rear seating is too low. Rear room for three is a bit tight and the middle passenger will be squeezed from both sides. The remote lock key fob is quirky: sometimes it refuses to unlock the doors.

COST				
List Price (firm)	**Residual Values** (months)			
	24	36	48	60
Accord DX Sedan:				
$23,000 (10%)	$19,000	$16,000	$13,000	$10,000
TECHNICAL DATA				

Powertrain (front-drive)	Head room F/R: 40/37.6 in.
Engines: 2.3L 4-cyl. (135 hp)	Leg room F/R: 42.1/37.9 in.
• 2.3L 4-cyl. (150 hp)	Wheelbase: 106.9 in.
• 3.0L V6 (200 hp)	Turning circle: 40 ft.
Transmissions: 5-speed man.	Cargo volume:14.1 cu. ft.
• 4-speed auto.	Tow limit: 1,000 lb.

Dimension/Capacity (sedan)	Fuel tank: 65L/reg.
Passengers: 2/3	Weight: 3,230 lb.
Height/length/width:	
57.2/188.8/70.3 in	

SAFETY FEATURES/CRASHWORTHINESS

	Std.	Opt.
Anti-lock brakes	■	■
Seatbelt pretensioners	—	—
Side airbags	■	—
Traction control	—	—
Head restraints	***	**
Visibility (front/rear)	*****	*****
Crash protection (front) D/P	****	****
Crash protection (side) D/P	****	****
Crash protection (offset)	***	
HLDI injury claims (model)	N/A	
HLDI injury claims (all)	N/A	

Prelude

Prelude

RATING: Above Average. **Strong points:** Powerful engine, easy handling, lots of standard features, and impressive reliability and quality control. **Weak points:** A bit hard-riding, difficult rear seat access, limited rear seat room, insufficient trunk space, and excessive road noise.

NEW FOR 2000: Nothing significant. If the S2000 sales really take off, the Prelude may get axed.

OVERVIEW: This fifth-generation Prelude sport coupe is complete, functional, and rational without any hint of aggression in its styling or performance components. In fact, most of its performance upgrades won't be noticed by the average driver. It comes with a standard 2.2L

200-hp VTEC engine. There are two trim levels available: the base Prelude and the Prelude Type SH.

Cost analysis/best alternatives: If you don't know it already, the 1999 Prelude is practically identical to this year's version, and is a real bargain if you can find a reasonably priced discounted leftover. Other worthwhile cars to consider are the Acura Integra, Ford Mustang, GM Camaro and Firebird, and Mazda Miata. **Options:** Try to get a free extra set of ignition keys written into the contract; Honda's anti-start, theft-protection keys may cost as much as $150 a set. **Rebates:** Not likely. **Delivery/PDI:** $300. **Depreciation:** Slower than average. **Insurance cost:** Higher than average. **Parts supply/cost:** Parts are easily found and moderately priced. Most corner mechanics are ill-equipped to service these cars, and the complex Automatic Torque Transfer System (ATTS) won't make their job any easier. **Annual maintenance cost:** Less than average. **Warranty:** Bumper-to-bumper 3 years/60,000 km; powertrain 5 years/100,000 km; rust perforation 5 years/unlimited km. **Supplementary warranty:** Not needed. **Highway/city fuel economy:** 8.2–11.2L/100 km. **Annual fuel cost:** 1,970L=$1,320.

Quality/Reliability/Safety

Pro: Quality control: Exceptional quality control. **Reliability:** No problems have been reported that would make the Prelude unreliable. **Warranty performance:** Better than average. **Owner-reported problems:** Preludes usually give their owners excellent service for the first five years. Even later on, the few problems that surface aren't difficult to diagnose or expensive to repair.

Con: Owner-reported problems: Air-conditioner condensers frequently need cleaning to eliminate disagreeable odours. Owners have complained about minor electrical problems and accessory malfunctions. **Service bulletin problems:** A clunking noise may be heard coming from the trunk area. **NHTSA safety complaints/safety:** Driver's airbag failed to deploy; without ABS, wheels tend to lock up easily during emergency braking; door locks frequently malfunction, causing the driver's door to lock unexpectedly and not unlock.

Road Performance

Pro: Emergency handling: Handling is excellent in all conditions. Suspension travel is long enough to reduce bottoming out when fully loaded or when encountering irregular terrain. Last year's suspension upgrade gives a better feel of the road while reducing throttle-lift oversteer, bump, and torque steer (high-performance enthusiasts, rejoice!). **Steering:** Direct and predictable. **Acceleration/torque:** Plenty of power (0–100 km/h: 7 sec.), but insufficient torque means you'll do a lot of shifting to keep pace in traffic or on the highway. The Automatic Torque

Transfer System (ATTS) is an interesting gizmo that transfers torque to the outside wheel in a turn, making for quicker high-speed cornering. **Transmission:** The manual and automatic transmissions are precise, smooth shifting, and require little effort. **Routine handling:** Very responsive. The ride is quite comfortable, due mainly to suspension refinements and four-wheel disc brakes. **Braking:** Better than average.

Con: Even though the 200-hp engine is ideal for sporty performance, this car cries out for a V6 powerplant that provides more torque in all gears. It could also use a 6-speed transmission to more efficiently harness the VTEC's high-revving engine.

Comfort/Convenience

Pro: Standard equipment: Lots of standard features. Height-adjustable bucket seat. Excellent visibility. **Controls and displays:** Greatly improved, user-friendly dash. **Climate control:** Competent climate control system is quiet and easy to adjust. **Interior space/comfort F/R:** Last year's extended wheelbase increased rear head room by 1.5 inches, knee room by 2.5 inches, and foot room by almost 3 inches. Comfortable front seats are well-padded and supportive.

Con: Driving position: All drivers may find head room lacking, especially with a sunroof. **Interior space/comfort F/R:** Insufficient rear passenger room. **Entry/exit:** Very difficult for both the driver and passengers. **Cargo space:** Rather limited. **Trunk/liftover:** Small trunk has a low liftover. **Quietness:** Some road noise is still present.

COST				
List Price (negotiable)	**Residual Values** (months)			
	24	36	48	60
Base Prelude: $27,900 (10%)	$19,000	$16,000	$13,000	$10,000

TECHNICAL DATA	
Powertrain (front-drive)	Head room F/R: 37.9/35.3 in.
Engine: 2.2L 4-cyl. (200 hp)	Leg room F/R: 43/28.1 in.
Transmissions: 5-speed man.	Wheelbase: 101.8 in.
• 4-speed auto.	Turning circle: 40 ft.
Dimension/Capacity	Cargo volume: 8.7 cu. ft.
Passengers: 2/2	Tow limit: 1,000 lb.
Height/length/width:	Fuel tank: 60L/reg.
51.8/178/69 in.	Weight: 2,950 lb.

SAFETY FEATURES/CRASHWORTHINESS		
	Std.	**Opt.**
Anti-lock brakes	■	❏
Seatbelt pretensioners	■	❏
Side airbags	—	—

Traction control	■	❑
Head restraints	**	**
Visibility (front/rear)	*****	*****
Crash protection (front) D/P	N/A	
Crash protection (side) D/P	N/A	
Crash protection (offset)	N/A	
HLDI injury claims (model)	N/A	
HLDI injury claims (all)	N/A	

Odyssey

BEST BUY

Odyssey

RATING: Recommended. Not perfect yet, but it will do nicely until the American automakers wake up and start building quality minivans. **Strong points:** Standard ABS and traction control (EX model only), car-like ride and handling, easy entry/exit, second driver-side door, quiet interior, lots of passenger and cargo room, impressive reliability, and an extensive list of standard equipment. **Weak points:** A high base price, premium fuel is required for optimum performance, and rear seat head restraints impede side and rear visibility.

NEW FOR 2000: An optional GPS navigation system.

OVERVIEW: When it was first launched in 1995, the Odyssey was a sales dud simply because Canadians and *Lemon-Aid* saw through Honda's ruse in trying to pass off an underpowered mid-sized, four-door station wagon with a raised roof as a minivan. However, last year the Odyssey was redesigned, and now represents one of the two best minivans on the Canadian market (Toyota's Sienna is the other top choice).

No longer simply an Accord masquerading as a minivan, the redesigned front-drive, Alliston, Ontario–built Odyssey is longer, wider, taller, and more powerful than last year's model. In fact, it compares well with the Ford Windstar as the longest front-drive minivan on the market. It has a leaner look than before, yet the interior is wide enough and long enough to accommodate a 4x8 plywood sheet laid flat. Sliding doors are offered as standard equipment and, if you buy the EX version, they will both be power-assisted.

You can only get one engine—the largest one among minivans, a powerful 210-hp V6 that easily handles most driving chores. Odyssey also offers an upgraded, fully independent suspension, front and rear AC, second-row captain's chairs that can be shoved side by side to create a bench seat, and a convenient third-row bench seat that folds into the floor when not in use.

Cost analysis/best alternatives: Despite its high price, the Odyssey is more reliable and handles more easily than its American competition. Forget about finding a bargain-priced '99 model, they're long gone—plus this year's model costs only $200 more. Incidentally, a fully loaded EX does run $3,000 more than the base model. However, for the additional money you get traction control, power rear doors, remote entry, a power driver's seat, fore-and-aft adjustment for the middle seats, a climate control system that's hard to access and calibrate (the LX version is more user-friendly), and an upgraded sound system. I suggest you bite the bullet and buy your Odyssey before the second round of price increases are announced early next year. There *is* room for some price negotiation, with savings in the $1,500–$2,000 range, but make sure you have a *specific* delivery date spelled out in the contract along with a *protected* price, in case there's a price increase while you're waiting for delivery. Also be wary of the '99 Isuzu Oasis; it's simply a carried-over '98 Honda Odyssey with none of the important performance upgrades that Honda's '99 Odyssey offered. The Nissan Quest is also worth considering if you plan mostly light-duty urban commuting. However, if you want better handling and reliability, the closest competitor to the Odyssey is Toyota's Sienna minivan. The Pontiac Montana and Chevrolet Venture from GM are good front-drive choices—they're less reliable, but still acceptable. If you're looking for lots of towing "grunt," then the rear-drive GM Astro, Safari, or full-sized vans would be good buys. **Options:** Traction control. **Rebates:** Are you kidding? The Alliston, Ontario, plant was scheduled to produce 60,000 units annually; it's now up to 120,000, with 40,000 more to be added by the end of 1999. All these efforts still haven't made a dent in the four-month waiting period. **Delivery/PDI:** $500. **Depreciation:** Slower than average. **Insurance cost:** Higher than average. **Annual maintenance cost:** Average. **Parts supply/cost:** Supply is better than average because the Odyssey uses many generic Accord parts. **Warranty:** Bumper-to-bumper 3 years/60,000 km; powertrain 5 years/100,000 km; rust perforation 5 years/unlimited km. **Supplementary warranty:** Not needed. **Highway/city fuel economy:** 8.5–13.2L/100 km. Premium fuel is recommended, but the Odyssey will run on regular, with a slight loss of power (about five horses). **Annual fuel cost:** 2,217L=$1,286.

Quality/Reliability/Safety

Pro: Quality control: Component quality and assembly are similar to the Accord: first class, although there are some buzzes, rattles, and rumblings. **Reliability:** Much better than average, but Honda still has a few problems to work out. **Warranty performance:** Comprehensive base warranty that's usually applied fairly with lots of "wiggle room" that the service manager can use to apply "goodwill" adjustments for post-warranty problems. **Safety:** Honda claims it's the only automaker to offer head restraints and three-point seatbelts at all seven seating positions. Plus, the body structure has been extensively reinforced to protect occupants from all kinds of collisions, including rollovers.

Con: Owner-reported problems: Premature front brake wear, excessive front brake noise, sliding side door frequently malfunctions, electrical glitches, and accessory items that come loose, break away, or won't work. Plastic interior panels have rough edges and are often misaligned. **Service bulletin problems:** Front brakes make a low-pitched moaning sound; constant tapping noise from the sliding side doors; power sliding door malfunctions. **NHTSA safety complaints/safety:** In a frontal collision, van caught fire due to a cracked brake fluid reservoir; while stopped on an incline of about 35 degrees, van rolled backwards; brakes made a loud screeching noise and lose effectiveness; sudden loss of brakes, preceded by a loud rumbling noise; loud squeaking noise from both front wheels, caused by premature wear (at 2,000 km) of brake pads and rotors; passenger side door window suddenly exploded while driving on the highway; erratic power sliding door that won't open with the remote control, opens and closes on its own, or fails to open and close properly; sliding door doesn't have a safety stop, allowing gas cap to get jammed; a faulty striker apparently causes erratic opening and closing of sliding door; rear seatbelt tightened up so much that a child had to be cut free; too much play in rear lapbelts, which won't tighten adequately, making it difficult to install a child safety seat securely; faulty speedometer and tachometer; placement of the gear shift lever interferes with the radio's controls; frequent static electricity shocks.

Many owners report that the rear head restraints seriously hamper rear and forward visibility and that early models had the only tether strap anchor for a child safety seat located behind the third row of seats (Honda's working on a correction).

Road Performance

Pro: Emergency handling: Predictable and well controlled. **Acceleration/torque:** Quiet yet powerful V6 engine performance with plenty of torque throughout the power band (0–100 km/h: just over 9 seconds). In fact, only the Toyota Sienna exceeds the Odyssey in powertrain refinement. **Transmission:** Smooth and quiet shifting, though a bit slow to downshift at full throttle. **Routine handling:** Better handling than most of the competition, with a short turning circle, making it quite nimble; akin to driving a large, quiet, sport family sedan. Steering is light to the touch and responsive on the highway. **Braking:** Better than average braking, with little fading after repeated stops. The ABS-equipped front disc/rear drum setup is the best you'll find among minivans; even with a full load and after repeated stops they perform quite well—most of the time (see "NHTSA safety complaints/safety").

Con: Steering: A bit heavy at low speeds; sometimes feels overboosted at highway speeds. Column-mounted shift-lever tends to slide past Drive into third gear when shifted out of Park. The taut suspension is a bit jolting over bumps, but the ride smooths out as the load is increased. Braking is often accompanied by front and rear brake squealing in low-speed stops.

Comfort/Convenience

Pro: Standard equipment: Well appointed. **Driving position:** Comfortable, commanding driving position. **Controls and displays:** Controls and displays are easy to reach and read. **Climate control:** Much improved. Quiet and efficient. Each seat has its own AC and heating vent. **Entry/exit:** Low step-up. The Odyssey provides car-like room in the front two rows of seats; getting in is no more difficult than climbing into an Accord. **Interior space/comfort F/R:** It's easy to strap a child seat into the Odyssey because there's far less lifting and reaching. The bench seat in the centre row is more practical than the captain's chairs, which can't be removed. It's more like a seven-seater station wagon than a minivan. All passengers have their own reading light, air vent, and power rear vent window controls. **Trunk/liftover:** There's space enough for groceries, and the edging around the storage area will help keep your apples from rolling around. **Cargo space:** Lots of little storage areas. A handy storage tray between the front seats folds down when not in use. If you need to expand the cargo area, the third seat folds flat into the floor. **Quietness:** The interior is quiet in most situations.

Con: Styling isn't to everyone's taste: colour and model selection are limited, carpeting looks cheap, and some find the Odyssey looks too bus-like. The sun visor extensions cover up the rear view mirror. Rear washer dribbles rather than squirts and doesn't have an intermittent setting. Standard issue winter wiper won't clean the front and rear windshields adequately (get upgraded wipers at Canadian Tire). **Driving position:** The driver's seat has backrest bolstering that is too padded for some, not enough for others (try before you buy). **Interior space/comfort F/R:** Front-seat passenger leg room is marginal due to the restricted seat travel; you can't slid your legs comfortably under the dash. Some passengers bump their shins on the glovebox. Third row seat is only suitable for children; the narrow back bench seat provides little leg room, unless the middle seats are pushed far forward, inconveniencing others. **Controls and displays:** Radio control access is blocked by the shift lever and it's difficult to calibrate the radio without taking your eyes off the road. Power outlet, located at the base of the centre console, is awkward to access. Sealed centre windows. Power-sliding doors are slow to retract. Huge interior is slow to warm up and rear side windows fog up with a full passenger load. **Climate control:** AC controls and pictograms on the EX aren't very user-friendly and are confusing to adjust. **Cargo space:** Stowing the "hideaway" third seat exposes metal sidewall anchors that can easily damage cargo. The storage well won't take any tire larger than a "space saver"—meaning you'll carry your flat in the back. **Quietness:** Some tire rumble and body drumming at highway speeds.

COST

List Price (negotiable)	Residual Values (months)			
	24	**36**	**48**	**60**
Odyssey LX: $30,800 (19%)	$25,000	$21,000	$17,000	$14,000
Odyssey EX: $33,800 (19%)	$26,000	$22,000	$18,000	$15,000

TECHNICAL DATA

Powertrain (front-drive)
Engine: 3.5L V6 (210 hp)
Transmission: 4-speed auto.
Dimension/Capacity
Passengers: 2/2/3
Height/length/width:
68.5/201.2/75.6 in.

Head room F: 41.2/R1: 40/R2: 38.9 in.
Leg room F: 41/R1: 40/R2: 38.1 in.
Wheelbase: 118.1 in.
Turning circle: 41 ft.
Cargo volume: 67 cu. ft.
GVWR: N/A
Payload: N/A
Tow limit: 2,000 lb.
Fuel tank: 65L/prem.
Weight: 4,245 lb.

SAFETY FEATURES/CRASHWORTHINESS

	Std.	Opt.
Anti-lock brakes (4W)	■	❏
Seatbelt pretensioners	—	—
Side airbags	—	—
Traction control	❏	■
Head restraints	**	*
Visibility (front/rear)	*****	*
Crash protection (front) D/P	*****	*****
Crash protection (side) D/P	*****	*****
Crash protection (offset)	*****	
HLDI injury claims (model)	N/A	
HLDI injury claims (all)	N/A	

HYUNDAI

Hyundai doesn't make top-quality cars—a fact repeated time and again by consumer groups on both sides of the border. But Hyundai quality is improving, its vehicles are now backed by a more comprehensive warranty, and they're reasonably priced—three reasons Canadians are giving Hyundai products more consideration, resulting in an almost 20 percent increase in sales during the first five months of 1999.

For its 2000 model year lineup, Hyundai has redesigned the Accent and freshened the Tiburon's styling. Its other cars are carried over without any significant changes.

Accent

RATING: Above Average. Think of it as a more refined Metro/Sprint from South Korea. **Strong points:** Reasonably priced and well appointed, adequate engine and automatic transmission performance in most situations, comfortable driving position with good visibility, cheap on gas, and a low base price. **Weak points:** Primitive manual transmission; passing power comes up short, especially with the automatic transmission; mediocre braking; excessive engine, road, and wind noise; and uncertain long-term reliability.

NEW FOR 2000: A total redesign will include a beefed-up 1.5L engine.

OVERVIEW: This front-drive 4-cylinder sedan retains most of the Excel's underpinnings while dropping the Mitsubishi powerplant in favour of its own home-grown 1.5L 4-cylinder. It's better than the old Excel, though, with its upgraded, smoother-shifting automatic transmission, stiffer, better-performing suspension, stronger and quieter-running engine, dual airbags, and optional ABS. The three-door matches the Excel in length; the four-door is six inches shorter. Interior space was increased by an inch last year.

Cost analysis/best alternatives: Get a year 2000 model made after March for a better-built product with the most upgrades. Other vehicles worth considering: the Chevrolet Metro, Ford Escort ZX2, Honda Civic, Nissan Sentra, Suzuki Swift, Toyota Corolla, and VW Golf. **Options:** An automatic transmission and power steering are essential. **Rebates:** Expect $1,500 rebates to clear out the '99 models as this year's improved cars are trucked in. **Delivery/PDI:** $350. **Depreciation:** Slower than average. **Insurance cost:** Average. **Parts supply/cost:** Parts aren't hard to find and they're reasonably priced. **Annual maintenance cost:** Average. Hyundai says the timing chain should be replaced every 100,000 km. **Warranty:** Bumper-to-bumper 3 years/60,000 km; powertrain 5 years/100,000 km; rust perforation 5 years/unlimited km. **Supplementary warranty:** A good idea, since every Hyundai redesign has brought with it a number of first-year factory-related deficiencies. **Highway/city fuel economy:** 6.1–9.0L/100 km. **Annual fuel cost:** 1,539L=$893.

Quality/Reliability/Safety

Pro: Quality control: Average. Repairs are straightforward because of a fairly simple design, and parts are less expensive than average. **Reliability:** Average. Accents have overcome a lot of the early bad karma caused by the failure-prone Excel. **Warranty performance:** Average. **Service bulletin problems:** Nothing published yet—an encouraging sign.

Con: Owner-reported problems: The engine cooling system and cylinder head gaskets aren't very durable; premature front brake wear and excessive noise when braking; wheel bearings, fuel system, and electrical components also fail prematurely. Body assembly is mediocre and paint is poorly applied. **NHTSA safety complaints/safety:** Airbags failed to deploy; fire caused by alternator failure; sudden transmission and brake failure; chronic stalling; premature suspension strut failure; electrical system failure caused by loose solenoid wire; horn controls may be hard to find in an emergency; the rear seatbelt configuration complicates the installation of a child safety seat; engine burning two quarts of oil a month.

Road Performance

Pro: Although the 1.5L engine is no pocket rocket, it performs adequately in city traffic. **Emergency handling:** Slow, but predictable. **Steering:** The non-power steering is precise and transmits plenty of road feedback at higher speeds. **Transmission:** Surprisingly, this is one car where the automatic transmission performs better than the manual gearbox. **Routine handling:** Above average. The Accent rides comfortably and handles responsively.

Con: Acceleration/torque: Last year's 1.5L engine provides glacial acceleration (0–100 km/h: 11.2 sec.). The manual transmission is hard to shift correctly due to its balky linkage and long lever movements. Uneven pavement makes for a busy, jittery ride that's accentuated as passengers are added. Steering without the power-assist option takes a lot of effort around town and when parking. **Braking:** Unacceptably long stopping distances (100–0 km/h: 139 ft.).

Comfort/Convenience

Pro: Driving position: Very good. Multiple front seat adjustments and a well-appointed interior make for a pleasant driving environment with a good view of the road. **Controls and displays:** Well laid-out dashboard and controls. **Climate control:** Efficient, easy-to-understand climate control system. **Entry/exit:** Front and rear access is impressively easy. **Interior space/comfort F/R:** Room for two adults in the rear. Plenty of front head room. Fairly comfortable but very firm and narrow front seats. **Cargo space:** Reasonable amount of luggage space, but the hatchback is more versatile with its folding rear seatbacks. **Trunk/liftover:** Average-sized trunk with a low liftover.

Con: Standard equipment: Few standard features, and there aren't a lot of options to choose from. Limited front leg room for tall passengers. Temperature controls aren't within easy reach. **Quietness:** Excessive engine, road, and wind noise.

COST				
List Price (negotiable)	**Residual Values** (months)			
	24	**36**	**48**	**60**
Accent L: $11,565 (11%)	$7,000	$5,500	$4,500	$3,500

TECHNICAL DATA	
Powertrain (front-drive)	Head room F/R: 38.7/38 in.
Engines: 1.5L 4-cyl. (92 hp)	Leg room F/R: 42.6/32.7 in.
Transmissions: 5-speed man.	Wheelbase: 94.5 in.
• 4-speed auto.	Turning circle: 35 ft.
Dimension/Capacity	Cargo volume: 11 cu. ft.
Passengers: 2/3	Tow limit: N/A
Height/length/width:	Fuel tank: 46L/reg.
54.9/162.1/63.8 in.	Weight: 2,100 lb.

SAFETY FEATURES/CRASHWORTHINESS

	Std.	Opt.
Anti-lock brakes	❑	■
Seatbelt pretensioners	—	—
Side airbags	—	—
Traction control	—	—
Head restraints	*	*
Visibility (front/rear)	*****	*****
Crash protection (front) D/P	***	****
Crash protection (side) D/P	N/A	
Crash protection (offset)	N/A	
HLDI injury claims (model)	*	
HLDI injury claims (all)	*	

Elantra

Elantra

RATING: Average. **Strong points:** Reasonably priced and well appointed, nimble handling. **Weak points:** Noisy, weak engine, passing power comes up short with the crude, automatic transmission, a jittery ride, mediocre braking, lots of wind noise, difficult entry/exit, hard rear seats, below average crashworthiness scores, and a high insurance claim rate for injuries.

NEW FOR 2000: Nothing significant; major changes will occur when the car is redesigned in 2001.

OVERVIEW: This Italian-designed, front-drive, conservatively styled sub-compact comes either as a sedan or wagon. It's only marginally larger than the discontinued Excel. Nevertheless, its powerful 2.0L 140-hp 4-cylinder powerplant supplies the much-needed power that you won't find with the Excel. The ride and handling are also improved, due mainly to the Elantra's longer wheelbase and more sophisticated suspension.

Elantra comes in two body styles: the base model and the GLS. As with most Asian cars, the Elantra is loaded with standard equipment, including standard AC and seatbelt pretensioners, intermittent wipers, full centre console, dual remote-control outside mirrors, remote fuel-filler door and trunk release, reclining bucket seats, and tinted glass. Upgrading to the GLS will get you more instruments, power accessories, better tires, a tilt steering wheel, and a premium sound system.

Cost analysis/best alternatives: Get a leftover '99 model if it's discounted by at least 10 percent. Other cars worth considering are the Ford Escort ZX2, Honda Civic, Nissan Sentra, and Toyota Corolla. **Options:** None. **Rebates:** Expect $1,500–$2,000 rebates to clear out the '99s. **Delivery/PDI:** $300. **Depreciation:** Faster than average. **Insurance cost:** A bit higher than average. **Parts supply/cost:** Easy-to-find and reasonably priced parts, with heavy discounting by dealers. **Annual maintenance cost:** Average. **Warranty:** Bumper-to-bumper 3 years/60,000 km; powertrain 5 years/100,000 km; rust perforation 5 years/unlimited km. **Supplementary warranty:** A wise investment. **Highway/city fuel economy:** 7.1–10.8L/100 km. **Annual fuel cost:** 1,827L=$1,060.

Quality/Reliability/Safety

Pro: Quality control: Few quality control problems, so far. **Warranty performance:** Average. Hyundai customer relations staff usually deal with customer claims in a fair and efficient manner. **Service bulletin problems:** Nothing important.

Con: Reliability: Overall reliability has been slightly below average after the fifth year of ownership. **Owner-reported problems:** Powertrain and electrical system failures. **NHTSA safety complaints/safety:** Airbags failed to deploy; accelerator pedal floored, but vehicle failed to pick up speed; chronic transmission failures; automatic transmission slips; transmission goes into low gear periodically and gets stuck there; vehicle rolled forward even though emergency brake was applied; clutch slave cylinder failure; transmission produces clunking and whining noises; brakes not very efficient; brake master cylinder failure; sudden steering failure; loose steering; low beam doesn't light up driver's view—instead, the light reflects outward to the left or right; AC circulates bad air; tire jack is too small and weak; defective side moulding.

Road Performance

Pro: Emergency handling: Better than average. **Steering:** Accurate and responsive. **Routine handling:** Independent suspension helps make for a pleasant ride with exceptional handling and control.

Con: Acceleration/torque: Leisurely acceleration (0–100 km/h: 10.5 sec.). Around town this is no problem, but highway cruising and hilly terrain bring out the worst in this low-torque engine. **Transmission:** The optional 4-speed automatic transmission robs the base engine of at least 10 horses, and it isn't as smooth as it should be. It shifts frequently, trying to keep up with the overburdened engine. **Braking:** Worse than average without anti-lock brakes (100–0 km/h: 146 ft.). Brakes are difficult to modulate.

Comfort/Convenience

Pro: Driving position: Good driving environment with excellent all-around visibility and comfortable front seats. **Controls and displays:** The attractive interior includes an easy-to-read dashboard with large analogue gauges that are complete and clear, and climate and radio controls that are effective and easy to operate. **Climate control:** The climate control system works without a hitch. Comfortable rear seating for two adults. **Entry/exit:** Good up front; difficult access to the rear. Rear seating is relatively roomy. **Cargo space:** Average. **Trunk/liftover:** Average, with a low liftover. **Standard equipment:** Reasonably well-equipped.

Con: Firm rear seats are uncomfortable for long trips. Small radio controls. **Interior space/comfort F/R:** Interior room is snug, and head room is particularly tight for tall drivers. **Quietness:** Excessive high-speed engine and road noise.

COST

List Price (negotiable)	Residual Values (months)			
	24	**36**	**48**	**60**
Elantra GLS: $14,875 (13%)	$9,000	$7,000	$5,500	$4,500

TECHNICAL DATA

Powertrain (front-drive)	Head room F/R: 38.6/37.6 in.
Engine: 2.0L 4-cyl. (140 hp)	Leg room F/R: 43.2/34.6 in.
Transmissions: 5-speed man.	Wheelbase: 100.4 in.
• 4-speed auto.	Turning circle: 36 ft.
Dimension/Capacity	Cargo volume:11.9 cu. ft.
Passengers: 2/3	Tow limit: N/A
Height/length/width:	Fuel tank: 55L/reg.
54.9/174/66.9 in.	Weight: 2,500 lb.

SAFETY FEATURES/CRASHWORTHINESS

	Std.	Opt.
Anti-lock brakes	❑	■
Seatbelt pretensioners	■	❑
Side airbags	—	—
Traction control	—	—
Head restraints	***	***
Visibility (front/rear)	*****	*****

Crash protection (front) D/P	***	***
Crash protection (side) D/P	***	*
Crash protection (offset)	***	
HLDI injury claims (model)	*	
HLDI injury claims (all)	*	

Sonata

Sonata

RATING: Average, but only with an extended warranty. **Strong points:** Well-equipped, stylish, and reasonably priced. **Weak points:** Base engine lacks sufficient torque for highway cruising, clunky automatic transmission, primitive ride and handling, substandard braking, uncomfortable rear seating, and excessive cabin noise.

NEW FOR 2000: Nothing significant. The V6 will get a horsepower boost in the 2001 model year.

OVERVIEW: Give Hyundai credit, it's trying to make more refined cars, and this year's Sonata, fresh from last year's redesign, is the best product to come out of South Korea to date. It has a more rigid structure, a double-wishbone front suspension (like the Accord), and more attractive styling. Unfortunately, this mid-sized sedan still lacks the powertrain, handling, and ride refinements to cut it in the Honda Accord, Mazda 626, and Toyota Camry league. Nevertheless, its recent upgrades and significantly longer, more comprehensive warranty make it a contender when compared to the second-tier mid-sized sedans represented by Ford's Taurus, Sable, '99 Contour, Mystique, and Chrysler's Cirrus and Stratus.

Like Hyundai's other models, the Sonata is loaded with standard features that are optional or not found on competitive makes. Some of those standard features include air conditioning, power steering, and a 2.4L 149-hp 4-cylinder engine. It also features an optional 2.5L twin-cam 170-hp V6 and ABS.

Hyundai has again put the accent on safety this year, giving buyers a lot more safety features for their money than competing models. Standard features include: side airbags, seatbelt pretensioners, an integrated rear child safety seat, and a "smart" passenger-side airbag that won't deploy if the passenger weighs less than 66 lb (30 kg). An optional ABS/traction control is also offered.

Cost analysis/best alternatives: Buy a deeply discounted second series '99 model (built after March) and plan to keep it at least five years to shake off the additional year's depreciation. Other cars worth considering are the Honda Accord, Mazda 626, and Toyota Camry. **Options:** The V6 engine; if you get the 4-banger version, keep in mind that good fuel economy means putting up with an engine that's rougher and noisier than the V6. Be wary of the sunroof; it eats up a lot of head room. **Rebates:** Expect $2,000 rebates to clear out the '99 models. **Delivery/PDI:** $300. **Depreciation:** Average. **Insurance cost:** Average. **Parts supply/cost:** Easy to find and relatively inexpensive. Large engine compartment for easy servicing. **Annual maintenance cost:** Higher than average. **Warranty:** Bumper-to-bumper 3 years/60,000 km; powertrain 5 years/100,000 km; rust perforation 5 years/unlimited km. **Supplementary warranty:** A good idea to get you through the critical fifth year of ownership, when major components start to self-destruct. **Highway/city fuel economy:** 7.7–11.4L/100 km with the 2.4L and 7.8–11.7L/100 km with the 2.5L engine. **Annual fuel cost:** 2.4L: 1,947L=$1,129; 2.5L: 1,989L=$1,154.

Quality/Reliability/Safety

Pro: Quality control: Much improved quality control. No serious problems reported with the 2.5L powerplant. Repair is straightforward because of the Sonata's simple design. **Reliability:** No serious reliability problems have appeared over the last several years. **Warranty performance:** Average.

Con: Owner-reported problems: Poor engine performance (hard starting, poor idling, stalling). Excessive front brake pulsation and premature wear. Steering defects (when the steering wheel is turned to either extreme, it makes a sound like metal cracking). Cruise control malfunctions and electrical short circuits, poor door and window sealing (water leaking into the interior when the car is washed), and premature paint peeling and rusting. **Service bulletin problems:** Faulty rear mirror defroster. **NHTSA safety complaints/safety:** Airbags failed to deploy; transmission shifter will not lock into place and slips into Neutral if bumped.

Road Performance

Pro: Emergency handling: Average. **Steering:** Very good. Predictable, with lots of road feedback. **Acceleration/torque:** Reasonably good acceleration, but the base engine's insufficient torque makes the optional V6 a prerequisite for highway cruising, especially over hilly terrain (0–100 km/h: 9.8 sec.). **Transmission:** The 4-speed automatic transmission with Overdrive (a fuel-saving feature) works smoothly and is well adapted to the engine's power range. An improved electronic automatic transmission uses "fuzzy logic" to make shifting smooth and predictable. **Routine handling:** Better than average. Hyundai has changed the suspension setting to provide a less bouncy ride.

Con: The V6 engine is still a bit rough-running and noisy despite last year's improvements. Harsh slow-speed or Forward to Reverse shifting. An overly soft, wallowing ride produces significant body roll. Ride quality deteriorates as load increases. **Braking:** Substandard braking accompanied by excessive brake fade—the 151 feet required for a 100 km/h stop is 10–15 feet more than the competition.

Comfort/Convenience

Pro: Standard equipment: Well equipped for the price. **Driving position:** Very good. Great visibility and fairly supportive front seats are set high off the floor. **Controls and displays:** Well laid-out dashboard and controls. Easy-to-read gauges. **Climate control:** Good heating-defrosting-ventilation system. **Entry/exit:** Easy front and rear access. **Interior space/comfort F/R:** Up front, this is one of the roomiest mid-sized vehicles around. **Cargo space:** Many storage bins.

Con: Trunk/liftover: Rear head room is tight for tall passengers and the low, short rear seat cushions forces occupants into a painful knees-to-chin position. Surprisingly shallow trunk has a low liftover. **Quietness:** Excessive wind, road, and suspension noise.

COST				
List Price (very negotiable)	**Residual Values** (months)			
	24	**36**	**48**	**60**
Base: $19,595 (15%)	$15,000	$13,000	$10,500	$8,500

TECHNICAL DATA	
Powertrain (front-drive)	Head room F/R: 38.5/37.7 in.
Engines: 2.4L 4-cyl. (149 hp)	Leg room F/R: 43.3/36.6 in.
• 2.5L V6 (170 hp)	Wheelbase: 106.3 in.
Transmissions: 5-speed man.	Turning circle: 38 ft.
• 4-speed auto.	Cargo volume:13.2 cu. ft.
Dimension/Capacity.	Tow limit: N/A
Passengers: 2/3	Fuel tank: 65L/reg.
Height/length/width:	Weight: 3,100 lb.
55.3/185/69.7 in.	

SAFETY FEATURES/CRASHWORTHINESS

	Std.	Opt.
Anti-lock brakes	❏	■
Seatbelt pretensioners	■	❏
Side airbags	■	❏
Traction control	❏	■
Head restraints	***	***
Visibility (front/rear)	*****	*****
Crash protection (front) D/P	N/A	
Crash protection (side) D/P	N/A	
Crash protection (offset)	N/A	
HLDI injury claims (model)	N/A	
HLDI injury claims (all)	N/A	

Tiburon

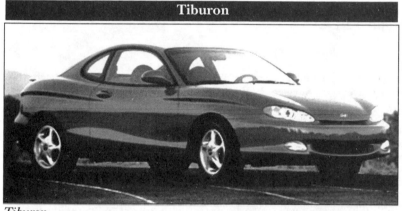

Tiburon

RATING: Average. **Strong points:** Well-equipped, impressive 2.0L performance with a manual gearbox, exceptional ride and handling. **Weak points:** Base 2.0L engine's passing power is seriously handicapped by the automatic transmission. Restricted rear visibility, uncomfortable seating, not for six-footers or portly occupants.

NEW FOR 2000: Body styling will be freshened and interior appointments upgraded.

OVERVIEW: Although the Tiburon (it means shark in Spanish) is a stylish, two-door spinoff of the Elantra sedan, it does deliver sports car thrills in a compact coupe. Powered by a base 140-hp 2.0L and mated to a 4-speed electronically controlled automatic or a 5-speed manual transmission, the Tiburon is a competent performer for both city and highway driving. It handles well, with gas-charged shocks inside coil springs at all four corners and front MacPherson struts. Steering is

light and responsive with a minimum of body flex. Standard brakes
consist of discs up front and drums in the rear; the FX package
includes four-wheel discs and ABS.

Cost analysis/best alternatives: Get the '99 model if it's discounted sufficiently. Other vehicles worth considering: the GM Cavalier, Sunfire,
Ford Escort ZX2, and Honda Civic. **Options:** The FX package with
better-gripping tires, four-wheel disc brakes, and ABS. **Rebates:**
Hyundai is expected to offer attractive rebates on the '99s early in the
year 2000. **Delivery/PDI:** $350. **Depreciation:** Average. **Insurance cost:**
Higher than average. **Parts supply/cost:** Parts aren't hard to find and
they're less expensive than average. Repair is straightforward because
of a fairly simple design. **Annual maintenance cost:** Average. **Warranty:**
Bumper-to-bumper 3 years/60,000 km; powertrain 5 years/100,000 km;
rust perforation 5 years/unlimited km. **Supplementary warranty:** A
smart buy. **Highway/city fuel economy:** 7.4–10.5L/100 km. **Annual fuel
cost:** 1,821L=$1,056.

Quality/Reliability/Safety

Pro: Quality control: Average, but much improved. **Reliability:** Better
than average. **Service bulletin problems:** Nothing published, yet.
Warranty performance: Average. **Safety:** Impressive headlight illumination (take heed, Chrysler).

Con: Owner-reported problems: Premature front brake wear and excessive brake noise. Some electrical glitches. **NHTSA safety complaints:** Airbag
deployed when it shouldn't have; airbag didn't deploy when it should have;
reflection of the sun on the dash distracts vision; horn controls may be hard
to find in an emergency; rear head restraints appear to be too low to protect occupants; the rear seatbelt configuration complicates the installation of a child safety seat. The rear spoiler is distracting and cuts
rearward vision.

Road Performance

Pro: The 2.0L gives respectable power (0–100 km/h: 9.1 sec.).
Emergency handling: Very good. Well-controlled, with minimal body
roll. **Steering:** The light, responsive steering is precise and predictable.
Transmission: The 5-speed manual transmission shifts smoothly and is
well adapted to the engine's power range. The ride is reasonably soft on
good roads. **Braking:** Acceptable, though not impressive (100–0 km/h:
132 ft.).

Con: Acceleration/torque: The 4-speed automatic transmission shifts
roughly under full throttle and is noisy at high revs. **Routine handling:**
Uneven pavement makes for a busy, jittery ride that's accentuated as
passengers are added. Poor braking on wet pavement.

Comfort/Convenience

Pro: Attractive styling and a well-appointed interior. **Controls and displays:** Well laid-out dashboard and controls (except for the radio). **Climate control:** Efficient, easy-to-understand climate control system. **Interior space/comfort F/R:** Comfortable seatbacks. Multiple front seat adjustments. Plenty of front head room. **Cargo space:** Average. **Trunk/liftover:** Reasonable amount of luggage space, but the hatchback is more versatile with its folding rear seatbacks. **Standard equipment:** Fairly well-equipped for a vehicle in this price range.

Con: Rear view is obstructed by the Tiburon's high tail and wide pillars. Tiny radio controls and temperature controls aren't within easy reach. **Entry/exit:** Front and rear access isn't easy. **Interior space/comfort F/R:** Low, firm, narrow, and short seat cushions give little thigh support. Limited front leg room for tall passengers, and rear head room is tight. Barely enough back seat room for two adults. **Trunk/liftover:** High liftover to the cargo area. **Quietness:** Plenty of engine, road, and wind noise.

COST

List Price (very negotiable)	Residual Values (months)			
	24	36	48	60
Base: $18,995 (15%)	$12,000	$10,000	$8,000	$7,000
FX: $20,500 (17%)	$14,000	$12,000	$10,500	$9,500

TECHNICAL DATA

Powertrain (front-drive)
Engine: 2.0L 4-cyl. (140 hp)
Transmissions: 5-speed man.
• 4-speed auto.
Dimension/Capacity
Passengers: 2/2
Height/length/width:
51.3/170.9/68.1 in.

Head room F/R: 38/34.4 in.
Leg room F/R: 43.1/29.9 in.
Wheelbase: 97.4 in.
Turning circle: 37 ft.
Cargo volume:12.8 cu. ft.
Tow limit: N/A
Fuel tank: 55L/reg.
Weight: 2,600 lb.

SAFETY FEATURES/CRASHWORTHINESS

	Std.	Opt.
Anti-lock brakes	❏	■
Seatbelt pretensioners	—	—
Side airbags	—	—
Traction control	—	—
Head restraints	**	*
Visibility (front/rear)	*****	**
Crash protection (front) D/P	N/A	
Crash protection (side) D/P	N/A	
Crash protection (offset)	N/A	
HLDI injury claims (model)	N/A	
HLDI injury claims (all)	N/A	

INFINITI

Infiniti has historically stressed performance over comfort and opulence. Lately, though, it's become a more mainstream luxury automaker and has lost its performance edge, particularly after dropping the J30 and J30t. When Nissan launched its Infiniti line, it promised that Infinitis wouldn't be merely restyled Nissans selling at a premium. It lied.

Infiniti makes three vehicles: the I30, an entry-level luxury sedan; the top-of-the-line Q45 four-door sedan; and the QX4 sport-utility. All Infinitis come fully equipped and offer owners the prestige of driving a reliable and nicely styled luxury car, with lots of standard features. Interestingly, though, Infiniti can't make head restraints that are deemed acceptable by the IIHS; its restraints are rated either "marginal" or "poor" by that insurance agency for their ability to protect occupants in a collision.

Infinitis are sold and serviced by dozens of dealers across Canada. This small number doesn't affect either the availability or quality of servicing, since any Nissan dealer can carry out most non-warranty maintenance work.

Except for the redesigned I30 and some cosmetic revamping of the other models, the Infiniti lineup is carried over this year relatively unchanged.

G20

RATING: Not Recommended. **Strong points:** Standard side airbags, ABS, competent steering and handling, well laid-out controls and instruments, good overall visibility. **Weak points:** Slow acceleration, mediocre automatic transmission performance, inadequate passenger head room and rear leg room, lots of engine and road noise, not very well appointed (want some plastic wood?), limited side and visibility, and a "marginal" head restraint rating by the IIHS.

NEW FOR 2000: No significant changes. This model may be dropped within the next two years.

OVERVIEW: After pulling its original G20 off the market in 1996 after a five-year run, Nissan has been lusting after the entry-level luxury car niche it abandoned. It hoped the $32,950 G20 launched two years ago would fit the bill.

It didn't.

Nissan's "spirited performance" claim is pure hype. Looking a lot like its poor-selling predecessor, this year's front-drive G20 is merely an entry-level Sentra disguised as a luxury car. Nissan should be ashamed of itself for attempting this automotive charade. The 145-hp 2.0L 4-cylinder engine (most entry-level luxury cars have V6s) and live-axle rear suspension are borrowed from the Sentra, and the rest of its underpinnings are derived from the European Nissan Primera. Owners have complained that the car has numerous squeaks and rattles (addressed by a service bulletin), and that the driver's seat reclines involuntarily when the vehicle is put into Reverse.

Slightly larger than its 1996 iteration, the G20 comes with additional features like four-wheel ABS, side-impact airbags, front seatbelt pretensioners, and a Bose 100-watt sound system. Interestingly, Infiniti doesn't charge for shipping or the pre-delivery inspection, and throws in a free tank of gas along with a comprehensive 4-year/100,000 km warranty. A G20t "touring" model adds a viscous limited-slip differential, foglights, and a spoiler starts—all for $29,950. Competitive models you may wish to look at are the Audi A4 1.8T and the Lexus ES 300.

I30

RATING: Above Average. Even though this is a redesigned model, Infinitis don't have as many "teething" problems with newly launched models as do other automakers. **Strong points:** Fully equipped with lots of innovative safety features, excellent engine and transmission match-up, comfortable ride, impressive handling, and first-class quality control. **Weak points:** An upscale, roomier, more conservatively styled Maxima, rear headrests obstruct visibility, and it has poor fuel economy (premium fuel suggested).

NEW FOR 2000: Redesigned along with the Maxima, the I30 is more conservatively styled, its V6 engine gets 37 more horses (five more than the Maxima), and the cabin is somewhat larger with most of the extra space, adding to rear leg room and trunk volume. This year's model also has a firmer suspension, bigger wheels, Xenon high-intensity headlights, and upgraded head restraints.

OVERVIEW: The I30's $41,350 base price makes it the world's most expensive Maxima, incorporating many of that car's chassis and drivetrain components, including the 227-hp 3.0L V6 engine and rear multilink suspension.

You can choose either the base or sportier I30t Touring models. The I30t gives you larger, 17-inch wheels, a firmer suspension, power moon roof and rear-window sunshade, a Comfort and Convenience Package, and Xenon high-intensity headlights. You won't get a manual transmission; it's been dropped this year.

Alternative vehicles that compete with the I30: those costing $40,000–$50,000, like the BMW 328, Lexus ES 300, Mazda Millenia, Mercedes-Benz C230, and Volvo S90; and those costing $50,000 or more, such as the BMW 5-series. For my money, the Maxima looks like the better buy.

Cost analysis/best alternatives: Get this year's models for the engine and cabin upgrades. The redesigned Maxima SE is a worthy competitor from a price/performance standpoint. **Options:** None worth the extra money. **Rebates:** Not likely. **Delivery/PDI:** $350. **Depreciation:** Faster than average for a luxury Japanese import. **Insurance cost:** Higher than average. **Parts supply/cost:** Moderately priced parts are available only from Nissan or Infiniti dealers. **Annual maintenance cost:** Much less than average. **Warranty:** Bumper-to-bumper 4 years/100,000 km; powertrain 6 years/100,000 km; rust perforation 7 years/unlimited km. **Supplementary warranty:** Not necessary. **Highway/city fuel economy:** '99 I30: 7.8–11.4L/100 km. **Annual fuel cost:** 1,956L=$1,134.

Quality/Reliability/Safety

Pro: Quality control: Excellent. **Reliability:** Much better than average. **Warranty performance:** Very good. **Owner-reported problems:** Nothing significant, although you can expect some electrical, fuel injection, and fit and finish problems to crop up on the first-series production.

Con: Service bulletin problems: Steering pull or drift at highway speeds; squeaks and rattles; hiss or fluttering noise along upper edge of windshield. **NHTSA safety complaints/safety:** ABS failure, sudden acceleration.

Road Performance

Pro: Emergency handling: Better than average. Little body lean or front-end plow during high-speed cornering. **Steering:** Exceptionally quick and precise. **Acceleration/torque:** First class for a car of this heft. The engine performs well throughout the power band (0–100 km/h: 8.9 sec.). **Transmission:** The automatic transmission is imperceptible, and the viscous limited-slip differential assists traction over slippery roads. **Routine handling:** Handles better than the '99 model due to this year's upgrades and provides a quiet, comfortable ride when cruising. **Braking:** Braking is acceptable, with little fading or loss of directional stability (100–0 km/h: 131 ft.).

Con: The I30t's suspension may be too firm for some. Rear headrests obstruct visibility.

Comfort/Convenience

Pro: Standard equipment: The I30 has many standard features that are optional on other cars in its class. **Driving position:** Excellent driving position with good front visibility. **Controls and displays:** Very well laid-out, accessible, and easy to understand. **Climate control:** Efficient and quiet. **Entry/exit:** Large door openings make access a breeze. Rear

passengers have a bit more leg room than before. **Trunk/liftover:** The
spacious trunk has a pass-through for carrying long items. **Cargo space:**
Lots of small storage areas. **Quietness:** Extra damping makes for an
exceptionally quiet interior.

Con: Interior space/comfort F/R: Rear middle passenger will still be
squeezed. Rear seat backrest is too inclined for comfort.

COST				
List Price (firm)	**Residual Values** (months)			
	24	**36**	**48**	**60**
I30: $41,350 (20%)	$33,000	$27,000	$23,000	$18,000

TECHNICAL DATA

Powertrain (front-drive)
Engine: 3.0L V6 (227 hp)
Transmission: 4-speed auto.
Dimension/Capacity ('99)
Passengers: 2/3
Height/length/width:
56.5/193.7/70.2 in.

Head room F/R: 40.1/37.4 in.
Leg room F/R: 43.9/34.3 in.
Wheelbase: 106.3 in.
Turning circle: 35.4 ft.
Cargo volume:14.9 cu. ft.
Tow limit: N/A
Fuel tank: 70L/prem.
Weight: 3,342 lb.

SAFETY FEATURES/CRASHWORTHINESS

	Std.	Opt.
Anti-lock brakes	■	❑
Seatbelt pretensioners	■	❑
Side airbags	■	❑
Traction control	■	❑
Head restraints	**	**
Visibility (front/rear)	*****	*****
Crash protection (front) D/P	****	****
Crash protection (side) D/P	****	***
Crash protection (offset)	***	
HLDI injury claims (model)	****	
HLDI injury claims (all)	****	

Note: The above data apply to only the '99 I30.

Q45

RATING: Recommended. A nice compromise between luxury and performance; a Japanese BMW with good rear seating. **Strong points:** Well-appointed, stylish, pleasant ride, quiet, plenty of rear leg room, excellent braking, and first-class workmanship. **Weak points:** Limited trunk space, below average offset crash rating, and requires premium fuel.

NEW FOR 2000: No significant changes; the Q45 will be redesigned next year when the 320-hp, 4.5L V8 returns.

OVERVIEW: Infiniti has shifted the Q45's emphasis from performance to luxury and comfort. This is unfortunate, because it reduces the distinction between the Q45 and Lexus LS 400. In fact, since the engine was downsized a few years ago from a 4.5 to a 4.1L, one wonders if the Q45 moniker isn't misleading advertising. Nevertheless, this luxury sedan is faster and more glitzy than many cars in its category in spite of its less powerful engine.

The Q45 uses a 32-valve 266-hp 4.1L V8 not frequently found on Japanese luxury compacts. It's a refined powerplant that has been both reliable and durable over the years. Standard safety features include side airbags for both driver and right front passenger, dual-locking shoulder belts, and front seatbelt pretensioners that activate in a crash to reduce belt slack. Additionally, you get electronically modulated shocks, upgraded headlights, an upgraded moon roof switch, a power-assisted rear-window sunshade, and a remote-closing trunk lid.

Cost analysis/best alternatives: Get the '99 model if it's sufficiently discounted, or wait until 2002 when the redesigned, more powerful Q45 arrives. **Options:** Forget about the active suspension option; it doesn't improve the handling or ride very much. **Rebates:** Not likely.

Delivery/PDI: $350. **Depreciation:** Much slower than average. **Insurance cost:** Much higher than average. **Parts supply/cost:** Parts may be more expensive than other cars in this class, and they're available only from Nissan or Infiniti dealers. **Annual maintenance cost:** Much less than average. **Warranty:** Bumper-to-bumper 4 years/100,000 km; powertrain 6 years/100,000 km; rust perforation 7 years/unlimited km. **Supplementary warranty:** Not necessary. **Highway/city fuel economy:** 9.2–13.5L/100 km. **Annual fuel cost:** 2,313L=$1,550.

Quality/Reliability/Safety

Pro: Quality control: High-quality components and superior workmanship. **Reliability:** No reliability problems reported. **Warranty performance:** Better than average. **NHTSA safety complaints/safety:** Nothing significant.

Con: Owner-reported problems: Tire thumping, some interior rattles, and excessive wind noise around the A-pillars. **Service bulletin problems:** Steering pull to the right; tips on troubleshooting interior squeaks and rattles.

Road Performance

Pro: Emergency handling: Very good. Standard traction control works well in preventing the car's rear end from sliding out on slippery roads. **Steering:** Precise, with plenty of road feedback. **Acceleration/torque:** Impressive acceleration and plenty of torque (0–100 km/h: 8.6 sec.). The car accelerates without a hint of noise or abrupt shifting. The engine supplies plenty of upper-range torque as well. **Transmission:** Smooth-shifting and quiet automatic transmission. **Routine handling:** Quite nimble handling for such a heavy car. **Braking:** Incredibly short stopping distances, thanks to four-wheel ABS (100–0 km/h: 121 ft.).

Comfort/Convenience

Pro: Standard equipment: Incredibly well-appointed, with lots of standard safety and convenience features. **Driving position:** Excellent. Unobstructed front and rear visibility. **Controls and displays:** Well-positioned and easy to decipher. Complete instrumentation. **Climate control:** Efficient, quiet, and very easy to adjust. **Entry/exit:** Both the front and rear seats can be easily accessed without undue acrobatics. **Interior space/comfort F/R:** Luxury seating both fore and aft. Rear seating is particularly comfortable. **Trunk/liftover:** Trunk has a low liftover. **Quietness:** Cocoon-like quiet.

Con: Cargo space: Limited room for storage of bulky items. **Trunk/liftover:** Small trunk.

COST			
List Price (negotiable)	**Residual Values** (months)		
	24	36	48	60
Q45t: $69,000 (21%)	$55,000	$45,000	$38,000	$29,000

TECHNICAL DATA

Powertrain (front-drive)
Engine: 4.1L V8 (266 hp)
Transmission: 4-speed auto.
Dimension/Capacity
Passengers: 2/3
Height/length/width:
56.9/199.2/71.7 in.

Head room F/R: 37.6/36.9 in.
Leg room F/R: 43.6/35.9 in.
Wheelbase: 111.4 in.
Turning circle: 40 ft.
Cargo volume: 12.6 cu. ft.
Tow limit: N/A
Fuel tank: 81L/prem.
Weight: 3,900 lb.

SAFETY FEATURES/CRASHWORTHINESS

	Std.	Opt.
Anti-lock brakes	■	❑
Seatbelt pretensioners	■	❑
Side airbags	■	❑
Traction control	■	❑
Head restraints	*	*
Visibility (front/rear)	*****	*****
Crash protection (front) D/P	N/A	
Crash protection (side) D/P	N/A	
Crash protection (offset)	**	
HLDI injury claims (model)	N/A	
HLDI injury claims (all)	N/A	

KIA

After going bankrupt in 1998, Kia has been bought by Hyundai (it's also partly owned by Ford through its Mazda affiliation) and continues to sell the Sephia and Sportage sport-utility in the United States. Unlike Daewoo, Kia has the money and backing to build a solid, stable dealer organization in Canada, but it'll take a great deal of time. Presently, it only has 24 stores in Canada.

What could stop its expansion? Kia's own low-quality cars and sport-utilities.

All of the consumer and government feedback I've seen paints a very poor picture of Kia's quality control. Add in that this is the company's first year in Canada, few dealers can be found outside of large urban areas, and its vehicles haven't been tested in our environment, and you have all the ingredients to make any Kia purchase a risky buy.

Sephia

RATING: Not Recommended during its first year on the market. The Sephia has sold its products in the States since 1994, and in Canada since the early '90s—the Aspire and Festiva—marketed under the Ford nameplate. **Strong points:** Cheap, cheap, and cheap. **Weak points:** Crude and weak engine performance, harsh ride, poor handling, noisy engine, lots of road and wind noise, sub-par fit and finish, and a small dealer network that may complicate servicing and warranty performance.

OVERVIEW: The front-drive, five-passenger Sephia is about the size of a Toyota Corolla, sells for $12,995, and comes with a twin-cam 125-hp 1.8L 4-cylinder engine hooked to a standard 5-speed manual transmission, and seated on a four-wheel independent suspension.

Kia's products, unlike Daewoo's, do have a track record—and it's not good. In fact, *Consumer Reports* says in its April 1999 New Car edition, "You'd have to search far and wide to find a car that's worse than this small Korean model."

LEXUS

Unlike cash-strapped Nissan—and Infiniti, which has just been acquired by Renault—this has been another year of record sales for Toyota and Lexus. Lexus has become a luxury automaker on its own merits, even though it started out selling dressed-up Camrys as upscale models (only the ES 300 fits that description now). But so did Acura and Infiniti, right? Unlike Infiniti, though, Lexus isn't morphing into anything other than what it's always been: the epitome of luxury and comfort, with a small dab of performance thrown in. While Infiniti engineers see the highway as a challenge, Lexus sees it as an irritant, successfully isolating the driver from the driving experience. And guess what? It's a winning formula. No matter how often car enthusiast magazines say that drivers want "road feel," "responsive handling," and "high-performance" thrills, the truth of the matter is that most drivers simply want to travel from point A to point B in safety and comfort, without interruption, in cars that are more than fully equipped Sentras or warmed-over Maximas.

Infiniti bucked that concept, and lost.

Don't get the impression that Lexus does everything right. Lexus has half as many dealers as Mercedes and BMW, yet its models and units sold have proliferated over the years to the point where servicing is strained. The automaker wants to add dealers, but the dealer body—mesmerized by high profits per dealer—is resisting. This has created a customer service crisis that will only worsen as sales continue to soar.

Although these luxury imports do set advanced benchmarks for quality control, they're not engineering perfection (they do average about half a defect per car during the first 90 days of ownership). Cheaper luxury cars like the Acura 3.0L CL, Mazda Millenia, Nissan Maxima, and Toyota Avalon give you almost as much comfort and reliability, but without the Lexus cachet.

Dealer service bulletins show that these cars are affected by some minor body fit and trim glitches. Most owners haven't heard of these problems, because Lexus dealers have been particularly adept at fixing many of them before they become chronic.

In summary, the Lexus lineup is geared more to the luxury cruiser crowd, which prefers comfort over performance thrills. All models come with such important standard safety features as ABS and side airbags, automatically adjusted head restraints, an automatic transmission shifter interlocked with the ignition and brakes, childproof door locks, and easily adjusted three-point seatbelts.

Holding a winning hand, Lexus won't make any major changes to its model lineup until next spring, when the IS 300, a V6-equipped, rear-drive sedan targeting BMW's 3-series, makes its debut.

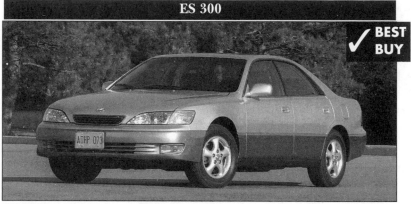

ES 300

RATING: Recommended. **Strong points:** Standard side airbags and ABS, good acceleration, pleasantly quiet ride, quiet-running, top-quality components, impressive crashworthiness ratings and favourable accident injury claim data, and excellent quality control and warranty performance. **Weak points:** Primarily a four-seater; three adults won't sit comfortably in the rear. Muted steering feel, some nosedive in panic stops, and overall handling isn't as nimble as its BMW or Mercedes rivals. Trunk space is limited (low liftover, though) and rear corner visibility is hampered by the high rear end.

NEW FOR 2000: A minor facelift and some interior upgrades.

OVERVIEW: A Camry clone with some additional features, this $43,995 entry-level Lexus front-drive returns relatively unchanged. The sole engine is a 210-hp V6 mated to an electronically controlled 4-speed automatic transmission that handles the 3.0L engine's horses effortlessly—making for 0–100 km/h times in the low 8s—without sacrificing fuel economy. All ES 300s feature dual front and side airbags, anti-lock brakes, improved double-piston front brake calipers, 60/40 split folding rear seats, and one of the rarest features of all, a conventional spare tire.

Cost analysis/best alternatives: Get the '99 model if you can find one discounted by about 10 percent. Other cars worth considering are the Acura TL, Audi A6, BMW 3-series, Infiniti I30, Mercedes-Benz E420, Mazda Millenia, Toyota Avalon, and Volvo's S70 and S90 series. **Options:** Traction control. I don't recommend the Adaptive Variable Suspension option; it's mostly a gimmick with little functional improvement. **Rebates:** None. Some discounting on the '99's MSRP by about 5–10 percent. **Delivery/PDI:** $350. **Depreciation:** Depreciation is much lower than average. **Insurance cost:** Much higher than average. **Parts supply/cost:** Average availability, and parts are moderately priced. **Annual maintenance cost:** Below average. **Warranty:** Bumper-to-bumper 4 years/80,000 km; powertrain 6 years/110,000 km; rust perforation 6 years/unlimited km. **Supplementary warranty:** Not necessary. **Highway/city fuel economy:** 8.4–12.5L/100 km. **Annual fuel cost:** 2,131L=$1,236.

Quality/Reliability/Safety

Pro: Quality control: Impressive; top-quality mechanical and body components. **Reliability:** Dependable reliability. **Warranty performance:** Excellent; Toyota is generous in interpreting its warranty and post-warranty responsibilities.

Con: Owner-reported problems: Some interior fit and finish deficiencies. **Service bulletin problems:** Brakes may make a groaning or grinding noise. **NHTSA safety complaints/safety:** Instrument panel lights aren't bright enough at night; middle rear shoulder belt locks up, making it difficult to get the occupant out from the middle seat.

Road Performance

Pro: Emergency handling: Very good, though not as nimble as the Acura TL. **Acceleration/torque:** Incredibly fast acceleration and lots of torque (0–100 km/h: 7.2 sec.); beats out the Infiniti Q45. **Transmission:** Shifts smoothly in all gear ranges. **Routine handling:** Capable handling, with little body roll. **Braking:** Better than average braking (100–0 km/h: 121 ft.).

Con: A bit numb and over-assisted.

COST				
List Price (firm)	**Residual Values** (months)			
	24	36	48	60
ES 300: $43,995 (20%)	$36,000	$32,000	$27,000	$22,000

TECHNICAL DATA	
Powertrain (front-drive)	Head room F/R: 36.8/36.2 in.
Engine: 3.0L V6 (210 hp)	Leg room F/R: 43.5/34.4 in.
Transmission: 4-speed auto.	Wheelbase: 105.1 in.
Dimension/Capacity	Turning circle: 40 ft.
Passengers: 2/3	Cargo volume: 13 cu. ft.
Height/length/width:	Tow limit: N/A
54.9/190.2/70.5 in.	Fuel tank: 70L/prem.
	Weight: 3,300 lb.

SAFETY FEATURES/CRASHWORTHINESS

	Std.	Opt.
Anti-lock brakes	■	❑
Seatbelt pretensioners	■	❑
Side airbags	■	❑
Traction control	■	❑
Head restraints	***	***
Visibility (front/rear)	*****	**
Crash protection (front) D/P	****	****
Crash protection (side) D/P	*****	****
Crash protection (offset)	N/A	
HLDI injury claims (model)	***	
HLDI injury claims (all)	****	

GS 300, 400

GS 400

RATING: Recommended. **Strong points:** Standard side airbags, ABS, and Vehicle Stability Control anti-skid system. Excellent high-performance powertrain setup, pleasantly quiet ride, superb handling and braking, and exceptional quality control and warranty performance. **Weak points:** Primarily a four-seater with limited head room for six-footers. High window line impedes rear visibility, poor fuel economy (premium fuel), some instruments hidden by the steering wheel, trunk and fuel-door releases hidden at the base of the dash, and the fuel gauge may give inaccurate readings (there's a service bulletin on this problem).

NEW FOR 2000: Carried over unchanged.

OVERVIEW: Redesigned last year, these rear-drives are shorter, the wheelbase is longer, the trunk is larger, and there's a lot more interior room. Two models are available: one carries the in-line 6-cylinder engine and the other is V8-powered. Both engines have VVT-i (Variable

Valve Timing with intelligence), a feature that continually changes the engine timing to achieve peak horsepower with low emissions and high fuel economy. Other innovative features include Vehicle Stability Control (VSC), dual side airbags, and dual-zone climate controls.

Cost analysis/best alternatives: It's a toss-up whether to buy a '99 or 2000 version, since they're identical. Choose whichever has been discounted the most. Other cars worth considering are the BMW 5-series, and Mercedes-Benz E-class. **Options:** 17-inch tires. Stay away from the in-dash navigator; it complicates the calibration of the sound system and climate controls. **Rebates:** Not likely. Look for discounting on the MSRP by about 5 percent. **Delivery/PDI:** $350. **Depreciation:** Much slower than average. **Insurance cost:** Much higher than average. **Parts supply/cost:** Parts aren't easily found outside of the dealer network, prices tend to be on the high side. **Annual maintenance cost:** Less than average. **Warranty:** Bumper-to-bumper 4 years/80,000 km; powertrain 6 years/110,000 km; rust perforation 6 years/unlimited km. **Supplementary warranty:** Not necessary. **Highway/city fuel economy:** 8.5–11.8L/100 km for the GS 300 and 9.0–13.4L/100 km for the GS 400. **Annual fuel cost:** GS 300: 2,063L=$1,382; GS 400: 2,284L=$1,530.

Road Performance

Pro: Acceleration/torque: Hot rod acceleration with lots of torque (0–100 km/h: 6.1 sec. with the V8). **Braking:** Exceptional braking for a car this heavy (100–0 km/h: 122 ft.).

COST				
List Price (firm)	**Residual Values** (months)			
	24	**36**	**48**	**60**
GS 300: $59,420 (30%)	$45,000	$39,000	$34,000	$29,000
GS 400: $68,910 (30%)	$49,000	$44,000	$39,000	$35,000

TECHNICAL DATA	
Powertrain (rear-drive)	Head room F/R: 39.2/37 in.
Engines: 3.0L 6-cyl. (225 hp)	Leg room F/R: 44.5/34.3 in.
• 4.0L V8 (300 hp)	Wheelbase: 110.2 in.
Transmissions: 5-speed auto.	Turning circle: 39 ft.
• 5-speed auto.	Cargo volume:15 cu. ft.
Dimension/Capacity	Tow limit: N/A
Passengers: 2/3	Fuel tank: 70L/prem.
Height/length/width:	Weight: 3,300 lb.
56.7/189/70.9 in.	

SAFETY FEATURES/CRASHWORTHINESS		
	Std.	**Opt.**
Anti-lock brakes	■	❏
Seatbelt pretensioners	■	❏

Side airbags	■	❑
Traction control	■	❑
Head restraints	***	***
Visibility (front/rear)	*****	**
Crash protection (front) D/P	N/A	
Crash protection (side) D/P	N/A	
Crash protection (offset)	N/A	
HLDI injury claims (model)	N/A	
HLDI injury claims (all)	N/A	

MAZDA

Although Mazda's Canadian sales picked up considerably last year, the company remains more vulnerable than other Japanese automakers to downturns because it doesn't have the huge cash reserves of Toyota (almost $30 billion) and has only one overseas plant (a Michigan plant co-owned by Ford) to which it can shift production. The company had been hit hard by a lack of new products and a softening in the entry-level market, both in North America and in Japan, that sent sales spinning downward. In an effort to improve its sales, Mazda has redesigned its MPV minivan this year and cut the exorbitant prices of its parts (see below).

Mazda eases price gouging
After years of being downgraded in *Lemon-Aid*'s ratings for expensive parts, Mazda has reacted. Last August, Mazda Canada announced lower prices on several categories of maintenance-related parts. The targeted groups, comprising 485 parts in total, include items such as bumpers, hoods, fenders, lamp assemblies, brake pads, brake rotors, and airbags. The price reductions range between 19 and 32 percent.

"This pricing action symbolizes Mazda's dedication to ensuring our customers throughout Canada find owning their Mazda vehicle a rewarding experience," said Serge Pannu, Director of Customer Service and Parts for Mazda Canada. "To that end, we are committed to providing competitively priced parts through our 155 franchised dealers and independent repair shops," he continued.

I'll monitor Mazda's prices throughout the year to see if this price reduction is fact or fantasy.

Protegé

✓ **BEST BUY**

Protegé

RATING: Recommended. **Strong points:** Good engine performance (manual transmission), comfortable ride, plenty of interior room, good fuel economy, and quality workmanship. **Weak points:** Limited highway passing power is further compromised by the automatic transmission; excessive engine, road, and wind noise; ride is a bit harsh in the SE version.

NEW FOR 2000: Optional side airbags.

OVERVIEW: Protegé is Mazda's least costly model. It shares platforms with the Escort and Tracer, but keeps its own sheet metal, engine, and interior styling. Powered by a standard, fuel-efficient 105-hp 1.6L engine mated to a manual 5-speed transmission, and offering an optional Miata-based 1.8L powerplant, the Protegé is one of the roomiest and most responsive small cars around.

Cost analysis/best alternatives: Get the '99 model if it's discounted by about 10 percent. Other cars worth considering are the '99 Ford Escort and Tracer (Protegé clones), Honda Civic, Hyundai Accent, Suzuki Swift, Toyota Corolla, and VW Golf and Jetta. **Options:** The 1.8L engine and anti-lock brakes. **Rebates:** $750–$1,500 on the '99s. **Delivery/PDI:** $400. **Depreciation:** Average. **Insurance cost:** Average. **Parts supply/cost:** Mazda parts costs are now more reasonable and they aren't difficult to find. Plus, these cars are easily serviced by dealers or independents. In fact, most Ford dealers have parts that can be used on Mazda products because the Ford Escort uses lots of Mazda mechanical components. This knowledge may be useful if you find your Mazda dealer jacking up parts prices to an now more unreasonable level. **Annual maintenance cost:** Below average. **Warranty:** Bumper-to-bumper 3 years/80,000 km; powertrain 5 years/100,000 km; rust perforation 5 years/unlimited km.

Supplementary warranty: A good idea while waiting for improved service. **Highway/city fuel economy:** 6.9–9.3L/100 km with the base 1.6L engine and an automatic transmission, and 7.1–9.7L/100 km with the 1.8L engine and an automatic transmission. **Annual fuel cost:** 1.6L: 1,644L=$954; 1.8L: 1706L=$989.

Quality/Reliability/Safety

Pro: Quality control: Very good. Few quality-control complaints. **Reliability:** Better than average. **Warranty performance:** Acceptable, though a lot depends on the dealer going to bat for you. **Service bulletin problems:** Nothing significant. ABS is standard on the ES and optional on the LX.

Con: Owner-reported problems: The front brakes tend to wear out quickly, and MacPherson struts and rear shock absorbers don't last as long as they should. Some complaints of poor fit and paint defects. **NHTSA safety complaints/safety:** Brake pedal pushed almost to the floor before brakes work, and they produce excessive noise; random hard shifting at moderate speed.

Road Performance

Pro: Emergency handling: Comfortable, firm, no-surprise ride doesn't deteriorate as passenger load increases or when cornering at high speed. **Steering:** Predictable, well-controlled, and transmits good road feedback. **Acceleration/torque:** Excellent overall performance with either engine. The 1.6L twin-cam 4-cylinder engine is surprisingly responsive and quiet. Impressive acceleration with the 1.8L optional powerplant. **Transmission:** Both transmissions shift smoothly. The 5-speed manual has a handy "Hold" feature that allows the driver to select and hold any of the three lower gears through the shift lever. Two other advantages: the automatic transaxle can be driven away in second gear, an asset on snow and ice; and you can lock out Overdrive with the push of a button, allowing you to traverse hilly terrain or urban traffic without constant shifting. **Routine handling:** Although the base suspension is less firm this year, handling is quite nimble.

Con: The automatic transmission robs the base engine of much-needed power. Some body roll in turns. SE suspension is a bit too firm for some. **Braking:** Average braking without ABS.

Comfort/Convenience

Pro: Driving position: Better than average. The driver and front passenger are pampered with firm, comfortable front bucket seats and multiple-seat steering wheel adjustments. Great all-around visibility. **Controls and displays:** Clear and well laid-out controls. **Climate control:**

Efficient, quiet heating and defrosting, although controls are not as user-friendly as they could be. **Entry/exit:** Large doors make for easy access to the front and rear. **Interior space/comfort F/R:** One of the roomiest small cars on the market, although the rear seating is better suited for two average-sized adults. **Cargo space:** Lots of interior space to store large and small items. **Trunk/liftover:** Trunk space is expanded with locking, folding rear seatbacks. A low liftover facilitates loading.

Con: Standard equipment: Cheap-looking, sober interior. The sunroof drastically reduces head room. Even with a tilt steering column, the steering wheel may be too low for some tall drivers. Others may find the gearshift lever a bit too far away when shifting into fifth gear. **Quietness:** Excessive engine, road, and wind noise intrusion into the interior.

COST

List Price (negotiable)	Residual Values (months)			
	24	36	48	60
DX: $14,995 (12%)	$11,000	$9,000	$7,500	$6,000

TECHNICAL DATA

Powertrain (front-drive)
Engines: 1.6L 4-cyl. (105 hp)
• 1.8L 4-cyl. (122 hp)
Transmissions: 5-speed man.
• 4-speed auto.
Dimension/Capacity
Passengers: 2/3
Height/length/width:
55.5/174/67.1 in.

Head room F/R: 37.9/36.7 in.
Leg room F/R: 42.2/35.6 in.
Wheelbase: 102.8 in.
Turning circle: 38 ft.
Cargo volume:13.1 cu. ft.
Tow limit: N/A
Fuel tank: 50L/reg.
Weight: 2,350 lb.

SAFETY FEATURES/CRASHWORTHINESS

	Std.	Opt.
Anti-lock brakes	❏	■
Seatbelt pretensioners	—	—
Side airbags	—	■
Traction control	—	—
Head restraints	**	**
Visibility (front/rear)	*****	*****
Crash protection (front) D/P	****	****
Crash protection (side) D/P	***	****
Crash protection (offset)	N/A	
HLDI injury claims (model)	N/A	
HLDI injury claims (all)	N/A	

626

626

RATING: Recommended. These sedans provide room for five along with a high level of luxury and comfort, making the 626 one of the best and most reasonably priced mid-sized cars on the market. **Strong points:** Strong V6 acceleration, pleasant handling, roomy interior, comfortable front and rear seating, easy entry/exit, and good overall reliability. **Weak points:** Sluggish 4-cylinder performance, jerky automatic transmission, and excessive road noise.

NEW FOR 2000: Cosmetic changes, horsepower boost, and optional side airbags.

OVERVIEW: Restyled two years ago to resemble the more luxurious Mazda Millenia, the 626 is a stylish front-drive compact sedan that does everything well. It comes in three trim levels with a choice of two engines, coupled to either a 5-speed manual or a 4-speed automatic transmission. The base DX is touted as the price leader, but you have to take the 4-cylinder engine and few standard features with the low price. The top-of-the-line ES has more bells and whistles in addition to a V6 engine. A good compromise model is the LX: it's cheaper than the ES, yet offers many of its amenities.

Cost analysis/best alternatives: Get the cheapest '99 model available; it's practically identical to this year's version. Alternative vehicles: Honda Accord and Toyota Camry. Now that there's so little difference between the 626 and the upscale Millenia, consider the 626 as a cheaper alternative. **Options:** The LX's V6 engine, traction control, and various power accessories. **Rebates:** Expect $1,500 rebates to clear out the '99s. **Delivery/PDI:** $400. **Depreciation:** Faster than average. **Insurance cost:** Slightly higher than average. **Parts supply/cost:** Reasonably priced parts aren't difficult to find, and the cars are easily serviced by dealers or independents. Keep in mind that most Ford dealers have parts that can be used on Mazda products. This knowledge may be useful if your Mazda dealer is too greedy when it comes to parts prices (cost plus 50 percent is the industry norm). **Annual maintenance cost:** Less than average. **Warranty:** Bumper-to-bumper 3 years/80,000 km; powertrain 5 years/ 100,000 km; rust perforation 5 years/unlimited km. **Supplementary warranty:** Not necessary. **Highway/city fuel economy:** 7.5–10.7L/100 km with the base 4-banger and 8.5–12.2L/100 km with the 2.5L. **Annual fuel cost:** 4-banger: 1,852L=$1,074; 2.5L: 2,107L=$1,412.

Quality/Reliability/Safety

Pro: Quality control: Few quality control complaints. Assembly and component quality are high. **Reliability:** Better than average. **Warranty performance:** Not generous, but fair.

Con: Owner-reported problems: Complex electronics cause trouble with age, air conditioning defects, head gasket leaks, automatic transmission malfunctions, excessive hydraulic lifter noise, sunroof rattles, and premature wearout of the front brakes. **Service bulletin problems:** Inoperative, binding, noisy sunroof. **NHTSA safety complaints/safety:** Surging and stalling; seatbelts don't secure a child safety seat properly; transmission shift shock; noisy fuel pump; knocking noise while driving.

Road Performance

Pro: Emergency handling: Very good. The 626 is sure-footed, responds well to sudden corrections, and has little body roll or front-end plow when cornering under speed. **Steering:** Power steering is a bit light, but very accurate and predictable. **Acceleration/torque:** The V6 powerplant is a road burner with a fair amount of torque once it gets up to speed (0–100 km/h: 7.8 sec.). **Transmission:** The manual transmission and clutch work very well, though downshifts are sometimes jerky. Handling is very good, but not quite as crisp and responsive as the Toyota and Honda competitors. The 4-speed Overdrive automatic shifts smoothly most of the time. **Routine handling:** Nimble handling, and the steady, soft ride doesn't deteriorate as passenger load increases. Overall, a less jittery ride than previous versions. **Braking:** Good braking (100–0 km/h: 119 ft.).

Con: The standard 2.0L 4-cylinder engine is smooth and peppy for urban duties, but it's at a disadvantage when pressed into more demanding service, like passing other vehicles on the highway or merging with fast-moving traffic. It works best with the manual gearbox. Equipped with the V6, power is channelled just a bit less smoothly than what you'd find with the Toyota Camry or Honda Accord.

Comfort/Convenience

Pro: Standard equipment: Many standard performance and convenience features. **Driving position:** The front seats are exceptionally comfortable, and there's lots of head and leg room for tall drivers. **Controls and displays:** Well-positioned gauges and instruments. **Climate control:** Heating and ventilation are above reproach. **Entry/exit:** Easy as pie. **Interior space/comfort F/R:** The rear seat will hold two adults easily and comfortably. **Cargo space:** The hatchback version has a versatile cargo area and lots of handy storage bins. **Trunk/liftover:** Large trunk can be easily expanded through the use of the sedan's locking, folding rear seatbacks. **Quietness:** Body rigidity has been increased, making the car more comfortable and preventing many of the creaks and groans common to all small cars.

Con: The driver's seat may be too low for some. Rear middle passenger will find it a tight fit. **Quietness:** Excessive road noise in the passenger compartment.

COST

List Price (negotiable)	Residual Values (months)			
	24	**36**	**48**	**60**
DX: $23,175 (17%)	$18,000	$14,000	$12,000	$10,000

TECHNICAL DATA

Powertrain (front-drive)
Engines: 2.0L 4-cyl. (125 hp)
• 2.5L V6 (170 hp)
Transmissions: 5-speed man.
• 4-speed auto.
Dimension/Capacity
Passengers: 2/3
Height/length/width:
55.1/186.8/69.6 in.

Head room F/R: 39.2/37 in.
Leg room F/R: 43.6/34.6 in.
Wheelbase: 105.1 in.
Turning circle: 39 ft.
Cargo volume: 14.2 cu. ft.
Tow limit: 2,000 lb.
Fuel tank: 60L/reg./prem.
Weight: 3,100 lb.

SAFETY FEATURES/CRASHWORTHINESS

	Std.	**Opt.**
Anti-lock brakes	❏	■
Seatbelt pretensioners	—	—
Side airbags	—	■
Traction control	❏	■
Head restraints	*	*
Visibility (front/rear)	*****	*****
Crash protection (front) D/P	****	*****
Crash protection (side) D/P	***	***
Crash protection (offset)	N/A	
HLDI injury claims (model)	N/A	
HLDI injury claims (all)	N/A	

Millenia

Millenia

RATING: Above Average. **Strong points:** Well-appointed, lots of power (S version), good handling and braking, comfortable ride, quiet-running, and top-quality, sophisticated mechanical components. **Weak points:** Just so-so acceleration with the base powerplant, some S-model throttle lag, limited rear seating room, and restricted rear visibility.

NEW FOR 2000: No significant changes.

OVERVIEW: Despite its late entry into the luxury market—Lexus and Infiniti have had years to fortify their position—Millenia has been a hit, with surprisingly strong sales.

Smaller than the Mazda 929, the front-drive Millenia carries the same 2.5L 170-hp V6 used by the 626. An optional 2.3L Miller-Cycle "S" 6-cylinder engine, although smaller than the base powerplant, still manages to pump out 210 horsepower. Both engines use a standard 4-speed automatic transmission.

As with all luxury cars, the Millenia comes with a wide array of standard features that would normally cost thousands of dollars more. Although billed as a five-passenger car, the middle occupant in the rear seat would be cramped and have to sit on a hump—a problem with which 929 owners are familiar.

Cost analysis/best alternatives: Get the '99 model for the discounted MSRP. From a performance standpoint, the Camry V6, with its less complicated powertrain, outruns the Millenia; and the redesigned 626 gives you practically all the same features for less money. Other cars worth considering are the Infiniti I30, Lexus ES 300, Mercedes-Benz E420, and Volvo S70 and S90 series. **Options:** Traction control. Get the dealer to change the limited spare tire for a full-service tire that can easily fit in the trunk well. Be wary of the sunroof option on the sedan if you're a tall driver; it takes away much-needed head room. **Rebates:**

Instead of rebates, Mazda has announced hefty price cuts of $2,450 for the base model and over $5,000 on the Miller version. **Delivery/PDI:** $600. **Depreciation:** Slower than average. **Insurance cost:** Higher than average. **Parts supply/cost:** Parts are costly and frequently back-ordered. **Annual maintenance cost:** Average. **Warranty:** Bumper-to-bumper 3 years/80,000 km; powertrain 5 years/100,000 km; rust perforation 5 years/unlimited km. **Supplementary warranty:** Not necessary. **Highway/city fuel economy:** 8.0–12.2L/100 km with the 2.3L, and 8.3–12.3L/100 km with the 2.5L. **Annual fuel cost:** 2.3L: 2,062L=$1,382; 2.5L: 2,100L=$1,407.

Quality/Reliability/Safety

Pro: Quality control: Assembly and component quality are high. **Reliability:** No serious reliability problems noted. **Warranty performance:** Acceptable. **Owner-reported problems:** Nothing of any significance. **Service bulletin problems:** Nothing published, yet. **NHTSA safety complaints/safety:** No safety-related incidents have been recorded.

Con: Some complaints of poor servicing affecting reliability because vehicle is sidelined for days at a time.

Road Performance

Pro: Emergency handling: Very good. Electronic traction control performs flawlessly. **Steering:** Smooth, precise steering. **Acceleration/torque:** The 170-hp V6 engine provides plenty of power in most driving situations, but the supercharged version is a real road burner (0–100 km/h: 8.3 sec.) that provides gobs of mid-range torque. **Transmission:** Quiet and smooth-shifting. **Routine handling:** Fun to drive due to the Millenia's crisp handling and comfortable ride, which doesn't deteriorate as passenger load increases. **Braking:** Relatively short braking distance without any fading after successive application (100–0 km/h: 130 ft.).

Con: The Miller Cycle engine is a bit slow to get up to speed.

Comfort/Convenience

Pro: Standard equipment: Plenty of standard amenities. Great sound system. Firm, comfortable driver's seat has lots of control for height and tilt. **Climate control:** Works well with little noise. **Cargo space:** Above average storage space in the passenger compartment. **Trunk/liftover:** Spacious trunk has a low liftover. **Quietness:** Very little engine or road noise intrudes into the interior.

Con: Bland exterior styling. Front seat may be too low for some. **Driving position:** Tall drivers may find head and leg room a bit limited. Insufficient thigh support with the bucket seats. **Controls and displays:** Controls aren't sufficiently lit. Radio controls aren't user-friendly.

Climate control: Erratic temperature control can't keep a consistent setting. **Entry/exit:** Narrow rear doors complicate rear seat access. **Interior space/comfort F/R:** Rear seating isn't very comfortable for three.

COST

List Price (negotiable)	Residual Values (months)			
	24	36	48	60
Base: $39,595 (21%)	$28,000	$22,000	$18,000	$14,000

TECHNICAL DATA

Powertrain (front-drive)	Head room F/R: 37.9/36.5 in.
Engines: 2.5L V6 (170 hp)	Leg room F/R: 43.3/34.1 in.
• 2.3L V6 (210 hp)	Wheelbase: 108.3 in.
Transmission: 4-speed auto.	Turning circle: 42 ft.
Dimension/Capacity	Cargo volume: 13.3 cu. ft.
Passengers: 2/3	Tow limit: 2,000 lb.
Height/length/width:	Fuel tank: 68L/prem.
54.9/189.8/69.7 in.	Weight: 3,400 lb.

SAFETY FEATURES/CRASHWORTHINESS

	Std.	Opt.
Anti-lock brakes	■	❑
Seatbelt pretensioners	—	—
Side airbags	—	—
Traction control	❑	■
Head restraints	*	*
Visibility (front/rear)	*****	**
Crash protection (front) D/P	*****	*****
Crash protection (side) D/P	N/A	
Crash protection (offset)	***	
HLDI injury claims (model)	**	
HLDI injury claims (all)	***	

MX-5 (Miata)

✓ **BEST BUY**

Miata

RATING: Recommended. An exceptional, reasonably priced roadster. **Strong points:** Good powertrain setup provides better than expected acceleration for such a small engine, nice handling, impressive braking, and a high resale value. **Weak points:** Limited passenger and cargo room, a firm ride, excessive road, wind, and engine noise intrudes, restricted rear visibility, and no crashworthiness or injury claim data available.

NEW FOR 2000: No significant changes.

OVERVIEW: The Miata is a stubby, rear-drive, two-seater sports car that combines new technology with old British roadster styling reminiscent of the Triumph, Austin-Healy, and Lotus Elan.

This is a fun car to drive, costing much less than other vehicles in its class. Built on a shortened 323 platform, the Miata is shorter than all other sports cars except the Porsche 911 (although it's almost eight inches longer than the old Honda CRX). The 1.8L twin-cam 4-cylinder engine, borrowed from the Protegé, is coupled to a 5-speed manual gearbox, and the rear suspension is a copy of the discontinued RX-7's.

Cost analysis/best alternatives: A discounted '99 (lucky fellow/girl) would be a great buy. Other cars worth considering are the BMW Z3 series Ford Mustang, GM Camaro and Firebird, Honda Prelude, and Toyota Celica. **Options:** Anti-lock brakes, power steering, and a limited-slip differential. Original equipment 185/60R14 winter tires are poor performers; go for the Sport Package's 195/50VR15 rubber, instead. **Rebates:** $1,500 on the '99s early in the year 2000. **Delivery/PDI:** $300. **Depreciation:** Much slower than average. **Insurance cost:** Higher than average. **Parts supply/cost:** Parts are easy to find, but often cost more than average. **Annual maintenance cost:** Less than average. **Warranty:** Bumper-to-bumper 3 years/80,000 km; powertrain 5 years/100,000 km; rust perforation 5 years/unlimited km. **Supplementary warranty:** Not needed. **Highway/city fuel economy:** 7.5–10.5L/100 km. **Annual fuel cost:** 1,830L=$1,061.

Quality/Reliability/Safety

Pro: Quality control: Excellent workmanship and exceptional quality. **Reliability:** Nothing reported that would take these cars out of service. **Warranty performance:** Average, although a lot depends on dealer servicing. **NHTSA safety complaints:** Well-designed head restraints; if you must carry an infant, the Miata has a factory-installed airbag cut-off switch.

Con: Owner-reported problems: Specialty replacement batteries have been hard to find and dirt and debris can clog up side door sill holes, allowing water to collect and corrosion to occur. Ask the dealer to drill larger drain holes. **Service bulletin problems:** Engine hard to start, and excessive cranking time; fluctuation in cruise control set speed; rattling noise at 3,000 rpm; rattle from the main silencer; console hole cover doesn't fit flush; paint damage caused by trunk rubber cushion. **Safety:** Shoulder belts may chafe your neck; seatbelt's low anchor causes the belt to pull down against the shoulder.

Road Performance

Pro: Emergency handling: No surprises. Performs emergency manoeuvres predictably and almost as quickly as the Porsche Boxster. Exceptionally responsive, with minimal body roll; the rigid chassis gives the car a solid feeling. **Steering:** Steering is crisp and predictable. **Acceleration/torque:** Brisk acceleration with a good amount of low-end torque (0–100 km/h: 8.5 sec.). **Transmission:** Easy, precise throws with the manual and smooth, quiet shifting with the automatic. The 6-speed gearbox is helpful in keeping the noise level down. **Routine handling:** Lightness and 50/50 weight distribution make it an easy car to toss around corners without tossing your cookies. **Braking:** Impressive braking performance on dry pavement with little brake fading after successive stops (100–0 km/h: 102 ft.).

Con: Although the ride is a bit choppy, it's not as harsh as previous versions. The rear end tends to swing out when cornering under speed.

Comfort/Convenience

Pro: Standard equipment: The base model is well equipped. The round dash air vents heighten the sports car image, giving the cockpit a 1960s British roadster allure. The convertible top is easily lowered from inside or outside of the car, and the optional hardtop is quite practical and easy to install. An innovative wind block flips up behind the rear seats. **Controls and displays:** Gauges are simple to comprehend and well positioned. **Climate control:** Efficient, quiet heating and defrosting system is easy to adjust. **Entry/exit:** Not difficult once you get used to stepping down into your Miata. **Cargo space:** Storage areas include a relatively large locking glove compartment and centre console bin (with cupholder), net pouches behind the seats, and small map pockets in each door. However, storage space for large objects is practically non-existent, and there's almost no room behind the rear seats. **Trunk/liftover:** A low liftover makes for easy loading, although the trunk itself is quite small and shallow.

Con: Driving position: Not for six-footers. The steering wheel is set too close to the driver, isn't height-adjustable, and blocks your view of the ignition switch and power mirror control. Seats are set too low for short drivers. Unusually small inside door releases are mounted too far back to be accessed comfortably. With the top in place, rear visibility is obstructed by the wide rear panels, the small rear window, and small side view mirrors. Small bucket seats give marginal lateral support and could use a bit more padding. **Interior space/comfort F/R:** Interior is a bit small for tall occupants, who must sit bolt upright when pushing their seat all the way back. Insufficient lower back and thigh support. Inadequate head and leg room for tall adults. If you have large thighs, you may need a month at Weight Watchers to fit them between the steering wheel and seat cushion. **Quietness:** Better get used to road, tire, and engine noise that increases as the Miata picks up speed.

COST				
List Price (negotiable)	**Residual Values** (months)			
	24	**36**	**48**	**60**
Base Miata: $26,995 (19%)	$18,000	$15,000	$12,000	$10,000

TECHNICAL DATA	
Powertrain (rear-drive)	Head room: 37.1 in.
Engine: 1.8L 4-cyl. (140 hp)	Leg room: 42.7 in.
Transmissions: 5-speed man.	Wheelbase: 89.2 in.
• 4-speed auto.	Turning circle: 33 ft.
Dimension/Capacity	Cargo volume: 5 cu. ft.
Passengers: 2/0	Tow limit: N/A
Height/length/width:	Fuel tank: 45L/reg.
48.2/155.4/65.9 in.	Weight: 2,300 lb.

SAFETY FEATURES/CRASHWORTHINESS		
	Std.	**Opt.**
Anti-lock brakes	❏	■
Seatbelt pretensioners	—	—
Side airbags	—	—
Traction control	❏	■

Head restraints	*	N/A
Visibility (front/rear)	*****	*
Crash protection (front) D/P	N/A	
Crash protection (side) D/P	N/A	
Crash protection (offset)	N/A	
HLDI injury claims (model)	N/A	
HLDI injury claims (all)	N/A	

MPV

✘ RISKY BUY

MPV

RATING: Not Recommended. This underpowered, lumbering, under-sized, and overpriced minivan is an Odyssey wannabe that simply comes across as odd. **Strong points:** Comfortable ride and easy handling, good driver's position, responsive steering, and lots of gadgets and innovative storage spots. **Weak points:** The small V6 engine is performance-challenged; it gives the impression that there's nothing in reserve, with barely enough power for highway use and leisurely acceleration from a stop (like the first Odysseys). Smaller than most of the competition. Dealer servicing and head office support have been problematic in the past.

NEW FOR 2000: An entirely new mini-minivan; rumour has it that Ford didn't want Mazda competing in the lucrative, red-hot large minivan market where Ford has its own Windstar If the MPV's latest redesign doesn't catch on, which I predict it won't, you'll soon see Mazda selling re-badged Windstars.

OVERVIEW: Mazda's only minivan quickly became a bestseller when it first came on the market in 1989, but during the past few years its popularity has fallen off. Mazda sales bounced back last year as a result of price cutting and the popularity of the automaker's small cars and pickups. This infusion of cash has allowed the company (33 percent owned by Ford) to put additional money into its MPV redesign. Mazda hoped to get a fresh start with its redesigned MPV, thus ending a minivan drought that has plagued the company for almost a year.

Unfortunately, the latest MPV iteration appears to embody all the mistakes made by Honda's first Odyssey—its 170 horses aren't adequate for people-hauling and it's too expensive for what is essentially a smaller van than its predecessor. For example, the MPV is over a foot shorter than the Ford Windstar and a half-foot shorter than the Toyota Sienna and Nissan Quest.

Manufactured in Hiroshima, Japan, this redesigned seven-passenger minivan switches from rear-drive to front-wheel drive and includes a number of innovative features, like "theatre" seating (rear passenger seat is slightly higher), and a third seat that pivots rearward to become a rear-facing bench seat—or folds into the floor for picnics or tailgate parties. Another feature unique among minivans is Mazda's Side-by-Slide removable second-row seats that move fore and aft as well as side-to-side while a passenger is seated. Sliding door crank windows are standard on the entry model and power assisted on the LS and ES versions.

All-wheel-drive models have been dropped, and this year's MPV comes equipped with a standard Ford 170-hp 2.5L V6, assembled in Ohio and shipped to Japan (a homegrown 3.0L V6 is scheduled for 2002). A 4-speed automatic transmission is the only gearbox available— which is unfortunate, because it shifts erratically and robs the MPV engine of power it badly needs.

Standard DX equipment includes AC, dual sliding doors, intermittent rear wiper/washer, 100-watt audio system, and tilt steering wheel. The higher trim levels don't offer much of value, except for power windows and door locks and an ignition immobilizer/alarm/keyless entry system. Side airbags are optional on the LX and standard on the ES model. This being their first year in service, buyers should be wary of these airbags until their reliability and safety have been ascertained.

Cost analysis/best alternatives: There weren't many '99 MPVs produced, so your chance of finding one is slim. Plus, they aren't recommended buys. Actually, the 2000 model is $700 cheaper than the '99's base price and you'll find lots of discounting as the year progresses. This should play well in your plans, because you wouldn't want the glitch-ridden first-series MPVs, anyway. Other minivans worth considering are the Chrysler Caravan/Voyager, Honda Odyssey, Nissan Quest, and the Toyota Sienna. **Options:** Higher trim option includes an ugly, orange fake wood dash. An integrated child safety seat isn't available. Rear AC and seat height-adjustment mechanisms are recommended convenience features. **Rebates:** Expect $2,000 rebates by spring as dealer inventory piles up. **Delivery/PDI:** $900. **Depreciation:** Predicted to be worse than average. **Insurance cost:** Likely to be higher than average. **Parts supply/cost:** Likely to be back-ordered and cost more than average. **Annual maintenance cost:** Too early to say. **Warranty:** Bumper-to-bumper

3 years/80,000 km; powertrain 5 years/100,000 km; rust perforation 5 years/unlimited mileage. **Supplementary warranty:** An extended warranty is worth having, particularly in view of the fact that this is a totally redesigned vehicle that's in its first year on the market. **Highway/city fuel economy:** 9.9–13.6L/100 km. **Annual fuel cost:** N/A.

Quality/Reliability/Safety

Pro: Quality control: High-quality workmanship and rugged construction. **Service bulletin problems:** Nothing, yet. **NHTSA safety complaints/safety:** No complaints registered.

Con: Reliability: Expect transmission failures, ABS malfunctions, and premature wearout of the front and rear brakes. **Warranty performance:** Inadequate base warranty. Mediocre past servicing will likely be put to a severe test as the new model's problems emerge. **Owner-reported problems:** Too early to report. This new model will likely have some engine, transmission, and brake problems judging by the mechanical specs given out at press time. Rear visibility obstructed by high seatbacks.

Road Performance

Pro: Ford's Duratec V6 (essentially the same engine that powers the Mercury Cougar) has plenty of power for in-town use. Excellent steering feedback. **Routine handling:** Acceptable at low speeds. **Braking:** Adequate.

Con: Emergency handling: This minivan's highway performance doesn't inspire confidence. Some brake fade after successive stops. **Steering:** Fights to stay on-centre, even when trying to make a turn. **Acceleration/torque:** Insufficient power for highway use. Slow acceleration makes merging with traffic and passing other cars a bit scary. Not much low-end torque. Excessive engine whine and vibration when passing the 4,500 rpm mark. **Transmission:** The primordial automatic transmission shifts roughly and constantly. It lumbers through first and second gear, and then bangs when going from second to third.

Comfort/Convenience

Pro: Standard equipment: Lots of standard features, but the 180-watt, nine-speaker audio system that stores up to six CDs is particularly impressive. **Driving position:** Driver sits comfortably high with excellent forward visibility and lots of head room. **Controls and displays:** Instrumentation is easy to read, with large gauges, buttons, and knobs. Controls are within easy reach. **Climate control:** Good heating/defrosting/ventilation system. **Entry/exit:** Easy entry/exit up front. **Interior space/comfort F/R:** Without a doubt, the MPV manages its limited interior space far better than the competition. All seats are well bolstered with plenty of head room in all seating positions. Middle row seating converts easily from bench, with an aisle on each side, to buckets, with an aisle down the middle. Third row seat flips and folds into a floor well. Side doors have windows that drop down, rather than swing out, which tends to be rattle-prone. **Cargo space:** Adequate; large door bins. Seats can be easily removed for additional cargo room and they weigh 13 lb. (6 kg) less than the Odyssey's seats. **Trunk/liftover:** Easy to load or unload.

Con: The sliding side door openings are narrow and doors only operate manually. **Interior space/comfort F/R:** Elbow room is at a premium and it takes a lithe figure to move down the front- and middle-seat aisle. Don't believe for a minute the MPV will hold seven passengers in comfort—six is more like it. The flip and fold third-row seat, when flipped 90 degrees backward for tailgate parties, puts the passenger side occupant dangerously close to the hot exhaust pipe and leaves adult legs dangling uncomfortably. **Quietness:** Excessive engine and road noise.

COST

List Price (negotiable)	Residual Values (months)			
	24	**36**	**48**	**60**
DX: $24,555 (20%)	$16,000	$12,000	$10,000	$8,000

TECHNICAL DATA

Powertrain (rear-drive)
Engine: 2.5L V6 (170 hp)
Transmission: 4-speed auto.
Dimension/Capacity
Passengers: 2/2/3
Height/length/width:
68.7/187/72.1 in.

Head room F: 41/R1: 39.3/R2: 38 in.
Leg room F: 40.8/R1: 37/R2: 35.6 in.
Wheelbase: 111.8 in.
Turning circle: 37.4 ft.
Cargo volume: 54.6 cu. ft.
GVWR: N/A
Payload: N/A
Tow limit: N/A
Fuel tank: 70L/reg.
Weight: 3,662 lb.

SAFETY FEATURES/CRASHWORTHINESS

	Std.	Opt.
Anti-lock brakes (4W)	■	❑
Seatbelt pretensioners	■	❑
Side airbags	■	■
Traction control	—	—
Head restraints	N/A	
Visibility (front/rear)	*****	***
Crash protection (front) D/P	N/A	
Crash protection (side) D/P	N/A	
Crash protection (offset)	N/A	
HLDI injury claims (model)	N/A	
HLDI injury claims (all)	N/A	

NISSAN

Nissan is one sick puppy. The company is saddled with a debt of about 3 trillion yen ($37.2 billion), a larger debt load than that of the U.S. Big Three combined. This debt hasn't been reduced much by Nissan's unsuccessful attempts to buy market share by offering rebates and free air conditioning and automatic transmissions.

On the positive side, Nissan makes good cars, trucks, and minivans. Its Tennessee manufacturing plant is running at full capacity to meet demand for its new Xterra sport-utility and Crew Cab pickup. Most of the 1999 production of both vehicles has been sold and orders for the Crew Cab, with its four full-sized doors, represent 28 percent of pickup sales, whereas Nissan predicted only 12 percent.

On the other hand, Renault France's acquisition of a controlling interest in Nissan may not be the godsend that was first thought. The French automaker is known for making lousy marketing decisions and producing low quality vehicles (think back to the Alliance, Encore, Premier, and Medallion).

Independent of Renault's plans, Nissan intends to gain market share and increase profits by taking four simple steps this year: cut the number of variations per model; slow down the model-change race to better amortize development costs; standardize parts so that 55 percent will be interchangeable; and offer innovative six-year leasing plans to bolster sales and service.

This year will see the Xterra's debut and the arrival of a redesigned Sentra and Maxima. Instead of changing its product lineup, the company is standing firm on prices and pushing its comprehensive warranty to lure buyers into showrooms.

Sentra

RATING: Average, primarily for city commuting. **Strong points:** Cheap to buy and run, acceptable ride and handling, and good quality control. 2.0L-equipped versions provide much better acceleration, handling, and ride. **Weak points:** Sluggish base engine is clearly inadequate for merging into traffic with the automatic transmission; poor braking without ABS; poor high-speed handling; limited rear passenger room; difficult rear access; excessive engine, tire, and road noise; SE requires premium fuel; rear corner pillars impede rear-side visibility; only average crashworthiness, but much higher than average accident injury claims.

NEW FOR 2000: A redesigned Sentra is due out in the spring of 2000. It will resemble a low-budget version of the Audi A4 and carry Nissan's 1.8L and 2.0L powerplants.

OVERVIEW: Nissan's entry-level small sedans come in three trim levels: the XE and GXE, housing an anemic 1.6L 4-cylinder engine, and the sporty SE Limited, carrying a perky 2.0L engine, larger wheels, an upgraded chassis, wider tires, aero body cladding, and foglights. Unlike many bare-bones economy cars, entry-level Sentras offer dependable motoring at little cost.

Cost analysis/best alternatives: It's a toss-up as to which model year is the better buy. If you wait until the spring of 2000, you'll pay top dollar for a better performing, upgraded Sentra that will likely have lots of factory glitches during its first six months of production. On the other hand, if you can live with the '99 version's deficiencies and want a much cheaper car, then you may wish to wait a few months, and purchase the '99 Sentra just when the new model arrives and rebates along with dealer incentives are at their peak. Other worthwhile cars to consider are the '99 Ford Escort, GM Cavalier and Sunfire, Honda Civic, Mazda Protegé, and Toyota Corolla. Fully equipped '99 Sentras sell for much less than many other Japanese subcompacts, making them particularly good buys for city use. **Options:** Spend extra money for anti-lock brakes and better-grade, quieter tires. **Rebates:** $2,000 to clear out the leftover '99s by next spring. **Depreciation:** Average. **Insurance cost:** Average. **Parts supply/cost:** Inexpensive parts can be found practically anywhere. **Annual maintenance cost:** Less than average. Uncluttered under-hood layout makes servicing easy. **Warranty:** Bumper-to-bumper 3 years/80,000 km; powertrain 5 years/100,000 km; rust perforation 5 years/unlimited km. **Supplementary warranty:** Not needed. **Highway/city fuel economy:** 6.0–8.8L/100 km with the 1.6L and an automatic, and 7.3–10.2L/100 km with the 2.0L and an automatic. **Annual fuel cost:** 1.6L: 1,508L=$875; 2.0L: 1,779L=$1,032.

Quality/Reliability/Safety

Pro: Quality control: Sentras are almost trouble-free. First-class body assembly. Sentra production has been moved to Mexico—however, this isn't likely to affect quality control. **Reliability:** Overall reliability is better than average. **Warranty performance:** Average. **Service bulletin problems:** Nothing published, yet.

Con: Owner-reported problems: Some reports of 1.6L engine cylinder head and gasket failures. Clutch, exhaust system, and fuel system problems are fairly common after the first three years. Front brakes aren't very durable either. **NHTSA safety complaints/safety:** Airbag failed to deploy; ABS brake failure.

Road Performance

Pro: Steering: Steering response is predictable, but slow. **Acceleration/torque:** The 2.0L 4-cylinder provides plenty of power for all driving situations. **Transmission:** Both manual and automatic transmissions shift very smoothly under normal circumstances. **Routine handling:** Good manoeuvrability around town. Firm but well-mannered ride on most roads.

Con: The base engine is woefully inadequate for highway driving. Full-throttle shifting is jerky at times. Some third and fourth gear "hunting" with the automatic transmission. **Emergency handling:** High-speed handling is a bit sloppy, and emergency handling is sluggish. Very sensitive to side winds. Standard tires perform poorly while cornering. **Braking:** Unacceptably long braking distances (100–0 km/h: 147 ft.).

Comfort/Convenience

Pro: Driving position: Spartan, though acceptable instruments and controls. **Controls and displays:** Easy-to-read dash gauges and convenient controls. Neatly finished interior. **Climate control:** Efficient and uncomplicated heating, defrosting, and ventilation. **Cargo space:** Average for this size of car. **Trunk/liftover:** Spacious trunk has a low liftover.

Con: Standard equipment: Antiquated, boxy styling. Just the bare necessities, in keeping with this car's entry-level pretensions. Seats a bit thinly padded. Hard to see through the rear quarter panels. **Entry/exit:** Small rear doors make access a bit difficult. **Interior space/comfort F/R:** Don't believe Nissan's claim of five-passenger seating: the four-door sedan only accommodates four people comfortably. The front driver's seat is set a bit too low. Cramped rear seating. All seats could use extra padding. **Quietness:** Excessive road and engine noise in the passenger compartment.

COST

List Price (very negotiable)	Residual Values (months)			
	24	36	48	60
Base: $14,998 (12%)	$11,000	$9,000	$7,500	$6,500

TECHNICAL DATA

Powertrain (front-drive)
Engines: 1.6L 4-cyl. (115 hp)
• 2.0L 4-cyl. (140 hp)
Transmissions: 5-speed man.
• 4-speed auto.
Dimension/Capacity
Passengers: 2/3
Height/length/width:
54.5/170.1/66.6 in.

Head room F/R: 39.1/36.5 in.
Leg room F/R: 42.3/32.4 in.
Wheelbase: 99.8 in.
Turning circle: 38 ft.
Cargo volume: 11 cu. ft.
Tow limit: 1,000 lb.
Fuel tank: 50L/reg./prem.
Weight: 2,450 lb.

SAFETY FEATURES/CRASHWORTHINESS

	Std.	Opt.
Anti-lock brakes	❏	■
Seatbelt pretensioners	—	—
Side airbags	—	—
Traction control	—	—
Head restraints	**	**
Visibility (front/rear)	*****	**
Crash protection (front) D/P	***	****
Crash protection (side) D/P	***	***
Crash protection (offset)	***	
HLDI injury claims (model)	**	
HLDI injury claims (all)	*	

Altima

RATING: Average. **Strong points:** Handles well, good braking, reliable, and better than average craftsmanship. **Weak points:** Sluggish acceleration with the automatic transmission; delayed, harsh shifting; limited rear seat room; and disappointing crashworthiness scores and accident injury claim data.

NEW FOR 2000: A facelift, reduced levels of noise vibration and harshness, and an upgraded suspension.

OVERVIEW: Nissan's latest mid-size sedan, this yuppie-mobile is a four-door, front-drive, 4-cylinder aimed at Chrysler's LH series and GM's best-selling Cavalier/Sunfire. The engine is a spinoff of the discontinued 240SX's 16-valve 150-hp 2.4L 4-banger.

Cost analysis/best alternatives: For the money, the upgraded 2000 is your best choice. Other cars worth considering are the Honda Accord, Mazda 626, and Toyota Camry. **Options:** Nissan tends to option-load its Altimas, forcing you to take a number of unwanted, unnecessary optional features along with the one you want. Can you get by without the optional automatic transmission? I say it's not refined enough for pleasurable shifting; however, test-drive an Altima yourself to judge your own tolerance for its shifting eccentricities. **Rebates:** $2,000 to clear out the leftover '99s. **Delivery/PDI:** $500. **Depreciation:** A bit slower than average. **Insurance cost:** Higher than average. **Parts supply/cost:** Parts are easy to find, but dealer prices can be steep. Independent suppliers often sell them at discount prices. **Annual maintenance cost:** Less than average. Uncluttered under-hood layout makes servicing easy. **Warranty:** Bumper-to-bumper 3 years/80,000 km; powertrain 5 years/100,000 km; rust perforation 5 years/unlimited km.

Supplementary warranty: Not needed. **Highway/city fuel economy:** 7.1–9.9L/100 km with the manual transmission and 7.2–10.6L/100 km with an automatic. **Annual fuel cost:** Automatic: 1,814L=$1,052.

Quality/Reliability/Safety

Pro: Quality control: Good body assembly and powertrain components. **Reliability:** No reliability problems have been reported. **Warranty performance:** Average. Nissan staffers aren't particularly generous in handling premature brake wear complaints or in giving out post-warranty "goodwill."

Con: Owner-reported problems: Minor electrical glitches and excessive brake wear, noise, and pulsations. **Service bulletin problems:** Front door window rattling. **NHTSA safety complaints/safety:** Fire ignited in fuse box area; the driver hit a telephone pole head-on and neither airbag deployed; design of door caused consumer to hit eye on sharp door edge; malfunctioning power door locks re-lock doors; rear seatbelts malfunction; front passenger shoulder/lapbelt won't pull out of seatbelt assembly; tiny horn buttons may be hard to locate in an emergency.

Road Performance

Pro: Emergency handling: The Altima's sporty handling is way overrated, but it does handle sudden corrections quite well, if with just a bit too much body roll. **Steering:** Responsive, with good road feedback. **Routine handling:** Good manoeuvrability around town, and highway cruising isn't as jarring as before. **Braking:** Better than average (100–0 km/h: 120 ft.).

Con: Acceleration/torque: Slow acceleration (0–100 km/h: 9.8 sec.). Engine performance is smoother this year, but it's still noisy and rough-running. The 4-banger has insufficient top-end torque and gets buzzier the more it's pushed. This car cries out for a V6 like the one used in the Maxima. **Transmission:** The automatic transmission hesitates, and then shifts abruptly. The 5-speed manual transmission is sloppy. The more softly sprung suspension results in poor body control when passing over highway bumps and dips.

Comfort/Convenience

Pro: Standard equipment: Fairly well appointed. Infiniti J30 styling. **Controls and displays:** A major improvement. User-friendly controls, and instruments are easy to read and understand. **Climate control:** Good heating, defrosting, and ventilation. **Interior space/comfort F/R:** Comfortable, supportive seats. Up front, there's good all-around head room and leg room. **Cargo space:** Acceptable. Trunk pass-through allows for storage of long items. **Trunk/liftover:** Average size with a low sill to facilitate loading.

Con: Driving position: Only the GLE offers a height-adjustable seat. Drivers may find that the pedals are set too close and the steering wheel is too far away. Rear roof pillars and high-tail styling obstruct rear/side visibility. **Entry/exit:** Rear seat access is difficult to master due to the slanted roof pillars, inward-curving door frames, and narrow clearance. **Interior space/comfort F/R:** The small cabin seats only four comfortably, with limited rear leg room. Although Nissan enlarged the interior, rear space hasn't been improved. **Quietness:** Too much engine, road, and tire noise intrudes into the passenger compartment. Trunk loading is made difficult by the wide bumper shelf; trunk lid hinges can damage cargo.

COST

List Price (very negotiable)	Residual Values (months)			
	24	**36**	**48**	**60**
XE: $19,998 (15%)	$14,000	$11,000	$9,000	$7,500

TECHNICAL DATA

Powertrain (front-drive)
Engine: 2.4L 4-cyl. (155 hp)
Transmissions: 5-speed man.
• 4-speed auto.
Dimension/Capacity
Passengers: 2/3
Height/length/width:
55.9/183.5/69 in.

Head room F/R: 39.4/37.7 in.
Leg room F/R: 42/33.9 in.
Wheelbase: 103.1 in.
Turning circle: 41 ft.
Cargo volume: 14 cu. ft.
Tow limit: N/A
Fuel tank: 60L/reg.
Weight: 3,050 lb.

SAFETY FEATURES/CRASHWORTHINESS

	Std.	Opt.
Anti-lock brakes	❑	■
Seatbelt pretensioners	—	—
Side airbags	—	—
Traction control	—	—
Head restraints	**	**
Visibility (front/rear)	*****	**
Crash protection (front) D/P	***	**
Crash protection (side) D/P	***	***
Crash protection (offset)	N/A	
HLDI injury claims (model)	**	
HLDI injury claims (all)	**	

Maxima

Maxima

RATING: Recommended. A high-quality, reasonably priced luxury sedan that's hidden by all the Infiniti hype. Even though this is a redesign, Nissans don't have as many "teething" problems with newly launched models as do other automakers. **Strong points:** Impressive powertrain performance, comfortable ride, pleasant handling, and above average reliability. **Weak points:** Loose clutch and stiff shift with the manual transmission, cramped rear seating, poor fuel economy, and missing some standard safety and convenience features like ABS and side airbags.

NEW FOR 2000: This year's redesigned Maxima is larger, has more power, and comes with additional standard features. It gets 32 more horses (the I30 gets five more), standard anti-lock brakes, a bit more interior space (mostly rear leg room) and trunk volume, and a standard engine immobilizer anti-theft system. Optional side airbags are available for the first time, the sportier SE offers a firmer suspension, an optional spoiler, 17-inch wheels, and traction control.

OVERVIEW: The front-wheel drive mid-sized Maxima soldiers on as Nissan's luxury flagship, one step removed from the briefly discontinued and recently resuscitated Infiniti G20. The 222-hp 24-valve DOHC V6 is a real dazzler. With its impressive array of standard features, the Maxima becomes a full-fledged member of what Nissan calls the "executive sports" luxury sedan class that includes the base Infiniti and Lexus models, as well as European entries like the Volvo 900/S90, Audis, and smaller BMWs. In fact, the Maxima "borrowed" its aerodynamic shape from BMW's 5-series.

There's not much risk involved in buying a Maxima; it's a pleasure to drive and much cheaper than most of the competition.

Cost analysis/best alternatives: Get the 2000 model for the upgrades. Other cars worthy of consideration are the BMW 3-series, Ford Crown Victoria and Grand Marquis, Lexus ES 300, Mazda Millenia, Toyota Camry and Avalon, and Volvo S70 and S90 series. **Options:** Side airbags, anti-lock brakes, and the form-fitting SE seats. The optional sonar suspension found on the GXE is an unnecessary gadget; it will give the average mechanic nightmares. Be wary of the sunroof option (it eats up head room) and don't buy the optional instrument panel: it's distracting, confusing, and more suitable to a video arcade than a luxury automobile. **Rebates:** $2,500 to clear out the leftover '99s. **Delivery/PDI:** $500. **Depreciation:** Average. **Insurance cost:** Higher than average. **Parts supply/cost:** Reasonably priced parts aren't hard to find from dealers or independent suppliers. **Annual maintenance cost:** Less than average. **Warranty:** Bumper-to-bumper 3 years/80,000 km; powertrain 5 years/100,000 km; rust perforation 5 years/unlimited km. **Supplementary warranty:** Not needed. **Highway/city fuel economy:** 7.7–11.4L/100 km with the 3.0L engine. **Annual fuel cost:** 1,947L=$1,129.

Quality/Reliability/Safety

Pro: Quality control: Outstanding. **Reliability:** Maximas have always had an impressive reliability history. **Safety:** Integrated child safety seat anchors have been added to the rear parcel shelf.

Con: Warranty performance: The company's claims handlers can be rather obtuse in interpreting Nissan's warranty obligations to Maxima owners. (I'm reminded of the ongoing battle that some customers are waging in order to get the company to pay for exhaust manifold components.) **Owner-reported problems:** Scattered reports of automatic transmission and electrical system malfunctions, as well as paint defects and assorted body rattles. **Service bulletin problems:** Interior squeaks and rattles; steering pull or drift when driving at highway speeds; wind noise, hiss, or fluttering along the upper edge of the windshield. **NHTSA safety complaints:** While driving, the front wheels locked up, causing extensive undercarriage damage; airbags failed to deploy; the trunk lid and latch are hazardous when raised.

Road Performance

Pro: Emergency handling: A bit slow, but well controlled. **Steering:** Accurate and predictable. **Acceleration/torque:** The powerful and smooth standard V6 engine provides substantial power without excessive noise (0–100 km/h: 8.7 sec.). This year's engine upgrade doesn't make the car accelerate faster from a stop, but it does get better mid-range passing ability. **Transmission:** The smooth-shifting automatic transmission has an Auto position that switches the transmission from normal to power mode when accelerating. It also has a switch to let you lock out fourth gear to assist in trailer towing and to prevent frequent gear changes over hilly terrain. **Routine handling:** Very good, with lots of control. The ride is fairly firm but comfortable, due to the refined suspension that handles rough roads well if the car is lightly loaded. The SE's sport suspension makes the handling a bit crisper. **Braking:** Good braking with or without ABS (optional on last year's models) thanks to rear disc brakes (100–0 km/h: 131 ft.).

Con: Manual transmission's clutch action is vague and the shifting is a bit stiff. Some torque steer (a steering wheel tug upon acceleration) is still present.

Comfort/Convenience

Pro: More rearward seat travel for tall drivers, power seat controls are more user-friendly, and a lower windshield line adds to fore and aft visibility. Impressive theft deterrent system sounds an alarm, flashes the lights, and disables the car if the vehicle is disturbed. The system is automatically armed whenever the Maxima's doors are locked with a key. **Driving position:** Very good. Firm, supportive, and comfortable front seating, plenty of head and leg room, and good all-around visibility. **Controls and displays:** Although some controls are a bit fussy, the dashboard is designed well, with easily read analogue gauges that don't wash out in sunlight. **Climate control:** Efficient and quiet. **Entry/exit:** Easy front and rear access. **Interior space/comfort F/R:** Lots of front and rear head room and leg room. **Cargo space:** Lots of little storage bins for odds and ends. **Trunk/liftover:** Trunk has a low liftover to facilitate loading and is a bit larger this year. **Quietness:** Much improved this year, with little wind and road noise invading the passenger compartment.

Con: Rear visibility is blocked by rear side pillars. **Standard equipment:** Disappointing. High-tech luxury interior with emphasis on electronic gadgets. Head restraints in the rear are too low for average-sized adults. **Interior space/comfort F/R:** Only two adults will fit comfortably in the rear; three adults will adopt a knees-to-chin posture. Low, flat seats give inadequate thigh support, and obtrusive side wing bolsters push passengers into the middle. **Trunk/liftover:** The trunk isn't very deep.

COST				
List Price (negotiable)	**Residual Values** (months)			
	24	**36**	**48**	**60**
Maxima GXE: $28,590 (20%)	$23,000	$18,000	$15,000	$13,000

TECHNICAL DATA	
Powertrain (rear-drive)	Head room F/R: 40.1/37.4 in.
Engine: 3.0L V6 (222 hp)	Leg room F/R: 43.9/34.3 in.
Transmissions: 5-speed man.	Wheelbase: 106.3 in.
• 4-speed auto.	Turning circle: 39 ft.
Dimension/Capacity	Cargo volume: 15 cu. ft.
Passengers: 2/3	Tow limit: N/A
Height/length/width:	Fuel tank: 70L/prem.
55.7/187.7/69.7 in.	Weight: 3,050 lb.

SAFETY FEATURES/CRASHWORTHINESS

	Std.	Opt.
Anti-lock brakes	■	❏
Seatbelt pretensioners	—	—
Side airbags	❏	■
Traction control	■	■
Head restraints	***	**
Visibility (front/rear)	*****	*****
Crash protection (front) D/P	****	****
Crash protection (side) D/P	****	***
Crash protection (offset)	***	
HLDI injury claims (model)	***	
HLDI injury claims (all)	***	

Note: The above scores apply to the '99 Maxima only.

Quest

Quest

RATING: Above Average. Nissan reliability and Ford styling. **Strong points:** Plenty of passenger and cargo room, and a comfortable ride with lots of seating choices. **Weak points:** Adequate powertrain setup trails Windstar and Odyssey in acceleration and passing. Soggy base suspension, difficult rear seat access, horrendous gas consumption.

NEW FOR 2000: Minor trim items. The Mercury Villager, the Quest's twin, was dropped last year, as Ford Canada continues to close down Mercury dealerships.

OVERVIEW: Smaller and more car-like than most minivans, this minivan is built by Ford at its truck factory in Avon Lake, Ohio, and sized comfortably between the regular and extended Chrysler minivans. This front-drive, five- or seven-passenger minivan comes without aero-styling gimmicks, having adopted a bit of Chrysler's boxy look and interior dimensions.

Of all the small minivans, the Nissan Quest is the most economical to maintain and the most fun to whip around the city in. Its strongest assets are car-like handling, modular seating, and reliable mechanical components that have been tested for years on the Maxima.

The 170-hp 3.3L V6 engine gives this minivan car-like handling, ride, and cornering. Nissan borrowed the powertrain, suspension, and steering assembly from its Maxima, mixed in some creative sheet metal, and left the job of outfitting the sound system, climate control, dashboard, steering column, and wheels to Ford. This has resulted in an attractive and not overly aero-styled minivan.

Cost analysis/best alternatives: Get either the '99 or 2000 model—they're practically identical. Expect some discounting on the '99s that may go as high as $2,000. Try to find an SE version for the improved suspension setup. Other minivans worth considering are the Chrysler minivans, the Honda Odyssey, or the Toyota Sienna. **Options:** The integrated child safety seat is a must-have and the seat height adjuster will benefit short drivers. A separate rear air conditioner/heater and power side windows are also worth considering. The optional performance handling equipment makes little improvement to the standard suspension. **Rebates:** $1,000 on the '99s. **Delivery/PDI:** $900. **Depreciation:** Average. **Insurance cost:** Above average. **Parts supply/cost:** Good supply and reasonable costs. **Annual maintenance cost:** Average. **Warranty:** Bumper-to-bumper 3 years/80,000 km; powertrain 5 years/100,000 km; rust perforation 5 years/unlimited km. **Supplementary warranty:** An extended warranty isn't needed. **Highway/city fuel economy:** 8.9–13.8L/100 km. **Annual fuel cost:** 2,319L=$1,345.

Quality/Reliability/Safety

Pro: Quality control: Good quality control—Nissan designs and develops the minivans while Ford manufactures them. **Reliability:** The engine and drivetrain are borrowed from the Nissan Maxima, a very reliable vehicle. Excellent fit and finish. A large dealer network means that servicing and parts are readily available. According to CAA, parts are less expensive than most other cars in this class. Plenty of glass provides excellent front and rear visibility.

Con: Warranty performance: Below average. **Owner-reported problems:** Most owner-reported problems involve interior and exterior noise and driveline vibrations. **Service bulletin problems:** Rear suspension rattling. **NHTSA safety complaints/safety:** ABS failures; brake and accelerator pedals are the same height, so driver's foot can easily slip and step on both at the same time; 22-month-old child was able to pull the clasp apart on integrated child safety seat; rear window on liftgate door shattered for unknown reason (dealer was aware of problem and replaced window under warranty); power steering fluid leakage due to O-ring at rack gear splitting; door hinge allows the door to damage the fender during average wind storms; windshield wipers are noisy when put in the "high" mode. Safety investigators are also looking into reports of electric door lock and power window failures that have trapped occupants in their vehicles.

Road Performance

Pro: Emergency handling: Impressive highway stability. **Steering:** Precise steering makes the Quest quite responsive at highway speeds and in emergency manoeuvres. **Acceleration/torque:** Upgraded V6 engine delivers plenty of power for city and highway driving needs (0–100 km/h: 11.5 sec.). **Transmission:** The 4-speed automatic transmission is much quieter and smoother this year—you can switch from Economy to Power shift mode by pressing a dashboard button. Fourth gear can be locked out to prevent constant gear hunting when going over hilly terrain. **Routine handling:** Handles and manoeuvres like a large station wagon. Agile (the short wheelbase and revised suspension help in this area) and easy to drive. The smooth, quiet ride on the highway isn't compromised by a full load. **Braking:** Braking performance is excellent, because four-wheel ABS improves directional control by eliminating wheel lockup (100–0 km/h: 138 ft.).

Con: Long-legged drivers may find the leg room a bit short. Not the minivan for high-speed cruising or carrying lots of cargo or passengers. Rough terrain or uneven pavement makes for a busy to rough ride. Don't make too much of the Quest's car-like handling pretensions. Sure, it handles much better than truck-based minivans like the GM Astro and Ford Aerostar, but it isn't superior to other front-drive minivans. It requires a rather wide turning circle. Towing capacity of 3,500 lb. (1,590 kg) is possible only with an optional towing package.

Comfort/Convenience

Pro: Standard equipment: Comfortable and well-appointed interior. The standard radio gives great sound. The Quest offers a large array of standard safety features that include airbags, side-impact beams, reinforced centre pillars, front and rear impact absorbing zones, rear outboard three-point safety belts, ABS, and a childproof door lock in the sliding door. An integrated child seat is optional. **Driving position:** Car-like driving position and comfortable seats, which include a power lumbar support in the driver's seat. **Controls and displays:** Most controls and instruments are generally easy to use and read. **Climate control:** Efficient, powerful system; you can turn on the AC and control the air outlet location separately. All side windows can be opened for maximum ventilation. **Entry/exit:** Easy. Helpful assist grab handles over the front and sliding doors. The front captain's chairs are easily removed, and the modular interior allows 14 possible seating and cargo configurations, making for better seating for three adults in the rear than with most other small vans or wagons. An additional 4.8 inches in length gives second row passengers an extra inch of leg room and two more inches of cargo space. **Cargo space:** Expanded this year. Flexibility and the easy-to-use sliding rear seat make up for the Quest's modest cargo-carrying capacity. Middle seatback folds flat, and the rear seats have tracks that allow them to slide forward all the way to the front. **Trunk/liftover:** Low liftover height makes for convenient loading from the rear.

Con: Interior space/comfort F/R: Front seats could use more lateral support. **Quietness:** Some wind and road noise.

COST				
List Price (negotiable)	**Residual Values** (months)			
	24	**36**	**48**	**60**
$24,295 (20%)	$17,000	$14,000	$12,000	$10,000

TECHNICAL DATA	
Powertrain (front-drive)	Head room F: 39.7/R1: 39.9/R2: 37.6 in.
Engine: 3.3L V6 (170 hp)	Leg room F: 39.9/R1: 36.4/R2: 36.3 in.
Transmission: 4-speed auto.	Wheelbase: 112.2 in.
Dimension/Capacity	Turning circle: 39.9 ft.
Passengers: 2/2/3	Cargo volume: 56.5 cu. ft.
Height/length/width:	GVWR: N/A
64.2/194.8/74.9 in.	Payload: 1,200–1,290 lb.
	Tow limit: 2,000–3,500 lb.
	Fuel tank: 75L/reg.
	Weight: 3,850 lb.

SAFETY FEATURES/CRASHWORTHINESS		
	Std.	**Opt.**
Quest ABS (4W)	■	❑
Seatbelt pretensioners	—	—
Side airbags	—	—
Traction control	—	—
Head restraints	**	*
Visibility (front/rear)	*****	**
Crash protection D/P	****	***
Crash protection (side) D/P	N/A	
Crash protection (offset)	*	
HLDI injury claims (model)	N/A	
HLDI injury claims (all)	N/A	

Note: NHTSA crash rating applies to '97 models; no tests done on redesigned '99 versions.

SUBARU

Subaru's overall product lineup for the year 2000 reinforces the company's return to its four-wheel drive roots with a continued emphasis put on its 4X4 capabilities and Outback versatility. (Half of all Legacys sold are Outbacks.) This year the entire Legacy line is redesigned and the Outback is spun off as a separate model.

Are Subarus good buys? Absolutely.

They provide reliable, reasonably priced 4X4 capability, but most Subaru owners could care less about the Outback's off-road prowess; only 5 percent will ever use their Subaru for that purpose. The other 95 percent just like knowing they have the option of going wherever they please, whenever they please. Even if they stay home.

Impreza

RATING: Above Average. If you don't need the AWD capability, you're wasting your money. **Strong points:** One of the most refined and reliable AWD drivetrains you'll find. Good acceleration with the 2.5 RS, excellent handling, lots of storage space, and better than average quality control. **Weak points:** 2.2L engine has little reserve power for highway cruising, especially when hooked to an automatic transmission; both engines are rough-running and noisy; limited rear seat room; difficult entry/exit, and very dealer-dependent for parts and servicing.

NEW FOR 2000: Nothing significant.

OVERVIEW: The full-time four-wheel drive Impreza is essentially a shorter Legacy with additional convenience features. It comes as a two-door coupe, a four-door sedan, a wagon that resembles the old

American Motors Pacer, and an Outback Sport wagon also powered by the 2.2L engine and dressed more aggressively in GT cladding.

The base engine is a peppy (with a manual transmission) 2.2L 142-hp 4-cylinder, but the optional 2.5L powerplant provides an extra dose of power for highway passing and additional torque when traversing rough or hazardous terrain. Buyers may choose either a 5-speed manual or a 4-speed automatic transmission.

Cost analysis/best alternatives: Get a discounted '99 model. If you really don't need a 4X4, here are some front-drives worth considering: '99 Ford Escort, Honda Civic, Mazda Protegé, and Toyota Corolla. **Options:** Anti-lock brakes. The RS version's safety and performance upgrades are well worth the extra cost. **Rebates:** $500–$1,000 rebates to clear out the '99 models. **Delivery/PDI:** $500. **Depreciation:** Slower than average. **Insurance cost:** Higher than average. **Parts supply/cost:** Parts aren't easy to find and can be costly. **Annual maintenance cost:** Higher than average. Mediocre, expensive servicing is hard to overcome because independent garages can't service key 4X4 powertrain components. **Warranty:** Bumper-to-bumper 3 years/60,000 km; powertrain 5 years/100,000 km; rust perforation 5 years/unlimited km. **Supplementary warranty:** A good idea. **Highway/city fuel economy:** 7.5–10.7L/100 km with the 2.2L engine and 7.7–10.5L/100 km with the 2.5L. **Annual fuel cost:** 2.2L: 1,852L=$1,074; 2.5L: 1,848L=$1,072. Interesting that the larger engine is $2 cheaper to run than the 2.2L.

Quality/Reliability/Safety

Pro: Quality control: Better than average. Above average quality mechanical components. **Reliability:** Powertrain components should be durable, and there are few mechanical problems that take these Subarus out of service. **Warranty performance:** Base warranty is fairly applied, but servicing quality is spotty. **Service bulletin problems:** Nothing significant. **Safety:** Huge, fold-away side mirrors.

Con: Body panel and trim fit and finish is inconsistent. **Owner-reported problems:** Poor engine idling, frequent cold weather stalling, manual transmission malfunctions, premature exhaust system rust-out and brake wear, minor electrical short circuits, catalytic converter failures, and paint peeling. **NHTSA safety complaints:** Driver burned from airbag deployment.

Road Performance

Pro: The 2.5L is the engine of choice. It's smooth and powerful with lots of low-end torque if you really need to go off-roading. The 2.2L engine is quite peppy with a manual gearbox when travelling over level terrain or darting in and out of city traffic. **Emergency handling:** Better than some sport-utilities. Tight cornering at highway speeds is done with minimal body lean and no loss of control. **Steering:** Precise and predictable. **Transmission:** The automatic transmission shifts smoothly. The all-wheel drive system is a boon for people who often need extra traction, and it works well with either a manual or an automatic transmission. The manual transmission's "hill holder" clutch prevents the car from rolling backwards when starting out. **Routine handling:** Smooth and nimble. Hurtles through corners effortlessly with a flat, solid stance and plenty of grip.

Con: Acceleration/torque: The 2.2L lacks sufficient mid-range torque to traverse hilly terrain without straining. When harnessed to an automatic transmission, it quickly loses steam. Uncomfortable ride with a full load. Larger tires would improve handling. Non-assisted steering requires maximum effort when parking. **Braking:** Average braking (100–0 km/h: 133 ft.). Barely adequate with the L models. Non-ABS braking may lead to loss of directional stability that causes the car to spin out of control.

Comfort/Convenience

Pro: Standard equipment: Well-appointed base models have a nice array of standard safety and convenience features. **Driving position:** Very good. Comfortable front seat and plenty of head and leg room. **Controls and displays:** Clear and simple dashboard and gauges. Very firm and supportive front seats. Versatile hatchback design. **Trunk/liftover:** Trunk has a low liftover.

Con: The coupe's narrow rear window and large rear pillars hinder rear visibility. Radio has awkward-to-access, poorly marked, tiny buttons. **Climate control:** The heater is insufficient and air distribution is inadequate. Tiny, confusing radio controls. **Entry/exit:** Small doors and entryways restrict rear access. **Interior space/comfort F/R:** Front shoulder belts are uncomfortable and rear seatbelts are hard to buckle up. Front and rear seat leg room may be insufficient for tall drivers. Rear seating is uncomfortable and limited to two small passengers. **Cargo space:** Not exceptional. Even though the wagon has extra storage capacity, overall capacity is a bit limited. **Trunk/liftover:** Small trunk. **Quietness:** This is not a quiet car. The clutch pedal and the dash click, the engine roars, and the fan whirs.

COST				
List Price (negotiable)	**Residual Values** (months)			
	24	36	48	60
Base Impreza:				
$21,995 (18%)	$15,000	$12,000	$10,000	$8,000

TECHNICAL DATA

Powertrain (AWD)
Engines: 2.2L 4-cyl. (142 hp)
• 2.5L 4-cyl. (165 hp)
Transmissions: 5-speed man.
• 4-speed auto.
Dimension/Capacity (Outback
  Sport)
Passengers: 2/3
Height/length/width:
60/172.2/67.1 in.

Head room F/R: 39.2/37.4 in.
Leg room F/R: 43.1/32.4 in.
Wheelbase: 99.2 in.
Turning circle: 36 ft.
Cargo volume: 19.5 cu. ft.
Tow limit: 1,500 lb.
Fuel tank: 50L/reg.
Weight: 2,900 lb.

SAFETY FEATURES/CRASHWORTHINESS

	Std.	Opt.
Anti-lock brakes	❑	■
Seatbelt pretensioners	—	—
Side airbags	—	—
Traction control	—	—
Head restraints	N/A	N/A
Visibility (front/rear)	*****	**
Crash protection (front) D/P	****	****
Crash protection (side) D/P	N/A	
Crash protection (offset)	N/A	
HLDI injury claims (model)	*****	
HLDI injury claims (all)	***	

Note: Rear visibility rating applies only to the coupe.

Legacy Outback, Forester

Legacy

RATING: Above Average. The AWD is what this car is all about. Without it, the Legacy is just a mediocre, middle-of-the-road sedan or wagon that would be lucky to get an average rating. **Strong points:** A refined and reliable AWD system, a comfortable ride, and better than average crashworthiness ratings, as well as fewer than average accident injury claims. **Weak points:** The reworked 2.5L is only a so-so performer (its additional torque is miniscule), problematic manual and automatic transmissions, mediocre handling, excessive engine and road noise, cramped back seat, and very dealer-dependent for parts and servicing.

NEW FOR 2000: Redesigned this year with the following improvements: a larger cabin, a small torque boost for the 2.5L engine, and anti-lock brakes. For the GT: front side-impact airbags and a standard limited-slip differential. Forester gets the same standard limited-slip differential.

OVERVIEW: A competent, full-time 4X4 performer for drivers who want to move up in size, comfort, and features. Available as a four-door sedan or five-door wagon, the Legacy is cleanly and conventionally styled, with even a hint of the Acura Legend in the rear end.

Owners who prize Subaru's rugged reliability and distinctive styling may find the Legacy too "modern." Nowhere is there any sign of the excessive reliance upon chrome moulding and oddball styling that has turned off buyers in the past. Another plus is that the Legacy's interior dimensions are similar to the Accord's—the benchmark for comfortable four-door sedans.

The Legacy Outback is a marketing coup that stretches the definition of sport-utility by simply customizing the AWD Legacy wagon to give it more of an outdoorsy flair. American Motors tried the same marketing approach with the Eagle several decades ago and failed miserably due to poor quality control, lousy marketing, and a passive public whose concept of off-road thrills was a night at the drive-in.

Another Subaru spin-off, the Forester, is a cross between a wagon and a sport-utility. Built on the Legacy's platform, the Forester uses the Legacy Outback's 2.5L 165-hp engine coupled to a 5-speed manual transmission, or an optional 4-speed automatic.

Cost analysis/best alternatives: Get this year's model for the upgrades. Front-drives worth considering: Honda Accord, Toyota Camry, and VW Passat. Worthwhile 4X4s: the Honda CR-V, second-series Nissan Xterra, Suzuki Grand Vitara, and Toyota RAV4. **Options:** ABS. **Rebates:** $750 rebates to clear out the '99s. Matching dealer incentives are also applicable. **Delivery/PDI:** $500. **Depreciation:** Slower than average. **Insurance cost:** Higher than average. **Parts supply/cost:** Parts aren't easily found and can be costly. **Annual maintenance cost:** Average. **Warranty:** Bumper-to-bumper 3 years/60,000 km; powertrain 5 years/ 100,000 km; rust perforation 5 years/unlimited km. **Supplementary warranty:** A good idea. **Highway/city fuel economy:** 7.6–10.5L/100 km with the 2.2L and 8.2–11.4L/100 km with the 2.5L engine. **Annual fuel cost:** 2.2L: 1,839L=$1,067; 2.5L: 1,992L=$1,155.

Quality/Reliability/Safety

Pro: Quality control: Average, though powertrain defects have begun cropping up. Above average body assembly and finish. **Service bulletin problems:** Nothing important.

Con: Reliability: Powertrain defects can sideline the car for days. Engine and transmission problems keep showing up. One owner of a '98 Legacy Outback has replaced his engine twice, at 800 km and 4,000 km. There are several reports of the transmission jumping out of first gear, or using first gear to slow down or to descend a steep grade. **Warranty performance:** Servicing quality is spotty. **Owner-reported problems:** The above-mentioned powertrain deficiencies and minor electrical, fuel system, and automatic transmission problems are common. Owners report that the front brakes require more attention than average. Premature surface rust and exhaust system rust-out are common. Servicing can be awkward because of the crowded engine compartment, particularly on turbocharged versions. Small horn buttons may be hard to find in an emergency. **NHTSA safety complaints/safety:** Igniter failure allowed unburned gasoline to flow into catalytic converter and resulted in chronic stalling; ABS brake failure; cruise control failed to disengage when brake pedal was depressed; fuel sloshes in fuel tank due to the absence of baffles; during a collision, airbags deployed but failed to inflate; the suspension's design causes severe pulling to one side; engine failure due to a cracked #2 piston; frequent surging from a stop; rear centre seatbelt prevents the secure attachment of child safety seats.

Road Performance

Pro: Steering: Acceptable steering response and average handling at moderate speeds. **Acceleration/torque:** The 2.5L engine is a competent performer only with a manual gearbox (0–100 km/h: 9.7 sec.). **Transmission:** The electronically controlled automatic has a power mode and a manual button that holds the lower gears a bit longer to reduce irritating gear hunting. **Routine handling:** Fairly soft and comfortable ride. The GT's firmer suspension exhibits above average handling. **Braking:** A bit better than average (100–0 km/h: 126 ft.).

Con: Engine is noisy and rough-running. The automatic transmission shifts into too high a gear to adequately exploit the engine's power and is reluctant to downshift into the proper gear. Manual transmission's shift linkage isn't suitable for rapid gear changes. **Emergency handling:** Rear end tends to swing out during high-speed cornering and there's too much body lean in turns at lesser speeds.

Comfort/Convenience

Pro: Standard equipment: Well appointed. **Driving position:** Low but comfortable driving position, with plenty of head and leg room. Good fore and aft visibility. The left foot rest prevents cramping. Adjustable driver's seat on the deluxe model. **Controls and displays:** Well designed, sweeping dashboard (similar to the Accord's) and control layout. Easy-to-read analogue gauges. **Climate control:** Excellent climate control system that's both efficient and quiet. **Entry/exit:** Tall doors make for easy front and rear access. **Interior space/comfort F/R:** Seating for four adults offers good front and rear head and leg room. Comfortable cloth-covered seats with plenty of side and shoulder support. **Cargo space:** Better than average cargo capacity. **Trunk/liftover:** The wagon's cavernous trunk is expandable with split rear seatbacks.

Con: It's a tight fit for the middle rear seat passenger. Power window and lock switches aren't easily accessible. Limited-service spare tire. Sedan has a small trunk, which is expandable only through a rear-seat pass through. **Quietness:** Excessive engine noise.

COST

List Price (firm)	Residual Values (months)			
	24	**36**	**48**	**60**
Forester: $26,695 (20%)	$20,000	$17,000	$13,000	$11,000
Legacy Outback:				
$31,395 (20%)	$22,000	$19,000	$15,000	$13,000

TECHNICAL DATA

Powertrain (AWD)
Engines: 2.5L 4-cyl. (165 hp)
Transmissions: 5-speed man.
• 4-speed auto.
Dimension/Capacity ('99)
Passengers: 2/3
Height/length/width:
55.3/180.9/67.5 in.

Head room F/R: 37.2/36.5 in.
Leg room F/R: 43.3/34.6 in.
Wheelbase: 103.5 in.
Turning circle: 38 ft.
Cargo volume: 13 cu. ft.
Tow limit: 1,500 lb.
Fuel tank: 60L/reg.
Weight: 2,400 lb.

SAFETY FEATURES/CRASHWORTHINESS

	Std.	Opt.
Anti-lock brakes (4W)	■	❑
Seatbelt pretensioners	■	❑
Side airbags	■	❑
Traction control	■	❑
Head restraints	**	**
Visibility (front/rear)	*****	*****
Crash protection (front) D/P	****	****
Crash protection (side) D/P	***	N/A
Crash protection (offset)	***	
HLDI injury claims (model)	****	
HLDI injury claims (all)	****	

SUZUKI

As GM's sales decline, Suzuki's sales have been less than stellar over the past several years (down almost 20 percent for the first half of 1999), although its Vitara and Grand Vitara sport-utilities launched last year are quite popular. Actually, with the exception of its ill-fated X-90 sport-utility, Suzuki has been making very good entry-level small cars and sport-utility vehicles for over a decade. But most buyers aren't familiar with the company's products because they're mostly sold under GM's name. In fact, the company makes only three mainstream vehicles: the Swift (GM's Metro twin), the Esteem, and the Vitara—a vehicle sold by General Motors of Canada as the Tracker.

Vitara, Grand Vitara/Tracker (GM)

Vitara

RATING: *Vitara/Tracker:* Below Average; *Grand Vitara:* Average. These truck-based sport-utilities' lack of refinement relegates them primarily to off-road use. A more comprehensive rating is given in *Lemon-Aid 4X4s, Vans, and Trucks 2000.*

OVERVIEW: The Vitara/Tracker is longer, wider, taller, and handles much better (read: less tippy) than the Sidekick it replaced. Essentially an entry-level version of the Grand Vitara, the Vitara carries a smaller 2.0L 127-hp 4-cylinder engine, less standard equipment, and a smaller price tag. It's Canadian-built at Suzuki's CAMI factory in Ingersoll, Ontario, alongside its Tracker twin.

Suzuki's top-line entry, the Grand Vitara, is an import that arrives with a competent, though not very powerful, 24-valve, 2.5L 155-hp V6 powerplant coveted by GM for its Vitara. In fact, GM is reportedly seething after its request for a V6-equipped Tracker was turned down.

Other standard features include a full-sized spare tire and four-wheel ABS on any "+" model.

Selling for $23,995, the Grand Vitara is a versatile truck-base, body-on-frame sport-utility that may not provide as much car-like handling as the Honda CR-V and Toyota RAV4, but neither Honda nor Toyota can offer V6 power and shift-on-the-fly capability. Furthermore, its plastic lower body and wheel-well covers effectively ward off rust and parking-lot dents. Inside, there's plenty of head room, arm room, and leg room, but like the RAV4, the interior is somewhat narrow—hips and thighs are pressed uncomfortably against the armrests. The rear seats and seatbacks fold flat, adding to cargo capacity, and there are plenty of small trays, bins, and compartments in which to store things.

Neither model has been crash-tested by NHTSA. However, the Vitara was given an "acceptable" rating by the IIHS for offset-impact collision protection.

COSTS

List Price (negotiable)	Residual Values (months)			
	24	36	48	60
Tracker 4X4 convert.:				
$19,995 (15%)	$14,000	$12,000	$10,000	$8,000
Vitara 4d: $20,795 (13%)	$16,000	$14,000	$12,000	$10,000
Grand Vitara JLX:				
$23,995 (13%)	$18,000	$16,000	$14,000	$11,000

TECHNICAL DATA

Powertrain (rear-drive/part-time 4X4)
Engines: 1.6L 4-cyl. (97 hp)
• 2.0L 4-cyl. (127 hp)
• 2.5L V6 (155 hp)
Transmissions: 5-speed man.
• 3-speed auto.
• 4-speed auto.
Dimension/Capacity (Vitara)
Passengers: 2/3
Height/length/width:
66.3/162.4/66.7 in.

Head room F/R: 39.9/39.6 in.
Leg room F/R: 41.4/35.9 in.
Wheelbase: 97.6 in.
Turning circle: 37 ft.
Cargo volume: 30 cu. ft.
GVWR: 3,373–3,593 lb.
Payload: N/A
Tow limit: 1,000 lb.
Fuel tank: 66L/reg.
Weight: 2,450 lb.

SAFETY FEATURES/CRASHWORTHINESS

	Std.	Opt.
Anti-lock brakes (4W)	❑	■
Safety belt pretensioners	—	—
Side airbags	—	—
Traction control	—	—
Head restraints	****	****
Visibility (front/rear)	*****	*
Crash protection (front) D/P	N/A	
Crash protection (side) D/P	N/A	

Crash protection (offset)	***
HLDI injury claims (model)	N/A
HLDI injury claims (all)	N/A

Esteem, Swift

Esteem

RATING: Average. Both the Swift and Esteem are best used as urban commuter cars. **Strong points:** Nice handling, plenty of cargo room (wagon), good fuel economy, nimble handling, and better than average quality control. **Weak points:** Weak, noisy engine; poor rear visibility; poor braking and ride; excessive engine, road and wind noise; rear seat room limited to two passengers in comfort; and insufficient crashworthiness and accident injury claim data.

NEW FOR 2000: Both vehicles return this year relatively unchanged. The Swift will be dropped at the end of the 2000 model year, while the Esteem is scheduled to receive a standard 122-hp 1.8L four by the end of the year.

OVERVIEW: The Esteem is Suzuki's small four-door imported sedan; Swift is its Canadian-made two-door hatchback twin. Smaller than the Honda Civic and Dodge Neon, both cars have a fairly spacious interior, offering comparable or better rear accommodation for two full-sized adults than many cars in their class.

The base GL and upscale GLX come loaded with standard features that cost extra on other models. The GL, for example, comes with power steering, rear-window defroster, remote trunk and fuel filler door releases, tinted glass, and a fold-down rear seat (great for extra cargo space). GLX shoppers can look forward to standard ABS, power windows and door locks, and a host of other interior refinements.

Cost analysis/best alternatives: Forget the cheaper '99 model; buy this year's model for the power boost. Other cars worth considering are the GM Metro and Firefly, Honda Civic, Hyundai Accent, and Nissan Sentra. **Options:** Think twice about adding an automatic transmission; as with so many other small cars with small engines, it shifts harshly and cuts fuel economy. Also, ditch the 13-inch tires for ones that are larger. Rear-wheel lockup when braking is a certainty without ABS. **Rebates:** $500 on the '99 models. **Delivery/PDI:** $450. **Depreciation:** Slower than average. **Insurance cost:** Average. **Parts supply/cost:** Suzuki parts are occasionally expensive, but not that hard to find. **Annual maintenance cost:** Average. Servicing can be done by any independent garage, and maintenance is made simple by an uncluttered under-hood layout. **Warranty:** Bumper-to-bumper 3 years/80,000 km; rust perforation 5 years/unlimited km. **Supplementary warranty:** A good idea is you plan to keep the car longer than three years. **Highway/city fuel economy:** 6.4–8.6L/100 km. **Annual fuel cost:** 1,522L=$883.

Quality/Reliability/Safety

Pro: Quality control: Better than average. **Reliability:** Many of the mechanical components have been used on Suzuki's other models with few reliability problems reported. **Warranty performance:** Average. **Service bulletin problems:** Nothing published, yet.

Con: Body panels and trim are flimsy, and wind and water leaks may be a problem. **Owner-reported problems:** Problems include noisy front metallic brake pads, wind and water intrusion into the passenger compartment, and fragile body panels and trim items. **NHTSA safety complaints/safety:** Sudden acceleration from a stop.

Road Performance

Pro: Acceleration/torque: The ugraded engine delivers respectable acceleration. **Emergency handling:** Average. **Steering:** Predictable and precise. **Transmission:** The manual gearbox performs flawlessly. **Routine handling:** Better than average, thanks to the Esteem's 4-wheel independent suspension, which gives just the right balance between a comfortable ride and no-surprise handling.

Con: Small tires compromise handling. Power steering doesn't transmit much road feedback. The Esteem's automatic transmission shifts harshly and vibrates excessively between gear changes. **Braking:** Terrible braking for cars this light (100–0 km/h: 149 ft.).

Comfort/Convenience

Pro: Standard equipment: Many standard features that would cost extra on other small cars. **Driving position:** Very comfortable. Everything's within reach and there's plenty of head and leg room. **Controls and displays:** Nicely laid-out instruments and controls. **Climate control:** Efficient, quiet-running heater, defroster, and AC. **Interior space/comfort F/R:** Despite sitting on a small wheelbase, the interior space beats out most of the competition. Roomy cabin has lots of front and rear head room and leg room for four adults. **Cargo space:** Fairly good with the sedan; exceptional with the wagon's rear seats folded. **Trunk/liftover:** Average trunk space; a low sill makes for easier loading.

Con: Boring, bland styling. Vinyl upholstery. A narrow windshield and thick pillars hinder rear visibility. Thinly padded rear bench seat. **Entry/exit:** Narrow rear doors complicate rear seat access. **Trunk/liftover:** Sedan's trunk opening is a bit small. **Quietness:** Excessive wind, road, and engine noise.

COST

List Price (negotiable)	Residual Values (months)			
	24	36	48	60
Esteem GL: $15,495 (10%)	$11,000	$9,000	$7,000	$6,000
Swift DLX: $11,595 (9%)	$8,500	$7,000	$5,000	$4,000

TECHNICAL DATA

Powertrain (front-drive)
Engines: 1.0L 3-cyl. (55 hp)
• 1.3L 4-cyl. (70 hp)
• 1.8L 4-cyl. (122 hp)
Transmissions: 5-speed man.
• 4-speed auto.
Dimension/Capacity (Esteem)
Passengers: 2/3; 2/2
Height/length/width:
53.9/165.2/66.5 in.

Head room F/R: 39.1/37.2 in.
Leg room F/R: 42.3/34.1 in.
Wheelbase: 97.6 in.
Turning circle: 35 ft.
Cargo volume:12 cu. ft.
Tow limit: N/A
Fuel tank: 51L/reg.
Weight: 2,200 lb.

SAFETY FEATURES/CRASHWORTHINESS

	Std.	Opt.
Anti-lock brakes	❏	■
Seatbelt pretensioners	—	—
Side airbags	—	—
Traction control	—	—
Head restraints	**	**
Visibility (front/rear)	*****	**
Crash protection (front) D/P	N/A	
Crash protection (side) D/P	N/A	
Crash protection (offset)	N/A	
HLDI injury claims (model)	N/A	
HLDI injury claims (all)	N/A	

TOYOTA

There's no longer much difference between Toyota and Honda when it comes to the overall reliability and durability of their products. True, Toyotas hold up very well over the years, but Honda has more competitive prices, and is on the cutting edge of new technology relating to fuel economy and performance. Both automakers make vehicles that are especially forgiving of owner neglect and cost very little to service at independent garages. Also, warranty performance is outstanding—Honda and Toyota customers are treated generously even after the warranty has expired. But the kicker for most buyers is how little their vehicles depreciate; it's not unusual to see a five-year-old sedan selling for almost half its original selling price—a value reached by most Big Three American vehicles between the second and third year of ownership.

As for customer dissatisfaction with arrogant and ill-informed salespeople and service managers—a *Lemon-Aid* criticism for the last few years—the company has taken remedial steps that have apparently improved relations with its dealers and their customers in both the showroom and service bay. Now when you call Toyota's customer relations staff, you can rest assured that your claim will be handled more professionally and competently than in the past. Hopefully, this trend will continue.

Believe it or not, there *are* some generic factory-related problems with Toyotas, but they're all mostly minor glitches affecting the front brakes, electrical system, AC, and accessories like the sound system and trim items.

Apart from launching the Echo (a Tercel replacement) and Tundra, and redesigning the Celica, this year's product lineup remains practically unchanged.

Echo

Echo

RATING: Not Recommended during its first year on the market. Although Toyotas don't have as many "teething" problems with newly launched models as do other automakers, you'll get a better-made vehicle six months down the road.

OVERVIEW: Toyota scrapped its stripped-down Tercel in favour of the $13,835 Echo, a new entry-level model that the company says uses some of the same engine technology as the Lexus. Both two- and four-door models will be available, and the car will cost substantially less than the Corolla and a bit more than the discontinued Tercel. Echo will offer about the same amount of passenger space as the Corolla, thanks to a high roof and low floor height.

Cockpit controls and instrumentation will be particularly user-friendly, located high on the dash and more toward the centre of the vehicle, rather than directly in front of the driver, where many gauges and controls are hidden by the steering column. Toyota says the repositioning of the instrument cluster farther away from the driver requires less refocusing of the eyes from far to near, which produces less driving fatigue and eye strain.

Echo will be powered by an all-new, 100-plus horsepower, 1.5L 4-cylinder engine featuring Variable Valve Timing cylinder head technology. It's the same design used in Lexus to combine power and fuel economy in a low-emissions vehicle. **Best alternatives:** Other cars worth considering are the GM Metro and Firefly, Honda Civic, Hyundai Accent, Mazda Protegé, and Nissan Sentra.

Corolla

Corolla

RATING: Above Average. **Strong points:** Effective powertrain setup, pleasant ride, good braking, better than average quality control, better than average crashworthiness scores, and a high resale value. **Weak points:** Few standard features, rear seating is not for three adults, clumsy emergency handling, some reports of airbags deploying inadvertently or failing to deploy, only hard-to-find stripped versions are reasonably priced.

NEW FOR 2000: Five more horses; a facelift is scheduled for next year, prior to a 2003 redesign.

OVERVIEW: The Corolla has long been Toyota's standard-bearer in the subcompact sedan class. Over the years, however, the car has grown in size, price, and refinement to the point where it can now be considered a small family sedan. All Corollas ride on a front-wheel-drive platform with independent suspension on all wheels. Four-wheel drive has been dropped as an option on the four-door sedan.

Cost analysis/best alternatives: Except for an insignificant power boost on the 2000, the '99 models are identical to this year's version and represent the better buy if discounted by about 10 percent. Other small cars that represent good investments are the '99 Ford Escort, Honda Civic, and Mazda Protegé. **Options:** The optional 4-speed automatic is worth consideration. Stay away from the 3-speed; it's mainly for rental agencies and driving schools. Also, consider the built-in rear child seat. Air conditioning saps horsepower considerably; test-drive an AC- and automatic transmission-equipped Corolla before making a final decision. For better steering response and additional high-speed stability, order the optional 185/65R14 tires that come with the LE. **Rebates:** Not likely. **Delivery/PDI:** $500. **Depreciation:** Much slower than average. **Insurance cost:** Higher than average. **Parts supply/cost:** Parts are easily found and reasonably priced. **Annual maintenance cost:** Lower than average. **Warranty:** Bumper-to-bumper 3 years/60,000 km; powertrain 5 years/100,000 km; rust perforation 5 years/unlimited km. **Supplementary warranty:** Not needed. **Highway/city fuel economy:** 6.8–8.5L/100 km with the 1.8L and an automatic transmission. **Annual fuel cost:** 1,547L=$897.

Quality/Reliability/Safety

Pro: Quality control: Better than average component and assembly quality. **Reliability:** The Corolla is one of the most reliable cars sold. **Warranty performance:** Fair and generous in interpreting warranty obligations, even after the base warranty expires.

Con: The Corolla has fallen from its Recommended status, due mainly to the flurry of safety complaints reported to government safety officials. Makes one wonder if this isn't an early warning that Toyota went too far in "decontenting" the Corolla several years ago. **Owner-reported problems:** Premature exhaust system rusting, front brake wear, and electrical glitches are the more common problems. **Service bulletin problems:** Steering column noise. **NHTSA safety complaints/safety:** When the vehicle was parked the parking brake was released and both airbags deployed; both airbags deployed right after driver turned on the ignition switch; airbags deployed after car passed over a bump in the road; side airbag failed to deploy in a side impact; faulty seatbelt wiring could cause a fire; brake failure when decelerating; when brakes are applied, pedal goes soft, resulting in extended stopping distances; sudden collapse of the rear axle; rear control arm broke while driving at 110 km/h; vehicle pulls to the left or right at moderate speeds; rear seatbelt is not compatible with securing a child safety seat.

Road Performance

Pro: Acceleration/torque: Good, but not impressive, acceleration times. **Transmission:** Both manual and automatic transmissions shift smoothly. The automatic permits you to lock out fourth gear for towing or when climbing long grades. The manual transmission gives the Corolla extra pep and uses a light clutch for effortless shifting. **Routine handling:** Average handling under normal driving conditions; the ride is busy, but comfortable. This is characteristic of Toyota products where handling takes second place to comfort. **Braking:** Better than average performance without ABS (100–0 km/h: 123 ft.).

Con: AC and an automatic transmission can seriously reduce engine horsepower. **Emergency handling:** A bit clumsy, with some body roll, and sometimes the car plows straight ahead in hard cornering. Ride quality deteriorates as the load increases. **Steering:** Not much road feel. The sedan's ABS braking isn't impressive—too much weaving and veering to one side.

Comfort/Convenience

Pro: Standard equipment: Fairly well-equipped, with many past optional features standard this year. **Controls and displays:** The instrument panel and control layout are exceptionally user-friendly. **Climate control:** First-class heating, defrosting, and ventilation system. **Entry/exit:** Wide rear doors facilitate access to the rear. **Interior space/comfort F/R:** Comfortable front seating; the wagon's rear seat will hold two comfortably. **Cargo space:** Spacious cargo area on the wagon. The rear seatback can be folded down. **Trunk/liftover:** Large trunk on the sedan has a low sill for easy loading. **Quietness:** Very little noise intrudes into the passenger compartment.

Con: DLX models don't have a deluxe interior. **Driving position:** In models equipped with a sunroof, tall drivers may find the front head room, thigh support, and leg room inadequate. Short drivers may have trouble seeing over the wagon's hood. Rear seating is compromised by insufficient toe and leg room. **Climate control:** Climate controls aren't user-friendly and there's no automatic shutoff for the rear defroster. **Interior space/comfort F/R:** Tight rear seating and limited rear foot room. Trunk lid hinges can damage luggage. Base models don't have the handy split folding seatbacks that increase storage space.

COST

List Price (very negotiable)	Residual Values (months)			
	24	36	48	60
Corolla: $15,625 (9%)	$12,000	$10,000	$8,500	$7,000

TECHNICAL DATA

Powertrain (front-drive)	Head room F/R: 39.3/36.9 in.
Engine: 1.8L 4-cyl. (125 hp)	Leg room F/R: 42.5/33.2 in.
Transmissions: 5-speed man.	Wheelbase: 97 in.
• 3-speed auto.	Turning circle: 34 ft.
• 4-speed auto.	Cargo volume: 12.1 cu. ft.
Dimension/Capacity	Tow limit: 1,000 lb.
Passengers: 2/3	Fuel tank: 50L/reg.
Height/length/width:	Weight: 2,400 lb. (est.)
54.5/174/66.7 in.	

SAFETY FEATURES/CRASHWORTHINESS

	Std.	Opt.
Anti-lock brakes	❏	■
Seatbelt pretensioners	■	❏
Side airbags	❏	■
Traction control	—	—
Head restraints	***	***
Visibility (front/rear)	*****	*****
Crash protection (front) D/P	****	****

Crash protection (side) D/P	****	***
Crash protection (offset)	***	
HLDI injury claims (model)	N/A	
HLDI injury claims (all)	N/A	

Camry, Solara

Camry

RATING: Recommended. Strong points: Excellent powertrain setup
(V6), 4-cylinder is also a competent performer, pleasant ride, quiet
interior, well-laid-out instrumentation and controls, legendary reliability, and a high resale value. *Solara:* More attractively styled than the
sedan. **Weak points:** Suspension may be a bit too soft for some and
noisy at times, limited over-the-shoulder visibility, little steering feedback, inadequate rear seating for three adults due to insufficient head
and shoulder room, and annoying windshield reflections at night. Also,
an unusually large number of safety-related complaints registered by
government safety investigators may show that Toyota went too far in its
cost-cutting, "decontenting" strategy adopted several years ago. *Solara:*
Tricky entry/exit, and trunk has a small opening and high sill.

NEW FOR 2000: No significant changes, except for a slight restyling
and sound system upgrades. A redesign is scheduled for the 2002
model year. A convertible Solara will debut for the 2001 model year.

OVERVIEW: The Camry is available only as a four-door sedan—gone
is the station wagon variant and the coupe has been designated the
Solara (see below). The Camry is powered by a peppy 2.2L 133-hp
16-valve 4-cylinder engine (taken from the Celica), and an optional
3.0L 24-valve V6 that unleashes 194 horses. Either engine can be coupled to a 5-speed manual or an electronically controlled 4-speed automatic. The suspension features MacPherson struts up front, dual-link
mounted struts at the rear, gas-pressurized shocks for better damping,

and stabilizer bars in the front and rear. Control is further maintained through speed-sensing variable power steering.

Camrys have fallen behind in the standard equipment offered in its base models, obviously a result of Toyota's "decontenting" its products to keep prices down. For example, all 4-cylinder Camrys still use rear drum brakes while most of the competition use disc brakes; variable intermittent wipers are found only on top-of-the-line Camrys while the competition spread them throughout their lineup; the Camrys' MacPherson strut suspension is no match for the Accords' double-wishbone suspension at all four corners; and Camrys now have single-seal doors while Accords use double seals—and the Taurus uses triple.

But there is a nice array of safety features: ABS and traction control are standard on all V6-equipped models, rear seats have shoulder belts for the middle passenger, low beam lights are brighter, headlights switch on and off automatically as conditions change, and front side airbags are optional.

The Solara's small, but it's not cheap. Built in Cambridge, Ontario, a base model Solara costs $26,655, but put in the Sienna and Lexus ES 300's V6 powerplant and you can expect to pay thousands more.

Introduced in the summer of 1998, the Solara is essentially a longer, lower, bare-bones, two-door Camry with a sportier powertrain and suspension and a more stylish exterior. But don't let this put you off. Most new Toyota model offerings, like the Sienna, Avalon, and RAV4s, are Camry derivatives.

You have a choice of either a 4- or 6-cylinder powerplant. Unfortunately, if you choose the V6, you also get a gimmicky rear spoiler and a head room-robbing moon roof. The stiff body structure and suspension, as well as tight steering, make for easy sports car-like handling, with lots of road feel and few surprises.

Cost analysis/best alternatives: A 1999 model Camry or Solara would be your best bet if discounted by about 10 percent. Prices are at their highest during the fall, and most of the initial supply will be snapped up by leasing agencies and rental car firms, creating delays of 90 days or more for everyday buyers (make sure you have a *specific* delivery date spelled out in the contract along with a *protected* price, in case there's a price increase while you're waiting for delivery). Other cars worth considering are the Honda Accord, Lexus ES 300, and Nissan Maxima. **Options:** The built-in child safety seat ($150). Stay away from the optional sunroof; it robs you of much-needed head room. Toyota's base radio and tape player have been failure-prone in the past; buy a better sound system from an independent supplier. **Rebates:** Not likely. **Delivery/PDI:** $500. **Depreciation:** Slower than average. **Insurance cost:** Higher than average. **Parts supply/cost:** Parts are easily found and moderately priced. **Annual maintenance cost:** Less than average. **Warranty:** Bumper-to-bumper 3 years/60,000 km; powertrain 5 years/100,000 km; rust perforation 5 years/unlimited km. **Supplementary warranty:** Not needed. **Highway/city fuel economy:** 7.2–10.4L/100 km with the 2.2L and automatic transmission, and 7.8–11.9L/100 km with the 3.0L and an automatic transmission. **Annual fuel cost:** 2.2L: 1,792L=$1,039; 3.0L: 2,011L=$1,166. Transport Canada says there is no fuel savings difference between the Camry and the Solara.

Quality/Reliability/Safety

Pro: Quality control: Exceptional. First-class body assembly and component quality. **Reliability:** One of the most reliable cars on the market. **Warranty performance:** Much better than average. Customers usually get a fair shake, even if the warranty has expired.

Con: Owner-reported problems: Chronic braking problems even though pads and calipers are replaced repeatedly; suspension failures, and body/accessories glitches. The unusually large number of safety-related complaints during the past two years raises concerns that Toyota's last Camry redesign has cheapened the product. **Service bulletin problems:** Front brakes may make a groaning or grinding noise; troubleshooting other brake noises; improvements affecting the centre console compartment door latch. **NHTSA safety complaints/safety:** Under-hood fire (left-side) while vehicle was parked overnight; airbags failed to deploy; inadvertent airbag deployment; faulty cruise control caused vehicle to suddenly accelerate; sudden acceleration without braking effect; excessive grinding noise and long stopping distances associated with ABS braking; pedal went to floor but no braking effect; defective rear brake drum; vehicle tends to drift to the right at highway speeds; excessive steering wheel vibrations at speeds over 100 km/h; suspension bottoms out too easily, damaging the undercarriage; too-compliant shock absorbers make for a rough ride over uneven terrain; car rolled backwards after put into Park and ignition key was removed; vehicle parked overnight has its rear window suddenly blow out; windshield distortion is a strain on the eyes; floor-mounted gear shift indicator is hard to read; seatbelts are too tight on either side and tighten up uncomfortably with the slightest movement; leaking suspension struts and strut rod failure; faulty driver's window track; driver-side door latch sticks; fuel tank makes a sloshing noise when three-quarters full.

Road Performance

Pro: Emergency handling: Very good. Minimal body roll and front-end plow. Responds well to sudden steering corrections. **Steering:** Quick to respond and predictable. **Acceleration/torque:** Better than average (0–100 km/h: 8.7 sec. with the V6), with sufficient reserve torque for passing. Both the 4- and 6-cylinder powerplants are more powerful and offer better fuel economy than do previous years' engines. The smooth and flexible 2.2L 4-cylinder engine is best mated to the 5-speed manual transmission and should be relegated to city commuting, although it's surprisingly peppy in the lower gear ranges. This car shines on long

drives, and for that you must have the exceptionally quiet-running 3.0L
V6. **Transmission:** Smooth-shifting automatic gearbox with a dual-mode
feature that allows the driver to choose either a power or economy setting. **Routine handling:** Nimble and predictable handling. Supple but
steady ride on all but the worst roads. **Braking:** Better than average braking with the optional anti-lock brakes (100–0 km/h: 128 ft.).

Con: Neither the 4-banger nor the V6 are high-performance engines,
but the Camry doesn't pretend to be a high-performance car. The
torque converter disengages noisily when traversing hilly terrain.
Overly compliant suspension makes for a busy ride when passing over
bumps, even for the more tightly sprung coupes. Little road feel with
power steering.

Comfort/Convenience

Pro: Standard equipment: Fully equipped. **Climate control:** Heater and
climate controls are well-situated and easy to use, with large buttons
and logical placement. Firm and supportive seats. **Controls and displays:** Well-designed instrument layout is both practical and attractive.
Climate control: Efficient heating, defrosting, and ventilation.
Entry/exit: Front and rear seats are easily accessible. **Interior
space/comfort F/R:** Roomy interior includes comfortable front seats
and large rear seats will easily accommodate three adults, though rear
head room is a bit tight for six-footers. **Cargo space:** Better than average. Huge glove box and lots of little storage bins and door map pockets. Huge but narrow cargo area on the wagon. **Trunk/liftover:**
Reasonably sized trunk has a low liftover sill and carries a full-size spare
tire. All models have split folding rear seatbacks with in-trunk security
locks.

Con: Standard equipment: Squarish, angular, and conservatively styled,
the Camry lacks distinctiveness. Rear taillights look to be the wrong size
for the allocated space. Side-view mirrors don't spring back (if you clip
your garage door, kiss your insurance deductible good-bye). You can
get the manual transmission and V6, but only with the CE model.
Driving position: The side-view mirrors can't be adjusted from inside
unless you go for the power option. Front seat centre console armrest is
set too far back to be comfortable. Limited over-the-shoulder visibility,
worse with the Solara. **Entry/exit:** Difficult with the Solara's narrow rear
passageway and the lack of a driver's seat slide-forward mechanism.
Cargo space: Tall rear suspension towers cut into luggage space. Trunk
hinges can damage cargo. Solara's trunk isn't user-friendly with its
small opening and high sill. **Quietness:** Noisy suspension transmits lots
of shock absorber clunk and tire rumble into the passenger cabin.

COST

List Price (negotiable)	Residual Values (months)			
	24	**36**	**48**	**60**
Camry CE: $24,070 (12%)	$19,000	$17,000	$14,000	$12,000
Solara: $26,655 (12%)	$20,000	$18,000	$15,000	$13,000

TECHNICAL DATA

Powertrain (front-drive)
Engines: 2.2L 4-cyl. (133 hp)
• 2.2L 4-cyl. (135 hp)
• 3.0L V6 (194 hp)
• 3.0L V6 (200 hp)
Transmissions: 5-speed man.
• 4-speed auto.
Dimension/Capacity (Camry)
Passengers: 2/3
Height/length/width:
55.4/188.5/70.1 in.

Head room F/R: 38.7/37.6 in.
Leg room F/R: 43.5/35.6 in.
Wheelbase: 105.2 in.
Turning circle: 40 ft.
Cargo volume: 14.1 cu. ft.
Tow limit: 2,000 lb.
Fuel tank: 70L/reg.
Weight: 3,200 lb.

SAFETY FEATURES/CRASHWORTHINESS

	Std.	Opt.
Anti-lock brakes	■	■
Seatbelt pretensioners	■	❏
Side airbags	❏	■
Traction control	❏	■
Head restraints	***	***
Visibility (front/rear)	*****	*
Crash protection (front) D/P	****	*****
Crash protection (side) D/P		
Camry	***	***
Solara	***	*****
Crash protection (offset)	*****	
HLDI injury claims (model)	***	
HLDI injury claims (all)	***	

Note: Injury claim data and front and offset crash test scores apply only to the Camry.

Avalon

Avalon

RATING: Recommended. Essentially an all-dressed Camry or an entry-level Lexus. **Strong points:** Excellent powertrain performance, a roomy interior with plenty of storage space, and easy access to comfortable rear seats. Exceptional reliability, quiet interior, and a high resale value. Sportier handling than the Camry. **Weak points:** Rear corner blind spots, a bit fuel-thirsty.

NEW FOR 2000: The wheelbase has been lengthened to make for a roomier passenger compartment, the V6 gets 10 additional horses and the more fuel-efficient Variable Valve Timing first used on the Lexus, and standard ABS will be enhanced by offering optional traction control and skid control.

OVERVIEW: Toyota's largest model, this six-passenger near-luxury four-door offers more value and reliability than do other cars in its class that cost thousands of dollars more. A front-engine, front-drive, mid-sized sedan, based on a stretched Camry platform, the Avalon is similar in size to the Ford Taurus and bigger than the rear-drive Cressida it replaced.

The Avalon offers a 210-hp version of the Camry's 3.0L V6 power-plant coupled to a 4-speed electronically controlled automatic transaxle. Base models give a nice array of standard comfort and convenience features, including air conditioning, power windows, power door locks, cruise control, and an AM/FM cassette sound system. Safety features include standard ABS and a three-point shoulder belt for the rear centre seat passenger.

Cost analysis/best alternatives: Forget about bargain-hunting for a discounted '99 Avalon; you'll miss too many important upgrades found on this year's model. If you want a more driver-involved experience in a

Toyota/Lexus, consider a Lexus ES 300 or GS 300. Other cars you may wish to look at: the Ford Crown Victoria and Mercury Grand Marquis, Mazda Millenia, Nissan Maxima, and Toyota Camry V6. **Options:** The engine immobilizing anti-theft system. **Rebates:** $2,000 on the '99s. **Delivery/PDI:** $500. **Depreciation:** Slower than average. **Insurance cost:** Higher than average. **Parts supply/cost:** Parts are relatively inexpensive and easily found. **Annual maintenance cost:** Less than average. **Warranty:** Bumper-to-bumper 3 years/60,000 km; powertrain 5 years/ 100,000 km; rust perforation 5 years/unlimited km. **Supplementary warranty:** Not needed. **Highway/city fuel economy:** '99 Avalon: 7.4–11.4L/100 km. **Annual fuel cost:** 1,920L=$1,114.

Quality/Reliability/Safety

Pro: Quality control: Top-quality powertrain and body components. Much-improved brake durability. **Reliability:** The Avalon uses conventional mechanical components employed on Toyota's other models, which explains why there are no major reliability or durability problems. **Warranty performance:** Better than average. Warranty claims are handled in a fair and professional manner.

Con: Owner-reported problems: Owners report excessive wind noise intruding into the passenger compartment and some fragile trim items. **Service bulletin problems:** Front brakes may make a groaning or grinding noise; troubleshooting other brake noises. **NHTSA safety complaints/safety:** Sudden acceleration with no brakes; airbag deployed for no reason; side airbags failed to deploy in a side impact; transmission failure; fuel dampener and fuel pump failure caused fuel leak and fumes to enter interior; Bridgestone tire failure; upper steering knuckle broke; steering turned to the right, yet fails to respond.

Road Performance

Pro: Emergency handling: Slow, but sure-footed. **Acceleration/torque:** Brisk acceleration with the smooth, powerful, and quiet V6 engine; and there's plenty of torque for passing and traversing hilly terrain (0–100 km/h: 7.8 sec.). **Transmission:** The electronically controlled 4-speed automatic transmission is well matched to its power without any performance penalty. In fact, the powertrain setup is one of the smoothest, best-integrated combinations available. **Routine handling:** Better than average handling, thanks to the stiffened suspension. Ride quality is flawless, providing living-room comfort on virtually any kind of road. **Braking:** Better than average (100–0 km/h: 130 ft.).

Con: Steering: Power steering is over-assisted at all speeds, and the car has a tendency to oversteer. Tends to plow ahead when cornering at high speed.

Comfort/Convenience

Pro: Standard equipment: Loaded with standard safety and convenience features. **Driving position:** Plenty of room and comfortable, supportive seating. **Controls and displays:** Well-designed instrument layout is both practical and attractive, with controls that are both easy to see and well within reach (instruments are similar to the Camry's, with controls placed in all the familiar places). **Climate control:** Powerful climate control system—efficient heating, defrosting, and ventilation. User-friendly controls. **Entry/exit:** Easy access to both the front and rear seating areas. **Interior space/comfort F/R:** Roomier than the Camry; front and rear seats are exceptionally comfortable with plenty of thigh support and more room as a result of this year's lengthened wheelbase. Large rear seat will easily seat three people. **Trunk/liftover:** Enormous trunk has a low liftover sill. **Quietness:** Lots of sound insulation makes for an interior that's quieter, generally speaking, than the Camry's.

Con: Bland styling, with a hint of Lexus' GS 300. Limited rear corner visibility. **Controls and displays:** Radio controls are busy, with lots of identical buttons that are difficult to operate while driving. The cupholders are flimsy, and the fuzzy headliner has a cheap appearance. **Cargo space:** The Avalon doesn't have fold-down rear seats for trunk access and hauling long objects.

COST				
List Price (negotiable)	**Residual Values** (months)			
	24	36	48	60
Avalon XL: $37,000 (15%)	$28,000	$23,000	$19,000	$16,000

TECHNICAL DATA	
Powertrain (front-drive)	Head room F/R: 39.2/37.8 in.
Engine: 3.0L V6 (210 hp)	Leg room F/R: 44.2/38.3 in.
Transmission: 4-speed auto.	Wheelbase: 107.1 in.
Dimension/Capacity	Turning circle: 40 ft.
Passengers: 3/3	Cargo volume: 15 cu. ft.
Height/length/width:	Tow limit: 2,000 lb.
55.9/190.2/70.3 in.	Fuel tank: 70L/reg.
	Weight: 3,300 lb.

SAFETY FEATURES/CRASHWORTHINESS		
	Std.	Opt.
Anti-lock brakes	■	❑
Seatbelt pretensioners	■	❑
Side airbags	■	❑
Traction control	❑	■
Head restraints	***	*
Visibility (front/rear)	*****	**

Crash protection (front) D/P	****	*****
Crash protection (side) D/P	*****	****
Crash protection (offset)	**	
HLDI injury claims (model)	***	
HLDI injury claims (all)	****	

Celica

Celica

RATING: Recommended. This year's redesign addresses almost all of the Celica's earlier shortcomings. **Strong points:** Exceptionally well-matched engine and transmission, comfortable front seating, impressive reliability, and a high resale value. **Weak points:** Difficult rear seat access, rear seating not for three adults, pricey, no crashworthiness data, and a higher than average rate of accident injury claims.

NEW FOR 2000: A major redesign offers the following improvements: lighter weight, a shorter overall length set on a longer wheelbase, and a powerful 180-hp 1.8L 4-cylinder engine, a variant of the base 140-hp powerplant.

OVERVIEW: The front-wheel drive Celica offers benchmark reliability, good handling, and great fuel economy in an attractive sports car package. The GT and GTS have a firm suspension, well-equipped interior, ABS brakes, and a more sporting feel than do other versions. All handle competently and provide the kind of sporting performance expected from a car of this class. The extra performance in the higher-line versions does come at a price, but this isn't a problem given the high resale value and excellent reliability for which Celicas are known. Overall, it's one of the best choices in the sporty car field.

Cost analysis/best alternatives: Buy the upgraded year 2000 model for the engine and body upgrades. If you miss the GT version, try the Acura Integra or Honda Prelude. Other cars worth considering are the Ford Mustang, GM Camaro and Firebird, and Mazda Miata. **Options:** Not much worth buying. The Celica comes fairly well equipped. **Rebates:** Expect sizeable mid-year rebates on the '99s. **Delivery/PDI:** $500. **Depreciation:** Slower than average. **Insurance cost:** Higher than average. **Parts supply/cost:** Parts are relatively inexpensive and easily found. **Annual maintenance cost:** Less than average. **Warranty:** Bumper-to-bumper 3 years/60,000 km; powertrain 5 years/100,000 km; rust perforation 5 years/unlimited km. **Supplementary warranty:** Not necessary. **Highway/city fuel economy:** *'99 Celica:* 7.7–10.6L/100 km with the 2.2L and an automatic transmission. **Annual fuel cost:** 1,859L=$1,078.

Quality/Reliability/Safety

Pro: Quality Control: The best among automakers. **Reliability:** The Celica uses the same mechanical components that are employed on Toyota's other models, and this explains why there are no major reliability or durability problems. **Warranty performance:** Warranty claims are dealt with in an efficient, professional, and fair manner. **Service bulletin problems:** No defects reported.

Con: Owner-reported problems: The front brakes are troublesome; some audio systems and trim items have also been failure-prone. **NHTSA safety complaints/safety:** Rear glass may shatter when lowering the convertible top; water leaks through the sunroof.

Road Performance

Pro: Emergency handling: Better than average. **Steering:** Responsive, predictable power steering also transmits plenty of road feel. **Acceleration/torque:** The 2.2L powerplant coupled to the smooth-shifting 5-speed manual gearbox is a good choice for overall performance. However, the 180-hp 1.8L engine is just the ticket for high-performance thrills. **Transmission:** Silky smooth, quiet shifting. **Routine handling:** Nimble and predictable handling in all conditions. Sportier handling on GT and GTS models makes for a firm but not uncomfortable ride. **Braking:** Excellent performance (100–0 km/h: 120 ft.).

Con: Suspension may be too firm for some.

Comfort/Convenience

Pro: Standard equipment: Long on standard, innovative features. For example, the 10-speaker 200-watt "System 10" radio is one of the most advanced systems currently on the market. Restyled exterior resembles a

Lexus coupe from the front and a Supra from the rear. **Driving position:** Very good. The driver's seat has a manual adjustment that's easy to use. **Controls and displays:** Complete and well-designed controls. **Climate control:** Works well and is easy to calibrate while driving. **Interior space/comfort F/R:** Basically a two-seater, front seats are particularly comfortable, especially on the GT and GTS. **Quietness:** Fairly quiet, well-insulated interior, with a bit of road noise and transmission whine.

Con: Entry/exit: Very poor rear access forces you to practically crawl into the cramped back seat. **Interior space/comfort F/R:** Models equipped with the sunroof offer minimal head room for tall front-seat passengers. Limited outward vision. The high beltline and low seating position induce claustrophobia. **Cargo space:** Rather limited. **Trunk/liftover:** Small trunk has a high liftover.

COST				
List Price (negotiable)	**Residual Values** (months)			
	24	36	48	60
Celica GTS: $34,825 (15%)	$28,000	$25,000	$21,000	$18,000

TECHNICAL DATA	
Powertrain (front-drive)	Head room F/R: 38.6/33.2 in.
Engines: 1.8L 4-cyl. (140 hp)	Leg room F/R: 43.2/29.2 in.
• 1.8L 4-cyl. (180 hp)	Wheelbase: 99.9 in.
• ('99) 2.2L 4-cyl. (130 hp)	Turning circle: 38 ft.
Transmissions: 5-speed man.	Cargo volume: 16 cu. ft.
• 4-speed auto.	Tow limit: N/A
Dimension/Capacity ('99 Celica)	Fuel tank: 60L/reg.
Passengers: 2/2	Weight: 2,400 lb.
Height/length/width:	
51/174.2/68.9 in.	

SAFETY FEATURES/CRASHWORTHINESS		
	Std.	**Opt.**
Anti-lock brakes	❏	■
Seatbelt pretensioners	—	—
Side airbags	—	—
Traction control	—	—
Head restraints	***	**
Visibility (front/rear)	*****	*****
Convertible	*****	**
Crash protection (front) D/P	N/A	
Crash protection (side) D/P	N/A	
Crash protection (offset)	N/A	
HLDI injury claims (model)	**	
HLDI injury claims (all)	**	

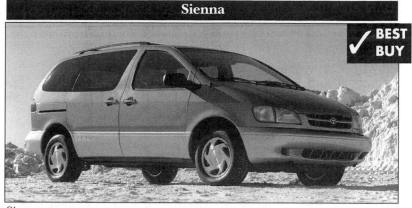

Sienna

Sienna

RATING: Recommended, but still outclassed by the brawnier, more innovative Odyssey. **Strong points:** Incredibly smooth powertrain; a comfortable, stable ride; a fourth door; quiet interior; better than average fit and finish; and bulletproof reliability. **Weak points:** V6 performance compromised by AC and automatic transmission power drain; lacks the trailer-towing brawn of rear-drive minivans; poor rear visibility.

NEW FOR 2000: Nothing significant.

OVERVIEW: Toyota's Camry-based front-drive Sienna replaced the Previa two years ago. It's built in the same Kentucky assembly plant as the Camry and comes with lots of safety and convenience features that include side airbags, anti-lock brakes, and a low-tire-pressure warning system.

Sienna abandoned the Previa's futuristic look in favour of a more conservative Chevrolet Venture styling. It seats seven, offers dual power sliding doors with optional remote controls and a V6 powerplant. As with most minivans and vans, you can save money by buying the Sienna's cargo version, but you won't get as many features.

Cost analysis/best alternatives: Chances are slim that any '99 models remain in stock, but if you can find one discounted by at least 10 percent, go for it. Other minivans worth considering are the Chrysler Caravan/Voyager, Honda Odyssey, and Nissan Quest. **Options:** Remember, a fourth door costs over $4,000 more. Power windows and door locks, rear heater, and AC unit. **Rebates:** Not likely. Toyota favours discounts instead. **Delivery/PDI:** $900 (est.). **Depreciation:** Much slower than average. **Insurance cost:** A bit higher than average. **Parts supply/cost:** Excellent supply of reasonably priced parts taken from the Camry parts bin. **Annual maintenance cost:** Like the Camry, much lower than average. **Warranty:** Bumper-to-bumper 3 years/60,000 km;

powertrain 5 years/100,000 km; rust perforation 5 years/unlimited mileage. **Supplementary warranty:** An extended warranty isn't really necessary. **Highway/city fuel economy:** 8.8–12.7L/100 km. **Annual fuel cost:** 2,189L=$1,270.

Quality/Reliability/Safety

Pro: Quality control: Benchmark quality workmanship and construction. **Reliability:** Legendary. **Warranty performance:** Above average.

Con: Owner-reported problems: Premature brake wear, power sliding door malfunctions, interior squeaks and rattles. **Service bulletin problems:** Creaking sliding door. **NHTSA safety complaints/safety:** Vehicle constantly pulls to the right, even after several alignments; the power sliding door can close on children because it requires too much pressure to stop when closing; next to the power sliding door there's a power door switch that continues to operate even if the child door lock is on—a child can easily activate the switch; power sliding door doesn't latch properly and warning light short-circuits; reflection of the dashboard on the windshield impairs visibility; when turning the steering wheel to the left, the steering wheel doesn't return smoothly; rear seatbelts can't be adjusted; slope of the windshield makes it hard to gauge where the front end stops.

Road Performance

Pro: Emergency handling: No problem. Sienna can change course abruptly without wallowing or losing directional stability. **Steering:** Excellent steering feel and quick response. **Acceleration/torque:** Toyota's V6 handles most driving chores effortlessly without noise or vibration (0–100 km/h: 10.2 sec.). **Transmission:** Quiet and smooth shifting. **Routine handling:** A pleasure. Handling is crisp and effortless. **Braking:** Excellent for a minivan (100–0 km/h: 139 ft.), with minimal brake fade after successive stops.

Con: Engine struggles a bit when carrying a full load uphill. **Braking:** Rear drum brakes cheapen the vehicle and will surely require early replacement—they should be discs.

Comfort/Convenience

Pro: Standard equipment: Very well appointed. **Driving position:** Comfortable seating with excellent visibility fore and aft. **Controls and displays:** Easy-to-read displays and user-friendly controls. **Climate control:** Easy to adjust and operates efficiently. **Entry/exit:** Easy entry/exit up front. **Interior space/comfort F/R:** First-class seating with plenty of head and leg room. **Cargo space:** Adequate. Seats can be easily removed for additional cargo room. **Trunk/liftover:** Easy to load or unload. **Quietness:** No engine or road noise.

Con: There's a confusing array of stalks sprouting out from the steering column. Radio speakers are set too low for acceptable acoustics. **Interior space/comfort F/R:** The wide centre pillars make for difficult access to the middle seats. **Cargo space:** Third-row seats lack a fore/aft adjustment to increase cargo space. **Trunk/liftover:** The rear hatch is inordinately heavy. **Quietness:** Some rattles.

COST

List Price (negotiable)

	24	36	48	60
Sienna 3d: $26,590 (15%)	$20,000	$17,000	$14,000	$12,000
Sienna 4d: $30,705 (16%)	$22,000	$19,000	$16,000	$14,000

Residual Values (months)

Note: Price includes a full tank of fuel.

TECHNICAL DATA

Powertrain (front)
Engine: 3.0L V6 (194 hp)
Transmission: 4-speed auto.
Dimension/Capacity (LE)
Passengers: 2/2/3
Height/length/width:
67.3/193.5/73.4 in.

Head room F: 40.6/R1: 39.9/R2: 37.7 in.
Leg room F:41.9/R1: 36.6/R2: 34 in.
Wheelbase: 114.2 in.
Turning circle: 44 ft.
Cargo volume: 63.5 cu. ft.
GVWR: 3,730–3,945 lb.
Payload: N/A
Tow limit: N/A
Fuel tank: 79L/reg.
Weight: 3,990 lb.

SAFETY FEATURES/CRASHWORTHINESS

	Std.	Opt.
Anti-lock brakes (4W)	■	❑
Seatbelt pretensioners	■	❑
Side airbags	■	❑
Traction control	—	—
Head restraints	*	*
Visibility (front/rear)	*****	**
Crash protection (front) D/P	*****	*****
Crash protection (side) D/P	****	*****
Crash protection (offset)	*****	
HLDI injury claims (model)	N/A	
HLDI injury claims (all)	N/A	

European Vehicles

European hatchbacks, sedans, convertibles ("cabriolets"), and sport-utilities are hot in Canada. For the most part (Lada excepted), they are more fun and comfortable to drive than most American vehicles, they're loaded with high-tech gadgets, most have a relatively slow rate of depreciation, and they're not much more expensive than the Japanese and American competition.

Volkswagen and Audi have managed to do relatively well as a result of their comprehensive warranties, improved quality control (remember the Rabbit?), price cuts, and the launching of less expensive entry-level models (for example, Audi's A4 1.8T, a spinoff of the A4 2.8).

On the other hand, some European automakers have abandoned the U.S. and Canadian markets altogether, while others are barely hanging on. Fiat, Renault, and Peugeot were the first to turn tail, while Jaguar, Rover, and Saab continue to struggle with losses that have drained GM, Ford, and BMW's cash reserves. Why? Because buyers are still wary of European automakers' reputation for poor quality, high parts and servicing costs, and weak dealer networks. As heretical as it sounds, some of the luxury makes have indeed proved to be surprisingly problematic. One MIT report, for example, concluded that European automakers fail to build quality into every step of the production process, as do Japanese manufacturers. Instead, they waste time and money correcting mistakes at the end of the assembly line rather than preventing them at the beginning.

This conclusion is echoed by Canadian drivers. *Lemon-Aid* readers who own pricey European imports invariably tell me of nightmarish electrical glitches that run the gamut from the annoying to the life-threatening. Other problems noted by owners include premature brake wear and excessive brake noise, AC malfunctions, faulty computer modules leading to erratic shifting, poor driveability, hard starts, and frequent stalling.

Although the servicing problem is usually more acute with vehicles that are new on the market, it has long been the Achilles heel of European importers. Owners give them low ratings for mishandling complaints, inadequate service training, and hiring an insufficient number of service representatives—not to mention the abrasive, arrogant attitude typified by some automakers and dealers who bully customers because they have a virtual monopoly on servicing in their region. Look at their dealer networks and you'll see that most European automakers are crowded into Quebec and Ontario, leaving their eastern and western Canada customers to fend for themselves. This makes the chance of finding competent repairs somewhat akin to winning the lottery.

In light of all these shortcomings, why are European vehicles still so popular? Because they make driving so much fun and so comfortable that you quickly forget about Franz, Ingmar, and Luigi waiting for your return for servicing at Marquis de Sade Motors Inc.

AUDI

Sudden acceleration? That phrase is now only used to describe Audi sales over the past five years. Audi sales plummeted in the '80s amid controversy over the 5000's reputation for sudden, unintended acceleration, poor reliability, and sky-high maintenance costs. But Audi refused to follow Fiat and Peugeot back to Europe and has staged a spectacular comeback in North America with well-built, moderately priced front-drive and AWD Quattro sedans. Through a limited lineup of just three vehicles (the A4, A6, and A8), Audi has gained a reputation for making sure-footed, all-wheel drive luxury cars that are loaded with lots of high-tech bells and whistles. This reputation will no doubt be enhanced when the S4, a high performance version of the A4, hits the streets by year's end along with an AWD Quattro TT Coupe, and a redesigned A4 sedan.

As with most European makes, Audis excel in comfort and performance. But servicing and warranty support remains problematic, especially now that VW/Audi has closed down its Canadian headquarters and runs its Canadian operations from the U.S. and Germany.

TT Coupe

TT Coupe

RATING: Not Recommended during its first year on the market. Wait for next year's more powerful engine. **Strong points:** Competent acceleration, first-class handling, very well-appointed and tastefully designed interior, comfortable, supportive seats, plenty of passenger and cargo space (especially with rear seatbacks folded), standard ABS and side-impact airbags, "smart" dual front airbags, and a predicted high resale value. **Weak points:** Poor rear and side visibility, ride may be too firm for some, and lots of engine and road noise invade the cabin.

NEW FOR 2000: Next year will see the addition of Quattro AWD, a 225-hp engine, and a two-seat convertible.

OVERVIEW: Costing an estimated $50,000 the TT Coupe is a new sporty front-drive hatchback with 2+2 seating and set on the same platform used by the A4, Golf, Jetta, and New Beetle. The base 180-hp 1.8L engine (lifted from the A4) is coupled to a manual 5-speed transmission (an automatic won't be offered until the end of next year). It's a bit shorter and more firmly sprung than the A4, however.

A6

RATING: Above Average. **Strong points:** Standard ABS and side airbags, "smart" dual front airbags, superb handling, comfortable seating, plenty of passenger and cargo room (beats out both BMW and Mercedes in this area), easy front and rear access, and very good build quality. The Avant wagon performs like a sporty sport-utility with side airbags and intense HID Xenon headlights. The IIHS considers head restraint protection to be "acceptable," and accident injury claim rates are far lower than average. **Weak points:** Firm suspension can make for a jittery ride, some tire thumping and engine growling, low-mounted climate controls aren't user-friendly, outside mini-mirrors make side and rear vision a bit tricky, the wagon's two-place rear seat is rather small, door-mounted stowage compartments frequently open inadvertently, and servicing can be problematic.

NEW FOR 2000: Two new engines will be offered next summer: a bi-turbo, 250-hp 2.7L V6 and a 300-hp 4.2L V8.

OVERVIEW: The $48,880 A6 is essentially a larger, fully equipped A4. It's a comfortable, spacious, front-drive or all-wheel drive luxury sedan or wagon that comes with standard dual front side airbags and ABS. It uses the same V6 powerplant and platform as its smaller sibling and exhibits similar driving characteristics. Its Tiptronic automatic transmission also has a manual gearshift capability.

Cost analysis/best alternatives: Choose the upgraded year 2000 model for the better-performing engines. Other vehicles worth taking a look at: the BMW 328, Infiniti I30, Lexus ES 300, Mazda Millenia, Mercedes C-class, Toyota Avalon, and the Volvo C70 and S70. **Options:** All-wheel drive. Think twice about getting the power moon roof if you're a tall driver. **Rebates:** Look for $2,000 rebates by late spring as Audi clears out dealer stocks in preparation for its new arrivals. **Delivery/PDI:** $600. **Depreciation:** Slower than average. Audi values no longer plummet when the base warranty expires, and high repair costs have been brought under control. **Insurance cost:** Higher than average. **Parts supply/cost:** Very dealer-dependent and expensive. Independent suppliers carry few Audi parts. **Annual maintenance cost:** Low during the warranty period, then it climbs steadily. **Warranty:** Bumper-to-bumper 3 years/80,000 km; powertrain 3 years/80,000 km; rust perforation 10 years/unlimited km. **Supplementary warranty:** A prerequisite to Audi ownership, and it guarantees a good resale price. **Highway/city fuel economy:** 7.8–13.5L/100 km and 8.4–13.9L/100 km for the Quattro version. **Annual fuel cost:** Base: 2,187L=$1,465; Quattro: 2,285L=$1,531.

Road Performance

Pro: Acceleration/torque: Much improved acceleration and more torque with this year's engine enhancement (0–100 km/h: 9.6 sec.). **Braking:** Better than average braking performance (100–0 km/h: 125 ft.).

Con: NHTSA safety complaints/safety: Low-beam headlights are too narrow to provide proper illumination (same complaint heard from A4 owners); anti-theft alarm self-activates when the vehicle is parked; loose steering wheel airbag; front seatbelts don't retract properly; faulty gas tank sensors transmit wrong remaining fuel indication; can't read instruments because windshield angles sunlight upon their display; front bumper is too low and vulnerable.

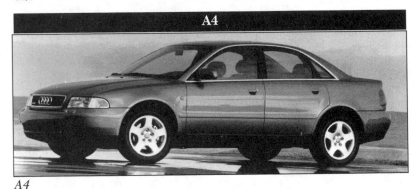

A4

RATING: Recommended. Strong points: Standard side airbags, "smart" airbags, ABS, traction control (front-drive 2.8), optional AWD, powerful and smooth-running base engine, comfortable ride, exceptional handling, front and rear seatbelt pretensioners, and impressive build quality. **Weak points:** Not as fast as its rivals; plain, functional interior; an obtrusive centre console limits leg movements; limited rear seat room; climate controls mounted too low; some tire drumming and engine noise; and servicing remains Audi's Achilles heel.

NEW FOR 2000: An all-new S4 version featuring a 250-hp 2.7L turbocharged V6.

OVERVIEW: The A4 bills itself as Audi's family sport sedan and targets the BMW 3-series and Volvo S70 customer by featuring a roomy interior, standard multi-link suspension, an efficient automatic climate control, a light body, low-speed traction enhancement, an optional 5-speed automatic/manual transmission, and all-wheel drive—all for about an extra $2,000. Equipped with standard dual and side airbags, ABS, and a 150-hp 1.8L turbo or a 190-hp 2.8L V6 engine coupled to an electronic 5-speed Tiptronic automatic transmission, this entry-level four-door is reasonably powerful, easy to handle, and holds its value very well.

Cost analysis/best alternatives: Get the '99 model if the MSRP has been discounted by at least 10 percent. Other vehicles worth taking a look at: the BMW 328, Infiniti I30, Lexus ES 300, Mazda Millenia, Mercedes C-series, Toyota Avalon, and the Volvo C70 and S70. **Options:** An automatic transmission and all-wheel drive. Think twice about getting the power moon roof if you're a tall driver. **Rebates:** Not likely; instead, Audi gives out dealer incentives to encourage discounting. **Delivery/PDI:** $500. **Depreciation:** Very slow. Audi values no longer nosedive when the base warranty expires, and repair costs become the owner's responsibility. **Insurance cost:** Higher than average. **Parts supply/cost:** Often back-ordered and expensive. Forget about saving money by getting parts from an independent supplier; they carry few Audi parts. **Annual maintenance cost:**

Higher than average, but not exorbitant. **Warranty:** Bumper-to-bumper 3 years/80,000 km; powertrain 3 years/80,000 km; rust perforation 10 years/unlimited km. **Supplementary warranty:** Don't leave home without it. **Highway/city fuel economy:** 7.0–11.4L/100 km with the 1.8L, and 7.4–13.1L/100 km with the 2.8L. **Annual fuel cost:** 1.8L: 1,884L=$1,262; 2.8L: 2,107L=$1,412.

Quality/Reliability/Safety

Pro: Quality control: Better than average. Overall quality control has improved markedly over the past several years, with fewer body, trim, accessory, brake, and electrical glitches than exhibited by previous models. **Reliability:** No major headaches. Electrical problems have taken these cars out of service for extended periods in the past. The jury is still out on the new 2.8L's long-term reliability. **Warranty performance:** Better than average over the past few years. **Service bulletin problems:** Nothing for this model year.

Con: Owner-reported problems: Long servicing delays and minor brake, electrical, and powertrain glitches. **NHTSA safety complaints/safety:** Total loss of power when coming to an intersection and depressing the accelerator pedal; sudden acceleration when backing up and brakes failed to respond; headlights don't provide sufficient illumination on low or high beam; defective front windshield.

Road Performance

Pro: Emergency handling: Better than average. **Steering:** Crisp and predictable, with lots of road feedback. **Acceleration/torque:** Surprisingly, the base 1.8L engine provides gobs of low-end torque and accelerates better with the automatic transmission than with the manual gearbox. The turbocharger works well with no turbo delay or torque steer. The 2.8L V6 engine needs full throttle for adequate performance. Nevertheless, it provides respectable acceleration times and plenty of torque for passing and traversing hilly terrain (0–100 km/h: 8.7 sec.). **Transmission:** Both the manual and Tiptronic automatic transmission perform flawlessly. AWD is extended to entry-level models at a time when most automakers are dropping the option on passenger cars. **Routine handling:** Handling is exceptional, with no passenger discomfort. **Braking:** Impressive braking performance (100–0 km/h: 118 ft.).

Con: The A4's rivals provide better acceleration. The ride is a bit firm, and the car still exhibits some body roll and brake dive under extreme conditions. Braking is a bit twitchy at times.

Comfort/Convenience

Pro: Standard equipment: A nice array of functional, though not lavish, features. **Driving position:** Acceptable. Comfortable, firm seating and a telescopic steering column help you easily find the right driving position. Excellent visibility fore and aft. **Controls and displays:** Most major controls can be easily reached and the instrument layout is both practical and complete. **Climate control:** Efficient climate control system, although some of the controls take getting used to. **Entry/exit:** Easy front and rear access. **Interior space/comfort F/R:** Plenty of head room and interior space for passengers up front. **Cargo space:** Average cargo space for a vehicle this size. **Trunk/liftover:** Large trunk is easy to load and unload. **Quietness:** Exceptionally quiet interior.

Con: Don't mistake Audi's automatic locking differential for traction control. It's not as effective. The wide centre console robs the driver of much-needed leg and knee room, and the optional power moon roof cuts head room by almost two inches. Rear passenger room is a bit limited. **Controls and Displays:** Radio and climate controls aren't intuitive; keep the owner's manual handy.

COST

List Price (negotiable)

	Residual Values (months)			
	24	36	48	60
A4 1.8: $32,990 (21%)	$22,000	$18,000	$14,000	$12,000

TECHNICAL DATA

Powertrain (front/AWD)
Engines: 1.8L 4-cylinder (150 hp)
• 2.8L V6 (190 hp)
• 2.7L V6 (250 hp)
Transmissions: 5-speed man.
• 5-speed auto.
Dimension/Capacity
Passengers: 2/3
Height/length/width:
55.8/178/68.2 in.

Leg room F/R: 41.3/33.5 in.
Head room F/R: 38.2/36.8 in.
Wheelbase: 103 in.
Turning circle: 36 ft.
Cargo volume: 14 cu. ft.
Tow limit: 2,000 lb.
Fuel tank: 62L/prem.
Weight: 3,000 lb.

SAFETY FEATURES/CRASHWORTHINESS

	Std.	Opt.
Anti-lock brakes	■	❑
Seatbelt pretensioners (F/R)	■	❑
Side airbags	■	❑
Traction control	❑	■
Head restraints	***	***
Visibility (front/rear)	*****	*****
Crash protection (front) D/P	****	*****
Crash protection (side) D/P	N/A	
Crash protection (offset)	N/A	
HLDI injury claims (model)	****	
HLDI injury claims (all)	****	

BMW

While Audi improves its product mix, BMW continues to build well-appointed cars that excel at handling and driving comfort. Its vehicles have excellent road manners, depreciate slowly, and have an *"I got mine!"* cachet that buyers find hard to resist. Unfortunately, they also have limited interior room (except for the high-end models) and are difficult and expensive to service. But these drawbacks haven't discouraged BMW's loyal following of young professionals and people who want something prestigious, but not priced entirely beyond reach.

Tapping this growing popularity over the past several decades, BMW has brought out a larger and much more expensive line of sedans known as the 3.0, the Bavaria, and (since 1976) different combinations of the 5-series, 6-series, 7-series, and 8-series. Over the past few years, however, BMW has concentrated its efforts to trim its model lineup, introduce a sporty entry-level roadster, produce larger interiors, introduce wagon versions of its best-selling 3- and 5-series, and engineer handling improvements to give their vehicles better traction on slippery roads. The company is also making lots of dough on bullet-proofed versions of its 7-series; two new light-armoured 7-series will be launched this fall equipped with either a V8 or V12 engine and run-flat tires—just the thing for the next British Columbia NDP leader's convention.

There are three good reasons for buying one of these German cars: high-performance road handling, prestige value, and a low rate of depreciation. Keep in mind, though, that there are plenty of other cars that cost less, offer more interior room (Passat and Audi come to mind), and are safer, more reliable, and better performing. So if you're buying a BMW, remember that the entry-level versions of these little status symbols are more show than go, and that just a few options can blow your budget. The larger, better-performing high-end models are more expensive and don't give you the same standard features as do many Japanese imports. Also, be prepared to endure long servicing waits, body and trim glitches, and brake, electrical, and accessory problems. And finally, don't be overly impressed by BMW's high-tech safety features: the company is still struggling to make head restraint systems that will earn an "acceptable" or "good" rating for head and neck protection from the Insurance Institute for Highway Safety.

Z3

RATING: Recommended. **Strong points:** Attractively styled, standard traction control, impressive acceleration, excellent handling, exceptional braking, top quality fit and finish, and a "good" rating for head restraint protection by the IIHS. **Weak points:** Some rear-end instability upon acceleration and when cornering; excessive engine, road, and wind noise filters through the soft top; difficult rear access; and limited rear leg room.

NEW FOR 2000: Nothing significant, except for slight restyling touches.

OVERVIEW: BMW's Z3 is an attractive, rear-drive, $45,900 roadster made with parts cobbled together from the 318ti hatchback. Its modern interior, head-turning body, and affordable base price makes the Z3 a tough competitor in a market niche heretofore monopolized by the cheaper and less distinctive Mazda Miata. It comes with a 170-hp 2.5L inline six, borrowed from the 3-series, and an optional 193-hp 2.8 six, coupled to either a 5-speed manual or 4-speed automatic transmission. The M roadster and coupe come with a high-performance 3.2L 240-hp 6-cylinder powerplant.

On the plus side are the Z3's generally excellent handling and braking, a firm ride, and its uniquely German styling. Safety features include smart airbags and three-point seatbelts with pretensioners. Accident injury data shows far fewer claims than the average for this type of vehicle and for small vehicles overall.

The base 2.5L six is slower than the 2.8L inline six, but it's more fuel-efficient. Unlike some other convertibles, the Z3 has few body rattles and groans; the climate system works well; and lowering the top, assisted by an electric motor, is a breeze. Resale value remains high, primarily because the Z3 is still relatively rare in Canada.

Some of the Z3's less impressive features: a handling problem all too familiar to Mustang owners—the rear end can slide out upon acceleration or during hard cornering; braking performance is about 20 feet longer than what the Miata can do; and the transmission is slow to upshift when cold.

The small interior also has its minuses. For example: six-footers will find the seats don't retract far enough and the low windshield blocks their view of overhead traffic lights, and other drivers may have difficulty seeing over the non-adjustable steering wheel. Visibility is further hampered by side mirrors that are set too far back on the doors and by the plastic rear window, which is easily damaged and lacks a defroster. As with many convertibles, there's plenty of noise that intrudes into the interior at highway speeds, and storage capacity is limited to a small glove compartment and mini storage bins.

Service bulletins highlight the following two problems: engine runs rough after a cold start and the fuel tank reads one-quarter when it's full. Other deficiencies mostly concern poor ergonomics, a surprising oversight for a German-engineered car. Examples are: inside door handles are located too far back on the doors, getting the spare tire from under the vehicle is a chore, and shoulder belts are uncomfortable.

Best alternatives: Mazda Miata, Mercedes-Benz SLK230, and Porsche Boxster.

3-Series

328

RATING: Recommended. **Strong points:** Standard traction control, good acceleration (except for the 318ti), excellent handling, impressive braking, and top-notch quality control. **Weak points:** Limited rear seat room and cargo area; tricky entry/exit, even on sedans; and excessive tire noise.

NEW FOR 2000: The 323Ci and 328Ci coupes will come with the 2.5L and 2.8L 6-cylinder engines used in BMW's entry-level sedans and standard Sport suspension. These new four-seaters will also be lower, longer, and wider than their four-door equivalents, use different body panels, and present a more aero appearance. Convertible versions will be made over in a similar fashion sometime early next year, about the same time the 3-series wagons debut. The entry-level 318ti has been dropped. Cockpit improvements include a standard tilt/telescope steering wheel and optional power memory seats, power lumbar adjustments, an in-dash CD player, and steering wheel audio and cruise controls.

OVERVIEW: With BMW's recent mechanical upgrades, styling changes, and increased exterior and interior dimensions, the 323i and 328i have come to resemble their more expensive big brothers with super-smooth powertrain performance and enhanced handling. The 2.8L 4-valves-per-cylinder 193-hp inline 6-cylinder engine is borrowed from the 525i. The less expensive 318i is powered by a 16-valve DOHC inline 4-cylinder with 138 horsepower. Its convertible twin is a budget version of the 328 convertible. It has a manual top and a smaller 1.9L engine (waiting for a mid-year upgrade).

Cost analysis/best alternatives: Get the '99 sedans, which haven't been reworked this year—only if you can find them sufficiently discounted. As for the coupes and convertibles, wait until mid-2000 to buy the latest versions embodying engine, body, and handling improvements. Other cars worth considering are the Audi A4, Lexus ES 300, and Mercedes-Benz C-Class and SLK. **Options:** If you buy the 325i convertible, invest $1,500 in the rollover protection system that pops up from behind the rear seat. Don't spend money on the optional Sport suspension. It produces an overly harsh, jiggly ride on rough pavement. **Rebates:** Not likely. **Delivery/PDI:** $500. **Depreciation:** Slower than average. **Insurance cost:** Higher than average. **Parts supply/cost:** Parts are less expensive than for other cars in this class. Unfortunately they aren't easily found outside of the dealer network, where they're often back-ordered. **Annual maintenance cost:** Average, until the warranty runs out; then your mechanic starts sharing your pay cheque. **Warranty:** Bumper-to-bumper 4 years/80,000 km; powertrain 4 years/80,000 km; rust perforation 6 years/unlimited km. **Supplementary warranty:** A prerequisite to Beamer ownership. **Highway/city fuel economy:** *318i:* 6.9–10.3L/100 km; *Base 323:* 7.8–12.3L/100 km. **Annual fuel cost:** *318i:* 1,754L=$1,175; *Base 323:* 2,055L=$1,377.

Quality/Reliability/Safety

Pro: Quality control: Better than average. Body assembly and workmanship have improved lately. **Reliability:** No serious reliability problems have been reported. **Warranty performance:** Average. BMW usually resolves disputes through individual "goodwill" settlements. **Service bulletin problems:** Nothing reported on this year's models. **Safety:**

All 3-series models are pre-wired for an alarm system and use a Coded Driveaway Protection system that won't allow the car to start unless the ignition key matches the ignition switch code, which changes each time the car is started.

Con: Parts are scarce outside major metropolitan areas, and independent mechanics are rare. **Owner-reported problems:** Brakes, electrical system, and some body trim and accessories are the most failure-prone components. **NHTSA safety complaints:** *318:* Sudden acceleration; gas and brake pedals are so close together, driver can easily confuse the two; airbag safety light keeps going off. *320:* Premature transmission failure. *325:* Brake rotors warp every 5,000 km, causing excessive vibration and pulsation. *328i:* False deployment of the passenger and driver's side airbag; when pulling out of a parking space with both feet on the brake pedal, vehicle started moving forward; vehicle lurches forward in Drive as well as in Reverse; water leaks into the vehicle from all doors in rainy weather; bent aluminum wheels cause the vehicle to shake at cruising speed.

Road Performance

Pro: Emergency handling: No-surprise suspension and steering makes for crisp high-speed and emergency handling. Much better rear-end stability. **Steering:** Exceptionally accurate and sensitive. Lots of road feedback. **Acceleration/torque:** Impressive off-the-line acceleration with the 1.9L 4-cylinder engine, and a manual transmission oriented toward driving enthusiasts. The 2.5L and 2.8L inline 6-cylinder engines and transmissions are the essence of harmonious cooperation, even when coupled to an automatic transmission; there's not actually that much difference between the two from a performance perspective. **Transmission:** Light and precise gear shifting with easy clutch and shift action. **Routine handling:** Competent and predictable handling on dry surfaces. **Braking:** Incredibly short stopping distances with the 318ti (100–0 km/h: 107 ft.), and the 328i does almost as well (100–0 km/h: 120 ft.).

Con: The 318ti's acceleration is embarrassingly slow with an automatic transmission. The ride is firm and occasionally uncomfortable on rough roads.

Comfort/Convenience

Pro: Driving position: Comfortable driving position enhanced by firm, supportive seats, a tilt/telescope steering wheel, nice ergonomics, and good all-around visibility. **Controls and displays:** Excellent control layout and design, though it could use additional gauges. Wiper action automatically drops from constant to intermittent when you slow down or stop. All power windows have an express down and up. **Climate control:** The 325i's additional room and separate driver and passenger climate controls make for a more hospitable interior. **Entry/exit:**

Acceptable, but tight. The four-door model offers marginally improved access to the rear seat. **Interior space/comfort F/R:** Plenty of space and comfort for four occupants—not five, as BMW would like you to believe. More toe, leg, and knee room for rear occupants this year. **Trunk/liftover:** Trunk has a low liftover for easy loading. **Quietness:** A rigid body design keeps rattles and clunks to a minimum.

Con: Standard equipment: Bland styling and very austere interior. Interior plastics look tacky. **Controls and displays:** Confusing switches on the dual climate-control system. **Interior space/comfort F/R:** Limited head room when equipped with a sunroof. Centre console cuts into driver's leg and knee room. Seats are too firm for some. Rear seating is comfortable only for two adults. **Cargo space:** At a premium. **Trunk/liftover:** Limited trunk space. **Quietness:** Noisy high-performance tires.

COST

List Price (firm)	Residual Values (months)			
	24	**36**	**48**	**60**
'99 318ti: $27,800 (16%)	$22,000	$18,000	$15,000	$12,000
323: $35,900 (18%)	$27,000	$23,000	$19,000	$16,000

TECHNICAL DATA

Powertrain (rear-drive)
Engines: 1.9L 4-cyl. (138 hp)
• 2.5L 6-cyl. (168–170 hp)
• 2.8L V6 (193 hp)
• 3.2L V6 (240 hp)
Transmissions: 5-speed man.
• 4-speed auto.
Dimension/Capacity (328i)
Passengers: 2/3

Height/length/width:
55.7/176/68.5 in.
Head room F/R: 37.2/36.7 in.
Leg room F/R: 41/34 in.
Wheelbase: 107.3 in.
Turning circle: 36 ft.
Cargo volume: 15 cu. ft.
Tow limit: 1,000 lb.
Fuel tank: 62L/prem.
Weight: 3,100 lb.

SAFETY FEATURES/CRASHWORTHINESS

	Std.	Opt.
Anti-lock brakes	■	❑
Seatbelt pretensioners	■	❑
Side airbags	■	❑
Traction control	■	❑
Head restraints	**	*
Visibility (front/rear)	*****	*****
Crash protection (front) D/P	N/A	
Crash protection (side) D/P	N/A	
Crash protection (offset)	N/A	
HLDI injury claims (model) 318Ti	****	
HLDI injury claims (all) 318Ti	***	

MERCEDES-BENZ

You can't lose money buying a Mercedes-Benz if you keep it long enough. The German automaker has long made it a point to design and engineer cars at the forefront of technology and safety, and to clothe them in conservative, though attractive, garb.

In an attempt to respond to critics' charges that its cars were priced out of most buyers' reach and that its styling was antiquated, Mercedes tried out its own new aero look in the beginning of this decade with the entry-level 190 ("baby Benz") series. It was a flop.

But the aero look was retained and refined, and is now what makes these luxury imports distinctive, along with a revamped model lineup full of high-tech safety and convenience features. During the past few years, Mercedes has introduced three new models (SLK, CLK, and M-Class), enhanced or revised its existing model lineup, and dropped the hot-rod C36 and SL320.

Mercedes' 2000 model year lineup includes the following: C-Class, E-Class, S-/CL-Class, M-Class sport-utilities, CLK, SL, and the SLK. This year, the C-Class will return with few changes; the E-Class gets a facelift; S-Class vehicles will be redesigned and joined by a coupe version; the CLK also gets a redesign along with a CLK430 Cabriolet; and the SLK returns unchanged.

C-Class, CLK, SLK

CLK320

RATING: Recommended. **Strong points:** Standard "smart" airbags, side airbags, traction control (optional on the C230), "brake assist," and ABS. Good powertrain match-up enhanced with a supercharger. Comfortable ride, easy handling, good braking, excellent quality control, innovative anti-theft system, and a high resale value. **Weak points:**

Limited rear seat and cargo room; small, oddly shaped trunk; tight entry/exit; a choppy ride; some tire thumping, engine, and wind noise.

NEW FOR 2000: C-Class cars will be carried over unchanged this year until their redesign for the 2001 model year. An AWD wagon will debut at that time.

OVERVIEW: The CLK320 coupe and convertible are styled a bit like the larger E-Class and use a 3.2L version of the C280 6-cylinder as the base engine. A 275-hp 4.3L V8 equips the CLK430, and the C230, redesignated as the C230 Kompressor, and uses a 185 hp supercharged 4-banger, taken from the SLK roadster.

CLK

The $57,750 CLK 320 is a stylish, four-passenger, roomy coupe that's both practical and well-appointed, with technically advanced features that enhance high performance and comfort. Standard safety features include front and side airbags, a BabySmart sensor that disconnects the passenger airbag when a special child seat is in place, and a "smart" passenger airbag that won't deploy if no one is seated, cutting repair costs. An innovative brake assist feature is tied into the anti-lock brake system to provide an extra boost upon hard braking. Surprisingly, the CLK has been given a "marginal" rating for head restraint protection by the IIHS.

In addition to a high degree of comfort and safety, the CLK's 215-hp V6 engine posts a 0–100 km/h time of less than seven seconds—with an automatic 5-speed transmission. The multi-link suspension and optional Electronic Stability Program (ESP) allow for high-speed, sure-footed cornering in quiet comfort.

SLK230

Taking its cue from BMW's 318ti and Audi's 1.8t, the SLK230, Mercedes-Benz's entry-level model, returns this year with few changes. This rear-drive roadster isn't cheap ($57,550), but you can get one for almost half the cost of M-B's other roadsters. In addition to a great price, there are a number of amenities one would expect to find only with a far costlier SL, including a one-button full-power top, rollover protection, side airbags, ABS, and traction control. Add to this a 185-hp 2.3L supercharged inline four hooked to a 5-speed automatic transmission pulling only 3,000 pounds (1360 kg), and you can expect swift performance and superb handling. Additionally, the SLK has earned an "acceptable" rating for head restraint protection by the IIHS.

Cost analysis/best alternatives: Get a discounted '99 model if you can find one. Other cars worth considering are the Audi A4, BMW 3-series, and Volvo C70, S70, or V70. Rivals to the CLK and the SLK230 would be the BMW Z3, Chevrolet Corvette, Mazda Miata (OK, I *am* reaching a bit here), and other models in the Mercedes-Benz SL-Class stable.

Options: Seriously consider the traction control option. **Rebates:** Not likely. **Delivery/PDI:** $600. **Depreciation:** Average. **Insurance cost:** Higher than average. **Parts supply/cost:** Limited availability, but CAA says parts aren't that expensive. **Annual maintenance cost:** Less than average. **Warranty:** Bumper-to-bumper 4 years/80,000 km; powertrain 4 years/80,000 km; rust perforation 5 years/unlimited km. **Supplementary warranty:** Not needed. **Highway/city fuel economy:** 7.6–11L/100 km with the 2.3L; 8–11.2L/100 km with the 2.8L V6; 9.6–13.1L/100 km with the 4.3L. **Annual fuel cost:** 2.3L: 1,894L=$1,269; 2.8L V6: 1,952L=$1,308; 4.3L: 2,305L=$1,544.

Quality/Reliability/Safety

Pro: Quality control: Above average. **Reliability:** Major components that would affect reliability are relatively trouble-free. **Safety:** Standard three-point seatbelts, side airbags, and anti-theft alarm (thieves just adore these cars; they steal the badges from the grille and rear panel, and there are a dozen thieves for each Blaupunkt radio).

Con: Service bulletin problems: Tips on correcting hesitation following a cold start. **NHTSA safety complaints:** *230:* Rear window shattered; instrument panel control module failed; automatic transmission replaced; brakes won't work for the first 30 seconds after startup; fuel gauge reads more than what's in the tank and Mercedes is apparently aware of the problem, but doesn't yet have a fix. *280:* Sudden acceleration while in Reverse.

Road Performance

Pro: Emergency handling: Excellent. Hard cornering produces very little body roll and sudden corrections don't compromise handling or comfort. **Steering:** Quick, precise, and predictable. **Acceleration/torque:** The supercharged 2.3L engine is quite competent in handling most driving chores with plenty of low-end torque. And speaking of grunt, the 2.8L powerplant is a real powerhouse in this small car. Although its power is used most effectively when coupled to a 5-speed manual transmission, its performance with the 5-speed automatic is quite acceptable. **Transmission:** Smooth and quiet shifting. **Routine handling:** Exemplary. The C-Class combines superb handling with enhanced passenger comfort. **Braking:** First-class braking that produces incredibly short stopping distances (100–0 km/h: 106 ft.) for a car of this heft.

Con: The ride is a bit choppier than what you would find with the E-class.

Comfort/Convenience

Pro: Standard equipment: These cars are lavishly equipped with safety, convenience, and high-performance features. **Driving position:** Very good, with everything within easy reach. **Controls and displays:** Well laid-out displays and complete instrumentation. **Climate control:** Efficient, quiet, and innovative. Large buttons calibrate the system; a "rest" setting circulates warm air with the engine off. **Entry/exit:** Easy access to the front seats. **Interior space/comfort F/R:** Has as much room up front as the E-Class sedan. Comfortable, supportive front and rear seats. **Cargo space:** Average. **Trunk/liftover:** Average-sized trunk has a low liftover. **Quietness:** Better than most cars.

Con: CLK's wide rear roof pillars obstruct visibility. **Interior space/comfort F/R:** Rear seat is a squeeze for three adults and access is a bit tricky. The coupe's rear seat is configured for two adults only. **Quietness:** Some road noise intrudes into the passenger compartment.

COST				
List Price (firm)	**Residual Values** (months)			
	24	**36**	**48**	**60**
C230 Kompressor:				
$38,900 (21%)	$27,000	$22,000	$18,000	$15,000

TECHNICAL DATA

Powertrain (rear-drive)
Engines: 2.3L 4-cyl. (185 hp)
• 2.8L V6 (194 hp)
• 3.2L V6 (215 hp)
• 4.3L V8 (302 hp)
Transmissions: 5-speed man.
• 4-speed auto.
• 5-speed auto.
Dimension/Capacity (C230)
Passengers: 2/3
Height/length/width:
56.1/177.4/67.7 in.

Head room F/R: 37.2/37 in.
Leg room F/R: 41.5/32.8 in.
Wheelbase: 105.9 in.
Turning circle: 35 ft.
Cargo volume: 13 cu. ft.
Tow limit: 2,000 lb.
Fuel tank: 62L/prem.
Weight: 3,200 lb.

SAFETY FEATURES/CRASHWORTHINESS

	Std.	Opt.
Anti-lock brakes	■	❑
Seatbelt pretensioners	■	❑
Side airbags	■	❑
Traction control	❑	■
Head restraints	***	**
Visibility (front/rear)	*****	**
Crash protection (front) D/P	****	****
Crash protection (side) D/P	***	****
Crash protection (offset)	N/A	
HLDI injury claims (model)	**	
HLDI injury claims (all)	***	

E-Class

E-Class

RATING: Recommended. **Strong points:** Standard "smart" airbags, side airbags, traction control, "brake assist," and ABS. Excellent engine and transmission combo, easy handling, good braking, comfortable ride, roomy interior, innovative anti-theft system, excellent quality control, a high trade-in value, and an "acceptable" rating for offset crashworthiness and head restraint protection by the IIHS. **Weak points:** A surprisingly small trunk, poor fuel economy (E430), and tall drivers may be bothered by the knee bolsters.

NEW FOR 2000: These cars return with a minor restyling to make them look more aerodynamic, the 4Matic AWD system is extended to the E430 sedan, and the diesel engine will be dropped.

OVERVIEW: Most of the mid-sized E-Class sedans offer inline 6-cylinder engines, but a V8 powerplant is offered on the E300D ($59,950) with its 134-hp 3.0L turbodiesel, the E320 ($67,150) with a 217-hp 3.2L, and the E430 ($74,750) with its 275-hp 4.3L V8.

Redesigned twice in the past seven years, the E-Class is considered to be state of the art in German auto technology. These cars do everything well, and manage to hold five people in relative comfort. They're first class in combining performance, road manners, and comfort. True, they're not the best riding, handling, or accelerating cars available, but they're able to perform each of these tasks almost as well as the best cars in each specific area without sacrificing some other important element in the driving equation.

The E-Class continues to offer standard traction control that prevents wheelspin upon acceleration. Another interesting feature is the remarkably smooth and quiet base 24-valve 217-hp high-performance version of the inline 6-cylinder engine that powers the 300 series.

Mercedes E-Class models have front and side airbags for both driver and right front passenger, plus dual-locking shoulder belts. The front airbags are designed to deploy at higher crash speeds when occupants are belted than when they're unbelted. Belts in the front seat have tensioners that activate in a crash to reduce belt slack. Sensors in the seat and belt deactivate the airbags and belt pretensioner on the passenger side if no occupant is riding in this seat. The middle back seat has a lap/shoulder belt. Energy-absorbing padding between the footwell and floor carpet is designed to reduce the forces on drivers' legs in serious frontal crashes. The IIHS has given the E-Class an "acceptable" rating for offset crash protection.

All these safety and luxury features have their price, though. If you'd like to drive one of these cars but are of an economical frame of mind, choose a leftover 280; it offers everything the E320 does but for much less. The E300CE is a coupe version, appealing to a sportier crowd, while the E300TE is the station wagon variant. Both the 300E sedan and 300TE station wagon carry the 4Matic all-wheel drive.

Cost analysis/best alternatives: Get the '99 model if you want a diesel engine. Leaving aside the question of the engines, the restyled 2000 models don't cost much more than last year's versions and represent the better buy. Other cars worth considering are the Audi A6, BMW 5-series, Lexus GS 300 or 400, or Volvo S90 and V90. **Options:** None. **Rebates:** Not likely. **Delivery/PDI:** $500. **Depreciation:** Slower than average. **Insurance cost:** Higher than average. **Parts supply/cost:** Hard to find outside of the dealer network, but CAA reports that parts aren't expensive. **Annual maintenance cost:** Less than average. **Warranty:** Bumper-to-bumper 4 years/80,000 km; powertrain 4 years/80,000 km; rust perforation 5 years/unlimited km. **Supplementary warranty:** Not needed. **Highway/city fuel economy:** 7.5–11.4L/100 km with the 3.2L V6 engine, and 6.1–8.9L/100 km with the 3.2L V6 diesel powerplant. **Annual fuel cost:** 3.2L V6: 1,929L=$1,292; 3.2L V6 diesel: 1,528L=$840.

Quality/Reliability/Safety

Service bulletin problems: Transmission may slip, disengage, or go into Neutral by itself. **NHTSA safety complaints/safety:** *320:* Vehicle pulls hard to the right when driven at any speed; stalling whenever vehicle passes over a bump; cruise control and turn signal stalks are too close together; fuel pump failure; the starter relay intermittently misreads the vehicle's key code; airbag cover on passenger side is exposed and distorted; blurred images from rear view mirror and rear windshield; bumpers crack from minor impacts.

Road Performance

Acceleration/torque: Better than average acceleration with the base engine, but the 4.2L V8's performance is dazzling (0–100 km/h: 8 sec.). **Braking:** You won't find better braking with any other car in this class (100–0 km/h: 114 ft.).

VOLKSWAGEN

Like most European cars, Volkswagens are practical and offer excellent handling and great fuel economy without sacrificing interior comfort. While overall reliability isn't spectacular (particularly after their fifth year of ownership), the entry-level models are reasonably priced. And they're not all that difficult to service at independent garages, which have grown increasingly popular as owners flee more expensive VW dealerships. Although parts are fairly expensive, independent repair agencies usually have no trouble finding them.

The only continuing concern is how the closure of its Canadian headquarters will affect Volkswagen's supply of new vehicles, warranty administration, and parts availability. In a recent Canadian Federation of Automobile Dealer Associations dealer survey, done before VW relocated, VW dealers blasted Volkswagen management for being insensitive to their concerns.

So far, the company's move to the States hasn't showed VW to be insensitive to its Canadian customers' concerns: its toll-free, bilingual customer service line is easily accessed and the few staffers I spoke with were friendly, helpful, and forthcoming.

This year, Volkswagen brings back most of its products unchanged, except for slight restylings of the Passat and EuroVan.

New Beetle

RATING: Average. The New Beetle is an expensive ($21,950) trip down memory lane. Personally, I don't think it's worth it—with or without its speed-activated spoiler and dash-mounted bud vase. **Strong points:** Powerful 1.8L turbocharged engine; standard side airbags; easy handling; sure-footed and comfortable, though firm, ride; impressive braking; most instruments and controls are user-friendly; comfortable and supportive front seats with plenty of head and leg room; cargo area can be expanded by folding down the front seats; and top-quality mechanical components and workmanship. The Insurance Institute for Highway Safety has given the Beetle a "good" rating for offset crashworthiness and front seat head restraint protection, and an "acceptable" rating for the rear. **Weak points:** Serious safety defects reported by owners; base engine runs out of steam around 100 km/h; diesel engine lacks pep and produces lots of noise and vibration; delayed shifts from Park to Drive; easily buffeted by crosswinds; optional ABS; high-mounted side mirrors; large head restraints, and large front roof pillars obstruct front visibility; limited rear leg and head room; difficult rear entry/exit; excessive engine noise; awkward to access radio buttons and door panel-mounted power switches; skimpy interior storage and trunk space.

NEW FOR 2000: Sound-system upgrades and standard traction control (1.8T GLS and GLX).

OVERVIEW: The New Beetle was a hands-down marketing and public relations winner when the model was re-introduced last year after being absent since 1979. By the end of March 1998, over 56,000 were sold, and sales for '99 versions are tracking first-year sales.

Why so much emotion for an ugly German import that never had a functioning heater, was declared "Small on Safety" by Ralph Nader and his Center for Auto Safety, and carried a puny 48-hp engine? The simple answer is that it was cheap, and it represented the first car most of us could afford as we went through school, got our first job, and dreamed of getting a better car. Time has taken the edge off the memories of the hardship the Beetle made us endure—like having to scrape the inside windshield with our nails as our breath froze—and left us with the cozy feeling that the car wasn't that bad, after all.

But it was.

Now VW has resurrected the Beetle and produced a competent front engine, front-drive, compact car—set on the chassis and running gear of the Golf hatchback—that's much safer than its predecessor, but oddly enough is still afflicted by many of the same deficiencies we learned to hate with the original.

Again, without the turbocharger, the 115-hp base engine is underwhelming (the 90-hp turbodiesel isn't much better) when you get it up to cruising speed, there's still not much room for rear passengers, engine noise is disconcerting, radio buttons and power accessory switches located on the door panels aren't user-friendly, front visibility is hindered by the car's quirky design, and storage capacity is at a premium.

On the other hand, the powerful, optional 1.8L turbocharged engine makes this Beetle an impressive performer; the heater works fine; steering, handling, and braking are quite good; and the interior is not as spartan or tacky as it once was.

Cost analysis/best alternatives: Don't bother looking for a second-series '99 model, they're long gone. Other cars worth considering are the Honda Civic, Mazda Protegé, Nissan Sentra, Toyota Corolla, and VW Cabrio. **Options:** A turbocharged engine is essential if you plan lots of highway use. **Rebates:** Look for some substantial price cuts next year as the originality wears off. **Delivery/PDI:** $525. **Depreciation:** Much slower than average, especially during the first two years. **Insurance cost:** Higher than average. **Parts supply/cost:** Not hard to find since they're taken from the Golf/Jetta parts bin, but they may be more expensive than parts for most other cars in this class. **Annual maintenance cost:** Less than average during the first three years. After this, expect repair costs start to climb dramatically. **Warranty:** Bumper-to-bumper 2 years/40,000 km; powertrain 5 years/80,000 km; rust perforation 6 years/unlimited km. **Supplementary warranty:** A good idea. **Highway/city fuel economy:** 4.8–6.9L/100 km with the 1.9L turbodiesel, 7.9–10.5L/100 km with the 1.8L, and 7.7–10.5L/100 km with the 2.0L. **Annual fuel cost:** 1.9L: 1,191=$655; 1.8L: 1,866L=$1,250; 2.0L: 1,848L=$1,072.

Quality/Reliability/Safety

NHTSA safety complaints/safety: Driver's head restraint sits too high and can't be lowered, seriously restricting rear visibility; excessive brake noise; oil pan hole leaked oil and caused vehicle to stall; sudden loss of power while driving 100 km/h, forcing driver to reset computer by restarting the vehicle; while driving at any speed, vehicle goes into emergency mode and suddenly slows down to about 20 km/h; instrument cluster failure; vehicle was smoking under the hood because a faulty hose leaked oil onto the engine; while stopped at a traffic light, vehicle just exploded into flames and was a total loss (see following photo).

This New Beetle's owner says that if he had been carrying passengers in the rear, they wouldn't have made it out in time.

COST

List Price (firm)	**Residual Values** (months)			
	24	**36**	**48**	**60**
Base model: $21,950 (17%)	$16,000	$14,000	$11,000	$9,000

TECHNICAL DATA

Powertrain (front-drive)
Engines: 2.0L 4-cyl. (115 hp)
• 1.9L TD 4-cyl. (90 hp)
• 1.8L TD 4-cyl. (150 hp)
Transmissions: 4-speed auto.
• 5-speed man.
Dimension/Capacity
Passengers: 2/2
Height/length/width:
59.5/161.1/67.9 in.

Head room F/R: 42/34 in.
Leg room F/R: 45.5/23 in.
Wheelbase: 98.9 in.
Turning circle: 36. ft.
Cargo volume:12 cu. ft.
Tow limit: N/A
Fuel tank: 55L/reg.
Weight: 2,769 lb.

SAFETY FEATURES/CRASHWORTHINESS

	Std.	Opt.
Anti-lock brakes	■	❑
Seatbelt pretensioners	■	❑
Side airbags	■	❑
Traction control	■	■
Head restraints	*****	****
Visibility (front/rear)	**	*

Crash protection (front) D/P	****	****
Crash protection (side) D/P	N/A	
Crash protection (offset)	*****	
HLDI injury claims (model)	N/A	
HLDI injury claims (all)	N/A	

Golf, Jetta, Cabrio

Cabrio

RATING: Above average. Price hikes are putting these cars out of most people's reach. **Strong points:** Superb all-around front-drive performers that offer power to spare with the manual shifter (GTI VR6, GLX), first-class handling, a comfortable ride, and good fuel economy. **Weak points:** Poor acceleration with the 4-cylinder engine, powerful V6 produces excessive torque steer, harsh automatic transmission downshifts, difficult entry/exit, restricted rear visibility, limited rear leg room, and a high number of safety-related complaints. Keep in mind that maintenance costs increase dramatically after the fifth year of ownership.

NEW FOR 2000: Brake wear indicator, anti-theft device and sound-system upgrades, and standard traction control on some models.

OVERVIEW: Practical and fun to drive. That pretty well sums up the main reasons why these VWs continue to be so popular. Yet they offer much more, including lots of front interior room, a peppier engine than what you'll find in most cars this size, responsive handling, great fuel economy, and better than average reliability over the first three years.

The Jetta is a more expensive Golf with a trunk (probably why Jettas outsell Golfs five to one), and the Cabrio is a much more expensive Golf without a roof. The Golf GTI V6 is a sporty performer that comes with lots of standard equipment, including air conditioning, an upgraded sound system, and a split folding rear seat. Jettas offer standard cruise control, power mirrors, and alloy wheels.

Three engines are available: a 115-hp 2.0L base 4-cylinder, a 90-hp 1.9L turbo diesel variant, and a 174-hp 2.8L V6 borrowed from the

Corrado and Passat. A manual 5-speed transmission is also offered as a standard feature, along with an optional 4-speed automatic. Power steering is optional on base-level models. Although the entry-level Golf's engine is no tire burner, it's well mated to the base manual transmission and handles most driving conditions with ease.

Cost analysis/best alternatives: These vehicles were extensively redesigned last year and this year's models are coasting on those upgrades. Still, the 2000 versions don't cost much more and represent the better buy, considering the few upgrades they get this year. Other cars worth considering are the Honda Civic, Mazda Protegé, Nissan Sentra, and Toyota Corolla. Cabrio shoppers might also want to test-drive a convertible Chevrolet Cavalier or Sunfire. **Options:** Stay away from the electric sunroof; it costs a bundle to repair and offers not much more than the well-designed manual sunroof. Plus, you lose too much head room. The Jetta TDI isn't a good idea. Why in the world would you invest in a diesel engine, unless you want to get your gas at truck stops? Granted, there are fewer things to go wrong with diesel engines, but gasoline-powered VW engines already have an excellent track record. Less fuel cost isn't a strong enough argument to weigh against the extra noise and smellier emissions associated with diesel engines. And there's no guarantee that diesel prices won't get boosted again this year. **Delivery/PDI:** $525. **Rebates:** Not likely, but look for some substantial end-of-the-year price-cuts on the '99s. **Depreciation:** Slower than average, especially the Jetta and all Cabriolet versions. **Insurance cost:** Higher than average. **Parts supply/cost:** Not hard to find, but parts can be more expensive than most other cars in this class. **Annual maintenance cost:** Less than average while under warranty. After that, repair costs start to climb dramatically. **Warranty:** Bumper-to-bumper 2 years/40,000 km; powertrain 5 years/80,000 km; rust perforation 6 years/unlimited km. **Supplementary warranty:** A good idea. **Highway/city fuel economy:** 4.8–6.9L/100 km with the 1.9L TDI; 7.7–10.5L/100 km with the 2.0L; and 8.4–12.6L/100 km with the 2.8L V6. **Annual fuel cost:** 1.9L: 1,191L=$655; 2.0L: 1,848L=$1,072; 2.8L: 2,142L=$1,242.

Quality/Reliability/Safety

Pro: Quality control: Better than average. Major components are relatively trouble-free. **Reliability:** Good overall reliability (that's why so many are used as taxis) during the first few years. **Warranty performance:** Slow, but fair treatment of warranty claims by customer service staff located in the States. **Safety:** Standard three-point seatbelts and anti-theft alarm (thieves just adore these cars).

Con: Now made in Mexico, the quality control on these vehicles isn't comparable to German workmanship. Apparently, reliability deteriorates about the same time as the warranty expires, and ownership costs rise dramatically after the fifth year of ownership. **Owner-reported problems:** The brakes and the electrical, fuel, and exhaust systems are especially troublesome. Owners report that doors are poorly hung, rattles are omnipresent, and dashboard controls and interior and exterior trim items aren't very durable. Paint defects and premature rusting have been common. **Service bulletin problems:** Windshield wiper intermittently stops wiping after one sweep. **NHTSA safety complaints/safety:** *Golf:* Intermittent stalling; uncomfortable driver's seat creates excessive fatigue on long trips; horn can't be located when wheel is turned; improper lug nuts allow wheel to separate from the car. *Jetta:* When the brakes are released, vehicle suddenly accelerates; airbag warning light comes on for no apparent reason and shuts down the airbag system; ABS failure; driver's seat faulty wiring caused a fire; passenger-side airbag deployed seconds after impact; exhaust pipe extends underneath the bumper, revealing raw edge of pipe; car hit the curb and airbag deployed, hitting driver's head and killing him; fuel tank leaks; adhesive that secures the brake light in the rear window can melt in sunlight; shoulder and lapbelt disengaged during a collision; restraints failed, allowing driver to hit the windshield even though the airbag deployed; vehicle was hit from all sides and neither front nor side airbags deployed; intermittent stalling; when vehicle is driven at speeds over 35 mph (57 km/h), tachometer registers 4,700 rpm before downshifting; gear console gives an inaccurate gear reading; interior and instrument lights fail intermittently. *GTI:* Corner front wheel hit curb at 10 mph (16 km/h) and was severely damaged.

Road Performance

Pro: Emergency handling: Acceptable, despite the softer suspension creating additional body roll. **Steering:** Precise and predictable steering. **Acceleration/torque:** The standard 2.0L 4-cylinder engine is acceptable for city driving and leisurely highway cruising with the manual gearbox, thanks mainly to the car's light weight and improved fuel injection. The V6 is the prerequisite engine for performance thrills (0–100 km/h: 8 sec.). **Routine handling:** Excellent handling. Ride quality is less firm than with previous models. **Braking:** Acceptable (100–0 km/h: 130 ft.).

Con: The base 4-cylinder engine provides sluggish acceleration when hooked to an automatic transmission. Excessive torque steer with the V6. Diesel engines equipped with cruise control can't handle small hills very well, and usually drop 10–15 km/h. **Transmission:** Manual 5-speed transmission is imprecise and requires long lever throws to change gear. Harsh automatic transmission downshifts at full throttle. The soft suspension produces lots of body roll when cornering under power.

Comfort/Convenience

Pro: Standard equipment: Adequate. Although you don't get a lot of lavish standard features, the essentials are all there. **Driving position:** Excellent driving position. Comfortable and versatile front bucket seats help to make driving a pleasure. Front seat head room is adequate for most drivers, even with a sunroof. Ergonomics are impressive. **Controls and displays:** The dash is well laid-out and gauges are easy to read. Most controls are easy to find and use. **Climate control:** Generally works well and is easy to adjust. However, some owners have complained that heating is barely sufficient. Check this out on the dealer's lot before accepting delivery. **Interior space/comfort F/R:** Although the interior is very austere, it's well finished and fairly spacious up front. The rear seats include headrests. **Cargo space:** The Golf's hatchback design is a bit more versatile for diverse cargo. **Trunk/liftover:** Spacious trunk has a low liftover.

Con: Rear visibility somewhat restricted. The front seats are too firm for some and the low-profile tires make small bumps unusually harsh. The rear seats are too narrow and there's not enough knee room. Radio and power window buttons are too small. The lack of a centre console cuts down on storage space. The Cabrio's trunk is too small. The odd way the trunk opens compromises loading. **Entry/exit:** A bit tricky. **Quietness:** Despite additional sound deadening, the TDI's engine is fairly noisy and tends to produce excessive vibrations.

COST				
List Price (firm)	**Residual Values** (months)			
	24	36	48	60
Golf 2d: $18,950 (13%)	$13,000	$11,000	$9,000	$7,000
Golf 4d: $21,170 (14%)	$15,000	$13,000	$11,000	$9,000

TECHNICAL DATA	
Powertrain (front-drive)	Head room F/R: 37.1/36.5 in.
Engines: 2.0L 4-cyl. (115 hp)	Head room F/R: 37.9/36.5 in.
• 1.9L 4-cyl. diesel (90 hp)	Leg room F/R: 41.3/33.3 in.
• 2.8L V6 (174 hp)	Wheelbase: 98.9 in.
Transmissions: 5-speed man.	Turning circle: 36 ft.
• 4-speed auto.	Cargo volume: 18 cu. ft.
Dimension/Capacity (GTI VR6)	Tow limit: 1,000 lb.
Passengers: 2/3	Fuel tank: 55L/reg.
Height/length/width:	Weight: 2,723 lb.
56.7/163.3/68.3 in.	

SAFETY FEATURES/CRASHWORTHINESS		
	Std.	**Opt.**
Anti-lock brakes	■	❑
Seatbelt pretensioners	■	❑

Side airbags	■	❏
Traction control	■	■
Head restraints	**	*
Head restraints (Cabrio)	*	*
Visibility (front/rear)	*****	**
Crash protection (front) D/P	***	***
Crash protection (side) D/P		
Jetta	***	**
Crash protection (offset)	N/A	
HLDI injury claims (model)	N/A	
HLDI injury claims (all)	N/A	

Passat

Passat

RATING: Recommended. **Strong points:** Well-appointed, with standard side airbags, traction control, and ABS. Refined road manners, quiet-running, plenty of passenger and cargo room, exceptional driving comfort, and top-quality construction and mechanical components. **Weak points:** Mediocre acceleration (automatic transmission-equipped GLS 1.8T and TDI), rear corner blind spots, serious safety complaints, and poor fuel economy.

NEW FOR 2000: A slight restyling, brake wear indicator, anti-theft and sound-system upgrades, and standard traction control.

OVERVIEW: Volkswagen's largest front-drive compact, the Passat is an attractive mid-sized car that rides on the same platform as the Audi A4, giving it a three-inch larger wheelbase and more passenger room. It has a more stylish design than the Golf or Jetta, but still provides a comfortable, roomy interior and gives good all-around performance for highway and city driving. The car's large wheelbase and squat appearance give it a massive, solid feeling, while its aerodynamic styling makes

it look sleek and clean. Most Passats come fully loaded with air conditioning, tinted glass, power-assisted disc brakes on all four wheels, front
and rear stabilizer bars, full instrumentation, and even a roof rack with
the wagon.

Engine offerings include a new 150-hp 1.8L turbocharged inline
four and a 190-hp 2.8L V6 hooked to either a 5-speed manual or a
5-speed Tiptronic automatic transmission.

Cost analysis/best alternatives: Get the 2000 model for the upgrades.
Other cars worth considering are the BMW 3-series, Honda Accord,
and Toyota Camry. **Options:** The 2.8L V6 and a good anti-theft system.
Rebates: Not likely. **Delivery/PDI:** $500. **Depreciation:** Slower than
average. **Insurance cost:** Higher than average. These cars are favourites
with thieves—whether for radios, wheels, VW badges, or the entire car.
Parts supply/cost: Not hard to find. Parts and service are much more
expensive than average, reports CAA. **Annual maintenance cost:** Higher
than average. **Warranty:** Bumper-to-bumper 2 years/40,000 km; powertrain 5 years/80,000 km; rust perforation 6 years/unlimited km.
Supplementary warranty: A must-have. Maintenance costs are higher
than average once the warranty expires, which is all the more reason to
buy the optional warranty from VW. **Highway/city fuel economy:**
7–11.4L/100 km with the 1.8L engine, 7.5–13.3L/100 km with the
2.8L, and 8.2–13.7L/100 km with the 2.8L Synchro. **Annual fuel cost:**
1.8L: 1,884L=$1,262; 2.8L: 2,138L=$1,432; 2.8L Synchro:
2,245L=$1,504.

Quality/Reliability/Safety

Pro: Quality control: So far, so good. The new Passat uses mechanical
parts and underpinnings borrowed from Audi, so overall reliability and
problem areas should be similar to those of the Audi A4. **Reliability:**
Predicted above average reliability during the first three years. **Warranty
performance:** Apparently good. VW staffers in the States (there's no
office in Canada) have been particularly sensitive to Passat complaints.

Con: Owner-reported problems: Some electrical malfunctions, premature brake wear, and noisy braking. **Service bulletin problems:** Chronic
engine misfiring, and windshield wiper intermittently stops wiping after
one sweep. **NHTSA safety complaints/safety:** Airbags failed to deploy;
rack and pinion steering cap fell out causing leaking steering fluid to
ignite; clutch remained depressed and gear stayed engaged; clutch
pedal wouldn't spring back and car continued to accelerate; vehicle
accelerated forward when the emergency brake was released; steering
wheel locked up when turning at 10 mph (16 km/h); chronic hesitation; power steering rack failures; brake booster failure; passenger side
airbag isn't fitted properly; driver's seat has excessive fore and aft movement; optically distorted windshield; rear window defroster power button

failure, only works when held in the "on" position; map light and sun-roof failures; burnt caramel odour whenever the heater is on.

Road Performance

Pro: Emergency handling: Better than average. **Steering:** Quick, precise, and predictable. **Acceleration/torque:** Decent acceleration with the base 1.8L turbocharged engine, unless saddled with an automatic transmission. Better acceleration times with more torque can be wrung from the V6 (0–100 km/h: 7.9 sec.). Diesel power is relatively quick and quiet. **Transmission:** Smooth and quiet shifting with the automatic gearbox. The Synchro 4X4 shifts effortlessly into gear. **Routine handling:** Suspension is both firm and comfortable; precise handling outclasses most of the competition.

Con: Braking: Less than impressive (100–0 km/h: 141 ft.).

Comfort/Convenience

Pro: Standard equipment: This is VW's most luxurious car, so it comes fairly well-appointed. Heated outside mirror. **Driving position:** Very good. Comfortable seating and good fore and aft visibility. Fairly good dashboard layout. **Controls and displays:** User-friendly instrument panel. **Climate control:** Efficient and quiet operation. Includes a dust and pollen filter. **Entry/exit:** Relatively easy front and rear access. **Interior space/comfort F/R:** Spacious interior seats four in comfort, as long as the rear passengers aren't too tall. All seats are supportive and comfortable. **Cargo space:** Average for the sedan. Many small storage spaces. **Trunk/liftover:** Large and accessible trunk has an innovative latch and low liftover. **Quietness:** Additional sound-deadening material keeps interior noise to a minimum.

Con: Rear visibility is compromised by the styling of the rear pillars. Limited rear head room. **Quietness:** Excessive tire noise.

COST				
List Price (firm)	**Residual Values** (months)			
	24	36	48	60
Passat GLS 1.8:				
$29,500 (18%)	$23,000	$19,000	$16,000	$13,000

TECHNICAL DATA	
Powertrain (front-drive)	Head room F/R: 39.7/37.8 in.
Engines: 1.8L 4-cyl. (150 hp)	Leg room F/R: 41.5/35.3 in.
• 2.8L V6 (190 hp)	Wheelbase: 106.4 in.
Transmissions: 5-speed man.	Turning circle: 38 ft.
• 5-speed auto.	Cargo volume: 15 cu. ft.
Dimension/Capacity	Tow limit: 1,000 lb.
Passengers: 2/3	Fuel tank: 47L/prem.

Height/length/width: 57.4/184.1/68.5 in.	Weight: 3,250 lb.	

SAFETY FEATURES/CRASHWORTHINESS

	Std.	Opt.
Anti-lock brakes	■	❏
Seatbelt pretensioners (F/R)	—	—
Side airbags	■	❏
Traction control	■	❏
Head restraints	**	*
Visibility (front/rear)	*****	**
Crash protection (front) D/P	N/A	
Crash protection (side) D/P	N/A	
Crash protection (offset)	*****	
HLDI injury claims (model)	N/A	
HLDI injury claims (all)	N/A	

VOLVO

In the past, Volvo distinguished itself from the rest of the automotive pack through its much-vaunted standard safety features, crashworthiness, and engineering that emphasized function over style. But unfortunately these noteworthy features were eclipsed by bland styling, ponderous highway performance, inconsistent quality control that compromised long-term reliability and drove up ownership costs, and chancy servicing by a small dealer network.

Well, you can forget about bland styling and mediocre highway performance now. Volvo's latest models are rounder, sleeker, and more attractively styled than anything the Swedish automaker has put out in the past three decades. In addition to the new C70 high-performance luxury coupe, Volvo has copied Subaru's successful marketing strategy and brought out an AWD wagon variation of its popular 850/S70/S80.

As far as quality control and dealer servicing are concerned, Volvo has improved service and warranty relations by accelerating service training programs and allowing its dealers to carry out most warranty and extra-warranty repairs without obtaining prior authorization from the company.

The downside to all this good news?

Volvo, like VW, is pushing new car prices through the roof. Now owned by the Ford Motor Company, one gets the impression that Ford will milk the company for all it can get and keep prices high to do so. Furthermore, Ford's involvement may mean some sharing of components—a good idea for Jaguar, a bad idea for Volvo. Such a scheme will likely make Fords safer and more reliable and Volvos less so (I doubt Ford's ubiquitous aluminum forward clutch piston or 3.8L biodegradable engine head gaskets would have ever found their way onto a Volvo assembly line).

Volvo S40 and V40
A Mitsubishi Volvo? That's right, the S40/V40, Volvo's new small sedan and wagon that go on sale at the end of September, are built in the Netherlands through a joint venture with Mitsubishi. Priced about $4,500 less than the S70, Volvo's entry-level model, the cars will arrive with a 1.9L 150-hp turbocharged 4-cylinder engine coupled to an automatic transmission. Two side airbags, anti-lock brakes, air conditioning, cruise control, and power windows are also standard. One option sure to please "cyber" cruisers: a small personal computer table that mounts on the passenger's seat.

C70

C70

RATING: Above Average. **Strong points:** Good acceleration with lots of torque, exceptional steering and handling, first-class body construction and finish, predicted better than average reliability. **Weak points:** Difficult rear-seat entry/exit, some engine turbo lag, excessive engine noise, and a jarring suspension.

OVERVIEW: Seating four comfortably, this $54,695 luxury coupe and convertible is based on the 850 (pardon, S70) platform, and marketed as a high-performance Volvo. It comes with two turbocharged engines: a base 2.4L 190-hp inline 5-cylinder, and a 2.3L 236-hp variant. Either engine can be hooked to a 5-speed manual or a 4-speed automatic transmission. Of the two engines, the 190-hp appears to offer the best response and smoothest performance.

Acceleration is impressive, despite the fact that the car feels underpowered until the turbo kicks in at around 1,500 rpm—a feature that drivers will find more frustrating with a manual shifter than with an automatic. Steering and handling are first class, fit and finish above reproach, and mechanical and body components are top quality.

The only things not to like are a high base price, turbo lag, tire thumping caused by the high-performance tires, excessive engine and wind noise, and power-sliding rear seats that require lots of skill and patience.

Safety features include dual driver/passenger airbags, side airbags, ABS, traction control, and a platform designed to give maximum passenger protection in a collision. The IIHS has awarded the C70 its highest rating for front and rear seat head restraint protection.

S70

RATING: Recommended. Strong points: Practical to the extreme, with plenty of power; good handling; lots of carrying capacity; top-quality mechanical and body components; many standard safety features; and impressive crashworthiness ratings and accident injury claim data. **Weak points:** Some serious safety defects reported by owners; limited rear visibility; excessive engine, wind, and road noise; fuel-thirsty (turbo models); and soaring base prices with little room for negotiating.

NEW FOR 2000: The 2.4L engine gets six more horses and variable value-timing. Naturally aspirated cars get a new five-speed gearbox and an optional stability-enhancement system.

OVERVIEW: There are three variants of the S70 and V70: base, GLT, and T5. The base sedan uses a 2.4L 24-valve 162-hp 5-cylinder engine hooked to a front-drive powertrain. Wagons use the same base powerplant, hooked to a 5-speed manual or optional 4-speed electronic automatic. GLTs have a torquier, turbo variant of the same powerplant that boosts horsepower to 190. A 247-hp turbocharged 2.3L engine powers the V70R.

The T5 "sports" sedan is a rounder, sportier-looking successor to the 850R model. It delivers honest, predictable performance but comes up a bit short on the "sports" side. Volvo's base turbo boosts horsepower to 222, but its new T5R variant uses an upgraded turbocharger that boosts power to 236 horses—for up to seven seconds.

Cost analysis/best alternatives: Buy the 2000 version for the upgrades. Other cars worth considering are the Acura TL, Audi A4, Infiniti I30, or the Lexus ES 300. Other wagons you may wish to consider: the BMW 5-series Touring and Mercedes-Benz E-class wagon. **Options:** Integrated child safety seats, seat heaters, and a full-sized spare tire. The turbo's traction control and additional 22 horses aren't worth the extra cost. **Rebates:** Are you kidding? These cars are so hot that dealers are refusing to budge from the MSRP—and some are tacking on unwarranted "administrative" fees and inflated PDI/destination charges. **Delivery/PDI:** $700. **Depreciation:** Slower than average. **Insurance cost:** Higher than average. **Parts supply/cost:** Parts are highly dealer-dependent. Volvos are well serviced by the small dealer body, and parts aren't hard to find. **Annual maintenance cost:** Average. Higher than average predicted after the fourth year. **Warranty:** Bumper-to-bumper 4 years/80,000 km; powertrain 4 years/ 80,000 km; rust perforation 8 years/unlimited km. **Supplementary warranty:** A toss-up. This latest generation of Volvos hasn't shown any reliability weakness yet, but it's still too early to tell how they'll perform on a long-term basis, now that Ford owns the company ("Have you driven a Ford, lately?"). If you plan on keeping your Volvo longer than the standard warranty, the extra protection would make your trade-in easier to sell at a higher price. **Highway/city fuel economy:** 7.7–11.6L/100 km with the 2.4L, and 8.1–12L/100 km with the turbocharged engine. **Annual fuel cost:** 2.4L: 1,969L=$1,319; turbocharged: 2,049L=$1,373. AWD will cost about $100 per annum in extra fuel.

Quality/Reliability/Safety

Pro: Reliability: No serious reliability problems have been encountered. **Warranty performance:** Much better than average. Many warranty claims are settled through "goodwill" on a case-by-case basis. **Safety:** Standard side-impact airbags and standard traction control with the T5R version are a nice touch. Other safety features include rear head restraints, reinforced anti-roll bars, front and rear crumple zones, a practical, roof-mounted interior cargo net that protects passengers from being hit by objects stored in the rear, and rear three-point seatbelts. As with Volvo's other two models, the IIHS has awarded the S70 and V70 its highest rating for front and rear seat head restraint protection.

Con: Body assembly and paint quality are better than average, but they can't match the Japanese competition. **Owner-reported problems:** Problem areas are limited to the front brakes, electrical system, and minor body faults. Some servicing delays decried. **Service bulletin problems:** Rear axle whine. **NHTSA safety complaints/safety:** *S70*: Car suddenly accelerated and brakes locked up at the same time; airbags failed to deploy; a piece of the vacuum brake system came loose, causing an increase in the engine rpms and locking up the brakes; vehicle suddenly loses power and the CHECK ENGINE light comes on; when making a left turn vehicle shut down, causing loss of control; extended tailpipe length caused child to burn his leg; dashboard causes excessive windshield glare which makes for serious eyestrain. *V70*: Fuel leaks badly from the fuel tank area; fuel odour in vehicle after a fillup; brakes grind when applied, then fail completely; shoulder portion of the rear seatbelt won't retract; with a child safety seat installed in the rear centre seat, the buckle for the right rear passenger seatbelt is blocked; passenger exited rear door and exhaust pipe burned his leg.

Road Performance

Pro: Emergency handling: Better than average, with minimal body roll and good control. **Steering:** Predictable, rapid steering response. Handles sudden steering corrections very well. **Acceleration/torque:** Plenty of high-range power with the base engine, especially with a manual gearbox. With an automatic transmission, the normally aspirated base engine has a 0–100 km/h time of 9.5 seconds. No turbo lag. The 190-hp engine posted better than average acceleration times (0–100 km/h: 8.8 sec.) with plenty of torque. **Transmission:** Smooth and quiet automatic and manual gearboxes. **Routine handling:** Nimble handling doesn't sacrifice passenger comfort. **Braking:** Excellent braking performance (100–0 km/h: 115 ft.) on dry or wet pavement.

Con: Moderate torque steer when accelerating. Both the wagon and the sedan's soft ride deteriorates progressively as the road gets rougher and passenger weight is added.

Comfort/Convenience

Pro: Standard equipment: Lots of standard safety and performance features. **Driving position:** Excellent driving position and plenty of seat adjustments to accommodate almost any size of driver. **Controls and displays:** Everything is in plain sight, accessible, and intuitive. **Climate control:** Excellent. The system operates flawlessly and is simple to comprehend. **Entry/exit:** Easy front and rear access. **Interior space/comfort F/R:** Passenger space, seating comfort, and trunk and cargo space are unmatched by the competition. **Cargo space:** The wagon's rear seatbacks fold flat and the seat cushion can be removed for additional cargo space. **Trunk/liftover:** Spacious trunk has a low liftover.

Con: Three rear head restraints limit rear visibility. **Quietness:** Excessive engine noise upon acceleration, as well as some wind and tire noise at highway speeds.

COST

List Price (firm)	Residual Values (months)			
	24	**36**	**48**	**60**
Base S70: $34,995 (20%)	$25,000	$20,000	$15,000	$13,000

TECHNICAL DATA

Powertrain (front-drive/AWD)
Engines: 2.4L 5-cyl. (162 hp)
• 2.4L 5-cyl. turbo (190 hp)
• 2.3L 5-cyl. turbo (236 hp)
• 2.3L 5-cyl. turbo (247 hp)
Transmissions: 5-speed man.
• 4-speed auto.
Dimension/Capacity
Passengers: 2/3

Height/length/width:
 56.2/185.9/69.3 in.
Head room F/R: 39.1/37.9 in.
Leg room F/R: 41.4/35.2 in.
Wheelbase: 104.3 in.
Turning circle: 38 ft.
Cargo volume: 15 cu. ft.
Tow limit: 2,000 lb.
Fuel tank: 73L/prem.
Weight: 3,750 lb.

SAFETY FEATURES/CRASHWORTHINESS

	Std.	Opt.
Anti-lock brakes	■	❏
Seatbelt pretensioners	■	❏
Side airbags	■	❏
Traction control	■	❏
Head restraints	*****	*****
Visibility (front/rear)	*****	**
Crash protection (front) D/P	*****	*****
Crash protection (side) D/P	****	N/A
Crash protection (offset)	*****	
HLDI injury claims (model)	****	
HLDI injury claims (all)	****	

S80

S80

RATING: Recommended. **Strong points:** Powerful turbocharged engine, generally comfortable ride, quiet-running, handles well, and many standard safety features. **Weak points:** Base engine a so-so performer, driving position not for everyone, ride comfort deteriorates as load is increased, steering feels over-assisted, fuel-thirsty, and high base prices demanded by dealers who won't negotiate.

NEW FOR 2000: Carried over practically unchanged. A wagon will appear late next summer.

OVERVIEW: Volvo has dropped the wagon version and replaced the rear-drive S90 sedan with the front-drive S80, equipped with a twin-cam 2.9L straight-six engine. Selling for about $5,000 more, the S80 T6 employs two turbochargers to boost the 2.8L engine's power to 268 horses and mate it to a 4-speed automatic transmission equipped with a Geartronic manual-shift feature.

Both models are well-equipped with safety and convenience features that include standard ABS, front side airbags and Inflatable Cushion side airbags that extend from the front to the rear roof pillars, seatbelt pretensioners, traction control, a "WHIPS" seatback and head restraint whiplash protection system, and an optional Dynamic Stability and Traction Control System. Furthermore, the IIHS has awarded the S80 its highest rating for front and rear seat head restraint protection.

Cost analysis/best alternatives: Beat the dealers at their own game and opt for an almost identical, though cheaper, '99 leftover—if you can find one left over. Other cars worth considering are the BMW 5-series or Lexus GS 300 and 400. **Options:** The turbocharged engine is the better performer for highway driving. Also consider built-in child safety seats and seat heaters. **Rebates:** Not likely. Get ready for some real sticker shock. These cars are so hot that dealers are tacking on unwarranted "administrative" fees and inflated PDI/destination charges. **Delivery/ PDI:** $700. **Depreciation:** Average. **Insurance cost:** Higher than average. **Parts supply/cost:** Parts availability is very dealer-dependent; a high-volume dealer is your best bet. Volvos are well served by the small dealer body, and parts aren't generally hard to find and they're reasonably priced. **Annual maintenance cost:** Average during the warranty period; expected to rise when the warranty expires. **Warranty:** Bumper-to-bumper 4 years/80,000 km; powertrain 4 years/80,000 km; rust perforation 8 years/unlimited km. **Supplementary warranty:** You can go either way with this option. This latest generation of Volvos hasn't shown any major reliability weaknesses yet, but it's still too early to tell how they'll perform on a long-term basis. If you plan on keeping your Volvo longer than the standard warranty, the extra protection would make your trade-in easier to sell at a higher price. **Highway/city fuel economy:** 8.0–12.2L/100 km with the 2.9L 6-cylinder, and 7.9–12.8L/100 km with the turbocharger. **Annual fuel cost:** 2.9L 6-cylinder: 2,062L=$1,382; Turbocharger: 2,119L=$1,420.

Quality/Reliability/Safety

Pro: Quality control: Volvo's quality control is better than most European automakers'. **Reliability:** Nothing that would sideline these cars for an extended period of time. Body assembly and finish is comparable to the Japanese competition. **Warranty performance:** Better than average. Volvo staffers have been fair and professional in handling warranty claims. **Service bulletin problems:** Nothing important. **NHTSA safety complaints/safety:** Nothing recorded.

Con: Owner-reported problems: Failure-prone air conditioning, premature brake wear and noisy braking, and electrical and fuel system malfunctions. Parts shortages and delivery delays are commonplace.

Road Performance

Pro: Emergency handling: Very good. The multi-link rear suspension and front engine placement make for crisp handling. **Steering:** Good steering response, although it sometimes feels over-assisted and road feel is a bit muted. **Acceleration/torque:** The 2.9L 201-hp 6-cylinder puts out lots of low-end and mid-range torque that meets all driving conditions with a minimum of strain or engine noise (0–100 km/h: 9.2 sec.). The turbocharged version is the engine of choice, however. It delivers plenty of high-speed cruising power and torque. **Transmission:** Smooth and quiet automatic transmission. **Routine handling:** Acceptable handling prioritizes passenger comfort. **Braking:** Better than average. Braking is short and straight with minimal fading after successive brake application (100–0 km/h: 120 ft.).

Con: Some torque steer upon acceleration. Comfort and handling diminishes as passenger/cargo load increases.

Comfort/Convenience

Pro: Very good driving position for most. User-friendly cockpit. **Controls and displays:** Well laid-out dash and analogue gauges are easy to read. Controls are within easy reach. **Climate control:** Climate control system is efficient, quiet, and unobtrusive. **Entry/exit:** Easy front and rear access. **Interior space/comfort F/R:** Capable of carrying five people in comfort, and the wagon variant provides lots of cargo space. Front and rear seats are supportive and comfortable. Three passengers can sit in the rear in comfort. **Cargo space:** Plenty of cargo space. **Trunk/liftover:** Spacious trunk has a low liftover. **Quietness:** Whisper quiet.

Con: Not enough room for driver's left leg to stretch. Small trunk opening. **Standard equipment:** Bland exterior and interior styling. **Driving position:** Short-statured drivers may find it necessary to lower the seat in order to extend the leg room to reach the accelerator comfortably. This makes it difficult to see over the steering wheel.

COST				
List Price (firm)	**Residual Values** (months)			
	24	**36**	**48**	**60**
S80: $50,995 (22%)	$36,000	$30,000	$24,000	$20,000

TECHNICAL DATA	
Powertrain (front-drive)	Head room F/R: 39.1/37.9 in.
Engine: 2.9L 6-cyl. (201 hp)	Leg room F/R: 41.4/35.2 in.
• 2.8L 6-cyl. (268 hp)	Wheelbase: 109.9 in.
Transmission: 4-speed auto.	Turning circle: 40 ft.
Dimension/Capacity (S80)	Cargo volume: 14 cu. ft.
Passengers: 2/3	Tow limit: 2,000 lb.
Height/length/width:	Fuel tank: 73L/prem.
57.2/189.8/72.1 in.	Weight: 3,630 lb.

SAFETY FEATURES/CRASHWORTHINESS		
	Std.	**Opt.**
Anti-lock brakes	■	❑
Seatbelt pretensioners	■	❑
Side airbags	■	❑
Traction control	■	❑
Head restraints	*****	*****
Visibility (front/rear)	*****	*****
Crash protection (front) D/P	N/A	
Crash protection (side) D/P	*****	*****
Crash protection (offset)	N/A	
HLDI injury claims (model)	N/A	
HLDI injury claims (all)	N/A	

Appendix I
24 HELPFUL INTERNET GRIPE SITES

Websites come and go. Please email *lemonaid@earthlink.net* if you find a site has closed down or moved. Also let me know if you have discovered a website that should be included in next year's *Lemon-Aid* guide.

1. BMW Lemons (*www.bmwlemon.com/*)
Yes Virginia, BMW makes lemons, too. This site covers most of the problems owners on three continents have experienced with their 3-, 5-, and 7-series BMWs. There are lots of servicing tips and detailed information on some of the more common defects, like engine head gasket failures. One owner gives a blow-by-blow description of how he filed suit in an Ottawa small claims court and forced BMW to settle out of court.

2. Chrysler Warranty Review Committee (email *RAR17@chrysler.com*)
No, you won't read about this consumer complaint committee in your owner's manual or see it touted anywhere at your local dealership. Chrysler's Review Committee was set up in February 1998 in response to the bad publicity and threats of court action coming from *Lemon-Aid* and about six hundred Chrysler owners who helped form Chrysler Lemon Owners Groups (CLOG) in British Columbia and New Brunswick.

These groups submitted the names of irate owners to Chrysler and have succeeded in getting sizeable refunds for brake, transmission, and paint repairs. If you have had any of these problems and want "goodwill" repairs or a refund for repairs already carried out, go through Chrysler's regular customer relations hot line. If you're not satisfied by the response you get, phone or fax Mr. Lou Spadotto, National Service Manager, at telephone: 519-973-2300 (Bob Renaud's old line) or 519-973-2890; fax: 519-973-2318. If you cannot get in touch with Lou Spadotto, phone or fax Mr. Larry Latta, Vice President, Sales and Marketing, at telephone: 519-973-2947; fax: 519-973-2799. They use the Review Committee to take a hard look at all claims, including those that were previously rejected.

Up to now, I can say the Review Committee has treated most consumer complaints diligently and professionally. It is still paying off customer claims that had been refused when presented through Chrysler's regular channels. I wish Ford had the good sense to create a similar mechanism for its aggrieved customers.

Three suggestions if you plan to contact the Review Committee:
• Send Chrysler copies of all your repair bills or independent garage estimates.
• Don't accept a refusal based on the fact that you're not the first owner.

• Don't let Chrysler turn your claim down because the repairs were carried out by an independent repair facility.

3. Chrysler Products' Problem Web Page (*www.wam.umd.edu/~gluckman/Chrysler/*)
This page was designed to be a resource for Chrysler owners who have had problems in dealing with Chrysler on issues such as peeling paint, transmission failure, the Chrysler-installed Bendix-10 ABS, and other maladies.

4. Jeep Paint Delamination/Peeling (*www.goofball.com/keane/badpaint/*)
Jeep paint and other body defects are covered. Useful links to other sites.

5. Ford Insider Info (*www.blueovalnews.com*)
Set up by a Ford Mustang enthusiast living in the Detroit area who has contacts with lots of Ford employee whistleblowers, this website is the place to go for all the latest insider info on the company's activities. The website is still operating although Ford got a temporary restraining order preventing it from publishing certain internal documents that Ford considers to be confidential. Why did Ford pick on this website when websites such as *Lemon-Aid*'s go unchallenged? Insiders tell me that Ford is particularly incensed over *www.blueovalnews.com* spilling the beans that the 1999 Mustang SVT Cobras have exhaust problems that cut as much as 50 horsepower from the 320 horsepower advertised. Ford had to recall 5,300 Cobras to fix the problem.

6. Dead Ford Page (*www.mindspring.com/~ics_mak/deadford.html*)
An amusing and informative gathering place for Ford car, sport-utility, minivan, van, and truck owners, who discuss common problems and solutions. A fun site just to see the FORD VENT page where an animated character walks across the screen, drops his shorts, and takes a leak up against a thinly disguised Ford logo.

7. Ford Paint Delamination/Peeling (*www.ihs2000.com/~peel*)
Everything you should know about the cause and treatment of Ford paint delamination. It has useful links to other sites and tips on dealing with Ford and GM paint problems.

8. Ford Contour/Mystique Gripe Site (*www.contour.org/FAQ/*)
Similar to the Nissan site listed below, except that this one provides a more comprehensive listing of major problems affecting the Ford and Mercury Contour and Mystique.

9. Ford Taurus, Sable Automatic Transmission Victims (*members.aol.com/MKBradley/index.html*)
A great site for learning about Ford's biodegradable automatic transmissions (1991–97).

10. Ford Windstar Engine Head Gasket/Automatic Transmission Site (*www.fordwindstar.com/*)
This site was constructed by a 1995 Windstar owner who collected complaints from three dozen other Windstar owners who experienced similar powertrain problems.

11. GM Paint Delamination/Peeling
Unfortunately, there's no longer a single website that relates to the above GM problem. (One awesome site existed for two years and then was taken down. A GM payoff? Who knows?) Nevertheless, there are many sites where the problem is discussed. Simply access any search engine and type in "GM paint delamination" or "GM peeling paint."

12. Nissan Gripe Site (*129.22.253.156*)
For dissatisfied owners of most Nissan vehicles, this site is particularly helpful in providing useful links to groups and government agencies that will take your complaint. It also covers in detail what it calls Nissan's "silent recall" of defective engines.

13. "Lemon Aid or How to Get Car Manufacturers to Call You and Beg You for Mercy" (*www.saabnet.com/aas/1997.W26/1344522661.26426.html*)
Although not affiliated with the *Lemon-Aid* car guides, this site contains a hilarious listing of tactics to use in getting auto manufacturers to return your calls, listen to your complaints, and give you compensation. For example, here's how you're advised to deal with the automaker's customer relations rep:

> This is what you should do. DENY THAT YOUR CAR HAS ANY PROBLEMS, and try to sell the car to the person who answered the phone. They will absolutely hate this. When you see that you are going nowhere with this, then ask the customer service rep to go around the office to take up a collection to pay for the car. Say outrageous things; take my word for it, they will remember your name! Alternatively, demand to know the telephone number of the rep's mother. When the rep asks you why you want his/her mother's telephone number, say you have a piece of metal to sell and you feel that his/her mother deserves it.

14. Canadian Law Resources on the Internet (*mindlink.net/drew_jackson/mdj.html*)
If you have to take a dealer or automaker to court and need a lawyer or additional jurisprudence, this is an excellent site to find both. Lots of case summaries, articles, and links to Canadian lawyers and experts. There are a number of discussion groups where lawyers will field your questions for (gasp!) free.

15. *Perez-Trujillo v. Volvo Car Corp.* (*www.law.emory.edu/1circuit/mar98/ 97-1792.01a.html*)
This U.S.-initiated lawsuit provides an interesting, though lengthy, dissertation on the safety hazards that airbags pose and why automakers are ultimately responsible for the injuries and deaths caused by their deployment.

16. *Lemon-Aid* Feedback (*www.lemonaidcars.com*)
The official site of the *Lemon-Aid* guides. Comments and critiques are welcome, particularly if you have an experience to relate that can help other *Lemon-Aid* readers.

17. U.S. NHTSA (*www.nhtsa.dot.gov/cars/problems/*)
Run by the Big Daddy of federal government auto safety regulators, the National Highway Traffic Safety Administration, this site has a comprehensive database covering owner complaints, recall campaigns, defect investigations initiated by the department, and automaker service bulletins that may be helpful. Best of all, this data is easily accessed by typing in your vehicle's year, make, and model. Additionally, there's lots of pro and con information and updates relative to ABS, airbags, child safety seats, and frontal and side crash tests.

18. Transport Canada (*www.tc.gc.ca/roadsafety/Recalls/search_e.asp*)
After two years of doing nothing, Transport Canada's Road Safety Branch set up a more user-friendly recall database in March 1999. Cybersurfers can now access the recall database for 1970–2000 model vehicles, but unlike NHTSA's website, owner complaints aren't listed, defect investigations aren't disclosed, and service bulletin summaries aren't provided.

Nevertheless, this site is a useful guide to Canadian university accident research teams and has plenty of links to provincial transport bureaucrats, auto clubs, and other safety organizations. Too bad it continues to churn out lots of "establishment" auto safety info that promotes the traditional namby-pamby road safety dialectic. For example, after its two-year site makeover, Transport Canada re-released a December 1996 joint press release with the Rubber Association of Canada to "advise motorists to think about safe driving in winter"—and it had the *cojones* to label the info "new."

Buyers wishing to know if a vehicle can be imported into Canada from Europe or the States can get a list of admissible vehicles (those that conform to Canadian federal safety and pollution regulations) at *www.tc.gc.ca/roadsafety/rsimp_e.htm#US*, or can call the Registrar of Imported Vehicles at 1-800-511-7755.

19. Insurance Institute for Highway Safety (*www.hwysafety.org/*)
A dazzling site that's long on crash photos and graphs that show which vehicles are the most crashworthy. Lots of safety info that eschews the

traditional "nut behind the wheel" dialectic. (Let owners deactivate their airbags if they feel at risk. And beware of driving schools: they don't make kids better drivers.)

20. Alldata Service Bulletins (*www.alldata.com/consumer/TSB/yr.html*)
Automotive recalls and technical service bulletins are listed by year, make, model, and engine option. Select a year and then a manufacturer to see a summary list of recalls and technical service bulletins for your car or truck. The only drawback is that you can't see the contents of individual bulletins.

21. Automobile News Groups
These news groups are compilations of email raves and gripes and cover all makes and models. They fall into four distinct areas: *rec.autos.makers.chrysler* (you can add any automaker's name at the end); *rec.autos.tech; rec.autos.driving;* and *rec.autos.misc.*
   The following news group bulletin board is particularly helpful to owners with minivan problems: *www.he.net/~brumley/family/vanboard.html.*

22. The Auto Channel (*www.theautochannel.com/*)
This website gives you comprehensive information useful in choosing a new or used vehicle, filing a claim for compensation, or linking up with other owners. Lots of background info on ABS defects and paint delamination/peeling, with an update as to where the paint class actions are before the courts.

23. Automobile Protection Association (*www.apa.ca/apa-services.html*)
APA is a Canadian non-profit auto industry watchdog that works for improved legislation, industry sales practices, and automobile safety. It mediates complaints and provides lawyers for its members. For $25, plus provincial and federal sales taxes, APA will mail or fax you the dealer's cost or invoice price for any vehicle you are considering buying. It will also provide any information on rebates and interest-rate promotions. No credit card requests are taken, but the Invoice Request Form can be printed from the group's website and mailed to the association with the $25 fee.

24. Center for Auto Safety (*www.autosafety.org*)
Consumers Union and Ralph Nader founded the Center for Auto Safety (CAS) in 1970 to provide consumers a voice for auto safety and quality in Washington and to help lemon owners fight back across the United States. CAS has a small budget but a big impact on the auto industry. It collects complaints and provides a lawyer referral service to its members.

Appendix II
SURVEY AND BULLETIN SEARCH

Rate your vehicle

The information found in this book has been garnered from motorists' responses to surveys, like the one on the following page. Your answers help us protect others from sales scams and bad products. Include any photographs (especially of paint defects), diagrams, contracts, or work orders that expose a defect or dishonest practice. If you order a bulletin summary, your survey comments will also help me to zero in on bulletins that may be useful to you.

I pull the computer bulletin summaries myself (it keeps me in touch with readers like you) and usually have them faxed back within a few days. Sorry, I can process only Visa cards.

Phil Edmonston
Email *lemonaid@earthlink.net*

**Cut Repair Costs • Fight Fraud and Incompetence
with ...
Lemon-Aid's $15 Bulletin Summary**

If you plan to buy a used vehicle, have just bought one, or want to know what to check before the warranty expires, you'll need a bulletin summary computer printout. Nothing gives you a stronger argument with a mechanic than pulling out a confidential bulletin (DSB) that says a failure is factory related or is covered by an extended warranty.

Fill out the request on the next page. You'll receive an exhaustive summary of the DSBs (published in the U.S.) that concern your 1982–99 vehicle. (It's too early for 2000 models.)

Bulletins show repair shortcuts, labour time, lists of upgraded parts, probable defects, recall campaigns, and secret warranties. As well, we'll list your vehicle's present wholesale and retail value.

Order by fax or mail. There's no difference in price, although faxing is much faster. Expect 5–10 faxed pages. You may email your request, but be sure to give a fax number or mailing address because I can only fax or mail the summary.

- **FAX** (Visa only): 954-563-2448 (24 hours a day). Replies by fax should take only a few days—unless I'm on vacation or way behind in my work. You may fax your request and have the bulletin summary mailed. That takes about a week.

- **MAIL:** Make your cheque payable to "DSB" (2805 E. Oakland Park Blvd., PMB 211, Ft. Lauderdale, FL, 33306–1813, U.S.A.). Allow a total of 2–3 weeks for reception and delivery.

LEMON-AID SURVEY/DSB SUMMARY REQUEST

❑ I don't need a DSB summary; my survey comments are below.

❑ Please fax ❑ mail ❑ me a DSB summary for my vehicle (CDN$15 fee enclosed) and an estimate of its worth. (From the DSB summary, individual bulletins may then be ordered for an additional CDN$5 per bulletin.)

Fax #: _____

VISA (ONLY) #: _____

(It will be used once and then destroyed.)

Signature: _____

Name: _____

Address: _____

_____

MY VEHICLE'S PROFILE

Make: _____ Model: _____

Year: _____ Engine (litres): _____ Mileage: _____

GENERAL COMMENTS

Include a photo, diagram, or bill. If you decorated your vehicle with lemons or other signs, please send a photo for the *www.lemonaidcars.com* website or next year's *Lemon-Aid.*

Safety: _____

Reliability: _____

_____

_____

JOY OF OWNERSHIP

(Recommended ⑤, Above Average ④, Average ③,
Below Average ❷, Not Recommended ❶)

Overall Reliability

Air conditioning	Ignition system
Automatic transmission	Rust/Paint
Body integrity	Steering
Braking system	Suspension
Electrical system	**Dealer service**
Engine	**Maintenance**
Exhaust/Converter	**Parts availability**
Fuel system	**Repair costs**